D0927878

JOHN
BUCHAN

JOHN BUCHAN

Model Governor General

J. WILLIAM GALBRAITH

Foreword by His Excellency
the Right Honourable David Johnston,
Governor General of Canada

Foreword by Lady Deborah Stewartby

DUNDURN
TORONTO

Copyright © J. William Galbraith, 2013

All rights reserved. No part of this publication may be reproduced, stored in a retrieval system, or transmitted in any form or by any means, electronic, mechanical, photocopying, recording, or otherwise (except for brief passages for purposes of review) without the prior permission of Dundurn Press. Permission to photocopy should be requested from Access Copyright.

Project Editor: Allister Thompson
Editor: Dominic Farrell
Design: Jennifer Scott
Printer: Marquis

Library and Archives Canada Cataloguing in Publication

Galbraith, J. William, author
    John Buchan : model governor general / by J. William Galbraith ; foreword by Lady Deborah Stewartby.

Includes bibliographical references and index.
Issued in print and electronic formats.
ISBN 978-1-4597-0937-9 (bound).--ISBN 978-1-4597-0938-6 (pdf).--ISBN 978-1-4597-0939-3 (epub)

    1. Buchan, John, 1875-1940. 2. Governors general--Canada--Biography. 3. Authors, Scottish--Biography. 4. Statesmen--Great Britain--Biography. I. Title.

PR6003.U13Z593 2013   823'.91209   C2013-900840-3
                                         C2013-900841-1

1   2   3   4   5   17   16   15   14   13

We acknowledge the support of the **Canada Council for the Arts** and the **Ontario Arts Council** for our publishing program. We also acknowledge the financial support of the **Government of Canada** through the **Canada Book Fund** and **Livres Canada Books**, and the **Government of Ontario** through the **Ontario Book Publishing Tax Credit** and the **Ontario Media Development Corporation**.

Care has been taken to trace the ownership of copyright material used in this book. The author and the publisher welcome any information enabling them to rectify any references or credits in subsequent editions.

J. Kirk Howard, President

Printed and bound in Canada.

Visit us at
Dundurn.com | @dundurnpress | Facebook.com/dundurnpress | Pinterest.com/dundurnpress

Dundurn	Gazelle Book Services Limited	Dundurn
3 Church Street, Suite 500	White Cross Mills	2250 Military Road
Toronto, Ontario, Canada	High Town, Lancaster, England	Tonawanda, NY
M5E 1M2	L41 4XS	U.S.A. 14150

For my wife, Kate, and my children,
David and his wife, Sarah, and Karen, and James

Contents

Acknowledgements

Foremost, I must thank my very good friend Dr. Paul Benoit, who encouraged me to begin thinking about my disparate articles and research in terms of a larger, more coherent whole. His intellect, interest, and thoughtful perspectives challenged and encouraged me to look at my subject in different ways. His framework provided a more meaningful way to examine Buchan's time as governor general. Our conversations were made all the more enjoyable by the many delectable and intellectually stimulating lunches along the way

Another good friend, Allan E. Jones, provided many and varied comments on early draft chapters — all very helpful. His questions were sometimes key to me keeping a proper focus.

My wife, Kate, and many other friends and acquaintances over many years provided me with references and leads to Buchan material or information they happened across. I must also thank Deborah Stewartby for her support and friendship, and for articulating so well in her foreword what I have tried to achieve with this book.

The co-operative and friendly staffs of the many libraries and archives, listed in the bibliography, where I have conducted research over very many years, by correspondence or in person, are deserving of a huge and sincere thanks. Without their expertise and patience, my work would have been immeasurably more arduous, slower, less productive, and less complete.

For ultimately making this book a reality, I owe sincere thanks first to the president of Dundurn, Kirk Howard; to my editor, Dominic Farrell, whose knowledge extends far beyond editing to awareness and sensitivity of the subject and the time period, which made working with him a great pleasure; to those involved in the design and technical production that made the whole work so wonderfully presentable; and to the marketing team at Dundurn, led by Margaret Bryant, particularly publicist Karen McMullin, whose communications and ideas would not let me leave inactive my desire to make known more broadly John Buchan's contribution to this country and to Western civilization.

Finally, I would like to thank my life partner, Kate, and our children, whom I owe irrecoverable time for my absences, both physically and in spirit, as I retreated into what my daughter, Karen, called my "Buchan bubble."

There is much more material I could have included in this book; if readers find it unsatisfying or incomplete, or if there are errors, they are wholly my responsibility. If readers find interest, enjoyment, learning, or inspiration in this book, it is due to the inspiring subject.

Foreword by His Excellency the Right Honourable David Johnston, Governor General of Canada

As the 28th governor general of Canada, I continually draw ideas and inspiration from my predecessors. Each governor general brings to the role their own love for Canada and their own sense of the great promise of this country, and in this Lord Tweedsmuir — better known to the world as the writer John Buchan — was truly exemplary.

Buchan held office during a crucial period in Canada's history and constitutional development. A strong believer in the critical role of the citizen in a democratic society, he travelled widely in Canada and regularly met with ordinary Canadians. He was deeply interested in the possibilities of this country as a diverse, multicultural society, encouraging Canadians to retain their various identities while at the same time embracing national unity. Buchan was also especially sensitive to and supportive of Canada's complex relationship with the United States, and he did much to strengthen friendships between the people and leaders of that country and those of Canada and the United Kingdom.

A man of culture and learning, Buchan was also a prodigious writer and the founder, in 1936, of the Governor General's Literary Awards, which continue to celebrate and foster excellence in Canadian literature. In fact, being the author of several books on the law myself, I am in awe at the number of volumes Buchan published, the range of their subject matter, and his capacity to inspire, stimulate and delight his audience. His writing was as varied and imaginative as his life.

During his time in office, John Buchan quietly established a new model for the position of governor general. His considerable impact on Canada has not been fully recognized, so it is with pleasure that I welcome the present volume. I encourage all Canadians to learn more about this remarkable individual and his contribution to the progress of our country.

— David Johnston

Foreword by Lady Deborah Stewartby

I was proud to be asked, as a granddaughter of John Buchan, 1st Lord Tweedsmuir, to write this foreword to William Galbraith's commentary on my grandfather's tenure as the fifteenth governor general of Canada since Confederation. The book is the more remarkable because by the time William Galbraith was born, "JB," as he is known in the family, had been dead for more than a decade.

My father, JB's second son, wrote in his book *John Buchan: A Memoir*: "to anyone who cares for JB only as the author of highly acceptable, exciting and amusing adventure stories, my insistence on the fundamental seriousness of his purpose may seem odd." William Galbraith has taken that comment and set out to explore the last phase of my grandfather's life — as governor general of Canada — which is the manifestation of his "seriousness of purpose."

JB would have been amazed and delighted that, nearly a century after it was written, his novel *The Thirty-Nine Steps* is universally remembered and reproduced in drama and film. But he should not be remembered for his "shockers" alone. The "fundamental seriousness of purpose" is evident in his poetry, his biographies, and, indeed, his novels, as his concern grew about the survival of Western civilization — physical, moral, and, above all, spiritual. His appointment as governor general in

1935 was the culmination of a career of public service — he served as a soldier, lawyer, propagandist, publisher, businessman, and member of Parliament. A man who was himself adventurous, industrious, instructive, inspiring — he celebrated finding all of these qualities also in the people of Canada.

The research evident in this long-overdue study has produced insights into JB's character, and images of Canada in the 1930s and on the brink of war. The book shows how JB and Canada came to love and respect each other. They grew richer together. He felt the Scotsman's affinity for Canada and could identify with their sensitivities and pride. I am sure this book will rekindle interest in Lord Tweedsmuir the statesman to march beside JB the writer.

My father ends his memoir of his father with these words: "There is nothing in the day brighter than his eye, nor greener than the hope which, untarnished, has sustained him throughout his extraordinary pilgrimage." I welcome William Galbraith's contribution to a deeper understanding of the "seriousness of purpose" of my grandfather's time in Canada, the culmination of his "extraordinary pilgrimage" and of the significant part he played at a critical time in Canada's history.

— Deborah Stewartby
Scottish Borders, May 2013

Preface

He is the author of *The Thirty-Nine Steps*. This spy thriller and chase novel is the most oft-cited identifier for the man noted as a source of the genre. John Buchan's novel remains in print almost one hundred years after its debut in 1915; it has also been the subject of three movies and a television production, and it is the source for a popular current play showing on theatre stages in Britain and North America.

That was not all he wrote, however. Buchan was a prolific writer, producing more than one hundred books — novels and history — in addition to writing about current and foreign affairs in innumerable newspaper and magazine columns. Not surprisingly, most references and writing about John Buchan are about his writing, but there is so much more.

Apart from being a renowned author, John Buchan was a member of the British Parliament; before that he had been a lawyer, publisher, journalist, director of Reuters, and head of the British information and intelligence departments during the Great War, among many other accomplishments and contributions. He was appointed governor general of Canada in March 1935; King George V subsequently granted him a peerage and John Buchan became Lord Tweedsmuir. This was his culminating role of public service, one that would call upon his accumulated breadth and depth of experience and character. An individual of exceptional qualities, he arrived at an exceptional time in Canada's development.

The decade from 1926 to 1935 was arguably the most important period in terms of Canada's sovereignty and constitutional history. More than half a century of Britain's growing confidence in Canada and the other self-governing Dominions of the British Empire, particularly as a result of their roles in the First World War, led to recognition that greater autonomy was called for. This realization, and pressure from the Dominions, led to the Imperial Conference of 1926, which resulted in highly significant changes to the status quo: governors general would no longer represent the government of the United Kingdom but, instead, would act for the sovereign alone; and the Dominions would not only be responsible for their internal affairs but for their external affairs as well — that is, they would be responsible for their own foreign policy. These developments took legal form in the 1931 Statute of Westminster that made Canada and the other Dominions constitutional equals with the United Kingdom — sovereign states freely associating under a common Crown in what was now referred to as the British Commonwealth — and the sovereign was now also sovereign of Canada. These developments were especially significant at this juncture because of the increasing threat, ultimately existential, to democracy from European dictators and their violent ideologies. The first governor general to be appointed after the Statute of Westminster was John Buchan.

His role as governor general has been an inspiration to a number of his successors. Vincent Massey, the first Canadian-born governor general (1952–1959), wrote: "I greatly admired his work as governor general and learnt much from it. No one among my predecessors had a clearer insight into Canadian life. He travelled as widely as he could and with imagination and courage."[1] General Georges Vanier, governor general from 1959 to 1967, shared many traits in common with Buchan. Many of the themes of Vanier's time in office echoed those of Tweedsmuir, in particular national unity and the importance of French-English relations, for the latter of which Vanier explicitly referenced Tweedsmuir.[2]

More recently, Adrienne Clarkson, governor general from 1999 to 2005, wrote, "I always felt close to Buchan, who had become Lord Tweedsmuir, because he was a writer, because he began the Governor General's Literary Awards, and because he truly loved Canada and travelled all over the North and the West."[3] Elsewhere in her memoirs, she refers to Buchan's approach as a basis for her own time as governor general: "... Lord Tweedsmuir called to Canada 'to [make] her own music,' and that was an unquestioned and firmly established part of the vice-regal function while I held the office."[4]

The current governor general, David Johnston (from October 2010), "has been drawn to John Buchan," who, Johnston says, was "a man of many parts and I think he was a quiet man ... who derived his joy from serving well."[5]

These are compelling reasons to write about John Buchan's time in Canada.[6] But how best should the subject be approached? A straightforward chronological recounting of more than four years did not seem satisfactory. Rather, I have adapted a framework developed by Dr. Paul Benoit that is built around various roles that a governor general plays and that fall into two broad areas — governmental and cultural.[7] The governmental involves certain functions a governor general performs as the Crown-in-Parliament, such as reading the Speech from the Throne, giving royal assent to legislation, and proroguing or dissolving Parliament. This governmental side also includes the governor general as Crown-in-Council, meeting with the prime minister and ministers, dealing with the administration of government, and working, as statesman, to strengthen governmental institutions, as well as the sovereignty and the broader, international interests of the country.

The cultural side involves the governor general reaching out to Canadians through travel and speeches, meeting and "forging emotional ties with people from all parts of society."[8] These are actions that create a sense of greater community and contribute to unity. It is in this area as well that the governor general encourages excellence, "celebrating in public," to help build pride in, and encourage service to, one's country, and to humanity, in and through "all forms of cultural endeavour."[9]

The "Introduction" consists of a biographical sketch of John Buchan and a sketch of Canada in the 1930s. The objective of the five sections is to compose a rich and meaningful picture of this individual of many talents and accomplishments, converging with this emerging sovereign country of many resources and opportunities.

A Fortuitous Convergence

"His Majesty the King has been graciously pleased to approve the appointment of Mr. John Buchan, Companion of Honour, Member of Parliament, as Governor-General of Canada, upon the retirement in the fall of this year of His Excellency the Earl of Bessborough."[1] Acting Prime Minister Sir George Perley, standing in for a seriously ill Richard B. Bennett, read this official announcement in the House of Commons on Wednesday, March 27, 1935. The leader of His Majesty's Loyal Opposition, Mackenzie King, rejoined: "I think the appointment is an excellent one."[2]

The brief, routine-sounding statement signalled a significant change. A "Mr." was replacing an earl; that is, an untitled man was replacing the traditional lord. The ordinariness of the announcement also belied momentous changes that had occurred in the British Empire and in Canada's constitutional status. And even though R.B. Bennett, as prime minister, officially proposed John Buchan's name to King George V, it was the opposition leader, Mackenzie King, who tingled with delight.[3]

The reading public at the time knew that John Buchan was a famous author and, from the announcement at least, that he was a member of Parliament. But most knew little else. Who was this man who was coming to Canada to represent the king, and what was the country like that he was coming to?

Part I: A Superbly Cumulative and Integrated Life

When he arrived in Canada, the writer with the immense reputation surprised many people by his small stature.[4] He had a wiry toughness about him, formed in part from a stoicism in the face of poor health but also from his love of the outdoors, of fishing, hiking, and mountaineering. A high forehead, with a prominent and rather large round scar on the left of it, the result of a childhood accident, was accented by high cheekbones. Drawing a straight line across the lean visage was a thin, set mouth that spoke silently of determination. His step was described as a "springy gait [that] suggested he was walking on sponges."[5]

Apart from the accident that had left him with the scar and bedridden for almost a year at five years old, John Buchan had had a happy childhood.[6] He was born on August 26, 1875, in Perth, Scotland. His father, also John Buchan, was a Free Church of Scotland minister. His mother, born Helen Masterton, was the daughter of a sheep farmer at Broughton Green in the Scottish Borders.

Shortly after the younger John's birth, the family moved to Pathhead, a small town on the north side of the Firth of Forth, opposite Edinburgh, where the family lived for the next twelve years. Mrs. Buchan ran a disciplined household and the religious routine was what one would expect living in a manse in the late nineteenth century. From his father, though, John heard more than Bible verse. Old Scottish ballads, folktales, and adventure stories filled the house. The imagination fired from these stories was stoked even more by the natural environment that surrounded his youth. His summers were spent with his maternal grandparents in Broughton Green, where he played freely among the hills and streams of the surrounding countryside, which had seen battles long past.

The family moved to Glasgow when John was thirteen. His father served a parish in the Gorbals, a working-class area and a social challenge to the minister. Here the young John attended Hutchesons' Grammar School. It was a formative period and one that left a lasting link. In future years, whenever he travelled he always took delight when he met other "Hutchies." Here he learned much of the basis of his civilization, studying Greek and Latin literature under the influence of a teacher that Buchan biographer, Janet Adam Smith, describes as "outstanding," a teacher who transmitted the "intrinsic greatness" and "continuing significance" of the humanities.[7] In October 1892 Buchan's promising future was signalled when he was admitted to Glasgow University with two bursaries, for a general Master of Arts degree, covering Latin, Greek, mathematics, logic, moral philosophy, natural science, and history.[8]

It was at Glasgow University that Buchan came into contact with several more outstanding professors, including Gilbert Murray, the professor of Greek, who had been appointed to the position while still only twenty-three years old. Murray subsequently went on to a long and distinguished career, maintaining contact with this student who had impressed him as "obviously a treasure." The student had asked him why Francis Bacon had quoted the Greek philosopher Democritus in Latin; the seventeen-year-old student was working for a London publisher, editing a book of Bacon's essays![9]

Buchan became imbued with the classics. His imagination and initiative took hold of his energy and channelled it into writing. He published stories and articles in the university magazine and elsewhere. His first book, the collection of Bacon's essays, was published in 1894. The next year, he published his first novel, *Sir Quixote of the Moors*, which he dedicated to Gilbert Murray. A reputation was being established.

From Glasgow a scholarship to Brasenose College, Oxford, followed in October 1895. It was here that Buchan's writing began to blossom. In 1896 he published a book of essays, *Scholar Gypsies*, followed by two more novels, *John Burnet of Barns* in 1898, and *A Lost Lady of Old Years* in 1899, as well as a collection of short stories, *Grey Weather*, that same year. He also published short stories in *The Yellow Book*, a quarterly, bound publication and one of the best known and avant-garde literary magazines of the time.[10] From his first year at Oxford, he was a paid literary advisor to publisher John Lane. Not only was his reputation as a writer growing, but he was now starting to have an income that paid his way. This was all on top of his regular academic work and social life at the university, which included long hikes to London and Cambridge. These were early indicators of his capacity and capability.

It was also at Oxford that Buchan came in contact with many individuals who would become lifelong friends or colleagues. Most of Buchan's friends at university were from middle-class, professional backgrounds, but his circle was wide, including Raymond Asquith, son of a prime minister, writer and poet Hilaire Belloc, and Tommy Nelson, a future business partner in publishing. His continuing literary work in London for John Lane put him in contact with an even wider acquaintance and with business life. In his third year, he was elected president of the Union, Oxford's debating society, in which he had participated since his first year. He graduated with a "First in Greats," that is, top of his class in a humanities program.

Buchan set objectives for himself in writing and his career. On leaving Oxford he set his sights on the law. This period was, however, not without setback. He had applied for a fellowship in history at All Souls College, Oxford, a position that would have been "a tremendous help to a young man starting at the [b]ar."[11] He was not accepted. It was a bitter blow, and he tried a second time the next year. He was rejected again. Both times he received many letters of support, including, for his second attempt, from Cosmo Lang, ten years his senior and future archbishop of Canterbury.[12] He let it go and moved on in 1900 to work at a law office in London. That year, he published another novel, *The Half-Hearted*.

He was called to the bar in 1901. During this period he began editing and writing for *The Spectator*, bought in 1898 by John St Loe Strachey. Among the many commentaries Buchan wrote, one in July 1901 dealt with Canada, including a prescient description of what would captivate him completely when he arrived in Canada as governor general: "Canada is essentially a country of the larger air, where men can still face the old primeval forces of Nature and be braced into vigour, and withal so beautiful that it can readily inspire that romantic patriotism which is one of the most priceless assets of a people."[13] His commentaries in *The Spectator* included one about the refugee camps established by the British during the Boer War: "We have to remember that our charges, while they are the relatives of our enemies, are also the stock of our future citizens. We have to preserve good temper, patience and humanity, knowing that every misfortune will be only too readily interpreted as a crime."[14] He was able to take what seemed a small, if controversial, issue and place it in a strategic context — the characteristics of a statesman were developing.

Not long after being called to the bar, Buchan's life took an adventurous turn. Lord Milner, high commissioner for Southern Africa and governor of Cape Colony, had taken notice of *The Spectator* article and Buchan's views on the refugee camps, and inquired about the author. He asked the twenty-six-year-old lawyer, journalist, and author to join his staff. Buchan accepted the offer and spent two formative years in South Africa. He was assigned responsibility for the refugee camps, over which Milner had secured civilian administration from Lord Kitchener's army. The camps were filled with Boer women and children whose husbands and fathers had surrendered to the British, and who now were at risk of retribution, from Boers still fighting and from Africans; other camps were for Africans. Conditions in both were appalling and death rates high.

Milner was satisfied with Buchan's work, which dramatically reduced the death rates, and subsequently gave him responsibility for land settlement, buying farms in the Transvaal and providing land for British settlers.[15] It was done through the Crown Lands Disposal Act, which, Smith notes, was "mainly Buchan's work."[16] He was gaining experience of British policy being implemented and was learning first-hand from the master administrator, Milner. He also watched how visiting politicians, such as Joseph Chamberlain, the colonial secretary, approached the issues. It was the richest kind of experience for the young men who were dubbed Milner's "kindergarten."[17] Here Buchan also came in contact with troops from the Dominions, learning about their perspectives. It helped to shape his views of the Empire. He learned about war and human suffering, about recovery from war, about living in the outdoors.

As part of his job, he rode horseback across wild terrain, experienced the beautiful ruggedness of the country, and met a wide variety of humanity. It was physically challenging. While these experiences had specific purpose, they also fired his imagination. He delighted in it all.[18] He wrote of many of his experiences in *The African Colony*, published in 1903, and would use those experiences and his accumulated knowledge of the country, the characters, and legends in many of his adventure novels. His principal character, Richard Hannay, had been a mining engineer in South Africa. When Hannay returned to England, he discovered how staid it was and how stark was the contrast between life in England and his former life in the far reaches of the Empire.[19] It wasn't unlike Buchan's own sentiments on his return to London where he picked up his legal work and writing for *The Spectator* again.[20]

Four years after his return to England, Buchan published *A Lodge in the Wilderness*, a discussion of Empire by a group of British citizens, nine men and nine women, staying at a lodge in East Africa.[21] The host was modelled on Cecil Rhodes. One of the nine men was Canadian. The book was intended to be "a means of revivifying the cause [of Empire]," and has been cited and analyzed as a key to Buchan's understanding and evolving views of the British Empire.[22] His time in South Africa, where he first really was able to meet individuals from all the Dominions in any numbers, had a profound impact on his views. "I realised," Buchan wrote, "that Britain had at least as much to learn from them as they had from Britain.... I began to see that the Empire ... might be a potent and beneficent force in the world."[23]

His barrister's life in London dealt with less exhilarating subjects. He published *The Law Relating to the Taxation of Foreign Income* in 1905. This period was relieved, however, by holidays to Switzerland and Scotland, mountain climbing, and hiking. He was elected to the Alpine Club in 1906, as a result of recounting his experiences in *The African Colony* and of articles he had written in *Blackwood's Magazine*.

It was also during this period, in 1905, that he met Susan Grosvenor, the daughter of a cousin of the Duke of Westminster and grand-nephew of the Duke of Wellington. As he thought about marriage, he also thought about income, and so spoke with his friend Tommy Nelson, who had suggested he join their publishing firm, Thomas Nelson and Sons, as editor and literary advisor. His task was to revive the firm's fortunes, which he did with great success. John and Susan were subsequently married, in July 1907, by the then bishop of Stepney, Cosmo Lang. A honeymoon trip took them through Austria to northern Italy and Venice. Their first child, Alice, was born a year later, in June 1908.

At Nelson's, Buchan also edited the weekly *Scottish Review*, contributing to each edition articles on a wide range of issues, from domestic politics to international relations and the Empire. His interest continued in the evolving sentiments of the Dominions and the issue of sovereignty. In one contribution, written in 1908, he wrote of Canada's desire to conclude her own treaties.[24] At this same time, he also continued to write for *The Spectator* and contributed to the *The Times Literary Supplement*. More novels and short stories flowed from his mind and pen, sometimes stimulated by foreign trips: to Constantinople (now Istanbul), Greece, and the Aegean in 1910; to Bavaria in 1911 to visit with Moritz Bonn and his wife; 1912 to Norway; and 1913 to the Azores. In each of those years, a book was published.[25]

It was also during this period that Buchan finally acted on an option he had considered since South Africa — politics. He was selected in the spring of 1911 as a candidate for the Unionist party in the Scottish riding of Peebles and Selkirk. The Unionists were Scottish conservatives who wanted to preserve the union with England. That suited him, but his intellect and independence of mind did not allow him to blindly accept politically partisan policies.[26] As with any of his endeavours, he undertook it enthusiastically and seriously. It was a large constituency and his canvassing of it became a strain on his health.

Through 1910 and 1911, Buchan's parents had serious health problems that weighed on him, too. But happier events arrived with the birth of the Buchans' second child, John, in 1911. The following year, however, Buchan's brother Willie, who had returned from administrative service in Bengal, died. It was a blow because the two had been great friends as well as brothers.

It was around this time, too, that the "sporadic attacks of indigestion" he had formerly suffered from only occasionally became more serious.[27] Amidst these personal and emotional challenges, he continued to work the political ground in Peebles and Selkirk, and to write and to work for Nelson's. It was not a schedule to alleviate his digestive problems, which forced him to bed more often for rest. It was during one of these prescribed rests, this one a cruise to the Azores in 1913, that "he determined to amuse himself ... by 'writing a real shocker.'" *The Power-House*, a story of a master criminal who insinuates himself into the governing class of Britain, was serialized in *Blackwood's Magazine* in December that year.

It is in this novel that a recurring theme, one that was of importance not just in his novels but to the man himself, too, is neatly phrased: "You think that a wall as solid as the earth separates civilization from barbarism. I tell you the division is a thread, a sheet of glass."[28]

In the late summer of 1914, John, Susan, and their two children retreated to Broadstairs, east from London, on the Kentish coast. The purpose was to have a rest for Alice, who had just had surgery, and for John himself, who was suffering from his digestive disorder. At Broadstairs he began writing another shocker. It would not be completed until another bedrest had been ordered for him in November, after the war had started. He sent *The Thirty-Nine Steps* to *Blackwood's* at the beginning of December. It was a spy novel in which the unassuming hero, Richard Hannay, is falsely accused of murder, having stumbled on a German plot to steal British naval plans. It was serialized in *Blackwood's* beginning in July 1915, then published in book form. Sales took off immediately.

Buchan had not been able to enter the army because of his poor health, an acute point of frustration for him. The war brought other stresses, also. His political aspirations were blown up by the war, and Nelson's business began to suffer as a result of the war. The firm decided to publish a readable history of events as they occurred. Buchan wrote it, all of it, in twenty-four volumes, the first published in February 1915. The profits and the author's royalties went to a fund for families of Nelson's employees who were serving in the military. Buchan's commitment to, and huge volume of work for, the firm was rewarded with a directorship in the company in 1915.

In the spring of 1915, Buchan started giving lectures on the war. His clear and concise way of explaining the complexities attracted the attention of the *Times*, and he was asked if he would be their special correspondent to report from the Front on the Second Battle of Ypres. He did, starting in May 1915, and it brought him in contact with General Sir Douglas Haig and other senior military leaders, including Julian Byng, whom he had met in South Africa and who would later become governor general of Canada (1921–1926).

When he had completed his work in Belgium, Buchan returned to England and continued his writing and lectures. By this time both the War Office and the Foreign Office became interested in using his talents. He was commissioned as a lieutenant in the Intelligence Corps and returned to France. Buchan's writing and analytical abilities and understanding of the strategic dimensions were recognized, and he was promoted to the rank of major in early 1916 and worked for General Headquarters under General Charteris. In June he was charged with heading up the Information Department, responsible to the foreign secretary, Sir Edward Grey. It was a short tenure, because Haig, now commander in chief of the British Expeditionary Force, requested that the Foreign Office allow Buchan to serve on his headquarters staff in France until the end of the year. It was done.

All the while, Buchan had been writing another novel, *Greenmantle*, a war adventure about Richard Hannay uncovering a German attempt to direct an Islamic uprising against the British. It was published in 1916 (*The Power-House* was published in book form the same year). A third child, William, was born in January 1916.

Dissatisfaction with the conduct of the war prompted a change of government, and in December 1916 Lloyd George became prime minister. Shortly thereafter a decision was taken to establish a department of information to deal with propaganda. Buchan returned to England in January 1917. He was appointed director of information in early February and began engaging staff. At the same time, he was promoted to lieutenant-colonel.

His approach was to base information for the public on facts, not fabricated stories. It was his gift for quick analysis and his ability to translate the complexities of strategy and tactics into understandable language that continually increased his value to the war effort. Charteris wrote, "Now that we have Buchan in charge in London, things, I think, will gradually improve in the Press Bureau."[29] The department's productions, both the fact-based articles, which were usually accompanied by photographs, and the films, were important components to help maintain morale at home and at the Front. However, Buchan was anxious to strengthen the role of the department even more. He established a British Information Bureau in New York. Speakers from Britain lectured in the United States. The objective of these initiatives was to strengthen American support for Britain.

In late February 1917, he underwent surgery to alleviate what had been diagnosed as a duodenal ulcer. He ignored recuperation and kept working.

In March of that year, his long-time friend and business partner, Tommy Nelson, was killed, and in April, his brother Alastair. Even before this, he had come to detest war for its brutality and tragedy.[30] The films and photos produced by his Department of Information brought the reality of the horror before the public.

With changes in the administration of the War Cabinet, Buchan was having difficulties accessing Prime Minister Lloyd George. The situation became acute and Buchan recommended that a ministry be established so there could be representation at Cabinet level, to better look after the interests of information and propaganda. In February 1918 a Ministry of Information was created, with Lord Beaverbrook (the Canadian Max Aitken) as minister and Buchan as director of intelligence, reporting to him. The ministry thrived under Beaverbrook. Buchan's work was made less frustrating. Following the Armistice on November 11, 1918, Buchan was instructed to wind down the ministry, transferring to other ministries any activities that were not discontinued. The war had exhausted him, as it had many others, as well as the country. It was time to reconstruct and to heal.

Buchan looked forward to a new life. To his young family was added another son, Alastair, born in September 1918. As a central part of the new life, he wanted country serenity. He and Susan bought a manor house in the Cotswolds, near Oxford, an area where they had taken a short holiday in the early fall of 1917. Given his position at Nelson's, he needed to have easy access to transportation to London. They found the manor house of the village of Elsefield to be ideal. It was a short distance from Oxford. He could settle in to a life of publishing, writing, and spending time with his family in the country. His income allowed him to have staff to look after the grounds and house.

In 1919 he was appointed to the board of directors of Reuters, a news organization he had had dealings with during the war. That year he also published another Richard Hannay novel, *Mr. Standfast*, and completed *Nelson's History of the War*.

Elsefield became a stopping place for many people, and he was not far from other old friends, including Gilbert Murray and Fred Oliver, who had worked for him in the Department of Information.[31] T.E. Lawrence would stop by unexpectedly on his motorcycle. Other guests were regularly there: Violet Markham, Leo Amery, and Robert Cecil, as well as professors and young students from Oxford. He spoke to various groups at Oxford and delighted in his exchanges with the undergraduates. It was a pleasant life, but the problem with his duodenal ulcer had not been eliminated by the surgery. As Smith wrote: "He had in the end to face the fact that a constant carefulness about his food, a constant slight discomfort and, every few months, a crippling bout of pain, were the conditions upon which his life had to be lived."[32]

For the next eight years, Buchan's output was prodigious: history, fiction, contemporary commentary. Fifteen books were published in these years, including a memoir of Lord Minto (1924), another Scottish borderer, who had been governor general of Canada from 1898 to 1904. Through this book in particular, Buchan learned about the viceregal role, though it would be changing significantly in the mid-1920s. His earlier knowledge of Canada was expanded and his appreciation deepened about its growing national sentiment. The Buchans' close friend, Violet Markham, was a long-time friend of the now Canadian prime minister, Mackenzie King. She had in fact introduced them in 1919, when King travelled to Britain, before he had re-entered Canadian politics. In conversations with Buchan, she would undoubtedly have discussed Canadian matters and referred to Mackenzie King. Buchan's continuing interest in the Empire, particularly after the war, would have to incorporate new information and attitudes. During the war the Dominions had demanded more say about policies and decisions affecting them. They attended the Treaty of Versailles negotiations and subsequently became independent members of the League of Nations.

In September 1923 Buchan was appointed deputy chairman of Reuters. In that capacity, the following year, he planned to travel to New York and Boston. Aware of this, likely through Violet Markham,

Mackenzie King invited the Buchans to Ottawa on their way to the States. It was an enchanting visit for King and "raised [his] emotional and spiritual attraction to John Buchan."[33]

From Ottawa the Buchans travelled to Boston, where they were hosted by Ferris Greenslet, whom Buchan had met during the war and who was now a partner in the publishing firm of Houghton Mifflin, Buchan's American publisher. Greenslet accompanied the Buchans to Washington, where John Buchan met President Wilson. Aside from Reuters business and his time with Greenslet, Buchan had been invited to give an inaugural address at Milton Academy in Massachusetts, a boys' school, where a foundation had been established for an annual lecture to honour those graduates who had been killed in the Great War.[34] The Buchans also spent ten days touring Civil War sites, an event of keen interest to Buchan.[35] It was clearly an opportunity for Buchan to know better this country he admired and to contribute to the "transatlantic relationship." This is a theme Michael Redley accurately describes as "among Buchan's most important articles of faith in his adult years."[36]

After their lengthy sojourn to the States, the Buchans returned to Canada, first travelling to Ottawa, where they visited with Governor General Lord Byng. Montreal was next, where Buchan met with former Canadian prime minister Sir Robert Borden and General Sir Arthur Currie, chancellor of McGill University. Finally, they travelled to Toronto, where Vincent Massey hosted them, visiting Hart House at the University of Toronto, a centre for undergraduate and graduate students the Masseys established and funded. Throughout his visits Buchan made numerous speeches, to Canadian clubs in the major cities and to other groups. He received high praise. Indeed, the visit was such a success, and Mackenzie King was so taken with the Buchans, that Violet Markham suggested to her prime ministerial friend in 1925 that Buchan might succeed Byng as governor general.

Any thoughts of that would have to be postponed, however, for Buchan was soon to find himself occupied with a new, if familiar, calling. Having long abandoned aspirations to enter politics, Buchan found his interest was rekindled in 1927. At that time there were constituencies for universities. A seat for the Scottish universities was vacated by the death of the incumbent and the Unionist Association approached Buchan. Here was an ideal opportunity. In his memoir, Buchan wrote: "It was the kind of constituency which suited me, for I was warned that my health would not stand the ordinary business of electioneering."[37] The by-election was held in April 1927 and he won with the widest of margins.

Buchan's political career has been amply described by his biographers and others, but some points merit highlighting.[38] His absence of thirteen years from political life had not modified his approach to party politics. He could still not be a partisan politician. His belief in democracy had strengthened after the war. He had faith in "the ordinary man" and his "hard sense."[39] He defined democracy as "a spiritual testament, and not an economic structure or a political machine"; it was a testament with basic beliefs: "that the personality was sacrosanct, which was the meaning of liberty; that policy should be settled by free discussion; that normally a minority should be ready to yield to a majority, which in turn should respect a minority's sacred things."[40] And he believed in the Empire, but his views had evolved into a strong belief in the new Empire as it was defined by the Imperial Conference of 1926 and the 1931 Statute of Westminster. The Empire, or Commonwealth when referring to Britain and the self-governing Dominions, was now a body of constitutionally equal nations, "a community of free nations ... under one King."[41] He had long ago, in 1908 in fact, recognized that the "Colony [Canada] is becoming a nation, and wants national attributes."[42]

In Parliament he had as colleagues old friends like Leo Amery, Walter Elliot, and Robert Cecil, and would associate with new colleagues like Ramsay MacDonald, Harold Macmillan, and Victor Cazalet. Over the years he enjoyed the company and discussion of members from all parties, and particularly the Scot "Red Clydesiders."[43] He looked forward to his parliamentary career, especially since his "outlook and temperament" were in sympathy with Stanley Baldwin, whose politics were described as "progressive Conservatism."[44] Buchan's maiden speech in the House — a Labour vote of censure on government measures to reinstate certain powers to the House of Lords — was received with acclaim.

Buchan never attained the Cabinet, though he desired it, but he became a confidant to Prime Ministers Baldwin, Conservative, and Ramsay MacDonald, Labour. This is, Lord Stewartby remarks, "an enormous testament to the wisdom and judgement which people at the top of the Government, whatever their party, thought about JB."[45] His life in Parliament was, nonetheless, the culmination of his belief that service to the public good through politics was "the greatest and the most honourable adventure."[46]

Buchan's participation in parliamentary debate and his activities covered a wide range of topics, from his expected constituency interests of universities and education, including adult education, through unemployment and local government, to defence and the importance of air power.[47] He also had great sympathy for many Labour issues, and, indeed, would at times vote against his own party.[48] During a debate in May 1932, on a Sunday Entertainments Bill, he proposed that 5 percent of the Sunday revenues from cinemas be provided for establishing a film institute. The British Film Institute was established the following year in October and Buchan became a governor and chairman of its advisory committee.[49] He was chairman of the School Age Council and campaigned to raise the school-leaving age to fifteen.[50] He chaired the parliamentary Palestine Committee, committed to assisting Jews settle in Palestine. He also made contributions to "the shaping of Conservative Party institutions," including political education.[51] He was chairman of the executive committee of the Conservative and Unionist Educational Institute and was involved in planning for a Students Unionist Federation. In 1934 he was a member of a Conservative Party committee responsible for choosing two candidates to represent the Oxford University seat in Parliament. And at Oxford itself, he was inaugural president of the Oxford Exploration Club, an association he continued after becoming governor general.[52]

If continuing to write at least a book a year, including major biographies of Sir Walter Scott (1932) and Cromwell (1934), was not enough for the active MP, around 1930 he also began writing a regular column in a biweekly magazine called *The Graphic* and writing the Atticus column for the *Sunday Times*. The same year (1930), Buchan and Baldwin were involved with the establishment of the Pilgrim Trust, financed by an American of British descent. They were allowed to interpret their mandate broadly and included relations between Britain and America.

In 1933 Prime Minister Ramsay MacDonald asked Buchan to be lord high commissioner to the General Assembly of the Church of Scotland. Buchan had maintained his connection to the Church as an elder for more than twenty years and had written a history with George Adam Smith, *The Kirk in Scotland*. As commissioner he represented the Crown during the ten-day assembly, accompanied by much ceremony and pomp. It was a role he filled with aplomb, such that he was reappointed the following year. It was a demonstration of his ability to carry out public ceremonies with dignity and sincerity. Stanley Baldwin, then leader of the opposition, and Mackenzie King, via Violet Markham, took notice. Mackenzie King, for his part, revived Violet Markham's decade-old idea of having Buchan as governor general.

Part II: A Promised Land Beset

On his visit to Canada in 1924, John Buchan made a remark to Prime Minister Mackenzie King, from a vantage point in the Gatineau Hills overlooking the Ottawa valley, that suggested Canada was a promised land. The 1920s certainly held promise after the disruption of the Great War, a war the British Empire had fought as one, but which also saw countries of the Empire demanding more say for themselves. Canada was still in a chrysalis-like state, however, emerging from the cocoon of the "Mother Country." It was a period in which the country was trying to define itself as capable of full autonomy, especially after its sacrifices during the war. At the same time, it was feeling the ever stronger gravitational pull of the economic and cultural giant to the south. By the time John Buchan arrived as governor general in November 1935, however, the country was sorely challenged, its earlier promise obscured by economic depression, Prairie drought, and federal-provincial discord.

Through the period before World War One, the Dominions had achieved control over their domestic affairs, but some, including Canada, were looking to extend that to aspects of their foreign relations, which remained largely an Imperial prerogative. Canada's prime minister through the first decade of the twentieth century was the Liberal Sir Wilfrid Laurier, who was loyal to the Crown and Empire but who was also giving greater voice to Canada. When Britain declared war in 1914, the Dominions were automatically at war also, but they asserted some autonomy by having their parliaments determine the extent of their participation.

As the war progressed, the Dominions claimed greater participation in policies that affected them. As Margaret Macmillan wrote, by 1916 "[t]he dominions knew how important their contribution was, ... they now expected to be consulted, both on the war and the peace to follow."[53] When the Armistice was signed and negotiations begun that culminated in the Treaty of Versailles in 1919, Canada insisted on a seat at the table.[54]

One of the key outcomes of those meetings was the League of Nations, created to avoid war and promote peaceful settlement of disputes. Canada and the other Dominions became League members in their own right. However, the United States was not a member, because its president at the time, Woodrow Wilson, who had been a leading advocate of such a concept, could not counter the strong isolationist current in his country. Nazi Germany and militarist Japan withdrew from the League in 1933. Japan had invaded and occupied Manchuria two years before that.

After the Great War, there followed several years of the push and pull between those who believed in a full-blooded form of Imperialism and those pushing for a greater degree of Dominion autonomy in foreign relations. There were attempts to formulate a common Imperial foreign policy. These attempts were put to rest as a result of what became known as the Chanak Incident in 1922.

The British government acted to commit troops to defend neutral territory along the Dardenelles Strait from the new, revolutionary Turkish government under Kemal Ataturk. It did so without consulting the Dominions.[55] Canadian prime minister Mackenzie King replied to his British counterpart, Lloyd George, that the Canadian Parliament would have to authorize the commitment of any troops. This effectively sealed a new relationship within the Empire. Canada, and the other Dominions, would no longer automatically be bound by any decision of the British government. This was the beginning of what Canadian historian MacGregor Dawson described as the period of decentralization, which culminated in the Imperial Conference of 1926 and the beginning of a "period of equal status."[56]

The 1926 Conference established a committee to examine inter-Imperial relations, under the chairmanship of a former prime minister, Arthur Balfour. The committee issued a report in November that year, acknowledging the "very different stages of evolution" of the Empire's component parts. In particular, it noted that the Dominions "are autonomous Communities within the British Empire, equal in status, in no way subordinate one to another in any aspect of their domestic or external affairs, though united by a common allegiance to the Crown, and freely associated as members of the British Commonwealth of Nations."[57]

This was a recognition of the reality of how the Dominions had evolved through periods of violent international affairs. John Buchan later wrote that Balfour had seen the "inevitable development of the Empire."[58] Buchan also believed this conference was "the most important event in the history of the Empire."[59]

The Balfour report also dealt with the role of the governors general, recalling that the previous June, Canadian prime minister Mackenzie King, leading a minority government, had clashed with Governor General Lord Byng over a request for the dissolution of Parliament. That controversy, known as the "King-Byng affair," was a catalyst to discussions during the 1926 Conference.[60] Balfour's report noted that "an essential consequence of the equality of status [is that] the Governor-General of a Dominion is the representative of the Crown ... he is not the representative or agent of His Majesty's Government in Great Britain or of any Department of that Government."[61]

Four years later, in November 1930, another Imperial conference was held in London, essentially to discuss preparation of legislation dealing with inter-Imperial relations, and to give effect to resolutions from the 1926 Conference. Additionally, it passed resolutions regarding the primacy of Dominion legislation — from that point forward, laws passed in the United Kingdom did not apply to the Dominions. On this issue there were special representations made to the Canadian prime minister from some provinces concerned their rights under the British North America

Act might be negatively affected. The report also picked up the issue of appointing governors general and provided detail as to the procedure. Specifically, it noted that the only "interested parties" were the king and the Dominion, and that His Majesty would be advised by and act on the advice of his ministers in the Dominion.[62]

In July of 1930, however, five months prior to the November 1930 Imperial Conference, the Liberals under Mackenzie King were defeated by R.B. Bennett's Conservatives in a federal election. Bennett was therefore the one attending the Imperial Conference that fall. However, he did not deviate from the path of declaring Dominion autonomy that was now established.

With these changes now in place, it fell to Bennett to make a decision on who should serve as successor to Governor General Lord Willingdon, whose term was due to end. Bennett received unsolicited advice. An organization called the Native Sons of Canada had branches across the country. They sent letters and formal resolutions to Prime Minister Bennett requesting that a "native son" be governor general.[63] Australia had Sir Isaac Isaacs, an Australian, as their governor general. The newspapers discussed the implications of the 1930 Imperial Conference that officially cut the British government out of the process of nominating the king's representative.[64] Bennett was also receiving letters from private individuals who suggested Canadian-born individuals such as Sir Robert Borden or Sir Arthur Currie.[65]

The politician Bennett did not deviate from the established path at the 1930 Imperial Conference, and neither did the imperialist Bennett deviate from nominating peers of the United Kingdom. In fact, there was no desire on Bennett's part to imitate Australia. Rather, he believed it preferable to have a governor general from Britain to ensure detachment from Canadian politics, should the constitutional need arise to exercise the viceregal powers.[66] As a result Lord Bessborough, a member of Parliament until he inherited his father's earldom in 1920, as well as a businessman (he was a deputy chairman of De Beers Mines), was appointed by King George V on February 9, 1931.

Even though Bennett recommended another British lord for governor general, a new practice was established with the simultaneous announcement from Ottawa and Buckingham Palace of Lord Bessborough's appointment.[67] It emphasized that the appointment was between the sovereign and his Canadian government. Bessborough was sworn in on his arrival at Halifax in April 1931.

On the eleventh of December that year, the British Parliament, with the agreement of the Dominions, passed "an Act to give effect to certain resolutions passed by Imperial Conferences held in the years 1926 and 1930," known as the Statute of Westminster, 1931. It was a brief document, of only twelve articles.[68] The preamble notes the United Kingdom and the six Dominions "did concur in making the declarations and resolutions set forth in the Reports of the said Conferences," which thus gave a legal basis to the Dominions' advising their sovereign on whom to appoint as governor general.[69] The preamble also proclaimed "that no law hereafter made by the Parliament of the United Kingdom shall extend to any of the said Dominions as part of the law of that Dominion otherwise than at the request and with the consent of that Dominion."

There was also a paragraph that stated that "any alteration in the law touching the Succession to the Throne or the Royal Style and Titles shall hereafter require the assent as well of the Parliaments of all the Dominions...."[70] The drafters could not know this paragraph would take centre stage in a crisis a short five years later.

Article 3 of the Statute gave the Dominions "full power to make laws having extra-territorial operation," that is autonomy over their external, or foreign, affairs.[71]

A new constitutional chapter remained to be written for Canada in the wake of the Statute, but it would take time before many Canadians would become aware of or fully appreciate its significance for the country and for its role in the world.

In the meantime a looming European crisis would distract Canada — indeed, the whole world — for many years to come. As Canadian historian Blair Neatby has noted: "European crises were like remote earthquakes or famines; they made the headlines but they were soon forgotten."[72] By 1935, however, some politicians and interested Canadians had begun to take note of what was happening across the Atlantic. There was concern about the rise of dictators in Europe and fear that another European war in which Britain would be involved would also drag Canada into it. This sentiment was shared by pacifists throughout Canada, but was nowhere more significant than in Quebec, where the life of the majority French-speaking population was dominated by the Catholic Church and business largely dominated by the English-speaking elite in Montreal.

In Parliament, debate was expanding. Minister of Justice Hugh Guthrie, responding in the House of Commons to J.S. Woodsworth, leader of the Commonwealth Co-operative Federation (CCF), during a lengthy debate on international affairs in the House of Commons on April 1, 1935, stated that Canada would from now on "have to assume an international view of many questions which a few years ago we considered as entirely foreign to [our] interests."[73]

The respected London-based weekly *The Economist* welcomed the wide-ranging Canadian debate, commenting that England recognized that the United States "must play a determining part in Canada's foreign policy [but] by the same token, Canadians will understand that Great Britain is a European country and can no more contract out of Europe than Canada can contract out of America."[74]

Canadians may have been content to some extent to rest on their new status, as Neatby noted, but he also noted another factor contributing to Canadians' inward-looking tendency. The 1930 Imperial Conference and passage of the Statute of Westminster followed the onset of the Great Depression, heralded by the stock market crash in the United States in October 1929. The Depression "had forced Canadians to turn inwards, to concentrate on Canadian problems and to try to raise themselves from the slough of economic stagnation by their own bootstraps."[75]

Bread lines, "Bennett buggies," and beggars knocking on doors to ask for food and lodging in exchange for performing chores.[76] These words evoke just a few images of the desperation and the forced poverty of the Great Depression.

The country's population stood around 10.2 million people in 1930. Montreal was Canada's largest city, with over 800,000 residents;

it was followed by Toronto, which had over 600,000 inhabitants, and Vancouver, with just a quarter million. The trend to urbanization meant that almost 30 percent of the population lived in seven cities by 1931, but Maritime cities stagnated.[77] There were 1.2 million automobiles registered and 1.4 million telephones in use, the numbers of both of which declined as the Depression dragged into middle of the decade.[78] More than one quarter of the working population was unemployed by 1933, feeding the bread lines that were common sights in the cities.[79]

On the East Coast, the "Atlantic fishing industry remained troubled."[80] In the West, the Prairies were parched from drought. Farms were abandoned and the wooden structures that were once active family homes and full barns were transformed into skeletal reminders of the misery. The situation was desperate, with two-thirds of the rural population in Saskatchewan, for example, on some form of government relief. Provincial government finances couldn't support the requirements for adequate relief.[81] The consequent impact on federal-provincial relations was harsh. It was a time that forced greater government involvement in the economy and the lives of Canadians to mitigate the circumstances that were taking such a toll in human and social terms.[82]

Mackenzie King's Liberals ran the government through the "Roaring Twenties" until both the decade and the Liberals crashed into the Great Depression. King, the central Canadian politician, labour specialist, and advocate of correcting the ills of industrialization, didn't seem to understand the seriousness of the darkening environment, including the unemployment, and would not offer financial support to provincial governments, particularly Conservative-led ones. He "would not give them a five-cent piece."[83]

King called an election but subsequently regretted it. The Conservatives, under Bennett, won that July 1930 election, the first election in which radio was a major tool for campaigning.[84] Indeed, radio was emerging as a significant social and cultural vehicle. A royal commission set up in 1928 resulted in the creation by Bennett's government in 1932 of the Canadian Radio Broadcasting Commission. It would be replaced four years later by the Canadian Broadcasting Corporation.

In response to the devastating economic conditions and their potentially dangerous social consequences, the Bennett government established
relief camps to provide shelter and some form of work for unemployed
young men. The relief camps, initially run by the Department of National
Defence, provided food and crude lodging for the men, putting them to
work building, repairing, or improving infrastructure such as roads, dig-
ging ditches, or planting trees, for twenty cents a day.

Canada was not suffering alone, of course. The United States and
Britain were also grappling with the impact of the Great Depression. U.S.
President Franklin Roosevelt, elected in 1932, had introduced various
programs that became known as the "New Deal," designed to alleviate
some of the economic and social suffering.

With a greater sense of urgency, the British Empire rescheduled an
Imperial conference, a conference that had been postponed, to deal with
economic issues. Canada was host in July 1932 to the prime ministers
from the United Kingdom and the other Dominions. Bennett was an
ardent Imperialist and he supported conference attempts to restore and
strengthen trade within the Empire through reducing tariffs amongst
themselves while setting up tariffs to the outside. Preparation, however,
was slow. This has been attributed to the weakness, i.e., inexperience, of
the Canadian civil service at the time, but it also was a result of organizers
having to wait for Bennett, who wanted to be involved in the preparation.[85] The conference did not achieve the desired goals, though it was
not a complete failure, because bilateral agreements resulted, including
one between Britain and Canada benefitting Canadian exports.[86]

Internationally, the increase in protectionist tariffs by many countries during the years following the Depression exacerbated conditions
even more. As export prices fell, governments promoted export production through increased debt, but the export production growth
was held back by tariff restrictions. As the Rowell-Sirois Report noted,
this situation "place[d] an increasing strain on public finance and
consequently on Dominion-provincial relations."[87] Wheat exports in
particular had performed well during the previous year and had in fact
been "the strongest dynamic factor making for east-west integration."[88]
This positive economic force now turned negative, with the federal

government having to prop up the Prairie provinces because of the effects of the Prairie drought and declining export markets for wheat.

In these dismal conditions, another political party germinated at the federal level: the Co-operative Commonwealth Federation (CCF). It was formed in 1932 in Alberta by a combination of individuals with socialist views, labour groups, and farmers' organizations.[89] At a meeting of the party in Regina in 1933, J.S. Woodsworth, a Methodist minister, was elected leader. Woodsworth had been a member of Parliament since 1921, representing a Winnipeg riding for a party he helped organize, the Independent Labour Party.[90] The CCF policy platform was outlined in their "Regina Manifesto," which advocated greater government involvement in the economy to temper the excesses of industrialism and capitalism through, for example, the nationalization of certain industries, and the creation of universal pensions, and health, welfare, and unemployment insurance programs. In Quebec nationalists, under Abbé Groulx, were becoming more vocal, and fascists, under Adrien Arcand, were a not insignificant factor in the province.

Around this same time, and quite independent of the economic issues, another dimension of Bennett's Imperial orientation surfaced. It was symbolic of the continuing tension that existed between Canada's British heritage and its North American reality. In 1933 Bennett reintroduced the practice of recommending Canadians to the king for honours — including knighthoods, which came with the title "Sir." It was a practice that had been discontinued in 1919, following a recommendation from a parliamentary committee chaired by W.F. Nickle, Conservative MP for Kingston, Ontario. The recommendation requested that His Majesty "refrain hereafter from conferring any title of honour or titular distinction upon any of his subjects domiciled or ordinarily resident in Canada."[91] In the House of Commons, which then had a Unionist government led by Sir Robert Borden, a motion was passed on May 22, 1919, to give effect to the recommendation. It was not, however, statute. The establishment of the committee was in part due to a reaction to the surfeit of knighthoods awarded during the war — "as common as snowballs in Canada"[92] — and to unwarranted peerages, one given to Sir Hugh Graham, owner of the *Montreal Star*, who became Lord Atholstan.[93]

There was strong sentiment in Canada that equated titles with the class structure of Britain. For the most part, Canadians did not believe them appropriate in Canada, particularly hereditary titles. It was a characteristic embodied in United Empire Loyalists who had fled the American colonies during the revolution against Britain. There was no contradiction in remaining loyal to the Crown while not wanting to replicate class-layered British society here.[94]

Mackenzie King was ideologically opposed to titles and abhorred them.[95] This strong opinion ensured that no Canadians received titles while he was prime minister. Bennett's reinstatement of the practice of recommending Canadians for honours-conferring titles took into consideration the disrepute the process had accrued during the war. Care was taken in who was recommended. No one begrudged the two knighthoods announced in the king's New Year's Honours List, January 1, 1934, to the chief justice of Canada, Lyman Duff, and to the chief justice of Quebec, Joseph M. Tellier, nor criticized subsequent knighthoods, which included Dr. Frederick Banting and the composer Ernest MacMillan.[96]

Into the fourth year of Bennett's mandate, the effects of the Depression were taking their toll on support for the Conservatives. The situation of many provinces, particularly the Prairies and British Columbia, was continuing to deteriorate, taking federal-provincial relations down with it.[97] By the fall of 1934, the leader of His Majesty's Loyal Opposition, Mackenzie King, increasingly offered the partisan political view that the government had no right to govern because it lacked the confidence of the people, having lost in recent by-elections. King expected to win the next election and began to act like it.

In Ontario a June 1934 election saw voters elect a Liberal government, the first since 1905. In Quebec, under Liberal Premier Taschereau in the early 1930s, political change was bubbling. The Quebec Conservatives had elected Maurice Duplessis as leader in 1933. In 1935 Duplessis joined with disenchanted Liberals and nationalists to fight the election that year, but lost. He then formed a new party, the Union Nationale, and won a landslide victory in 1936.

The CCF and the Union Nationale were not the only new parties of the era. The social agitation and activism fomented by the Depression resulted in other alternative solutions to the economic and social problems. Another political party was formed out of the social credit movement in Alberta, under the Reverend "Bible Bill" Aberhart. The Alberta Social Credit Party went on to win a provincial election in August 1935, but the social credit concept of finance and banking dealt with areas of federal jurisdiction, creating an area of confrontation between the new provincial government and its federal counterpart.

Political unrest took other forms, too. The relief camps that had been established and that were filled with young, able-bodied men, began to boil over. In Vancouver, with support from organized communist workers, plans were set in motion for what has become another well-known image of the times, the "on-to-Ottawa trek."[98] The protesters left Vancouver on June 3, 1935, riding in and on railway freight cars. They were a couple thousand strong by the time they reached Regina. There the Dominion government determined to stop them. A *Toronto Star* reporter was accompanying the trekkers and reported on the event and the people in eye-witness detail as it progressed.[99] In Regina the protesters rallied downtown on Dominion Day. Violence broke out. A Regina policeman died and there were many injuries — a black eye for the Bennett government.

During this period the Bennett government made attempts to help mitigate the disastrous conditions on the sprawling, drought-stricken Prairies. In the spring of 1935, it set up the Prairie Farm Rehabilitation Administration (PFRA).[100] The PFRA Act was passed by Parliament in April 1935, and a year later was headquartered in Regina, researching, planning and building dams and irrigation canals and trying to prevent soil erosion. The same year the Bennett government created the Canadian Wheat Board to formalize support for Prairie wheat farmers and guarantee the Board's payments to farmers. With the reduction in wheat exports, the railways, those iron lines that had bound the country together east to west, suffered financially and the Dominion government was required to guarantee their survival. The Dominion government was also required to make transfers to provincial governments, to assist with relief and to prevent defaults, which in turn would have cut essential services, compounding social problems.[101] It was a desperate time indeed.

In the continuing search for solutions to the economic problems, the Bennett government realized that trying to find a solution for Canada solely within the Empire was not in Canada's best interests. Bennett opened trade negotiations with the United States. Canada's total trade in 1934 was valued at just over one billion dollars, from which Canada enjoyed a surplus, with almost $580 million in exports and $434 million in imports.[102] The United States already figured more prominently than the United Kingdom in Canada's trade. Over half the value of Canada's imports were from the United States, while only a quarter came from the United Kingdom. Even if all of the Empire were included, its imports still only comprised a third of the total value.[103] The United States was also ahead, though just slightly, in terms of the value of Canada's total exports to it: 41 percent went to the United States, and 39 percent went to the United Kingdom.[104] And whereas Britain had been the primary source for investment in Canada since before Confederation, helping to build the railways and the canals, by 1922 the United States had surpassed Britain as the primary source of foreign direct investment.[105] The economic realities of geography were taking hold, with all that that entailed for other domains, such as, for example, culture, with more and more in the way of magazines, movies, and even education, emanating from the United States.

The Depression that had brought Bennett into power also showed him out; the Liberals won an impressive victory, 173 of 245 seats, in the election on October 14, 1935. The increasing orientation toward the United States would be emphasized by Mackenzie King after. The trade negotiations with the United States begun by Bennett were accelerated and concluded within weeks of King forming a new government.

The role the Dominion government played was gaining in scope and size as a result of its fiscal powers and the leverage it gained through financial transfers to destitute provincial governments. Foreign policy was a less certain field because it was new. Italy's invasion of Abyssinia in October 1935 was forcing Canada, as a member of the League of Nations, to think through what its policy should be. It could no longer just rest on its new status from the 1931 Statute.

John Buchan, now Lord Tweedsmuir, an individual of exceptional qualities, was arriving at an exceptional time in Canada's constitutional history, a difficult time in its social and economic history, and a dangerous time in the world's history. It is time to explore the fortuitous convergence of this superbly cumulative and integrated life and a promised land beset.

PART I

A Refreshing Change
The Model Takes Shape

Chapter 1

A Noble Soul

On a spring evening in late May 1919, a chance meeting occurred at 76 Portland Place in London, a meeting with significance for Canada. The address was the home of John and Susan Buchan, where a close friend of theirs, Violet Markham,[1] had gone while waiting for the delayed arrival of a friend from Canada, Mackenzie King. King was travelling to England to study the impact of the war and the effects of industrialization on workers. His arrival had been delayed. Rather than meeting King at the train station, Markham had communicated with him that he should come to the Buchan's home.

When Mackenzie King finally arrived at Buchan's home, he "was much impressed with Mr. Buchan's personality … scholarly appearance and … delightful quiet English manner."[2] It was an instance of what Buchan himself might have described as the "casual," rather than the "causal," in history.[3]

The next time John Buchan met Mackenzie King, the latter was prime minister of Canada and attending a Dominion prime ministers' meeting in London in the fall of 1923.[4] The following year the Buchans were King's guests during a stopover en route to the east coast of the United States. Buchan was, at the time, travelling on business as deputy chairman of Reuters, the British-based international news agency, but while in the United States he would also meet with his American publisher. They spent one night at Laurier House, King's green-trimmed, mansard-roofed residence in Ottawa's Sandy Hill area, and one night at Kingsmere, King's Gatineau Hills estate, on the Quebec side of the Ottawa River.

On the Sunday, after lunch, King and the Buchan couple took to the outdoors, climbing a hill near Kingsmere. Just before the crest, the host blindfolded the couple, guiding them gently up the remaining steps to the top. There he removed the blindfolds to reveal before them a panoramic view of the Ottawa valley. Buchan spontaneously described it as "a real Pisgah's heights."[5] The Biblical reference would have struck an immediate chord with the religious Mackenzie King. In the Old Testament, Pisgah was a point atop the mountain of Nebo, which Moses climbed and from where God showed Moses the Promised Land. Buchan's graciousness and sincere compliments regarding places and ideas that Mackenzie King took pride in evoked an effusive response from King and further strengthened King's attraction to his visitor.

On Monday, before departing, Buchan gave King a copy of his memoir of Lord Minto (governor general of Canada, 1898–1904), inscribing it, "with affectionate regard, from your friend." It was a gesture Mackenzie King treasured. "I cannot be too proud of that," he confided to his diary.[6] After bidding his guests farewell at the train station, King reflected that there was no one he would rather have as a friend. He could not find enough words to describe this "beautiful noble soul, kindly and generous in thought and word and act [and] informed as few men in this world have ever been."[7]

In the autumn of the following year, spurred on by the glowing reports of the Buchans' visit to Canada, Violet Markham proposed to Mackenzie King that Buchan succeed Lord Byng as governor general (1921–1926).[8] It would be, she commented, "such a healthy change from 'the correct and conventional peer usually selected for these posts.'"[9] Her political principles were in harmony with Mackenzie King's, and he approached Buchan to obtain his permission to place his name on the list of those to be considered for the position. At this point, however, the changes from the 1926 Imperial Conference were not yet in play, and Lord Willingdon, a former governor in India (Bombay (now Mumbai) and Madras), was appointed (1926–1931).

Mackenzie King's Liberal government was succeeded by R.B. Bennett's Conservatives in July 1930. Lord Willingdon was succeeded as governor general by Lord Bessborough, who arrived in Canada in April 1931. As the Great Depression continued, dissatisfaction and anger grew against the Bennett government. By the fall of 1934, the leader of His Majesty's Loyal Opposition, Mackenzie King, increasingly offered the view that the government had no right to govern because it lacked the confidence of the people, having lost in recent by-elections. In September both King and Bennett were in England and had separate talks with King George V's private secretary, Sir Clive Wigram, about Bessborough's successor, since it was now the Canadian government that was responsible for proposing names to the king for the position of governor general.

With a hint from Bennett, Bessborough provided a confidential list of possible successors, all lords.[10] Bennett's meeting with Sir Clive resulted in instructions that he (Bennett) should discuss matters with the governor general on his return to Canada, after which the king's private secretary expected to "hear something on the subject of [Bessborough's] successor."[11]

When Mackenzie King met with Sir Clive, however, the opposition leader set out his interpretation of the political situation. King stated that he would oppose any significant proposals by Bennett or his government, including advice to His Majesty regarding a successor to the governor general. Wigram was taken aback by this attitude, which placed King George in a potentially difficult constitutional position, whereby a newly elected prime minister did not approve of the governor general who had only just been appointed before the election. Mackenzie King's opinion was that Bennett could avoid any potential embarrassment by calling an election early enough for a new government to make a decision that "would meet the needs and wishes of all," in particular Bessborough's desire to leave early.[12] Wigram replied that His Majesty had told Bennett he should confer with the opposition leader, and Bennett had agreed. Sir Clive emphasized that King George V would not appoint a new governor general before a general election without the opposition leader agreeing with the prime minister about who the successor should be.

Back in Ottawa, a week before Christmas 1934, there were a few snow flurries and temperatures were falling past the ten degree Fahrenheit mark, as a hopeful opposition leader made his way through the cold, darkened streets to the warm ambiance of Rideau Hall, arriving at five o'clock for tea, for a "personal and private" discussion with the governor general. It concerned, of course, the governor general's successor and the correspondence Bessborough had had with His Majesty. Mackenzie King, however, repeated that he would oppose any major proposals by the Bennett government. Reflecting the concern of Buckingham Palace, Bessborough explained that the most important consideration was to avoid any embarrassment for His Majesty, primarily due to some disagreement among Canadian politicians.

This type of situation had been foreseen by King George himself in Australia in 1930. The Australian prime minister of the day, J.H. Scullin, had wished to exercise the newfound autonomy given the Dominions by the Imperial conferences, and, controversially, had decided that it was important therefore to appoint an Australian as governor general.[13] While King George reluctantly accepted the advice, he expressed concern that such an appointment might, following an election, lead a new government to want a new governor general.[14] The Australian appointment was commented on widely in Canadian newspapers, with mixed opinion for and against having a "native son" appointed as governor general.[15]

Mackenzie King repeated the points to Bessborough that he had made to Wigram, then moved on to the timing of an election. Ever persistent, King continued to push for an early election, and raised the spectre, if not outright threat, of the appointment becoming "a grave issue" in Parliament, and more generally in the country, if it were made before an election, whether or not he had been consulted!

Bessborough picked up the last point, leading him to ask who should be governor general. King stated that he "did not think it would be wise" to have a member of the royal family as governor general, or, for that matter, a peer in Rideau Hall.[16] His rationale was that doing so helped to protect the Crown, by keeping it out of politics — a danger inherent in the position, he believed, based on his disagreement with Lord Byng over the dissolution of Parliament in 1926. King had other reasons, too: the "radical movements" making headway in other countries had counterparts in Canada, he maintained, and adding a title at Rideau Hall "would perpetuate a feudal system" and give "ammunition to such parties as the CCF" (the Co-operative Commonwealth Federation, the predecessor to today's NDP). Bessborough was not convinced, and noted that Lord Athlone was a very good governor general in South Africa. King was polite in his response, stating, it "would not be wholly satisfactory, but that it was a matter I would want to consider very carefully if called upon to do so."[17]

Mackenzie King's subtle threats caused George V to express privately his great displeasure with the Canadian opposition leader's attitude. The king believed such an approach undermined legitimate government; an expected electoral defeat should not preclude the prime minister or the government from continuing the business of the country.[18] Amidst the political battle that Mackenzie King firmly believed he was winning, the question of the governor general's successor was left aside for a time; but timing was becoming critical. If Bessborough was to leave by October and King George's silver jubilee celebrations were to be held in May, it was important that an announcement be made no later than April. Efforts, including those by the Palace, were redoubled to get Bennett and Mackenzie King together.[19]

On Thursday, February 21, with less than two hours' notice, Bennett's secretary called Mackenzie King's office to make an appointment for the the prime minister to meet the opposition leader.[20] Bennett arrived at King's office and appeared to be very tired — not without justification, as an imminent, lengthy illness would prove. After some pleasantries, Bennett stated that his purpose was to ask if King would serve on a committee to draw up plans for King George's silver jubilee. As they talked, King wondered whether what Bennett really had in the back of his mind was the issue of the governor general's successor. Bennett finally delivered the pregnant topic by speaking of Bessborough's determination to leave sometime during the year.

After reviewing their respective conversations with the Palace and Bessborough, and Mackenzie King repeating his earlier statements that he would oppose any appointments by the government, Bennett searched for receptive ground, laying out his government's program, which reflected many Liberal policy themes. King just repeated his point about Bennett's government not having the support of the people.

At this juncture Bennett asked King to think over some names for governor general, but kept his own orientation to a candidate from the House of Lords. He speculated aloud that the Liberal leader would "no doubt wish to have a Liberal peer." Bennett knew there were those who preferred to have a Canadian and wanted to pre-empt the possibility that his political foe would raise the issue. He therefore turned the conversation to the experiences of Australia and South Africa. Following the Imperial conferences, Australia had been the first to appoint one of their own as governor general, but, Bennett qualified, they later thought they had made "a great mistake." As for the South Africans, they had decided they were ready to appoint one of their own, but were having difficulty settling on whom it might be. The two leaders in the National Party coalition, J.B.M. Hertzog, the premier, and Jan Smuts, the justice minister, were both willing to nominate each other but neither was willing to give up the government!

After expressing his limited suggestions, but with no particular name in mind, Bennett then essentially gave King carte blanche. "I tell you what I will do, King," the inveterate diarist recorded of their conversation. "If you will name your man, I will take your nominee." Perhaps it was Bennett's poor health, or perhaps political fatigue, combined with the pressure from the king, Sir Clive Wigram, and Bessborough, that caused Bennett to surrender such a key nomination. Initially, Mackenzie King was cautious. He stated that he would have to "consider the whole matter carefully." He then appeared to reach for compromise, suggesting to Bennett that "it would be a fortunate thing if someone could be selected in whom there would be equal confidence on the part of all." It was all part of King's strategy of preparing his opponent in steps that could be recognized as making good, logical sense.

King continued, recalling an idea he had had some time ago and which might commend itself now. He related that perhaps the time had come for the country to have someone appointed in a similar circumstance to that of James Bryce, the British ambassador to the United States (1907–1913). The fact that Bryce had not been a member of the House of

Lords when he was appointed "created the most favourable of all impressions in the United States."

It struck a chord. Bennett rejoined that Bryce's *American Commonwealth*, published in 1888, was "the best thing the Americans had ever had."

Having set the stage with reference to a non-peer and an intellectual author, and despite Bennett being apparently receptive, King still did not wish to appear to be too anxious. He wondered aloud "whether a man like John Buchan might not be a very good choice." It was clear, however, from the attributes King began to list in Buchan's favour, that he had carefully planned his approach with Bennett.

First, being a member of Parliament, Buchan was familiar with parliamentary procedure. The fact that Buchan was a Conservative MP was not objectionable to the Liberal leader because, as he told Bennett, he believed Buchan would be above partisan politics. King explained that it was important to consider the people of Canada, too; they would, he was certain, find someone as distinguished as Buchan "very acceptable." He would appeal also to journalists, having been one himself. Speculating on his high expectations for Buchan, King suggested that with some leisure time and visits to different parts of Canada, Buchan might be inspired to write books that "would help to bring the country, more than ever, before other countries of the world." Additionally, and equally important, he was well known throughout the Empire, and beyond, and would be a good host for people of distinction "from the Old Country" who might also stay at Government House. Here was a couple who "would understand what was required." He was referring to Buchan in the highly ceremonial post of lord high commissioner to the Church of Scotland, representing His Majesty, and to the social connections of his wife, who King thought was related to the Duke of Wellington.[21]

Bennett appeared to be attracted to the suggestion. What struck him was the possibility of finding someone from outside the House of Lords. King recalled Bennett saying he "never thought of looking into the other House of Parliament but," he added, "the idea commends itself to me very strongly." Bennett believed that Buchan was also "just the right age." The conversation continued, with King repeating some of the arguments he'd made to Bessborough about the dangers of encouraging the political fringes by having royalty or aristocrats at Rideau Hall. Toward the end of their meeting, Bennett mentioned again that he thought Buchan was "an excellent idea," but that he would keep it confidential for the moment. King was quietly very pleased at Bennett's receptiveness.

After Bennett left, King remembered another fact that commended Buchan for the post: his biography of Lord Minto. Then his political conscience began niggling him. What would others think of him, a Liberal, wanting a Tory for governor general? To assuage his conscience, he thought of another British writer and journalist, but this time a well-known Liberal — John Alfred Spender. Spender, however, was seventy-one years old, compared with Buchan's fifty-nine years. Spender would be "a guide and help to one in public life, [and King could] not think [of another] person in the British Empire equal to Spender." On the other hand, he could think "of no one preferable to John Buchan ... as a friend and delightful companion in an office of the kind." Whether King thought of it consciously or not, providing another name to Bennett would give the prime minister options and make King seem more balanced, leaving him a winner regardless! What a gift his political opponent had given him!

Bennett and King were both back in the House of Commons for the afternoon session at 3 p.m. The House recessed at six o'clock, having just begun debate on a Depression-related bill to establish an unemployment and social insurance commission. The opposition leader crossed over to Bennett's desk in the front row.[22] The prime minister listened to Mackenzie King's afterthoughts of their earlier conversation: the additional reasons in Buchan's favour and the attributes of another possible name, J.A. Spender. Bennett was quite familiar with Spender but did not appear to respond as enthusiastically as he had to Buchan, at least in King's interpretation. The two bachelors then discussed "the wife feature," though they came to no specific agreement except that it was an important consideration. They then retired from the Commons for the remainder of the two-hour recess, returning to continue their verbal sparring in the Commons until almost eleven o'clock that night.

King's observation regarding how tired Bennett had looked over the past while, and particularly at their last meeting, would be confirmed the next week when Bennett did not return to the House. The

PM was confined to bed in his "palatial suite," as King described it,[23] at the Chateau Laurier hotel, with what was originally believed to be the flu. Talk spread through political circles about how exhausted he was. King imagined, though, that Bennett would be back soon, "and as rude as ever." It was, however, only the beginning of a lengthy illness, including a respiratory infection and heart problems. In Bennett's absence Sir George Perley became acting prime minister.

Before Bennett became ill, however, he had had the opportunity to mention to Lord Bessborough that John Buchan was a name he was considering as a possible successor as governor general. It appears Bennett only mentioned Buchan's name and not Spender's, which would be consistent not only with the fact that the latter name was mentioned only as an afterthought to discussions between the two political leaders, but also with the likelihood that Bennett would have preferred the Conservative Buchan to the Liberal Spender. Less than a week after the prime minister was confined to bed, Bessborough wrote to him to express his concern about the illness and discuss some of the business of the House. He also noted briefly that "J.B. sounds an excellent idea" and informed Bennett that he had written His Majesty, asking for a reply, before he and Lady Bessborough left on their trip to western Canada, about when he might depart Canada.[24]

On March 1 Mackenzie King attended a dinner at Government House, along with a number of other leading politicians, and had an opportunity to speak privately at some length with the governor general, whose concerns, among other things, included Bennett's poor health. In the library, following dinner, Bessborough repeated to King what he had written to Bennett, but enthused more about the suggestion of Buchan, describing it as "a very good brain wave."[25] Again, there was apparently no reference to Spender, firmly reinforcing Buchan's position as *the* candidate. The fact that Buchan was a "Mr." seemed to preoccupy Bessborough, who spoke of "peerage as an essential feature" for a representative of the king. It is likely that Bessborough was reflecting views from the Palace and that George V was firm in wanting a peer as his representative in Canada.[26]

By mid-March the Palace had communicated to Bennett that the king was prepared to appoint Buchan and raise him to the peerage. The Palace wished, however, to confirm the opposition leader's concurrence before proceeding. Sir George Perley relayed this information to Mackenzie King on the afternoon of Thursday, March 14, when the two met in the House of Commons. Perley also told King "frankly" that Bennett's plans were to keep the House in session until after the king's silver jubilee celebrations, which Bennett hoped to attend in London, then return to close the business of the House before calling an election. It would have been disheartening to King to hear this news. He nonetheless recalled his previous protest and told Perley he preferred to wait to name the governor general until after an election.

The reply from Perley was similar to what King had heard from Bessborough just before Christmas. Despite an aching desire to have an early election, King resigned himself to losing that battle and gave Perley his agreement, solacing himself with the knowledge that "Buchan will be a true friend, … a Scotchman and a presbyterian to begin with, and one who understands history and politics."[27] The fact that George V wanted to grant Buchan a peerage would surely have added to Mackenzie King's disappointment, though.

The issue of Bessborough's successor was resolving itself as a classic Canadian compromise. Despite having to cede ground to the traditionalists, King could take comfort that he had, in effect, determined who the next governor general would be. The traditionalists could rest more easily knowing that, despite an unfavourable political climate for them, Canada would have a former Conservative MP, and a peer, however recently appointed, as governor general.

As these matters were being settled, Bennett's health was the subject of increasing concern. Mackenzie King in fact wondered if they would ever see Bennett in the House again. Doing what he considered his Christian duty, King wrote a note to Bennett on March 5, expressing regret at the latter's sickness. Bessborough continued to write notes to his prime minister, for which Bennett was grateful. Replying to His Excellency, as the governor general prepared to leave on his last western tour, Bennett wrote: "Of course, my occupancy of [the] office may be terminated by my being called upon to pay 'the debt to nature,' which we must all pay, in which event Your Excellency would have to return immediately to Ottawa."[28]

Bessborough wrote to Bennett again on March 18, stating that the king "telegraphed personally to ask after you," and adding "H.M. responded very quickly and favourably to your proposal about J.B., which shows how little worry or trouble your recommendation gave him."[29]

Now that the Palace had received the name put forward by the Canadian first minister, and he had consulted the opposition leader as requested, Sir Clive Wigram approached Buchan in mid-March. He met with some initial hesitancy because Buchan preferred South Africa, given that he spoke Afrikaans and knew the country well from the three years he had spent there as a private secretary to the governor, Lord Milner. Violet Markham had also expressed a wish for the Buchans to go "to our beloved South Africa" for the job, though she conceded Canada was "the greater distinction."[30]

Buchan was informed, however, that South Africa was not likely to be offered to him.[31] On March 21 he wrote to Wigram: "I shall be grateful if you will inform His Majesty, with my loyal and humble duty, that, if a post of governor general of Canada is offered to me, I am willing to accept it."[32] Bennett later received word that the king had invited Buchan to see him in the south of England to offer him the post.

The day after Wigram received Buchan's reply, he sent a cyphered telegram, marked "Secret and Personal," from Compton Place, Eastbourne, to Lord Bessborough in Ottawa: "Buchan has accepted and [the k]ing gladly approves appointment."[33] Knowing the possibilities of rumours and leaks, Wigram emphasized the importance of making the announcement as soon as possible. He therefore requested that the governor general ask his prime minister to submit the nomination using a cyphered cable for his reply. The king's approval would then be telegraphed back, also by cypher. This was the procedure followed in 1931 for Bessborough's own appointment.

The actual document, signed by Bennett on his sick bed and sent to the Palace for the king's approving initials, was dated March 23, 1935, while the cable was sent the next day at 5:35 p.m. from the Code Section at the fledgling Department of External Affairs, accommodated in the East Block of the Parliament Buildings: "The Prime Minister humbly petitions His Majesty graciously to approve of the appointment of John

The Prime Minister of the Dominion of Canada presents his humble duty to His Majesty the King.

The Prime Minister humbly petitions His Majesty graciously to approve the appointment of John Buchan, Esquire, Companion of Honour, Member of Parliament, as Governor General of His Dominion of Canada.

The Prime Minister remains His Majesty's most faithful and obedient servant.

Ottawa, 23rd March, 1935.

(R.B. Bennett Papers/Library and Archives Canada)

King George V approved the recommendation of Canadian prime minister Richard B. Bennett to appoint John Buchan as governor general — an appointment that sparked controversy in Canada as to who should be governor general.

Buchan, Esquire, Companion of Honour, Member of Parliament, as Governor General of His Dominion of Canada."[34] Bennett then asked Sir George Perley to inform the opposition leader of the news.

The cyphered reply telegram from the king, informing his Canadian prime minister that he approved of the appointment of John Buchan, was sent on Tuesday, March 26.[35] Sir Clive Wigram then sent a secret telegram to Bennett the same day, proposing to announce the appointment on Thursday, March 28, at 3 p.m., and requesting Bennett's approval.

A short time later that day, however, another coded telegram arrived from Wigram, noting that reports of the appointment were appearing in the press.[36] Wigram assured Bennett the leak was not from his office, but it seemed that Sir Clive's concerns about leaks had been well-founded! He was "disgusted" by the leak, believing that it had first appeared in the *Glasgow Herald* on the 24th and then in the *Daily Express* in a later edition the next day.[37] Max Aitken, known better as Lord Beaverbrook, the well-connected, New Brunswick–born press baron who owned the *Daily Express*, was suspected, although it was clear, also, that a journalist by the name of Stevenson, of the *Times*, had caught wind of the story.

Reacting to the rumours, the Canadian Press correspondent in London approached John Buchan, MP, in the corridors of Westminster; he was met, however, by discreet silence. In the circumstances, Wigram asked Bennett if he could announce the appointment a day earlier instead, at the same time. Bennett agreed.[38]

That same Tuesday, as spring temperatures warmed to almost fifty degrees Fahrenheit, Mackenzie King sat in his office making telephone calls. One of his contacts, a Mr. Lambert, informed King he had just received a call, from Stevenson of the *Times* in London, saying that John Buchan had been appointed governor general. The *Ottawa Journal* sent a note to King's office asking for comment on the rumour. King made no reply, but his mind was in a febrile and anguished state. His source of relief was his diary, into which he applied copious amounts of ink.[39]

He had kept his discussions with Bessborough and Bennett confidential, but he was concerned that two people in particular would feel slighted that he had held back on them: his Quebec lieutenant, Ernest Lapointe; and the president of the National Liberal Federation, Vincent Massey. Massey, however, frequently got under King's skin, and so King dismissed him as trying too hard to be the "kingmaker" in appointing the next governor general. In a mixed mood, King saw Massey's motivation as purely personal, for his own glorification, rather than stemming from more noble goals, such as serving His Majesty or the country, which King no doubt believed were his own motivations. He was also certain that Massey had promised Lord Halifax the post, and would therefore be doubly disappointed, especially since King was aware Massey had spoken strongly against Buchan.[40] Vindictively, he was quite satisfied.

King ran over in his mind many of the events of the past months, anguishing again over the loss of Spender, but concluding with a very self-satisfied tone in the "divine justice of it all." Regardless of the fact that Bennett's friends had not wanted the appointment of Buchan, Bennett himself had taken quite favourably to it. "It remains the suggestion was my own [and] had not occurred to others," King smugly noted.[41] Bennett, the big-money man, had had to go to his political opponent, and then had accepted his suggestion. What pleased King most was that he had "broken the precedent of going to the Lords … [and] … had a commoner selected." The certainty now stirred King to reflect on the origins of his first meeting with John Buchan.

King's memory over fifteen years, however, transformed that first meeting from the sparsely recorded one of an evening in May 1919, into a more emotional one suited to how he now saw himself and Buchan — a morning, Buchan's desk "near the window, the long, hanging curtains, the painting or two over the mantel and on the wall, both of us standing there, Violet so happy."[42] He gave credit for that meeting where it was due. His "thoughts went naturally to Violet Markham, to her the appointment is due, for through her we met."[43] By now the newspapers had already begun to speculate on what the appointment meant for Canada.

CHAPTER 2

Untitled but Uncommon

When the rumours about John Buchan's appointment began circulating publicly in Canada, they offered a hint of the excitement, and controversy, to come. Commenting on the rumours, the editors at the *Globe* in Toronto suggested "Canadians will have reason to count themselves fortunate if the unadorned name of John Buchan is added to the list of Canadian Governors-General."[1] "Fortunate" and "unadorned" because he was a self-made man of many talents and accomplishments, not being appointed because of a title. "A very pleasant innovation" was how John Dafoe's Liberal-oriented *Winnipeg Free Press* described the rumoured appointment.[2] While Buchan was a commoner, he was an uncommon choice for governor general.

The official announcement was made simultaneously in London and Ottawa on March 27, a day earlier than had been planned, because of the leak in London. While Acting Prime Minister Sir George Perley was making the announcement in the House of Commons at three o'clock, however, the upper chamber remained officially in the dark. The government leader in the Senate, former Conservative prime minister Arthur Meighen, who was a minister without portfolio in Bennett's Conservative government, was asked whether the report in the morning *Ottawa Journal* about John Buchan's appointment was true.[3] Meighen had to apologize for his inability to give an answer but speculated that "if the information should prove true, I can commend the appointment on the ground of Mr. Buchan's position in English literature."[4] Meighen soon obtained confirmation of the appointment and duly informed his Senate colleagues but was livid at having been put on the spot, exchanging accusatory correspondence with Sir George.[5]

Back in London Buchan was now free to speak to the London-based Canadian Press reporter. He was "proud to be given a chance of serving Canada," adding it was a country with which he was already familiar.[6] He also revealed to Canadians that one of his favourite pastimes was fishing and that he had fished in the Maritimes. In this regard Canada was made for him!

Bennett ordered a cable sent to congratulate Buchan on his appointment and expressed the hope he would see him in May during the king's silver jubilee celebrations.[7] Buchan delayed his reply for almost two weeks because it seemed "a shame to bother" the prime minister with letters while he was ill.[8] When he did reply, he added a bit of flattery with wishes that the prime minister's ill health would not impede his public life because "the Empire cannot afford, at a time like this, to be deprived of the services of such a man as you."

Now that the rumours were confirmed, Canadian newspapers were quick to print a Canadian Press story, sourced in London, that Buchan was the first commoner to be governor general. A number of editorial writers developed the theme and lauded this constitutional first, but a subsequent CP article corrected the previous one, citing a document put before the Judicial Committee in London.[9] The first commoner, in fact, was Canada's second governor general after Confederation. Although Sir John Young was a commoner when he was appointed in 1869, he was granted a peerage two years later, becoming Lord Lisgar. Not all the papers that had included the "first commoner" story printed the correction, thus perpetuating a popular notion that can still be heard or read today.[10] The significant point, though, is that Buchan was both a commoner and untitled, and that was just fine with the many Canadians who believed titles were inappropriate for Canada, Mackenzie King foremost among them. The *Globe* in Toronto asked, in a rather tongue-in-cheek fashion, whether the capital city could bear up without its lord.[11]

The untitled governor general–designate did indeed unsettle some people. Individuals concerned about social status and the more traditionally minded were disappointed, recalled G.E. Beament, a young partner in his family's prominent Ottawa law firm and a lieutenant in the militia.[12] Invitations to Government House just wouldn't be the same anymore! And indeed, the Buchans would make clear when they arrived that they would not be a part of "society" life in Ottawa.[13]

It was not, however, just the capital city with its high society activities that this applied to. In Winnipeg Earl Johnson, then a young enlisted man who would later serve as one of Lord Tweedsmuir's drivers during a visit to that city, observed that some people were more concerned with the question of whether or not the governor general wore a cocked hat than with the fact that he was a famous writer.[14] In Aylmer, Ontario, twenty-year-old Strome Galloway remarked to his mother that it seemed Canada had been snubbed when he heard Lowell Thomas announce on the radio that his old friend, Colonel John Buchan, had just been appointed governor general of Canada.[15] The view of this young militia lieutenant in the Elgin Regiment was representative of a segment of the population that was strongly attached to Britain. They were to a large degree imperialists by sentiment,[16] and remained traditional in their outlook toward the position of governor general. Many of them were, therefore, shocked by "Mr." Buchan's appointment. That the Canadian prime minister, as a result of the Imperial conferences and the 1931 Statute of Westminster, now advised the king directly on who should be governor general was likely not fully known or appreciated, or, if it was, it was not necessarily accepted. What concerned traditionalists was the result, which in this case was a change from what they were familiar with, and it unsettled them.

Mackenzie King may have masked his own delight in a commoner governor general by his muted reaction in the House of Commons, but he could not restrain some Liberal senators he considered "loose cannons."[17] Raoul Dandurand and Rodolph Lemieux pushed the idea of a commoner for governor general even further during a debate in the upper chamber — on the day of the announcement no less![18]

Septuagenarian Liberal leader in the senate, Raoul Dandurand, prefaced his remarks in the upper chamber by stating he was speaking on his own account. One of the longest serving senators (since 1898), and a rather regal figure, with his full, squared-trimmed white beard, Dandurand added that the nomination of a Canadian for the position of governor general would be in keeping with Canada's new status "of absolute equality," alluding to the Statute of Westminster. It would cause Canadians to feel they had grown up. After all, Dandurand pointed out, Australia had a few years earlier appointed one of their own as governor general.[19] Transposing the example to Canada, possibly with the aim of trying to win over some Conservative support for his idea, Dandurand suggested the respected former prime minister, Sir Robert Borden, as a suitable candidate. But with a sentiment as noble as his looks, Dandurand asserted that his thoughts did not prevent him from joining others in recognizing that the appointment of Buchan was "a happy one," and that Mr. Buchan has "all the qualifications necessary to adorn the post."

Rodolphe Lemieux, a former minister in Sir Wilfrid Laurier's government, who had put Arthur Meighen on the spot in the Senate on the day of the announcement, remarked that the idea of having "a full-blooded Canadian as governor general" was one that had been in the public mind for some time already. Indeed, their colleague Senator Béland suggested that Dandurand and Lemieux would see the day when a Canadian was appointed governor general. But as for himself, Béland declared he was entirely satisfied.[20] Mackenzie King's strong political senses and his qualified loyalty to the "old country" would not have allowed his personal involvement in a debate on this theme, even though he privately thought that "we have certainly got pas[t] the day of really needing a governor general coming out from England to Canada."[21]

Arthur Meighen, on the other hand, supported governors general coming from the "Mother Country," regardless of the changed political scene in the post-Statute of Westminster Empire. But his comments in reaction to the announcement, once he was informed of it officially, were surprisingly similar to those of his bitter political rival, Mackenzie King. Meighen, a superb parliamentary debater, was also known as unpretentious and "totally unimpressed by age, wealth, or social position," preferring to judge people on their merits.[22] He was glad, he stated to his Senate colleagues, that the post had been offered to one who, "though not ennobled, is noted for his high achievements, who has risen to a distinguished position by his own efforts and genius."[23]

Outside the privileged confines of the Senate, the French-language editorialists in Quebec City, Montreal, and Ottawa echoed the Canadianizing views of Dandurand and Lemieux, but not all for the same reasons. In Quebec City, even after Buchan's appointment was announced, *Le Soleil* nonetheless made it known that it too favoured a Canadian for the viceregal post. It emphasized, like Senator Dandurand, that this opinion was in no way intended as a personal criticism of John Buchan, whose writings were popular in Quebec.[24] The more conservative *La Presse* in Montreal, though, just stuck to observing that the political and press reactions in the rest of Canada signalled that Buchan was likely to be a success as governor general. Other opinion in Quebec, however, had different motivations.

The world situation weighed on many people's minds. Newspaper coverage reminded the reading public on a regular basis of the threatening situation overseas, not just in Europe but also in Asia, where Japanese militarism was on the march in China. As the European situation intensified, it revived memories of Canada's participation in the Great War and of the divisive issue of conscription, particularly in Quebec. This set the context for some leading opinion-makers in Quebec, who believed that the presence of a British governor in Ottawa implied Canada's automatic involvement should another European conflict erupt.[25]

In an editorial prepared prior to Buchan's appointment but which it decided to print even though the appointment was a fact, *Le Devoir* wrote: "*Nous demandons un homme du pays*" (We are asking for a man from our own country) to be governor general.

Supporting this view in the House of Commons was the former editor of *Le Devoir*, Henri Bourassa, an influential advocate of neutrality and an Independent member of Parliament for the Quebec riding of Labelle. Bourassa spoke of the increasingly dangerous situation in Europe. He qualified his major point by emphasizing a theme he had raised well over thirty years before.[26] The best homage he could pay to Britain was to act as a free British subject and support the policy he believed best for his

country: "We should signify politely but firmly to the British government … that we are prepared … to stay at home if England chooses to go
to war for causes which are foreign to Canada."[27]

Prime Minister Bennett was well aware of the political sensitivities
surrounding Canada's sovereignty and of any potential involvement
in another European war. When he finally returned to the House of
Commons on Monday, May 20, 1935, after his illness and having attended
George V's silver jubilee celebrations in England, he reported that "the
European situation is one of great difficulty, and at times it gives evidence
of being very dangerous."[28] He assured the House that "no commitments
were sought [from Britain] … nor were any given."

The Quebec City daily *Le Soleil*, despite expressing a desire to have
a Canadian as governor general, wished the Buchan family a happy and
useful time in Canada and included similar wishes for the link with the
British Crown. Virtually everyone recognized the value of that link,
although there was a great deal of division over the significance of the
untitled status and British origin of the governor general and what they
might mean regarding whether or not Canada followed Britain into any
possible European conflict.

In the rest of Canada, there were others who shared this desire to
have a Canadian-born governor general. Curiously, however, there were
those who, while they may have been traditional in their approach and
disliked the change represented by Buchan's appointment, were nonetheless pushed by a certain logic to consider other possibilities — other
possibilities that ironically aligned them with the Liberal senators and
editorialists from Quebec!

Lieutenant-Colonel C.R. Hodgins, a retired officer of the Royal
Artillery, living comfortably in Colwood, on the edge of Victoria, B.C.,
was unsettled by the news. He wrote a letter to the *Globe* in Toronto and
one directly to the Rt. Hon. R.B. Bennett.[29] Hodgins was indignant at the
appointment, which he described as "a smack in the eye for us Canadians."
His ignorance of Buchan's background led him mistakenly to chide the
new appointee for his lack of administrative experience compared to the
previous British peers, who were trained, he commented, in the best traditions of English schools. "What an awful comedown for us! From Lord

Dufferin to a novelist!" he wrote Bennett. If Canada was going to give up having these well-qualified British peers in exchange for a commoner, then that commoner might as well be Canadian, he continued. Are we not, he asked, equal subjects of the king? If ignorant of Buchan's background, Colonel Hodgins was at least knowledgeable about the impact on Canada of the Statute of Westminster. Others from that generally very British part of Canada joined in and called for Canadians to "wake up [and] protest to Ottawa against this unwarranted appointment"; one John Taylor suggested Canadians should consider the appointment "a direct insult to their Canadian nationality."[30]

These individuals were, though, only the most recent and informal of the popular protest against Buchan's appointment. A group formed in 1922 and calling itself the Native Sons of Canada, "*Fils natifs du Canada*" in Quebec, had for several years already been arguing for a Canadian as governor general. They were not, however, hostile to the monarchical system itself, which was an accepted part of Canadian life. The group represented a cross-section of the population, and included amongst its members in 1935 a number of prominent citizens with entries in the *Canadian Who's Who*.[31] The group had "assemblies," or branches, across the country and had lobbied the government at the time of the previous governor general's appointment.

This time, however, the Native Sons had no lead time to react. They "learned with alarm" about the appointment of John Buchan after the fact, but carried their protest formally to the government with as much, if not more, vigour as they had the last time. On the day of the announcement, March 27, 1935, George J. Smith, the organization's national president, sent a telegram from Toronto to Acting Prime Minister Sir George Perley.[32] In it Smith argued that "the country which did produce the Canadian Expeditionary Force in the last war is able to produce at least one man fit to fill the office of His Majesty's representative in Canada." He noted he was sending by regular mail a copy of a resolution to this same effect which had been sent to Prime Minister Bennett "some time ago."

The Native Sons' lobbying included an open letter to members of the House of Commons and the Senate, repeating the text of the telegram to Sir George Perley as well as incorporating a resolution. The resolution's first proposal was to change the name of the position of governor general to viceroy. It went on to suggest that in a period of economic depression, expenditures for the governor general were unwarranted. They accumulated their estimate over ten years, totaling five million dollars, and recommended that the post remain vacant for that length of time.[33] The functions could be carried out by the chief justice of the Supreme Court, who would act as administrator of the Dominion in the absence of the governor general.

Perley replied to Smith's telegram two days later. He stated he was as strong a believer as the Native Sons of Canada in the capacity of individual Canadians and of Canada as a whole. Perley could not agree, however, "that the choice of a resident of Great Britain in any way conflicts with this view." Expressing an accepted opinion of the time, he explained that such a choice ensured the necessary detachment from political and party prejudices required for the effective working of Canada's form of government. It was also, he added, "a symbol of the connection between Canada and the other members of the British Commonwealth of Nations, which I trust you do not desire to see broken."[34] Another resident of Victoria, B.C., was more blunt, describing the Native Sons approach as betraying "a dog-in-the-manger conception of nationhood," noting that as a member of a larger body, the Commonwealth, he had not heard that the British had protested when the Canadian Bonar Law became prime minister in the U.K.[35]

The *Globe*, too, taking great pride in the untitled man who had been appointed, concurred and chided the immaturity of those calling for a Canadian-born governor. Canadians have "no need to sit up nights nursing a sickly and juvenile national self-consciousness."[36]

If some Canadians opposed John Buchan's appointment outright, either because of ignorance or because of a belief it reflected a new sovereign status, the majority of others who lobbied for a Canadian as governor general, like the editorialists at *Le Soleil* and *Le Devoir*, still welcomed the appointment, recognizing in the *fait accompli* a very talented individual. Much of Canada's arts community, as might be expressed through *Saturday Night* magazine, took satisfaction, at least, in the appointment of a literary man and offered a comforting word to those advocates for the Canadianizing of the governor generalship. "[T]hose who claim that the governor general should be a Canadian [are] almost entitled to say that [John Buchan] is at least a step in the right direction."[37] Recognizing the trend, the *Leader-Post* editors in Regina offered, rather presciently, that "a precedent had been set … It may well be a step towards the nomination ultimately of a Canadian-born Governor."

Eventually, even those opposed realized that the appointment was now a *fait accompli*, which helped shift the focus from Buchan's status and origin to his qualities as an individual, a man who had been named, regardless of some wishes of what might have been.

Buchan's knowledge of the French language attracted obvious attention and was commented on favourably by the French-language newspapers. One eminent Quebecker, the Honourable Justice Camille Pouliot of the Quebec Superior Court, was excited enough about a note, handwritten in French, he had received from Buchan that, with a hint of vanity, he shared it with Montreal's *La Presse* editors. They, in turn, reproduced it prominently in their paper, not two weeks after Buchan had penned it on May 8![38] The note expressed warm thanks to Justice Pouliot, who had written some books himself and which he sent to the governor general–designate. Describing the note as *une pièce inédite et fort intéressante*, the editors stated it was with *infinniment de plaisir* that they shared with their readers this *précieux souvenir* of Justice Pouliot.

The note to Justice Pouliot demonstrated Buchan's astuteness, sensitivity to, and knowledge of, Canada. It was perhaps not surprising, largely because this type of respect for others was in his very nature. He had also been given "wise advice" when he received his appointment personally from the king in March. George V had counselled his new representative "to be sympathetic to the French people of Canada, and jealously to respect their traditions and their language."[39]

For the Canadians of French origin, there was, in fact, an affinity with Buchan's Scottish origins, as Senator Lemieux articulated on the day of the announcement: "If we are not to have a Canadian … I think His Majesty the King has been well advised in selecting a son of Scotland." Recalling his history and the old alliances between Scotland and France, the senator explained that the Scots have "always been a good interpreter, an *agent de liaison*, between the English and the French." He was certain, therefore, and so assured his Senate colleagues, that John Buchan would be well received by all parts of the Dominion and particularly by Quebec. This view was fairly widespread and echoed by Fulgence Charpentier, a journalist who was working for the city of Ottawa at the time but who had been a former president of the Press Gallery during Lord Byng's time at Rideau Hall.[40] The reasons the French generally got on better with the Scots than the English were those old alliances and a certain sentimentality. Also at play, though, was the common experience of a smaller ethnic group living next to a much larger, dominant culture.

According to some people, there was not a happier lot of men to be seen than the Presbyterians, especially in Ottawa, when they learned of the appointment.[41] Some of them were concerned, however, when they learned later that the new governor general would preside at the anniversary of the new United Church, which included some Presbyterian congregations, and that he might be drawn away from the old Presbyterian Church. There was no chance that this governor general would be drawn into the church debates in Canada. St. Andrew's Presbyterian Church in downtown Ottawa, where Lord and Lady Aberdeen had attended and that Mackenzie King attended, would also be the church attended by the new governor general. The Scottish connection led as well, though, to lighter conclusions. One humorous advisor asked if anyone had warned the governor general–designate that "being who he is," he would not be able to escape making St. Andrew's Day and Burn's Nicht addresses, warning fairly that the "full perils of his situation should be made known to him!"[42]

While many in the general public expressed great satisfaction that an untitled individual had been appointed governor general, others fully expected that Mr. Buchan would be granted a peerage by King George V. Mackenzie King remained in the dark about what King George would do. But to press his own preference that Buchan remain untitled, he wrote to Violet Markham asking her to speak with Buchan and let Buchan know that he, Mackenzie King, believed there was nothing more Buchan could do "to win for him a stronger place in the admiration and affection of the people of this country than to forego its [a title] acceptance till after his return from Canada."[43]

Public anticipation and speculation grew over who was to be included in George V's Jubilee Honours List, expected to be made public on Monday, May 6. A certain suspense developed in the public over whether Canada's next governor general would remain plain Mr. Buchan, "or something more ornate."

The announcement that John Buchan was to receive a barony from the king was made on May 15. The exact title, though, was a debate within the Buchan family. The governor general–designate finally settled on Baron Tweedsmuir of Elsefield: Tweedsmuir after the region in the borders area of Scotland where he had spent so much of his childhood; and Elsefield after his home near Oxford. Letters and comments arrived from friends, acquaintances, and literary colleagues. One, from Ezra Pound writing from Venice, stood out if only for its spacing, handwritten corrections, and eclectic messages on international, economic, and British political affairs as well as the war of 1812 and books on finance, adding in the middle, "I shall call you J.B. until I can spell it right? Tweedsmuir?"[44]

Those who were excited that Buchan was coming as governor general, as well as those who were disappointed about the peerage, generally agreed he deserved the honour that the title signalled. In fact, one opinion held that Buchan's peerage should be viewed not only as a compliment to his achievements but as a compliment to Canada as well. Going further, it could even be looked upon as "refreshing the peerage" after the harm done "by grasping governments who have debased themselves by elevating the unworthy."[45]

When Mackenzie King did hear the news, he resigned himself to it, reflecting in his diary that "[Buchan] is right perhaps, in feeling that he cannot oppose the King's wishes, if he is to be the King's representative."[46] But he could not resist working out in his own mind how it might otherwise be: "[S]till, in strict constitutional procedure, [Buchan] would be fully justified" in not taking a title if the king's Canadian advisor "desired it." King, however, was not yet that advisor.

Since the more traditional Bennett was prime minister he would certainly not advise Buchan to refuse the title. It is clear, though, that had some slight twists in events occurred, it may well have been "Mr." Buchan who arrived as governor general. Had Bennett not taken ill, perhaps Mackenzie King's pressure to have an election earlier would have succeeded. The opposition leader's arguments to King George V and Lord Bessborough, to wait until after the election to name the new governor, would, with Violet Markham's encouragement, have placed Mackenzie King as the king's advisor in Canada. King would have insisted Bessborough's successor be "Mr." Buchan, with the compromise that he be granted a peerage only after his time in Canada.

The *Globe* in Toronto, representing advocates of common-ness, wrote "there are regrets" the commoner was to become titled. "'Lord Tweedsmuir' cannot but fall flatly on the ear."[47] There was even the suggestion of insensitivity on Buchan's part, noting he should have considered his public who were so well acquainted with John Buchan. A title carrying a different name would only cause confusion for the public who knew John Buchan. His name was "world wide" and "no title can ever add to the honour and fame of John Buchan," Violet Markham had argued in a letter to her friend.[48] At the time, for those people who couldn't figure out peerage names or for those not paying attention to all the fuss in the newspapers, there was indeed confusion, and it would increase with the years.[49]

Regardless of this possible confusion and the suggested insensitivity to his reading public, "Canada must just get used to her disappointment [and] try to give this new member of the peerage as warm and eager a welcome when he comes as she had reserved for Mr. Buchan."[50] This theme of a double identity was one which had already flowed through many commentaries and would continue with Lord Tweedsmuir's arrival. It was a theme reflecting that defining characteristic of Canada, torn between Canada's British heritage and its North American geography. Leonard Brockington, who would be named the first chairman of the Canadian Broadcasting Commission the next year and who was near the centre of political and cultural life in Canada, had a view similar to that of Mackenzie King and Arthur Meighen. Canada, he recalled, "like the rest of North America, feels a sort of family pride in a man who without wealth or privilege or influence, hews his own path through the forests of the frontier."[51]

Whatever the criticism or expressions of dissatisfaction with the appointment and peerage, the overwhelming opinion of Canadians welcomed Buchan's appointment and eagerly awaited his arrival. And none more so than Mackenzie King, who recorded in his diary at the beginning of April, "the more I read and think of Buchan, the better in every particular I think his appointment is."[52] And the more he thought about it, the more intense his emotions became, especially on receiving a reply from Buchan on May 7.[53] King delighted in what he read as "Buchan's expressed views re titles, peerages, etc. so completely in accord with my own." King was in for a rude shock, but so was Buchan when he learned how quickly King's emotions could shift. At this point, however, King was looking to the future through idyllic lenses. "I feel we shall be able to sit together here at Laurier House and at Government House, and talk as intimate friends and fellow workers in affairs of State and Church — that he will be immensely helpful to me, an incentive in literary and public work."[54]

The current Parliamentary session kept King fully occupied for the next two months, until he could at last write his desired, very lengthy, and sometimes gushing, letter to Buchan. "Perhaps, for the last time," King wrote, "I may be permitted to address you by your ancient Scottish name."[55] King was "perhaps imprudently expressing" his feelings on a number of subjects, but his anticipation was intensifying and needed an outlet. He repeated his views that much would have been gained from Buchan coming as a commoner and noted that had Bennett shared King's view, they would have advised King George V that a peerage wait until after Buchan returned to Britain. Mackenzie King believed Buchan's appointment was "an historic milestone [on] ... the path to a new order," an expression he had used in the House of Commons against Bennett's revival of titles for the king's subjects resident in Canada. He congratulated Buchan on the choice of the name for his title and wrote that, should he win the next election, "no single factor ... will begin to afford me the same comfort and satisfaction as that I shall have you at my side as a counsellor and friend [and that] our paths have been brought together through the guidance of Providence."

The stage was set. The country's emotions had been convulsed, first by the break with tradition in appointing a commoner, and then disappointing those who favoured the commoner by the granting of a barony. None doubted, however, the appointment was significant for Canada. It was now time to prepare for his arrival and to speculate on what he would contribute.

CHAPTER 3

Double Arrival

The intervening months between John Buchan's appointment and his planned date of departure from the United Kingdom were filled with preparations for the move and with continuing business matters. Buchan viewed the screening of the film version of his highly popular novel *The Thirty-Nine Steps*, which debuted in New York at the beginning of April.[1] He had sold the film rights to Gaumont British Studios the year before, and had spent time consulting with a young film director, Alfred Hitchcock, on what was to become a classic black-and-white film, still one of the best of its genre. Numerous books by Buchan were also published throughout 1935, including some new collections of his novels, and some reprints of others. More significant, however, was a tribute to George V in his silver jubilee year, *The King's Grace*, published in April.

In Canada there was no doubt that interest, and sales, in John Buchan's books would increase. Canadian bureaucrats and administrators, for their part, were occupied with readying themselves for the expected fall arrival of His new Excellency.

At the beginning of July, as the Canadian government prepared official documents and the new governor general's Privy Seal, the External Affairs Department asked the Canadian High Commission in London to inquire as to Lord Tweedsmuir's proper title and to obtain a copy of his coat of arms. Tweedsmuir had just received his grant of arms from the Court of the Lord Lyon in Edinburgh. At the High Commission, one of the senior members of the staff, Lt.-Col. Georges P. Vanier, who, a quarter century later, would be the second Canadian-born governor general, consulted Tweedsmuir, who included in his reply a copy of his arms with a description written in the unique and colourful language of heraldry: "Azure, a fess argent between three lions' heads erased of the same."[2] His crest was a "sunflower proper," an image he had long used on many of his books.[3] The following day Vanier sent the requested information to the External Affairs Department. But there were other, more practical considerations.

The current governor general, Bessborough, wrote to Buchan in April to discuss their respective departure and arrival dates, noting that "[it] is not wise or convenient for an Administrator [the Chief Justice of Canada] to have to be acting in the absence of the Governor-General for longer than is necessary."[4] The issue of the administrator was, however, of more particular concern for Prime Minister Bennett after his experience the last time. In February 1931 Bennett had written to British prime minister Ramsay MacDonald to express concern that he would have to open Parliament with the administrator rather than a governor general. This will, Bennett wrote, "cause some comment in Canada amongst those who are seeking for the appointment of a Canadian."[5]

A general election had been called for October 14. Free trade — in particular, negotiations the Bennett government had undertaken with the United States — played a significant part in the election campaign, but the Depression played an even greater part. It had created financial and unemployment problems, and at least one and a quarter million people were receiving some form of public relief out of a total population of 10.8 million. This strained provincial and municipal resources and generated dissatisfaction with the governing Conservatives. The election results, not surprisingly, yielded a strong Liberal majority. Mackenzie King was elected prime minister again, as he had expected.[6]

Bennett and Mackenzie King met in King's parliamentary office at five o'clock, the day after the election.[7] The first issue of discussion was the arrival of the governor general. Tweedsmuir's departure from England was scheduled for October 19, later than Bessborough had proposed. Bennett's earlier concern, about minimizing the absence of a governor, returned, but this time it was aired by King, who observed threateningly "that there is a danger of the people of the country saying that if the governor general could not be on hand for the opening and closing of Parliament, and at a time of the general elections, there could be no great necessity for the office."[8] Notwithstanding those concerns, they agreed the arrival should be postponed by a week to allow the new government time to be installed.

A series of telegrams then crossed between Ottawa and London. The code section of the Department of External Affairs was instructed to send an urgent telegram from Bennett to Canada's high commissioner in London, Howard Ferguson, to request that Lord Tweedsmuir postpone his departure until October 25.[9] There was polite resistance in Tweedsmuir's response. Changing at this late date would be "extremely difficult.... However, if postponement [was] considered imperative this [could] be arranged, if necessary."[10] Bennett consulted King again, then regretfully telegrammed a reply that, under the circumstances, the delay was indeed imperative.[11] Tweedsmuir could not but agree. This first direct exposure to Canadian politics in general and indirectly to King as a partisan politician in particular was a foretaste of some of the challenges that lay ahead.

On October 25 Their Excellencies and their youngest son, Alastair, who was seventeen at the time, boarded the *Duchess of Richmond* and quickly became part of the floating community.[12] Tweedsmuir got on well with all the assorted personnel on board. He was described as "friendly" and "democratic." These characteristics, along with his natural curiosity and interest in others, ensured a pleasant voyage. For example, while on board Tweedsmuir made the acquaintance of Roy Tash, an Associated Screen News cameraman. Tash enjoyed the opportunity to explain the technicalities of his profession to Tweedsmuir, who donned headphones and peered through the viewer of the large moving camera apparatus.[13]

As the *Duchess of Richmond* steamed across the Atlantic, uncooperative weather and fog impeded her progress. The delay caused several changes to the program, and no doubt caused unreported headaches for protocol personnel and several chefs! The Dominion government's plans became as foggy as the weather. First, the state luncheon that was

Associated Screen News/Library and Archives Canada/PA-67251

Roy Tash, a pioneer cameraman employed with Associated Screen News, demonstrates an Akeley camera for the governor general.

to be held in welcome was cancelled. It was replaced by a dinner, which in turn was cancelled; finally, plans were finalized, with the government settling for a late evening buffet. As the ship approached Canada, Prime Minister King sent a wireless message to Tweedsmuir, noting that he and his colleagues "looked forward with delight to greeting you in person upon your arrival at Canada's ancient capital."[14]

The *Duchess of Richmond* docked just after sundown on Saturday, November 2, amidst the celebratory sounding of other ships' whistles echoing off the water in the harbour.[15] The Dominion administrator, Chief Justice Sir Lyman Duff, the prime minister, and Secretary of State Fernand Rinfret, in that order, were escorted into the drawing room to meet, unofficially, Lord and Lady Tweedsmuir. This moment was, as Mackenzie King recorded in his diary, "the realization of a vision to which I have looked forward for years."[16]

After a greeting, the first words the new governor spoke to his prime minister, as King noted them, were ones that Tweedsmuir would have planned in advance, to ensure he got off on the right, official, foot: "Prime Minister, I have no voice but yours; are you prepared to 'vet' my replies to the addresses [at the installation ceremony soon to be held] without seeing them."[17] King replied he would trust him in everything. Lady Tweedsmuir told King she had a gift for him from Violet Markham and would give it to him at the first opportunity. After about ten minutes, Duff, King, and Rinfret left the ship to take their places on the quay for the official welcoming.

The Tweedsmuirs met briefly in the ship's lounge with Canadian journalists who had come on board with the river pilot as the ship entered the mouth of the St. Lawrence. When reporters asked him to say a few words, he spoke of his pleasure of having finally arrived and welcomed the opportunity of serving Canada.

The man who stepped off the gangway of the SS *Duchess of Richmond* in Wolfe's Cove and onto the quay contrasted not only in achievements and background but physically as well with many of his predecessors, the immediate one of whom, Lord Bessborough, stood much taller and with a more imperial bearing. This new governor was slender, of medium height, and clean shaven. Mackenzie King's impression of his friend was that he looked "very fragile," with "nothing to spare in the way of flesh on his bones."[18] His complexion and wiry features reflected an individual toughened by a love of the outdoors. "Small, rugged, durable," is how one young man, who became a friend of the Tweedsmuir's son Alastair, described him.[19] Buchan was, despite his sixty years, an incurable walker and sport fisherman, as well as a mountaineer; Canada could provide opportunities for him to pursue all of these pastimes in abundance.

In the brightly lit Cove Terminal building, which was decorated with red, white, and blue bunting, Lord Tweedsmuir was officially greeted by the Dominion administrator, the prime minister, and eight Cabinet ministers, followed by Quebec lieutenant-governor Patenaude, Premier Taschereau, and two of his ministers.[20] The guard of honour, the red-tunicked Royal 22nd Regiment (the "Van Doos") awaited inspection.

Subsequently, in the receiving line, there was a meeting of historic interest. Vincent Massey, who had met Buchan on the latter's 1924 visit to Canada, surprised the newly arrived governor, who blurted out

"Vincent!"[21] Massey became the first Canadian-born governor general in 1952. He was on his way to London to be Canada's high commissioner,[22] replacing Howard Ferguson. Massey had just recently been appointed by Mackenzie King after a particularly trying time in their relationship.[23]

Leaving Cove Terminal, and likely glad to be seated for a while in the relative quiet of their car before the next stage of their arrival, the Tweedsmuirs could see the lit streets lined with Union Jacks and fleur-de-lys flags. The cavalry escort and torchlight made an "extraordinarily romantic" drive for the new governor general as his car wound its way up the hill toward the Quebec legislature, its architecture proudly proclaiming its French heritage. People along the route removed their hats in a respectful gesture as the car passed.

The swearing-in ceremony started at 8:30 p.m. When everyone was in place and the chamber had fallen silent, Shuldham Redfern, the governor general's private secretary, read the Canadian government's request of King George V, from Prime Minister Bennett. Redfern then read out the commission, given at the Court of Saint James on August 10 and by which George V appointed "Our Right Trusty and Well-beloved John, Baron Tweedsmuir ... to be, during Our pleasure, Our Governor-General and Commander-in-Chief in and over Our Dominion of Canada."[24] E.J. Lemaire, clerk of the Privy Council, then handed a Bible bound in black morocco leather to Supreme Court Justice Thibaudeau Rinfret, older brother of Fernand, secretary of state. Justice Rinfret, with Tweedsmuir standing, administered first the Oath of Allegiance, followed by the oath as governor general and finally the oath as keeper of the Great Seal. Now formally governor general, Tweedsmuir signed the oath book and remained standing while all the Supreme Court justices, save one who was ill, signed the book, along with the prime minister. The Great Seal was then handed to His Excellency, who, as custom had established, handed it back to Secretary of State Fernand Rinfret with the words, "I hand you the Great Seal of Canada for safe keeping." The singing of "God Save the King" ended the formal part of the ceremony, an hour after it began.

Tweedsmuir sat on the throne, with a huge Union Jack draped vertically behind him. Mackenzie King, dressed in his braided Privy Councillor's uniform, stood before him. His "few words" were by far the

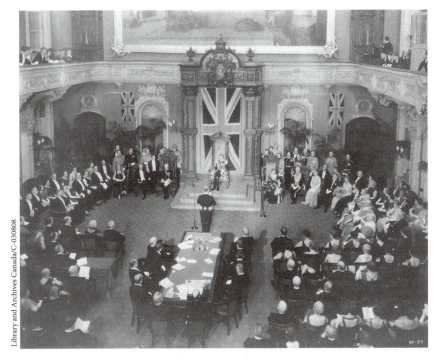

Library and Archives Canada/C-030808

Prime Minister Mackenzie King stands before the new governor general on his arrival in Quebec City: "It is as John Buchan, commoner, that you will find the warmest welcome and abiding place in the hearts of the Canadian people."

longest of all the speeches that evening, but they would appeal to many of the French Canadians present and to many others across the country who had engaged in the debate over Buchan's appointment.

Recalling His Excellency's humble origins and "loyalty to ancient virtues and traditions," Mackenzie King didn't wait long to cut through the initial formalities and publicly state his personal opinion. The man before them had "shown wherein industry, integrity, and ability are the surest and most honourable paths to high recognition.… It is as John Buchan, commoner," King emphasized, that "you will find the warmest welcome and abiding place in the hearts of the Canadian people."[25] He noted what the new governor would find in Canada and the expectation of the benefit that Canada would "derive from [his] wide knowledge, wealth of experience, and great understanding in dealing with the human world problems with which, in the fields of industrial and international relations, our own and other nations are faced."

Beginning his reply with the common courtesy of thanks for the kind words, the new governor general referred in admiring tones to King George V's silver jubilee year. He and his wife already knew and loved this country and had many friends here, "one of the oldest and most valued" of whom was the prime minister. "By virtue of Canada's adoption," he said, "we can now proudly call ourselves Canadian."[26] He was committed to the country as one of its own. He then alluded to the unsettling situation in Europe and Canada's future, using the weather during his Atlantic crossing as a metaphor. Their ship left England in a gale, which did not abate until approaching Canadian shores, when the winds fell but were replaced by fog. He continued, saying that Canada lay out of the hurricane area, "but the visibility is still not good and the future is a little misty." The problems confronting this nation were "intricate and incalculable," but she had even greater possibilities and powers. Continuing with a theme he would carry through his entire time in Canada, he spoke of the country's greatest asset: her people. He admired what they had done already and expressed confidence in what they would do. He concluded that he would be proud to think that at the end of his time in Canada his "mite of effort" might have contributed to the fulfillment of the country's destiny — security, prosperity, and a "leading position among the nations."

The speech drew praise across the country, not just for the eloquence that was expected of John Buchan, but for its expression of faith in the Canadian spirit. If Tweedsmuir continued to put words so powerfully to Canadian hopes, the editors of the *Globe* wrote, continuing its theme from the previous spring, he would not have to envy any of the popularity that would have been John Buchan's. While Buchan's expressions of faith in Canada would have pleased Mackenzie King, the latter thought some of his expressions of loyalty were "the old stock in trade," a loyalty to tradition on Buchan's part, perhaps a link with British convention and public opinion, which would "receive modification here on his part as time goes on."[27] King was intent on shaping post-Westminster Canada as he believed it should be, but he overestimated his ability to shape Buchan and Buchan's belief.

Premier Taschereau's speech of welcome, delivered in French and then in English, referred to the birth of the Canadian nation in Quebec. Tweedsmuir's reply paid tribute to "the merits of [his] predecessors" and amplified the role that history played in his own orientation. "I am naturally drawn," he said, "to a race who have history in their bones and who jealously conserve the heritage of their fathers." Briefly touching on the historical fact that Scotland had been for centuries an ally of France, he concluded by saying how much he looked forward to returning and getting to know the people better. It was significant that he gave his speech in "excellent French,"[28] a point that was a subject of favourable comment and reinforced earlier references to his speaking in French.

"He simply captivated the hearts of the French Canadians," according to Mackenzie King. The senior Quebec Cabinet minister, Ernest Lapointe, when asked by King a short time later whether they had the right man, confirmed with an emphatic "Oh gosh, yes."[29]

Finally, it was the turn of Mayor Grégoire to welcome the new governor general, in French then English. Tweedsmuir again replied, also in French and with no notes. "For beauty of natural situation, for diversity of design, for historic interest, I know of no capital which excels yours — not even my own city of Edinburgh — and I assure you from a Scotsman that is no small tribute." The speeches ended and the chamber broke into spontaneous and prolonged applause, an expression of how successful and appreciated his speeches, and the ceremony, had been.[30] The handshaking that followed took almost an hour, before everyone removed to the Legislative restaurant for the late buffet supper.

The viceregal party left the Legislature among a cheering crowd despite the late hour. They were driven to their train, which they boarded close to midnight, likely tired but content with such a good beginning to their time in Canada. Later that evening, Mackenzie King reflected that it had been "a real triumph" and "most impressive."[31] He was particularly taken by what he saw as the "naturalness and simplicity" of both His Excellency and Lady Tweedsmuir, titles he used in his diary with seeming acceptance, despite his pride that he welcomed John and Susan Buchan.

Comments in the newspapers reflected the excitement over the new governor general, just as they had on his appointment in March.

There was something "intriguingly and attractively different" about him.[32] From Halifax to Victoria, opinion was virtually unanimous in its praise, but for those who preferred Mr. Buchan to Lord Tweedsmuir, like Mackenzie King, there was still a tinge of disappointment. Even within the Buchan family, there was regret, though not for the same reasons as those of Mackenzie King. Buchan's middle son, William, wrote that they wondered whether anyone would recognize him "under the [to most people] impenetrable guise of a peerage."[33] These family musings were similar to the *Globe*'s opinion that suggested John Buchan hadn't considered his readers when he accepted the barony.

In Quebec City, on the very day the Tweedsmuirs arrived, *Le Soleil* unabashedly headlined their editorial "*Bienvenue au Gouverneur*," but began their welcome: "*Même s'il devait être le dernier Gouverneur anglais envoyé au Canada*" (Even if he should be the last English governor sent to Canada). Like many in the country who wanted to give concrete expression to the Statute of Westminster, however, there was no intention to insult the new governor. He was deserving of high consideration for his own achievements as much as for the royal authority vested in him.

Newspaper readers on the Prairies read words in praise of the new governor general as having been appointed "for his own sake"[34] and "by personal achievement."[35] On Vancouver Island, the conservative *Daily Colonist* in Victoria, B.C., wrote of high expectations for the new resident of Rideau Hall, who "has profound learning, something that brings in its train balanced judgement, and when he speaks it is in vivid and vigorous English and with a display of unfailing good taste."[36] It described him as "one of the most brilliant Scots of modern times."

Canada's leading literary magazine, *Saturday Night*, under the respected managing director Bernard K. Sandwell, proffered the view that the appointment had "an experimental side."[37] There was rejoicing in the raised status for writers, given the "discovery that a Scottish poet, novelist, and historian of good but not titled family can become a representative of the king in Canada is having a good effect in circles where money was hitherto the only thing that could compete with blue blood."[38] There was, certainly, an expectation that Tweedsmuir would have a beneficial influence on Canadian literature, arts, and education.

Canadians knew the new governor primarily because, as a writer, he was "a man self-revealed in his art."[39] More Canadians came to know him as their interest was piqued from the time of his appointment and they began buying the books of their governor general-to-be. John O. Herrem, a middle-aged Norwegian immigrant who had arrived in Canada in 1910 and who, more than two decades later, had become a successful, independent businessman and community leader in Fort Frances, in northwestern Ontario, bought *The King's Grace*. It was a demonstration of loyalty and of a desire to learn more about his king and the king's new representative.[40] For many others, like Roger Rowley, who was twenty-one at the time and living in Ottawa, "you felt a companionship, a kinship, with [him] because we all read his books."[41]

Dr. H.L. Stewart, a professor of philosophy for twenty-two years at Dalhousie University in Halifax, commented, "[T]his time, it is more than the conventional interest attendant on all such arrivals that is aroused in the public mind."[42] The symbolism evoked by the governor general's arrival and the familiar oaths that would be administered had new meaning, and comfort, in a world where old forms of government were jettisoned by people finding relief in dictatorships. Stewart's thoughts paralleled Tweedsmuir's. He was not alone in extolling Tweedsmuir's interests and intellectual capacity which gave good reason for high expectations.

The governor general's train finally turned northwest away from the St. Lawrence valley and up into the Ottawa valley on Monday, November 4, headed for the nation's capital. The city prepared for His Excellency's expected three o'clock arrival by shutting down the administration. Government offices were closed at one o'clock and city employees were allowed to leave work at two, to allow as many people as possible to participate in the welcome. The weather, however, was not welcoming. Overcast and windy, those waiting around Union Station were forced to turn up their collars.[43] The upper windows of buildings around Connaught Place and Confederation Square, adjacent to the station, were crowded with people taking advantage of the better view, from inside. The station itself was decked out in flags and coloured bunting. Adding to the anticipation and colour were two hundred men of the Cameron Highlanders who marched to the station, in step with the traditional tunes being squeezed out of the accompanying bagpipes. The men and horses of the Princess Louise's Dragoon Guards, with their shiny helmets and lances topped with small pennants, stood like equestrian statues outside the station with an open carriage, awaiting the emergence of Their Excellencies.

When the train arrived at Union Station, Prime Minister King boarded it and again greeted His Excellency. They exchanged a few words, both expressing delight at the prospect of working together during the next few years.[44] The party then stepped down onto the platform and the new governor general inspected a unit of his foot guards before proceeding into the station. They came to a halt and the assembly broke into strong applause, which echoed loudly in the cavernous hallway of the station. The governor general removed his top hat and gloves and handed them, along with his cane, to an attendant. He was now ready to be presented to the Cabinet and the various waiting diplomats, who included ambassadors from Japan, France, and the United States.

His Worship, Mayor P.J. Nolan, bedecked with his chain of office, was handed an awkwardly large sheet of paper on which his welcoming speech was written. He began to read from the paper in a very stilted manner, sometimes stumbling over his words. The Tweedsmuirs listened. No one appeared to react to the small errors and mispronunciations the nervous mayor made, beginning with the usual listing of the governor general's titles, referring to him as a member of "the Order of the Champions [sic] of Honour" (instead of Companion of Honour). Continuing, he noted that His Excellency was "no stranger to us" and Ottawa "no stranger to you." Echoing a by then familiar theme, Mayor Nolan proclaimed that the governor general was known to thousands of people who had never seen him before but who enjoyed "that literature written by the pen of John 'Bue-can.'"[45]

Tweedsmuir, clearly in his element and with no notes, gave the impression of complete ease, looking as though he were gathering up more thoughts for what seemed to be a spontaneous and gracious reply to the mayor's welcome. With hands behind his back and a casual swivel to address now the mayor, now the crowd of invited guests, he exuded a comfort and confidence that was reflected in the satisfied smile of Mackenzie King, standing just behind him. It was an address that could only have strengthened the expectations that people had already set in their own minds about their unique new governor general.

For some who dwelt on the Scottish dimension, there may have been some surprise that his accent was very much Oxford English, with only the odd, very slight, rolling "r" that hinted at the speaker's roots.

Sensitive to the fact that he and his wife and son would be residing much of the time in Ottawa, Tweedsmuir addressed himself to Ottawa at a local level as well as to its role as the seat of government, then going on with a few words aimed at the national level. He accepted a gift from the mayor, expressing the hope that he might take it "as a symbol that you may accept me as one of yourselves." It was with "most complete sincerity and resolute determination" that he and his wife would "devote all the talents we possess to the service of Canada and it is my ernest hope that by the help of God … I may not fail in the great trust which it is permitted to me by His Majesty and by this great Dominion." As he finished, he gave a deep bow, symbolic in itself of respect and an expression of his willingness to serve the people of Canada. The speech struck just the right chords at so many levels, and the silent crowd broke into loud applause again. Mackenzie King, in the background, quite accurately thought the speech "had a ring of great sincerity and ability of heart and mind."[46] The new governor general was handed his top hat, gloves, and cane, then he and Lady Tweedsmuir were led out by two army officers.

Their Excellencies spent the next fifteen minutes in the waiting room of the station shaking hands with the almost 250 specially invited guests who were presented to them by forty-nine-year-old veteran aide-de-camp, Colonel Willis-O'Connor. The Canadian aide-de-camp and the new governor general were not complete strangers. They first met during the Great War, when Major John Buchan was working in the Intelligence Corps, attached to General Headquarters in France, and Willis-O'Connor was aide-de-camp to General Arthur Currie.[47] The handshaking finished, the couple finally emerged from the stout, pillared, stone railway building, where a large crowd waited eagerly and broke into applause as the viceregal couple emerged. The *Ottawa Evening Citizen* journalist cleverly described

Library and Archives Canada/PA-148539

Official portrait of Lord and Lady Tweedsmuir, taken shortly after they took up residence at Rideau Hall, Ottawa, November 1935.

the double arrival: "Lord Tweedsmuir was warmly welcomed by a great crowd of Ottawa people who went to the station to see John Buchan."[48]

The Princess Louise Dragoon Guards, lances vertical with pennants fluttering in the cool, late fall breeze, held their horses steady as Their Excellencies stepped up into the open carriage, acknowledging the crowds. The procession circled round in front of the station and the Château Laurier Hotel across the street and proceeded along Sussex Drive toward the Tweedsmuir's new Canadian home. As they drove, Tweedsmuir could hear repeated calls of "Good luck, John."[49] The arrival at Rideau Hall continued its ceremonial form as the horse guards drew up under the front-entrance portico. Entering their home was not an escape from the bustling activity of the world outside. A short while later, the prime minister arrived with James Garfield Gardiner, a former Saskatchewan premier and loyal Liberal, who had been brought to Ottawa by Mackenzie King and appointed minister of agriculture.[50] In his first administrative act, Tweedsmuir conducted the swearing-in ceremony of the new minister.

After three days of living "like goldfish in a bowl," the Tweedsmuirs were quite tired.[51] The governor general's physician gave him a complete going-over the day after his arrival in Ottawa, setting out a dietary regime to help him put on some weight and recommending he rest for two hours every afternoon.[52] The new occupants of Rideau Hall began settling in and the governor general took up this new role with his usual energy and imagination.

PART II

Making the Statute of Westminster a Reality

Statesman in Canada

CHAPTER 4

Counsellor

Desired, Trusted, and Suspected

On his first day as governor general in Ottawa, November 4, 1935, Tweedsmuir repeated to his prime minister what he had said to him on board the *Duchess of Richmond* on his arrival at Quebec City: "You are my only voice."[1] He knew, and wanted to emphasize, his constitutional role, acting on the advice of the first minister.

Tweedsmuir was certainly aware of what Walter Bagehot described as the "trinity of rights" due the sovereign, or his or her representative — to be consulted, to encourage, and to warn. John Buchan had researched, studied, and written about previous Governor General Lord Minto. In that work, published in 1924, he quoted Canadian prime minister Sir Wilfrid Laurier's observation that a governor general "need not be the mere figurehead ... [h]e has the privilege of advising his advisors and, if he is a man of sense and experience, his advice is often taken."[2] While this statement was made prior to the passage of the 1931 Statute of Westminster, and Buchan knew his formal constitutional role, he was a man of considerable experience, who could offer intelligent exchanges with the prime minister.

Mackenzie King, however, had a narrower view and had written to Buchan subsequent to his appointment, describing their respective roles: "the one of accepting, and the other of tendering, advice."[3] Their different conceptions of their relationship made it unclear what the road ahead would be like.

Their first business meeting occurred the day after the new governor's arrival in Ottawa. When they met, King's emotional state was evident. He drew Tweedsmuir's attention "to the shadow of light above his head in the photographs taken at Quebec, and of what had passed through [his] mind when [he, i.e., King] looked at it."[4] Could such high expectations be sustained?

Prior to leaving London, Tweedsmuir had been asked by the Palace to raise with the Canadian prime minister the possibility of a knighthood for the departing Canadian high commissioner in London, Howard Ferguson.[5] This first business meeting presented the opportunity. The governor general noted that it was English custom to allow an outgoing government to propose a number of knighthoods. Acknowledging that King opposed titles, Tweedsmuir nonetheless suggested responsibility for such a decision should lie with the former prime minister — Bennett, in this case.

Mackenzie King rejected those, and other, arguments, believing that a title for Ferguson would land him (i.e., King), the governor, and the king all into trouble when the issue was raised in Parliament.

Tweedsmuir remained insistent. He did not seem to fully appreciate the intensity of King's views, even though they had been made evident in a letter to Buchan the previous July — that much would have been gained from Buchan coming to Canada as a commoner.[6] King became irritated. He asked if His Excellency "might be interested in knowing the detail[s] of his own appointment."[7] It was, of course, a not so subtle way of telling Buchan that he really owed his appointment to King, not Bennett.

Undeterred, and likely believing he was being helpful, Tweedsmuir told Mackenzie King that he might "find it necessary to adopt titles," as a way to reward civil servants, and suggested that Canada might wish to create its own order of knighthood, "something in the nature of the Order of St. Lawrence."[8] He advised his prime minister to consider the issue.

That was it for King. He believed it was not the governor's place to advise but rather to accept advice. King was now thinking that Buchan was too conscious of being the king's representative.[9] How bittersweet the arrival of this dream governor general was becoming!

After that first meeting, there was only minor contact between the two men until they both attended the Armistice Day ceremony. Apart from the ceremony, they discussed the successful conclusion of the trade negotiations with the Americans. Tweedsmuir congratulated the prime minister "in a quite sincere and downright way," saying it was "a great achievement," that it was what the world needed, and that it would have "a fine effect on conditions in Europe."[10] A few days later, as a goodwill gesture, Buchan had his book *Men and Deeds* sent to King, with good wishes for his trip to Washington to sign the trade agreement.

They did not meet again until the first week of December, after Mackenzie King had been in Washington and Tweedsmuir had travelled to Montreal and Toronto. Surprisingly, Tweedsmuir again raised the issue of honours. King was annoyed at the topic's return, though he acknowledged an order of merit "for our own country" might be a possibility at some point. Then, transposing his own strong sentiments, he doubted Parliament would favour even that.

King began to think he had made a mistake having a governor general and his wife "from Tory stock," but, despite their run-ins so far, he declared that he had "not yet lost faith in the Governor."[11] Still, the annoyance King had felt regarding Tweedsmuir's championing of the honours was now compounded by what he saw as his excessive formality. Hoping that that might change, writing on the subject in his diary, King noted bluntly to himself that "a year or two may help to get this knocked out of him."

Tweedsmuir continued, unknowingly, to irritate his prime minister. December 17 was King's sixty-first birthday. Whether Tweedsmuir knew this or not was beside the point. Mackenzie King did not receive congratulations from his governor general. This failure helped to make King's frustration with what he saw as Buchan's other lapses even more pronounced: "It has been a real shock to me to lose the John Buchan I had known, and discover a [T]ory ... [with] ... a sort of royalty complex, which is damnable in my eyes. I cannot abide by it!" King now seemed to be confusing John Buchan, the man he knew, with the king's new representative who was attempting to come to grips with his new job. King sent Lord and Lady Tweedsmuir each a book as a gift for Christmas, but his disappointment grew when he received no greetings in return.[12]

The prime minister ended the year with an entry in his diary that the "disappointment of the Governor General has been a very deep and bitter one."[13] Fortunately, there was some light from other issues, to be discussed shortly, that would allow King to qualify his disappointment. As he noted in his diary that New Year, "the year is not going out without evidence of a better condition there."[14] But the original issue sparking disappointment in King continued.

Three months later Tweedsmuir again raised the issue of awards for civil servants that would include titles.[15] The prime minister was furious and was now categorical. The government's policy was clear and would not include recommending anyone in Canada for any order or award involving a title. A long discourse by King ensued, about their relationship and how hurt he was that this subject was continually being raised and that they had not been able to have the kind of discussions King had anticipated. The next day he wrote to Tweedsmuir, stating that had he not valued their personal friendship more than the official relationship, he would "not have ventured to say a word last night."[16] The issue was at an end. Tweedsmuir learned that he would have to be more sensitive and choose his battles. The following day he wrote to King that he would not raise the issue of honours again.[17] His contrition, and a small, bound collection of speeches for the king's jubilee as "a gift for a gift," helped him to redeem himself and evoked an effusive, even gushing, response from Mackenzie King.[18]

These exchanges over the subject of honours give us a glimpse of King's character and of what the new governor general had to deal with. Tweedsmuir had been trying to put his constitutional role, and what he believed to be the general interests of Canada, first, but he had misread the strengths of King's opinions and moods. This attempt undoubtedly contributed to King finding "JB" too formal, a sentiment that would return repeatedly.[19] Fortunately, other matters at hand helped heal the wounds of their first collision.

In mid-December Tweedsmuir had written to his prime minister to thank him for "a most extraordinarily kind letter."[20] The governor general observed "how desperately busy" King was and offered to "do anything to help in [his] heavy task," a task that also raised concerns about King's health.

In Tweedsmuir's letter to King, he had stated that he was looking forward to a time when King's "duties [were] less urgent" so that they could talk about things "that concern our peace," a reference to the increasing threat from the violent dictators in Europe. King was indeed busy, in fact, becoming exhausted from the volume of work he was dealing with.

Attempting to better inform himself of the situation, Tweedsmuir invited one of the prime minister's long-time assistants, E.A. Pickering, to dinner at Government House just before Christmas. While Tweedsmuir no doubt learned about Pickering's experience and his duties, Pickering may have used the opportunity to discreetly express his concern about the state of relations between his boss and the governor general, and to propose to Tweedsmuir suggestions on how to improve it. Whatever the instigation or motivation, Tweedsmuir invited Mackenzie King to Government House on Boxing Day, the day before King had planned a dinner for Lord and Lady Tweedsmuir at Laurier House. Tweedsmuir's mid-December letter may have helped begin to salve King's hurt from initial disappointments. When the two men met on Boxing Day for a discussion, Tweedsmuir repeated his offer of help, which seems to have been received by King for the first time.[21]

During the meeting the prime minister and governor general enjoyed a wide-ranging discussion, which included the European situation, the Dominion-provincial conference, and the financial situation, about which they agreed there was "the necessity of getting a picture which would show the situation in its entirety."[22] This was more the type of meeting King expected, and thus enjoyed.

The topic then turned to the prime minister's workload and the organization of his office. When Tweedsmuir mentioned that he had had Pickering to dinner, King was "non-plussed" and embarrassed at not having heard of the event previously. King rationalized Tweedsmuir's motivation, and believed it "apparent from the way in which the [g]overnor spoke that he had done so largely to be able to speak to me of the staff generally, and undoubtedly thought I would have expressed some word of appreciation to him."[23] Pickering had obviously taken a risk, but how could he have refused the invitation? As it was, he was at his wit's end in dealing with his boss's business because by early January he was off the job, having "broken down."[24]

Tweedsmuir again offered to assist King in any way he could, to which King replied he "would deeply appreciate anything he could do toward helping me to discover the right type of person" who could help organize King's work more efficiently and relieve him of some of the burden of his office. Tweedsmuir essentially stressed that it was in the national interest that the prime minister be "kept free from anything in the way of detail and anxiety."[26] King reflected that Tweedsmuir was, in contrast to earlier encounters, "very natural ... [and] ... could not have been friendlier."[26] This was one of the first significant manifestations of why the arrival of "JB" had been so anticipated by King.

The next day, after the dinner at Laurier House, Tweedsmuir again brought up the subject of King's office. He asked King to "reduce to writing" the duties that he thought should be assigned to the individual who would fill this new position. Tweedsmuir added that he wanted King to "feel he [Tweedsmuir] was acting, not as [g]overnor [g]eneral, but as an old friend." Tweedsmuir told King he would do what he could, "in communication with others, to find the right kind of man ... which could be," he added, "of help to each of us."[27]

The following two days, King had a bad cold. Tweedsmuir telephoned to ask how King was, and the following day sent "exquisite spring flowers." The call compensated for the lack of birthday and Christmas greetings. King was touched by the kindness and saw "a new note" in their relationship.[28] It appears that someone, perhaps Pickering, had indeed whispered something to Tweedsmuir as to how he could get his relationship with King on the right road.

On the last day of the year, King received "a very kind communication" from Tweedsmuir, setting down his "first impressions" and "some suggestions about the reorganisation of [the prime minister's] office."[29] He divided his note into two parts.[30] The first was "a short outline of the British practice" that he thought might be useful for comparative purposes. It included how he had worked in a "very private" but unofficial manner as a personal assistant over eighteen months to Prime Ministers

Ramsay MacDonald and Stanley Baldwin, finally recommending to them "something like a *chef du cabinet*," The second part contained "suggestions for the position of a *chef du cabinet*" but his "first impressions" were qualified, he wrote, because of his still limited knowledge of Canadian administration. He was aware, however, that there was no one person with the "permanent reservoir of knowledge," like Sir Maurice Hankey, who was the first, and the longest-serving, secretary to the British Cabinet, nor was there a developed civil service from which to second good people into this type of job. Finally, the Canadian prime minister had the additional load of being responsible for external affairs, which demanded ever more time as Canada searched to develop an independent foreign policy in the wake of the Statute of Westminster.

King had known about Hankey. In May 1927 he had invited a respected academic to set out a proposal to "begin the work of slowly building up a Cabinet office." Professor Burgon Bickersteth, warden of Hart House at the University of Toronto, produced a lengthy memo on the subject after spending time in London to study the workings of the Cabinet office there. During his stay in London, he met with Cabinet ministers and senior officials, but most significantly, with Sir Maurice Hankey. After considering the report, King offered Bickersteth the position of Cabinet secretary.[31] Before accepting, however, Bickersteth consulted with Hankey; he then declined the offer, in no small part because of confirmation that King was mixing up the political and civil service functions, a critical issue.[32] King was gracious with the rejection but made no apparent offers to anyone else.

There was, however, no point in "finding the right man" until the duties were defined. Tweedsmuir set the duties of this man at three: i) head the Prime Minister's Office, with the help of, perhaps, two assistants, to schedule the prime minister's day, make all appointments, and deal with correspondence, the most important of which would be prepared by the head, who would, however, never accompany the prime minister to political meetings; ii) serve as the prime minister's "intelligence officer," identifying what the prime minister should read in terms of books and articles, monitoring the press, and preparing memos on "special questions" the prime minister should be informed of; and iii) serve as the principal liaison officer for the prime minister with all departments, including External Affairs — this latter function required someone who knew and understood not only the machinery of government but also the country. Such a position would lighten the prime minister's burden and, just as importantly, would provide "a permanent continuing administrative machine" that would continue to function even if the prime minister were away for any reason.

For King, however, it came down to the "right kind of assistance." Tweedsmuir seems to have recognized that King still had not really defined the role. Even if he had chosen to do so then, and even if Tweedsmuir had suggested a name, King did not think he could have accepted it — Buchan was, after all, a Tory! King called his under-secretary of state for external affairs, Dr. O.D. Skelton, whom he trusted on some matters but not others.[33]

At some point, someone, perhaps King himself or Pickering, informed Tweedsmuir about Bickersteth's work, because the governor general contacted the professor to request a copy of his 1927 memo.[34] This was duly sent on January 4, along with an accompanying "confidential" letter summarizing his work, as well as a candid assessment of the current situation.[35] Bickersteth noted bluntly that the fact that, three months after taking office, King still only had H.R. Henry and E.A. Pickering as his long-suffering assistants was "pathetic," because their abilities were limited. This led Bickersteth to the cynical assessment that public men failed to surround themselves with "really able assistants" and that it "would almost seem as if the P.M. and Cabinet Ministers were suspicious of brains in this capacity." The failings fell largely into Mackenzie King's lap because he had not seized opportunities and did not effectively use the assistants he did have.[36]

It was at this point in his confidential letter that Bickersteth expressed his belief that Tweedsmuir "could do much to encourage the P.M. to think out this problem." The governor general's approach, which Bickersteth endorsed, was to try to draw out Mackenzie King on this issue and get him to move it forward by making him think it was his idea. It was in any case perhaps what Tweedsmuir had hoped to achieve by having King "reduce to writing" his activities.

The prime minister attended the governor general's New Year's levee and enjoyed a short walk with him. Their relationship was improving. But King's depressed mood continued, his anxiety heightened by the anticipated increased activity in preparation for the opening of Parliament on February 6.

On January 6 King met with Tweedsmuir at Government House and gave him the requested written copy of his activities.[37] It incorporated points Tweedsmuir set out in his "first impressions" and listed in considerable detail the various activities and needs of the prime minister, in three categories — public, political, and personal. On reviewing the document, Tweedsmuir remarked, "it was impossible for any human being to cope with this amount of work [and] ... a complete organization is necessary."[38] They also raised the question of names again; obviously King and Skelton had not been able to come up with any satisfactory potential candidates.

Their discussion was extensive. King was opening up and providing valuable additional details with which Tweedsmuir could further assess the situation.[39] For his part Tweedsmuir was frank in his comments and shared some of his own experience with King. He told King he should be "giving his time to thought and study" and emphasized "the need for leisure to think out problems."[40]

Over these couple of weeks, amidst the discussions about the organization of the Prime Minister's Office, Tweedsmuir emerged as a senior statesman and counsellor to King — proving himself to be a man of considerable experience, capable of advising his advisor. Tweedsmuir understood the seriousness of the situation and was concerned for the good governance of the country. The lack of organization in the Prime Minister's Office was a serious impediment. Despite Tweedsmuir's best efforts, however, King did not act on the matter, even though his situation was deteriorating. The prime minister told his Cabinet on January 8 that he "could not keep up." Discussions were held involving giving some responsibilities to others, but there was nothing on the core issue. On January 20, King George V died. Parliament opened on February 6. King was caught up in it all and paid no attention to the organization of his office affairs.

In October that year (1936), Tweedsmuir returned from Toronto, where he received an honorary doctor of laws from Victoria University. He was accompanied by Professor Bickersteth, who stayed at Rideau Hall.[41] No doubt, discussions concentrated on how to revive the by then ten-month-old initiative with Mackenzie King. They were not successful, as there appears to have been no activity through 1937, other than some changes in personnel.[42]

With the arrival of 1938, the prime minister's situation again appeared to be reaching a critical point, even attracting the attention of the Palace. At the beginning of February that year, Alexander Hardinge, George VI's private secretary, commented in a letter to Tweedsmuir about Mackenzie King's health and that it seemed advisable to drop "this particular tradition" of the prime minister also acting as secretary of state for external affairs, and the sooner the better.[43]

The status quo continued into the summer, when one of King's long-time secretaries, E.A. Pickering, left. King's general health was not good and he lamented in a letter to Tweedsmuir, who was himself in Britain at a health clinic for a rest, that because several of his ministers were away for much of the summer, "the Departments [were] loading more and more on [his] shoulders until [he] reached the point where now [he was] quite unable to carry their burdens longer."[44] The situation has been described as "the increasingly chaotic way of dealing with government business" and was contributing to King's periodic poor health.[45] Ill, and with time to reflect, King was finally compelled to seriously consider how better to organize his activities. With much of the groundwork done and duties defined by Tweedsmuir and Bickersteth, King could focus on who could fill the job. A candidate was at hand; someone King had first met five years earlier.

Arnold D.P. Heeney was the son of a prominent Anglican minister originally from Winnipeg. The younger Heeney was a Rhodes scholar and an increasingly successful lawyer in Montreal. He had first met Mackenzie King when he and his father visited Kingsmere in 1933. King was impressed at that first meeting. Canon Heeney visited Kingsmere each summer. He and King talked much of spiritual matters, but also of other topics as well, including family. King saw them as "a lovely and loving family," which would only enhance his impressions of Arnold.[46]

In July 1938 the prime minister wrote to Arnold Heeney offering him the position in his office and describing it as a sort of Canadian Hankey.[47] On August 24 Arnold Heeney accepted a post titled principal secretary to the prime minister, corresponding to the rank of deputy minister. He would start October 1.

In early September Tweedsmuir, who was still in Britain at a health clinic, received a letter from Mackenzie King, who was at his Gatineau Hills home, suffering from sciatica. King believed he had found the right person to manage his office: "an immense relief."[48] Tweedsmuir described Heeney as "excellent"; it is likely they would have met and he would certainly know him through conversations with King. The prime minister returned to Ottawa on September 19 for the first time in three weeks, as he informed Tweedsmuir, with relief from the sciatica and from hiring a principal secretary.[49] The timing was fortuitous, allowing Heeney to become familiar with the job, and with King, before the very strenuous labours of the war descended on them a year later.

Two years after his appointment, Heeney was made clerk of the Privy Council Office (PCO) and secretary to the Cabinet.[50] He wrote in his memoirs: "I realize once more how great is the debt which the embryonic cabinet secretariat in this country incurred to Britain."[51] The debt Heeney could not know, though, was the influential role played by Tweedsmuir, who applied his experience, intellect, and initiative to King's problem, and engaged with Burgon Bickersteth. All this prepared the ground for the prime minister to create, but ultimately only when he was forced to, what would become a key part of Canada's modern machinery of government.[52]

King George V died on January 20, 1936. Tweedsmuir wrote that he "never realised before the influence that simple goodness and dutifulness could have in the world." [53] He received a sincere and personal note of sympathy from Mackenzie King.[54] Indeed, George V had inspired Tweedsmuir as an exemplar of constitutional and personal propriety, as well as being a strong unifying force for the Empire, all reflected in John Buchan's 1935 book, *The King's Grace*, celebrating King George's silver jubilee.

The mourning period for George V, though, had a silver lining for Tweedsmuir. With no formal functions and very little entertaining during this period, it provided "a wonderful chance of seeing people."[55] Three mornings a week, he held a reception for members of Parliament at his office in the East Block of the Parliament Buildings. There was never a lack of members, from all political parties, who wanted to see him. Some no doubt came to meet John Buchan, but they would very soon likely be talking about their interests and activities as parliamentarians and about the region of the country they were from, or about the domestic and international issues raised in the Speech from the Throne.[56] The impression he formed of the MPs was that they were perhaps more confidential with him than with their own leaders, because his office was "now blessedly free of any ordinary political colouring," compared to the period before the Statute of Westminster.[57]

He also met some of the younger officials within the civil service. "There is uncommon good stuff in Canada among the youth," he wrote.[58] Who were these young men, "the youth," who impressed him?

Many would have been the bright young men, as historian Jack Granatstein describes them, that Dr. Oscar D. Skelton, the nationalist under-secretary of state for external affairs, hired from the universities into the nascent Department of External Affairs.[59] The External Affairs offices were located in the East Block of the Parliament buildings. The names of the young men illumine the early decades of the department. Among them are Loring Christie, Lester Pearson, Charles Ritchie, Norman Robertson, and Hume Wrong. It was also in the East Block that the office of the governor general was located. It is here that Tweedsmuir would run into them or, likely, arrange to have many of them stop in during his morning receptions. Writing to his wife in England about Charles Ritchie, one of the young men who was posted later that year to the Canadian mission in Washington, Tweedsmuir noted that his departure would "be a great loss to Ottawa."[60]

As with the MPs, Tweedsmuir thought these young civil servants too seemed to be "very confidential" with him. Perhaps it was because, as Tweedsmuir explained, "they have no one else to go to."[61] It is likely that at least one of them made that statement to him. "I hope I may be of some use to them," he confided to Baldwin.[62]

His travels were also an opportunity to meet civil servants. In Winnipeg, aboard his railway car, he met Leonard Brockington for the first time. Brockington was counsel on a public inquiry into grain commerce and was shortly appointed chairman of the Canadian Broadcasting Corporation (CBC).[63] Brockington recalled that first meeting: Tweedsmuir "knew the history of all preceding inquiries [and there had been many] and the gist of the one in progress."[64] It was a reflection of both his capacious memory and his great intellectual curiosity. Writing after Tweedsmuir's death, Brockington summed up what others had told him as well about their meetings with Tweedsmuir: "So many others have told me of the breadth of his interest, the depth of his knowledge and the subtle way with which he encouraged those with whom he spoke."[65]

Parliament prorogued for the summer of 1936. Tweedsmuir had offered to return to Ottawa from Quebec City, but the prime minister, appreciating Tweedsmuir's respect for his role in Parliament, indicated it was not necessary.[66] Tweedsmuir replied graciously that "you have been extraordinarily considerate towards me," and then congratulated him on the first session, commenting that King had "managed it brilliantly" and had gotten through a lot of valuable work.[67] At the end of his letter, Tweedsmuir turned from business to suggest that King join him for a relaxing week at the end of August, yachting and fishing with the lieutenant-governor of British Columbia.[68] King was not to be caught, though, declining for reasons of business, specifically preparation for the League of Nations meetings he would be attending in Geneva in October.

While King was in Geneva, Tweedsmuir met with many of the other ministers, "who," he remarked, had "suddenly discovered a passion for my society";[69] perhaps because the prime minister was absent. Heads of government departments and senior civil servants also sought increasingly to meet with the governor general.[70]

In 1936 fascist Italy consolidated its brutal conquest of Abyssinia (Ethiopia); in October of that year, the League of Nations met in Geneva to try to make good on its mandate, and resolve the crisis between these two member countries. Elsewhere, in the spring of that year, Hitler reoccupied the Rhineland, unopposed. These events were but portents of more dire ones to come. For the British and Dominion governments, though, there was a more immediate, festering crisis.

Throughout the summer and into the autumn of 1936, British prime minister Stanley Baldwin and a few other individuals became aware of a relationship between the new king, Edward VIII, and an American woman, Wallis Simpson, who was in the process of divorcing her second husband in the United States. The relationship was troubling because of the potential constitutional complications, and because of adverse public perceptions in an age when divorce was a social stigma. It was more so because it involved the king himself, who was also head of the Church of England! Complicating this was the new context of the Statute of Westminster, which meant the issue was not Britain's to deal with alone but required the consideration of the Dominion governments as well.

The British papers remained respectfully silent, but this was not the case in the United States. In the middle of October, King Edward's private secretary, Alexander Hardinge, wrote a "Private and Personal" letter to Tweedsmuir, setting out a "distasteful request" for information about Canadian public opinion and the impact of American newspaper coverage of His Majesty's "domestic affairs."[71]

Tweedsmuir replied two weeks later, "with profound unwillingness," but scrupulous about his position: he stated that he would provide information, but added that it would be "improper for me to have any view."[72] Tweedsmuir noted the country had "retained more of the Victorian tradition in thought and conduct" than had the United States, and would not reprint what appeared in the American papers. In addition, the young King Edward, who had been popular as Prince of Wales, had visited Canada in 1919 and now owned a ranch in Alberta. His appeal was strong, especially among younger people.

The seriousness of the situation forced Baldwin to meet with the king. On October 20, he "broke the ice," requesting that Edward conduct himself with more discretion and asking Mrs. Simpson to "put off her impending divorce proceedings."[73]

At this same time, Mackenzie King was in London, on his way back to Canada from the League of Nations meetings in Geneva. Susan Tweedsmuir was also in London, having returned to England earlier in October to visit family. They met each other and each met separately with Baldwin, who was eager to hear first-hand accounts of Canadian opinion. Mackenzie King also met with Edward VIII but was not prepared to advise him in any particular direction. He believed that if he did, Canada could then be blamed for causing His Majesty's actions, which, if perceived to be unpopular in any way, would have negative consequences for Canada. He had a suspicion of British motives, especially those of a "Tory" government, feeling that they would use Canada "to pull their chestnuts out of the fire for them."[74]

After the flurry of meetings, Baldwin wrote directly to his old friend and confidante, John Buchan, who was in Ottawa between travels to the West. He expressed concern about King Edward's situation and confided that he had broached the issue with the king himself.[75] Concern grew dramatically during the next few weeks.

Immediately after Mackenzie King returned to Ottawa in early November, he met with Tweedsmuir over tea at Rideau Hall, disappointed again by what he perceived as Tweedsmuir's apparent formality. While the League of Nations meeting and the Abyssinian crisis were topical, the primary subject was the perilous situation into which Edward was casting the Throne.

Tweedsmuir told his prime minister about Hardinge's request but not, it seems, about Baldwin's letter, aware by now of King's sensitivities regarding his contact with the British government. Tweedsmuir said he believed there was a general view in England that Canada was key in terms of being an influence on Edward because he "had a real love for Canada."[76] It was a statement of fact obtained from the highest levels, but it was interpreted by Mackenzie King as confirming his suspicions about British motivations and indicating that Tweedsmuir might think of Britain's interests first.

At the end of their meeting, Tweedsmuir stated he was glad King was back. With King's perception of Tweedsmuir's formality, he offered "to communicate with the Governor-General in an official way" but in a self-satisfying reflection he thought "Buchan" didn't "seem to wish to encourage this."[77] King's evident inconsistency in his relationship with Tweedsmuir is also revealed in his diary — King used the familiar reference, "Buchan," and almost in the same breath, the more formal "Governor-General," regardless that the entire subject was official business.

The next day, after hearing the prime minister's version of his talks in London, Tweedsmuir wrote to Stanley Baldwin to explain Mackenzie King's "sagacious" words during the latter's meeting with Edward VIII, attempting to ensure better mutual understanding between the two prime ministers. [78] Always encouraging in the circumstance, Tweedsmuir told Baldwin both he and Mackenzie King had taken the "right line" by emphasizing to Edward the important role he could play. Tweedsmuir believed Edward was "perfectly competent to play [the role] brilliantly" and was convinced of Edward's "essential soundness." The former confidante to Baldwin also recommended who should and shouldn't be allowed to advise the king, adding that he, Baldwin, was "the only man with sufficient purchase," because of Edward's attachment to him. He concluded by emphasizing his own delicate situation as the king's representative, and stated that if Baldwin wanted an official opinion about Canadian feeling on the matter, it would have to come from Mackenzie King.

Amidst this intensifying crisis, the governor general left Ottawa by train on November 18 for his second trip west. A week later, while Tweedsmuir was in Edmonton, Edward VIII met with Baldwin again, this time with a proposal for a morganatic marriage, in which he would marry Wallis Simpson and remain king but she would not be queen. The information was transmitted to the Dominions. Mackenzie King made clear in a despatch to Britain that Canada would not be involved and would neither agree nor disagree with the proposal, something that one way or another might result in forcing Edward to abdicate.[79] Remaining suspicious of Britain's motives, he insisted on keeping Canada apart from the issue, and referred to the Statute of Westminster that stated an Act of Parliament in Britain would only apply to a Dominion if that Dominion "requested and consented" to it.[80]

The crisis finally broke publicly in Britain on December 3. Canadian newspapers, having been discreet on the subject over the past two months, began publishing articles but focused mainly on the constitutional and political dimensions.[81] On December 4, Baldwin addressed the British Parliament outlining an ultimatum to King Edward — drop his plans to marry or abdicate. English law, he said, did not allow a morganatic marriage.

Tweedsmuir arrived back in Ottawa on Sunday morning, December 6, with the crisis building to a crescendo. Mackenzie King confided to his diary that he was happy the governor general had not been present for the past weeks, consistent with his earlier suspicions that Tweedsmuir might push British government interests ahead of those of Canada.[82] Once the governor general had a few hours to settle in, King dutifully arrived at Rideau Hall. The two men were sequestered for a couple of hours in the late afternoon and again that evening, discussing the crisis, its possible constitutional implications, and scenarios for dealing with various outcomes.

It was a long, meandering conversation, which, despite King's suspicions, ironically led to the kind of discussion he had dreamed about. They talked generally about Canada and about Tweedsmuir's approach to Canada. At one point Tweedsmuir told King he wanted "to reveal Canada to herself," a remark revealing the potential he saw for the country.[83] King wrote in his diary in a self-congratulatory manner that that was "exactly what I said would be the effect of his coming."[84]

The discussion refocused on the crisis at hand. King was being as candid as he could be, but seeming always to try to strengthen his own hand. He relayed information he had received from London, and said that he was sharing it, "as between two friends not as Prime Minister in any way advising him."[85] He later cautioned, though, that what Tweedsmuir had "to say as John Buchan was different from what he had to say as Governor-General, that ... [he] was always speaking as the representative of the Crown."[86] King expressed his concern that Buchan's training as a journalist caused him to see the dramatic side of events and overrode "the caution which was needed in weighing words" as governor. Tweedsmuir must have bitten his tongue hard with this rather condescending talk from King, but he could only acquiesce and thanked his prime minister for pointing this out.

As Victoria Wilcox has concluded, in Tweedsmuir's judgment a governor general had to work in harmony with his prime minister, and if this meant giving in to Mackenzie King's wishes, then Tweedsmuir was willing to do so.[87]

King, however, wasn't finished. The prickly constitutional past of Governor General Lord Byng was raised and seemed, at least to King, to evoke some slight but muted reaction in Tweedsmuir.[88] King cited Byng's problem of listening to advisors other than his prime minister, a situation that Edward VIII was also repeating, he said. Again, it was for Tweedsmuir but to take heed at this not so subtle hint for himself.

After what must have felt like a cathartic talk for King, and in contrast to his thoughts a couple of days ago that he was glad the governor general had been away, he believed their "conversation together was extremely interesting and helpful … [and] a strong bond has been established as a result of it."[89] It helped that Tweedsmuir had the patience of Job, listened, and thanked his prime minister for his advice. What likely made the most positive impact for King, however, was the intellectual dimension of their discussion, of which he had dreamed.

The prime minister left around 6 p.m. for Laurier House and dinner, during which time he received more messages from the British high commissioner Sir Francis Floud, most significantly that Baldwin would make a statement in the British Parliament the next day. He returned to Government House around eight o'clock that evening, bringing papers with him to show Tweedsmuir. Mackenzie King asked if Tweedsmuir would consider it awkward viewing them under the circumstances since these papers were correspondence between ministers about the king. The governor general simply recalled his prime minister's remark earlier in the day and replied that "it would be understood that [King] was only showing them as between friends."[90] In what undoubtedly took Tweedsmuir aback, King chastised him with an emphatic, "No!" It would be as prime minister he did this, and lectured Tweedsmuir on his "dual-relationship [first] to the king as his representative …; [second] to the Ministers, [House of Commons] & Senate."

Over the next week, the intensity of the situation resulted in Tweedsmuir being in frequent telephone and telegraph contact with Stanley Baldwin.[91]

These were communications Tweedsmuir undoubtedly valued but could not let Mackenzie King know of without risking King's suspicion or worse. With some understatement Tweedsmuir wrote: "My own situation has been horribly delicate."[92]

Tweedsmuir prayed for a solution to the perplexities of the Palace crisis. He believed the British throne was the "most stable thing in the world," but he also believed that it had to be based solidly on righteousness and honour, which was the antithesis of what it had become under Edward — "shabby, shoddy, [and] raffish."[93] This was a far cry from the optimistic and supportive views of Edward he had expressed a mere month earlier. Does it reveal a contradiction? The earlier views must be taken in context. Tweedsmuir tried to make the best of a given situation. He considered how popular Edward was in Canada, especially among young people. His positive outlook would not have considered that the unthinkable — abdication — would become reality so soon.

News of the impending abdication was received by the governor general in a secret cable on December 9. The official dénouement followed on December 10 when Baldwin announced King Edward's intention to abdicate. The following day, the Abdication Bill made its way quickly through the lower and upper houses of Westminster and Edward broadcast to the Empire that he was giving up the throne for the woman he loved.

With the end of the crisis, there followed assessments of what impact the outcome would have and what it had revealed as it had run its tortured course. The constant communications between the Dominions and London, by cable and especially by telephone, demonstrated for Tweedsmuir "an inner mechanism of policy [within the Empire] which we had hardly suspected."[94] Tweedsmuir agreed with his old Scottish friend, the Conservative politician, peer, and privy councillor Lord Crawford, who wrote that the quick communication among Commonwealth leaders during the abdication crisis was demonstrating how efficient Imperial co-operation and relations had become.[95] Indeed, at the accession of Edward, developments in transportation and communication had caused excitement and anticipation that during the new monarch's reign "improved lines of communication" would advance the unity of the Commonwealth.[96] Tweedsmuir was impressed as well at how the Dominions had "risen to the situation." Others shared similar observations and optimism with Tweedsmuir.[97] After the abdication, Tweedsmuir and King talked philosophically at length about the issue. King repeatedly suggested Buchan write "a history of the conditions which led up to the present situation and the moral forces which were holding the Empire together."[98] Tweedsmuir replied he had been thinking about it, but that is as far as it went.

The intensity of the abdication crisis also revealed more of the characters of Buchan and Mackenzie King to each other. The crisis did, in its way, result in a stronger bond, but it was a heavily qualified one. King's approach to the relationship was more emotionally charged, conflicted between a desire for friendship and officialdom. Tweedsmuir's approach was more practical and without the emotional need.

If the abdication crisis helped to reveal more of Buchan and King to each other on a personal and official level, it also revealed Tweedsmuir, for the first significant time, as interpreter between Canada and Britain, a role he had earlier suggested to Mackenzie King that he could play. It was a role he would play often during the next few years.

CHAPTER 5

Stirrings in Foreign and Defence Policy
Controversy and Helpful Observations

By the autumn of 1935, the world beyond Canada's borders was increasingly threatening. A number of European countries, including Austria, Romania, Portugal, and the Baltic states, had fallen under authoritarian regimes by the early 1930s. The Nazis came to power in Germany in 1933. When fascist Italy's troops began their conquest of Abyssinia (Ethiopia) in October 1935, it was a crisis for the League of Nations, since both were member countries. The international organization began discussions on a process to apply sanctions against Italy, but the lack of universal membership rendered sanctions ineffective. A member of the League and newly responsible for its own foreign policy in the post-Statute of Westminster world, Canada had to consider what its policy would be regarding the Abyssinian crisis and sanctions.

This crisis had a positive, catalytic effect for Canada, according to Tweedsmuir. What he perceived to be a slowness in reaction to international events reflected the newness of the field for the country. He observed that Canada "has been stirred out of her apathy about international affairs and has been really anxious."[1] He hoped this was the beginning of "a serious attempt on Canada's part to consider her whole international and imperial position."[2]

By the spring of 1936, the struggles of the League demonstrated to Tweedsmuir that the organization was not workable in its present form. He shared his views for short- and long-term solutions with his prime minister.[3] In their discussion they both agreed with a speech by Neville Chamberlain, then chancellor of the exchequer, recommending the lifting of sanctions against Italy. The governor general commented that he had written about the situation to Baldwin and the former Labour prime minister Ramsay MacDonald. King seemed not to take exception to Tweedsmuir's direct communication with Baldwin, possibly because he believed Tweedsmuir had arrived at his view as a result of his "observations in Canada and talks with myself and others here."[4] King's comment did not take into consideration Tweedsmuir's experience and wide range of contacts in Britain where various options were being discussed as well.[5]

On June 18 the prime minister spoke at length in the House of Commons about sanctions against Italy, about whether to maintain, expand, or discontinue them, and about why the League had failed thus far. He set this in a broader discussion about what Canada's role in the world was and what it should be. Tweedsmuir thought the speech "a great performance," and complimented Mackenzie King, saying the speech was "the best and wisest thing said on the subject — better than anything said at home, because far more fully reasoned and more perfectly phrased."[6] The speech was articulate; it balanced divergent views and set out factors influencing Canada's foreign policy, many of which remain valid.[7]

As a way of encouraging Canada "to consider her whole international and imperial position," Tweedsmuir suggested that the speech be published as a pamphlet.[8] There is no record that it was, but both men agreed on the need for such encouragement. King attributed the lack of such discussion to Canada's recent emergence from a colonial attitude, its immunity from invasion, and a preoccupation with economic development and national unity. The economic depression of the 1930s had unquestionably focused much of the population's outlook. The situation was changing, however, as they both observed, with international issues being discussed more in the press and by concerned groups of citizens.[9]

The attitude of the Dominions toward the League of Nations and the issue of sanctions against Italy caused concern for the governor general's British friends and former government colleagues, such as the Earl of Crawford and Colonial Secretary Malcolm Macdonald. The primary focus, Macdonald had written to Tweedsmuir in early May of 1936, was to "maintain co-operation within the Commonwealth of Nations."[10] The concern was not just about the potential impact on Commonwealth co-operation but also unity.

By July 1936 the international situation had deteriorated further. Civil war in Spain erupted. General Franco, supported by Germany, Italy, and Portugal, was fighting the Republicans, supported by France, the Soviet Union, and the International Brigades, in which some Canadians participated. Cabinet ministers and other members of Parliament who returned from trips to Europe through the summer of 1936 spoke of the gravity of the situation. The people they had spoken with overseas, and the writers in the magazines and newspapers that they had read, "irrespective of country," all seemed to agree: war was inevitable.[11]

The spectre of another European war reignited for King, and others, concerns about the possibility of British involvement and what that might mean for Dominion unity, and, by extension, Commonwealth unity. The prospect of war immediately summoned the prospect of conscription, a policy that had produced a crisis in the last war that nearly split the country apart. King knew that it would be just as divisive a policy were it contemplated anew. The views on the subject recently expressed by certain opinion-makers in Quebec, as well as those offered by English-Canadian pacifists, confirmed those concerns. It is little wonder, then, that King was anxious to avoid war at all costs.

However, despite its newly acquired control over foreign policy, Canada was still irrevocably tied to Britain and the other members of the Commonwealth. King might wish to insulate the country from what was looming in Europe, but to guarantee it would not be compelled to go to war, he needed to consider strategies that Canada and Britain could pursue jointly to protect themselves. Tweedsmuir acted as a useful sounding board for the prime minister as he pondered the possibility of the Empire remaining outside a European war. In formulating his rationale,

King explained to Tweedsmuir that such a policy had two objectives: "to restrict the area of conflict and to assist in its termination."[12]

Tweedsmuir was more than sympathetic to King's concerns about unity, and shared his desire to stay out of any European conflict, but believed the situation was "wholly different" from the last war.[13] Neither Canada nor Britain, he wrote, had an interest "in this miserable struggle of Communism and Fascism in Europe."[14] Despite this, Tweedsmuir did not discount war completely, having in mind three scenarios that could bring Britain into war. The first, but most unlikely, scenario would involve a direct attack on British territory. Tweedsmuir was certain there would be from the Dominions the "same rush to defend [Britain] as there was in 1914."[15] The second scenario would involve a direct threat to the Netherlands or Belgium, "which are Britain's front door," and a constant in British foreign policy.[16] The third scenario would involve an "unprovoked" attack on France. He qualified this because he wasn't certain that France, "in her present neurotic condition," would not enter some agreement with Russia that could give Germany a pretext to attack France. Germany's concern about encirclement was touted as a reason for not pursuing certain alliances.

Discussions over defence policy became more frequent. It was reported that Canada spent far less than most countries on armaments, a fact that was stated with pride by a number of individuals. Indeed, Henri Bourassa, in the Commons foreign policy debate on April 1, 1935, took the extreme position that Canada should "proclaim to the world that we are disarming, as the best means of defending Canada" and that the country should look to Britain and the United States for its security.[17] Tweedsmuir viewed such an extreme attitude as jeopardizing the country's nascent sovereignty. Likewise, Mackenzie King could not accept the extreme step proposed by Bourassa, though he was ever-sensitive to all manner of political opinion, seeking to gauge what his room for manoeuvre was. Both Tweedsmuir and King realized that in the current, deteriorating international context they could not insulate the country from what was generally accepted now as an interdependent world.

Despite Mackenzie King's abhorrence of war and his belief that spending on armaments was immoral, he had included in his summer reading the war memoirs of Lloyd George. He was going through them "pretty carefully" so he could "anticipate as largely as possible, the matters to be given consideration prior to or in the event of war."[18]

Coincident with King's reading of Lloyd George's war memoirs and the dismal outlook from Europe, the time must have appeared propitious to the prime minister's advisors. Defence Minister Ian Mackenzie submitted a memo by General McNaughton — prepared the previous year! Mackenzie King read it one evening that late August as he sat before the fire in his library at Laurier House. It disclosed "a complete lack of any real defence," prompting King to reflect on the need to acquire aircraft equipment and become "prepared to mobilize industry."[19] At a mid-week Cabinet Defence Committee meeting on August 26, 1936, army, navy, and air force reports reinforced this state of affairs and left the prime minister with an impression "of the complete inadequacy of everything in the way of defence."

King's focus was, however, still limited to defending Canada's coasts and its neutrality. The tinder for a public debate was dry. The first spark to set it alight was struck by a visiting Scottish peer.

Viscount Elibank was on a cross-Canada speaking tour on his way to New Zealand to chair meetings of the Federation of Chambers of Commerce of the Empire. Obviously, trade matters figured prominently in the speeches of this "outstanding Empire figure," as one newspaper described him.[20] He also spoke about the possibility of war in Europe implicating Britain and the Empire. It was, though, his comments in Toronto about Canada's lack of air defences and lack of general military preparedness that made headlines, both critical of him and supportive. By the time Elibank reached Vancouver, in the latter part of August, his criticisms of Canada's defence spending had evolved into taunts for the country to make up its mind whether to stay in the Empire or get out of it. Not surprisingly, the government took exception to the man and his remarks.[21] Defence Minister Ian Mackenzie acerbically responded: "[W]e are Canadians here and don't want any peregrinating imperialists to dictate our defense policies."[22] It hadn't helped that the premier of New South Wales, Australia, who was also in Canada at the time, commented factually that Australia was spending more on defence.

It was against this backdrop that the governor general set out by train on August 6, 1936, on his first trip to western Canada, looking "better but none too strong."[23] The domestic and international contexts, along with discussions he had had with the prime minister, suggested to Tweedsmuir that it would be appropriate to address international and defence issues in some of his speeches, since he was also Canada's commander in chief.

In Vancouver, on Wednesday, August 26, the very day the government's Defence Committee was receiving military reports on the inadequacy of defence matters, Tweedsmuir spoke to the Canadian Club. He emphasized that the "world has shrunk today and there is no part of the globe which can say that its geographical position renders it immune from danger."[24] He acknowledged that his subject "is in a sense political," but in the same breath added that it "is also beyond party politics." The distinction is critical and demonstrates Tweedsmuir's acute awareness of his position, its limits, but also its possibilities.

The governor general expounded on the "new Empire," referring to the Statute of Westminster, and applauded "how great a part Canada ... played in its making," alluding to the roles of Laurier, Borden, and King, Liberal and Conservative prime ministers. He then addressed the question of the League of Nations, arguing for a revised League as the preferred means of collective security. His rationale for continuing to focus on that organization rested on the limitations of the Empire. As powerful as it was, he said, the Empire "is not potent enough to stand alone in the world," adding that if it could speak "as a whole [it] would have infinitely more weight." From this latter point, he called for "some apparatus of common action," which recalled his pre-departure speech in London. Tweedsmuir emphasized, though, that such a development must not be attempted too fast; the Imperial machinery must grow organically. He supported, in fact encouraged, the new sovereignty of the Dominions, and he envisaged them in free co-operation, acting from their own policies which would be similar, he believed, because acting from a common constitutional and cultural heritage. It was an ideal objective.

Regardless of Tweedsmuir's qualification of his neutral position, it was not enough to prevent partisan interpretations of his words. A Vancouver paper remarked that it was "an address which in directness and factual content was decidedly different from most vice-regal public expressions."[25] Newspapers in the East, however, interpreted the speech as a prescription for policy. The *Mail & Empire* declared, "Empire Defence Plan Questioned By Tweedsmuir," while the *Globe* front page headlines ran: "Tweedsmuir Sees Common Defense as Unattainable; Empire as a whole cannot guarantee security of every part, he says Canada needs foreign policy."[26]

Sensitive to his prime minister's sensitivities, Tweedsmuir wrote to him on August 31 in what reads like an attempt to assuage any concerns. The governor general pointed out that he and the prime minister had often discussed the theme of his speech. "I felt that at some time or other I was bound to talk on this subject," but, he wrote reassuringly, his speech had been well received by the press and he believed he had been discreet.[27] Surprisingly, there was no reaction from King.[28] It was fortuitous that Tweedsmuir had sent the explanatory letter shortly after his Vancouver speech.

On September 3, in a speech to the Alberta Military Institute in Calgary, the governor general explained that in the context of the disappointment of the League of Nations, every nation had to give some attention to defence matters, whether they wanted to or not. He emphasized that he felt it was his duty, as commander in chief, to interest himself in these matters. Canada and Britain were, he stated, martial but not military nations, and thus their defence policies should be limited to what was only absolutely necessary. He lauded the "stupendous achievements" made by Canadians as "the spearhead of the British army" in the Great War, reflecting an event that had just been commemorated in the unveiling of the Vimy Ridge memorial in northeast France on July 26. Canada, he declared, "has to think out a defense policy and implement it," adding that "neither Britain nor Canada could afford an inefficient and poorly equipped militia."[29] He concluded with a tribute to the militia for its efficiency and public spirit. The speech poured fuel on the controversy sparked by Elibank. It produced major headlines the next day: "Tweedsmuir Urges Defense Policy!"[30]

The following morning, Mackenzie King received a phone call at his Gatineau Hills home about the Calgary speech from one of his assistants. Later, he received "a strong letter" from Defence Minister Ian Mackenzie.[31]

Another letter of protest arrived that evening from his Quebec lieutenant, Ernest Lapointe. King's initial impression is interesting in that he did not express anger over the political implications in the way his cabinet colleagues did, but, rather, focused on the person: "Buchan," he felt had "hurt himself irreparably" with this "very indiscreet" speech.[32] There were two factors, though, that would help mitigate his overall reaction.

The first and most important factor was the strength of King's long-standing attraction to Buchan, combined with almost a year of working together, though it had already had its ups and downs. The other factor was Buchan's letter. When it arrived it helped convince King that "[Buchan] did not mean either to reflect on the government or to be dictating the need for a policy."[33] It was this type of very frequent communication between the two men, even while they travelled extensively, that ensured their relationship could never be completely darkened by political shadows.

Once again, as with the first disappointment King experienced with the governor general, partisanship fixated King: "[Buchan's] mistakes are errors of judgement due to his innate Toryism."[34] He thought the seriousness of the incident might adversely affect Buchan's health because Buchan was "sure to be perturbed," knowing what political turmoil he had caused. "I really believe in him still," he wrote in his diary, adding a revealing note of his own philosophy: in "politics it is what we avoid more than what we do that counts for most."[35] In the circumstances he felt the need to write immediately, balancing the personal touch of a handwritten letter with the use of the more business-like address of "My dear Governor-General," instead of "JB," and signing, equally more formally, "Yours very sincerely, Mackenzie King," instead of, "affectionately, Rex."[36]

King's letter was to-the-point but consistent with his inner thoughts. He cited the problematic passages, and told Tweedsmuir they were certain to have been misconstrued and, thus, to draw the governor general into public controversy. "I shall not attempt to review the situation at the moment," he wrote, adding, "it will of necessity have to await consideration between us until after my return from Geneva." He added, in perhaps a purposefully conflicted statement, "[I] hope that if attacks should be made upon Your Excellency by the government, these should be permitted to pass unnoticed so far as you are concerned, at least until we have had an opportunity to confer together."

The following day, Saturday, the controversy deepened. The *Globe* in Toronto had canvassed local members of Parliament regarding the governor general's speech, and then, with the headline, "Tweedsmuir Backed by MPs in Toronto," noted that four of the six MPs supported the remarks. The paper's editorial used the remarks, as well as those by Lord Elibank and the comments by the New South Wales premier, as the basis for "An Open Letter to Ottawa" to highlight its opinion that public opinion was leaderless.[37] Mackenzie King felt betrayed, not by Tweedsmuir but by the *Globe*. By Monday the paper was reporting, "Seven MPs Back Defense Policy."

King wrote again on September 8, addressing his letter more familiarly this time to "My dear J.B.," and signing it, "With my renewed thanks and good wishes, Ever sincerely yours, Rex." Clearly, King had taken the incident in stride. Amongst his other news and queries about JB's family, he inserted a reference "to the matter touched upon in my letter of September 4th." He hoped "J.B." hadn't been caused "undue concern," but in a tone of vindication noted how fairly accurate he had been in his assessment of how the governor general's words would be interpreted to raise controversy. King was quite clear in what he wanted, i.e., "at all costs" to avoid any controversy involving the king's representative. This was a familiar theme.

King did not send the letter immediately, adding a handwritten note two days later. In a somewhat defensive manner, as if to answer criticisms of the government resulting from the governor general's comments, King seemed obliged to explain what his government had been doing in the defence policy field. He pointed out that his Cabinet colleagues were quite perturbed over the reported statements, especially the defence minister, who had, in fact, King wrote, been working hard on defence policies. Several weeks earlier, King explained, he had named a special Cabinet committee to discuss details of a policy to which they had been giving consideration since the beginning of the year and which had tentatively been agreed upon. King acknowledged that it would be a difficult policy to carry out, but he hoped to garner support for it when

Parliament resumed. In closing King gave a reassuring note: "I am sure it will all work out all right in the end."[38]

On the same day that King began writing his second letter, Tweedsmuir was replying to the prime minister's first, handwritten, one of September 4. Tweedsmuir was "greatly distressed" and apologized for the anxiety he had caused, especially when the prime minister had so much else to think about just before leaving for Europe and the League of Nations assembly.[39] Tweedsmuir summarized his Calgary speech, explaining that since he was speaking to a group of soldiers, he had to deal with defence. He thought he was "helping to hold up the hands of your Government," which really only implicated him further, but at least on the side of Mackenzie King. He knew full well that he could not be seen criticizing government policy, and stated that it was the "very last thing I should dream of." He asked Mackenzie King to explain this to the defence minister, but still made arrangements to meet with the minister and Lapointe on his return to Ottawa.

Almost four weeks after the event, a still contrite Tweedsmuir attempted in a letter to Mackenzie King, then overseas, to minimize the consequences. He didn't think the "unfortunate mis-reporting" of his Calgary speech had done much harm. As far as he could discern, the fuss appeared to have been only the product of some "mischievous Toronto papers," including the *Globe*, which had tried to use his speech to criticize the government's defence policy.[40]

In London Mackenzie King raised the speech with Malcolm Macdonald, secretary of state for Dominion affairs, but did not seem entirely comfortable with it, noting this was all in the strictest confidence.[41] He was, however, more critical of Tweedsmuir with Lord Halifax, then minister without portfolio. King stated that the government had been embarrassed and that Tweedsmuir did not have a proper appreciation of the limits of a governor general involving himself in defence matters, despite being familiar with the Dundonald incident.[42] Even though the issue was entirely Canada's, in light of the Statute of Westminster, it was a demonstration of King's inconsistency in dealing with the governor general that he shared this with British ministers. Perhaps he did so because he thought their knowledge of his views might prove useful at some future point should he have difficulties with the governor general.

Tweedsmuir wrote to Mackenzie King while he was still in London, putting the troubling speech past him and moving on to the issues to be discussed in Geneva. Sounding very much an advocate for Canada, he advised his prime minister to "[h]ammer into the British Cabinet's head that the most loyal people of Canada will refuse to return to the old eighteenth[-]century game in Europe."[43] It was a propitious point, and common ground between Tweedsmuir and King, on which to recover from the recent difficulties.

Written on October 2, from the desirously named Hôtel de la Paix, King's reply reflected both his wished-for personal relationship with John Buchan as well as his professional relationship with the governor general.[44] Reinforcing views the two men had shared previously, King then explained that in this type of international meeting, "no country can too frankly express in advance what its position at the moment of crisis is pretty certain to be."[45]

The crisis in the League was also exposing differences between countries of the Empire and raised concerns about Empire unity. A number of Tweedsmuir's correspondents relayed their concerns to him.[46] The situation was exploited by King, who told British leaders that if Britain were to go to war, it would mean the breakup of the Empire, because Canada was not united in its view to participate in another war.

Co-operative Commonwealth Federation (CCF) leader J.S. Woodsworth expressed concern about proposed increases in defence expenditures, which, he argued, "foreshadow the possibility of Canada being drawn into another European war," putting unity at risk.[47] The defence minister defended the proposed increases by arguing that if Canada were to maintain its neutrality, it must be able to protect it.[48] Sovereignty was at stake. What would the United States do if, for example, Japanese ships entered Canadian waters and Canada did not have the capability to force the ships out or defend its own coastline?[49]

As for the concern about unity, Prime Minister King was explicit in a statement in Parliament, on February 19, 1937, that unity was the guiding principle in formulating Canada's foreign policy. If Canada could not be kept united, little else in its foreign policy was relevant. Providing external validation in his speech, King cited an article published by Escott Reid in the *University of Toronto Quarterly* the previous month which, he said, "gives in a concise form certain phases of that policy," and set out seven brief points.[50] A second guiding principle for Canada's foreign policy, according to King, was that "in the main, [it was] not a matter of Canada's relations to the league [of Nations], but of Canada's relations to the United Kingdom and the United States." King continued: we must "safeguard our own neutrality ... [so that] no belligerent can come and operate from that base [Canada's coasts] against some other country with which it may be at war," an allusion to some country using Canadian coastal waters to attack the United States.

The governor general's private secretary attended the debate and returned to Government House "raving" about the prime minister's speech, which prompted Tweedsmuir to read it in Hansard the next day. For Tweedsmuir the speech had set in perspective Canada's position with respect to the United States and its place in the British Empire. "I cannot express too highly," he wrote to King, "my delight in a really brilliant and statesmanlike performance."[51] Coming from someone King respected so much, he was both encouraged and reassured by this confirmation of his approach.[52]

The Canadian context was little comfort for a concerned Britain. Defence assessments in Britain also exposed a lack of preparedness for a potential war against Nazi Germany — a situation with graver consequences if war should also be engaged in with Italy and Japan at the same time. Given American isolationism, support from countries of the Empire — that is, Empire unity — was a critical, strategic consideration for Britain. Unfortunately, it was not something that could be assumed. As Lord Halifax wrote in his memoirs: "In the event of war in 1938 South Africa had decided to remain neutral, a powerful opposition in Australia had declared against participation, and the attitude of Canada was, to say the least of it, uncertain."[53] These factors, among others, contributed to underpinning the policy of appeasement of Germany.

In May 1937 a fatigued Stanley Baldwin stepped down as prime minister and Neville Chamberlain replaced him. Chamberlain would therefore preside over the Imperial Conference organized for London in May and June, timed to coincide with the coronation of George VI and allow Commonwealth prime ministers to attend both.

At the beginning of April 1937, Tweedsmuir wrote several short notes for his prime minister in anticipation of his travels to London for the coronation and the Imperial Conference. He thought they might prove useful to King in suggesting points, knowing "how barren one begins to feel when one has many speeches to make on the same topic."[54] King often fretted about making and delivering speeches, depending on his level of mental or physical fatigue. The upcoming prospects were of particular concern.[55] Tweedsmuir was aware of King's concern, which prompted him to use the opportunity to provide notes appropriate to the occasion. There were six themes, befitting the context of the excitement of the coronation and the Imperial Conference, each spelled out in a concise two pages: "Canadian Imperialism"; "The Future of the Empire"; "What Canada Can Give to the Empire"; "What the Empire Can Give to Canada"; "Emigration"; and "The Canadian North."[56] Tweedsmuir knew King had an attachment to Britain, despite views to the contrary.[57]

The prime minister, refreshed from his Virginia Beach holiday, was gushingly grateful for them, because, as he confessed to his governor general, he had "become so terrified at the thought of being obliged to make speeches when over there ... and without opportunity of preparation."[58]

Enhancing Tweedsmuir's themes was a resolution of loyalty by the Canadian House of Commons on April 10. King described it as "a stirring scene," which revealed a "real feeling for the Throne."[59] Based on Mackenzie King's diary entries and on newspaper reports of his speeches, Tweedsmuir's notes appear to have influenced King, but King took some of the themes and, in his inimitable way, filtered them through his unique outlook.

Tweedsmuir's emphasis on Canadian sovereignty and how Commonwealth co-operation could only be based on the same purpose and ideals, rather than "artificial rules," would ensure King's attentive reception. But Tweedsmuir also linked to sovereignty his own views of the importance of the Crown, the Commonwealth, and British values, such as "unselfish public service" as having a spiritual dimension. In London, however, King did not emphasize the value of public service as Tweedsmuir had suggested it, but, rather, incorporated the ideal of service as he saw it through the role of his rebel grandfather, William Lyon Mackenzie.[60] That year, 1937, was the centenary of the Upper Canada Rebellion, in which King's grandfather was a leader. King believed the rebellion was at the core of "Canada's position in the establishment of responsible government throughout the Empire."[61]

Tweedsmuir followed the proceedings of the Imperial Conference in London with keen interest. He encouraged King in his approach, an approach they agreed upon in general terms, though not in emphasis. "I am glad," he wrote, "that you are resisting any suggestions for a centralised Imperial machinery."[62] It was consistent with his view of the Empire and its evolution into a partnership of sovereign states, "which involve[d] the pooling of interests and ideas and the linking together of energies."[63]

During the conference Tweedsmuir encouraged King to promote a trade agreement with the United States, "the most important problem before the Empire at the moment."[64] Britain had adopted a new agricultural policy, something that might make it hesitate to pursue an agreement. Again, Tweedsmuir emphasized the importance of such an agreement, stating that it contributed to the maintenance of peace by drawing Britain and the United States closer together and presenting a stronger front to the dictators. King was under no illusions as to the importance of the trade agreement, but he was also keenly aware of the difficulties such an agreement would pose for Canada, since Empire preferences would be diminished and Canada's market in Britain would give way to U.S. goods, allowing them to invade the Canadian market.[65]

Themes Tweedsmuir had set out in his notes for the prime minister were stated publicly by both men that same month. On May 12, before a crowd of some fifty thousand people on Parliament Hill celebrating the coronation, the governor general said: "The Crown is the emblem of sovereignty to which the British people pay homage and in which they recognize all that they cherish most — their national and family traditions, their common heritage of individual and collective freedom and their love of peace and order."[66] And the coronation itself, he continued, "reminds Canadians that Canada is not only a free sovereign nation but a partner in a great alliance of free sovereign nations," where "unity in spirit and in ideals" is "[f]ar more important than unity in forms of government." Later that month, on May 25, in a broadcast for Empire Day, the prime minister spoke about Commonwealth unity being based not only on common political institutions but also on a "common spirit," "common ideals," and "common allegiance to the [C]rown."[67]

After two and a half years in Canada, Tweedsmuir had gained an appreciation of political currents and sentiment in the country. He appreciated the implications of the Statute of Westminster both for Canada and for Britain. In April 1938 he wrote a summary impression of Canada to former British prime minister Stanley Baldwin. He noted he found that while the "spirit of the country" was excellent, Canada was "a very puzzled country."[68] Puzzled because it was not certain about its position within the Empire or internationally. But there had been progress in the last two years. There was now at least some reflection and discussion of these larger issues, which was the biggest change he had observed since arriving. Through his speeches, particularly the ones that, intentionally or not, stirred controversy, Tweedsmuir had contributed to this change in some measure.

Tweedsmuir had the impression, though, that officials in Britain "do not seem to understand the real delicacy of the position of the self-governing Dominions, especially of Canada."[69] In particular, the British Air Ministry was trying to get Canada to commit to assisting Britain with its aircraft production.[70] Toward the end of the previous year (November 1937), Anthony Eden, the British foreign secretary, had been arguing with Prime Minister Neville Chamberlain about the need to increase the pace of rearmament, including purchasing abroad if need be. In May 1938 a British mission was sent to Canada to examine aircraft manufacturing capacity as well as possibilities for training pilots.[71]

When news of the British mission became known, the concern for many in Canada was that it again implied participation in a war should Britain become involved in one. On this point, however, Tweedsmuir was well aware of Canadian sensitivities, and of Mackenzie King's in particular. King was discreet, thinking always of his varied domestic political audience. Not wishing to commit to Canadian participation in any eventual war, he would not commit to help Britain with air production. Nor, however, did he accept suggestions that Canada make a declaration of neutrality. To give him his due, King's reasoning for the latter recognized the

Dressed in full uniform, Governor General Lord Tweedsmuir fulfills his role of the Crown-in-Parliament as he reads the Speech from the Throne on January 27, 1938, preceding a session that included discussion of Canada's defense relations with Britain.

reality that "such a declaration ... would be an unwise encouragement to potential aggressors."[72] This latter point accorded with Tweedsmuir's views.

A planned trip to Britain in the summer of 1938 provided Tweedsmuir an opportunity for talks with the British prime minister and other members of Cabinet on these issues, as well as to pursue the idea of a visit to Canada by King George VI. The main purpose of Tweedsmuir's trip was his installation as chancellor of Edinburgh University on July 20. He would also take the opportunity to undergo a medical checkup. Before he left, however, King discussed with him concerns about the British Air Ministry's efforts to establish pilot training schools in Canada.[73]

The opposition Conservatives had raised the British air training proposal in the House of Commons, and Bennett continued his criticisms of government defence policy into July, after Parliament prorogued. The attacks forced the prime minister to state explicitly the government's position, because the press, in particular the *Gazette* in Montreal and the Toronto *Globe and Mail*, were seen to be misrepresenting the situation.

There was a huge distinction to be made between the British establishing their own pilot training schools on Canadian territory and Canadian establishments providing facilities for training British pilots. While in Britain Tweedsmuir wrote to King to criticize "Bennett's foolish attack," and noted that King's proposal for maintaining Canadian government control over any training on Canadian soil was "the only possible one."[74]

King expected that Tweedsmuir would pass on the Canadian view to the British prime minister, Neville Chamberlain, emphasizing how the Air Ministry position had made the situation rather difficult for the Canadian government. He thought British ministers would listen to Tweedsmuir more than they would to himself or another Canadian Cabinet minister.[75] The prime minister then heard that Senator Arthur Meighen had received information about the government's position privately through a Canadian newspaper owner, who had in turn received it from the British minister for coordination of defence, Sir Thomas Inskip.

King was indignant. Such a leak of confidential information, he said, was "perfectly outrageous," since Canada was, in fact, trying to co-operate with the British. Through his viceregal conduit, King made a veiled threat to pass on to the British government: "Unless the best of good faith can be kept between Governments ... political controversy will develop to a point where anything in the nature of co[-]operation will be wholly frustrated," adding that the whole business was prejudicial to British interests everywhere.[76] He wanted Tweedsmuir to let members of the British government know how difficult it was for him to avoid a political discussion in Canada that would prove embarrassing to the British.

Tweedsmuir did talk with several members of the British Cabinet, including the prime minister, though we are unaware of the details of those talks.[77] Tweedsmuir was playing both messenger and interpreter, but the former only because it was King's wish; otherwise, his contact with the British government had to be very circumspect, as we have read previously.

Tweedsmuir subsequently heard from King that the latter had received a request from British high commissioner Sir Francis Floud concerning the construction of warships at Montreal. While King was reticent politically, he acknowledged, "the time is coming, if it is not already here, when we should, perhaps, begin at Montreal or elsewhere, construction of an establishment for warships of different kinds."[78] Again, King asked Tweedsmuir to let the British prime minister, foreign secretary, and minister for coordination of defence know "how difficult a problem" this type of proposal was for the Canadian government and that he therefore could not accommodate British needs "at this particular time."[79] Later King noted that until the Canadian Parliament had an opportunity to debate and vote on necessary appropriations, whether for aircraft or for destroyers, the government could not promise that it would place any orders. Such orders were, King explained, a matter for the individual governments, British or Canadian, to negotiate separately with the companies involved.[80]

The situation ultimately worked out satisfactorily, Tweedsmuir was informed, when the British government contracted with Canadian companies.[81] King had won on two counts: he was relieved of the need to go to Parliament to ask for appropriations for military purchases, which would have been politically controversial — he did not have to make a decision; and he was still able to see Canadian industries build military capacity by fulfilling the British orders.

As Canada anguished over its defence policy and searched to determine its role in the world, how to give meaning to the Statute of Westminster, it exposed the strong currents of sentiment running through the country — nationalist and imperialist. The challenge Tweedsmuir took on was to moderate and reconcile those currents, ensuring a sovereign and loyal Canada.

CHAPTER 6

A Canadian's First Loyalty

As Tweedsmuir travelled throughout Canada, he was always meeting Scots, a good number of whom were originally "Borderers," including some from around Broughton and Peebles, where Buchan had spent summers at his maternal grandparent's farm. Whenever a Scottish immigrant with connections to Peebles appeared, his staff knew to introduce them. They knew that the village of Peebles "was one of his great loyalties."[1] Loyalty was a concept that emerged early in Buchan's life and played a constant role, evolving into a critical one for his governor generalship.

A happy childhood involved playing freely among the hills and surroundings of the Scottish Borders region. Indeed, his earliest memories were of his environment, rather than of himself.[2] He wrote in his memoir that it was this great sense of "place" that helped to develop a first sense of loyalty — loyalty to the land, the area where one was born and raised.[3] If one casts one's mind back to childhood, Buchan suggests, there is likely some "modest-sized place that lingers most in your recollection, the wood where you played, a corner of the sea-shore, the field which you regarded as your special property."[4] "We begin with a loyalty to little things," he said, adding that these are loyalties we "should never relinquish."

It is important as we grow older, however, he explained, that "we should acquire also wider loyalties."[5] He cited as examples loyalty to the academic institution we attend, to the profession we choose, to the province in which we live, to the nation, and ultimately to our fellow human beings.[6] This latter, ultimate, loyalty was natural for someone of Buchan's strong Christian background. And the "wider loyalty," he explained, "can only exist if the smaller loyalty is strong and deep."[7] Using patriotism as a synonym, he emphasized that there was nothing inconsistent "between the local patriotism and a patriotism of humanity."[8] It was a broad concept into which could fit several key levels of loyalty that would help fulfill his objectives in Canada.

In his early career John Buchan was aware of the growing national sentiment in Canada (and the other Dominions). In 1908 he described Canadian criticisms of the Imperial government and certain demands made by some Canadian politicians as demonstrating that the "Colony is becoming a nation, and wants national attributes."[9] That same year Canada was celebrating the tercentenary of the founding of Quebec. Buchan lauded "the work of men who may be French or may be British, but are first and foremost Canadians," adding that the French and English in Canada had "achieved union without sacrificing local patriotism."[10] Later, however, he became familiar with the divisions in Canada. Confederation had apportioned responsibilities between the Dominion and provincial levels of government, building in potential points of contention. The French and English union in Canada that he lauded in 1908 revealed a rift when conscription was introduced in the later years of the Great War; much of the French-speaking population of Quebec was opposed to conscription.

It was also in 1926 that member of Parliament John Buchan addressed the Westminster House of Commons, saying that to be a good citizen of the Empire, one had also to be a good Australian, a good New Zealander, and a good Canadian. It was a statement that reflected his long held knowledge of the growing national feeling in the Dominions and that was in harmony with the outcome of the 1926 Imperial Conference. What emerged, he said, was "the tremendous meaning of the Crown," leaving only as yet to be found "the means of giving expression to its unity of spirit."[11] For Buchan it was a given that citizens should be loyal to their Dominion, but that national loyalty was in no way incompatible with loyalty to the Commonwealth and Empire, nor with loyalty to their particular region or province.

It did not take long in Canada, however, for him to be reminded of the obstacles to unity, or of the intensity of some of them. Toward the end of March 1936, less than five months after his arrival in Canada, he was lamenting what he perceived to be a limited vision for the country: "everybody thinks in compartments."[12] Based on this approach, and after his first year as governor general, Tweedsmuir's assessment of the situation in Canada might best be described as an unbalanced loyalty. While in Winnipeg in November 1936, he addressed the St. Andrew's Society. After extolling the virtues, as well as the less virtuous past, of Scotland and the Scots, he focused on "our duty to do more" in a world where the need is for "co-operation instead of rivalry," "unity instead of antagonism."[13] "We need," he ventured to say, "in this Dominion of ours, a closer unity where national interests are supreme above local interests."[14]

Tweedsmuir continued to reflect on the question of unity, informed by his travels, meetings, discussions, and readings. In March 1937 he stated publicly: "I want to see Canadians prouder of Canada — of all Canada — and if, during my term of office, I can do something to foster that pride then I shall feel that my work has not been in vain."[15] Loyalty to Canada, a strong, sovereign Canada, would contribute to a strong Commonwealth, the focal point of which was the Crown. He promoted the wider loyalty, to the Commonwealth, because he believed it was a positive force in the world and particularly important as the violent ideologies took hold and spread in Europe, threatening the hard-won and long-evolved freedoms of Western civilization.[16] Those ideologies were nationalist, exclusive, and antithetical to the multiple loyalties John Buchan promoted and pursued.

While Tweedsmuir had been in Winnipeg in late 1936, he received an honorary doctorate from the University of Manitoba. He would have had discussions with John Dafoe, chancellor of the University of Manitoba and editor of the *Winnipeg Free Press*. Dafoe was a strong Canadian nationalist, and was known to be even opposed to the office of governor general.[17] Buchan knew of Dafoe's reputation and had referred to him in an article in 1926 about the national election in Canada that year, the "new doctrine of Empire" and the various sentiments in Canada.[18] He wrote at that time, reassuringly but perhaps naively, that "most nationalists are perfectly sound Imperialists."[19] It was these two strong sentiments that he had to try to reconcile and put on equal footings of loyalty, so they did not become exclusive.[20]

As a result of Canada's involvement in the 1914–1918 war and the increasingly perilous state of international affairs through the 1920s and 1930s, concerned citizens, including many prominent individuals, became engaged in organizations established to discuss international affairs and Canada's role in the world. In 1921 the League of Nations Society (LNS) had an organizational meeting in Sir Robert Borden's office, but it wasn't until 1925 that it was officially founded. Curiously, the YMCA was one of the earliest existing groups to take an active interest in international affairs. In 1924 an international YMCA meeting in Austria expressed concern over tensions in Asia. As a result of attending that meeting, several Canadians attended a conference held in Honolulu the following summer at which the Institute of Pacific Relations (IPR) was launched.[21]

There were also Canadian members of a group established in Britain in 1920, the British Institute of International Affairs (BIIA), chaired by Lord Robert Cecil, a future Nobel Peace Prize winner. The BIIA recognized the extent to which public opinion was increasingly influencing government policy, and believed that, therefore, public opinion should be as well informed as possible. Canadians members of the BIIA discussed the formation of a Canadian branch or separate institute but based on the same principles: namely, the non-partisan collection and dissemination of knowledge about international affairs. Toward the end of 1926, there were branches being organized in Montreal, Toronto, Winnipeg, and Vancouver, but it wasn't until 1927 that the Canadian Institute of International Affairs (CIIA) was founded, in agreement with what was now called the Royal Institute of International Affairs (RIIA) in Britain. Sir Robert Borden was one of three Canadians amongst the original members of the BIIA. He became the first president of the Canadian Institute. The executive council included General Sir Arthur Currie, the

Hon. Newton Rowell (chief justice of Ontario and future chairman of the Royal Commission on Dominion-Provincial Relations), and John Dafoe (editor of the *Winnipeg Free Press*).

"[N]ever before have Canada's foreign relations been so exhaustively discussed in public," noted the introduction to a 1936 publication entitled *Canada, The Empire and The League*.[22] The publication was the result of an annual conference held at Lake Couchiching during the first two weeks of August, organized by the Canadian Institute on Economics and Politics. The proceedings were published under the auspices of the National Council of YMCAs of Canada. The various presentations examined the world situation, and Canada's position in and policies toward it. One Quebec academic, Professor Jean Bruchesi, alluding to the Statute of Westminster, asked: "[C]an the fuller independence of the Dominions be reconciled with the requirements of a closer co-operation [in the Commonwealth]?" He dealt with his question, however, with a rather paranoid, overt criticism of the governor general, whom he accused of being part of a group, working in secret toward the goal of "reviving the project of Imperial Federation"![23] Bruchesi based his remark on a quote from Tweedsmuir's pre-departure speech in London the previous year, in which the governor general–designate referred to the desire for "a common policy on the questions which interest the Commonwealth." It would be "a common policy" arrived at by sovereign nations based on a shared heritage and shared values, not policy resulting from a centralized source. Nonetheless, Bruchesi's remark reflected the deep concern, even suspicion, held, especially in Quebec, of the imperial connection and, ultimately, of its potential for drawing Canada into another European conflict. It was a view confirmed by Professor Arthur Lower, who suggested that many in Quebec suspected many English-speaking Canadians thinking of the Empire first, before Canada.

At the 1936 conference, Professor Frank Underhill, an anti-imperialist and a founder of the Co-operative Commonwealth Federation (CCF) political party, noted that "the essence of Canadian policy must always be to maintain a delicate and quickly adjustable balance between Great Britain and the United States.... But if we are to perform that function so dear to our sentimental after-dinner speakers of interpreting the Americans and the British to one another, we must be genuinely independent of both."[24] Tweedsmuir would have been aware of these Couchiching conferences and would have been more than interested in the discussions.

In this context of growing interest in what was happening beyond Canada's borders, the CIIA invited the governor general to address its tenth anniversary dinner at the Ritz Carlton Hotel in Montreal on October 12, 1937. Tweedsmuir saw this as an important opportunity to speak to the reality of the Statute of Westminster and to promote his concept of the Empire as a grouping of sovereign nations with the same institutional heritage and values, centred on the Crown, discussing, then acting together, to address common problems. He also had in mind the challenge from Canadian nationalists, some of whom would be at the dinner. In fact the CIIA president was one of them.

The president was John Dafoe! He was known to view the post of governor general as "a symbol of colonialism,"[25] but this governor general was clearly different. As Dafoe's newspaper expressed on John Buchan's appointment: "A very pleasant innovation."[26] Dafoe would have been attracted to Buchan, in part because Buchan was, like himself, a self-made man, though their educational backgrounds were very different. Their respect was undoubtedly mutual. Tweedsmuir would certainly have appreciated discussing issues with Dafoe to learn about his type of nationalism. A challenge for the governor general, aside from having to be cautious not to wade into partisan policy issues, would be how to address both nationalist and imperialist sentiment represented in the room. The prospects would be daunting. Could the two sentiments be reconciled?

By the middle of September, Tweedsmuir had completed a second typed draft of his speech. He asked his private secretary to forward it to the prime minister, with a request to let him know "if there are any alterations you think would be desirable," and a request to quote words from a speech King had made previously.[27] King replied four days later that he would "not think of altering one word" of the speech, and that he was "sure this address will be greatly appreciated."[28] King then expressed thanks to His Excellency "for his too kind inclusion" of his remarks. However, he subtly corrected him by noting that the remarks were not recent, but were "what I said after my return from Geneva a year ago," a European trip during which he met with Hitler; they were not remarks that would survive inclusion in a reprinted version of the speech after the war with the Nazis had begun.[29]

Tweedsmuir continued to modify the typed draft with handwritten notations, deleting and adding words. Certain of his words would be key to expressing his opinion about Canada's place in the British Commonwealth, and would spark another controversy.

The crowd of more than 130 at the CIIA dinner was a who's who of Canadian politics, business, and law. In addition the U.S. Council on Foreign Relations was represented, as was the Royal Institute of International Affairs. Many of those present were members of the CIIA or the League of Nations Society, or had participated in various international delegations.[30] They also represented the two strong currents in Canadian opinion, nationalist and imperialist, which Tweedsmuir had to address and try to reconcile. The governor general was introduced by John Dafoe.

Tweedsmuir began his relatively brief, after-dinner address by reminding his audience that he had "to walk warily." In domestic affairs the governor general, he said, "can have no views on policy except those of his Ministers."[31] Even on questions of international affairs, he added, with what could only have been an oblique reference to the controversy sparked by his Calgary speech the year before, he was "in a position of some delicacy," because "international problems have the unhappy knack of also becoming domestic problems and dividing people into party groups." He stated explicitly that his audience would not hear "any views on international policy" from him. He acknowledged he had views, but stated that they could not be published "at present." There was an area, however, about which he could speak frankly, namely, the purpose of the CIIA: "a forum for discussion … to acquire expert knowledge about the data on which policies must be framed."

Describing how the "world has been telescoped [and] distances shrunk," the governor general noted that international affairs could no longer be the preserve of the government's foreign affairs department or some small social class. What happened across an ocean "may have a direct effect upon the safety and prosperity of the private citizen," and, therefore, "the foreign policy of a democracy must be the cumulative views of individual citizens." In turn the citizens' views must be "the consequence of a widely diffused knowledge." The allusion, of course, was to organizations like the CIIA that discussed and helped to diffuse knowledge of international affairs. He noted, with implicit advice, that the "purpose which your Institute sets before itself is not merely to provide a limited number of cultivated men and women with accurate knowledge ... [but to] help ... to create that spirit without which a true internationalism is impossible." Undoubtedly thinking about the "ultimate loyalty" to humanity, he urged "a truer understanding by the nations of each other." It was necessary because of "the interconnection of nations." No country, he said, "is prosperous because of its neighbours' misfortunes, but only because of its neighbours' well-being." "We want to understand their point of view," but that did not mean, he cautioned, that we would or should share it. And if, he added, "we have to fight it we shall fight it all the better for understanding it."

The internationalist ideal, as embodied in the League of Nations, had failed, he explained, "because it had not an adequate spiritual force behind it." To succeed, the world needed "the proper temper of mind," an analogy to the steel of a blade, which must be hard and flexible to be most useful; it complemented his earlier point about the need for an informed citizenry. He would return to this theme in his conclusion, challenging his audience by stating that to "create and maintain this temper is the first duty of every civilised man." But it was not, however, this challenge that most people at the dinner, or readers of the following day's newspapers, would take away from the fifteen-minute speech.

Midway through his address, Tweedsmuir raised a theme heard in Canadian parliamentary debates and in conferences about international affairs and Canada's position in relation to Britain and the U.S.[32] The governor general emphasized that Canada was "a sovereign nation and cannot take her attitude docilely from Britain, or from the United States, or from anybody else." "A Canadian's first loyalty," the governor general continued, was "not to the British Commonwealth of Nations, but to

Canada, and to Canada's King, and those who deny this are doing, to my mind, a great disservice to the Commonwealth."

Conservative Senator Charles Cahan, leading Montreal businessman James Macdonnell, and other Tories "did not like [what the governor was saying] any too well," and were observed as being clearly uncomfortable.[33] That Tweedsmuir had referred to loyalty to Canada's king, a key phrase he had inserted by hand in a version after the one Mackenzie King had seen, had not assuaged the imperialist and Conservative discomfiture.

Tweedsmuir continued, advising that if the Commonwealth was to speak "with one voice" in a crisis, which he clearly desired, "it will only be because the component parts have thought out for themselves their own special problems, and made their contribution to the discussion, so that a true factor of policy can be reached." Increasingly, for him now, was the fear that a crisis might erupt in Europe. The Commonwealth needed to be ready to respond in a unified way.

When the speech was over, Mackenzie King was "struck by how accurate [Tweedsmuir's] memorization of it was," but he thought the delivery to be "very 'sermonizing.'"[34] Nonetheless, he was pleased with the speech, as were Dr. Skelton and John Dafoe, but even King thought Tweedsmuir "went very far as G.G. in speaking of Canada as a 'sovereign country' & our loyalty to Canada first."[35]

Trying to explain why the governor "went very far" with his words, Mackenzie King thought it certain that "Buchan had Dafoe's presence in mind." This is, however, both a slight to and a misunderstanding of Buchan's more profound thoughts about the Empire, the Statute of Westminster, and Canada's role. Tweedsmuir would not have chosen his words because of the presence of a nationalist like Dafoe. He knew and appreciated the significance of the Statute of Westminster and the evolving sovereignty of the Dominions in the Commonwealth, "free sovereign nations, monarchies of which King George is King."[36] In his two and a half years, he had developed a deep understanding of Canada, and wanted to guide its burgeoning sovereignty within the Commonwealth *and* its loyalty to the Crown, to Canada's king. It was a manifestation of his concept of multiple loyalties.

Tweedsmuir was aware of the potential reaction he might evoke. The draft version of the speech he had provided to Mackenzie King included the sentence that made Cahan and others flinch, but it did not include the phrase that was key for Tweedsmuir and which he subsequently wrote in by hand. That sentence read: "A Canadian's first loyalty is not to the British Commonwealth of Nations, but to Canada, and those who deny this are doing, to my mind, a great disservice to the Commonwealth." To reconcile his promotion of sovereignty, and reassure imperialists and those with a strong attachment to Britain, Tweedsmuir wrote in, *and to Canada's King*, after "A Canadian's first loyalty is … to Canada." This phrase was key to his belief in the centrality of the Crown. But most of the newspapers across the country reporting on the speech, and virtually all of them did, did not include the key phrase "and to Canada's King," which would have left imperialists elsewhere in the country, reading this version, even more offended.

Despite the absence of the key phrase, "and to Canada's King," in much of the reporting of the speech, we know that Tweedsmuir did in fact include it in his verbal address because the Montreal newspapers, English and French alike, who would have had reporters there, included this key phrase. The difference in reported versions is due to newspapers outside Montreal receiving the Canadian Press (CP) wire story, which most likely was based on a copy of the typed text, which did not include the key phrase subsequently written in by hand. The version that appeared in *Canadian Occasions*, a collection of Tweedsmuir's speeches published after his death in 1940, did include the key phrase.

In the newspaper reporting of the speech, there were two main themes, varying widely between the two reactions of the audience at the Ritz Carlton but not restrained by the decorum dictated in that formal forum. Many of the headlines across the country were not unlike those sparked by the controversial speech in Calgary the year before, which quoted the governor general as saying, or implying, that "Canada needs foreign policy."[37] Even though Tweedsmuir had said in his introduction that "he can have no views on policy," he was perceived as having given another speech in which he did just that. There was suspicion and uncertainty, however misconstrued, over whether the governor general was issuing a warning or advice, perhaps with the tacit approval of the British government, but numerous writers suggested that it was necessary for His Excellency to "amplify" his points.[38] Others delved into how it was that Canada could afford to take an independent stand, noting that it was "the strength and policy of the United States [that] furnish[ed] a guarantee of protection to us even should we choose to stand aloof from Great Britain in any emergency of world affairs."[39]

The other main theme produced generally consistent headlines across most of the country — "First Loyalty to Dominion." It was this theme that divided opinions. The governor general's comment offended imperialists and many conservatives, but encouraged, in equal measure, and ironically, those who advocated for a Canadian to represent the sovereign, by placing emphasis on Canada first. Neither of these opinions reflected an appreciation of Tweedsmuir's position. His focus was on the meaning of the 1931 Statute of Westminster — loyalty "to Canada's King" reflected that.

Nor was there consensus in the French-language newspapers, but they were for the most part supportive of a separate Canadian way, echoing to a certain extent reactions to John Buchan's appointment.[40] *Le Devoir's* front-page editorial repeated in its headline the governor general's words *"Le Canada est une nation souveraine,"* and colourfully described the governor general who *"d'un pied dédaigneux, pousse à l'abime le cadavre du colonialisme"* (disdainfully booted the corpse of colonialism toward the abyss). The paper was faithful to its long-time editor, Henri Bourassa (then, a sitting MP), who likely attended the dinner, and reflected the content of his speeches in Parliament during the April 1935 debates on Canada's foreign policy.

Other comment pointed out the hypocrisy of those people who had last year claimed the governor was interfering in Canada's affairs with his Calgary speech on defence but were now lauding his words as "a great declaration of independence."[41] They sarcastically noted that while these critics may have heard of the Statute of Westminster, they did not know that it gave Canada its independence from Britain, and were still fighting the old anti-colonial battles, which some are still fighting today! The editors would be surprised if they could have known that the legacy of these views would continue on into the next century!

It is unlikely Tweedsmuir planned that his speech would spark such a high level of controversy, but he was aware of the potential and would not have been opposed to the debate. Tweedsmuir himself was proud of the speech, reflecting implicitly his support for the debate it engendered. He wrote to his mother that "every paper had a leader on it."[42] He would, however, have regretted or thought much less of any perspective that might diminish the role of the Crown and the linkage to Britain and the Commonwealth. Whatever the reaction to it, the speech was certainly a catalyst to discussion about Canada's position in the world.

The reaction to this speech was not dissimilar to the one Tweedsmuir gave in Calgary the previous year, but it stirred an opposite reaction. Whereas the Calgary speech was criticized by the Liberal government but supported by conservatives in the country, the Montreal speech was criticized by conservative opinion but applauded by Liberals and nationalists. For Tweedsmuir, however, there was a consistency. The tone, content, and intent of the Calgary speech, as the subsequent correspondence between the prime minister and governor general showed, was meant to encourage a stronger military and, through that, sovereignty. The Montreal speech was intended to encourage the sovereignty of Canada while at the same time promoting loyalty to the Crown and the Commonwealth.

Echoes of the speech continued years after, its promotion of sovereignty still rankling imperialists. Five years later, in June 1942, during a speech in London that dealt with, among other issues, relations within the Commonwealth, former Canadian prime minister R.B. Bennett made specific reference to Tweedsmuir's CIIA speech, commenting that he "wholly disagree[d] with that view."[43] The context of the war and the resultant closer relations with Britain that came with it, not to mention the character of the audience he was addressing, would have been factors in Bennett's statement. Knowing Bennett's strong imperial leanings, it is interesting to speculate how Tweedsmuir and Bennett, if the latter had been re-elected prime minister in 1935, might have gotten along and how it may have affected Tweedsmuir's approach to some of the more contentious issues.

Tweedsmuir's concept of multiple loyalties, not being mutually exclusive, were integrated with his knowledge of the origins and implications of the 1931 Statute of Westminster. During his last year as governor general, he initiated an event that encompassed all these dimensions.

CHAPTER 7

The Royal Tour
Sovereignty and Loyalty

Never before had there been such excitement right across Canada, such colour, such pride, such crowds. It was an exceptional, historic moment for Canada when King George VI and Queen Elizabeth stepped onto Canadian soil on May 17, 1939, the first visit to a Dominion of a reigning monarch. The king and queen travelled from one end of the country to the other. Hardly a soul in the land did not know about or try to catch a glimpse of the blue, silver, and gold royal train that carried Their Majesties. The tour was as memorable as it was precedent-setting, on many levels.

The origins for the idea of a visit to Canada by a reigning sovereign had curious and conflicting reasons. But this first royal visit of the sovereign and its impact were largely attributable to Tweedsmuir. This was the crowning achievement of his efforts to make the Statute of Westminster a reality.

"Startling news has just been divulged by my Prime Minister on his arrival," Tweedsmuir wrote to his wife, who was in England visiting family. It was early November 1936.[1] What news could possibly provoke the normally imperturbable Tweedsmuir to describe it as "startling"? It was, in fact, historic. King Edward VIII had proposed to visit Canada, the first time a reigning monarch would do so.

Mackenzie King had been in London on his way back from the League of Nations meetings in Geneva. Near the end of October, he met with his British counterpart, Stanley Baldwin, and with Edward VIII's private secretary, Alexander Hardinge, in preparation for his meeting with the king. Edward's relationship with Mrs. Simpson, the American divorcee, was causing serious concern at this point, as we have read. Mackenzie King and Hardinge agreed that just a couple of positive events, even as small a thing as Edward attending Evensong, might help divert the public's attention. It was at this point the Canadian prime minister suggested that "if [the king] could come out to Canada and other parts of the Empire ... the people would completely forget the other."[2] Edward was popular, having made very successful tours to Canada in 1919 and 1927. He also owned a ranch in Alberta.

The news of the king's proposed visit was announced by the prime minister on November 3. Edward VIII would visit Canada the following May, soon after his coronation.[3] Edward was also the king of Canada, and when he was in Canada, Tweedsmuir saw it as his duty to disappear — "the Arctic will be my refuge!" he proclaimed.[4] However, with British government leaders becoming ever more concerned about Edward's choice of partner, its potential negative constitutional consequences, and its implications for the Crown itself, expectations had to be managed down. The news was amended a week later. The visit would not be earlier than 1938.[5] However, the announcement by British prime minister Baldwin on December 10 that King Edward VIII would abdicate brought the matter to an end. The natural flow of subsequent events, the succession, which was followed by the coronation of George VI, and the Imperial Conference in Spring 1937, kept all minds occupied on other matters.

In early 1938, however, Tweedsmuir learned that a planned visit by King George VI to India had been cancelled. India was a special question for the British government, but the cancellation presented an opportunity. Tweedsmuir sent a letter to Alexander Hardinge in February, noting that the king would have to visit the Dominions soon and wondered if Canada could be first.[6] Hardinge's reply, received over six weeks later, was non-committal, indicating that they would have a better sense of where the Indian political situation might be headed over the next year when the viceroy, Lord Linlithgow, returned.[7] That would give them a sense of whether a visit by the king to India in the winter of 1939 would be possible. Since the question about the king visiting the Dominions had not "been seriously discussed," Hardinge suggested that he and Tweedsmuir could discuss it when Tweedsmuir came to England that summer, for his installation as chancellor of the University of Edinburgh. Tweedsmuir, who would have had to discuss this issue with his prime minister beforehand, responded immediately. Canada, he wrote to Hardinge, "would take [the visit] as a great compliment," and the situation in India that had caused the king to postpone his visit there might, in any case, last for some time to come.[8] He set himself the goal when he was in England of trying to convince the Palace, and the king himself, to come to Canada.[9]

In preparation for his talks in England, Tweedsmuir discussed possible approaches with his prime minister at the end of May, over tea at Kingsmere. He expressed his strong desire to have King George and Queen Elizabeth visit Canada.[10] To overcome some of Mackenzie King's reticence, caused by the possibility of an election and concerns over "expenditures on royalty while [the] poor [are] starving," Tweedsmuir struck a point that he believed strongly himself and that he was sure would appeal to Mackenzie King — the visit "would have a 'unifying' effect on Canada."[11] King agreed.[12] Tweedsmuir also said that he wanted the king to visit the United States and the New York World Fair. The idea indeed appealed to the prime minister, who believed it would be "helpful to relations of democracies."[13]

In June the governor general took up residence at the Citadel in Quebec City. In late June he returned to Ottawa to prorogue Parliament because he did not like to "omit even the most formal duties" of his office "at this time," referring to the unsettled international situation and the need to observe all established form to give the impression of stability.[14] The parliamentary session was longer than usual, and the prime minister, anticipating this, had earlier requested the governor general delay his trip to England.[15] King explained to the House of Commons that "His Excellency ... is quite prepared to prorogue parliament at three or four in the morning ... to postpone his sailing another week should his not being present to prorogue parliament occasion any disappointment." King added, however, that he assumed he had the support of the House "at this late time" to advise the governor general not to alter his plans, and to leave July 1 for Quebec City and sail from there to England. Parliament was duly prorogued by the chief justice of Canada, the Rt. Hon. Sir Lyman Duff.[16]

The main publicly known reason for Tweedsmuir's return to Britain was his installation as chancellor of the University of Edinburgh, but he was also there to have a medical checkup and he was looking forward to a rest. His key, non-public objective, however, was to secure agreement from King George VI, and the British government, of course, to visit Canada.

Tweedsmuir arrived at Elsefield, his home near Oxford, finding it "very beautiful." He spent his first few days there, arranging a medical appointment and speaking with former colleagues and members of the British government. In his first letter to his prime minister, Tweedsmuir emphasized that the "important question for me is, of course, the king's visit to Canada."[17] In discussions with British prime minister Neville Chamberlain and Foreign Secretary Lord Halifax, he found they were "very strong about the importance of the thing."[18] He informed Mackenzie King that, at a garden party hosted by the king and queen, he had had the opportunity to speak to King George and subsequently heard that His Majesty was "very sympathetic about the idea of coming to Canada next year."[19] He was to see the king on July 25, and hoped to "clinch [then the king's] resolution."[20]

Tweedsmuir's appointment with Dr. Lord Dawson resulted in a prescription to spend four to five weeks at a clinic, Ruthin Castle, in Wales. His leave from Canada had to be extended, as was his stay at Ruthin Castle. While at the clinic, he followed a very strict dietary and rest regime. He filled his time productively, however, with reading, writing a speech for the king, and, more importantly, working on how to persuade Their Majesties to visit Canada — an objective he pursued with, as he termed it, "the persistence of a horse-leech."[21] Despite the concerns of the European situation, Tweedsmuir found the king's private secretary supportive of the idea of the visit. The British government were next.

That soon followed. "As soon as I got Neville on my side," Tweedsmuir wrote, "I knew it would be all right, for the King was most sympathetic."[22]

In mid-September, while still at Ruthin Castle, Tweedsmuir received a telegram from Alexander Hardinge stating that the king would like to see him before he left for Canada, suggesting he come from September 24 to 26.[23] The recuperating governor replied that he would arrive at Ballater Station (near Buckingham Palace) on Saturday morning, September 24.[24] The king informed his representative that he would indeed visit Canada!

Tweedsmuir sailed from Liverpool on October 1, arriving in Ottawa on October 7. He must have felt very good; not only did he carry the positive news about the king's visit but he was enjoying the best health for a long while. In fact he had gained sixteen pounds and was experiencing much less in the way of gastric problems.[25] The morning after his arrival, Mackenzie King visited him at Rideau Hall and heard all the details, including the news of the proposed visit to the United States, and the wish of the king to hold a meeting of the Privy Council in Ottawa.[26] Shuldham Redfern telephoned to Balmoral Castle in the afternoon, requesting permission to make the announcement, which had been drafted by Tweedsmuir and approved by the prime minister. Shortly thereafter the announcement was made, with the Palace suggesting the replacement of "about three weeks" with "a month" for the duration of the visit.[27] Over the coming winter and spring, the planning of the visit would consume much of his time and energy. But it was the positive impact of reinforcing a pan-Canadian perspective, countering the provincialism, that Tweedsmuir believed was most important.[28] To achieve this objective, however, his challenge would be to ensure that the Canadian and English organizers understood each other as best as possible.

The excitement generated by the announced visit would, Tweedsmuir noted, likely result in many vetoed plans and consequent disappointments. Not wanting criticism to be aimed at Rideau Hall or the prime minister, a committee outside of Rideau Hall and the Prime Minister's Office was set up to be responsible and take any criticism that resulted from the planning.[29] Shuldham Redfern worked hard with the committee. They hoped to have a draft itinerary to the Palace in the early part of December, an accomplishment that Tweedsmuir wrote would "be entirely due to Redfern's perpetual pushing."[30] The itinerary was finally published in newspapers on January 4, 1939,[31] but there had been much activity, angst, and agitation before arriving at that point.

Alexander Hardinge emphasized that the visit should not be too strenuous so that the royal couple could enjoy the entire time. This was advice Tweedsmuir ensured was followed by Redfern, working with the committee.[32] As for Tweedsmuir himself, he was rather anxious, given the significant objectives he believed the visit could contribute to achieving, both domestically and internationally.[33] One source of anxiety was that the U.S. leg of the tour could not be controlled the way the Canadian portion could be. He also prayed that nothing would happen with the situation in Europe or with Their Majesties' health that would prevent the visit. His own health, though, was a concern for friends, one of whom cautioned him over the strenuous time ahead, especially since he was so much improved from his rest and prescribed regime from Ruthin Castle.[34]

The very early planning stages revealed just how "extraordinarily ignorant," in the governor general's expression, even well-informed people in Britain were about the status of the Dominions, alluding to the Statute of Westminster.[35] One stark example was the assumption the *Times* newspaper made in its reporting that the king would be accompanied by a British minister, when, in fact, the king's only advisors in Canada were to be his Canadian ministers.

One issue that appeared rather straightforward when it was raised in November 1938 was the question of who should meet the king on his historic arrival at Quebec City. Tweedsmuir seems to have taken for granted that he would be there, to symbolically hand the mantle of the sovereign's authority back to its source, the authority he was representing, that is, the king, thus emphasizing that it was the king of Canada who had arrived. Drawing attention to this was part of his prime objective for the visit. He also had the impression that his prime minister agreed with his views.[36] How mistaken he was! On meeting King, who had just returned from a holiday in the West Indies, he learned that King thought it would be more convenient and dignified for the governor general to await Their

Majesties in Ottawa, something King suggested would also be preferable based on the spurious grounds that he was considering Tweedsmuir's health. In fact, King was adamant as to who should meet His Majesty.[37]

In subsequent communications with the Palace, Tweedsmuir appeared to want to keep the debate open. He tried soliciting Hardinge's views but concluded that he would do as he was told.[38] Tweedsmuir informed Mackenzie King of his cable to the Palace. King was surprised at Tweedsmuir's position, and suspected him of being too ambitious in wanting to meet Their Majesties. Remarking on the matter in his diary, he noted, "I shall be very firm with Tweedsmuir on this matter, if the necessity arises."[39]

After some reflection over the next two weeks, however, Tweedsmuir again wrote to Hardinge, stating that the "more I think about it the more I feel that perhaps it would be right for me to meet Their Majesties at Quebec."[40] In this case he indicated that he would afterward immediately return to Ottawa and leave the provincial officials as hosts. Without waiting for a reply, he also broached the matter again with his prime minister. King's previous polite and suggestive reasons were displaced by the political, and, for King, constitutional arguments he would always bring out when he wanted to get his way with a governor general. His Majesty "should be met on Canadian soil by the elected representative of the people."[41] Tweedsmuir cabled the Palace immediately and followed up with a letter, commenting that this was "quite good sense," and that he was, in any case, bound to accept the prime minister's view.

At the beginning of January, however, Tweedsmuir's private secretary received a letter from the Palace that gave the governor general "some anxiety," since it proposed reopening the matter. King George VI wanted the governor general to meet him on board his ship, the *Repulse*, to hand over his stewardship. While he may have wanted to agree, Tweedsmuir replied that the matter was "more delicate than it appears."[42]

He explained to Hardinge that he did not think there was much in his prime minister's most recent argument, but that it was important because the prime minister thought it was. Tweedsmuir's concern about the possibility of this issue marring the royal visit plans led him to advance arguments to persuade the Palace to accept them. He interspersed them, though, with a deferential tone, perhaps in the suppressed hope that, "if His Majesty desires me to meet him on the *Repulse* then it [would be] a command, and my prime minister would at once fall into line." This was not guaranteed, though, and Tweedsmuir would have known this after three and a half years of dealing with King. He then continued his argument that his prime minister would likely be "very much disappointed and disturbed" if, indeed, the king did order his representative to meet him at Quebec. "Most respectfully," therefore, he urged that his prime minister's view be accepted, emphasizing they were setting precedents for the future, not only for Canada but for the other Dominions as well. Then, trying to respond, impossibly, to all parties, Tweedsmuir closed his tortured letter with "a possible alternative," but pleaded at the end: "I should be greatly relieved if His Majesty would permit me to await him in Ottawa."[43]

Whether Tweedsmuir wanted it or not, Hardinge pursued the matter in a reply that cited his own concerns as well as certain cases in England that supported the governor general meeting the king.[44] Hardinge added at the end of his letter that he hoped the prime minister "will not think that we are being deliberately obstructive and trying to lower his status." Helping to ensure he would not be completely caught in the middle, Tweedsmuir forwarded the letter to King on February 21, with his own accompanying explanations. He portrayed his own views as those of King, but also provided two possible courses of action.[45] The Palace was concerned about the issue and, perhaps on advice from Tweedsmuir, arranged to send King George's assistant private secretary, Tommy Lascelles, to Ottawa. Lascelles arrived in late February, and met with King.

Prior to Lascelles's arrival, however, King replied to Tweedsmuir's note in a formal and detailed letter, noting the situation was without real precedent and that the opinion of "Law Officers of the Crown in Canada," as the Department of Justice lawyers were then known, supported his view.[46] The prime minister concluded his letter with a reminder that he had already provided his advice and that it "should definitely stand." Four days later King met with Tommy Lascelles at Laurier House. The first item they discussed was who should meet the king. The prime minister listened to Lascelles's view that they believed the governor general should. King then laid out his arguments about the Statute of Westminster and "our determination not to be put back into any Colonial status," which could, he stated, cause a separation from Britain and also make it more difficult to use the good offices of Canada in relations with the United States; privately, he viewed matters in a very partisan, and almost paranoid, way.[47] Lascelles responded that he had not seen the situation in that light. It was a lengthy discussion but ultimately Lascelles agreed.

Tweedsmuir sent a final note to the Palace on March 1. Hardinge replied by telegram on March 17: "The King is pleased to accept the advice of Prime minister that he should meet Their Majesties in Quebec on board *Repulse* as suggested, while your Excellencies remain in Ottawa."[48]

This drawn out issue reinforces what we know of Mackenzie King and the intensity of his national sentiments. It also reveals, though, how persistent, but in this instance also conflicted, Tweedsmuir could be, in certain delicate situations, trying to challenge his prime minister but not antagonizing him unduly. When Their Majesties arrived at Quebec City two months later, it was King, in his gold-braided Windsor court uniform, who met them, while the governor general waited in Ottawa. According to one close observer, Tweedsmuir had handled the controversy "with his invariable urbanity … What mattered were the King and Canada, not himself."[49]

Apart from this episode, Tweedsmuir had long ago determined — indeed, he had settled the issue in his mind when King Edward VIII first proposed to visit Canada — that in the event of a royal visit to Canada, he would stay in the background. This would be certain, Tweedsmuir believed, to make it Canada's show and emphasize that George VI was the king of Canada. It would also bolster the position of the lieutenant-governors, who Tweedsmuir thought were being treated too cavalierly by provincial governments.[50]

The status of the lieutenant-governors was, however, an issue of concern to King. The Table of Precedence lists the highest positions in the governance structure, in order of rank or authority. The Table had been revised in 1923 (when King was also prime minister), and the revision raised the status of the lieutenant-governors to second place, after the governor general.[51] In light of the upcoming royal visit, the desire was to emphasize "the national aspect of the occasion," as the under-secretary of state for external affairs noted to Shuldham Redfern.[52] Tweedsmuir approved of the recommendation to revise the Table on this basis because it supported emphasizing the national dimension. Whether it affected one way or another the cavalier treatment of lieutenant-governors by provincial governments would have to be a secondary consideration.

The American portion of the tour raised another sensitive question, concerning who should accompany the king on his visit to the United States. This subject will be dealt with in the next chapter in the context of relations with the United States.

While all of this and the other aspects of the planning were going on, the international situation deteriorated, nourishing anxiety. "[G]rievous times," Tweedsmuir described them, because they also created a certain unreality in arranging details for a royal visit that might never occur.[53] Regardless of the gravity of the international situation, which suggested to some that the royal visit should be cancelled, Tweedsmuir believed it should go ahead. Only a declaration of war should prevent the king and queen departing England, he felt. Should war break out during the tour, it could, in fact, be very positive, he believed, a point echoed by a number of Tweedsmuir's correspondents.[54] Hardinge wrote to Tweedsmuir that they should continue with their preparations, "but [noted that] no man alive can say with any certainty that we shall sail," adding that the move of the German fleet into the Atlantic was just another complicating factor.[55]

The looming problems on the international scene paralleled another kind of deterioration for Tweedsmuir, who could feel the strain of his office and this additional activity. He was recuperating from the flu but felt that "as one grows older one's bodily resilience declines."[56]

During the king's visit, he would obviously have to make some speeches. Tweedsmuir inquired about this to the Palace and offered to try his hand at them. At the same time, he gave specific recommendations as to the number (four) and length (very short), conscious of the king's speech impediment. Four were agreed upon: one on His Majesty's arrival, in

English and French; another in Ottawa during the dedication of the National War Memorial; a third in Vancouver or Victoria; and a farewell speech at Halifax. Tweedsmuir sent drafts of the speeches to the prime minister for his comment, noting that "the primary law of our constitution [is] that the King's words must be the words of his Prime Minister."[57] Tweedsmuir pointed out that he had tried to keep the topic of each speech a little different: at Quebec, Canada's long history; at Ottawa, the lessons of war; in the West, the possibilities of Canada's development; and at Halifax, the usual farewell reflections. When Tweedsmuir received the speeches back, he made, for all but the War Memorial one, some additional slight changes "to make the rhythm a little more easy to the spoken voice," always mindful of the king's handicap. Tweedsmuir politely indicated to the prime minister that he could disregard the additional changes if he thought fit. At the same time, he forwarded a draft of the queen's speech for the laying of the corner stone of the Supreme Court building.[58] A few days later, Mackenzie King said he wanted more time to consider the War Memorial speech and wanted to discuss the significance of the changes.[59] King spent a morning revising the speech as well as the one for the queen, then delivered them to the governor general's office.[60]

The texts having been completed, the governor general sent them off the next day to the Palace, noting he had made them short and the language simple, but he noted that the draft of the War Memorial speech had been largely written by the prime minister. Respectfully, he noted the speeches would provide a good foundation for Their Majesties, who would undoubtedly wish to alter them.[61] Alexander Hardinge acknowledged Their Majesties' thanks to Tweedsmuir and gracefully expressed the hope that he would not "take it amiss" if Their Majesties changed the speeches to suit their individual styles.[62]

At the same time that he was considering the speeches, Tweedsmuir moved to deal with a related, practical aspect, one that could work toward larger objectives of his governor generalship. He was now well aware of the effectiveness of radio broadcasting, based on his own experience. He undertook, therefore, to ensure the broadest diffusion possible for the king's speeches. There were, however, not only technical issues but a sovereignty issue at stake if the king's speeches were to be broadcast, particularly beyond Canada.

The current Canadian broadcasting facilities were not judged adequate for the type of coverage envisaged. The nascent Canadian Broadcasting Corporation was considering building a short-wave transmitter because broadcasts from Canada overseas had to either go through the U.S. system or through the "beam telephone ... booked at high rates."[63] Tweedsmuir argued that "it would not be very dignified for the [k]ing to make his Empire Day broadcast through an American system."[64] He had spoken with Gladstone Murray, the first general manager of the CBC, about having a transmitter in Canada. Murray was happy to have the occasion of the king's visit to support the project because he had been advocating a Canadian transmitter for some time.

Inaugurating a Canadian short-wave broadcasting service would not only provide more adequate coverage of the royal visit, but would also form part of a larger scheme to increase information exchange within the Empire, which up until then was largely one way, from Britain outward, through the BBC's short-wave service, which had only been in operation six years by that time. The BBC's director general, F.W. Ogilvie, through an informal talk with Tweedsmuir, offered their experience and expertise to the CBC, should the Canadian agency decide to proceed with the project. In any case the BBC had already offered to make facilities available for a proposed speech by the king for Empire Day, in May, when he would likely be in Winnipeg.[65] It would, however, obviously be better if Canada had its own transmitter. This became Tweedsmuir's objective.

In a letter to C.D. Howe, minister of transportation, who was responsible for the CBC, Tweedsmuir expressed his wish that the CBC acquire the transmitter, "for a very obvious reason — one of the responsibilities of my post here is to secure the fullest possible publicity in Great Britain for Canada and Canadian activities."[66] This was a task Tweedsmuir took seriously, but which had also previously landed him in trouble with the Palace.[67] He asked Ogilvie to send him an informal letter setting out the views of the BBC, which the governor general then passed on to C.D. Howe. By the time of the visit, all was in place and the broadcasts were made, including that of the Empire Day speech from Winnipeg.

But however important the newer medium was to Tweedsmuir for achieving particular objectives, he did not ignore the role of the newspaper reporters. Having worked as a journalist himself and worked with journalists through his varied careers, Tweedsmuir respected the role of the profession. He proposed to Alexander Hardinge the benefits of having His Majesty recognize the journalists as part of his entourage by hosting them at Rideau Hall, for a glass of sherry and talking informally with them. It was also a way, he believed, of recognizing the more professional status and regard for journalists that existed in North America, in contrast to the situation in England. Such an event would have been unknown in England. A precedent was in the planning stage.

"[I]t would be a real compliment to the profession," Tweedsmuir proposed, and suggested that something similar could be done in Washington, but deferred on that point to the British ambassador's opinion.[68] He added encouragement by noting that there would be no speeches or interviews, keeping the affair as informal as possible. The king readily agreed to the plan, indicating he would receive the "press representatives" after the ambassadors and high commissioners. Ultimately, the reception at Rideau Hall was attended by almost 120 journalists and "clinched the relations between the Sovereign and the newspapermen," according to R.K. Carnegie, a senior Canadian Press and parliamentary press gallery veteran who was selected by the government to accompany Their Majesties from England and back again.[69] Carnegie wrote subsequently that in "no phase was [Tweedsmuir's advice] more [valuable] than in the relations between Their Majesties and the press."[70] A similar event would be arranged in Washington.

Tweedsmuir had found it was difficult to get organizers in Canada to understand English etiquette while at the same time trying to get the Palace staff to appreciate and understand Dominion sentiments and sensibilities.[71] Now he was playing the role of interpreter again, successfully, in planning this informal gathering with the journalists.

In Britain, on Saturday, May 6, the royal couple boarded the *Empress of Australia* in Portsmouth harbour, to set sail for Canada. As they approached "the new world," fog and ice-fields caused a delay that meant the cancellation of a large government dinner and an afternoon tea at Spencerwood, the residence of the Quebec lieutenant-governor. Lady Tweedsmuir lamented the cancellation, thinking of all the people involved in the planning and preparation.[72] The governor general drew an apt description of the forces of nature. "What," he joked, "induced the North Atlantic suddenly to go Nazi?"[73]

When George VI and Queen Elizabeth arrived, Tweedsmuir remained in the background: "I cease to exist as [v]iceroy, and retain only a shadowy legal existence as [g]overnor general,"[74] the same approach he expressed when Edward VIII's visit to Canada was broached. As a result, the principal architect of this precedent-setting visit was not in attendance at one of the most significant events in Canadian constitutional history up to that time: the king in Parliament personally granting royal assent to nine bills.[75] The official history made a special point of noting the absence.[76] Throughout the febrile activity, especially at Government House, Lord and Lady Tweedsmuir brought an element of calm; they "were their eminently sensible good selves."[77]

The royal arrival in Ottawa was captured dramatically by the official historian of the tour, Dominion Archivist Gustave Lanctôt: "When Their Majesties walked into their Canadian residence, the Statute of Westminster had assumed full reality: the King of Canada had come home."[78] It was the realization of Tweedsmuir's objective. There were a number of other constitutionally significant activities that His Majesty would undertake that would emphasize his constitutional position as king of Canada, as well as prompting changes that enhanced Canada's now almost ten-year-old sovereign status, such as using the Great Seal of Canada to ratify a number of international agreements.[79]

In the past if the king ratified a Canadian treaty, the Great Seal of the United Kingdom would normally have been used. However, if the king, as king of Canada, were to ratify a treaty under the Great Seal of Canada, the Justice Department opined that "it would seem to be necessary to secure the enactment by the Parliament of Canada of appropriate legislation to authorize [its] use … for such purposes." It was determined that the Canadian Parliament was competent to

Library and Archives Canada/C-33278

"[S]lowly, with a solemnity born of the dignity of centuries-old pageantry, mingling historic and present significance, ... His Majesty made an inclination of the head indicating assent." The king of Canada granted royal assent to nine bills, May 19, 1939.

pass such legislation. The Seals Act of 1939 was duly passed, allowing His Majesty to ratify international agreements under the Great Seal of Canada. Presiding over a meeting of his Canadian Privy Council, the prime minister presented His Majesty the two agreements for ratification.[80] This legislation, a direct result of the prospect of the king's visit, added to the sovereign status already granted to Canada by the Statute of Westminster. The new Seals Act allowed Canada to put its stamp, as it were, on its international relations. The event symbolized, in one action, Canada's sovereignty and her status as a constitutional monarchy with its own king.[81]

An event the governor general did attend was the unveiling of the National War Memorial on May 21, at which a spontaneous event occurred that gave national feeling a very public, additional boost. After the playing of "God Save the King," the band played "O Canada." His Majesty remained at the salute, following the precedent of Edward VIII at the dedication of the Vimy Ridge Memorial in July 1936. The royal visit historian commented that this royal recognition virtually raised the status of "O Canada" to that of the Dominion's national anthem.[82]

Tweedsmuir watches the king and queen walk amongst the crowd in Ottawa, May 1939.

Library and Archives Canada/PA-800469

The royal tour of 1939 was a memorable and precedent-setting visit of which Tweedsmuir was largely the author. It breathed life into the Statute of Westminster and brought the "King of Canada" home. From it flowed new practices and legislation that consolidated and confirmed Canada's sovereign status and her loyalty to the Crown. The royal visit to the United States helped strengthen the relations between that country and Britain at a time of increasing threats to democracy from the dictators. These were all objectives Tweedsmuir strove to achieve.[83] The increased sense of pride, patriotism, and loyalty was also a fortuitous and timely gift for a country that would be at war only three months later.

Courtesy the Galbraith family

The king of Canada and Queen Elizabeth among Canadian veterans at Redditt, northwestern Ontario, May 1939.

PART III

"The Best Bridge"
Statesman Beyond Canada

CHAPTER 8

Bridging Britain and America

Tweedsmuir had a "hopeless prejudice" toward the United States — that is what the *New York Times* delighted in telling its readers when describing the Canadian governor general–designate's attitude to America.[1] Recalling John Buchan's visit to the United States in 1934, the *New York Times* commented how fortunate the appointment was for their country.[2] The attraction was reinforced by Buchan having expressed views coinciding with a basic American principle: "No State mechanism, however perfect, can get rid of the initiative and responsibility of the ordinary individual." Such was the importance of the appointment for America that, just before his arrival in Canada, the editors of *Time* decided to put Buchan also on the cover of the magazine.[3]

Expectations among Buchan's friends in England focused on the transatlantic dimension as well. Violet Markham wrote to Susan Buchan that she thought her husband "may play a very great part in molding opinion on the American continent...."[4] She then wrote to Buchan himself, explaining that she believed he could "play a part as great as Bryce [James Bryce, British Ambassador to the United States 1907–1913] did in making England and America intelligible to each other."[5]

Buchan's admiration for the United States was well known and had been publicly referenced frequently, as alluded to by the *New York Times*.[6]

But he also had an understanding of America. In an articulate assessment in *The Graphic* magazine in May 1930, John Buchan, MP, described "The Two Americas."[7] He not only highlighted the differences that existed between Britain and the United States, but also observed that there were two Americas, an older one in the East and South, which understood Britain, better in fact than Britain understood the older America. But there was also a younger America, one that included many different immigrants, who neither understood nor even cared about Britain. If the two countries were to work together, which Buchan strongly believed they should, they had to understand how they were different and how, internally, America itself had differences.

There was, of course, another, pressing reason for the transatlantic focus: the increasingly threatening international situation. There was a growing realization in Britain and the United States that Britain, while it was still a dominant power, had been weakened by the Great War, and would need the assistance of the United States to protect freedom against the spreading tyrannies. It was for reasons like these that the *Times* described Buchan as "'the best bridge' between the two continents."[8]

Tweedsmuir's bridging role started almost immediately after his arrival in Ottawa. He provided a short, official message to Mackenzie King to give to the president when King travelled to Washington to sign a trade agreement. The message contained a reference to the "strengthening of bonds of friendship" between the two nations, but, more importantly, it stressed the hope that the president would be able "to pay him an official visit" in the near future.[9] Tweedsmuir also confided to a correspondent that Prime Minister Stanley Baldwin had "entrusted [him] with some very confidential things to say to the president of the U.S.A." We don't know what these "very confidential things" were, but we can surmise that they related to Britain's relations with America. This reveals Baldwin using Buchan as an unofficial, trusted channel to President Roosevelt.[10]

Once the new governor general settled into Rideau Hall, he began work on arranging a meeting with President Roosevelt, initially scheduled for June. Regardless of what Baldwin had entrusted to him, this was also a personal strategic priority for Tweedsmuir, who believed relations with the United States to be "the most important thing in the world at this moment."[11] He had recognized the significance of the Anglo-American linkage since the First World War, when he was involved in intelligence and headed the Department of Information. Aside from affecting the outcome of the war and shortening it, the arrival of the American Expeditionary Force in 1917 brought with it the beginnings of what became a unique relationship in intelligence.[12] Now, with the deteriorating international situation, strengthening the overall relationship was a priority.

Since the governor general takes up residence in Quebec City at the Citadel during the summer, Tweedsmuir suggested that Roosevelt visit him there.[13] The president found the suggestion "most appealing."[14] Tweedsmuir preferred Quebec City because it would emphasize the personal aspects of the visit, removed, as it was, from some of the more formal and bureaucratic aspects of life in Ottawa, the capital. It would connect Roosevelt with the Crown and with the Commonwealth, not with the Government of Canada.

The visit had to be postponed, however, because of congressional business. The U.S. under-secretary of state, Bill Phillips, dined at Rideau Hall at the beginning of June 1936, likely to discuss the president's visit, which was rescheduled for the end of July, and perhaps also to lay the ground for "confidential things."[15] Tweedsmuir kept the prime minister apprised of the changes but did not emphasize the personal nature of the visit.[16]

In preparation for Roosevelt's visit, Tweedsmuir wrote his own speech, as he most always did. He sent a draft to Mackenzie King for comment. "It is a case where one must weigh every word," Tweedsmuir wrote.[17] Exercising caution, despite the trust King had expressed in him on his arrival in Canada, Tweedsmuir was likely surprised at the extent of King's comments, which were longer than the speech itself![18] The prime minister did indeed "weigh every word," and proposed changes prompted by his political senses. King concluded that what he suggested "may appear to be hypercritical," but he argued it would be unwise to risk a single word that could be misinterpreted. For different reasons both men appreciated the significant potential impact of the visit.

When the president landed at Wolfe's Cove on July 31 and drove up the steep streets to the Citadel in Quebec City, the hillsides were covered with U.S. Secret Service men — perhaps to their misfortune. "We shall hear nothing but their howls, as the hill is covered with poison ivy," one of Tweedsmuir's staff quipped.[19]

"Providence was very kind" to the two statesmen, providing beautiful weather for the visit, between two blustery days.[20] The speeches were broadcast in England over the BBC. The significance of this meeting between "the Great Republic" and Canada, an integral part of the British Commonwealth of Nations, was reflected in the speeches. They spoke of the co-operation and friendship that existed between the two North American nations, demonstrating "how civilized neighbours should live together."[21] Emphasizing that he knew his "earnest hope" was also that of the president, Tweedsmuir concluded: "It is my prayer that not by any alliances, political or otherwise, but by thinking the same thoughts and fulfilling the same purpose that the Republic of

F.C. Tyrell/National Film Board of Canada. Photothèque/Library and Archives Canada/PA-130312

President Roosevelt's visit to Governor-General Tweedsmuir at Quebec City, July 31, 1936.

the United States and the British Commonwealth may help restore the shaken liberties of mankind."[22]

John Reith, a fellow Scot who was the founding father of the BBC in the 1920s, cabled Tweedsmuir afterwards to note the broadcast had "come through perfectly and that England had been deeply impressed."[23]

Yousuf Karsh, Library and Archives Canada/PA-164243

The U.S. president's visit to Canada "must do this present world much more good than any meeting of the Assembly of the League of Nations." Tweedsmuir speaks with Roosevelt on the terrace at Quebec City, while Mackenzie King looks on.

Reith's message suggests that Tweedsmuir may have been involved in making arrangements for the broadcasts.

Learning of the reception in Britain, Tweedsmuir believed the day had been very positive, for he had stressed that "the whole thing must work for good, both in America and in Europe."[24] Tweedsmuir's friend Lord Crawford could see the benefits and hoped Roosevelt would win the presidential election in November. "Roosevelt is a wonderful man ... who in a second term of office," Crawford predicted, "may become a really great statesman, with a worldwide outlook and influence as well."[25] Three weeks later, "echoes of Quebec" appeared in the *New York Times*, which noted that Roosevelt's visit to Canada "must do this present world much more good than any meeting of the Assembly of the League of Nations."[26]

Mackenzie King was thrilled with the visit. Unrestrained, he described it as "a joy too great to describe."[27] On his return to Kingsmere, he penned an eight-page letter, "not an 'official' communication," to congratulate both the governor general and Lady Tweedsmuir on "the great success" of the visit.[28] King's letter gushed, but he did recognize that much of the significance of the visit lay in the impression it must have given to the world, which was Tweedsmuir's objective.[29] His emotion carried him away, causing him to exaggerate Canada's status in his description of the nature of the relationship between the three countries: [One can only remark on the] "friendliness between [these] three great powers, to which the relations of others to one another, just at this time, present a sorry contrast. We speak of 'the blessings of peace' — where were they ever more completely or significantly portrayed!" In an understated manner, Tweedsmuir described the letter as "profoundly emotional."[30]

During the November 1936 U.S. presidential election, Tweedsmuir and his family listened to the results on the radio. Roosevelt won the election and would now be in a powerful position. Tweedsmuir hoped he might "be able to do something for the peace of the world." A return visit for the governor general to Washington was assured with Roosevelt's re-election.

After an absence of communication, reflecting his preoccupation during the period of the election campaign through to the State of the

Union Address in January 1937, Roosevelt sent a handwritten note to Tweedsmuir, inviting him and his wife to Washington at the end of March, which confirmed Roosevelt had not only enjoyed the Quebec City visit with Tweedsmuir but had found it useful.[31] While it would be a personal visit for the two couples, "rewarded with a good time," Roosevelt indicated there was "much ... to talk over with you — nice things as well as the world situation."[32]

In the meantime, in mid-March, King stopped over in Washington on his way to Virginia for a holiday. After meeting both President Roosevelt and Secretary of State Cordell Hull, King informed Tweedsmuir there was no doubt about the Americans' "desire to have the English-speaking peoples drawn more closely together."[33] This would have been encouraging indeed for Tweedsmuir. King's informal conversations focused on the European situation and left him with the impression that Roosevelt would take "action of a kind which will make clear his desire to effect an appeasement of conditions in Europe by lending good offices toward that end."[34]

Roosevelt would have known that he had to talk with Mackenzie King but, while the talks with King might have been useful, it was Tweedsmuir who could give him better access to British leaders while allowing him to not be seen as dealing directly with them, something which carried significant political risks.

In the United States it was expected that during the visit by Canada's governor general to the president, the two men, who had "been friends for many years," would discuss both the political and economic relations of the two countries, as had occurred during the Canadian prime minister's visit a few weeks earlier.[35] They seemed to make little distinction between the two positions. The *New York Times* noted there would be a focus on political relationships, "in view of the approaching Imperial Conference in London because of the role Canada has long played as an interpreter of the United States to the Empire."

Lord and Lady Tweedsmuir departed Ottawa by special train early Tuesday morning, March 30. Their welcome was "extraordinary," with large crowds in the streets and escorts of cavalry and armoured cars. During the visit Tweedsmuir and Roosevelt would have ample opportunity to continue their personal conversations because the Tweedsmuirs were staying at the White House, which was a first and signaled their close relationship. The viceregal couple carried out the expected activities: a visit to Arlington National Cemetery and laying wreaths at the Tomb of the Unknown Soldier and at the Canadian Cross; a visit to Washington's Tomb; luncheons and formal dinners. More importantly, however, would be the very public attendance by the governor general at the U.S. Congress and his private discussions with the president. The president was intent on discussing what he described as a "bread-and-butter problem for his country," the international situation and efforts to preserve peace.[36]

On the second day of the visit, the governor general, in full dress uniform and medals, held a press conference with the president in the White House. It was described as an innovation because a governor general does not usually hold press conferences. He was introduced individually to all the reporters present, and then Roosevelt introduced him to the group as "an old newspaperman."[37] Tweedsmuir "immediately dispelled any sense of formality," observed the reporter for the *New York Times*. He noted that he could not comment on public affairs, since "an official in his position has no politics." Not deterred, one journalist asked if he and the president had yet had any personal conversations. Tweedsmuir repeated his previous comment, and then the president interjected. Because of the position of his guest, he explained, there could be no official talks, but, he continued, the two of them could "sit on a sofa and soliloquize, and [of course] each could not help overhearing the other." Roosevelt added they had done some of that and that there would be more of the same later. It was a brilliant response. Britain was, as Roosevelt biographer Freidel notes, "the nation Roosevelt most courted," but he had to be wary of criticism from isolationists in his country who feared being drawn into European troubles.[38]

On Thursday, April 1, the governor general was scheduled to pay a visit to Capitol Hill; unexpectedly, according to Tweedsmuir, he was invited to address the Senate and then the House of Representatives. He improvised his short speeches, a feat which even he described as "not very easy," particularly given the significance and political sensitivity which would attach to such a prestigious event in terms of the

Commonwealth-U.S. relationship. To Tweedsmuir's knowledge, it was the first time a Briton had ever addressed both houses of Congress.

Shortly after three o'clock, Vice-President Garner introduced His Excellency the Governor General of Canada to the Senate. Tweedsmuir expressed thanks for the great kindness and honour he had been given. He humorously noted his "curious position," no longer being like those in his audience, "a free and independent politician."[39] Despite his being "unable to express [his] views upon any public question of any real importance, at least not for publication," he nonetheless touched on what was for him the most critical issue. He expressed great admiration for the country and then struck a strategic note: "I have always believed," he said, "that the secret of the future of civilization lies in the hands of the English-speaking people." There was much in common, he suggested, but it was important "that my country and yours … should be different … [that] the strength of an alliance between two nations lies in the fact that they should be complementary to each other." While the reference to "my country" technically might have been considered to refer to Canada, it was clear that the reference was broader.

A short time later, to the House of Representatives, he made a qualification similar to the one he had made to the Senate, saying that he "spen[t] his time walking on thin ice," since he could not express an opinion related to politics, even though almost everything did. Again he underlined the special bond that he felt existed with the United States. "Your nation and mine," he said, "are today in a special sense the guardians of that great form of government which we call democracy, and of which I think the truest definition is a true mixture of law and liberty."[40] Following each address, he was introduced to each member, often stopping to speak with someone he knew. He then spent a few minutes with the Speaker.

The following morning Tweedsmuir visited the Naval Academy at Annapolis, in full uniform, and spoke to over two thousand midshipmen. He highlighted the close friendship of Britain and the United States, and again emphasized their common interests: "The American and British navies are united in the same purpose — the preservation of liberty and peace. Every addition to your navy is an extra addition to the security of the world."[41]

When Tweedsmuir and Roosevelt finally were able to talk, there were two main subjects.[42] The first was Roosevelt's idea to propose a conference dealing with economic issues, which it was believed were largely behind the turbulence in Europe. The president believed the time propitious for such a proposal, because it would reinforce other factors that would give the dictators reason to pause. Some of these factors included the British defence program, the "fiasco of the German aeroplanes and the Italian troops in Spain," the strong stand of the Vatican, and a demonstrated closer understanding of the Western democracies. Roosevelt was committed to being at such a conference.

The second key subject the two men broached was a trade agreement between Britain and America. The United States had much to offer in terms of tariff reductions on British industrial exports, but it had to have, obviously, something in return, particularly for western farmers, who were great supporters of the president. There were significant difficulties inherent in such a bilateral agreement, because it implied adjustments to the imperial preferences, which affected the Dominions. The preferences were a target of U.S. negotiators. Tweedsmuir was confident that King would "take the long view," and be able to bring the country along with him on adjusting imperial preferences. Tweedsmuir's efforts received a boost when, next month, he received a visit in Ottawa from another enthusiast for an Anglo-American trade agreement, the financial editor of the *Daily Telegraph*, who had just met with Roosevelt and Hull in New York.[43]

Roosevelt's parting words to Tweedsmuir were to the effect that he hoped the visit would show the dictators how close Britain and the United States were. Tweedsmuir admired what he saw in the president — greatness, courage, and a productive mind. It reinforced his "natural liking for Americans."[44] He and Lady Tweedsmuir boarded their train and arrived back in Ottawa during the evening of Friday, April 2. It had been a visit of significant firsts.

Tweedsmuir was well satisfied with the visit, believing Britain and Canada, on the one side, and the United States, on the other, "have never been closer," which is why he believed the timing could not be better for conducting trade negotiations. The day after he returned, he wrote to Colonel Arthur Murray, a British Liberal who also knew Mackenzie

King but, more importantly in the current context, knew Roosevelt. Tweedsmuir described his welcome in Washington as "really unbelievable," giving him the impression that his visit had "done some good," in terms of enhancing U.S.-Empire relations.[45] It was indeed this relationship that mattered most to Roosevelt, who had told Tweedsmuir that, while their two countries had much in common and were thinking together to address common problems, "Canada was of very little importance to the U.S.A. except as part of the British Empire."[46] Tweedsmuir believed that "Canada [was] therefore the great liaison between the U.S.A. and the Empire" and this was where he also believed his most important work was to be done.[47]

The visit was seen widely as a tremendous success. Indeed, the *New York Times* gave it extensive text and photo coverage, including both the ceremonial and the social aspects, and speculated about the topics discussed by the Canadian governor general and the president.[48] In London, newspapers hailed the visit as well. The *Evening Standard* in London carried an article highlighting the United States as "sharing with us ideals, traditions, kinships, habits of mind, and instincts of heart."[49] It also praised Canada, implicating significantly of course the role of Tweedsmuir, as "the natural interpreter of Great Britain and the United States to one another."

The visit would add to the perception that the United States was supportive of Britain, an important element in trying to deter the dictators.[50] The British ambassador in Washington, Ronald Lindsay, wrote to congratulate Tweedsmuir on the success of the visit, which he felt "has done much to draw the United States closer both to Canada and to Great Britain."[51] Tweedsmuir's former parliamentary colleagues in London observed with interest the good work he was doing for Anglo-American relations.[52] But it was at a personal price.

After Tweedsmuir returned to Ottawa, Prime Minister Mackenzie King visited him late Sunday afternoon, April 4, 1937. He found him resting in bed and "looking quite frail," making King wonder whether he would be able to complete his time as governor general.[53] They discussed at length Roosevelt's proposal for a world conference to be held in Geneva. Tweedsmuir offered flattering encouragement to King, saying he thought that both the president and Secretary of State Cordell Hull wanted the Canadian prime minister to "help forward the whole movement between the United States and Britain when at the Imperial Conference" in London in June.[54]

Over the next several days, Tweedsmuir reflected on the discussions in Washington and composed a lengthy letter to Baldwin, making clear in this recorded correspondence that he had "no official standing" and was "reporting to [Baldwin] as to a private friend."[55] While no reference is made in the letter that this involved the "very confidential things" Baldwin had entrusted him to say to Roosevelt, it is certainly possible.

Tweedsmuir suggested to Baldwin that the president's presence at an economic conference would have "a great moral effect" and would undoubtedly be intended to offer encouragement. Roosevelt's desire to contribute to preserving the peace was based on his assessment that while this was something he could persuade the country to be part of, America's participation in another war "would probably mean something in the nature of a domestic revolution."[56] As for the conference, Roosevelt hadn't yet worked out the details over how best to introduce the proposal, its timing, or the best location. While Tweedsmuir assessed that there were many difficulties, he believed that it was in Canada's and Britain's best interests, and that they should "meet any proposals halfway," urging the British government to give it serious consideration.[57] He informed Baldwin that the Canadian prime minister would be able to provide him with more details when he arrived in London in early May to attend the coronation ceremonies for King George VI and the Imperial Conference.

Tweedsmuir sent a memo to President Roosevelt following their talks. It contained a detailed, eight-part background analysis for convening a conference, an initiative, Tweedsmuir wrote, that "can be taken only by the president of the U.S.A."[58] Tweedsmuir sent a copy to King, noting that the president had requested he do so.[59] King in turn believed Tweedsmuir's memo dovetailed beautifully with his own, which he had prepared at the White House.[60]

While Tweedsmuir was in Washington, he had been given information by Ambassador Lindsay, which he shared with King.[61] It was a confidential memo Lindsay had prepared for Foreign Secretary Anthony Eden, setting out what help might be expected from the United States in the case of war erupting in Europe. King viewed the very existence of such a memo as "ominous," and shared "the inside information" with his Cabinet a week later, though he did not record where or from whom he had obtained it. King speculated that the British government let him see the note because it would allow him to see how they assessed the European situation and, also, "the significance of the part Canada may be able to play in bringing the United States and Great Britain into closer relation with each other."[62]

There were other topics Tweedsmuir had discussed, about which Mackenzie King informed his Cabinet in August, but this time he did note his source. King talked about the possible U.K.-U.S. Trade Agreement: "I told my colleagues ... of the conversation I had subsequently had with the governor general after his return from Washington, and of the communication sent to him by the British ambassador, which His Excellency had given me to read."[63] Obviously, Tweedsmuir's connections were important to King, at least when they provided useful information and did not disagree with King's views or cause real or perceived potential political problems.

The links with the United States continued to be forged. On June 17 Tweedsmuir addressed a luncheon of the American-Canadian Conference in Kingston, Ontario. Prefacing his remarks with the statement that in his official capacity he was confined to "governor generalities," he picked up and elaborated on his theme offered to the American Congress in the spring: "On a close understanding between the British Commonwealth and the Republic of the United States depends the peace and freedom of the world."[64] In working toward those noble ends, however, he stressed that common ideals and thinking along the same lines were more important than a formal treaty. He wove into that theme other ideas on the relationships between Britain, America, and Canada, and the prospects of the latter two to develop themselves and their resources "for the purposes of a civilized life."

According to Tweedsmuir, it was an "interesting comment" on the evolving relationship with the United States that the American broadcasting companies had carried his speech in honour of the coronation of King George VI in May 1937.[65] This was followed by President Roosevelt broadcasting a message to Canada on July 1, the seventieth anniversary of Confederation. From his country home in Hyde Park, New York, the president stated, in a clear message intended not only for North American consumption, that the friendship between Canada and the United States was "secure from every hazard of destruction or misunderstanding because it [was] based upon a common aspiration to maintain, to defend, and to perpetuate the democratic form of constitutional, representative government."[66] It was a theme reflecting Tweedsmuir's words at Quebec City and to the U.S. House of Representatives. Roosevelt closed by congratulating Canadians "on the successful achievements of free institutions" and sent his "affectionate greetings."

With the government's approval, Tweedsmuir replied to Roosevelt's message from aboard a British cruiser in the harbour of Quebec City, reciprocating the president's greeting and setting a historic and historical context.[67] He emphasized that both countries had a living European tradition "which must be the basis of" a new civilization, of which the making was "in our hands." Alluding to the contemporary situation, he opined that both countries were "coming to realize that [they had] certain responsibilities to the world at large which may be difficult to define but which it [was] probable [would] have much in common." Addressing these difficulties would, he expressed hopefully and allegorically, see both countries pooling "our ideas about the problems of the road." Then, bringing the reference specifically to Canada, he offered "one reflection," which was effectively a challenge to Canadians. The Fathers of Confederation, he said, had given Canada union but they could not give the country unity. "Unity," he advised, "comes only by the slow assimilation of different points of view and different traditions." Canada must have, he continued, "a sincere identity of purpose and a true homogeneity of spirit." He concluded with his vision that Canada's destiny was "not to be a mere territorial expression ... not ... merely nine Provinces, but to be a single and indivisible nation."

Tweedsmuir saw these broadcasts as precedent-setting and another indicator of the drawing together of Canada, the United States, and Britain. Indeed, newspapers noted that it was the first time such a public exchange had occurred. The *New York Times* special correspondent in Montreal noted that Roosevelt's reassurances were particularly comforting for Canadians, who were troubled by developments in Europe. He also perceptively pointed out that Tweedsmuir had departed from his usual self-described "governor generalities" to address the question of unity and the aspiration of common goals with the United States.[68]

The idea for these broadcasts was likely given birth during the previous two meetings between Tweedsmuir and Roosevelt. Over this period letters between them appear to indicate a growing comfort and appreciation for each other's respective situation. Tweedsmuir's belief, expressed later that year, that "almost the most useful work I can do is in connection with the U.S.A.," was clearly manifesting itself.[69]

As Roosevelt travelled across the American West aboard the "Presidential Special," he replied to a letter from Tweedsmuir describing his trip to the Arctic that summer. Exchanging quips about fishing and finally comparing personal situations, Roosevelt wrote: "I am, as you know, an impatient soul, and it is especially difficult not 'to speak loudly in meeting.' I like to think that you also occasionally suffer in silence in the presence of expert and wise counsellors!"[70] He ended his letter, "I do wish that I might see you more often." There is an intimacy in the sentiments shared between these two statesmen. The tone can be read as a deepening of the understanding and the relationship between them. While the Presidential Special returned east, Roosevelt was working on a speech with which he hoped to move public opinion, the theme of which was likely discussed with Tweedsmuir. Influencing both him and public opinion was a revulsion over reports of ruthless Japanese attacks on China.

On October 5, 1937, in Chicago, Roosevelt used the opportunity of dedicating a new bridge and thirty miles of lakefront boulevard as the unlikely venue to deliver a major foreign policy speech. In it, he emphasized the primacy of international law for "removing injustices and well-founded grievances; but at the same time ... putting an end to acts of international aggression."[71] Treading carefully, because of the very strong isolationist opinion, but determined to lead it in his direction, Roosevelt ventured that the American people needed to "give thought to the rest of the world," because threats to peace would ultimately affect America.[72] "The peace-loving nations," he said, "must make a concerted effort in opposition to those violations of treaties and those ignorings of humane instincts which today are creating a state of international anarchy, international instability from which there is no escape through mere isolation or neutrality." If a disease begins to spread, he explained, to subsequent spontaneous applause, "the community approves and joins in a quarantine of the patients in order to protect … against the spread of the disease." His Chicago address was dubbed "the quarantine speech."

The speech made a major impact, throughout the United States and most of the concerned world.[73] Roosevelt biographer Frank Freidel noted that most American opinion endorsed the president's tone, but as reporters subsequently pressed him to explain what he meant by quarantine, skepticism grew.[74] The fact that the president believed he could make such a speech was aided by public opinion shifting as a result of reading about the Japanese atrocities and bombing in China. But the tone of the speech applied as well to aggressive authoritarian regimes everywhere. For those looking to the United States for support against European dictators, Tweedsmuir expressed the hope that perhaps there would now be "a good chance of the United States coming into direct alliance with the European democracies."[75]

Tweedsmuir described the speech to his old professor, Gilbert Murray, as "the culmination of a long conspiracy" between himself and the American president.[76] He added a bracketed comment that his comment must be kept secret. There are no explicit references to this in the Roosevelt papers nor in any of the major Roosevelt biographies. It is clear, however, that Tweedsmuir believed his contact and discussions with the president contributed to the speech — how directly or indirectly, we cannot know. There is little doubt, however, that Roosevelt appreciated his discussions about the world situation with a statesman and master of words like John Buchan, who could provide perspective, ideas, and rhetorical inspiration. What is clear is that Tweedsmuir recognized the influence of public opinion and the need to arouse it in favour of Britain and against the tyrannical ideologies. If the dictators recognized that the speech Roosevelt gave at Chicago that October represented increasing concern and shared purposes among the democracies, then, it was believed, they might be dissauded from further aggression.

Later that month the U.S. secretary of state, Cordell Hull, travelled to Ottawa with a proposal for a Nine-Power Treaty conference to deal with Japanese aggression. The treaty had been signed in Washington in 1922 to ensure stability for China's borders and, more generally, stability for the Far East.[77] Tweedsmuir knew of the American proposal and wanted to suggest to King that he say something at the Canadian Institute of International Affairs dinner in Montreal on October 11 in support of it. Wary of King's sensitivities, Tweedsmuir first complimented him on his refusal thus far to speak to the press, but then inquired whether, since the British prime minister had formally approved of the American proposal, King thought it might be a good idea "for Canada to give some indication of her approval."[78] King listened, respecting the statesman in Tweedsmuir, but consulted his under-secretary of state, Dr. O.D. Skelton. Ultimately, he thought it better to defer such a pronouncement to later in the month, when he would give a speech at the University of Toronto, since Cordell Hull would also be there (the latter was to receive an honorary degree from the university).[79] Tweedsmuir agreed with the reasoning, but there would have been no point in arguing with his prime minister in any case, especially since it was just a matter of postponing by a couple of days Canada's expression of support for the American initiative.

Hull arrived by train at noon in Ottawa on October 20 and went straightaway to Government House. We know that King went to Government House to meet Hull officially, then returned home to Laurier House, where he awaited the leading U.S. diplomat for tea at five o'clock. Hull was accompanied by the U.S. minister (ambassador) to Canada, Norman Armour. After a few pleasantries, which included Hull relaying how fond President Roosevelt was of the Canadian prime minister and King responding in kind,[80] Hull broached the subject of the international situation. As a reflection of how seriously the Roosevelt administration viewed the world situation, Hull expressed concern that the populations in the United States, Canada, the Empire, and France "did not realize how terribly dangerous the whole situation was."[81] Hull also described the complexity of whether or not to apply sanctions against Japan.[82]

Tweedsmuir described his talks with Hull as "most successful," though we do not know the specific details.[83] His personal objective was to provide support for the American proposal and encouragement for the thrust of the president's "quarantine" speech. Before the end of October, he communicated the essence of his exchanges with Roosevelt and Hull to Neville Chamberlain, encouraging the British prime minister to show support for Roosevelt's approach.[84]

Chamberlain, who had formally approved of the proposal put forward by Hull,[85] seemed appreciative of Tweedsmuir's information, but noted in a lengthy reply the following month that he had indeed been trying, in his recent speeches, to encourage "a more complete community of purpose between [Britain and the United States]," and was going

© National Film Board of Canada. All rights reserved.

Tweedsmuir and U.S. secretary of state Cordell Hull at the University of Toronto, October 22, 1937. Hull expressed concern that the populations in the U.S., Canada, the Empire, and France "did not realize how terribly dangerous the whole situation was".

out of his way "to encourage those sections of American opinion that seem to have welcomed the president's Chicago speech."[86] But public opinion would take time to develop, he thought, and the current U.S.-U.K. trade issues would divert attention from other international matters. Nonetheless, Chamberlain committed himself to doing what he could to improve future relations. It was not a solid commitment, though, given Chamberlain's disdain for the Americans.[87] A year later he would ignore it completely when he assessed that his own initiatives, as well as Britain's national interests, were at stake in dealing with Hitler. Chamberlain closed by noting he greatly appreciated Tweedsmuir's description of his discussions with Roosevelt and Hull, adding that he appreciated how careful Tweedsmuir had to be as governor general not to expose himself to accusations of meddling in politics.[88]

A few days later Tweedsmuir told his prime minister of the letter he had written to Chamberlain about Hull's visit. This was another instance where King took exception to Tweedsmuir's actions but did not say anything. Privately, however, he vented, and generalized, that "governors general from England cannot do other than regard themselves as first and foremost agents of the British Government."[89]

Through 1938 and 1939, three diplomatic posts were being filled, namely those of the U.S. ambassador to London and Ottawa, and that of the British ambassador in Washington. All three were of interest for Tweedsmuir because of the implications for Anglo-American relations in an increasingly dangerous time.

In January 1938 the U.S. ambassador to Ottawa, Norman Armour, a career diplomat, and his wife, a Russian princess whom he had met during a posting to Petrograd (St. Petersburg) from 1916 to 1918, were given a farewell dinner. Tweedsmuir described the couple as "our closest friends here," a superlative that reflected his affinity for America.[90] The departure of Armour made him anxious about who the new American representative would be. Given the deteriorating world situation, he viewed this appointment as "tremendously important."[91] It would be four months before former Secretary of Commerce Daniel Roper was appointed.[92]

At about the same time, in February 1938, a new American ambassador was arriving in London. Joseph P. Kennedy, father of future president John F. Kennedy, had been a long-time supporter of Roosevelt, but he was also an isolationist and was now grating on the president's nerves. As Roosevelt biographer Conrad Black notes, the president wanted to get the "bumptious" Kennedy out of the country and, in the process, "repay Chamberlain for the haughty refusal of his invitation to visit the United States."[93] On February 20, 1938, Anthony Eden was replaced as British Foreign Secretary by Lord Halifax.[94] Tweedsmuir immediately cabled him about the new American ambassador.

Specifically, he requested that Halifax and the Foreign Office give special attention to the new American ambassador. Subsequent to the cable, Tweedsmuir followed up with a letter wishing Halifax success, and asking that Kennedy receive a "proper sort of welcome" and that he be "sympathetically handled."[95] He explained that Kennedy was a man of great ability and independent character, but diplomatically described him as "rather different from the ordinary ambassadorial type." Kennedy was "clearly out of the diplomatic mould."[96]

Halifax replied promptly, noting that he had met with Kennedy and liked him, finding him "pleasantly unofficial."[97] To others he described Kennedy as "so representative of modern America," which included a rather colourful vocabulary, a down-to-earth approach but with behaviour that did not necessarily fit social protocols.[98] Halifax assured Tweedsmuir they would do "everything ... to make him feel welcome."

On the British side, the most significant diplomatic appointment was more carefully contextual. In early 1939 Tweedsmuir believed consideration was again being given to replacing Ronald Lindsay in Washington. There had been criticism of Lindsay for his failure in public relations, coupled with American criticisms of his arrogance in dealing with politicians and journalists.[99]

Tweedsmuir wrote to Chamberlain toward the end of January to pass on his own views about the choice of ambassador to Washington, views supported by Roosevelt, which he also passed on in his letter. Specifically, he suggested that "a career diplomat [was] not the proper choice at this time."[100] Tweedsmuir indicated this was an opinion that was also prevalent among most of his Canadian and American friends, and made a unique proposal. He suggested that if Chamberlain had not yet decided on the appointment, Stanley Bruce, the Australian high commissioner and former prime minister, would be an admirable successor to Lindsay.[101] It would have been a unique appointment, giving such an important British post to a Dominion representative. Was it realistic? Tweedsmuir was thinking beyond politics in Britain to ways he thought might also strengthen the Commonwealth. He believed the Americans would see the appointment as a compliment; it would also flatter the Dominions.

In a lengthy and detailed reply, Chamberlain noted that Roosevelt's opinion "has been duly taken account of," and that when the appointment was announced "it will command general approval on your side of the Atlantic."[102] The governor general passed the letter on to King, who was "deeply grateful" for the opportunity to read the letter, which he privately described as "comforting."[103] In this instance, King did not take exception to Tweedsmuir's direct contact with the British government; testimony, if it were needed, to King's inconsistency.

Toward the end of April, the British government announced the name of its new ambassador to the United States. And indeed it seemed to please Tweedsmuir, who wrote immediately to Philip Kerr, the Marquis of Lothian, to congratulate him. Lothian was a committed Atlanticist. Tweedsmuir complimented Lothian, noting that he was "one of the few Englishmen who really knew America," adding that, "above all you like the country; and there is no nation so sensitive to liking."[104]

Tweedsmuir's acquaintance with Lothian went back thirty-five years, when Kerr had been approached in the fall of 1904 to join Lord Milner's administration in South Africa. He was directed to speak with John Buchan, who had worked for two years in Milner's "kindergarten." Kerr attributed Buchan's advice as key to his decision to accept the offer.[105] The two men shared many views, most important of which was the need for close relations between the British Empire and the United States of America. In January 1939 Lothian, who was critical of Lindsay, had travelled to the United States and met with President Roosevelt, who had become irritated by what he described as a "we who are about to die salute you" attitude on the part of the British and their pleadings about the European situation.[106] After his U.S. tour, Lothian stayed at Rideau Hall to talk over what he had learned.[107]

While key diplomatic appointments were being made, watched, and commented on, non-diplomatic channels continued to be used. Trusted individuals could act as conduits for unofficial communication between leaders who didn't wish to risk overt contacts that might be seen in a negative political light. The conduits themselves sometimes had some advantages over the more official and diplomatic channels.[108] Tweedsmuir was one such individual. Another was one Tweedsmuir had already been dealing with, Arthur Murray.

The extent of Roosevelt's support for Britain and France was, as already noted, limited by the significant isolationist pressures within his country. He had to exercise caution in any contacts with Britain or France, or risk political damage. Despite this he looked for ways to help the two allies, recognizing that Hitler's threat to democracy meant as much for the United States as for Britain and France. Following Chamberlain's meeting with Hitler in Munich in September 1938, Roosevelt met secretly on October 19 with Jean Monnet, a French businessman (Monnet cognac) and a future "father" of a united Europe. Monnet was trusted by the French premier, Daladier, and some of his key ministers, who were alarmed at what they saw as French military deficiencies when compared to German rearmament, especially in aircraft. Monnet was sent to the United States for urgent talks with Roosevelt on how the United States might assist France.[109] Roosevelt pondered how France might circumvent the U.S. Neutrality Act in the event of war, and proposed having American companies shift parts to assembly plants in Canada.[110] Again, for Roosevelt's domestic political protection, there was no official French government link, thereby avoiding criticism or speculation about conspiracies.

A few days later, the president, at his home in Hyde Park, met with Arthur Murray for similar discussions. On leaving Washington Murray and his wife travelled to Ottawa and stayed at Rideau Hall. He had a message from the president and also relayed to Tweedsmuir the subject of his own discussions with Roosevelt.

Roosevelt's verbal message to Tweedsmuir consisted of a proposal to appoint an officer to liaise with a Canadian counterpart in order to exchange information on airplane design and manufacture and to keep contract prices down. Very significantly, the president had also asked Murray to convey to Prime Minister Chamberlain "assurance that the industrial resources of the United States would be behind him."[111] Roosevelt then wanted Murray and Tweedsmuir to prepare a memorandum for King on the discussions Roosevelt had had with Murray.

Tweedsmuir promised Roosevelt he would discuss these matters with King when the prime minister returned from holiday in the Caribbean at the beginning of November (1938).[112] When King did return, on November 7, the governor general sent him a note attaching two memoranda that he prepared with Arthur Murray.[113] Tweedsmuir also included in his letter to Roosevelt a request that he would like to arrange a meeting, because "there are many matters which concern our common peace."[114] After King had been consulted, Roosevelt indicated they could then deal further with "the preparedness problem."[115] Tweedsmuir was doing all he could to build on Roosevelt's already "tremendously pro-British" tendency and perceived him as "anxious to do all he can to help us."[116]

In June 1938 Tweedsmuir travelled as a private citizen, with the approval of King George VI and the Canadian prime minister, to the United States to receive honorary degrees from Harvard and Yale.[117] Tweedsmuir sent King copies of what he proposed to say, asking if there was "anything ... inappropriate" in his speeches.[118] King replied he was very pleased regarding the honours for Buchan, but advised Shuldham Redfern (Tweedsmuir's secretary) not to issue any public announcement, because it would raise questions as to why the governor general was leaving while Parliament was sitting.[119]

In New York during this visit, Tweedsmuir stayed at the iconic Waldorf-Astoria, organizing his time with maximum efficiency and meeting numerous Americans who would be able to inform his assessment of the economic and political situation of the United States and of public opinion concerning international affairs and American attitudes toward Britain. After a breakfast meeting, he had lunch on Wall Street, where he had "a valuable talk" with a number of partners of Morgans Bank and Colonel McCormick, who was publisher of the *Chicago Tribune* and a strong advocate of isolationism.[120] He also had "a very satisfactory talk" about the American financial situation, and, likely, Britain's war debt to the United States, with Owen Young, the chairman of General Electric and the deputy chairman of the New York Federal Reserve Bank.[121] Jan Morgan, a partner of Morgans Bank, had not been able to attend the lunch with Tweedsmuir but did attend the commencement at Harvard two days later, where they were able to speak.

On June 22 and 23, two beautiful, sunny days, Tweedsmuir received honorary doctorates of law from two of the most prestigious universities in the United States.[122] The events were given publicity in the press in both Canada and the United States. Tweedsmuir shared the stage with another popular personality: a thirty-seven-year-old Walt Disney, who was just hitting his animated stride at the time. His honorary degree from Yale was for having "created a new language of art."[123] Disney, of course, received a very warm welcome, but Buchan received an even warmer one. Canada's best-selling literary governor general received a standing ovation. While he admitted Walt Disney really "should have been the popular figure,"[124] the difference in their reception was a reflection of the predominance of books then and of the newness of film; John Buchan's novels and historical biographies were popular in the United States, particularly in the literary environment of the Ivy League universities.

When Harvard president Charles Seymour conferred the honorary doctor of laws on Buchan, before an estimated crowd of seven thousand people, he referred to the "brilliant historian and biographer, beloved novelist and distinguished public servant, [and] representative of a commonwealth of free peoples whom we trust."[125] The receptions he received at each university gave him the impression that he was more popular with the young people in the United States than he had thought. Quite apart from the personal satisfaction he derived from his honours, Tweedsmuir appreciated these ceremonies because they helped to

contribute to his strategic objective: showing co-operation and friendship between the United States and the Commonwealth, and inspiring
a younger generation of Americans to safeguard their inherited values
and look kindly toward Britain.

During this period Tweedsmuir and Roosevelt maintained their
correspondence also. In April Roosevelt sent Tweedsmuir an edition of
speeches he made in South America, which Tweedsmuir responded would
be "an invaluable addition" to his American library.[126] In May Tweedsmuir
suggested they try to arrange a meeting during the summer by coor-
dinating some events.[127] They were both to be involved in opening the
international bridge at the Thousand Islands over the St. Lawrence River
in mid-August. This could provide one opportunity, but Tweedsmuir was
also keen to have Roosevelt see the Canadian Prairies, where work and
innovative projects were countering the effects of drought.

As it turned out, however, Tweedsmuir's summer visit to Britain,
scheduled for July and early August, was extended after a medical examination and recommendation for total rest and a strict dietary regime,
which he followed at a clinic in Wales. The president officially opened
the Thousand Islands International Bridge on August 18, with Prime
Minister King. Roosevelt wrote that he missed Tweedsmuir at both
Kingston, where he gave a speech the same day, and at the dedication of
the Thousand Islands Bridge.[128] The president hoped the speech he gave
at Queen's University in Kingston might have some effect, however small,
in Berlin. At the end of the summer, Roosevelt wrote to Tweedsmuir, still
in Britain, inviting him and Susan to Hyde Park in October when Arthur
Murray and his wife were planning to be there as well.[129] Roosevelt
wanted discussions with his discreet unofficial contacts to Britain.

Tweedsmuir's role in initiating and organizing the royal visit to Canada
by King George VI and Queen Elizabeth has been described in the previous chapter, but it is noteworthy in the current context to look at the
U.S. portion of that visit.

Having the king and queen would be a very high-profile demonstration of the Anglo-American link for the European dictators to see, and to

this extent it would reinforce messages that Roosevelt had delivered consistently in the past. Roosevelt's reaction to the idea would no doubt be very positive. The anticipated significance of the royal visit to the United States was probably best summed up by a very perceptive Violet Markham, who wrote to Tweedsmuir that the three days in the United States would be more valuable than the three weeks in Canada in the grander scheme of things. She lauded her friend's role in arranging it. While he may not have been able to agree openly with her, she wrote, "you will send me a transatlantic wink at the same time!"[130] She particularly held out great prospects for "our little Queen," who had recently been a huge success in Paris and who she expected to take the United States by storm, erasing any residue remaining "of the hateful Simpson woman."

One of the sensitive issues arising around the U.S. portion of the royal visit was who should accompany the king as his principal advisor. Should he be British or Canadian? In November Alexander Hardinge wrote to Tweedsmuir that King George would take Mackenzie King with him, if he wished to go, in his capacity as minister of external affairs, and advisor on any matters affecting the Dominion.[131] His Majesty would, as well, Hardinge noted, be accompanied by the British Foreign Secretary, Lord Halifax, as advisor on European issues. He explained there were precedents for the sovereign taking two ministers on various trips, when matters would affect more than one department. Hardinge requested that Tweedsmuir not share this yet with his prime minister.

Tweedsmuir initially agreed with Hardinge, noting that it seemed "constitutionally correct" and that Mackenzie King would, if broached to accompany King George, be pleased.[132] After some reflection, however, Tweedsmuir believed it would not be wise for a British minister, especially the foreign secretary, to accompany the king to the United States. His concern was about the potential backlash from American isolationist opinion, which might well suspect there was some secret arrangement being made, which in turn could undermine the fairly good relations at the moment.

In January Tweedsmuir recommended that Mackenzie King, as minister of external affairs for Canada, accompany the king rather than a British minister. He supported his argument by unabashedly emphasizing to the Palace that he knew the United States "more than most Englishmen" and was "in constant touch with American opinion."[133] Mackenzie King had also given him correspondence received from President Roosevelt that supported this approach. Tweedsmuir indicated to the prime minister that he would use it in presenting his case to the Palace.[134] He explained to Alexander Hardinge that if Halifax accompanied His Majesty, Americans, the isolationists in particular, would suspect there was some political purpose, perhaps a secret alliance, which could jeopardize attempts to foster closer relations and would likely have potential adverse impact on Roosevelt's political life. He cited, as an example, conspiracies raised in even moderate newspapers over Anthony Eden's speaking tour in the United States.

It was to avoid raising this negative possibility that Tweedsmuir argued that Canada's "foreign secretary," that is, the prime minister, should accompany King George VI, because "no American has the slightest suspicion of Canada."[135] Tweedsmuir noted that while there was no set practice for this situation, the Dominions generally would view as very positive having one of their own advisors accompany the king on a foreign visit. It would also obviously "give great pleasure to Canada." Constitutionally, he added, it might be an anomaly, but it would be "a practical proof of the solidarity of the Empire," and after all, he concluded, "what is our Empire but a magnificent anomaly?"[136] Hardinge argued that having only a Canadian minister in attendance with the king in the United States might not go down well elsewhere in the Commonwealth.[137] The Palace would not make a final decision until it received information from British Ambassador Lindsay in Washington, after he had determined how the U.S. president felt about "this thorny problem."[138]

Given the strategic sensitivity of the issue, Tweedsmuir finally wrote to British prime minister Chamberlain in mid-March. He expressed concern about a backlash in American opinion if Foreign Secretary Lord Halifax accompanied His Majesty, as was the practice on foreign visits. Relations with the United States must be maintained for the "dark days before us," he appealed.[139]

At the end of March, Hardinge informed Tweedsmuir that the king was writing to the Canadian prime minister to ask him to come as minister-in-attendance for the U.S. leg of the tour; the British foreign secretary would not accompany the king.[140] Tweedsmuir's assessment had been accurate and his advice sound. After the visit the governor general received a note from Mackenzie King stating that "there can be no doubt about the extent to which a real friendship was formed between the king and the president."[141]

CHAPTER 9

Appeasement and Remembering Joseph

Throughout 1937 Tweedsmuir received news from correspondents and visitors about developments in Europe, particularly in Germany, that supported a more optimistic outlook. His friend, British MP Leo Amery, travelled to Vienna and Prague in March and spoke with the heads of government of both countries.[1] He commented to Tweedsmuir that both Austrian Chancellor Kurt von Schuschnigg as well as Czech President Eduard Beneš were encouraged by Britain's decision to rearm. They were focused at a strategic level and were particularly interested in seeing a strong British presence in the Mediterranean so as to persuade Mussolini that his interests lay more with Britain and France than with Germany. Beneš expressed optimism that the situation was improving after the events of 1936, a reference to Italy's conquest of Abyssinia and the concomitant failure of the League of Nations to deal with it, Germany's arms buildup, and the start of the Spanish Civil War.[2] It was this sort of first-hand intelligence that informed Tweedsmuir's assessments and undoubtedly shaped his discussions with Prime Minister Mackenzie King.

One visitor he received at Rideau Hall in May was a young German baron, a Rhodes scholar at Oxford on his way to the Far East for a year of study. He told the governor general that "there [were] many thousands of people like himself who [were] not Nazis and who [made] no secret of their opposition to Hitler and [were] left in peace."[3] The possibility exists that the student could have been a propaganda or intelligence agent, but his views were corroborated later that year when businessman Lord Bessborough apprised Tweedsmuir of similar information obtained from some of his friends who had spent two months in Germany.[4]

Optimism continued into that fall of 1937, when Tweedsmuir received cheering news from Britain about broad support for Prime Minister Chamberlain's approach to developments on the continent. In turn he helped to keep Chamberlain informed of information from a North American perspective. In October he wrote to Chamberlain about a pending visit to Ottawa by U.S. secretary of state Cordell Hull. He also included some of his thoughts about the proposed Nine-Power Treaty conference proposed for Brussels to deal with Japanese aggression against China.[5]

Tweedsmuir, with good intent, no doubt, shared the contents of his letter to Chamberlain with Mackenzie King.[6] King thought Tweedsmuir was venturing too far into politics — again. In the privacy of his diary, he criticized governors general from Britain who "cannot do other than regard themselves first and foremost [as] agents of the British government."[7] But here King was confusing someone acting as an agent with someone who simply continued to use his vast contacts to pursue common objectives and wanted to keep his prime minister informed. King was not consistent. In the spring, just a few months earlier, when Tweedsmuir shared information with him, he was appreciative and benefitted from the information. Fortunately, for the sake of their relationship, they shared many views in common regarding the situation in Europe and on Chamberlain's policies.

The Chamberlain government's foreign policy was the subject of debate in November in the House of Lords. Tweedsmuir received an account from Bessborough, who wrote that he approved of "the [British] government policy of seeking the appeasement of Germany."[8] He also approved of Edward Halifax's mission to Germany as a first step, referring to the latter's decision to accept an invitation from Herman Goering to attend a hunting exhibition, not as a British minister but as master of an English hunt club.[9] This was deemed to be a good cover for an informal meeting with the Nazi leadership. It was Bessborough's view that the

British government "had been ill-advised in the past in being too much guided by the French in refusing the various offers made by Germany in the last few years." The policy of appeasement was largely accepted as the best chance of preserving peace. But there were other considerations.

Tweedsmuir heard from John Simon, chancellor of the exchequer. The "entangling complications" of attempting to have countries reduce their armaments was not because of a lack of goodwill, Simon wrote, and certainly not due to resistance to the idea on the part of the British government, which Chamberlain had made very clear.[10] However, as a bit of a reality check, Simon added that "political and economic appeasement must go hand in hand and that neither the one nor the other is to be achieved unless Germany is a co-operating partner." Change could only come about, he argued, if Germany abandoned her closed economy, but that would raise questions about spending on armaments, something that would be good if it led to decreasing such expenditures, which the British Treasury was constantly monitoring. Tweedsmuir replied that Germany must be reaching a saturation point in armaments and that economically it must therefore be susceptible to an agreement to limit arms.[11]

By February 1938 tensions were again increasing, because of Germany's covetous eyes on Austria and Czechoslovakia, questions about Italy's position vis-a-vis Britain and Germany, and the ongoing Spanish Civil War. But British politics were soon to be distracted. Foreign Secretary Anthony Eden resigned on February 20. It was a shock to virtually everyone, from the more detached Canadians to the politically well-connected newspapers like the *Times* and the *Daily Telegraph*, and even to Eden's Cabinet colleagues.[12] Biographer R.R. James noted that Eden's propriety prevented him from exposing what had served as the "last straw" between himself and Chamberlain, leaving most observers to speculate on the differences they had witnessed or read about.[13]

In Canada Eden's resignation caused concern about the direction of British foreign policy. After reading Foreign Office despatches, Tweedsmuir was even more puzzled by Eden's resignation, because it appeared that just a week before he had agreed to do what Chamberlain had proposed, presumably with respect to an agreement between Britain and Italy.[14] Even Eden's successor, Edward Halifax, seemed puzzled, writing that one day he would tell Tweedsmuir what his opinion of the event was. Halifax simply wrote, "I suppose, as a result of difference of temperament and training, a point had been reached where the prime minister and Eden no longer saw eye to eye…."[15] The resignation was, in fact, triggered by a secret message from President Roosevelt to Chamberlain, proposing a meeting of representatives of certain European countries in Washington to discuss differences. Chamberlain replied that it might be better to postpone such a meeting because it could counter current British (i.e., Chamberlain's) efforts to appease Germany. The prime minister did not consult his foreign secretary, who was out of the country at the time.[16] Chamberlain's rebuff to Roosevelt's offer, coupled with subsequent developments, were seen by Eden as a blow to his efforts to improve Anglo-American relations and a demonstration of the fundamental disagreements between them.

In a letter to Chamberlain, congratulating him on his handling of the crisis, Tweedsmuir disdainfully put Eden in the same category as Churchill, arguing "more like a schoolboy than a man."[17] He also noted that he was "delighted" that Chamberlain seemed to have public opinion behind him; certainly he had Canada's support, with "no warmer admirer" than the Canadian prime minister. Eden biographer R.R. James notes, however, that the national mood was beginning to shift, even at this point, as was evidenced by the "extraordinary" public response, with cheering crowds outside Eden's house, and the increasingly frequent expressions of repugnance over the dictators' methods. But the majority of the population still supported Chamberlain's policy of trying to avoid war.

Given subsequent contacts with Eden, however, and shared views, especially as regards strengthening relations with the United States, Tweedsmuir's criticism may have been less an indication that he held a harsh view of Eden (he invited Eden to Ottawa when the latter came to North America later that year) than it was evidence that he felt that an encouraging word was needed for Chamberlain at a time of potential political stress.

Despite the shock of Eden's resignation, his departure was seen as an opportunity by some who wanted to enlist Tweedsmuir's assistance. Dr.

Chaim Weizmann, president of the Zionist Organization, had been trying to see Eden "for a long time ... but he never could spare the time."[18]
Up to February 1938, things had not been going well for Weizmann,
who was lobbying to ensure that British political leaders maintained
their commitment to the establishment of a Jewish state by the partition of Palestine. It was now over twenty years since the signing of the
Balfour Declaration (1917), in which the British government committed
to establishing a homeland for the Jews. Weizmann was worried about
Britain's commitment to honour its pledge; he was also concerned about
growing anti-Semitism in Britain, a trend that some of Tweedsmuir's
other, regular correspondents were also noting. This was the result,
in part, of the growing number of Jewish refugees from Germany and
Eastern Europe, which added to an existing current of anti-Semitism
in Britain. Two days after Eden's resignation and the appointment of
his successor, Lord Halifax, Weizmann wrote to his old acquaintance
who, as MP John Buchan, had been chairman of the parliamentary Pro-
Palestine Committee.[19]

Weizmann began his letter to Tweedsmuir with thanks for having
met with a friend of his, Dr. Bernard Joseph, a Montreal-born lawyer
who had settled in Jerusalem in 1921 and remained active in politics
there (he would do so all his life, continuing long after the creation of
the state of Israel). Weizmann then briefly outlined his concern that the
British government would make too many concessions to the Arabs in
negotiations over the partitioning and ignore the achievements of Jews
already in Palestine. He enclosed a copy of his lengthy letter to William
Ormsby-Gore, secretary of state for the colonies, who was responsible for
Palestine, a British protectorate at the time. Ormsby-Gore had promised
Parliament four months earlier that he would take the "most strenuous measures to conquer terrorism in Palestine," which, at the time,
primarily, but not exclusively, involved Arab terrorism against British
soldiers and the Jewish population.[20] The letter to Ormsby-Gore gave
Weizmann's detailed assessment of the situation and the various factors influencing the common interests of both the Jews and the British,
which he described as "inextricably bound up by a long tradition and
experience with the ideals of Justice and Democracy."[21]

Continuing to the main point of his letter, Weizmann lamented that "I find myself dealing with Pharaohs who 'know not Joseph,'" a reference to the story in the Old Testament Book of Exodus about Joseph, a Jew, who had been sold to the Egyptians by his brothers but who then became a trusted governor of the Pharaoh. After Joseph died, however, future Pharaohs forgot about him and were not so well disposed toward the Jews who had been allowed to live in Egypt.[22]

"I scarcely know Halifax," Weizmann wrote on February 22, "and I am afraid that much may depend on him in the near future in the negotiations which I shall have to carry on."[23] He added: "I would like to have a real chance of placing my case before him, and I am afraid that without some help I am not likely to get it." There was some urgency to respond, because Weizmann would soon be returning to Palestine. He suggested that Tweedsmuir send a telegram to Halifax. Tweedsmuir responded immediately after he received Weizmann's letter, cabling Halifax with the request on March 5.[24]

The same day as he sent the telegram, he wrote a short letter to Weizmann[25] to say he had done so, and sent another, "private and confidential," letter to Halifax confirming he had sent the cable but adding some additional comments.[26] In his letter Tweedsmuir picked up Weizmann's analogy of the story of Joseph, but he broadened it, from the leaders (Pharaohs) to "a generation has arisen which 'knows not Joseph.'" Weizmann's "good sense and judgement" were commended to Halifax. Tweedsmuir added: "I should be happier if I felt that [Weizmann] was in reasonably close touch with you."

Tweedsmuir's unease about the situation of the Jews was informed by many sources. Prior to receiving the February letter from Weizmann, he had had that visit from Weizmann's friend, Dr. Bernard Joseph, who had described some of the current situation. Tweedsmuir had also read from his well-informed correspondent Lord Crawford that "[a]nti-Semitism is growing apace here at home."[27] Tweedsmuir would have been one of those whom Weizmann described in his autobiography as being of the old school and "genuinely religious," and who "understood as a reality the concept of the Return [which] appealed to their tradition and their faith."[28] Weizmann noted in his letter to Tweedsmuir that he didn't want to suggest that the political leaders were "as hard of heart as Pharaoh," but, rather, that "their standards and their outlook unfortunately differ widely from those which animated Balfour and yourself — and which I know still animate you."[29]

Halifax, however, was not quite of the same character as Buchan or Balfour, though as a religious individual he might have been open to the concept of the Return. He was, his biographer Andrew Roberts writes, mildly anti-Semitic, "inexcusable, especially in a practicing Christian, ... [but] common to a number of his social contemporaries." He was, however, "genuinely revolted" by the brutality of *Kristallnacht* in Germany (which involved the murder of Jews, the arrests of many thousands, and the destruction of Jewish businesses and homes) that occurred later (November 9 and 10) that year, and therefore certainly not completely "hard of heart."[30]

Halifax responded positively to Tweedsmuir, and in contrast to Eden, met with Weizmann, on March 9. He liked Weizmann very much, he replied to Tweedsmuir.[31] Halifax made a hopeful impression on Weizmann.[32] During the talks Weizmann described Arab attitudes toward the partition of Palestine and made an alternative proposal for quickly establishing a Jewish state, which would compensate the Jews for the loss of certain parts of Palestine.[33] Halifax, for his part, apparently tried to determine what Weizmann's reaction would be if a government report found that partition would not work, perhaps tilling the ground for what he may have known, or suspected was coming, from a committee studying partition.[34] He subsequently asked Weizmann to write him a letter with some of the points they had discussed. This Weizmann did, on March 14, ending it on a positive note: "After my talk with you, I go with renewed confidence."[35]

Weizmann was to be disappointed, however, noting in a letter to a correspondent a few weeks later that he had received a reply from the foreign secretary, which was "the same old story."[36] Halifax had stated he couldn't impose his own views about Palestine, and defended the British diplomats in Cairo, who, Weizmann noted, expressed views that were contrary to information he was aware of.

If Weizmann's meeting was not successful, Halifax's apparent promptness in meeting Weizmann and his reply to Tweedsmuir were at least indicators of his respect for Tweedsmuir. It appears that the foreign secretary acted on Tweedsmuir's request. However, Weizmann makes no reference in his autobiography to Tweedsmuir's efforts on his behalf, nor is Tweedsmuir (or Buchan) referenced in this context in the various Weizmann biographies that exist.[37]

Rather, Weizmann states he met Halifax through Conservative MP Victor Cazalet, who was close to Halifax, and through Cazalet, he could meet with the foreign secretary more frequently and informally.[38] Weizmann had received a letter dated March 2 from Lord Hartington, who arranged for him to meet with Halifax. Halifax's reply to Tweedsmuir states that "Eddy Hartington got me to luncheon with him" (Weizmann). Historian Norman Rose states that "Sir Alexander Cadogan [permanent under-secretary at the Foreign Office] … agreed to arrange an interview with Halifax." Victor Cazalet knew Hartington.[39] Given the fact that Weizmann credits Cazalet with introducing him to Halifax, it may be that Cazalet spoke with Hartington and/or Cadogan. Or, it may just have been Weizmann's perception because of Cazalet's presence and frequent contact with him. We cannot know for sure, of course, with many people working to the same purpose.

The reality is, there were several interventions as a result of Weizmann pursuing his goals. To aid him in his efforts, he drew on the help of as many contacts as he could. Tweedsmuir was one of the contacts he could trust and who could assist him in gaining access to the new British foreign secretary. While Tweedsmuir's cable of March 5 to Halifax arrived subsequent to Hartington's March 2 letter to Weizmann, and probably subsequent to any request by Cadogan, these, and Tweedsmuir's letter to Halifax vouching for "the value of [Weizmann's] work," added weight to Weizmann's request. This view is supported by Norman Rose's assessment that "[e]xtra pressure was needed before the interview materialized," pressure that included both Hartington's and Tweedsmuir's requests.[40]

Despite the absence of acknowledgement in the autobiography, or the biographies, for the introduction to Halifax, Weizmann did acknowledge Tweedsmuir's role generally in a telegram to Susan Tweedsmuir on learning of her husband's death on February 11, 1940. "Jews everywhere," he wrote, "will mourn the loss of a great lover of freedom and tolerance and of a warm and proven friend of the work of restoration of the Jewish National Home in Palestine."[41] Norman Rose includes John Buchan among those "who gave of their best" in support of the Zionist cause.[42]

But regardless of who intervened on Weizmann's behalf, and despite Weizmann's arguments to Halifax, they were not enough to cause the British Cabinet to change its course with respect to partitioning Palestine. Even a year later, and despite Halifax's deep disgust over *Kristallnacht* in November 1938 and his "total about-face on appeasement" by the spring of 1939,[43] it was Weizmann's impression that Halifax remained "strangely ignorant of what was happening to the Jews of Germany."[44] Weizmann attributed Halifax's attitude possibly to a desire not to know "because the knowledge was inconvenient, disturbing and dangerous."[45] Weizmann's lack of impact can be largely explained by the government's policy of appeasement and its preoccupation about relations with Germany and Italy.[46]

Less than a month after assuming his new position, Halifax did indeed have "the wolf by the ears," as Tweedsmuir described Halifax's situation.[47] On March 12, 1938, German Nazi forces marched into Austria — the *Anschluss*. Tweedsmuir wrote to his sister Anna that he had always expected this German action, noting that it was "very largely our own blame."[48] As with the German reoccupation of the Rhineland, Tweedsmuir blamed the Treaty of Versailles, "the most half-witted thing ever perpetrated!"[49] Half-witted because it lay the seeds for the current problems they were facing. It was an assessment shared by many other politicians and statesmen, and by subsequent historians, with exceptions.[50] Tweedsmuir believed it would have been better to revise the terms of the Treaty, instead of revising the results by violence, as Germany was now doing.[51] It was wistful thinking.

In his statements Tweedsmuir seems to be engaging in a dangerous rationalization of the Austrian crisis by accepting it as probably inevitable. It seems inconsistent for someone who was increasingly recognizing the deception and madness of the Nazis. We cannot, however, take his opinion in isolation. It was shared by a majority of people, politicians and general public alike, in an emotional desire to avoid war. Why should they risk war for something that they believed was of their own making?

The impact in Britain was palpable. Leo Amery, who had met the year before with the now-imprisoned Austrian leader, wrote to Tweedsmuir at the end of March that he had never seen the British House of Commons so moved as it was over the "rape of Austria." This, despite the fact the British government's *realpolitik* policies advised Austria not to resist because Britain was in no position to give it protection, according to the Dominions' Office despatch that the Canadian government received.[52] There was a dawning for many, Amery wrote, that they were presented with a power that "might not hesitate to strike at us, regardless of any pledge."[53] Attitudes were continuing to shift, but Chamberlain and his policy of appeasement still remained solidly in favour.

In the Canadian House of Commons, by contrast, there were no questions about the *Anschluss*, though King was prepared to respond when the House sat on Monday, March 14.[54] That evening the prime minister stopped by Rideau Hall for a long talk with the governor general. Tweedsmuir shared with King a letter from Chamberlain, who noted that "the Austrian adventure was not premeditated."[55] Tweedsmuir remarked there were dangers of a ruler that acted so suddenly.[56]

A couple of days later, Tweedsmuir showed King a letter to Chamberlain from a British journalist who had access to the Nazi leadership and had met with Goering. King believed Chamberlain wanted him to see the letter, which relieved King's mind because "it seemed to make clear that it was possible for Britain and Germany to get together in a way which would help the peace of the world, without injuring any third country."[57] Chamberlain may indeed have wanted King to see the letter (to strengthen support from Canada for his policy of appeasement), but if so, King revealed no objection in this instance to the governor general's correspondence with the British government.

Tweedsmuir and King continued to share general views on the European situation and on the League of Nations, whose impotence was confirmed by the Austrian crisis. This situation only reinforced support for Chamberlain's approach from both Tweedsmuir and King.[58]

Tweedsmuir discreetly praised Chamberlain to his sister for doing and saying the right things.[59] To the British prime minister himself, he observed that Canada "wholeheartedly" supported his foreign policy.[60] Chamberlain, naturally, was pleased to hear of the support from Canada — support that included the backing of not only the current government but other important figures, such as the former Canadian prime minister R.B. Bennett.[61] These words and letters corroborated Chamberlain's belief that he had the Dominions' support, at least where avoiding war was concerned.[62]

The success of Chamberlain's strategy was still very much an open question, though, and the situation remained in flux. Constant updates were needed to remain apprised of the situation. By June 1938 Tweedsmuir was receiving secret telegrams daily about the situation.[63] He was also receiving frequent and lengthy notes from Alexander Hardinge, King George VI's private secretary, on domestic and foreign affairs and for which Tweedsmuir was appreciative.[64]

At the beginning of September 1938, Mackenzie King told his governor general, rather hopefully, that he believed Hitler would ultimately be for peace, adding in the appeasement vein, "unless unduly provoked."[65] In the worst case, however, he prepared plans to call Parliament.

On September 16, 1938, Chamberlain met with Hitler in Berchtes-gaden, having telegraphed him to propose he go see him to discuss his claims over Czechoslovakia. Believing Hitler could be satisfied with the Sudetenland of Czechoslovakia, Chamberlain again met with Hitler on September 22 in Godesberg in the Rhineland to present a British-French proposal that the Czechs had agreed to. Chamberlain returned to London on the 24, briefing his Cabinet and believing Hitler's territorial ambitions could be sated with the Sudetenland. After a series of messages between Britain, Germany, France, and Italy, Chamberlain flew to Germany on September 29, this time to Munich, for another meeting with Hitler, a meeting that also included Italian dictator Mussolini and French Premier Daladier. It was at this now infamous meeting that agreement was made to give over the Sudetenland of Czechoslovakia to Germany. The Czechs, however, were not present. An agreement was signed by Chamberlain and Hitler stating that the two countries would never go to war with each other again. Chamberlain returned to England to declare "peace in our time." He was hailed as a hero for avoiding war. The declaration had an elixir effect on almost everyone. There was, however, some criticism that Czechoslovakia had been betrayed — criticism that would grow louder.

At this apogee of appeasement, Tweedsmuir was still in Britain, having returned there in July for his installation as chancellor of Edinburgh University and to undergo medical examinations and treatment. He was not immune from the effects of Chamberlain's flying diplomacy, writing to his friend Stair Gillon in Scotland that he maintained the view that since Chamberlain's first visit to Germany, he had become convinced that "there would be no war, and I think I am going to be proved right."[66] King, joining the chorus in praise of Chamberlain, wrote to Tweedsmuir: "While it is not yet clear that war will be avoided, it is altogether certain that but for Chamberlain's meeting with Hitler, we all should have been in the throes of a world war today."[67]

Just before sailing for Canada, and on the same day that Chamberlain flew to Munich, Tweedsmuir wrote to him to express how profoundly he admired the prime minister's course of action over the past weeks. He expressed his admiration with a biblical-like statement from Lord Minto as viceroy of India, a statement he believed "to be a profound maxim of statesmanship": "No man is so strong as he who is not afraid to be called weak."[68] He was certain that this would "make one of the great episodes in our history." And indeed it did. The abhorrence of war made its avoidance a great source of relief. Chamberlain valued these words of encouragement in those difficult times, especially from "men of good-will," as he considered Tweedsmuir to be, addressing his reply to "My Dear John."[69] Less than two weeks after the Munich meeting, Hitler stated publicly that he would continue building his fortifications in the west. He also cautioned, in his propagandistic style, that Chamberlain, a statesman of peace, could be replaced by those like Churchill, Eden, and Duff Cooper (the First Lord of the Admiralty, who resigned over a disagreement with Chamberlain), whose aims were to start a world war. In the circumstances most of the British Cabinet now at least supported rearmament. Tweedsmuir, vacillating between a desire for peace and a recognition of the possibilities of conflict, was no exception.

At the end of October, he wrote again to Chamberlain, offering his opinion that the policy of legitimate appeasement and reasonable negotiation was the right one to follow.[70] But he added, inserting a recognition of the reality, we must be working at the same time "to make ready at home" to be able to talk with any enemy from a strong base. He focused particularly on air power, and in this respect, he was returning to views he had expressed as an M.P. and was coming more into line two men he had criticized earlier, Eden and, especially, Churchill. It was for now, though, more a matter of emphasis. Most everyone believed in some level of war preparations at home, though Churchill pushed much more vigorously and broadly for rearmament. And whereas Churchill believed there was a point at which it would have been wise to wage war before the dictators became too strong, Tweedsmuir fell in with the majority of opinion-makers and politicians who wished to avoid it to the extent possible.

To Chamberlain Tweedsmuir privately attacked some of the British press for their "fatuous criticism" of Chamberlain's policy.[71] In his own disgust of war, anything that avoided it was preferred. The Canadian press, in contrast to some of the British, was "wonderful" in its general support, with the exception of Dafoe's *Winnipeg Free Press* which, Tweedsmuir admonished, still held "romantic illusions about the League of Nations" as a means of achieving world peace and dealing with the worsening European situation. To a close friend, he used, for him, uncharacteristically strong language, calling Chamberlain's critics "donkeys" for their perceived stubbornness, and wondered if they ever considered "what the alternative was."[72] It was not an unusual reaction for many who had known war and lost family members and close friends.

During the first week of November 1938, a conference was held in New York at which British foreign secretary Lord Halifax spoke, along with Britain's First World War prime minister, Lloyd George, and Winston Churchill. The speeches were broadcast over radio. Halifax's talk, in particular, struck a basic chord with Tweedsmuir. He wrote immediately to let him know how significant an impact he believed it would have in strengthening British-American relations.[73] Tweedsmuir was comforted by the speech, which he believed gave a sense of stability and strength. In the still strong after-effect of Chamberlain's diplomacy, Tweedsmuir added hopefully that they might be at the "beginning of a new era in Europe, when war may steadily go out of the picture."[74]

In contrast to Halifax's speech, Tweedsmuir noted that Lloyd George's speech added nothing new, "merely his old Billingsgate,"[75] while Winston's "rhetoric exasperated everybody." Exasperation would have come as a result of Churchill's warnings about war, which were regarded by many as hyperbole, and which stood in sharp contrast to the still strong official commitment to appeasement. To those, like Churchill, who warned against the dangers of a policy of appeasement, Prime Minister Chamberlain had, only a few days earlier, countered by stating in Parliament that he did not "regard the Munich agreement as a defeat either for democracy or the cause of law and order," because "the only other solution appeared to be the use of force."[76] His beliefs were profound and sincere, as Churchill acknowledged respectfully in his history of the war.[77]

Opinion, however, continued to shift against Chamberlain's cornerstone policy of appeasement,[78] with many feeling increasingly concerned about future German plans. In Germany, too, there was some unease; for instance, Nazi propaganda from the period seems to reveal German concern about America. The Nazis were critical of American radio for broadcasting the British speeches in New York, and critical of the Roosevelt administration, which they decried as "sabotaging peace moves."[79] These were claims that confirmed for Tweedsmuir that Roosevelt's speeches were having an impact. The result would be, he wrote to Roosevelt, to make the dictators think twice and to help demonstrate a "massed commonsense of the civilised world."[80]

Adding to the Nazi's concerns was Roosevelt's announcement on November 4 from Hyde Park that he had initiated a survey of defence requirements with the results to be used in a defence program designed to facilitate military and naval expansion that would "be in full swing next year."[81] It was "an extensive resurvey of [defence] needs that was intensified by Europe's recent crisis," the Associated Press reported.[82]

The president was also reported to be intending to ask Congress to authorize "one of the world's mightiest air fleets, numbering 7,000 to 10,000 planes." At this same time, Tweedsmuir's correspondent, Lord Crawford, wrote that closeness with the United States would be reinforced if discussions about a side visit to the United States during the planned tour of Canada by the king and queen the following spring actually materialized.[83]

If certain members of the British press were increasingly critical of Chamberlain, establishment newspapers, such as the *Times* and the *Daily Telegraph*, continued to support him. Public reaction, however, continued to grow against the prime minister, particularly after *Kristallnacht*. The Earl of Crawford informed Tweedsmuir of the trend in one of his regular letters, in mid-November 1938.[84] Skepticism was growing about appeasement, Crawford reported. After the signing of the Munich accord, Hitler claimed he had no more territorial ambitions, but his planning continued all the same and his Nazi Party continued its sinister work against the Jews, sending anti-Semitic propaganda into Britain which Tweedsmuir heard about from his sister. Her local member of Parliament repeated accusations from these anti-Jewish pamphlets, pamphlets that had originally been mailed from Germany but by 1938 carried a British postmark. Tweedsmuir recommended to his sister that the electors should get rid of the MP, who he deemed must be "light-witted" if he gave currency to such "libels."[85] He added that the Jews were "suffering almost the cruellest persecution in history."

By the end of November, it was increasingly clear that appeasement was not working. Tweedsmuir rationalized that Chamberlain's policy was "the lesser of two evils." He explained, in absent expletive, that in any case it was difficult to have any clear policy when "dealing with an unknown X, like the temperament of a pseudo-Messiah!"[86] Tweedsmuir imagined that life for the average individual in Germany must be "hideously uncomfortable." The tensions within Germany, he thought, would result in the country either cracking internally or lashing out. He hoped for the former, based on an equally hopeful belief that the Nazi leader would "think twice" about lashing out or starting a war because world opinion, especially in the United States, was now moving so decidedly against Nazi Germany. But the signs were to the contrary. Hitler was indeed building his army to lash out, as Churchill continued to remind everyone with his comparative assessments of German military strength.

The deteriorating situation in Europe prompted Tweedsmuir to emphasize that Britain and Canada had to do something for the refugees, Jewish, and others as well.[87] It was perhaps because King knew Tweedsmuir's views and his support for the Jews that he told him, on his return from Washington later in November, "that on humanitarian grounds alone Canada should allow in some refugees."[88] It was likely the prime minister who made Tweedsmuir aware that Canada would have to "go very cautiously" on the Jewish refugee question. King's overriding concern was for national unity, and his key Quebec minister, Ernest Lapointe, did not want Jewish immigration. Tweedsmuir also wrote that he had the impression that anti-Semitism was a dormant factor in the Catholic Church in Quebec.[89] He understated the situation. Anti-Semitism was not dormant in the Church, nor in Quebec society generally, where fascists under Adrien Arcand were becoming more vehemently anti-Semitic as the 1930s progressed, an echo of what was occurring in Europe.[90]

Tweedsmuir is described in one history of the Jewish experience in Canada as the "most visible supporter" of the Jews in the country.[91] Both he and his wife "spoke publicly in favour of Zionism, lending the cachet of the Crown" to the cause of a Jewish homeland.[92] On April 11, 1938, Susan Tweedsmuir travelled to Montreal to address a Jewish audience, Montreal Hadassah, in a supportive activity that her husband described "in these times [as] very desirable."[93] She was "desperately touched by the Jewish meeting," he wrote to his sister. The overcapacity gathering in the Windsor Hotel's Rose Room heard Lady Tweedsmuir speak of the "kindness and generosity of the Jewish people."[94] They also heard details about her Prairie Library Scheme to which Hadassah members had contributed books. Rabbi Charles Bender, who introduced Lady Tweedsmuir, referred to the support she and Lord Tweedsmuir had offered the Jewish people. Susan was later presented with an illuminated certificate in recognition of her name being entered into the Golden Book, which records the names of great friends of the Jews. John Buchan's was already there. In Toronto the next month, the governor general attended the dedication of the new Temple for Holy Blossom Congregation, and remarked on the "untold misery and oppression" of Jews.[95] The very public support and encouraging words of both the governor general and his wife were welcome, but they would have no effect on a tragically intransigent government policy that excluded Jewish immigration.[96]

Tweedsmuir's preoccupation with the worsening news from Germany prompted him to think about how to gather more information. He proposed an idea to a family friend then living in England. Moritz Bonn was an eminent professor and economist who had been forced to resign as principal of the prestigious College of Commerce in Berlin in 1933, after the Nazis came to power, because he was Jewish. His vast experience included working in propaganda in the First World War and being an economic advisor with the German delegation to the Paris Peace Conference in 1919. He had travelled widely since then, which contributed to his being very well connected in Europe and the United States. His contemporary reputation was such that, of the more than a dozen professors forced to resign by the Nazis, it was he and Albert Einstein who were the subjects of international news stories.[97]

Tweedsmuir proposed a number of ideas to Bonn and asked for his help in starting an "organisation of information."[98] It is difficult to know precisely what Tweedsmuir had in mind, whether this was a personal initiative or had some unofficial link to the British government. The context of Bonn's reply, the month after *Kristallnacht*, implies Tweedsmuir's proposal included providing information from inside Germany to Prime Minister Chamberlain. Who better to assist with starting up such an organization than a German exile with myriad international contacts and experience in propaganda from the Great War. Bonn, however, was not optimistic about the idea, lamenting that the prime minister could not be counted on to support such a project because he believed he could "handle the situation satisfactorily by personal contact." It was reminiscent of Weizmann's assessment of Chamberlain.

If Tweedsmuir's proposal did not bear fruit, at least in the form he proposed to Bonn, it anticipated what later occurred. Bonn ended up working for the British cause, travelling to North America ten months later, in October 1939, from where he sent potentially critical information to Tweedsmuir and visited him in Ottawa in November 1939.[99] Bonn remained in the United States until 1945.[100] But Bonn's departure for the United States was still almost a year in the future. In the meantime, his contacts in Germany provided him with information that he assessed and passed on to Tweedsmuir, and presumably others. With exacting insight, he described the Nazi reaction to Chamberlain and how they could be stopped. The Nazis believed they had "bamboozled" Chamberlain completely, according to Bonn.[101] He believed Chamberlain did not understand who he was really up against.[102]

By the end of 1938, public opinion was thoroughly aroused against the repugnant events in Germany.[103] This buildup of anti-Nazi sentiment was likely why Tweedsmuir's opinion vacillated back toward the unlikelihood of war; he was "firmly convinced that every month that war [was] postponed it [became] less likely."[104] Some of his correspondents, however, were not so hopeful. Leo Amery relayed to him that the general view was that the Germans and Italians had "megalomania and war mania pretty badly," and that the spring could even bring the occupation of Holland.[105] The sense was that the dictators would enjoy proving to the Americans that they, the dictators, could do what they liked in Europe. Tweedsmuir's correspondent Lord Crawford provided some humour among other understated remarks about just how uncivilized the Germans were becoming.[106] He related a story making the rounds about the visit by the Hungarian leader, Admiral Horthy, to Berlin. When Hitler asked why a landlocked country like Hungary had a minister of marine, Horthy replied: "Well, the [Italian dictator] Duce has a Minister of Finance and you have a Minister of Justice, why should we not keep a Minister of Marine?"[107]

By now, with the many and varied accounts about the situation in Europe that Tweedsmuir was receiving, his views about what needed to be done continued to shift against appeasement. He was developing a sense that "something odd [was] happening inside Germany and Italy."[108]

Tweedsmuir now seemed prepared to dismiss all the behaviour of the dictators as "not sane on any conceivable principle."[109] The Earl of Bessborough wrote to him with news that talk of a general election in England had subsided, particularly from the government, because "the public [were asking how they could] vote for a policy of appeasement now, for you cannot appease a wild beast."[110] This after "one of the most ghastly events in history," referring to *Kristallnacht*.

At the end of 1938, Tweedsmuir wrote to Violet Markham: "I cannot feel that the work of defence preparation at home is being done sufficiently fast or sufficiently in earnest."[111] It was time for the government to actually lead and compel the nation to go in this direction. Even though he clung to his opinion that Chamberlain had played "the wise game," he was not certain he was the right person "to infuse the proper amount of vigour into his colleagues."[112] Adding a mild criticism of Chamberlain's handling of his Cabinet, he wrote that Neville was "not too respectful of mediocrity, but he is apt to be too slow in showing his disrespect." Opinion was indeed clearly shifting away from Chamberlain.

Regardless of the questioning of Chamberlain's leadership, Tweedsmuir entered 1939 ever hopeful, though still mixed in his outlook. He thought that international relations would go better in the coming year, though he had no strong logical reasons for this view. He did have some reasons, which included the widespread disapproval of the dictators, which he felt had to have some impact, except in Japan's case. In particular he thought that "there [was] no doubt that the strong feeling in America is making the Dictators pause and think."[113] Such a comment, shared with other correspondents, suggests that he believed that the dictators were rational, although a year earlier he had called them "semi-lunatics" and "lunatics."[114] So, it is clear that there was some confusion in his thinking. This confusion was understandable, of course, given the fact that there was a true sense of impossibility of knowing what may happen from day to day. Despite all of this, he tried to be positive; to his sister he commented that Britain and Canada were not as ill-prepared as they were in 1914. To his friend Stair Gillon, he wrote that "every week sees the Democracies stronger," while he maintained that Germany was not as well-prepared as many newspapers reported, since, he noted, the reports were based largely on Germany's own propaganda.

Chamberlain's confidence in his policy allowed him to assess that the changing of American opinion seemed, after being critical of his Munich visit, to "be developing a greater understanding of the position … [and a] … greater appreciation of the line the British Government has taken."[115] Chamberlain wrote to Tweedsmuir that he was "conscious of some easing in the tension," something, he believed, was not attributable to one fact but rather to "a number of impressions derived from various sources which somehow seem to fuse into a general sense of greater brightness in the atmosphere." Was this a basis for forming policy?

If such optimism was to be expected from Chamberlain, other of Tweedsmuir's correspondents were also somewhat optimistic, including Lord Bessborough and even Moritz Bonn. Others, however, were decidedly not. Leo Amery thought the situation "to be heading rapidly towards a crisis," and advised his friend "to warn Mackenzie King that trouble may come at any moment."[116] Amery saw it as probable that Britain would be dragged into a continental conflict because they could not abandon France. And France was likely to be threatened as soon as Hitler and Mussolini were certain of Franco's victory in Spain. Nor could Lord Crawford share the optimists' "illogical feeling" that the international situation would improve. The very reason Tweedsmuir cited for the dictators not acting — world opinion, especially in the United States — was exactly why Crawford thought they were more dangerous than ever. The dictators, he argued, could not afford to have world opinion "find an echo at home," and thus, "the worse their internal situation, the more menacing their foreign policy."[117]

Tweedsmuir remained unconvinced; he wanted to remain unconvinced. Nonetheless, the possibility of "dark days before us" made the realist in him continue to hold the relationship with the United States as the critical consideration.[118] To several of his correspondents, he added, humorously, but with a touch of pathos, the lament of a London charwoman trying to don a gas-mask: "If only Mr. 'Itler would marry and settle down."

The darkness intensified in March as Hitler dismembered what remained of Czechoslovakia, with Poland, to its discredit, taking a portion.

News from English people who had been in Prague at the time of the coup "found lots of evidence that it had been prepared with much detail many weeks if not months before," proving Hitler's intentions.[119] It was, for Tweedsmuir, as if the devil had been loosed in Europe again. He felt sorrow for Chamberlain, whose hopes for peace seemed to be crashing, though he faced it with candour in a speech that Tweedsmuir admired.[120]

From King George's private secretary, Tweedsmuir received another detailed note. "The rape of Czechoslovakia," Hardinge wrote, "has finally opened the eyes of those who hoped against hope that Hitler's word could be relied on."[121] Gloomily, he concluded that optimistic forecasts were a thing of the past. Reports of a possible German attack on Poland brought Prime Minister Chamberlain's warning to Germany that Britain would support Poland if such an attack occurred. The sobering result was that everyone at last realized that "he or she must prepare for a war which might be on us at any moment."[122] Only the timing of the "blow-up" was in question, Tweedsmuir wrote to his sister, but he hoped it would hold off "until the strength of the Democracies is so great that [the war] can be checked at the start."[123] To some extent it was a relief. He was "happier now that the British policy is clear and definite."[124]

Defence preparations continued apace in Britain, the United States, and Canada through 1939. Perhaps partly because of that, Tweedsmuir's optimistic nature could not be subdued. He wrote to "Rex" at the beginning of August that he didn't think war would erupt that year, believing that his reasoning supported his instincts.[125] King wholly sympathized with this view, and by August 10 the European skies were even "a little clearer" for Tweedsmuir.[126] Two weeks later, however, there was shock at the revelation that Stalin's Soviet Union and Nazi Germany had signed a non-aggression pact on August 23. The Allies — Britain and France — had waited too long and miscalculated Russia as their strategic, eastern hedge against further German aggression. On August 25, Britain signed a treaty with Poland, promising protection to it. The volatile situation forced the hopeful Tweedsmuir to change his metaphorical forecast. He wrote to his old friend in Scotland, Stair Gillon, on September 1 that "the skies seem to have darkened," adding that it didn't look like war could be avoided. He lamented the tragedy of a world "at the mercy of an inflamed and cracked-brain peasant!"[127] The thread by which peace hung was snapping as Tweedsmuir wrote.

Nazi Germany's military forces invaded Poland on September 1. British prime minister Chamberlain sent Germany an ultimatum to cease its aggression against Poland. On September 3, a solemn Neville Chamberlain broadcast to an attentive and tense nation that no undertaking had been received from Berlin and that therefore a state of war existed with the German Reich.

CHAPTER 10

The War

A Little Help in Connection with the U.S.A.

In the first dark hour of Sunday, September 10, 1939, an aide at Rideau Hall awoke the governor general to sign a parliamentary proclamation of Canada's participation in the war against Nazi Germany.[1] Significantly, though, Canada went a step further than the other Dominions.

The process for declaring war had been discussed during a special Cabinet meeting the preceding day, with the prime minister asking whether the king or the governor general should sign the declaration. His own opinion was that it should be the king. Cabinet agreed. It reflected the new constitutional environment created by the Statute of Westminster. This was only after Parliament had debated and declared its intention, a point insisted on by Mackenzie King, who stated that Canada's action was "not because of any colonial or inferior status vis-a-vis Great Britain but because of an equality of status."[2]

In other dominions, however, the governors general were signing the declaration of war, a point which gave King angst. He consulted Tweedsmuir following the Cabinet meeting. King was relieved to find the governor general was "quite enthusiastic," and believed "the more that could be done in the name of the king, the better."[3] The proclamation of war was sent via cable to Canada's high commissioner in London, Vincent Massey, to submit to King George VI, for approval as king of Canada.

This was the first time that Canada had acted on its own to declare war.[4] King George VI signed the declaration of war. The high commissioner cabled back to Ottawa and a special issue of the *Canada Gazette* was published just after noon in Ottawa: "George the Sixth, … Whereas by and with the advice of our Privy Council for Canada we have signified our approval of the issue of a proclamation in the *Canada Gazette* declaring that a state of war with the German Reich exists …"[5]

As people throughout much of the Dominion were on their way to morning church services, radio announcements began spreading the not unexpected news. Many newspapers on Monday noted the constitutional significance of Canada's declaration.[6] Some reported Tweedsmuir's signature, others King George's, and at least one used both versions in different articles.[7] The *New York Times* reported that this was the first time in history that the senior Dominion had "exercised the prerogative of nationhood by declaring a state of war on its own account."[8] The *Ottawa Citizen*, however, captured the concept of

National Film Board of Canada. Phototèque./Library and Archives Canada/PA-119438

The governor general reads the Speech from the Throne at a sombre special session of Parliament on September 7, 1939, called to debate declaring war on Nazi Germany.

the multiple Crown. It noted that the week's difference in Britain's and Canada's declarations of war disproved the theory of the indivisibility of the Crown, since the king had been, at the same time, at peace and at war.[9]

The fact that Canada's declaration followed Britain's by a week aroused the expected criticism from opposition politicians and the press. Canada should have declared war when Britain did, they cried.[10] There were, however, two significant considerations — demonstrating Canadian independence and national unity. The delay had also allowed Mackenzie King more time to try to build consensus, if not unanimity, and to assuage conscription fears, especially in Quebec.[11] King George VI expressed to Tweedsmuir that he understood the Canadian sensitivity regarding national unity.[12]

Canada's later declaration also had a practical benefit, however small. It allowed the United States, restricted by its Neutrality Act of May 1, 1937 from selling war materials to belligerents, to continue delivery of warplanes to Canada for another week.[13] Regardless of Roosevelt's sympathies with the Allies and his opposition to isolationism,[14] he was obliged to invoke the Neutrality Act, and on September 5 made such a proclamation, which included Britain, Australia, New Zealand, France, and Poland; he added South Africa three days later. A proclamation was prepared for naming Canada, but following a phone call by President Roosevelt to Mackenzie King, it was determined that Canada's inclusion could be delayed until its declaration of war was official.[15]

After the declaration of war, Tweedsmuir pondered the impact on his role as governor general. He surmised his duties would now largely be comprised of talks with his prime minister and flying around the country reviewing troops.[16] "My old work here is over," he wrote, and he saw additional new primary duties — watching over war charities "to prevent waste," and "holding the hands of Ministers."[17] He thought he might "also be a little help in connection with the U.S.A."[18] This modest statement, though, belied the strategic focus he had had since arriving in Canada. The new, formal wartime duties would be a "dull job," he admitted, though useful in their own way. All of it, he commented with stoic understatement, "is not made pleasanter by persistent minor ill-health."[19]

Tweedsmuir's immediate priority was to contact President Roosevelt. He knew much of America was suspicious of British imperialism, a sentiment that dated from the American Revolutionary War and continued through current concern over India, where Gandhi's actions to promote Indian independence caught international attention and American sympathy. This was compounded by other economic, cultural, and ethnic (e.g., Irish and German) factors "to create a strong anglophobia."[20] Many in the United States remembered British propaganda during the First World War, attributing American involvement, rightly or wrongly, to such propaganda.[21]

General skepticism of the British was strengthened between 1935 and 1939 by several publications dealing with British propaganda. The sensitivity of many Americans "verged on paranoia."[22] This sensitivity was reflected in various ways, such as by the passage of the Foreign Agents Registration Act in June 1938; this Act required all agents of foreign governments to register with the U.S. State Department, and stipulated that their published material be clearly labelled with an indication of who was issuing it.[23] Managing relations with the United States, to obtain both diplomatic and *matériel* support, would clearly require a subtle tact and a patient approach.

Tweedsmuir wrote to the U.S. president, ostensibly to take up a prior invitation to pay him a visit at the Roosevelt family home at Hyde Park, New York. In his message, he mentioned that "[t]here are many things I should greatly like to talk over with you."[24] But he was sensitive to Roosevelt's political situation. A visit from the governor general of a country whose sovereign was now at war could be politically damaging to the president because of the strong isolationist streak. The president had tried for much of the past year to repeal the Neutrality Act, but had had no choice other than to abide by it until his renewed efforts to repeal it could be successful. He argued bluntly with congressmen that the Neutrality Act supported Hitler.

The president believed he could assuage isolationist opinion by arguing that the best way for the United States to stay out of the war was to help Britain and France to defeat the Nazis. Britain's war declaration was a catalyst for Roosevelt to call a special session of Congress, beginning September 21, to try again to amend the Neutrality Act. It would be a huge challenge. In one biographer's analogy, Roosevelt's attempts were akin to those of a "navigator turning a large ship around in a narrow channel against a stiff current."[25]

The importance for Tweedsmuir of knowing the state of U.S. political and public opinion, to inform British policy, could not be overestimated.[26] He wrote to Roosevelt, suggesting he might "slip down inconspicuously" to Hyde Park while on a planned medical visit to New York City in October. As far as records indicate, there was no early reply, which, given the normal closeness of the two men and their frequent communication, suggests Roosevelt's political preoccupations at the time.

As the British government organized itself for war, a Ministry of Information, which had been in development for the better part of a year, was formally created to deal with news, censorship, and the information and propaganda flowing out of and into the country. Appointed as minister was a Scottish peer and judge. He was reportedly well known in Canada, having been appointed by the Canadian government to be its standing counsel in appeals before the British Privy Council, the court of last resort at that time, and had appeared several times on behalf of Canada.[27] On the face of it, the appointment of the thin and serious-looking Hugh Macmillan, the moving of someone from the judiciary to serve as the head of propaganda, may have been surprising, and it seemed to surprise none more than it did Macmillan himself.[28] He had, however, a connection to information and propaganda, and to John Buchan.

The association between the two men went back more than twenty years, to the latter part of the Great War, when they operated out of the Norfolk Hotel in London. When the Department of Information, which Colonel Buchan headed, was made a full Ministry of Information under Lord Beaverbrook, Buchan was appointed Director of Intelligence and Macmillan was one of his two assistant directors. They had also served

together from 1930 as trustees of the Pilgrim Trust in Britain, an organization dedicated to preserving Britain's heritage and to enhancing
relations between the United States and Britain.[29] Historian Nicholas Cull
described the Trust as "the most important" trans-Atlantic organization
for promoting Anglo-American ties.[30] Tweedsmuir was pleased about
the appointment and immediately wrote to Macmillan.[31]

Tweedsmuir described himself to Macmillan as "a close student of
American affairs," with "probably as large an American acquaintance as
any Englishman living."[32] Consistent with his focus on the importance
of the United States, his brief letter cautioned Macmillan to "walk very
warily" in conducting any "publicity" in the United States. At this point,
though, he did not offer anything other than assistance in providing
references for personnel, if Macmillan asked. As an initial offer, it was a
practical one, and was prompted by requests the governor general had
begun receiving almost immediately from young Britons in the United
States and from young Americans asking what they might do to help.

Tweedsmuir was, however, thinking also in broad policy terms,
about how, in practical terms, to address the threats facing Britain and
the Commonwealth. Macmillan, whose office was now set up in London
University's Senate House, was not yet settled into his new position, but
replied immediately with a note handwritten on his personal stationery
since he did not yet have official stationery. He was grateful to hear from
his friend, from whom he "learned a great deal" during their work in
the First World War.[33] Macmillan asked his former boss to send "any
guidance ... especially vis-a-vis Canada and the U.S.A."[34] The reply confirmed Tweedsmuir's opinion that his old friend would accept his advice
"in good part," knowing that they generally saw things "eye to eye."

The Ministry of Information, though, conceived in crisis and born
into a world of entrenched bureaucracy, was not having an easy time.
If it acted quickly, it was acting perhaps too quickly, according to some
news reports. Other reports criticized "its costly collection of highly
paid officials ... [who] reduced [Britain's] emissions of facts about the
war to the merest trickle."[35] Macmillan had to confront these criticisms,
and the fact that, though the war had only been underway a few days,
the Germans, who had been active on the propaganda front well before,

were perceived to be winning on that front.[36] The information minister, *malgré lui*, would certainly appreciate advice from an independent and trusted source that he knew well.

Before Macmillan's written request arrived, however, an anxious Tweedsmuir pre-empted it with a *"verbosa et grandis epistola."*[37] He wanted to recall to the new minister the "great many bad mistakes" they had made during the previous war in dealing with propaganda in the United States, and to suggest that the lessons learned from that experience would be valuable.[38]

After the United States had entered that war, the issue of propaganda was simplified, Tweedsmuir noted, but, he continued, the situation was "much more delicate now than it was then," alluding to U.S. isolationism and currents of anti-British sentiments. In a general remark, he believed that if U.S. isolationism could be explained in the British press, the Americans in turn might be more receptive in trying to understand the British perspective. He then divided his advice to Macmillan into negative and positive approaches, based on the lessons learned in the last war.

The most important point, he emphasized, was that there should be "no propaganda in the ordinary sense of the word," which meant no speakers touring the States, because they would be seen to be propagandists, regardless of their intentions. While this general approach was official British policy during the first two years of the war, it had been set as far back as 1924, most likely as a result of those lessons learned during the Great War, when attempts had been made to involve the United States in the conflict. At that time the Foreign Office stated that its policy as regards the United States was "to tell the truth ... and to let the facts speak for themselves."[39] Tweedsmuir had been at the centre of that experience, and he was now a forceful proponent of the policy. He added in his note to Macmillan that British news should "never deny a disaster," giving the example from the First World War of then Prime Minister Arthur Balfour, who was frank about the Battle of Jutland. Any attempt to "gloss over a setback," Tweedsmuir suggested, would result in American journalists exaggerating it. These were all points that isolationists and neutrals in the United States were aware of and tried to expose as part of the British efforts to bring the United States into the war. Particularly significant in this regard was the Institute for Propaganda Analysis, founded in 1937 by Professor Clyde Miller of Columbia University in New York, to provide analysis of an activity that they believed to be one of the reasons their country had been drawn into the First World War.[40]

The British government should also, Tweedsmuir added, avoid sending a flood of publications into the United States, since even a well-meaning book, like a well-intentioned speaker, could be disastrous. Books by private publishers should not be given a government imprimatur, as had been done in the last war. He cited a well-meaning book published in 1938, *Propaganda in the Next War*, by Sidney Rogerson, as having "had a quite disastrous effect."[41] But the role of writers was extremely important, as John Buchan had expressed in December 1918: "the great task of enlightening foreign countries as to the Allied cause and the magnitude of the British effort without the co-operation of our leading writers" would be "almost impossible" to state.[42]

Acting on their own, however, British writers could be quite useful, and so the Ministry of Information, through its American division, developed a program for propaganda in the United States based on their use, a program described so well by Robert Calder.[43] Confirming the soundness of this approach, Tweedsmuir set out his advice to Macmillan, and the Ministry reported in late October 1939 that it continued to discourage lecturers from visiting the United States.[44] They were, though, encouraging writers known in the United States, and who had already visited there, to do so now.[45] With no connection to the British government, writers could make still make a case for aiding the war effort, but allegations of propaganda would be minimized.[46]

Tweedsmuir continued his advice. The United States must receive only facts from which it could draw its own conclusions. He elaborated even more bluntly that Britain should not insult America's intelligence, and advised sticking to the truth to help ensure the United States did not become any more alienated from the British position than American isolationists had already made it. There were, he wrote, forces within the United States working to develop arguments that would ultimately support Britain, and their work should not be made more difficult by

Britain's failure to tell the truth. He was undoubtedly thinking foremost of Roosevelt.

What the American president faced, in addition to isolationism, was public fear, Tweedsmuir explained, fear that war would bring another round of economic problems, like the Depression. Rightly or wrongly, some in America blamed its current economic troubles on its involvement in the last war. Tweedsmuir had no doubt that Americans would realize sooner or later that they "may have to fight for the political faith in which [they believe]." His opinion was based on the arguable belief that he considered the Americans to be generally very well informed; though the reference was likely to those with whom he interacted. As for the fear in America, Tweedsmuir believed it would not last. Fear would be succeeded by anger, he wrote Macmillan, "and when America is angry she is very dangerous," implying that America's anger would resolve it to take action.

One of the challenges Britain faced in supporting its war effort was the necessity of obtaining financing in the United States. Adding to his what-not-to-do advice, Tweedsmuir cautioned Macmillan not to use only one bank as its financial agent, as Britain had used J.P. Morgan in the last war. The reasons, Tweedsmuir explained, had to do with Morgan's diminished size and prestige; it had "not quite the same size of men" among its partners, even though many of them were among "some of [his] oldest friends."[47] The world had changed, and the Great Depression had had a dramatic impact on the financial industry. Tweedsmuir acknowledged that this didn't fall within Macmillan's jurisdiction, but he may have considered Macmillan as the entré into government for his advice. Indeed, the minister forwarded that section of Tweedsmuir's letter to Sir John Simon, chancellor of the exchequer, another of Tweedsmuir's former parliamentary colleagues. Simon told Macmillan that his intention was indeed to use more than just Morgan's as Britain's financial agent in the United States.[48]

Tweedsmuir's complementary positive advice to Macmillan began with describing how the British government should provide news to the United States. The former long-time director of Reuters advised Macmillan to send out as much and as detailed "authentic news" as possible, following "the Reuter plan," which meant being as factual, as truthful, and as objective as possible.[49] Obtaining details for the "authentic news," Tweedsmuir knew, would prove problematic, because of War Office and Admiralty censorship. He did not have much patience with their "passion for babyish secrecy," arguing that 90 percent of what had been censored in the last war could have been "published with impunity." This may have been one of the reasons he was critical of the conceptual structure of the Ministry, saying it was a mistake to have included the contradictory activities of censorship and information/propaganda within the same Ministry. By the time Macmillan replied on September 23, he had already experienced what Tweedsmuir was warning about, writing that the Air Ministry could be added to the War Office and Admiralty.[50]

Overall, Macmillan was pleased that the policy approach they were taking was being reinforced "by the independent judgement of so experienced a student of American affairs." Indeed, the relatively new department was "staying as close to the 'truth' as possible," developing its message that a "special relationship" existed between Britain and America and using certain examples to highlight the "common historical and cultural legacy."[51] There was, however, one detailed suggestion in Tweedsmuir's positive approach with which Macmillan disagreed.

As part of his strategy both to help inform British policy and to help influence U.S. decision-makers and public opinion in support of Britain, Tweedsmuir proposed creating an informal, confidential network of leading individuals. He did not think it appropriate to have any formal organization at this early juncture. The eleven individuals he named would "have access to the inner circles in politics, law, journalism, finance, etc., ... friends who could hold a watching brief for our cause."[52] It was a variation on a theme from his intelligence and propaganda experience in the First World War, when he developed non-official mechanisms for information and propaganda purposes.[53] He would have believed that the eleven individuals could be counted on. In fact, at least three — Grenville Clark, Will Clayton, and William Allen White — would later become high profile advocates of American intervention in the fight against the Nazis, suggesting that America go to war herself or offer support for Britain, or do both.[54] The members of this network would "speak the right word in the right place," according to Tweedsmuir, give reliable views on the state of shifting American opinion, speak discreetly to sympathetic American opinion-makers and leaders, and counter misinformation from enemy propaganda, German sympathizers in the United States, or isolationists. They would both advise the British government and, where necessary, criticize it with respect to its relations with the United States.

The process of forming such a group could begin, Tweedsmuir advised, by contacting a Duncan M. Spencer of Fiduciary Trust Company, 1 Wall Street, in New York. He suggested they start with "a small informal nucleus," listing five of the eleven names: Walter Stewart, former Bank of England economic advisor; Douglas Freeman of Richmond, Virginia, "proprietor of the most powerful paper in the south," whom John Buchan had met on his trip to the United States in 1924;[55] William Allen White of Kansas, "the best known provincial journalist in the States," who knew Buchan from before 1919 and who corresponded closely with Roosevelt to help move American opinion;[56] Grenville Clark, a prominent New York lawyer; and V. Cameron of the Ford Motor Company, who was "responsible for the quite excellent broadcast which Ford issues."

Spencer was an "intimate friend," whom Tweedsmuir addressed as "Pat" and described like a character suitable for a John Buchan novel: a Scotsman by birth who had gone to school and college in the United States, joined the Royal Flying Corps in the First World War, and was now a highly respected and well-connected head of one of the main private banks in New York City. Tweedsmuir likely had already communicated with Spencer, and some of the others, either directly or indirectly.

Macmillan's disagreement about establishing this group was based on a belief that the very act of forming it could prove detrimental to British interests. After all, Tweedsmuir had warned about the need to deal so very carefully with the United States. Macmillan indicated it would be necessary to consult Ambassador Lothian in Washington, and so forwarded that part of the letter to him. Tweedsmuir could have asked for nothing more, since he and Lothian had known each other for thirty years and shared a strategic view about the importance of Anglo-American relations. Lothian was also psychologically prepared; in November 1936 he had predicted that there would be war in Europe.[57]

When Lothian was informed that Tweedsmuir would be in New York City for a medical visit, he wrote and asked if they might meet, inviting him down to Washington. Appearing in the American capital, however, was not something Tweedsmuir wanted to risk, because it would raise the same concerns that he had noted in his earlier correspondence with Roosevelt. Lothian indicated he would try to get up to New York.[58]

Having provided his immediate and practical concerns and advice to Macmillan, Tweedsmuir now turned his attention to British prime minister Neville Chamberlain.

In his first letter to Chamberlain, written on September 19, Tweedsmuir argued that it was important to issue "a statement of our purpose" to the Empire — maintaining morale must be a priority.[59] The statement should include the restoration of Poland and Czechoslovakia, and emphasize the desperate struggle ahead; in defending "all that is vital in civilisation and in Christian ethics," they would not yield until victory was achieved. Whether, in fact, it was wise to make a statement of war aims and, if so, what the content should be would remain a continuing subject of political discussion and editorial comment over the coming months. A letter a week earlier from Ambassador Lothian in Washington made it clear that it was not just for reasons of Empire morale that Tweedsmuir advocated a statement of purpose.

Lothian was concerned about negative opinions and stories circulating in the United States that suggested that Britain was not serious about the war, or that it was "just sitting back" and repeating a "Munich," but this time at Poland's expense. There was also concern that the lack of military action, this *drôle de guerre* or "phoney war," could cause the Americans, at least those not already isolationist, to not take Britain seriously, which would make it even more difficult to persuade them of the need for support. The ambassador explained to Tweedsmuir that he was "bombarding" the Ministry of Information with the importance of ensuring enough news and photographs of Britain's activities got through to America to help dispel such stories.[60]

Lothian believed strongly that positive messages must be conveyed to ensure that Britain's resolve was made clear, but at the same time, it was important that it not be seen, or even perceived, to be interfering in American opinion. Tweedsmuir suggested Chamberlain's statement could not be "too grave or too emphatic."[61] He added, likely because of Chamberlain's recognized deficiency in effective oratory skills[62] and his dislike for the Americans, that a statement of aims be supplemented with a broadcast by "somebody like Winston," referring to Churchill, who had been appointed First Lord of the Admiralty.[63] Having criticized Churchill's approach in the past, Tweedsmuir now recognized the extent to which "Winston" was the right person to communicate the right messages in the right way, especially to American ears.[64]

Chamberlain assured Tweedsmuir that he was doing what he could to develop relations with the Americans.[65] It was, however, a questionable claim, given his well-known contempt for them.[66] In his detailed reply, Chamberlain wrote that the suggestions were not "practical or desirable at the present moment."[67] He was already committed to making weekly statements in the House of Commons about the war, and believed he had well stated an overall purpose, quoting it in his letter: "Our general purpose in this struggle is well known; it is to redeem Europe from the perpetual and recurring fear of German aggression and enable the peoples of Europe to preserve their independence and their liberties."[68] Chamberlain also disagreed with the suggestion Tweedsmuir made that the restoration of Poland and Czechoslovakia should be primary objectives. He explained that such objectives would put the government in a situation where its foreign policy options would be seriously restricted. In this case making the restoration of Poland a condition for ending the war would now also involve war against Russia, which in August had signed a pact with Nazi Germany and had moved in to occupy the part of Poland that Germany hadn't.

Tweedsmuir accepted Chamberlain's arguments, then gave a two-fold explanation for his original, specific objectives. First, he had wanted to ensure Canada didn't lose its initial enthusiasm, and second, he wanted to dispel perceptions in the United States that Britain was not serious about the war.[69] In the short month since his first exchange of correspondence with Chamberlain, he thought the situation had improved, with two developments in particular sparking Canada's imagination and helping to maintain enthusiasm and morale. On the one hand, two Canadian infantry divisions were being prepared to be sent to England, and the Empire air training plan was being discussed, with delegations set to arrive in Canada shortly. Tweedsmuir also now believed that the United States realized that Britain was serious about fighting the war. The prime minister's negative response to Hitler's "impudent offer" to open peace negotiations had contributed significantly to this perception.[70]

British resolve was further confirmed by Churchill who, in an October 1 broadcast, described the events of the first month of the war, including the Royal Navy's activities against Nazi U-boats. The broadcast contained Churchill's now famous description of Russia as "a riddle, wrapped in a mystery, inside an enigma." Tweedsmuir described the speech as "very effective."[71] Even Chamberlain described Winston's broadcast as "excellent."[72]

Tweedsmuir continued to pursue ways to enhance American opinion of Britain, leveraging all sound possibilities, but brusquely dismissed a "second-rate" film that an American company was trying to sell the British government.[73] Hollywood, he replied to Lothian, who had consulted him, "is only too willing to make first-class films which would have an indirect propaganda effect."[74] The positive impact in the United States of Churchill's October 1 speech prompted another idea that strongly appealed to Tweedsmuir. The day after Churchill's speech, he wrote to the Palace with a proposal that the queen make a monthly broadcast. Such a speech would be aimed at the women of the Empire, but it would also, as with other broadcasts, be heard in the United States. Tweedsmuir would later counsel the British foreign secretary, Lord Halifax, that this was the only safe kind of propaganda intended for the United States.[75] He emphasized that the idea for a speech by the queen came "from many quarters in the United States," a point that added to its credibility.[76]

Following the royal visit to Canada and the United States the previous spring, the queen had become "a legendary figure," especially in the United States, where her charm and informality had seemed to seduce the Americans.[77] The governor general proposed that Her Majesty's first broadcast describe in simple terms what Britain was doing in these first months of the war, especially the women, "and speak words of comfort and encouragement." He offered, of course, to assist with the messages.

Six weeks later, during the evening of Armistice Day, Her Majesty made a radio broadcast for the first time since the royal visit. At the beginning of her speech, the queen referred directly to the United States and the kindly welcome she and the king received during their visit to Canada and the United States the previous spring. During her heart-felt seven-and-a-half-minute broadcast, she expressed sympathy for the women of Poland and of France, and called on the women of the Empire "to be guardians of [the] home front," while reminding them that their tasks now also included "every field of national service."[78] She stated near the conclusion of her address, that "amidst the trials of these days, I would give a message of hope and encouragement." Tweedsmuir's hand appears evident. This is supported by a letter from Sir Alexander Hardinge at the Palace, who expressed the hope that Tweedsmuir "approved of the Queen's broadcast."[79] It was a significant contribution to the war effort, to cultivating U.S. sympathies for Britain, and to demonstrating how useful such broadcasts could be.

Quite apart from the effect the broadcast had within the Empire, the impact in the United States was positive. The following day, the *New York Times* re-printed the full text, accompanied by a positive article.[80] The impact could not help but enhance the image and reputation of the queen in America, and also contribute to softening American opinion to Britain's situation. Such influences were critical to help counter pronouncements by personalities such as Charles Lindbergh, the famous aviator, and Father Coughlin, a popular radio commentator, both of whom were sympathetic to the Nazi regime or were even actively promoting their views.

Another prong of Tweedsmuir's strategy was to remain acutely aware of the state of public opinion in the United States and, with the "right messages" but no outright propaganda, to attempt to influence opinion in support of Britain's position. Ambassador Lothian shared the objective, observing that "[w]hat ultimately counts here is not the President or Mr. Hull [the secretary of state], but public opinion."[81] Even the slightest perception that Britain was attempting to sway opinion in the United States could produce an anti-British backlash. Despite Tweedsmuir's arguable impression that Americans were generally well informed, it could only be a limited generalization. As Conrad Black notes, it is difficult "to recreate the profound and prideful lack of foreign policy sophistication of the American voters and many of their representatives of this period."[82]

Tweedsmuir pursued his idea of a confidential group of Americans to keep a "watching brief" for Britain, despite the information minister's initial lack of enthusiasm for the idea. The main reason for pursuing the idea, he explained in a late October letter to Macmillan, was that "few Englishmen know all sides of American life."[83] If Britain was to be aware of American opinion toward it and the war in general, it had to be fully cognizant of all elements that could influence political decisions. Pursuing this strategic objective, Tweedsmuir would meet with the generally like-minded Lothian[84] during his planned medical visit to New York, but he would also meet with other prominent Americans.

In the meantime Roosevelt sent his long-delayed reply to the governor general's request to visit him. The prerequisite for the visit — an improved political climate — had of course not materialized. The chances were too high that the visit would find its way onto the front pages of the newspapers, fuelling conspiracy theories and jeopardizing his efforts to have the Neutrality Act repealed in the special session of Congress. Roosevelt believed that his "bill [had] a good chance of going through" and he was "almost literally walking on eggs ... saying nothing, seeing nothing and hearing nothing."[85] He knew Tweedsmuir would appreciate the delicacy of the situation.

Travel by the governor general to the United States, aside from the current complications and sensitivities the war presented, required the king's permission, with advice obviously from his Canadian prime minister. Once these steps were secured, the governor general's private secretary consulted on the details with the Department of External Affairs, which released a notice to the press on Saturday, October 14: "The Governor-General, acting on medical advice, proposes to go to New York on October 19th for special treatment. He hopes to return to Canada on October 25th."[86] That same day, the under-secretary of state for external affairs, Dr. O.D. Skelton, communicated the press release to Loring Christie, the Canadian minister in Washington, explaining that the notice was being issued "to avert the possibility of any political interpretation being given to the visit."[87]

Christie was aware of Tweedsmuir's pending visit and also of the political sensitivities that attended it; he had dined at Government House earlier in the month. In Washington Christie, who would have been sympathetic to Tweedsmuir's efforts, replied to Skelton's communication in a triply classified letter — "Secret, Private and Personal" — adding something he had neglected to tell the under-secretary before.[88] The governor general had informed Christie that he and Lothian wanted to meet, explaining the political difficulties of trying to do so in either Washington or Ottawa. Tweedsmuir undoubtedly saw his need to make a medical visit to New York and the fact that Lothian wished to make a personal trip there as providing good cover for the business the two men wanted to conduct. The bureaucrats, though, were left ignorant of the meeting's purpose; Tweedsmuir did not mention it to Christie "and of course [Christie] did not ask."[89] We know that each man had at least one major item to discuss; Tweedsmuir wanted to raise his proposal for a high level de facto intelligence network, while Lothian wanted assistance with his first important public speech, which he was due to deliver shortly.

The Tweedsmuirs would be staying at 107 East 70th Street, the New York residence of Thomas W. Lamont, a partner at J.P. Morgan's Bank, who had first met John Buchan in 1917 in London. Their network of common friends was a useful one at this juncture, and included Lord Lothian, Buchan's old professor Gilbert Murray, Lord Robert Cecil, and the American journalist William Allen White.[90] Significantly, Lamont was also a long-time friend, and former tenant, of Roosevelt.[91] The governor general and Lady Tweedsmuir arrived in New York on October 20 for their week-long visit.

During his stay, while not attending medical appointments, Tweeds-muir met with leading financiers and industrialists, such as John D. Rockefeller; journalists, including staff from the *New York Times*; academic leaders, such as Dr. James Conant, the president of Harvard University; and one of New York's most prominent lawyers, Grenville Clark, who had been on his proposed list of eleven men to keep a watching brief for the British government.[92] Clark was also on the board of Harvard. Tweeds-muir was surveying as widely as he could the tone of those who helped shape American opinion.

After Lothian had arrived from Washington, the two men met as scheduled, likely at Lamont's residence — for convenience but also because it was discreet. Tweedsmuir resurrected the idea he had first proposed to Lord Macmillan, to establish an informal group of Americans who could keep "a watching brief" for Britain. Macmillan, recall, had sent it on to Lothian. Having had time to reflect on Tweedsmuir's original proposal, the British ambassador explained that in a similar vein he was using British consuls around the United States to set up local committees to "act as information bureaux."[93] Lothian had hired John Wheeler-Bennett, a well-connected Englishman teaching at universities in the States, as his personal assistant and instructed him to travel widely. "I want you to be my eyes and ears," he wrote, "[b]etween us we know a great many people in America and we can use them to make further contacts."[94] Despite certain gaps in Lothian's connections in America, which Tweedsmuir had candidly noted to Hugh Macmillan, he was apparently satisfied that Lothian would be in touch "with every class" in America, and informed Information Minister Macmillan that the British government would be "properly fed with the right kind of 'dope.'"[95]

The use of the consuls, though, was more likely to assuage Macmillan's concerns; the fact that the information delivered would be coming from the British government's representative in the United States would also have been appreciated by Macmillan, who would have deemed recommendations provided by Lothian as being more trustworthy since the latter carried the risk with his official responsibility. The activities of the consulates would be less damaging, or at least more easily reprimanded, if exposed, than would any actions by a group such as the one Tweedsmuir suggested, which could be perceived as a more sinister British network attempting to clandestinely influence American politics and opinion. Lothian's local committees may not necessarily have included the prominent names in Tweedsmuir's list, but that list would have provided suggestions for Lothian and Wheeler-Bennett.

While Tweedsmuir's proposal did not materialize then, it foreshadowed developments that emerged midway through 1940, when similar, as well as other, tasks were given to a man known as "the quiet Canadian." Also known as "Intrepid," (later Sir) William Stephenson was appointed as British intelligence liaison with the United States (later known as British Security Co-ordination — BSC). Based in New York City, he operated with President Roosevelt's approval and the involvement of the FBI. Stephenson was given "no formal terms of reference," but his tasking from the British Secret Intelligence Service (MI6) included promoting public opinion in the United States in favour of aid to Britain.[96]

Lothian's "local committees" would also certainly have provided a basis for assisting Stephenson, who, according to one biographer, "worked closely with [Lothian]."[97] Lothian's personal assistant, Wheeler-Bennett, had "with the tacit cognisance of the Embassy, though not of the Ministry of Information, … maintained a fairly close contact with [Stephenson's staff]."[98]

The interconnections of Britons and sympathetic Americans continued to evolve and develop through the first half of 1940, and through these can be seen the links Tweedsmuir encouraged.[99] One such connection was developed by William Allen White, the nationally prominent Kansas journalist, who was one of the individuals on Tweedsmuir's list. In May of 1940, White and another colleague, Clark Eichelberger, formed a "Committee to Defend America by Aiding the Allies," establishing over three hundred branches throughout the United States within the first two months and actively promoting as much assistance to Britain as possible.[100]

One of the first members of White's Committee to Defend America was Tweedsmuir's friend Thomas Lamont. Another of Tweedsmuir's connections to join White's committee was Lewis Douglas, the former principal of McGill University in Montreal, who had left McGill at the end of 1939 to return to the United States.[101] Yet another leading member of the committee was the movie star, and anglophile, Douglas Fairbanks Jr., who had been in Ottawa in December 1938 at Tweedsmuir's invitation.[102] Fairbanks had met John Buchan in England when they discussed plans for making "a Highland costume film" involving Fairbanks's film company, Criterion, and again in 1934, maintaining correspondence in between and since.[103]

It was perhaps Lord Lothian's activities in establishing these connections and the local committees throughout the United States, activities encouraged by Tweedsmuir, that contributed to Lothian being described by *Time* in July 1940 as "the most popular British [a]mbassador" in Washington since James Bryce at the beginning of the 1900s.[104] Another contemporary assessment of Lothian comes from the authors of *War Propaganda and the United States*, published in May 1940 for the Institute for Propaganda Analysis, in which they noted that Lothian's "triumphs far outweighed his indiscretions."[105] Historians since then have noted that Lothian "was crucial in orchestrating British propaganda strategy, usually in the direction of providing more accurate information and greater access to American journalists," as well as the success of "the 'covert and effective' liaison work" it conducted within the United States.[106] Wheeler-Bennett described Lothian's activity as "a period of unqualified success" and inspiring "a campaign which attained remarkable proportions and had far-reaching effects."[107]

The links between Tweedsmuir, Macmillan, and Lothian, and between Lothian and Stephenson, reveal the connections and channels through which ideas could flow in the effort to build support for Britain and the principles for which it was fighting. Many individuals were involved in this work; some were involved in decision-making or in other official positions. Tweedsmuir did not hold a direct decision-making role in this field, but with his experience, ideas, and networks, he supported and influenced those who were making decisions; and both the British minister of information and the British ambassador to the United States sought his advice.

It is interesting to note also that the effectiveness of Tweedsmuir's approach, to establish a network of well-placed influential "friends," was confirmed by Lavine and Wechsler in May 1940. They noted that the British "were infinitely more successful in private meetings with 'keymen' in journalism, industry and society," than were the "British envoys," who were "not always triumphant" in their public appearances, a prescient point Tweedsmuir had included in his early advice to Macmillan in September 1939.[108]

The Tweedsmuir-Lothian meeting now moved on to an immediate interest of the ambassador. In just a few days, on October 25, Lothian was to deliver his first important public speech. As was traditional for British ambassadors, he would address the Pilgrims Society, dedicated to promoting relations between Britain and the United States, in this instance to their annual dinner at the Plaza Hotel in New York. Tweedsmuir worked on it with him, which appears to be the main reason Lothian came to New York. Tweedsmuir saw the speech as an opportunity to make Britain's policy "clear to America" and undoubtedly as a chance to implement advice he had given to Macmillan.

Both Tweedsmuir and Lothian had served as trustees of the Pilgrims Trust in Britain.[109] John Buchan had been honoured in New York at the Pilgrims' annual dinner in 1934. At that time the Trust was funding a new library for Columbia University, an institution that had bestowed an honorary degree on Buchan, who delivered a speech at the opening of the library. Dr. N.M. Butler, president of Columbia University, was chairman of the American Pilgrims. For his part, Lothian had spoken to the Pilgrims Society in London three months earlier, prior to leaving for Washington. The upcoming speech would be a link with that one. Many of those attending the dinner were people Tweedsmuir was meeting with in New York as part of his own efforts to plumb as many levels of American opinion as possible. Crafting the speech demanded immense political sensitivity, particularly since it was the ambassador's first since taking up his post. It would be a key opportunity to clarify Britain's policy to the Americans.

We can picture the two men, having much in common from their formative years spent in Lord Milner's South African administration and sharing similar views on the current international situation, sitting together at Thomas Lamont's residence in New York, discussing key strategic issues, how best to address American sensitivities, political and historical, and how best to communicate these issues. Could Roosevelt's views have been made known to Lothian and Tweedsmuir via Roosevelt's friend Thomas Lamont? Regardless, Tweedsmuir's existing knowledge of Roosevelt's views, the careful thought about British policy toward America he had already expressed to Macmillan and Chamberlain, and his eloquence of expression and keen mind would greatly assist in crafting this critical speech.

The Plaza Hotel ballroom was packed with an influential audience, including J.D. Rockefeller Jr., J.P. Morgan, Thomas Lamont, Count de Saint Quentin, the ambassador of France, U.S. secretary of the treasury Henry Morgenthau, Frank L. Polk, and many other prominent figures of business, industry, politics, finance, and education.[110] After a few introductory words, the ambassador set out, quite explicitly, the serious and sensitive context: "It is very difficult for a belligerent to address a neutral," particularly when there was legislation pending before Congress, to repeal the embargo of the Neutrality Act.[111] Nonetheless, he added, Britain had "a right, indeed a duty, ... to explain to you and all other democracies what we are doing and why we are doing it.... That is what we mean by saying the British Government conducts no propaganda." The ambassador continued: "We want to tell you the facts as we know them ... [and] are bound to leave you perfectly free to form your own judgement."[112] There was confidence, of course, in what that judgment ultimately would be. But they were sailing into the strong headwinds of American suspicion and anglophobia. British journalist Alistair Cooke's observation eight months later confirmed this: "Americans had not been reassured by the British Government's announcement that it was not conducting propaganda in the United States."[113]

The speech emphasized that this war affected values Britain shared with the United States. In attempting to overcome American suspicion of Britain as an imperialist power, the ambassador explained that the war was not a struggle of rival empires, but, rather, it was a war to decide whether the world would be democratic or totalitarian.[114] In trying to alleviate suspicion of Britain, Lothian recalled the visit of King George and VI Queen Elizabeth in the spring of 1939. The visit had demonstrated a more informal royal couple, countering perceptions that Britain remained the stuffy, class-bound country it had been at the time of King George III, that is, at the time of the American colonies' revolution against Britain.

Responding in a general way to American questions about British war aims, Lothian stated that there were two: the freedom of all countries in Europe, and the establishment of "some security against constantly renewed wars of aggression." The ambassador then turned the tables, stating to his American audience: "[W]e think we are entitled to ask you the same question." He continued, noting that Britain and France were fighting a defensive war, trying to "prevent the hordes of paganism and barbarism from destroying what is left of civilized Europe." "It is inconceivable," the ambassador emphasized, that the United States, "which has already done such immeasurable things for the freedom of mankind, ... should not have its own contribution to make to the solution of the greatest problem that has ever presented itself to the genius of man." To support his point justifying U.S. involvement in the shape of the post-war world along federal lines, he observed that the United States had found a successful federal basis but Europe had not.

The speech was a significant success. The following day, the *New York Times* gave it extensive and positive coverage in a front page article, and printed the entire text. After a day's reflection, the *Times*' editors confirmed the careful approach Tweedsmuir and Lothian had laboured to convey in the speech by commenting that "Lord Lothian violates no proprieties."[115] If the Hotel Plaza audience wished, the editorial noted, it "could read into the words the suggestion that there can be no new order unless this country and other neutral countries have a share in establishing it when the war is over." This was a theme Tweedsmuir likely raised with the *New York Times* staff when he met with them during his New York visit. There were those more skeptical, though, as represented by the popular *Saturday Evening Post*, which wrote that it did "not subscribe to any part of the argument."[116]

Phrases and words in Lothian's speech are familiar from Tweedsmuir's letters to Macmillan and Chamberlain. He had advised Macmillan that "there should be no propaganda ... Facts are the only argument that matter and ... that some chance should be taken of making clear to America that that is our policy — that we respect her intelligence too much to attempt to make her draw deductions from the data available — we leave her to do that for herself."[117] The speech had echoed this point in only slightly different words.[118]

Tweedsmuir's earlier prodding to Chamberlain and Macmillan to make a "statement of purpose," to the effect that Britain was fighting "for all that is vital in civilization and in Christian ethics," had also been reflected, and in historically laden descriptive terms such as John Buchan might have incorporated into one of his novels. This same theme was no doubt also discussed by Tweedsmuir and Mackenzie King, with the latter pushing it even further in a broadcast a week after the Lothian speech, calling the war a "crusade."[119]

Lothian's plea that America must be involved in the shape of the post-war world had been a point of considerable discussion between himself and Tweedsmuir. Lothian's previous reference, in his London speech in July 1939, to a role for the United States, was more general (the United States should have a contribution to the solution of "these vast problems"),[120] but became more focused in a relatively short time on organizing the post-war world along federal lines. The two men differed, however, on the scope of the federal basis and on the degree of sovereignty to be surrendered. Tweedsmuir focused on smaller, regional groupings, such as, for example, one based around the Danube basin, or groupings of countries with characteristics in common, such as those that "accept the Reign of Law." Lothian, on the other hand, looked to something on a much larger scale, approaching world government, which was closer to the ideas advocated by the prominent New York lawyer Grenville Clark, who subsequently shared his ideas with Tweedsmuir, as will be discussed in the next chapter.[121] Tweedsmuir's vision was closer to the future reality.

After arriving back in Ottawa, the day after Lothian's speech, and picking up on the theme of the shape of the post-war world, Tweedsmuir wrote to British information minister Macmillan that "if … reconstitu-tion must be [made] on some kind of federal basis it would be very acceptable to America who regards herself as the principal expert on federalism."[122] He made no reference to the speech, perhaps because he wanted to independently reinforce thinking about the shape of the post-war world.

From Ottawa Tweedsmuir followed Lothian's activities with evident interest, and in early February 1940, he congratulated the ambassador on his approach generally and on the content of his infrequent speeches specifically.[123] Subsequent to the Pilgrims speech, Lothian gave only five others over the next three months, repeating in various forms the main themes.[124] The infrequency was significant, Tweedsmuir believed, because it made each speech stand out as an event: "[W]ith you," he remarked, "every speech should be a landmark."[125]

In retrospect there is a certain pathos knowing that neither of these influential men, both of whom worked so hard to maintain and strengthen the Anglo-American relationship, would live beyond 1940. Tweedsmuir died on February 11 and Lothian on December 12; both would have had much more to contribute, but they left a legacy in their own spheres, as well as in other, overlapping spheres of influence, that helped lay the groundwork and set the tone for Britain's relations with the United States, thereby providing the critical basis for the defeat of Nazism. Both men were, however, replaced by individuals who much of the "New World" perceived as stereotypical members of traditional British class-based society — Tweedsmuir by Lord Athlone, a member of the royal family, and Lothian by Lord Halifax, the aristocratic former foreign secretary, whose beginnings in the United States only reinforced this impression.[126] Ironically, this was the very image that much of the British government's subtle propaganda in the United States had aimed to counteract.[127] Fortunately, the situation altered after the fall of France and the end of the "phoney war," creating a dynamic of necessity that helped counter American isolationist attitudes.

CHAPTER 11

The War

Interpreter of Canada and Britain; Post-War Order

The controversy over defence policy sparked by Tweedsmuir's speech in Calgary in 1936 was just one part of the larger context of growing concern about Canada's defence preparedness in the face of a deteriorating international situation. The economic depression, reduced revenues, heightened expenditures for relief, and transfers to bankrupt provinces had all taken their toll on the government's ability to finance the Department of National Defence, and other departments of course. Spending on the military had fallen as low as fourteen million dollars by 1932–1933.[1] In mid-1936 the press was reporting that the Defence Department had admitted the Dominion was not adequately prepared in the event of an attack by air, there being only ten fighter planes.[2] By early 1939 spending had risen by almost 250 percent from the lowest point, but it was still considered inadequate by many observers. Premier Duplessis's independent-minded Quebec, as well as isolationists and peace advocates in the rest of Canada, helped ensure the government focused on social issues and could not muster the political will to increase military expenditures more than they did.

As a result, in September 1939, the Canadian Militia (it was renamed the Canadian Army in 1940) had only 4,500 personnel in uniform, which was about 1 percent of the number of soldiers sent overseas in the First World War (425,000). The Royal Canadian Air Force had

1,800 personnel and the Royal Canadian Navy, 3,100.[3] After war was declared, however, mobilization occurred quickly, with almost fifty-five thousand volunteers enlisting in the first month. The task of rebuilding the militia to war readiness was complicated by an overabundance of obsolete artillery, coupled with an inadequate supply of military transport and of equipment such as light machine guns and helmets, and a shortage of instructors for training. The situation was not any better for the navy or the air force. Fortunately, there was little serious fighting in the first months, a period dubbed the "twilight war" by Churchill, a situation that allowed precious time to correct deficiencies. But the lack of fighting created its own problems in terms of maintaining morale and a fighting spirit.

With memories alive of how conscription had divided the country in the last great conflict, King's focus was, as always, the maintenance of national unity. It was for this reason that he emphasized the role of Parliament. He was explicit in his address to the House of Commons on September 8, stating that there was "general appreciation ... [of] the manner in which we have been able to hold our promise to let Parliament decide."[4] Partisanship must be set aside, he said, for the greater national good. He continued that he had no doubts that he and the leader of the opposition, despite sharp differences, would, "when the world should again be threatened, ... be found instantly side by side in an endeavour to unite this country."[5]

Along with the widespread anxiety about the country's state of military preparedness, there was also concern in many quarters, which was shared by Tweedsmuir, that there should be no profiteering from the war situation, as had occurred during the Great War. Prime Minister King made clear in a statement the week before the declaration of war that any war profiteering would be dealt with severely.[6] In this new mood of non-partisanship, patriotism, and propriety, the minister of defence, Ian Mackenzie, who had awarded a pre-war contract for the purchase of Bren guns in Canada without competing bids, was replaced on September 19 by Norman Rogers. Rogers had been labour minister and one of King's closest political colleagues. To further bolster public confidence that the military would be effectively managed, a non-partisan War Supply Board was established to help bring order to the chaos it was believed had enveloped the Department of Defence during recent years.[7]

Despite that situation Tweedsmuir was "proud of Canada" and of the initial actions the government had taken in the first two weeks since the declaration of war.[8] While there were administrative and logistical challenges to overcome, politically there was just one significant "fissure in Canada's war facade" to impede national unity. Maurice Duplessis, the premier of Quebec, had personal hatred of Mackenzie King, and for personal and political reasons his Union Nationale government was increasingly hostile toward Ottawa and opposed to participation in the war effort. Duplessis's attitude became even more antagonistic when Ottawa assumed control over credit. This made it impossible for the provinces to raise funds on foreign markets, a situation that posed serious problems for Quebec's finances. Exacerbating all of this was the provincial government's tolerance of fascist organizations within the province and its connections with their leader, Adrien Arcand.[9] There was a certain admiration in some Quebec opinion for Catholic Italy and Mussolini's reorganization of a previously inefficient country, and this admiration led to significant support in the province for the local fascists.

The federal government's problems with the Duplessis government were, according to the well-informed governor general, "not fair to the French Canadians" who were "enlisting magnificently."[10] His views were supported in a secret Department of National Defence memorandum two years later, stating that mobilization in September 1939 "provided a fair and just representation from Quebec."[11] The report, prepared in June 1941, noted "that all evidence points to a response from French-speaking active recruits, which is much more favourable than is generally appreciated, even in informed circles." It added that it had already been publicly stated that the first units to reach full strength after war started were *le Royal 22ème Régiment* and *les Fusiliers de Mont-Royal*. Overall, however, after the initial enthusiastic wave of militia enlistment, recruitment dropped off dramatically in the following months, from the almost fifty-five thousand in September, to well under five thousand in October and fewer again in November and December.[12] Both the limited capabilities to absorb large numbers and the lack of any major fighting in Europe contributed to this decline.

Another factor, however, made for a somewhat brighter outlook. In a personal note to British prime minister Chamberlain in mid-October, Tweedsmuir relayed that it appeared Duplessis would be defeated in the upcoming Quebec election. The expected result occurred on October 25, when the provincial Liberals under Adélard Godbout defeated Duplessis's Union Nationale. It was welcome news indeed to all those who were concerned about Canada entering the war united. This positive development was added to by other news of a significant project.

Tweedsmuir believed a plan to train Commonwealth pilots, navigators, air gunners, and ground crews in Canada would catch the public's imagination and help maintain morale during this period when there was little actual fighting. Negotiations would not be easy, however, with some

The governor general waits with Air Vice-Marshal G.M. Croil prior to leaving for RCAF Station Trenton. Tweedsmuir shared the view that air power was key to winning the war.

Department of National Defence/Library and Archives Canada/PA-063477 unchanged British imperial attitudes confronting the decade-old, fully sovereign Dominions.

As the negotiations developed, Tweedsmuir came to view the magnitude and potential for the project at several strategic levels: for the war effort; for the future of the Empire; and for Canada's future development. The expanded training and production of aircraft added to his belief that it was as "essential for our future that Britannia should rule the air as it is that she should rule the waves!"[13] He also described the air training plan to Chamberlain as "the most important step in imperial development since the Statute of Westminster."[14] It was a theme that related back to a point in his speech in Vancouver in August 1936, where he described the need for an "apparatus of common action" for the Empire. He was clearly excited, not only for what this plan would contribute to the war effort and Empire co-operation, but also for what it could contribute to Canada. He predicted the country would, by the end of the war, "be at the top of the [a]ir business."[15]

Negotiations of one sort or another regarding training or linkages between the Royal Air Force (RAF) and the Royal Canadian Air Force (RCAF) had been going on since the First World War. Through the early and mid-1930s, the RAF had accepted a few Canadians, because opportunities in the small RCAF were limited. By April 1937, as concern in Britain about Nazi Germany's increasing air power was growing, the British asked the Canadian government to increase the quota of Canadians who could join the RAF.[16] The number had previously been set at twenty-five, but the increase in Canadians interested in joining directly, along with the increasing desire of the British to expand the RAF, led to a request to raise the quota to 120. This was perceived, however, as a challenge to Canadian sovereignty, with potentially too many Canadians serving in the RAF.

In an attempt to address the concerns of sovereignty, the Visiting Forces Act (VFA) was introduced in the early 1930s. Having been passed under Bennett's Conservative government, the Act was consistent with King's protective view of Canadian sovereignty; whenever possible, Canadians serving abroad should serve in distinctly Canadian units and formations, under Canadian commanders.[17] This would serve as a basic principle for any negotiations. Despite these attempts to limit Canadian service in the RAF, however, by the time war did break out, there were more Canadian pilots serving in the RAF than in the RCAF, which had 235 pilots by August 1939.[18]

As British requirements increased, the RAF looked outward, to the Commonwealth, and began discussions about both recruiting and training in the Dominions. The British government concluded that Canada was the preferred location for the training of air and ground crews, because it was far enough away from the zone of conflict for safety but not so far as to present a major obstacle. A British mission was sent to Canada in May 1938 to examine aircraft manufacturing capacity; it was also tasked to discuss training.[19] King made it clear that any training and training facilities would be under the control of the Canadian government — this would form another basic principle for upcoming negotiations.

After Britain had declared war, but before Canada's own declaration, the British government informed the Canadians that they doubted whether the RAF would be able to meet its own manpower requirements and proposed that Canada contribute by training pilots, observers, and air gunners for service in the RAF. King bristled at the proposal, a response that surprised many of the British military leaders and others within the British government, who had not grasped the evolving attitudes in the Dominions, nor appreciated their internal politics, nor the transforming significance of the 1931 Statute of Westminster. The situation was an echo of what had occurred when that British mission examining aircraft production arrived in Canada a year and a half earlier. Then Tweedsmuir had noted that officials in Britain "do not seem to understand the real delicacy of the position of the self-governing Dominions, especially of Canada."[20]

In London informal discussions about a Commonwealth-wide air training plan took place between Canada's and Australia's high commissioners, Vincent Massey and Stanley Bruce respectively, and British Air Ministry officials. A lack of documentation, however, prevents knowing the details of the process, as F.J. Hatch noted in his comprehensive history of the British Commonwealth Air Training Plan (BCATP).[21] It is known, however, that "basic principles" were developed, and on September 26 a proposal was communicated to the Dominions. The aspect that attracted

King to the idea was that it would allow him to emphasize the important role Canada could play without necessarily requiring a large army being sent overseas, something that would limit the possibility of the divisive issue of conscription arising. The stage was now set for negotiations. Three weeks after sending the proposal, the British delegation arrived in Ottawa, followed by the Australians and New Zealanders at the beginning of November.

As the delegations arrived, the governor general's other activities carried on unabated. On November 2, wearing a khaki service uniform, he observed an air raid drill and defensive preparations at the RCAF repair depot at Ottawa, inspected a guard of honour, and toured the machine shops. But the arrival of the delegations and the start of formal negotiations revealed another role for Tweedsmuir. As he learned of the differences in negotiating positions that quickly manifested themselves, he felt compelled to engage himself in "smoothing over" differences, always behind the scenes, of course. The prime minister, aware of his contacts and the leverage provided by his official position, would also call upon him to help unblock negotiations.[22]

Neither the British mission nor the Canadian Cabinet "quite under-stands the other's point of view," the governor general observed.[23] Ever aware of King's sensitivities over sovereignty, Tweedsmuir cautioned Chamberlain at the very beginning of the negotiations that the British mis-sions "must be tactful in handling our sensitive government."[24] Tweedsmuir lauded the abilities of one of the British delegates in particular, Sir Gerald Campbell, who was contributing to a mutual understanding among the teams of negotiators and who would, in fact, succeed Sir Francis Floud, the British high commissioner to Canada, the following year.

Early in the negotiations, discussions between the British and Canadians became quite rancorous. On the last day of October, fol-lowing one particular incident between Lord Riverdale, head of the British mission, and the small group of Cabinet ministers led by King, Tweedsmuir felt compelled to intervene. Hoping to avoid additional misunderstandings as a result of the incident, Tweedsmuir wrote directly to Chamberlain, noting diplomatically that "his friend Lord Riverdale" was "not perhaps very much of a diplomatist."[25] He took great pains to describe the incident to Chamberlain, interpreting why certain things were said and placing them in context.

During initial discussions, Riverdale had referred to the aircraft from England (which would be sent over for the training plan) as "being a free gift to Canada."[26] The comment would have been made in the context of discussions about the financing of the plan, a major concern to the Canadians and an issue that Tweedsmuir had pointed out to Chamberlain as being a significant one. The British proposed, after their in-kind contribution of aircraft, that Canada pay half the estimated costs, amounting to about $375 million, an amount King and his colleagues found excessive.[27] The Canadians also expressed emphatically that Britain's in-kind contribution of aircraft and parts, valued at $140 million, was too small. Canada could not borrow funds in the United States, where financing would have been cheaper, and so, instead, negotiated on the basis of making Britain buy more Canadian wheat and of limiting credits to Britain for buying war-related material. It was in this context that King took exception to Riverdale's expression. "Free gift," he retorted, "but this is not Canada's war." King also objected strenuously to the "sort of taken-for-granted attitude" of the British and their proposal regarding Canada's role.[28]

The result of this incident was that Riverdale viewed King as being extremely difficult. Tweedsmuir explained to Chamberlain apologetically, and in what seems a bit of a forced manner, that what King really meant was that it was not Canada's own war but rather "a co-operative war of the whole Empire, and that it was impossible to talk of free gifts from one part to another."[29] He reassured Chamberlain that "no one could be more in earnest than [the Canadian prime minister] is." Tweedsmuir then stated explicitly that he was telling Chamberlain about this incident "in case it reaches you in a perverted form." For his part King believed that the reasonable position he and his Cabinet colleagues had set out to the British delegation may have avoided "a possible dismemberment of the Empire" as a result of the British "railroading" attitude.[30] These negotiations, Tweedsmuir wrote, make "severe demands upon patience!"[31]

By the end of November, with the negotiations all but concluded, the missions began to pack up. King was preparing to officially announce the plan over the radio on December 11. Before finalizing things, however, he was waiting for an answer to the letter Defence Minister Norman Rogers had sent to the British regarding how Canadian units would be identified and commanded, once Canadian servicemen had completed their training. The Canadians believed these questions had been settled several weeks before, but a difference of opinion had surfaced with the British Air Ministry, represented in the Ottawa negotiations by Air Chief Marshall Brooke-Popham. To complicate the issue further, the question of financing resurfaced.[32] Sir Gerald Campbell requested a meeting with King, who both refused to meet with him and to sign the agreement until he had an answer from the British to Rogers's letter.[33] Subsequent discussions took place, raising what was perceived as a "new question" of estimating Canada's financial costs, based on British ground crews servicing Canadian aircraft. King reflected privately on the "rather mean attitude [of the British] in the face of the enormous outlay" already made by Canada.[34]

By December 16, and with no word from Lord Riverdale, King "made up [his] mind this time that [he] must use every possible means of getting the agreement signed before morning."[35] He was concerned that if this didn't happen now, it would be overshadowed by an announcement about the arrival of Canadian troops in Britain. He wanted to shift the public's focus from that event to the air training plan — King's attraction to the air training plan was that he had seen it as a way of avoiding the need for a large army and thus the conscription issue. He also believed the agreement would have a positive impact on morale and send a strong message of Empire unity to the enemy. In his desperation he prevailed upon Tweedsmuir, brushing aside any consideration that this involved the governor general in a political sphere, knowing he could be a conduit to the British prime minister. He wanted to "get the whole situation placed before him as the representative of His Majesty, and as one who could give Chamberlain the true story," and thought the governor general "might be able to assist in bringing the others together."[36] King finally contacted Riverdale around nine o'clock that evening. He rejected as too late Riverdale's offer to see him the following morning. They agreed to meet at King's office. Riverdale then went off in search of Sir Gerald Campbell and King went off to Rideau Hall, where he found Tweedsmuir in bed, "propped on his pillows looking pretty frail."[37]

At Rideau Hall King described Air Chief Marshall Brooke-Popham's views, which seemed to contribute to the delays. According to King the governor general "on every point was 100 [percent] with me." Tweedsmuir apparently told the prime minister that this was "a matter of high policy," and that King should "pursue it on that line" and "make [Riverdale] sign at once."[38] Tweedsmuir said he would speak with him in the morning. Again, though, and notwithstanding how frail the governor general looked, King insisted that it be done now. Shuldham Redfern, Tweedsmuir's secretary, was tasked to contact Brooke-Popham and have him come to Rideau Hall.

Returning to his office, King was then joined by Lord Riverdale, whom he informed that they must "settle the matter themselves." After haggling over deleting a definite article, a point that had apparently been brought to Riverdale's attention by Brooke-Popham, and after some other minor consultations, they finally came to an agreement. In the end King achieved his objective, which was consistent with the principle of the Visiting Forces Act. Clause 15 of the agreement stated explicitly that "Canadian pupils when passing out from the training scheme will be incorporated in or organized as units of the Royal Canadian Air Force in the field."[39]

Prior to signing, however, Riverdale wanted to wait for Brooke-Popham, who had arrived from Rideau Hall just before midnight and who then had a brief word with Riverdale. Brooke-Popham was apparently satisfied with the changes. When they re-entered his office, King observed that he "never saw a man look more deflated in a way than Sir Robert Brooke-Popham did. His face was red and his manner very crushed. I think having the GG speak to him was something he had never anticipated, and ... would realize the significance of the word of a Governor in a self-governing Dominion."[40] King had used his ultimate resource to help move negotiations in his favour. He had also considered at one point having Tweedsmuir speak with Sir Gerald Campbell as well.[41]

As the clock struck midnight, King's principal secretary, Arnold Heeney, followed by Riverdale and Brooke-Popham, wished the prime minister a happy sixty-fifth birthday. The document was signed and dated December 17, which lent it added significance for the numerologically minded Mackenzie King. The prime minister went on radio that Sunday evening to announce the details of the plan, reporting that the negotiations "had proceeded in complete harmony," while Lord Riverdale, for his part, emphasized the "wonderful co-operation from your government."[42] King added that the "United Kingdom government has informed us that … the air training scheme would provide for more effective assistance towards ultimate victory than any other form of military co-operation which Canada can give."[43] The underlying message was that there was no requirement for a large army, a message that allowed the government to avoid the divisive issue of conscription, at least for now.

On Christmas Eve day, Tweedsmuir received a letter from King acknowledging his contribution to the negotiations. It was accompanied with a gift of an engraved inkwell shaped like a book. King thanked him "warmly for the help … in my effort to get the Air Training agreement signed in time to permit of some of its real advantages to the [A]llies.… What a mischief there would have been had there been another moment's delay!"[44] At the end of it all, Chamberlain confided to Tweedsmuir that King was "a bit difficult at times."[45]

With the agreement completed, Tweedsmuir once more wrote to Chamberlain, ostensibly offering "one line of greeting at the close of this year."[46] More importantly, however, his note gave him an opportunity to place the experience of the past months in context and reinforce earlier advice. He asked the British prime minister not to be impatient with the Canadian government "if now and then they seem a little pedantic."[47] Returning to a central theme of his time in Canada, Tweedsmuir explained that Canadian ministers "have the duty of interpreting for the first time many points in the new status of the Dominion." King George VI had watched developments of this "great Imperial project" with interest, both for its impact on the war effort and on Empire co-operation, expressing satisfaction when agreement was reached.[48]

Tweedsmuir derived considerable satisfaction from his contribution to the ultimate success of the negotiations and more generally to the state of morale in the country. He claimed privately to his sister that while much of Canada's war preparedness was attributable to King, who was "in tremendous form just now — better and younger than I have ever seen him," this state of affairs was due "a good deal to me" as well.[49] What is interesting here is to see finally revealed how this generally reserved and proper individual thought inwardly of his own contribution. The correspondence with his sister was an outlet for expressing those things he felt but would never say otherwise, certainly not publicly. He was genuinely proud of the country and of the role he was playing.

Waging war required materials, not just those related to aircraft. To make purchases in North America, British orders would go through "a non-partisan War Supply Board" set up by the Canadian government, and headed by fifty-seven-year-old Windsor native Wallace Campbell, president of Ford Canada, to ward off scandals of the type that led to the resignation of Defence Minister Ian Mackenzie.[50] Given that significant activity was expected in the United States once the amended Neutrality Act was passed, a British purchasing office located in New York was planned.

In close co-operation with the British, the Canadian government named an "eminent Montreal industrialist" as director general of the British Purchasing Commission in the United States to supervise purchases in the United States. Forty-nine-year-old Arthur Purvis had been president of Canadian Industries Limited (CIL) since 1924. He was selected not only for his business skills —Tweedsmuir described him in Buchanesque superlatives as "the most respected and … the ablest business man in Canada" — but also because he "knows the American scene intimately."[51] Both Purvis and Wallace Campbell would also become members of the British Supply Board, helping to ensure coordination.

Tweedsmuir focused his attention on the appointment of Purvis for a very specific reason. While the consensus seemed to be very positive regarding the appointment, he must have had some sense, perhaps from conversations with Purvis himself, that the respected Canadian businessman was not completely enamoured of the King government. He wrote to Chamberlain that Purvis had not been treated well, describing how he had chaired the National Employment Commission for a year and a half only to have his report "pigeon-holed and [to make matters worse, he was] scarcely thanked."[52] Additionally, accepting the position would entail a considerable sacrifice of time and money. It was in this context that Tweedsmuir requested Chamberlain's help, suggesting that a letter from the British prime minister would "greatly encourage" Purvis. Chamberlain agreed and sent a letter three days after Purvis's appointment was ratified by the British government on November 7.

The first orders placed by the British Supply Board were for aircraft, anti-submarine boats, gun barrels, and ammunition, though no further details were obviously reported publicly.[53] Purvis was "a tower of strength," Tweedsmuir heard, though he was concerned for Purvis's health, noting "he has no great margin of strength."[54] Purvis remained in the position in New York until his death in August 1941 in a plane crash on his way to Newfoundland to join the talks led by Churchill and Roosevelt.[55]

Nothing, however, could be purchased from the United States until the Neutrality Act was dealt with. When Congress finally approved amendments on November 3, purchases were on the basis of "cash and carry," so nicknamed because although armaments, equipment, and war-related supplies could now be sold to belligerents, it was with the condition that the buyers would have to pay immediately for the material as well as transport them on their own ships, the use of American ships being forbidden by law. American isolationists described the Act as the "road to war," a sentiment not disproved by the efforts of the U.S. government, which was involved at the time in the largest U.S. army recruiting effort in peacetime.[56] Canadian newspapers heralded the news with reports of the "tremendous arsenal now available" to the Allies, noting the British Purchasing Commission was ready to buy planes, 1,500 of which were for the training of Commonwealth pilots in Canada, and other war materials.[57]

The passage of the U.S. Neutrality Act sparked at least one demonstration of personal fervour. Just five days later, an old South African acquaintance of Tweedsmuir, another fellow border Scot, presented him with a cheque for $250,000 for war purchases![58]

When the issue of British payments for purchases became urgent, one of the people Tweedsmuir lined up for Purvis to contact was Duncan M. Spencer.[59] Tweedsmuir wrote to Spencer to say that Purvis hoped "to get a great deal of assistance from him" on the issue of British payments. Having facilitated this introduction, Tweedsmuir had another matter to raise with Spencer, which he also raised at the same time with Graham Towers, governor of the Bank of Canada, attaching a two-page document.[60]

Tweedsmuir had recently received news from an old friend, Moritz Bonn, that some senior decision-makers in the United States, including, apparently, members of the Federal Reserve Board, were suggesting their country should no longer purchase gold. Such a move by the United States could have had serious negative consequences for the Empire's ability to finance its war effort. With Canada and South Africa being major producers and sellers of the precious metal, the implications could indeed have been serious. The rumoured reasons for such consideration were that South Africa and Canada were artificially stimulating production, "to make the U.S.A. hold the baby," implying that the United States might be seen by isolationists as indirectly financing the war. Given Tweedsmuir would have considered his source as reliable, he forwarded it to those he believed should know such information, could confirm it through their own channels, and, if appropriate, act on it.[61]

The Tweedsmuirs' two sons who were in Canada at the time, the oldest and youngest, Johnnie and Alastair, both enlisted in the Canadian army. It is indicative of the family's attachment to Canada, and, especially, of Tweedsmuir himself, that his sons did not return to Britain to enlist. It also reflected Tweedsmuir's holistic view of the Commonwealth. In November Alastair was at Camp Borden to finish his training, which involved learning to drive a tank and doing his mechanical training.[62] Johnnie was preparing for qualifying exams on November 27 in ciphers, and was expected to ship out with the 1st Canadian Infantry Division. It is a testimony to the father's character, if there were need to show it, that he had "been very stiff about there being no kind of privilege given to the boys," a significant point, given the possibility of them being sent overseas. His positive and thankful attitude also shows through as he wrote to his sister that he considered it a "wonderful privilege to have had both boys with [them] for so long."[63] As for many parents, it was an anxious time. Johnnie was in the 1st Canadian Infantry Division, the first Canadians to arrive in England, in December 1940.[64] "Pray heaven," Johnnie's father wrote to a close friend, "he comes through the war safely, for he might be a great citizen."[65]

Shortly after the Canadian troops arrived in England, the War Office caught wind of rumours it considered as "anti-British propaganda" circulating among troops in training, but especially among the Canadians. Sensitive about dealing with a Dominion government wary of protecting its sovereignty, the War Office needed to consult someone they had confidence in and who had knowledge of that Dominion. In this case the director of public relations in the War Office, Major-General Ian Beith, went "to the fountain for advice."[66]

The sixty-three-year-old major-general, also known as John Hay Beith, was a well-known novelist and dramatist, writing under the pseudonym of Ian Hay. During the First World War, he had worked in John Buchan's Department of Information. He knew his letter to Lord Tweedsmuir, marked "personal" to sidestep the governor general's official position, would elicit a response. Beith noted he was "constantly receiving letters from the U.S.A. and Canada" asking what more could be done to counter German propaganda in those countries.[67] While this was really a matter for the Ministry of Information, Beith politely speculated that he received these letters instead because there was awareness of his involvement in this area in the last war. What he didn't state, however, was that it may also have been because of the perceived ineffectiveness of the Ministry of Information.

Beith broached the issue of how they could "take a more rigorous line" against the anti-British propaganda. Specifically, he wrote, "we have been asked not to send [to the United States] speakers and writers *ad hoc*," echoing advice Tweedsmuir had provided to the information minister in early September. Beith then gave details of the current rumours, which were based on a confidential letter received from a young captain of the Black Watch. This was the famous regiment the governor general had addressed two months earlier in Montreal, on the occasion of the regiment's two hundredth anniversary.[68]

"[R]ather disturbing reports" were circulating that the Royal Navy was losing ships "left and right," that the RAF was inadequate and their planes too slow, that rationing of just about everything was being forced on the civilian population, and, finally, that high-ranking British officials were telling the Americans not to "put too much money on the Allies" (meaning the British and the French). All or some of it may have been planted or encouraged by the Nazis, but the cynicism and negativism inherent in human nature could also have played a role. Beith set out possible responses, but asked whether sending out a "visitor" to address these issues was advisable, given their instructions not to send speakers to the United States.

As with his advice to Chamberlain and Macmillan in September, Tweedsmuir remained sensitive to offering counsel from his position. He wrote to Beith on January 9 that he was "shy of putting in my oar unless I am sure that it will be welcomed."[69] He was, however, more than willing to reply. He repeated his advice about dealing with the United States, specifically there should be no propaganda but only "authentic news." Regarding the concerns of the Black Watch officer, Tweedsmuir proposed that the experience must be "exceptional," and that he had not heard of any anti-British propaganda among the troops in training. It is questionable, of course, how much of this type of information would have made its way to the governor general, though he might have heard more through his two sons. There had, however, been one incident of which Tweedsmuir was aware, which he recounted to Beith. It involved "a foolish Canadian Air Force officer" who misunderstood what he saw of the RAF and had spread "mischievous reports." By the tone of Tweedsmuir's rejoinder to that incident — "but that won't happen again" — it was obvious that the matter had been dealt with quickly and decisively.

Tweedsmuir informed Beith that "Canadian feeling is perfectly sound," especially after the election defeat in Quebec in October of Maurice Duplessis.[70] Tweedsmuir was still concerned, however, about the potential for the "phony war" taking the edge off the Canadian spirit, which, he noted, "wants encouragement and nursing."[71] One example he gave for the resurfacing concern was that the army was not recruiting in large numbers and, as a result, there was "discontent among the younger people, who find no way of showing their ardour."[72] The only hopeful prospect at the moment, he felt, was the air training plan as it "gets into its stride."

As for the anti-British propaganda, one thing that Tweedsmuir felt might help was if "the right kind of people" were sent out from Britain to speak across the country, to catch the public's attention, help them to take the war more seriously, and help counter negative rumours about the abilities of the Allies. The need was for someone who could speak well and who could discuss issues with authority, from first-hand information, to the extent that it could be made public. Tweedsmuir suggested, as an example, the recounting of the successful battle against the German warship *Graf Spee* that Churchill had given in a radio broadcast on December 18. Tweedsmuir then gave specific suggestions to Beith, recommending three types of men from Britain to speak in Canada and giving some suggestions for each.[73]

The week after Tweedsmuir sent his letter off to Beith, King was at Rideau Hall, where Tweedsmuir mentioned he had received a letter from the literary figure at the War Office. Tweedsmuir seemed to put a particular interpretation on Beith's request, likely in case King reacted negatively to the suggestion of having lecturers from England to make its war effort better known in Canada.

King replied immediately that such an idea "would be a great mistake."[74] Ever watchful of Canadian sovereignty, King said, "it would be construed as an implication that Canada was not doing enough," and stated that General Crerar had told him Anthony Eden might come to Canada. For King this would have "the appearance of colonialism" and his Cabinet "were quite resentful and strong in their language in opposition." He added, "in this war, our pride is in our voluntary effort." Tweedsmuir apparently retorted defensively that he hadn't said Eden should come out, though King held in his memory that Buchan had "some time ago said … he hoped [Eden] would come."

The governor general changed the topic to compliment King on his "perfect health," having noted to friends how the prime minister seemed to have renewed energy in dealing with the war. The health reference somehow reminded King that Buchan had been a cause of earlier "serious disappointment and depression," which he felt as a result of his surprise at Buchan's attitude when he first arrived. Later that same day, King committed to his diary a brief balance sheet, noting that criticisms of Buchan's "little human weaknesses" were perhaps offset by his "soundness in the last resort." Even though Tweedsmuir understood the implications of the Statute of Westminster, perhaps better than anyone, he had a challenge at times in understanding the prime minister's motivations and moods, and thus anticipating his views.

The governor general remained concerned about the level of public support, but "precisely the kind of thing needed" came early in the new year from a surprising quarter.[75] On January 9, British prime minister Chamberlain spoke to the lord mayor of London's luncheon.[76] It was broadcast to the Commonwealth, but just as importantly, it was heard in the United States. Chamberlain described the continuous buildup of Germany's destructive power and warned against relaxing under the strain of a long vigil, while waiting for Hitler's war machine to be suddenly unloosed, in a war that was so far "in a form which is unfamiliar." To his credit Chamberlain tacitly acknowledged the error of his former policy of appeasement. He reached out to the United States, referring to Roosevelt's recent message to the pope that evil could only be overcome by the "friendly association" of the "seekers of light and the seekers of peace everywhere." Chamberlain concluded that "we … can await the future with unshaken confidence in the strength of our arms and in the righteousness of our cause."

The following day Tweedsmuir wrote to Chamberlain to compliment him on the speech, noting that it was just what was needed.[77] Even Mackenzie King, whom Chamberlain thought was "inclined to be persnickity and critical, call[ed] it the greatest utterance since the war began."[78] The speech had most, if not all, the main themes that Tweedsmuir supported. Chamberlain appreciated the accolades, including Tweedsmuir's letter, which not only was personally complimentary but also provided encouraging, first-hand news of the governor general's recent visit to Halifax. It must have helped salve the British prime minister's irritated sentiments about "the vile press" at home and the "more and more ill-tempered and unreasonable" House of Commons which depressed him.[79]

The public's demand for more information about Canada's war effort had been growing through the autumn and into the new year. The Cabinet agreed that something more should be done than was then being done through the Sub-Committee on Public Information, which had been established in September under Labour Minister Norman McLarty. It focused on how and what volume of information should be communicated to Canadians. At the beginning of December, the government announced the establishment of a Public Information Bureau, with a mandate to coordinate the activities of radio and film. Again the prime minister chose an individual from outside the public service to head an agency created for the war effort.

Walter S. Thompson was appointed director of public information, having been director of public relations for Canadian National Railways. Tweedsmuir judged him "a man of first-class ability," praising his "great energy and imagination" and predicting he would do "excellent work."[80] Rather than just issuing news releases to the press (which King hoped would act as a government counterweight to a press that he saw as too powerful), Thompson believed it was necessary to find out what the press wanted and then tell them how to get it.[81] King was equally laudatory of Thompson's abilities, perhaps due to the fact that Thompson's outlook coincided with King's, as their conversations had revealed. King could now anticipate proper publicity for the departure and arrival in England of the first Canadian troops.[82] King's conscience led him to include guidance to Thompson that "the government was not seeking to mislead anyone."[83] Unfortunately, illness caused Thompson to resign the following month, but the work he had initiated was now well underway, involving two other talented individuals, one from radio and the other from film: Leonard Brockington and John Grierson.

Through the autumn Brockington had tried, unsuccessfully, to assist the rather "wooden" prime minister with his rhetorical skills and his radio broadcasts.[84] King had apparently preferred Brockington to head up the Bureau but Brockington's past difficulties with the Associated Press precluded his appointment in that role. The Bureau's task would be to "collect, coordinate and disseminate to the public, information concerning all phases of the Canadian war effort," a role that would have entailed dealing with the Associated Press, as well as with other news agencies. After a meeting with the prime minister in December, Brockington was appointed as a counsellor to the War Committee of Cabinet, to be a "recorder of the war effort," and helped King prepare material for Parliament and the public.[85] John Grierson, a British government film producer, who had studied and reported on film production in Canada in 1938, was appointed the first commissioner (a paid employee) of the National Film Board, which had been legislated into existence just six months earlier.[86]

On New Year's Day, Tweedsmuir wrote to Lord Halifax to say that "we have got the beginnings of [an information] service," reflecting the initial work of Thompson, Brockington, and others. He added that he had been pressing King regarding the need for the "right kind of propaganda" in Canada.[87] King, however, understood the word differently. He acknowledged the need to provide the public more information, but he was intent on not having propaganda, "as that term is understood," because he was inclined to believe that the "lie of propaganda perhaps more than anything else accounts for the condition of the world today."[88] It was a principal difference of approach and understanding of the strategic importance of propagating information. Tweedsmuir's approach, as we have already read, was to stick as close as possible to the truth, to let the facts speak for themselves, to not gloss over failures, and to avoid that "passion for babyish secrecy." One objective of the information service was to maintain morale by communicating a sense of purpose, direction, and assurance, as Tweedsmuir had argued in his first letter to Chamberlain.[89]

The public had a huge appetite for information, and there was a need for reassurance. This was all-important in the information war and, from

November onwards, two elements for reassurance were aired. War aims as well as the shape of the eventual peace were being discussed publicly, reflecting work that was reported to be going on by "experts," as well as a department set up within the British Foreign Office "to pave the way for peace."[90] The renowned economist John Maynard Keynes outlined a plan in the *Times* of London.[91] Even the United States, though not a belligerent and wanting to maintain that status, viewed itself as a potential mediator and was thus looking at the future peace, which might include a reformed League of Nations and a reconstructed international monetary system.[92]

The end of the year was a time for reflection for the resident of Rideau Hall. To the former British prime minister Stanley Baldwin, Tweedsmuir wrote: "There has never been a clearer issue, for it is really between the forces of light and darkness, but the darkness is puzzling with so many twilight shades."[93] He was, though, by nature, always an optimist. The "complete unity" of Canada was a point for optimism for him, but his personal life contained apprehension. On New Year's Day, he wrote to his sister: "[H]eaven knows what 1940 may bring forth. I hope it means victory for the nation, and safety for our scattered family."[94]

On the evening of New Year's Day, 1940, the viceregal couple left by train for Halifax, the only part of Canada in the war zone, "solely in the interest of war service activities."[95] In the wartime port city, which the governor general described as one of the main strategic points in the Empire, dressed in his military uniform, he paid a relatively low-key visit to various facilities, including the Naval Dockyard, Admiralty House, and ships of the Canadian, British, and French navies, and went out to sea briefly in a destroyer. He also toured the RCAF base while Lady Tweedsmuir met with wives of RCAF officers. The two of them then visited a hospital. He also gave a short speech to a conference of merchant marine captains who were to be part of a convoy about to sail. He was so impressed by these skippers that he got "quite carried away."[96] "You never saw such magnificent fellows," he wrote, "engaged in one of the riskiest jobs on earth, and perfectly placid about it!"[97] Enthusiastically, he added that looking at "those old chaps I felt that nothing on earth could defeat the British Empire."

They returned to Ottawa on January 8. The Halifax visit had lifted Tweedsmuir's spirits and reinforced his pride in Britain and the Empire, but especially in Canada, which is, he wrote, "a magnificent answer to the German sneers at the Empire, and the doubts of some of our own people."[98] He urged the prime minister to visit Halifax, where he would find "real inspiration."[99] At a personal level, he felt the trip had been good for his health, though writing to his sister about his improved condition, he cautioned, "low be it spoken."[100]

The week following his return to Ottawa from Halifax, Tweedsmuir received a detailed memorandum from Grenville Clark in New York City, again drawing his attention to the shape of the post-war world. Clark was the fifty-seven-year-old founding partner of a large New York City law firm[101] and one of the eleven Americans Tweedsmuir had proposed to Information Minister Macmillan to keep a "watching brief" for Britain. Clark devoted much of his time to public affairs and world peace, though he was far from an "ivory tower" idealist since he had been an advocate of conscription in the First World War and would advocate it again during the Second World War.[102] The memo outlined in some detail Clark's thoughts about the post-war period, thoughts which evolved over the next two decades into a book entitled *World Peace Through World Law*.[103]

It is clear from the correspondence that the two men had spoken previously about this subject, possibly when Tweedsmuir was in New York in October. In early January 1940, Tweedsmuir "safely received [Clark's] memorandum and … read it with profound interest."[104]

This theme of how Europe and other countries in the world could diminish the possibility of future conflict was on the minds of many people.[105] As Tweedsmuir's thinking evolved, he drew on the models he knew best, Britain and the Commonwealth on the one hand, and the United States on the other. At the end of October, he had suggested to Information Minister Macmillan that if the "reconstitution of the world [were] on some kind of federal basis it would be very acceptable to America who regards herself as the principal expert on federalism."[106] It was clear that Tweedsmuir was counting on the formerly rebellious

British offspring to play an important role in the future of the world: "I am not particularly anxious that America should join in the war, but she must help us with the peace."[107] It was not quite two years later that Prime Minister Churchill and President Roosevelt — the United States still not in the war — met in Newfoundland to discuss what became known as the Atlantic Charter, involving "their respective war aims ... and to outline a post[-]war international system [and the] 'common principles' that the United States and Great Britain would be committed to supporting in the post[-]war world."[108]

The federalism Tweedsmuir envisaged would be on a limited, not a world, scale. The following month, he expressed his ideas to the Palace, drawing some skepticism. The king's private secretary, Sir Alexander Hardinge, interpreted these ideas as indicating that Tweedsmuir was "indeed a great idealist!"[109] Skeptical that surrendering national sovereignty to advance a form of federation, even if it was the "right solution for Europe," Hardinge didn't believe it would happen in their lifetime.[110] Tweedsmuir replied that what he foresaw were limited federations, necessary "in certain parts of Europe, particularly the Danube basin," to prevent conflict among the countries and to contain those who might otherwise become too powerful. He also suggested that another grouping could be composed of those who followed the reign of law, for example a federation of the Western democracies, a suggestion he had made to Chamberlain earlier.[111] That vision would surely have taken on a stronger conviction as time went on, but he could not foresee Germany being integrated into such a grouping. How, he speculated, could a nation that had shown such "a fundamental brutality" be included in peace arrangements? The Germans were, he wrote in an unforgiving mood, "past praying for."[112] His emotions of the moment were betraying his powers of reasoning.

By the time Grenville Clark's memo arrived in January, Tweedsmuir had given considerable thought to the subject. He agreed with Clark's main principles, though, he added, "some of the details might be open to argument."[113] What Grenville Clark proposed was an international federation with an original, limited membership, but which might be added to subsequently. This federation would have a military force, maintained by a congress, a proposal that was clearly an attempt to correct the past deficiency of the militarily impotent League of Nations that tried, and failed, to sanction Italy over its invasion of Abyssinia.

In his reply Tweedsmuir described for Clark his idea for two kinds of federation, the smaller regional ones, such as in the Danube basin, and a larger one, which was more toward the scale of Clark's proposal. Tweedsmuir agreed with particular points about a larger federation, enumerating and qualifying certain aspects: 1) initially, there could not be too much dilution of sovereignty, to avoid "any cataclysmic changes"; 2) "the mechanism must be simple and easily understood"; 3) the member countries must have the same political base; and, finally, 4) "America must take a leading part."[114] It was this last point that was becoming ever more critical in Tweedsmuir's thinking. "Without [America]," he cautioned, "nothing can be done." He recognized that Britain's leading role in the world as the protector and disseminator of institutions that guaranteed freedom and democracy was passing to Britain's republican offspring.[115]

Tweedsmuir went into greater detail, engaging Clark about his specific approach, particularly regarding the structure and how a new organization could enforce sanctions against a rogue nation. He admitted to Clark that his ideas were at this point all "very crudely" expressed, but believed that he might find time later to "work out the matter in more detail." He concluded by congratulating Clark on his "valuable piece of work" and requested a few more copies that he could send "to various people at home whose minds are now working upon this question." For Clark this was "badly needed encouragement," and was much appreciated, all the more so because Clark was also an admirer of John Buchan and an avid reader of his novels.[116]

The "various people" Tweedsmuir intended to send Clark's memo to included his old professor of classics, Gilbert Murray, Viscount Robert Cecil of Chelwood,[117] as well as Lord Halifax. All three were active in discussing the post-war order: Cecil had been a representative at the Paris Peace Conference in 1919 and had received the Nobel Peace Prize in 1937,[118] while Halifax had been discussing post-war reconstruction and economic federation in central and eastern Europe.[119]

In the same way that he was carefully selecting those to whom he would send the document, Tweedsmuir cautioned Clark not to distribute it too widely at this point. He complimented Clark on having wisely chosen to send it to just a few individuals, including Justice Evatt who, Tweedsmuir added, "understands the *arcana imperii* of the British Empire as well as anybody living."[120] Clark had already sent copies to the Carnegie Endowment for International Peace, an organization established in 1910 by industrialist Andrew Carnegie to "hasten the abolition of international war."[121] The Endowment apparently proposed to distribute Clark's paper more widely, an action Tweedsmuir advised against because he thought, at that point, "a false impression might be created," and possibly feared that its distribution could ultimately be counterproductive to the discussion by reinforcing the isolationist current in America.[122]

Tweedsmuir wrote to Robert Cecil on January 24 explaining how he was encouraged that "the wiser kind of American should be applying his mind to this question now."[123] Tweedsmuir was sure that Grenville Clark's memo would strike a chord with Cecil, given it was so similar in motive and objectives to Cecil's 1916 memo. Tweedsmuir asked both Murray and Cecil to provide him their criticisms, which he would pass on to Clark.

It is fitting that some of the last, major activities that Tweedsmuir was involved in had their sights on the future. He regretted that war had broken out again, but accepted that errors had been made at the end of the last war. He sorrowed still from losses in that Great War and feared for his own family, particularly for his sons who would be fighting. Nonetheless, his optimism, intellect, and energy remained focused. He could not know how the war would unfold, but there is no doubt he was confident in the ultimate outcome, victory of the democracies, and that the United States would play the major leadership role in the post-war order.

PART IV

"Never Be Off the Road"

Reaching Out to Canadians

CHAPTER 12

First Journeys

When John and Susan Buchan travelled to Canada in 1924, it was the same year that he published a memoir of Lord Minto, the man who served as governor general of Canada from 1898 to 1904. The memoir exposed him in a focused way and caused him to reflect on the role of a governor general. The visit to Canada, at least central Canada, exposed him in a more experiential, if limited, way to the country. It was enough, however, to make him want to see and learn more.[1]

When he was approached about being governor general, the possibilities must have been tantalizing. As a country known for its wilderness, it would also naturally attract an outdoorsman and an incurable fisherman like Buchan. Likewise, he had "always had a passion for travel and exploration,"[2] and he knew that the position would allow him to indulge those passions, since the vast geographic expanse of Canada commands a governor general to travel. In his memoir of Minto, Buchan had listed among what he termed the "*imponderabilia* of governorship," the fact that a governor general must visit every corner of the country and that he should be accessible so he can get to know the people and they him.[3] This would also enhance the visibility and role of the sovereign's representative and could in the process help promote loyalty to the Crown and strengthen the bonds within the post–Statute of Westminster Empire.

His arrival was, as described earlier, widely anticipated; it was a double arrival — of governor general and best-selling author. But perhaps no other group looked forward to his coming with more interest than did the country's many Scots immigrants, some of whom had known either John Buchan or his family in Scotland. Their presence in Canada helped make an instant connection and soften protocol. One, Alex Fraser, had been a school friend but took up farming on the Alberta-Saskatchewan border. He wrote to congratulate Buchan after his arrival.[4] Another was William R. Jeffrey, who had grown up in Haswellsykes. Though he was younger than Buchan, he and his older brothers had played with the Buchan children at nearby Peebles in the summers. From Montreal, Jeffrey wrote to congratulate Buchan on his appointment and received a reply with a promise to contact him in Canada.[5] The governor general was true to his word and renewed these old friendships.[6]

Buchan had a natural curiosity and delighted in meeting people from all walks of life and learning from them; his interest was sincere and profound,[7] and he eagerly looked forward to meeting as many different Canadians, from as many different regions and walks of life, as he could. But there was a concern that translated into another objective and that his travel could help achieve.

As dictators increased in number around the world, Buchan believed the basic principles of liberty, law, and democratic government needed to be refreshed and strengthened, to discourage people from becoming attracted to false prophets, that is to dictators and their violent ideologies. His travels would allow him to speak to these and related themes. It was with these initial objectives in mind that Lord Tweedsmuir settled into the nation's capital in early November 1935.

The Tweedsmuirs spent almost all of their first three weeks settling into Government House, the governor general's residence, more popularly referred to as Rideau Hall. The new governor's first travels had been predetermined and were, not surprisingly, to Canada's two largest cities. They also implicated two of Tweedsmuir's constant interests, education and youth. Both were subjects he involved himself in with a passion, since he believed the shape of the future depended on the quality of both. The principal universities in both Montreal and Toronto — McGill University in Montreal and the University of Toronto — had already offered to bestow honorary degrees on the new governor general.

On Saturday morning, November 23, John and Susan Tweedsmuir boarded their train for the short trip to Montreal, arriving at Windsor Station at 10:30 the same morning. The events on arrival and during the day were indicative of what would be repeated hundreds of times, with variations, of course, over the next four-plus years in Canadian communities of all sizes, from major cities to small villages.

The viceregal couple were met by the then two-time mayor, Camillien Houde, and other leading citizens.[8] After inspecting a guard of honour of the famous Black Watch regiment, the mayor and governor general were driven to city hall, where the mayor officially welcomed His Excellency with a lengthy address. Picking up on a theme raised in Quebec City at the governor general's installation, Houde described particular details of the historic Scottish-French link, referring to another "son of Scotland," who had been governor of Montreal and of New France during the reign of Louis XIV, Claude de Ramezay.[9] He summed up this theme by highlighting that "pour arriver au coeur des Canadiens-français … il ne pourrait y avoir de meilleur passeport que la qualité Ecossaise."[10] Tweedsmuir responded briefly in English and French, lauding the fact of the two cultures living side by side in Montreal. He quoted Sir Wilfrid Laurier, who had stated that a personal objective of his was to maintain harmony among the diverse elements that made up Canada. The Montreal French-language daily *La Presse* commented on the warm welcome, indicated by repeated spontaneous and vigorous applause, adding that what he said in French and about the French in Canada confirmed the high esteem in which he was already held. Tweedsmuir impressed his audiences with the clarity, simplicity, and discreet humour of his short speeches.

After the city hall welcome, the viceregal couple separated, he off to the Windsor Hotel to speak to the Canadian Club, and Susan to the Mount Royal Hotel to speak in praise of poets and modern poetry to the Women's Canadian Club. These clubs, with branches across Canada, had a founding objective of strengthening Canada by providing for learning about con-temporary issues of concern in or to the country and promoting pride in being Canadian. It was an objective Tweedsmuir appreciated, and it coin-cided with his approach as governor general.

At the Windsor Hotel, Tweedsmuir spoke about a subject of increas-ing concern to him. In a time of distress and confusion, he said, there was a tendency to try to divine the future and search for signs of renewal.[11] Hence also, the tendency to look to prophets. He described the confidence that British statesmen in the last century had had in democracy, as under-stood in England, believing it would become the model for all countries in the world. Now, he noted solemnly, it was a model rejected almost everywhere. The danger to democracy was evident. Lord Tweedsmuir, the statesman, could rely upon the resources, experience, and talents of John Buchan to raise awareness of that danger and re-emphasize the fun-damental principles of freedom, law, and democratic government.

Subsequent to his speech at the Canadian Club, the new governor gen-eral was driven the short distance to McGill University, where he was granted an honorary doctor of laws degree, the first of many. In his address to the large and mainly youthful audience, he outlined what he characterized as the "Western Mind." It was a speech that his classically trained mind might have given any time, but the advent of the fascists in Italy and the Nazis in Germany over the past decade made the message ever more important, especially for the young people. He described the Mediterranean tradition, descended from ancient Greece and Rome, expanded and adapted by the Christian Church in the Middle Ages: "... on it are based the thought and the philosophy, the art and the letters, the ethics and religion of the modern world. It is the foundation of civilisation, as we understand it. If I tried to describe it in one word, I should take the Latin word *humanitas*. It rep-resents in the widest sense, the humanities, the accumulated harvest of the ages, the fine flower of a long discipline of thought."[12]

Acknowledging that the Western mind "has often been unfaithful" to the moral code of Christianity, he compared it with "those strange people in Germany today who follow the cult of Thor and Odin and the gospel of naked force."[13] He noted that now, in all of Europe, the great tradition was only being defended by Britain and France. Canada, he suggested, with its French and English heritage, could be "the special guardian" of these values in the New World. This heritage, he continued,

> ... is the basis of our politics; it is the basis of our art; it is the basis of our thought; and it is the basis of our conduct. Today it has many critics. Because it involves discipline, it offends the natural rebel. Because it is based upon history, it is antipathetic to the *déracinés*, the rootless folk, who have no links with the past. Because it has balance and poise it is no creed for the neurotic. Because it is rich in spiritual ideals, it is no creed for the materialist. Because it is the faith of free men, it can never be a creed for the slavish and the timid. I have called it the central culture of civilization, and I believe that is a true description.[14]

On Wednesday, November 27, at the University of Toronto, he was granted another honorary doctor of laws and delivered the convocation address. His theme was consistent with that of Montreal but focused more on democracy and developments in Europe. "Popular forms of government have no value unless they foster in each individual the power of being himself, of standing squarely on his feet, and of living his life according to a law which is self-imposed, because it is willingly accepted. Let us consider for a minute or two the meaning of this spiritual democracy, without which no constitution, however liberal in form, is more than a tyranny and a bondage."[15]

These first official visits and the huge turnouts left Tweedsmuir with the impression that the "passion for the spoken word ... [was] remarkable."[16] There had been an estimated fifteen hundred people for one luncheon, two thousand for another, and at one university ceremony, there were some four thousand students who could not get in to hear his speech.[17] His reputation was growing steadily and strongly beyond his books.

Back in Ottawa, as the dull landscape and grey skies of November gave way to cold and snow, there was a sense of excitement. "The first snows are unbelievably beautiful" and the crisp air "wonderfully tonic," Tweedsmuir wrote to his old Oxford friend Stair Gillon.[18] Except for a period of minus twelve degrees Fahrenheit before Christmas, the winter stayed relatively mild until mid-January.[19] There were not a lot of travel commitments, so there was time to plan future trips, based on requests to visit various towns and cities, advice from others, or his own interests. It was also a period that gave him some time to recuperate, for, even though he had been "on the job" for only a month, his less than robust health had already been adversely affected. He wrote that he "was very seedy indeed when we started, and my first two functions here tired me a good deal."[20]

This first year was also a period when family members were anxious to visit. Just before Christmas, the Tweedsmuirs' daughter, Alice, and her husband, Brian Fairfax-Lucy, arrived for a month. In mid-January they boarded the governor general's train, destined for northern Ontario and a short visit to one of the northern mining areas.[21] The father was looking forward to showing them "a bit of wild Canada," which they saw, but at thirty degrees below zero Fahrenheit! At the mining settlements, Tweedsmuir was fascinated by the old-timers and their stories.

In the weeks that followed the departure of his daughter and son-in-law, Tweedsmuir made a couple trips to Toronto, one of which was so that he might be made an honorary member of the Bar of Upper Canada by the Law Society of Upper Canada, an honour that recalled the fact that he had been trained as a lawyer. His speech was peppered with wit and humour at lawyers' expense.

"I have heard the Latin tag: *nemo repente fuit turpissimus* — 'no one becomes very bad all at once' — translated, 'It takes five years to become a solicitor.' Gentlemen, just as hypocrisy is the tribute which vice pays to virtue, so I regard this popular ribaldry as the tribute which folly pays to wisdom."[22]

But he also had solemn purpose, referring to the law as "the chief bond of civilisation."[23] The growth of the law never stops, he explained; "it is an organic thing" and "should be regarded as an elastic tissue which clothes the growing body … too tight it will split, and you will have revolution … too loose it will trip us up."[24]

After only three months in Canada, Tweedsmuir wrote that the "vast country has enormously whetted my appetite for travel."[25] It was the people he wanted to meet, especially those beyond the receiving lines and behind the welcoming committees. "I think I shall be happier when I go on tour and feel that I am really getting my teeth into the country."[26] From the time he first arrived, his correspondence frequently commented about places he had been and seen and about future travel plans. And his fondness for fishing would be more than sated. He looked forward to trout fishing in Quebec, salmon fishing in the Maritimes, fishing anywhere, and shooting in the West, and "possibly a little mountaineering." It had not been a coincidence that a 1901 edition of Izaak Walton's seventeenth-century classic *The Compleat Angler* was republished in 1935, with an introduction by John Buchan.[27]

If he was off to a good start in fulfilling the objectives he set for himself through his travels, some of his initial experiences also began to open up additional possibilities. After his trip to northern Ontario, which he referred to as "a privilege," he spoke at a Canadian Institute of Mining and Metallurgy dinner in Ottawa, noting the importance of

The Beaver (now *Canada's History*) (September 1937), 17, Canada's National History Society. Print courtesy Hudson's Bay Company Archives/Provincial Archives of Manitoba

Ever the fisherman at heart, Tweedsmuir rarely missed an opportunity. Here he tries his hand off the pontoon of the Eldorado Silver Radium Express, August 1937.

their work for the future of the Dominion.[28] In part from these experiences, he believed he might "be able to do some good work in awakening Canada to the real meaning of its possessions in the northern wilds."[29] His own imagination about the North was just awakening. It seemed a promised land, where mineral exploration was just beginning to develop. From northern Ontario to the Far North, men were moving in to find and extract the earth's nickel, copper, silver, lead, zinc, gold, and uranium. Railroads were being built; steamships and, increasingly through the 1920s and 1930s, aircraft were all used to transport men and supplies into remote parts of the country.

On a brief visit to Montreal on February 15, the governor general wanted to make a private visit to the Osler Library at McGill University, a visit he had not been able to make in November because of some shortsighted university officials (not the librarian!).[30] John Buchan wanted to see certain antique books, one dedicated to an ancestor, "the mad Earl of Buchan," and another, a rare 1716 edition of *Christian Morals* by Sir Thomas

Eldorado Mining & Refining Ltd./Library and Archives Canada/C-24049

Tweedsmuir informed himself about developments in all industries and in all regions of Canada. At a mining dinner in Ottawa, he spoke with, among others, Harry Snyder, who would host the governor general on Great Bear Lake in August 1937.

Browne. He saw the books he wanted, but the librarian was subsequently reprimanded by the university registrar, its dean, and others for not informing them of his visit (these were the same men who had not the foresight in November to have the librarian on hand to respond to the governor general's request then). The librarian's confident reply to his critics was that he had been instructed by his guest not to! Tweedsmuir was on a private visit and wanted to avoid any official fuss.

In the first part of March 1936, the Tweedsmuirs had a "wonderful tour" in the Eastern Townships of Quebec, where most of the towns and villages had never before seen a governor general. Tweedsmuir gave what he described as "a terrible number of speeches in bad French!" though he was being unnecessarily modest. The "terrible number" was seventeen.[31] He had a sense that he "got fairly near the French-Canadian mind," perhaps because this was his first tour outside Montreal, into rural parts of the province.[32] These early impressions suggested to him that French Canada was "a most valuable element in Canadian life," and added that if Canada did "not possess it it would have to invent it, for, with all its parochialism and clericalism, it is an influence both for stability and gentility." While these characteristics were true of French Canada and appealed to his conservative nature, it was also true that they were at the root of other contradictory forces to which he would later find himself exposed.

An added delight on this visit, which tickled the historian in Tweedsmuir, was that he discovered he was entitled to enter a nunnery at any hour of the day or night as a result of his representing the king of France, a comment on the continuity of the Crown in Canada. The convents received the governor general with "the most wonderful ceremonies" and with his coat of arms and crest displayed everywhere.[33] Welcoming addresses were spattered with historical allusions to Scotland, and the ancient alliance with France.

Frequent references to his Scottish roots meant, of course, that invitations and speeches of welcome to His Excellency by civic authorities often included words of Gaelic. Not speaking the ancient tongue, he recruited Ian Mackenzie, the minister of defence, who was a Gaelic speaker. Thereafter, his replies to invitations that were written wholly or partially in Gaelic would in turn contain at least some Gaelic. While this undoubtedly reflected a courtesy and desire to please his correspondents, it raised expectations on his arrival. In explaining the result of his good intentions to a friend, he good-humouredly quoted Sir Walter Scott: "Oh what a tangled web we weave when first we practise to deceive!"[34]

Tweedsmuir's travels up to this point, and his intended travels, impressed his frequent correspondent the Earl of Crawford, who admired his courage in undertaking the expeditions he had planned through 1936, and the further plans he had outlined, such as his plans for travelling to the Arctic, Hudson's Bay, and the Yukon. All this left the Earl "bewildered," but looking forward to his friend's impressions of Canada's North and West.[35]

In mid-April Tweedsmuir's oldest son, Johnnie, twenty-four, arrived in a weakened state, ill with amoebic dysentery, from Uganda where he had been in the civil service. He was examined by his father's doctor, then sent fishing among the many lakes around Ottawa, in both Ontario and Quebec, where his father would often join him. The "Canadian air and fishing in the woods" did wonders, according to his father.[36] Johnnie was followed in a couple of weeks by Tweedsmuir's mother, and his sister, Anna, the latter of whom was also a writer, who used the pen name O. Douglas. While not as popular as her brother, she nonetheless had a following of readers in Canada. Their visit overlapped with one by the governor general's brother, Walter, who arrived in mid-June for a relatively short visit; he would return to Britain with Anna and Mrs. Buchan.

Mrs. Buchan and Anna accompanied their prominent son and brother on a tour of smaller cities in western Ontario, including Windsor, Chatham, Woodstock, St. Catharines, and Niagara Falls. Despite her eighty years, Mrs. Buchan turned out to be "a really wonderful traveller."[37] It was fortunate the governor general's railway car was "just as comfortable as any Government House."[38] Tweedsmuir made a point of getting beyond the train and what was visible only from the tracks, the stations, and the official ceremonies. Consistent with his objectives, he requested to be driven around the countryside so he could meet more people, see more of the land for himself, and give people in the small towns an opportunity to see and meet their governor general, as he had done in the Eastern Townships of Quebec. He was constantly being reminded of his earliest youth, with recollections of familiar place and family names from the Borders area of Scotland. At the end of this short trip, he wrote to a friend that "the underlying Scottishness of Canada requires to be seen to be believed."[39]

He found the small cities of western Ontario to be centres of "wholesome economics," where industries complemented agriculture. He noted to Mackenzie King that the industries were mainly owned by small proprietors, a situation that he believed was "socially ... far more valuable than branches of some vast mass-production show."[40] These comments reflected an outlook that would interest his prime minister, who had published *Industry and Humanity* in 1918.[41]

Passing through the Niagara Peninsula, Tweedsmuir was impressed by the "stalwart little cities full of memories of the 1812 war."[42] At Queenston he was interested to see the printing office of Mackenzie King's grandfather, William Lyon Mackenzie.[43] The house was now in decrepit condition, with a stone marker noting its former owner and indicating its significance as "the birthplace of responsible government."[44] In a letter to King, Tweedsmuir suggested that "a graceful act" might be to restore the office for the centenary of the 1837 Rebellion in Upper Canada (now the province of Ontario), which was led by King's grandfather.[45] It was a suggestion that could not have failed to appeal to King. That same year, 1936, the Niagara Parks Commission undertook restoration of the house. It was officially opened as a museum two years later, in the presence of the prime minister, who was "delighted beyond words at the appearance of the house, as reconstructed."[46] Whether it was Tweedsmuir's suggestion that prompted the initiative or whether his interest acted as a catalyst and support for local heritage advocates, we don't know, but his role seems evident.[47]

Having toured the smaller cities of western Ontario, he could not be seen to ignore the larger ones. So, a very short time after returning to Ottawa, he departed again for western Ontario, on May 25, this time bound for Hamilton, London, Kitchener, and other centres as well. Hamilton, he described as "a model of how a city can be industrial and yet beautiful," while London was a "city in a forest," and Stratford, a smaller city near Kitchener, "simply a little piece of England."[48] What impressed Tweedsmuir about all of them was their "stalwart municipal pride."[49]

In May, between the trips to western Ontario, Tweedsmuir spent three days fishing in the Gatineau Hills north of Ottawa in Quebec. Since at least March, he had anticipated the spring and the opportunities for fishing and birdwatching.[50] The fishing in the Gatineau was, in his word, "colossal" — but just as colossal were the number of blackflies! Tweedsmuir wrote that his left eye was almost swollen shut from the bites, and he "made a disreputable figure" when he gave a speech to the Royal Society shortly after.[51] But to his mother-in-law, he softened the image to note that despite the fly bites, he was "fairly respectable."[52] He expressed the hope that by the time she was scheduled to arrive, around the beginning of July, the plague would have passed, so it wasn't likely she would be "called upon to suffer."[53]

The beginning of June also brought the habitual summer migration of the viceregal household to the governor general's residence in Quebec City, the Citadel, with its historic stone walls overlooking the St. Lawrence River. While the comptroller, Colonel Mackenzie, moved the household and saw to the setting up of the living quarters in the Citadel, the Tweedsmuirs stayed at a hotel at Murray Bay (La Malbaie), a popular vacation area east along the river from Quebec City. The governor general and his convalescing son left to do some lake fishing north of Murray Bay.

Tweedsmuir used some of the quiet time away from official duties in Ottawa to plan a major trip to the Prairies and the West Coast. He wrote to King to ask if the prime minister would join him for a week at the end of August, yachting and fishing with the lieutenant-governor in British Columbia.[54] It presented a very good opportunity for a rest after a heavy parliamentary schedule and would "be a delightful holiday for us both." It was the sort of letter the solitary King absorbed with emotion, and which fulfilled his anticipatory reveries at the time of Buchan's appointment. It prompted an immediate and lengthy handwritten letter, fourteen pages on this occasion![55] In such letters King touched on many subjects, and he wrote that while he was glad that Tweedsmuir was pleased with the parliamentary session, it was the prospect of spending idyllic time with John Buchan that held the greatest appeal. It was all the more alluring since he could not go because he had to attend a meeting of the League of Nations in Geneva.

During the second week of July, with plans for a trip to the Maritimes imminent, a visit by U.S. president Roosevelt at the end of July, and plans for his western tour in August well in hand, the governor travelled to the Saguenay region, yet further east from Murray Bay, for more fishing. He would likely have hoped that the distraction of one of his favourite pastimes would provide relaxation with a resultant improvement in his general health. When he returned, however, he felt "very seedy indeed," as he described his state to certain family and friends. In fact, he noted he had felt "seedy" since the voyage over last fall. His condition, however, was now bad enough that, despite even his strong sense of duty and desire to see the country, he was forced to cancel his visit to the Maritimes.

One of the best-known doctors in Canada at the time, Dr. Jonathan C. Meakins, was called to Quebec City to examine the governor general.[56] Unable to do a complete examination away from his Montreal facilities, Meakins suggested the governor general return with him to Montreal, where he could undergo more extensive examinations. There, he was subjected to four days of intensive testing. Pumps were used to inflate his stomach to facilitate examination. He claimed he had been "x-rayed at least forty times in every conceivable attitude," and joked that "it is no light task to defy the laws of gravity and take a bismuth meal standing on one's head!"[57] His sense of humour in dealing with potentially debilitating health issues was indicative of his stoic character. He had great praise for "the magnificent clinic" in Montreal, noting there was "nothing like it … in Britain" that he knew of.[58]

Apart from a diagnosis and prescription for his troubled digestive system, Tweedsmuir quipped lightly that Dr. Meakins's examination also produced a "eulogistic" commentary about his heart, lungs, circulation, blood pressure, etc."[59] Tweedsmuir seemed satisfied with his treatment and the prescription of "a very easy and tolerable regime." It did require, however, that he rest after meals, on his left side. The governor general's general condition and the imposed rests later made an impression on one army officer, who had official equine duties at Government House in Ottawa. He recalled that the governor general seemed generally in ill health and spent considerable time in bed, sometimes complaining about the comfort of the bed, and sometimes cranky![60]

News of Tweedsmuir's health was significant enough to make it into the papers in Britain, causing concern among his friends there. Lord Crawford thought reports of Tweedsmuir's activities suggested "a degree of burden which sounds difficult to carry," and warned his friend that he needed to guard his health because his "program of public work is far-flung [and] has a long series of responsible years before it."[61] The news prompted his old Oxford roommate, John Edgar, himself suffering from a long-term illness, to write. Tweedsmuir replied he had not really been well since last Christmas.[62]

After the gruelling tests, when the governor general returned to Quebec City, Mackenzie King arrived from Ottawa to pay a visit.[63] King may also, though, have wanted to discuss the impending visit of U.S. president Roosevelt, particularly as it was billed as a personal visit to the governor general. The visit at the end of July was a huge success (described in Chapter 8). If Tweedsmuir's gastritis bothered him, it did not show publicly. The spare figure had an ample store of stoicism.

A couple of days after the president's visit, Lord and Lady Tweedsmuir were feted by the Huron First Nations at Loretteville, a short drive northwest of Quebec City. During the evening of August 3, His Excellency was made an honorary chief with the appropriate name of *Hajaton*, "the Scribe," and was presented with two addresses written on birch bark.[64] He arrived in full uniform, with aides-de-camp in attendance, wanting to demonstrate the importance he attached to this visit. It was a gesture deeply appreciated by the Hurons,[65] and was the first of several honours he was to receive from Canada's aboriginal peoples, a sign of their long-standing relationship with the Crown.

Subsequent to this honour, and the visit by President Roosevelt, Tweedsmuir admitted in a private and confidential letter to his prime minister that he had not really been well since Christmas. He tried to remain positive, by writing that his "tiresome gastritis" was "slowly mending."[66] He was by nature positive and had little choice but to express hope, given the persistence of his problematic health. He looked forward now, though, to his Western tour, to the change of scenery and atmosphere it would bring, but he was primarily motivated to see first-hand the difficulties faced by the drought-stricken Prairies and to show the people struggling there that they were not forgotten.

CHAPTER 13

Desperate Prairies, Gateway to the Pacific, and the Scotland of Canada

The anticipated journey west got underway at midday on Thursday, August 6, 1936. John and Susan, their eldest and youngest sons, Johnnie and Alastair, and Susan's mother, Caroline, all boarded the comfortable rolling home on rails. Three coaches, attached to regularly scheduled passenger trains, were painted black, a change from the previous royal purple. The governor general's car, however, was distinguished by the royal coat of arms painted on each side.

As they rolled over the Prairies from Winnipeg, Tweedsmuir was struck by the beauty of the landscape. Even man's intrusion did not necessarily detract from it. On the contrary, as he later observed, he found "a real beauty in the West in the grain elevators — with their white domes and towers, which carry the eyes from the immense Prairie levels to the blue Prairie sky."[1]

In Regina Tweedsmuir, among a few other activities, made time to meet with Archibald McNab, a candidate for lieutenant-governor whom Mackenzie King had asked him to meet.[2] Tweedsmuir sent King a brief note on this Buchan novel namesake (*John McNab*, published in 1925) who was subsequently offered, and who accepted, the post.[3]

Instead of continuing on directly to Alberta, the governor general travelled north, through Saskatoon to Carlton, where the Cree First

Nations honoured the king's representative by making him a chief, with the name *Okemow Otatowkew* — "Teller of Tales."[4] The name reflected Tweedsmuir's reputation, but also recalled the oral tradition in aboriginal culture. The Cree also presented the governor general "with a beautifully beaded robe as a coronation gift for His Majesty the King," a reflection of respect and of the strong link between First Nations and the Crown.[5]

The viceregal party reached Edmonton on August 13, where they were greeted by Lieutenant-Governor Walsh and Premier Aberhart. In his familiar way, Tweedsmuir complimented the people and their unique part of the country: "some of the finest scenery in the world," he said.[6] Then, alluding to the economic difficulties, he praised the courage and fortitude of the people in facing those difficulties.[7] While in Edmonton, as well as attending an official reception in the legislative building, which fatigued the governor general,[8] he unveiled a new war memorial and, later, met with another candidate for lieutenant-governor, Lieutenant-Colonel Phillip. In a note to his prime minister, Tweedsmuir provided the requested assessment of Phillip, who ultimately accepted the post, but his thoughts were dominated by Social Credit premier William Aberhart's politics, which he thought confused and a cause for chaos.[9] Prior to leaving the Alberta capital, he was taken on "a long motor-tour" to see for himself some of countryside suffering from the Depression and drought.[10]

Through the Rockies, what could otherwise have been a spectacular first journey was dampened by limited vision, due to what Tweedsmuir described as "real Scottish weather" — heavy rain and mist. The rains continued and became torrential, causing mudslides and a washout on the line, which in turn caused an eight-hour delay. They pulled into Vancouver around 5 p.m. (Saturday, August 15), but the planned official ceremonies and dinner had been cancelled because of the delay. The viceregal party were, instead, driven directly to the harbour where they boarded HMCS *Skeena* bound for Victoria, the provincial capital.[11] The press welcomed this first visit, commenting that "his demeanor as Governor-General has confirmed the reputation of John Buchan, student, soldier, story-teller, historian, statesman."[12]

The Tweedsmuirs were guests of Lieutenant-Governor Eric Hamber, who was a successful lumberman and corporate director. Tweedsmuir's impression was of "a first-class, … wise and far-sighted man," with a dedication to public service; he suggested that King keep him in mind for an ambassadorial post.[13]

On Monday the governor general addressed the Canadian Club in the stately Empress Hotel, overlooking the harbour. Bruce Hutchison, just launching in his journalism career, covered Tweedsmuir's visit.[14] The speech offered contrasting descriptions of prominent figures in British politics who Tweedsmuir had known personally, and whose names would have been then familiar to Canadians. Included also was mention of former Canadian prime minister Sir Wilfrid Laurier, whom Tweedsmuir had met at an event at Oxford University when he was a student. Laurier, he said, "more than anybody … blocked Joseph Chamberlain's scheme of imperial federation, [which he described as] a blind alley."[15] The speech was described as brilliant.[16]

The next day three automobiles left Government House, driving north. They stopped overnight in Qualicum Beach, and the next day Buchan and his party fished in the Stamp River. The governor general's "baptism as a Canadian fisherman" was duly recorded, with mention made that he had waded in too deeply, so that water poured into his boots, then slipped on a rock and fell in.[17] The dunking produced only smiles from the old fisherman; no steelhead were landed but fish are not essential to fishing, "as long as you have a well-balanced rod, a fast stream, and a good lunch in your creel."[18] "[A]way from crowds and reception committees," the day "was voted the best the governor general had spent since leaving Ottawa." His superlatives were his way of complimenting his hosts.

A little further north, in Courtenay, he addressed another Canadian Club luncheon, this one in a log hall of the Native Sons of Canada, which was, ironically, the same organization that had opposed his nomination as governor general. Among the crowd Tweedsmuir recognized a face and went over to talk. Bob Davis, a famous American newspaperman and the former editor of *Munsey's Magazine*, had met John Buchan before the war, attracted to his writing in *Prester John*.[19] Davis had paid Buchan "thousands of dollars for his stuff in the old days," telling others in the crowd that Buchan was "one of the real writers of the time … [and that his] stories of the Highlands [were] as good as Robert Louis Stevenson's."[20]

Returning to the podium, Tweedsmuir spoke of the inspiring natural beauty of Vancouver Island and extolled the virtues of conservation. He appealed to individual responsibility:

> It is the rank and file that must save everything in this country worth saving, and you have so much beauty here that is worth saving. Canadians are apt to think that their resources were inexhaustible, but this is not so. It is terribly easy, even in a great country like this[,] to ruin natural beauty and to destroy flora and fauna. It would be an awful pity if, through carelessness, you spoiled the natural charm of the country, if you allowed too many great trees to disappear, too many beauty spots to be ruined by cheap buildings; if through ineffectual administration of game laws you permitted the wild animals and fish to disappear.[21]

The following day the Tweedsmuirs sailed from Courtenay in the lieutenant-governor's yacht, *Vencedor*, to Campbell River, where "the big tyee" escaped the piscatorial governor and his wife. His Excellency did land a humpback salmon, though, after a twenty-minute fight. Bruce Hutchison wrote wishfully: "Undoubtedly a lot of this material will come out in a book by John Buchan."[22] In truth the author was never far. Indeed, while he was still on the island, a review of his most recent Richard Hannay novel, *The Island of Sheep*, appeared in the *Vancouver Daily Province*'s Sunday magazine.[23]

When the Tweedsmuirs left the island aboard the British warship HMS *Apollo*, they also left "a fine impression." The governor had met hundreds of people, "from millionaires to fishing guides [and all with] his democratic spirit and unassuming manner."[24] The viceregal couple had also visited institutions such as the Queen Alexandra Solarium for Crippled Children and the Fairbridge Farm School, which taught agriculture to British teenage orphans.[25]

With the return to the mainland, the pace and scale of activities picked up, and included much "speechifying," as Tweedsmuir described it. He appeared dapper, with his suit and tie finished with a pearl tie-pin and a sprig of purple heather in his lapel. The usual official events followed at the new city hall, but with another pleasant surprise.

Arriving at the cenotaph, the governor recognized an old, one-legged soldier on crutches, broke away from his party, and walked over to the man.[26] Hubert Burmester had worked in some capacity with John Buchan in South Africa. The two men smiled, shook hands, and walked away from the others, "still deep in conversation," then returned to their respective positions for the official wreath-laying and remembrance. After a rest in his rail car, Tweedsmuir made a brief appearance that evening at the Hotel Vancouver for a banquet of the "Old Contemptibles," the veterans' association of British regular army troops from the First World War.[27]

August 26 was John Buchan's sixty-first birthday. Mackenzie King sent a telegram. The *Daily Province* published a caricature of the governor general for the occasion, noting, among other things, that His Excellency, "contrary to reports, look[ed] exceedingly well and healthy."

It was a day of more official events, including the opening of the Seaforth Highlanders Armoury. At noon he attended a luncheon of the Canadian Club at the Hotel Vancouver and addressed the overflow gathering. In contrast to his Victoria Canadian Club character sketches, however, he focused on international relations and the Empire. He skated close to forbidden topics, but stated his was a subject "also beyond party politics," as he wrote to his prime minister and as has been previously described.[28]

The highlight of the afternoon was the official opening of the Pacific Exhibition. Lord Tweedsmuir offered a brief but uplifting speech that looked to the future and Vancouver's place in it. With "a rich full voice" that was easily heard by one of the largest crowds the Exhibition had seen, he said he agreed with Rudyard Kipling, who had expressed to him that he had found some places he admired, some he loved, but he had discovered only one earthly paradise and that was in British Columbia![29] "It is very clear," Tweedsmuir said, that as "the gateway to the Pacific," Vancouver may well become "the strategic vantage point in the economy of Canada and the Empire." "No Canadian," he said, "is prouder of his country than I am, or believes more devoutly in her future."

(Vancouver Daily Province, August 27, 1936)

Caricature of Lord Tweedsmuir following his speech at a Canadian Club luncheon in Vancouver, and in honour of his sixty-first birthday, August 26, 1936.

The next four days were filled with a variety of activities and visits, sometimes with the Tweedsmuirs splitting up: in beautiful Stanley Park, His Excellency dedicated the Shakespeare Gardens;[30] eight hundred Girl Guides greeted Lady Tweedsmuir at one location, while five hundred Cubs and Scouts surprised the Chief Scout as he entered a field elsewhere.[31] There were visits to factories; a three-hour boat tour of Burrard Inlet; a brief visit to New Westminster, promised when he met the mayor the previous week on Vancouver Island; and church, of course, on Sunday morning at the newly built St. James Anglican Church where His Excellency was invited to say a few words.[32]

It must have been with a feeling of satisfaction that the Tweedsmuirs re-boarded their train that Sunday evening. They were heading for Calgary, but would stop at Kamloops on Monday to allow an afternoon of fishing in the vicinity. They arrived in Calgary after dark, greeted by a crowd of some eight thousand. The next day the governor general spoke to the Alberta Military Institute, an address that caused a controversy we have already read about.

From Calgary Susan, her mother, and Alastair left to return directly to Ottawa, while the governor's return journey would be a zigzag through communities of all sizes and into remote parts of the western provinces. First was Waterton Lakes National Park, in the southwest corner of Alberta: "far more beautiful than Banff;"[33] then the nearby Blood Indian Reserve, where the governor general was made an honorary chief, "Eagle Head."[34] He also visited some of the farming areas on horseback, which was "a purgatory to [his] bare bones."[35] The vice-regal retinue then travelled northeast to Medicine Hat: "a curious little town" reeking with the smell of continuously burning natural gas.[36] They continued north by car to Alsask, on the Alberta-Saskatchewan border, to make a promised visit to an old boyhood friend, Alex Fraser, who could no longer farm due to an injury and a subsequent stroke.[37] From Alex, Tweedsmuir received a personal account of the difficult situation faced by farmers in the worst drought-stricken areas. It had been a touching visit, and Tweedsmuir subsequently helped the family in several substantial ways.[38] The car trip back to Medicine Hat was "a horrid experience," driving through a dust storm.

From his exposure to the Prairies thus far, Tweedsmuir admired "the courage and patience of the people in the face of adverse conditions."[39] He admired the beauty. The "immense landscape [of the Prairies] gives one the same feeling as the sea, and the effects of light and shadow are amazingly beautiful."[40] But he believed the "beauty of the Prairies has never been sufficiently recognised,"[41] which confirmed an impression he

Eagle Head, Honorary Chief of the Blood First Nation near Waterton Lakes National Park, Alberta.

Yousuf Karsh/Library and Archives Canada/PA-195664

had already formed: there seemed to be an ignorance of one part of the country for another. Another objective was added to his travels.

On to Moose Jaw, Saskatchewan. When Tweedsmuir arrived he learned that a popular local doctor had been killed in a car accident. He attended the funeral, sharing in the community's grief.[42] The following day his party continued eastward through Regina, and reached "a kind of miniature Grand Canyon" — the Qu'Appelle Valley. The journey continued its zigzag, now turning south to the coal-mining town of Estevan near the U.S. border, where on Sunday he read the lesson at a Presbyterian church.[43] From Estevan it was northeast, on to the Manitoba capital, where he met with John Dafoe, editor of the *Winnipeg Free Press* and chancellor of the University of Manitoba. Dafoe asked Tweedsmuir to accept an honorary doctor of laws; plans began for his return at the end of November.[44]

From Winnipeg the governor general headed north, to visit an Icelandic community, Gimli, on the shore of Lake Winnipeg, and a Ukrainian settlement to the west. In reaching out to Canadians, Tweedsmuir made a point to visit these immigrant communities, to demonstrate they were as important to the country as those in the established cities. In both places he was entertained by people in their colourful national costumes. In Gimli he praised the Icelanders, and Scandinavians generally, explaining how he believed a country of immigrants is made strong.

"You have become in the fullest sense good Canadians, and have shared in all the enterprises and struggles of this new nation, and at the same time I rejoice to think that you have never forgotten the traditions of your homeland. That is the way in which a strong people is made — by accepting willingly the duties and loyalties of your adopted country, but also by bringing your own native traditions as a contribution to the making of Canada."[45]

He continued, with a focus on certain of their particular traditions:

> There are two elements in your tradition, as reflected
> in the Sagas ... [which I hope] will never be forgotten.
> One is the belief in the reign of law. Everywhere in the

Sagas you find that insisted upon. The old Icelanders were not only great warriors and adventurers, but they were acute lawyers and mighty jurists.... The second element in the Saga tradition is still greater. As I see it, it is the belief that truth and righteousness must be followed for their own sake, quite independent of any material creed.... In these days when everyone is inclined to ask, in doing his duty, what he is going to get out of it, that noble spirit of un-self-regarding devotion is the true corrective.[46]

After "living laborious days" on the road and the rails for over six weeks, Tweedsmuir anticipated a reversal of direction, back west and north to Prince Albert, Saskatchewan. There, plans had been made to fly him in to Lake Waskesiu to meet Grey Owl, who was an impassioned conservationist.[47] From the float-plane, he had "never seen anything more lovely than looking down from the air upon rolling miles of bright gold [of the poplars and birch] with vast stretches of turquoise lake in between."[48] At Lake Waskesiu Tweedsmuir began to feel in touch with the North.[49] Lake Waskesiu enchanted Tweedsmuir, and not just for the eight-pound trout Grey Owl caught! During their discussions Grey Owl told Tweedsmuir that the First Nations could play an important role in the economy as stewards of the wilderness.[50] Tweedsmuir would remember the point.

Tweedsmuir returned refreshed to Prince Albert and rejoined his train for the journey to Ottawa. He believed this western tour had "made a very good popular impression," and that he had "got closer to the Canadian people ... than ever before."[51] As a bonus his health seemed to have improved, to the point where he was feeling "almost completely well."[52]

Back in Ottawa Tweedsmuir had a short time with Susan and Alastair before they left for England on October 10. The morning after their departure, he arrived at Ottawa's Union Station, under a light sprinkling of snow, to board a train for Toronto, where he would receive an honorary doctor of divinity from Victoria University, then celebrating its centenary. He gave, in his own words, a very solemn speech.[53]

"Well, the [w]ar, with its abysmal suffering and destruction, did achieve one thing. It revealed us to ourselves. It revealed how thin the crust was between a complex civilisation and primeval anarchy. If I were asked to name any one clear gain from the [w]ar — and here I am speaking of our own people — I would say that it was a new humility. We had our pride shattered, and without humility there can be no humanity."[54]

He encouraged the students to look at the world not as it has been, "but as it is and as it may be."[55] He laid out what he believed to be the intellectual, social, political, and moral gains made after the Great War, then continued:

> Our sufferings have taught us that no nation is suffi-
> cient unto itself, and that our prosperity depends in
> the long run not upon the failure of our neighbours,
> but upon their success[;] … that the dangers we were
> repelling were common to all the world, has done much
> to weaken what used to be our besetting sins, chau-
> vinism and racial pride. We know more about other
> peoples, and that knowledge has brought a sympathy
> not only of the head but of the heart. Such a patrio-
> tism of humanity (which is in no way inconsistent with
> national patriotism) is the only ultimate foundation for
> international peace.[56]

As a bequest a university can make to the youth of the future, he described a humanism, defined not by "man as the measure of all things and … his transient mundane interests," but rather its "true purport is that we set as our first aim the freedom and integrity of the human spirit."[57]

A brief trip to Montreal later in October was primarily for meetings at McGill University, with its chancellor, Sir Edward Beatty, who was also chairman of the Canadian Pacific Railway, and with the universi-ty's accountant. The discussions would inform his ideas for enhancing education and the intellectual life of Canada. As well as these meetings, he also took in a McGill football game against the University of Toronto; he thought Canadian football was better than the American version but "not nearly so good as ... [r]ugby."[58]

After their return to Ottawa, both father and eldest son underwent medical examinations.[59] The doctors were optimistic that Johnnie's dysentery was steadily improving. As for John senior, they proposed what one of his doctors in England suggested — pumping out his stomach, over a two-week period. The procedure was scheduled to be finished before he left for his return to the West.

Before that, however, on November 7, he travelled the short distance to Kingston, on the shore of Lake Ontario. In the morning, at Queen's University, he received an honorary doctor of laws. In a brilliant and lengthy address, he exhorted students just entering their careers to make it their duty, as honest and public-spirited individuals, "to endeavour patiently and resolutely to bring the world back to a saner mood and a wiser temper."[60]

Eldorado Mining & Refining Ltd./Library and Archives Canada/C-24050

"A new industry has been given to Canada, a new supply ground has been afforded the medical science of the world for one of its indispensable materials." Tweedsmuir addresses the Radium Dinner, Chateau Laurier Hotel, Ottawa, November 16, 1936.

"We are living in a confused and difficult world," he reminded them, "and in such time the human mind is predisposed to hasty conclusions. We are all inclined to look for some short cut out of our troubles, some violent course which will shift things suddenly into a new orbit. Patience, reasonableness, what we call commonsense, are apt to seem counsels of despair. The moderate man is at a discount. This morning I would venture to say a few words on his behalf."[61]

After a survey of the evolution of Western civilization, he explained an important distinction between the false and true moderate. The former appears tolerant because he is careless, believing "that every controversy can be settled by halving the difference." Not so the true moderate. The opposite of the moderate is found in the fanatic. Abraham Lincoln was offered as "a shining example of true moderation."

When he returned to Ottawa, his spirits were lifted because these weeks were ones of unusually good health for him; he felt invigorated by the November air, describing it as being like champagne.[62] Health and science was raised in one of his engagements in Ottawa. He addressed the Radium Dinner hosted by the Eldorado Mining & Refining Company at the Chateau Laurier Hotel, at which he noted that a "new industry has been given Canada, a new supply ground has been afforded the medical science of the world for one of its indispensable materials."[63] Attending the dinner, aside from company executives and the prime minister, was Harry Snyder, who would host Tweedsmuir on a journey to the Arctic the following summer.

After spending a little more than a week back in Ottawa, he boarded his railway car, bound for Toronto to attend the Royal Agricultural Winter Fair. From there, the car was attached to a transcontinental for his second trip west, to return to Winnipeg and to fulfill a promise of "a more personal" visit to Edmonton.[64]

The governor general steamed straight through to Edmonton, reaching the Alberta capital on Sunday, November 22, almost six hours late, but earlier than they might otherwise have arrived. A disabled freight engine had blocked the tracks near Rivers, Manitoba, a little more than halfway to the Saskatchewan border.[65] At Watrous, halfway through Saskatchewan, Tweedsmuir ordered a special train to run him from there directly to Edmonton in an effort not to disappoint the approximately 550 people, not to mention the organizers, who were gathering at Edmonton's Hotel Macdonald to hear him speak. It worked. He arrived one and a half hours ahead of the regular train. He immediately went forward to see the engineer and fireman to thank them for their efforts. The day he arrived, the *Edmonton Journal* proclaimed "Lord Tweedsmuir as 'One of Us.'"[66]

The luncheon was "believed to be the largest of its kind ever held in the city."[67] The hotel ballroom was packed, with adjoining rooms and loudspeakers set up to accommodate the overflow crowd, including various men's and women's service clubs, Premier Aberhart, Chief Justice Harvey, and Mayor Clarke. With a clear voice, Tweedsmuir delivered what the newspaper editors described as a "magnificent address," with an analysis of the "mental morality of public leaders."[68]

In an ever changing environment, he began, "we must constantly be adjusting ourselves to it … [but] there must be some continuity," for without that, he suggested, society would be like a weather vane, turning whichever way the wind blows.[69] Consistency is admired as a virtue, he continued. In fact "[i]t is no virtue at all," he argued, suggesting rather it is merely "laziness in most of us." Someone who changes and develops "presents a subtle problem and most of us dislike subtlety." Change and development is especially distrusted in a statesman, Tweedsmuir noted, since society tends to consider politicians who change positions as dishonest and, therefore, not to be trusted. As evidence that such beliefs were misguided, he gave three circumstances and examples in which change, or inconsistency, "is wholly right,"[70] then concluded by suggesting that it is vital that individuals be open "to new light and new ideas [because such openness is] a proof not only of a vigorous mind but of an honest character and a true sense of public duty."

After numerous other activities in the city, including a flight 250 miles over the Rockies, which gave him another elevated appreciation of the vastness and grandeur of this part of Canada,[71] the governor general's train departed for Regina, arriving Thursday evening, November 26.

At the Hotel Saskatchewan the next day, before a crowd of some 350, Tweedsmuir's address was playfully described by the press as "gossip."[72] The lunch was sponsored by the women's and men's Canadian Club, which he described as "an admirable organization and a power for good." His "gossip" consisted of character sketches of three prominent British leaders he had known: Field Marshal Lord Haig, the British military leader during the First World War; Lord Balfour, a former British prime minister; and the legendary T.E. Lawrence (of Arabia). Adding an element of controversy, Tweedsmuir criticized a recent book about Haig written by Lloyd George, prime minister during the First World War, which described Haig as an "inferior soldier."[73] Tweedsmuir strongly rebuked Lloyd George's criticisms, but his authority also betrayed his bias, recalling that John Buchan served in Haig's headquarters in France.

Later that afternoon he attended a joint meeting of the Saskatchewan Historical Society and the Saskatchewan Branch of the Canadian Authors Association. As the *Regina Leader-Post* commented, "in these days, he is in the public eye but Tweedsmuir's counterpart John Buchan is not far from their thoughts."[74] During the visit Tweedsmuir ignored the advice of police and met with Central European groups, including the "Red" Ukrainians.[75] He would not be cowed by the "communist bogey." There was no sign of socialist agitation; in fact, as he related, he was "nearly smothered in Union Jacks" and the roof was almost brought down by the singing of "God Save the King."[76] In Regina, he also visited ten institutions of various kinds, including schools, signing autographs for students along the way.

From Regina the governor returned to Winnipeg, the city looking clean with the gleam of new snow. It is significant that he started his visit in St. Boniface, the French-speaking municipality within Winnipeg. He acknowledged the heritage of the French explorers and settlers in several replies and speeches. After a visit to the city hall there, he toured St. Boniface Hospital, then attended a luncheon held by the Canadian Club at the Royal Alexandra Hotel.[77] His speech dealt with the importance of the written word, "which matters most," and the impact of radio on newspapers:

If we were to depend wholly upon the spoken word, ... our minds would be radically altered.... It was all very well in ancient Greece, in a small society, with a high standard of culture and ample leisure.... With us, in these hurried and furious days, if that became the only, or the main medium, we should become sciolists and *quid nuncs* and smatterers, the victims of constant misapprehensions, walking monuments of elaborate inaccuracy. The eye is a safer conduit-pipe to the brain than the ear, and the revival of the newspaper of opinion would, to my mind, be a substantial advance in that popular education without which democracy cannot endure.[78]

He cited the custom in French newspapers of "special signed articles by acknowledged experts." Looking into the future, he suggested to his audience that "one effect of broadcasting may be that while it may diminish the importance of the newspaper as a news carrier, it will enormously increase its importance as a vehicle of opinion."

Amusingly, his vocabulary created some "intensive nonsense." "[S]ciolist" (someone pretending to be knowledgeable) was heard by some people as "socialist!"[79]

The afternoon was filled with visits to medical facilities. He began with a trip to the Canadian Institute for the Blind, sitting in on a class of small children, and then continued to the Winnipeg General Hospital. The evening was reserved for an address to "contented exiles" at the St. Andrew's Society dinner.[80] He pleaded with his audience to maintain their traditions and linkages with Scotland, and recalled historic battles of the "two separate races," the Highlanders and Lowlanders, that ultimately, "with immense difficulty and with immense suffering," became one nation after 1745. He extended the theme of unity, calling on Scots to contribute to "the crying need of the world," unity, including "a closer unity" in Canada.[81]

The following day, December 1, at a special convocation of the University of Manitoba, the governor general received an honorary doctor of laws. Chancellor Dafoe stated that Lord Tweedsmuir, as John Buchan, "merits entrance to any sphere of learning."[82] The guest's address to the academic assembly was a "ringing summons to public service."[83] It was again a theme to reinforce the fabric of society and the foundation of Western civilization. He asked the students to remember that they were not only individuals, but citizens, and as educated young people they had a contribution to make.[84]

"Let me begin by paying a tribute to a certain British tradition. Heaven knows that some of our British traditions are foolish enough! but there is one which has now persisted for more than two centuries, and which has been of incalculable value to us in recent difficult days. That tradition is that the public service is one of the most honourable of all pursuits."[85]

Canada and the other Dominions, he said, had inherited from Britain "a free and orderly government, and a great literature of thought and imagination. But these gifts she has made to all the world, and they are no longer looked upon as her specific bequest, since they have become part of the common stock of civilisation."[86] The supreme duty of a citizen, Tweedsmuir told the students, was to offer their "thought and work to the welfare of the nation," and pay "close and vigilant attention" to public affairs. He cautioned, though, that if citizens neglect the State, meaning collective interests, in favour of private interests, "there will most certainly come a day when this neglect will react most seriously upon these private interests themselves."[87]

Later in the day, in the ballroom of Government House, an Italianate style structure situated on the same tract of land as the legislative building,[88] Tweedsmuir addressed a crowd of 150 at the inaugural meeting of the Western Canada section of the Association of Canadian Bookmen (ACB), an organization of which he was patron.[89]

The next day he lit a lamp intended to burn continuously at the Women's Tribute Memorial Lodge. It was a memorial to those women who did not return from the Great War and a tribute to those who did. He met the secretary of the Women's Memorial Tribute Foundation, a Mr. Raymond Large. In a statement that demonstrated his support for the active participation in society of the disabled, Tweedsmuir expressed "satisfaction that Mr. Large, although disabled, was the secretary of the Foundation."[90]

Sometime during his Winnipeg visit, he was asked to meet formally with a group of unemployed people. He refused, noting it was not his role. His humanitarian character could not, however, ignore them completely; so, likely again against official advice, he attended their noon meal. One of their leaders described him as a "grand guy."[91] It was a compassionate gesture of high impact.

Throughout this second, more informal, western trip, the weather had been superb, making it all the more pleasant. He had also gained four pounds, which signalled better health.[92] The whole experience was described by viceregal staff member Willis-O'Connor as "the nicest trip I have been on since the time of Lord Byng." It had been a great success, in large measure because of Tweedsmuir's enthusiasm. "His Excellency gets down so close to the people [and] is so frightfully interested in everything that happens."[93]

The first three months of 1937 were relatively quiet as far as travel was concerned, with short trips to Montreal and Toronto. At the end of February, as Chief Scout of Canada, he addressed the Boy Scouts Association annual dinner in Montreal. The importance of Scouting for Tweedsmuir was its cultivation of "the individual and the personality," and the way in which it "emphasize[d] initiative and encourage[d] self-development."[94] Partly, he said, this was achieved through keeping youth in touch with the wilderness and learning good comradeship. All of this was more important in the current circumstances, he added, when "a primary duty of every nation today [was] the ability to defend itself," but to do so without "the poison of militarism," a clear reference to Germany, Italy, and Japan. In the middle of March, he returned to Montreal, this time to speak for the second year in a row to the Canadian Institute of Mining, touching this time on "the development of the [N]orth"; the value of applied science; and the need for "a closer unity" if the country was "to rise to the height of her great opportunities."[95]

The Ontario Educational Association invited Tweedsmuir to address their meeting in Toronto on March 29. It was a chance to elaborate on one of his key themes — education and the making of good citizens.[96]

With deft touches of humour and reflections from his own broad experiences, he wove together the threads of academic and practical education. It was the job of education, he reminded his listeners, "to train the mind, not to crowd the memory." He praised the efforts of the vocational schools "to preserve an element of what I call the humanities." "By humanism in education," he explained, "I mean the study of man in all his relations, as thinker, as artist, as social and moral being ... the primary purpose of humane studies is the understanding of human nature, the broadening of the human interests and the better appreciation of human life."[97]

The vocational schools, by including an element of the humanities, he felt were "producing not only technicians, but men and women with minds," who were potential citizens, in the sense that they were better equipped to understand public affairs and to participate more fully in their society. He concluded with praise for Frontier College, which pointed the way to how "we must be prepared to go beyond the schools."[98]

The governor returned to Ottawa, to prepare for his official visit to the American capital beginning March 31, details of which have been previously described. The period following his return from Washington was relatively restrained, allowing Tweedsmuir a needed rest, which included four days of fishing on Lac Papineau in Quebec, with Sir George Perley and the American ambassador.[99]

The last week of May, he returned to western Ontario, to Guelph, Galt, Brantford, and "all that beautiful countryside."[100] The return included stops around Toronto, to open the new St. John Convalescent Hospital in Newtonbrook, operated by the Sisters of St. John the Divine,[101] and to attend the spring opening of Woodbine Racetrack. From Toronto his party skirted Lake Ontario, stopping at Gananoque in the Thousand Islands area of the St. Lawrence, which Tweedsmuir described as "a delightful little town."[102] He would have heard at the time of the plans to construct an international bridge there.

After ten days' rest in Quebec City, Tweedsmuir was on the road again, departing for a week-long tour of the Maritimes, to make up for the cancelled visit the previous summer. The viceregal couple arrived in Halifax late the following evening (June 7), and spent the night in their coach. The *Halifax Herald* welcomed the Tweedsmuirs to "the Scotland of Canada."[103] On June 8, the official welcomes played themselves out, though the guard of honour this time was, appropriately, from the Royal Canadian Navy. The dapper governor, dressed in top hat and morning coat, and outfitted with a cane, complimented the Nova Scotians as "a great industrious people," and highlighted the contributions of their famous ship builders and ship masters.

From Halifax the Tweedsmuirs entrained for Fredericton, the New Brunswick capital, for another round of official welcomes. Susan attended the closing of the twenty-fourth annual convention of the New Brunswick Women's Institutes.[104] An active member of the Women's Institutes in Britain, she remarked on the growth of the organization there, after its introduction from Canada.

While in the shipbuilding city of Saint John, New Brunswick, news arrived of the death of Sir Robert Borden. During his reply to the welcome of that city, Tweedsmuir included a tribute to "a great statesman and son of the Maritimes," whom he had first met in London during the war.[105] In a brief character sketch, much appreciated by his audience, the governor general described the former wartime prime minister as "a man who rose above petty things to become a figure esteemed by all." The eighty-two-year-old Borden, he said, "carried into great age the spirit and heart of a boy," recounting as one example how, a year earlier, Borden arrived unexpectedly by float plane on a bitterly cold morning at a fishing camp to join Tweedsmuir and others.

From Saint John Tweedsmuir and his party travelled north, stopping at Campbellton, the main town of northern New Brunswick, on the south bank of the Restigouche River. At the train station there, the governor general, likely wishing that he had more time to stop and fish, had the first of two "close shaves" in the space of two months. A large coping stone fell from the top of the station building onto the spot where Tweedsmuir had been standing only a few seconds earlier.[106]

His trip to northern New Brunswick concluded his trip to the Maritimes, and it was a relatively short run back to Quebec City after that. During the tour, he had met many of the region's political figures, listening to them and to their approaches for revising the relationship between the federal government and the provinces. It was at this time that discussions were concluding that would result in August in the establishment of the Royal Commission on Dominion-Provincial Relations under Ontario Chief Justice N.W. Rowell.

During the third week of June 1937, the governor general was in Montreal to speak at a dinner of the Engineering Institute of Canada. The Institute had previously made him an honorary member. He complimented their profession with the observation that it "has always been the foundation of every civilized society," going back to the Egyptians and the Romans.[107] He cautioned, though, that "the constructive powers of man must keep in some kind of harmony with nature."[108]

From Montreal the following day, Tweedsmuir travelled to Kingston, Ontario, to address the luncheon of the American-Canadian Conference on June 17, described in an earlier chapter. The following week, he returned to Montreal, where he addressed the "gigantic" Presbyterian Conference, then it was back to Ottawa for a talk to the Canadian Medical Association.

At the latter he acknowledged local and provincial medical societies but emphasized the importance of an "all-Canadian association" that reminds us "we are not only nine provinces but a single and indivisible nation."[109] He praised the physicians he had met on the Prairies, who, although they "often [had] a brilliant college record … [were] surrendering professional ambitions for the day-to-day work of relieving pain and sickness in poverty-stricken districts."

Tweedsmuir's theme of Canada being nine provinces but a single nation was challenged when he returned to Quebec City. He was already well aware of the "recrudescence of French nationalism in Quebec," a manifestation of discontent that he believed was largely economic in origin.[110] "[A] great deal of blame attaches," he assessed, "to the English population," which had "a good deal of arrogance and unfriendliness," and still contained, at least in Montreal, "a truculent Orange element."[111] The Orange Lodge was vehemently anti-Catholic, and Quebec was predominantly Catholic. The situation was compounded by business being run by the English, even though they constituted only a quarter of the population, while the education system was run by the Roman Catholic church, which, he observed, "is wholly classical and produces a vast number of young professional men for whom there are no jobs," because the demand was for commercial or technological work.[112]

At the *Congrès de la langue française* in Quebec City in June 1937, aimed at protecting the French language, he had the concentrated opportunity of meeting many and hearing their views. Here he believed he could contribute to the unity of the country in recognizing one of the founding cultures. He was also aware of the concern that "some of the extremists [would] turn it into a political demonstration."[113]

Throughout his address Tweedsmuir referred to French authors and poets, but highlighted that literature in French-speaking Canada had developed its own character and was only just beginning on its path. He spoke of the value of the French language and literature, "*qui constituent une richesse non seulement pour le Canada français mais encore pour le Canada anglais*." Sounding every bit as proud of French in Canada as anyone, Tweedsmuir noted: "*C'est de nous qu'il dépend de conserver la pureté du langage*," a language of which the glory "*repose sur sa pureté, sa précision, son exquise clarté*."[114] He concluded by saying that as an Englishman, as a Canadian by adoption, and as a long-time friend of France and of its cultural tradition, he offered them his wishes for success.

Tweedsmuir was encouraged that his speech in French was so well received.[115] Privately, to Mackenzie King, he noted that, with one exception, the "other addresses were unexceptional."[116] L'Abbé Groulx, an intellectual leader of Quebec separatism, spoke and was well received. Tweedsmuir offhandedly discounted that as owing to "a big claque of his followers in the audience." Perhaps too quickly, he downplayed Groulx's speech as merely "a string of rhetorical perorations," and equally discounted the impact as having "very little harm." The Quebec cardinal, however, recognized something quite different, more sinister to the established order, and was furious, Tweedsmuir relayed to the prime minister.[117]

The next day Premier Duplessis made what Tweedsmuir described as "a very courageous speech" against separatism.[118] The entire *Congrès* and the exposure of the separatists was all to the good, according to Tweedsmuir, because it "exposed the nakedness of the soil."[119] This would all be information valued by the prime minister, as the deteriorating situation in Europe raised anxieties, especially about Quebec, over possible Canadian involvement in any European war and potential implications for conscription and thus national unity.

Following his visit to Quebec, it was finally time for Tweedsmuir to begin his long-planned and greatly anticipated journey to the Arctic. On his way west, he intended to visit some of the drought areas again. Tweedsmuir believed, from experience now, that "personal visits do much good in such places."[120] As for his ultimate destination, he wrote to King that he sensed this trip to the Arctic would be valuable and he was "more and more impressed with the importance of the North in Canadian development."[121] The prime minister expressed his great appreciation for Tweedsmuir's travels generally: "I should like particularly to thank you for what, in so many ways, you have been doing toward promoting a feeling of good-will between the people in different parts of Canada."[122] He described as "providential" Tweedsmuir's visit to the drought-stricken Prairies, where he had offered words of encouragement.

The Tweedsmuirs departed the East during the second week of July, stopping in Kenora, in northwestern Ontario, for a day of fishing on Lake of the Woods. The following day, a brief stop in Winnipeg allowed the governor general to have "a most interesting talk with Jim Richardson," a prominent businessman, continuing to inform himself at every opportunity.[123]

There was a brief stop in Saskatoon, and then the fulfillment of a promise to return to Alsask to visit his ailing friend Alex Fraser, where he stayed for a day. As his train passed through one of the worst drought areas, Tweedsmuir gazed over the thousands of acres of yellow and brown vegetation, where it had recorded the longest period on record without precipitation.[124] Finally arriving in Calgary on July 9, the Tweedsmuirs spent the next several days in attendance at various Stampede activities.

An excursion was made by train from Calgary, north, to the town of Red Deer where Tweedsmuir attended numerous functions in a persistent rain,[125] making a brief public address and an impression on the residents, one of whom remembers his description of their town: "It is so pleasant to see your setting, with smiling green hills all around your town valley."[126]

From Red Deer, a lengthy and tiring one hundred kilometre drive eastward to the small community of Stettler and back took the better part of a day. At the Stettler arena, Tweedsmuir addressed a large crowd, including in his remarks that "the Governor-General should never be off the road."[127] His presence proved he hardly was!

After their return to Calgary, Tweedsmuir and his party travelled north to the provincial capital of Edmonton, where a garden party was held at Government House. There the governor saw Harry Snyder again, whom he had met in Ottawa and who had promised to host Tweedsmuir and his party at the Eldorado mines on the eastern end of Great Bear Lake on August 6 or 7.[128] Preparations were finalized in Edmonton for the voyage "Down North."

CHAPTER 14

"Lure of the Far North"

The North, as a place both physical and metaphysical, had long captured John Buchan's imagination. He was attracted to it by a sense of adventure and exploration, of danger and discovery. Northern lands had provided settings for several of his pre-Canada novels.[1] In 1924 Buchan published *The Last Secrets*, a book about "some of the main achievements" of exploration in the first two decades of the twentieth century, including the conquest of the North Pole.[2] It was, for him, the same as it was for the Polar explorer Nansen, whom he liked to quote on the subject: "the power of the Unknown over the mind of man."[3] It isn't surprising, then, that when an exploration club was formed at John Buchan's alma mater, Oxford University, in 1927, he should have been its first president.[4] He remained president, even through his time as governor general.

In the year prior to his appointment to Canada, the president of the Oxford University Exploration Club was approached for offers of support. He "helped considerably with introductions" for an expedition to Ellesmere Island, the most northerly point of land in Canada.[5] The Ellesmere Land Expedition, as it was called, was planned to take place over twelve months during 1934–1935, and was organized by the then twenty-three-year-old Edward Shackleton, son of the famous

Antarctic explorer Ernest Shackleton. Colonel Georges Vanier of the Canadian High Commission in London submitted the expedition plans to the Canadian government for approval and support. The government agreed, on the condition that the Royal Geographical Society also support the venture; they both did and provided "generous grants."[6] In the summer of 1933, Shackleton visited Canada to meet with officials, including RCMP Commissioner Sir James MacBrien, who subsequently assigned a Sergeant Stallworthy to the project.

The expedition lasted fifteen months, returning to England in October 1935, just as Buchan, now Lord Tweedsmuir, was leaving for Canada. Shackleton wrote a book detailing the expedition, for which Tweedsmuir wrote the "Preface." Buchan was pleased with the success of the mission, noting that those who had undertaken it had demonstrated that "the impulse towards adventure and discovery is as strong today in our young men as ever."[7] Knowing that a further adventure was planned, he added that he was "glad to know that another and a longer expedition is in prospect which will put fully on the scientific map Canada's most northerly territory."

Two and a half months after he arrived in Canada, Tweedsmuir received correspondence about organizing a second expedition, but this time with a request for more support from Canada. Making inquiries about the possibilities, he communicated with Thomas Crerar, the minister of mines and resources, and superintendent-general of Indian affairs. Crerar replied in mid-February 1936, stating that "in order to safeguard British sovereignty in these remote areas," there needed to be further exploration and investigation, as well as administrative acts.[8]

Edward Shackleton would have been encouraged when he received correspondence from Tweedsmuir. "Since I have come to Canada, I am completely captured by the lure of the [F]ar [N]orth."[9] That lure was stimulated further by individuals he met in Ottawa and during his first travels. At a luncheon given by the apostolic delegate at the end of April 1936, he met the vicar-general of the Arctic, "a magnificent old fellow with a long beard" who had spent almost twenty years with the Inuit.[10]

Certain visitors to Rideau Hall also sharpened his interest. A young Graham Rowley, who was just beginning his own northerly career, was the archaeologist of the British-Canadian Arctic Expedition, and had just come over from England in early 1936.[11] On board the transatlantic ship *Alaunia* was Johnnie Buchan, a friend of one of the other members of the expedition. When they arrived in Halifax, Susan Tweedsmuir was there to meet her son but invited all of them "to a delightful dinner in the viceregal coaches."[12] Rowley spent several weeks in Ottawa preparing for the onward journey to Churchill, Manitoba. He was invited to Rideau Hall for lunch and met Johnnie's father. Rowley recalls there was also present an American who had travelled in the Antarctic.[13] These were the sorts of guests — young explorers and adventurers — whose company Tweedsmuir enjoyed and from whom he drew inspiration at many levels. "All my life," he had recently told a group of surveyors, "I have been happiest among the men who spend their days on the outer fringes of civilization."[14]

Shackleton wrote to Tweedsmuir summarizing plans for the second expedition: "One or two flights would be made over the Arctic Ocean, north-west of Ellesmere Land, to search for new land close to the 'Pole of Inaccessibility,' and to claim it for Canada."[15] It is interesting that the Oxford student explorer seemed attuned to an emerging Canadian identity, talking of claiming land for Canada while the Canadian minister speaks of British sovereignty; it was a reflection of Canada's transition following the Statute of Westminster.

The slowness of the administrative process, however, concerned geologist Dr. Robert Bentham, who had been a member of the first expedition. He appealed to Tweedsmuir in late March 1936, to assist in any way he could "to expedite things a little."[16] Tweedsmuir wrote to RCMP Commissioner MacBrien, requesting assistance and asking which department he should approach.

At this point, however, it seems Tweedsmuir received advice concerning his involvement or had reconsidered his official position. A week later he wrote to Shackleton that he was "in rather a difficulty about these expeditions," since, as governor general, he could hardly recommend anything to his government.[17] He did say, however, there was much he could do "in private conversation, but I dare not make any official proposals." There is no record of the expedition taking place.[18]

Throughout 1936 the "lure of the [F]ar [N]orth" intensified. Tweeds-muir's travels west had taken him up to Lake Waskesiu to visit Grey Owl, where he began to feel in touch with the North. Through the winter of 1936–1937, he planned his most ambitious journey — a trip down the Mackenzie River, one of the longest in the world, to the Arctic Ocean, then back south into the interior of British Columbia. By the spring of 1937, he came to see the North "as one of the great unifying factors in the future of the Dominion."[19] By politically uniting the "different economic worlds" of East and West, the North could play a significant role in a country that defied geography's natural tendency to run north and south. The North is, he wrote, "common to both [E]ast and [W]est, [and] is a natural bridge to unite the two divisions."[20] The regionalism he had observed and heard up to now led him to consider that, as governor general, he was "the only *trait d'union* between the Atlantic and the Pacific, the St. Lawrence and the North Pole."[21] This, he believed, was why he had "to be constantly on the road."

Following final preparations in Edmonton, the viceregal group departed on July 20, travelling northward to Waterways, the "end of steel." Tweedsmuir noted that "at Lac LaBiche one begins to feel the North."[22] That "feeling" must have been in part personified by the colourful characters who shared the train with the viceregal party. They were described by one of the party, Dr. Thomas Wood, a composer and travel writer from England, as "trappers, hunters, miners, and prospectors, who eat, sing, chew, play poker, spit hard and true into burnished cuspidors, and seem free at any moment to tell you their plans, accept a cigarette, and applaud while the policeman chases another hobo off the roof."[23]

When they arrived at Waterways, Tweedsmuir's group became the guests of the Hudson's Bay Company (HBC), represented by a young official, Richard H.G. Bonnycastle. Bonnycastle feared the voyage would be a stifling exercise in formality, but his fears were immediately put to rest. He later described his few weeks' association with Tweedsmuir as one of the great privileges of his life, and described the man himself as "a most natural, friendly, and charming person."[24] From this point on, apart from fulfilling his objectives as governor general, one of Tweedsmuir's main tasks was to also record impressions and ideas about the work of the Hudson's Bay Company in the North, which HBC Governor Ashley Cooper had asked him to provide during a visit to Ottawa.[25]

From Waterways, where they visited the much-vaunted Abasand Oil Field, the party made its way by barge along a shallow Athabasca River to Fort McMurray. There they boarded a stern-wheeler, steaming their way to Lake Athabasca, with a brief, informal stop at Fort Chipewyan where, according to the Canadian Press report, Tweedsmuir received "a rousing welcome at the wharf."[26] It was a scene that would be repeated at each stop until they reached Aklavik; the special guest would be met by the local aboriginal leaders, RCMP officers, priests, traders, trappers, and other residents. The historian in Tweedsmuir did not miss the significance of Fort Chipewyan. It was from here that Alexander Mackenzie set out in the late 1700s on his major journeys of exploration, first to the Arctic and later to the Pacific.

Hudson's Bay Company Achives/Provincial Archives of Manitoba/1987/363-T-27/46

A relaxed governor general sits with HBC official Richard Bonnycastle on a barge being pushed in front of a steamer, July 1937. Bonnycastle described his time with Tweedsmuir as one of the great privileges of his life and described Tweedsmuir as "a most natural, friendly and charming person."

Down the Slave River from Chipewyan, the stern-wheeler pushed two barges. For part of the way, and with decent weather, Tweedsmuir sat in the bow of the first barge, reading. He had purchased six twenty-cent novels in Winnipeg on his way out.[27] He described this as "the most peaceful form of voyaging I have ever discovered," reading and also working on the index of his just completed historical biography of Augustus.[28]

The *Northland Echo* arrived at Fort Fitzgerald, about halfway down the Slave River, at which point the waterway became impassable because of a series of rapids with suggestive names like "The Mountain" and "The Rapids of the Drowned." The voyagers had to disembark and drive to Fort Smith in "a series of antiquated cars, of which the governor general's was the newest — it had only done seventy-two thousand miles,"[29] significant mileage in those days of bumpy, gravel roads.

The party reached Fort Smith, on the Alberta-Northwest Territories border, on Friday, July 23. They were finally "North of 60" (degrees latitude). Since Fort Smith was "the Northwest's biggest settlement" and "official headquarters of the Northwest Territories," there was a commissioned RCMP officer stationed there; a hospital; two day schools,

Tweedsmuir aboard the SS Athabaska River, *with Mrs. Redfern on his left and Mrs. G.A. Macdonald, July 1937.*

Lt. S.G. Rivers-Smith/Hudson's Bay Company Archives/The Provincial Archives of Manitoba/1988/6/539

one Roman Catholic and the other Anglican; the HBC store; and a wireless station manned by the Royal Canadian Corps of Signals.

The RCMP detachment was paraded for inspection. One young corporal, Stirling McNeil, didn't have to stand for inspection, however, because he was an engineer on the boats, although that day he had been tasked with related duties and put in charge of mowing the lawn on the grounds.[30] He was later introduced to His Excellency by RCMP Inspector D.J. Martin for a brief exchange of "How do you do, Sir."[31] Following the inspection, the governor general addressed the community's "civic reception committee" and repeated his optimism about the North. "So far," he began, "we have only scraped the edges of [the North], but I believe we are going to make it far more habitable than it is," then added, "[y]ou are at a gateway to what I believe is a great treasure house," referring to the potential natural resources being discovered.[32]

Finally, the viceregal party embarked on their second Hudson's Bay Company steamer, the SS *Distributor*, described as "simply a flat-bottomed wooden scow with two superimposed upper decks that looked very much like the verandahs of early Canadian and American houses."[33] Dr. Wood listed the special passengers boarding the steamer: Aide-de Camp (ADC) Lt. (Navy) Gordon Rivers-Smith; Private Secretary Shuldham Redfern and his wife; RCMP Inspector D.J. Martin; a sergeant of the Signals Corp; a minister of religion, Dr. George Macdonald; the Canadian Press reporter, Guy Rhoades; and the celebrated American photographer, Margaret Bourke-White. The latter was working for the year-old *Life* magazine, and had only just arrived by float plane on this last-minute assignment. She came with a collection of mourning cloak butterflies she was photographing through their life cycle.[34] Her presence may well have been Tweedsmuir's initiative, since it would fit his strategy to make Canada better known in the United States. Dr. Wood described Bourke-White as "American, dynamic, and femininity itself." There were, in addition, one horse, one cow, some sheep, two pigs, nine hundred tons of cargo and a pair of canaries.[35]

From Fort Smith, the stern-wheeler churned the water of the Slave River that cut its way through the vast green wilderness and emptied into Great Slave Lake, where Fort Resolution, the great lake's fur trade headquarters, was located. Hay River was next, a relatively short distance further west along the shore. The following day, Sunday, July 25, Reverend Macdonald held a service on board that, in the words of Shuldham Redfern "was of the type calculated to make an instant appeal … short … no sermon and … no collection."[36]

Continuing over calm waters along the western end of Great Slave Lake, they reached Fort Providence, "[twenty] families big," where they entered the mighty Mackenzie River. While talking with the Oblate missionaries, Tweedsmuir's memories of the Great War were rekindled because one of them "had been badly wounded at Verdun in an infantry regiment which I knew all about."[37]

On Monday, July 26, they reached Fort Simpson, where they put in for several hours, so cargo could be unloaded. There was a certain amount of excitement generated in the southern press by Guy Rhoades's article: "Lord Tweedsmuir saw wheat and vegetables growing on a farm 950 miles northwest of Edmonton. Even melons were grown there last year. Doesn't this give us a new idea of Canada?" ran one headline.[38] The popular impression contrasted, however, with more informed opinion that Tweedsmuir would certainly have been aware of from discussions with officials in Ottawa and his own reading. "Agriculture can play no important part in that future," wrote Lawrence J. Burpee, a noted historian, adding that "the awakening of the North can come only from the development of its mineral resources."[39] This view was shared by a "son of the North," Charles Camsell, the long-time deputy minister of mines and, from 1936, commissioner of the Northwest Territories.[40] Regardless, the government wished that "interest may be quickened and pride increased in a part of the Dominion which for so long has been considered by some as being of little value in our economic life."[41]

The HBC factor at Simpson, "LACO" Hunt, had been asked to organize a welcome. The question the townspeople asked was what kind of gift would be suitable for the king's representative. Hunt describes a generous piece of moosehide, beautifully tanned by Dené women, on which "Wilhelmina McGurran, our expert seamstress, worked in silk and beads a map of the Mackenzie District [and at] the bottom right-hand corner, she fashioned the arms of the Tweedsmuir family." "[O]n the momentous day,"

Hunt continued, "I made a short speech of welcome and presented the gift, pointed out that the work of art was the result of the spontaneous efforts of all the people of Fort Simpson: white, Metis and Indian."[42]

It was also at Fort Simpson that Tweedsmuir first heard of the rugged, almost inaccessible region of the South Nahanni River that flowed from the north into the Liard River. It was believed at the time to be an area of great mineral wealth. There were stories of men who had gone into the region to explore and prospect but who were never heard of again. Tweedsmuir noted that the "South Nahanni fascinates me, and I want to make a trip there … before I leave Canada." It was a wish he never realized, but one that provided inspiration for his last, Canadian novel.[43]

As they continued their journey, all on board waited for Bourke-White's butterflies to emerge from the chrysalis, with Tweedsmuir showing particular curiosity about them. She recalls "His Ex" asking her, while on his walks around the deck: "Hey Maggie, when is the blessed event coming?"[44] When it did, Tweedsmuir assisted by holding reflectors for Bourke-White, who took photographs, but only after an acquiescing captain stopped the engines so there would be no vibration to chance blurring the photographs.

Sailing on from Fort Simpson, into "a wonderful sunset," Tweedsmuir observed that the Liard's "muddy current pollutes the Mackenzie, which from the Great Slave Lake had been clear." It was, for him, "the only part of the river where the scenery is really impressive."[45] They continued their journey, making a brief stop at Fort Wrigley. Guy Rhoades reported the next day from "aboard SS *Distributor*" that the weather was "drowsy and hot and no one felt energetic, a contrast with last night's impromptu concert" when everyone had been singing "lustily after midnight."[46]

When they arrived at Fort Norman (known now as Tulita, which is Dene, and means, "where the waters meet") on Wednesday, July 28, their usual brief stop to unload cargo was prolonged so that the fires in the boat's boilers could be extinguished and maintenance performed. At the confluence of the Bear River, which empties from the east into the Mackenzie, there stands a solitary protrusion known as Bear Rock, rising about 1,300 feet. While it is not a snow-topped mountain, it revived the mountaineer in John Buchan. Age was no barrier for this sixty-two-year-old governor general. Several of the party joined him in a climb up the face of Bear Rock. But not Richard Bonnycastle, who later noted: "I had been up some years previously, and this time, avoiding the face of the mountain, which I knew was difficult, worked around to the wooded part of the slope [while] His Excellency insisted on going up the steep face.... I was uneasy about those climbing up the face because of its difficulty and danger.... The rock was so insecure and crumbling that one could not depend on any of it."[47]

Bonnycastle expressed his concern to Tweedsmuir's aide-de-camp, Rivers-Smith, who simply replied that the governor general was an experienced mountaineer, though the rest of them were not. The result of the day's climb confirmed the comment. Rivers-Smith and the reverend decided to follow Tweedsmuir but ended up having to be rescued.[48] When the governor general arrived at the top, with torn trousers, he remarked to Bonnycastle that "it was one of the nastiest climbs he had ever made and would make the blood of experienced Alpiners curdle."[49] The incident sparked titles in southern newspapers that reflected serious adventure: "Tweedsmuir Escapes Bad Fall on Mountain As Overhang Breaks," and "Nip and Tuck: Tweedsmuir Narrowly Escapes Fall While Mountain-climbing."[50]

After the *Distributor's* boilers had been cleaned, and all was ready for them to depart, high winds and rain prevented them from steaming on. The governor general used some of the extra time for working, but later on donned an oilskin and travelled in the *Distributor's* work-boat upstream to where a coal seam had been burning continuously since at least Alexander Mackenzie passed the point in 1789.

Finally underway from Fort Norman, the boat made a brief stop on Saturday at Fort Good Hope. That evening they celebrated crossing the Arctic Circle with an invented ritual similar to the one sailors "crossing the line" (the equator) play out involving King Neptune. A suitably grand speech was delivered: "[H]is enfrosted majesty, King Santa Claus [played by Bonnycastle], the first emperor of the snows, grand seigneur of the Aurora Borealis and warden of the midnight sun, in the name of the polar bear, the caribou, the teepee and the kayak, [gives leave to the governor general] to cross the Arctic Circle and be admitted into the most enviable order of seekers for the north."[51]

They reached Fort McPherson on Sunday, August 1. Among the residents Tweedsmuir spoke with was the legendary, eighty-seven-year-old John Firth, who had been a Hudson's Bay Company post manager for fifty years. He refused to leave the North. He disliked civilization, recalling that he had once gone to Winnipeg: "It was in 1908, and I stood on Portage Avenue watching the people rush here and there. Everyone seemed in a terrible hurry, chasing another dollar. I had three months' furlough and I had to come back in one. It was too monotonous."[52] But he must also have been a crusty character, because he was cited as the reason there was no Catholic mission at the post. According to what Shuldham Redfern heard, this post manager had always refused to give credit to Roman Catholics. Recalling a bit of economic history, Redfern noted: "As was discovered and practised by many Elizabethan adventurers, a little commercial bullying is worth any amount of sectarian propaganda."[53]

All along the settlements and posts of the Mackenzie, aside from leaving an autographed copy or two of some of his books, the governor general left an impression of someone special. The owner of one of the

A rest after the harrowing climb up Bear Rock, July 28, 1937. Tweedsmuir (sitting on gunwale) remarked to Bonnycastle (handing Mrs. Redfern a coat) that "it was one of the nastiest climbs he had ever made."

Hudson's Bay Company Archives/Provincial Archives of Manitoba/1987/363-T-27/29 float planes delivering mail to the *Distributor*, Walter E. Gilbert, described Tweedsmuir as someone who "fitted into the picture everywhere down North."[54] The reason, he thought, was "the happy combination of [Tweedsmuir's] own personality and — perhaps — his Scottish blood.... For everywhere on the Mackenzie you will find a Scot 'making good,' and the Governor-General was pre-eminently a Scot on that occasion."[55]

That Sunday evening (August 1), despite some earlier delays, the *Distributor* reached Aklavik, five days ahead of schedule. The headlines in the South proclaimed "Boat Sets New Record on 1,200-Mile Voyage Down Mackenzie River."[56] Everyone on board had agreed the eleven-day journey from Waterways to Aklavik was the fastest time, though nobody could recall the previous record. The entire journey was focusing attention on how much the North was changing. In a conversation recounted by Dr. Wood, one point was made emphatically: "You just wait ten years, then you'll see what flying is going to do for this country."[57]

Indeed, air transportation was becoming the primary tool for exploring and opening up the northern frontier. It was all part of the excitement generated by significant developments in the air that year. C.D. Howe, the minister of transport, made a cross-country flight to review the proposed route of a trans-Canada air service. It was equally big news when a flight from London to New York was publicized as just taking a day. There was also a report by the Dominion Bureau of Statistics that Canada led the world in airborne freight, the overwhelming proportion of which was in the North.

But there was a negative side to the airplane's increasing role in the North. Tuberculosis (TB) was a significant problem among the aboriginal populations in the North; and it would play a major role in John Buchan's last novel, *Sick Heart River*. According to what Tweedsmuir heard from the chiefs at various settlements, TB was attributed largely to malnourishment. Tweedsmuir included this particular concern in memoranda to HBC governor Cooper and to the prime minister. He cautioned about the white man's use of airplanes in the North. "[W]e must be very careful to see that [the Natives' malnourishment] is not due to the intrusion of the white trapper," resulting in less food for the native people. He noted that this was "strongly impressed upon [him] by everyone [he] met in the North who had given any thought to the question." And consistent with what he heard from Grey Owl, Tweedsmuir wrote that "the Indian *[sic]* is a natural conserver and will never over-trap, whereas a white man, especially with the assistance of the aeroplane, will trap a long line without regard to the future, since he can always shift his venue."[58]

The missionaries had also made a strong impression on Tweedsmuir. Their work was multifaceted. As a federal government booklet published that year explained: "Missionary work, education, and hospitalization ... are very closely interwoven by reason of the fact that all schools and hospitals in the Territories are owned by the Roman Catholic or Anglican missions, and are operated with the assistance of grants of money and school and medical supplies from the Dominion Government."[59] Despite these efforts Tweedsmuir observed that "medical services are very patchy," a recurrent theme in his notes.[60] "The right kind of missionary for the North is a medical missionary, for such will always have plenty of work to do," he wrote.[61] Recalling an administrative model used elsewhere in the Empire, he suggested the North have "a picked service, both medical and administrative, to which only the right kind of man is appointed, and not, as occasionally seems to happen, a discard from some other part of the country."[62] The Oblates struck him as particularly well suited. They could do everything from skinning a moose to building a boat, as well as ministering to the soul. He wanted to see the Anglican Church develop a similar group and would later correspond with the archbishop of Canterbury and Lord Halifax about the subject.[63]

The party spent a couple of days at Aklavik, a settlement that Tweedsmuir thought to be "a complete mistake," situated as it was in the middle of the delta, with "no proper sanitation, and the foreshore ... foul."[64] Tweedsmuir's impressions of the delta area also found their way into *Sick Heart River*, and were almost word for word his description recounted in the London *Sunday Times* in December 1937:

> The North is altogether beyond the human scale.... I
> expected bleak moors ... [and] instead I found a kind of
> coarse lushness ... too much coarse vegetation, an infin-
> ity of mud, and everywhere a superfluity of obscene insect

life.... The delta of the Mackenzie is ... the most sinister place I have ever seen.... It reminded me of nothing so much as the no-man's-land between the trenches in the war — but a colossal no-man's-land created in some campaign of demons — pitted and pocked with shell-holes from some infernal artillery.[65]

It had been the intention of the viceregal party to fly from Aklavik to Herschel Island in the Arctic Ocean, but the weather prevented them from doing so. Instead, when the Royal Canadian Air Force (RCAF) aircraft arrived, they flew the governor general to Tuktoyaktuk on the Arctic coast, which, when compared to Aklavik and the delta area, had "an open clean shore." "One had a wonderful feeling of space and peace," Tweedsmuir wrote.[66] During their return flight to Aklavik, they flew over a herd of reindeer, numbering in the thousands. The reindeer were being brought from Alaska on a three-year journey "to encourage the Eskimo to be a herdsman as well as a hunter."[67] This was part of the Dominion government's development efforts in the North.[68]

Hudson's Bay Company Archives/Provincial Archives of Manitoba/1987/363-T-27/40

"One had a wonderful feeling of space and peace." Tweedsmuir gazes out over the Arctic Ocean, August 1937.

The next day, Wednesday August 4, the viceregal party left Aklavik by air. Bad weather forced them to put down at Fort Norman, where temporary accommodation was made for the night. Fortunately, the next morning was clear, and they flew on to Cameron Bay (Port Radium) on the eastern end of Great Bear Lake, arriving in the evening. They were met by Harry Snyder,[69] as had been arranged when the two met at a dinner hosted by Eldorado Mining at Ottawa's Chateau Laurier Hotel the previous November where Tweedsmuir was guest speaker.

After an agreeable, if late, supper, Tweedsmuir retired to his cabin, while the others stayed up to talk and tell stories. It was quite late when the Mounties and a foreman from the Eldorado mine left by boat for the RCMP base back at Cameron Bay. As they were approaching the dock, a wave struck; the foreman slipped off the bow, fell into the water, and drowned. One of the Mounties jumped in to try and rescue him, but he, in turn, had to be rescued by the remaining officer. It was not reported in the press and we have no record of what His Excellency's reaction was. The tragedy was, however, recounted in a rather nonchalant manner by Snyder, in an article

Hudson's Bay Company Archives/Provincial Archives of Manitoba/1987/363-T-27/31

The governor general picnics on the shore of Great Bear Lake with Harry Snyder of Eldorado Mining (standing), Leigh Brintnell, president of Mackenzie Air Service, and Mrs. Brintnell, August 1937.

he wrote for *Canadian Geographic*: "It is generally accepted that if a man goes clear under in Great Bear Lake the chill of the water paralyzes him and he never comes up. Such are the risks and hazards of the North."[70]

The next morning Tweedsmuir toured the Eldorado mine, the world's main producer of radium, used in cancer treatment. A few years before, in 1930, international attention had been focused on the region by the discovery of pitchblende (from which radium was extracted) and silver deposits. That afternoon Tweedsmuir and his aide-de-camp were flown to Camsell River for some trout fishing and met with "splendid success" according to Snyder.

Perfect weather on the following day permitted Snyder to fly Tweedsmuir to Coppermine, where the river of the same name empties into Coronation Gulf. As they flew northward from the eastern end of Great Bear Lake, the trees diminished in size and faded into "the Barrens." Seen from the air, the Barrens appeared in marked contrast to the "sinister" Mackenzie delta, but the scale was similar: "The cloud shadows in these infinite plains, in constant motion, made a beautiful, fantastic world. It was all out of scale with humanity; but it is a good thing now and then if you manage to realize that the world was not created on your own scale. It sharpens the adventure of living."[71]

Before landing in Coppermine, Snyder delighted in flying forty miles out over Coronation Gulf which was still full of ice, "so His Excellency could see just what Arctic ice looks like."[72] Tweedsmuir later reflected: "I never thought, as a young man, that at sixty I should be flying over the Arctic."[73] When they departed Coppermine, they brought with them an Inuit woman who had to travel to Fort Smith for medical treatment.

On August 9 Tweedsmuir and his party flew from Eldorado, passed over Fort Rae, and went on to Fort Smith, where they spent the night, returning to Edmonton the next day. The strain of the trip, however, wreaked havoc with Tweedsmuir's health. Indeed, it had been quite evident at Fort Simpson, when Lord Tweedsmuir abruptly left a dinner aboard the *Distributor*, an event that caused LACO Hunt to wonder "if [he] had said something to offend." Shuldham Redfern assured him, no, saying in a soft voice, "ulcers, dear boy."[74] The governor's condition had at times also alarmed Guy Rhoades, who later wrote that Tweedsmuir told him: "You need not be afraid I am going to die.... I have been going on like this for years."[75] When he returned to Edmonton, where he rejoined Susan, he was tired, weak, and not at all well, but he also felt very content and fulfilled.

For several days Tweedsmuir rested in bed, but still spent the time productively, dictating notes to his literary secretary Lillian Killick, about his impressions of the journey. He had written almost daily accounts of his activities on specially printed note paper, with a map and place names along the left hand edge, marking where on the map they were. The typed notes were later sent to Mackenzie King.

Having rested and regained some strength, Tweedsmuir departed Edmonton on Saturday, August 14, to set out on a second major Canadian wilderness adventure, this time accompanied by Susan. They travelled on the CNR line through Prince George, British Columbia, and on to Burns Lake. With preparations made in advance, they left Burns Lake on August 15 to begin a trek into the 981,000 hectare Tweedsmuir Park which the provincial government had established and named in his honour just the previous year.[76] Again, Tweedsmuir would be following in the footsteps of Alexander Mackenzie, who had explored the area in 1793.

During the course of the journey by boat, canoe, pack-horse, and aircraft, the governor general visited some of the Native communities. The Babine and Bella Coola First Nations each made him an honorary chief, with the names "Chief of the Big Mountain" and "The Man from Above Who Has Come to Help Us," respectively. The latter suggests they had expectations, but we do not have a record of what those expectations might have been.

Tweedsmuir noted that he was particularly proud that his name was attached to "one of the most beautiful pieces of country in the world."[77] Susan recorded their experiences, which were later published in *National Geographic*.[78] It was all very exciting, especially for "His Ex," who, she described, "as an old mountaineer, becomes slightly lunatic at the sight of the high snows," and, with respect to flying, "is air-minded to the pitch of being light-minded"![79] Susan, herself, had to keep her eyes covered for much of the time to counter her fear of flying. It did not help that their flight toward the coast had some tense moments of "sensational flying," through foggy mountain passes. They came out through Dean Channel, and then made their way by "comfortable steamer" up to Prince Rupert, where they boarded the train for a five-day journey back to Ottawa.

Tweedsmuir spent time during the trip revising his initial note to the prime minister, and worked on his promised report for HBC Governor Ashley Cooper, as well as on a memo for George Allen, the company's senior official in their Winnipeg office. These reports demonstrate not only Tweedsmuir's relationship with his prime minister and the scope of his productive mind, but also his concern for the indigenous peoples, particularly their health, and his desire to promote responsible development in the North. In his note to George Allen, Tweedsmuir also wanted "to put on record" how much he thought of Richard Bonnycastle, "just the kind of man that any great organization, private or public, is always looking for."[80] He also wrote to Governor Cooper that Bonnycastle was "one of the best fellows I have met for many a day.... I congratulate you."[81] Tweedsmuir's judge of character confirmed HBC's selection of Bonnycastle. Bonnycastle, after a time with the Hudson's Bay Company went on to become a very successful businessman, owning among other companies, the publisher Harlequin; he was later appointed chancellor of the University of Winnipeg.

Settled again in the capital, Tweedsmuir arranged with the fledgling Canadian Broadcasting Corporation to read a heartfelt letter of thanks "to my friends in the North" who had helped make the journeys such a "wonderful experience."[82] He recalled that he had been able to follow the trails that Alexander Mackenzie blazed to the Arctic and to the Pacific 150 years earlier, but doing it in less than two months and "in conditions of extreme comfort." He conveyed his vision for "the new North," where he believed Canada's future development lay: "a large number of smallish industrial centres in close touch with civilization by radio and air," but realizing that vision depended, he observed, on a "chain of hypotheses, the most important being the cheapening of local oilfields." The key was the advent of air travel. "The North is not an easy problem for Canada," he said, "but it offers a wonderful chance."[83]

The journey continued to appear in the media on into the fall. Rivers-Smith had taken photos throughout the trip, a selection of which appeared in the October 1937 issue of the HBC magazine *The Beaver*.[84] Harry Snyder's article in *Canadian Geographic* included a detailed, diary-like section about the events that attended his stint as host of the governor general at Port Radium.[85] In October as well, Margaret Bourke-White's unique photographic record appeared in *Life* magazine,[86] and, in Britain, the *Times* carried a lively and detailed two-part account of the journey by Thomas Wood.[87] Finally, In London, Lord Kemsley's *Sunday Times* carried detailed articles in two successive issues in December, which were Tweedsmuir's account of the journey. The *Sunday Times* articles fit Tweedsmuir's objective of making Canada better known and understood in Britain, but it was not well received in one particular quarter.

George VI's private secretary, Alexander Hardinge, wrote to Tweedsmuir, emphasizing the importance of his message: "I happen to know that these views correspond to those held by the king."[88] They recognized Tweedsmuir's "laudable" objective, like that of his prime minister's, to make Canada "better known to the rest of the world," but they did not like the idea of the king's representative being "a [p]ublicity [a]gent for boosting a particular Dominion."[89] It was an undignified role and could set a precedent for other governors general, or lead to recriminations that other of the king's representatives were not as successful as Tweedsmuir in "the propaganda race" to promote their particular Dominion. Such actions were inconsistent with limitations on the king himself, and therefore must also apply to his representatives. Hardinge then took the opportunity to raise other criticisms. One *faux pas* in particular was Tweedsmuir's standing for election as chancellor of Edinburgh University. Hardinge also set out a firm reminder that he must avoid any possibility of controversy in his speeches.

Tweedsmuir replied promptly and contritely, addressing each of the criticisms.[90] He assured Hardinge that he would take great care that something similar to the "*Sunday Times* episode" should not happen again. As for the university chancellorship, when he discovered that he was not the only person proposed, he had "great difficulty in knowing what to do," then acknowledged he should have consulted the Palace.

He added that his prime minister encouraged him to accept this "very special honour," and that "[t]here was never ... much doubt that I would be elected."

The special journey to the Arctic was significant in three distinct ways. First, for the northern inhabitants — Dene, Inuit, and white — it was a very special and heartening event to meet the king's representative and see him amongst them, taking a sincere interest in their affairs and future. Second, for Lord Tweedsmuir, the governor general, the trip was important since it allowed him to reach out to those inhabitants and had helped southern Canadians from the East and the West to know and better understand a defining and developing region of their country, for which he saw potential economically and as a unifying force. He had reported his observations to the prime minister and the Hudson's Bay Company governor, and had called especial attention to the health and welfare of the aboriginal populations, for which he as "representative of the Crown feels a special responsibility."[91] Finally, for John Buchan, the writer, the scenery, the history, and the colourful characters he had met along the way had stimulated his creative mind and helped provide inspiration for *Sick Heart River*, and a children's book, *The Long Traverse*, by which he hoped to spark young people's interest in the excitement and adventure of the early explorers in their country.

CHAPTER 15

A mari usque ad mare — iterum

Despite having been away from Ottawa for two months on his spectacular northern and western journeys, Tweedsmuir had little time for rest in Ottawa. Within weeks of his return, he set out again. This time it was to make good on a promise to visit Prince Edward Island, after he had had to cancel the previous year due to illness. The governor general's train bypassed Halifax this time and carried him through to Cape Breton Island, which he described as being "more Highland than the Highlands of Scotland!"[1]

He crossed on the ferry to the provincial capital, Charlottetown. After official welcomes and a tour of Chester McLure's Silver Fox Farm, called Vimy Ranch, he addressed a large crowd in the capital. His speech bore largely on the objective he had added by the end of his first year — unity, which depended on loyalties beyond the provincial level. We explored Tweedsmuir's concept of loyalty in an earlier chapter, but he used the island's uniqueness as an opportunity to make his point. Describing the "peculiar pride" island inhabitants tend to have, he extolled the virtues of small places. But although this "patriotism of the small unit," as he phrased it, "is no less important to have [than] the patriotism of the bigger unit," there is nothing inconsistent between the two.[2] This country, he said, "is destined to be one of the greatest nations in the world," but only if, "in addition to your strong love of your home, you have also a pride and affection for the whole Dominion."

After his return to Ottawa, Tweedsmuir spent October and November making short trips to major centres of central Canada and indulging in more "speechifying." In early October, in Ottawa, he spoke to the annual civil service dinner, sketching the development of constitutional government and the creation of a permanent civil service, "essential to any government, but … especially necessary in a democracy." He outlined the required characteristics of a modern civil service, which reflected the world out of which it emerged in Britain: "it must be open to all; … offer a career to talents drawn from every class; … freedom from political bias; … security of tenure; … [and it must be] anonymous."[3]

In mid-October he was in Montreal, speaking to the Canadian Institute of International Affairs, an event dealt with in a previous chapter. The first week of November, he travelled to Hamilton to address the faculty and students at McMaster University on how dangerous it can be if quantity becomes our focus and is not inspired by quality.

> [Q]uantity is futile unless it can be permeated and dominated by quality.… We have acquired a new power over inanimate things, a power of which we cannot foretell the

Public Archives and Records Office of Prince Edward Island/Lena Caroline McLure fonds/Acc3387/Series1/19/P0004228

Tweedsmuir with Dutch children at Vimy Silver Fox Ranch, Prince Edward Island, September 28, 1937.

limits … [and] attain[ed] a speed of movement which a generation ago was unthinkable.… [We] can literally move mountains.… [We have] telescoped the world so that distance means little.… What value is our new control over physical force unless, by means of it, we can better the life of man? … We have created a gigantic machine, but unless we can use it, it will make use of us to our detriment.[4]

His philosophical address described practical examples to emphasize "what vain things mass and quantity were unless inspired by quality."[5] "We were prone to boast of an Empire on which the sun never set — but, as Mr. Chesterton once said, there is not much charm in an Empire which has no sunsets! … [Britain's] task is to use the discoveries of science in order to get from her vast estate the maximum value, … and to assist the varied peoples in their advance towards civilisation and self-rule.… Democracy … is the best method of government which the human mind has yet devised; but it is also the most difficult."[6]

Hudson's Bay Company Archives/Provincial Archives of Manitoba/1987/363-T-27/6

Tweedsmuir with Chester McLure, owner of the Vimy Silver Fox Ranch, Prince Edward Island, September 28, 1937.

He returned to Toronto at the end of November and then continued on to Montreal, for speaking engagements to poets and the Association of Canadian Bookmen respectively, talks that are described in a later chapter.

The first several months of 1938 were relatively quiet, for a reason, although there were still some brief trips to Montreal and Toronto. On top of the pain caused by his mother's passing in mid-December, the strain of the previous summer's journeys had wreaked havoc with his health. To his sister, Anna, he wrote letters in which his frustration was evident, but in them he also admitted what he would never say publicly: the Arctic journey had been "too heavy a job" for a man his age, and he was tired of having "no peace in the inward parts."[7] He also told her that he had to get "this wretched digestion of mine right."[8]

In early January he was back in Montreal to welcome McGill University's new principal, Lewis Douglas, an American businessman and sometime politician, but one with Canadian roots.[9] Both Sir Edward Beatty, the chancellor, and Douglas gave lengthy speeches on liberty, the international situation, and the role of the universities in meeting the challenges. Beatty was praised by *La Presse* for an admirable tribute to French culture; he had also reminded the new McGill president that he would be living in the second-largest French-speaking city in the world.[10]

For the first weekend in February, the governor general, as Chief Scout of Canada, travelled to Toronto, where he addressed for a third time the annual dinner of the Boy Scouts Association. He had two main points to impart. The first was a caution about how to treat young people. A combination of respectfulness and frankness best helps to prepare them as citizens, he felt, but he also believed that the respectfulness could be overdone. He described as "foolish" a current approach, which advised "that children must never be checked or reprimanded, or in any way repressed."[11] Recognizing that later life is full of checks, he thought this current "false and trashy psychology," which would make them less able to bear such experiences, ones not uncommon in real adult life.

His second point was a reflection on the miracle of Scouting, with its hundreds of thousands of members around the world, its absence of distinction with respect to class or religion, and its periodic meetings at international jamborees. The world of Scouting sounded, he suggested, like an idyllic world, where peace had been achieved, but the period of its existence was, he reminded his audience, the same thirty years in which the cruellest war in history had been fought. And the nations that had been involved in that war were still at odds. Despite that, the fact that an organization like Scouting existed, based as it was on "profound moral truths," allowed him to be optimistic.

While in Toronto Tweedsmuir made time to visit RCMP commissioner Sir James McBrien who was in hospital, dying of cancer. A month later, McBrien died — "a blessed release," Tweedsmuir reflected.[12]

He was back in Toronto a month later to open the Skating Carnival and do "other odd jobs."[13] More significantly, he addressed the University of Toronto Law Club Dinner on March 8, and proposed the toast to the memory of Lord Durham, as part of the commemoration of the centenary of Durham's famous report, a critical event in Canada's pre-Confederation development. Woven with touches of humour, Tweedsmuir's speech summarized both Durham's character and his work. As Tweedsmuir pointed out, though much criticized in his day, Durham was a reformer, who did much to alter the political landscape in his time. The groundbreaking work for which he is remembered was, surprisingly, the result of only a few months in Canada.

> The foundation stone of his structure was the gift of responsible government.... The kernel of the *Report* is to be found in the famous words, "The Crown must consent to carry the government on by means of those in whom the representative members have confidence.... Durham's achievement lay in the fact that he had the courage to give it a wider application, to shake off the dead hand of [C]olonial [O]ffice paternalism, and to trust the Canadian people.... Durham ... ruined his own career by his work in Canada, but he ... helped build a nation.[14]

Besides the issue of responsible government, perhaps the most significant question to bedevil Durham's brief tenure as governor was that of Protestant-Catholic relations. It was a source of contention for all of Canada's colonial history, and it remained one for the majority of its post-Confederation history as well. It was an issue that would almost certainly have been on Tweedsmuir's mind when he returned to Toronto on March 16, this time to attend the St. Patrick's Ball. It was more of a "special occasion," because the organizers were trying to get the Catholic and the Orange Irish to unite.[15] Their success, of course, was limited.

The next day Susan left Toronto by train, heading west to Winnipeg to visit with Johnnie, who had begun working for the Hudson's Bay Company, while her husband had a full day of commitments, including a visit to a girls' school and a meeting at the University of Toronto. That evening he addressed a crowd of about three thousand attending the Bible Society's annual meeting celebrating the four hundredth anniversary of Tyndale's version of the Bible. He was presented a copy of the Scriptures in Cree.

The following Monday Tweedsmuir was back in Montreal, again at McGill University, to address the twentieth anniversary of the Canadian National Committee for Mental Hygiene, of which he was patron.[16] He praised the increasing acceptance of health being considered in the broadest sense, because physical health was nothing without mental health. The younger generation, he said, was afflicted by strains uncommon in the past, but even older individuals were now suffering from sudden mental breakdowns "and a career of achievement often ended in darkness."[17] The effects of the war had not yet run their course either, he reminded them. He cited statistics for health care and social costs.[18] He then described three areas where improvement and help could be focused: research, administration, and education.[19] It was encouraging to those in the field to have support from the highest office in the land.

Tweedsmuir's own physical condition at this time, however, again came under serious siege, and for the next ten days he suffered constantly from nausea. He spent most of the time in bed, "living on slops," as he described his diet, and hoping his insides sorted themselves out.[20]

April was another relatively quiet month. Tweedsmuir required time to recover prior to another trip to the Prairies that was planned for May. On April 23 Susan departed for England, for a holiday and family visits. Two weeks after she left, Tweedsmuir wrote to her that he hoped his upcoming trip would have beneficial effects on his health, similar to their first trip west.[21] He added that Dr. Meakins had found another drug, not morphine, to help his digestive problems. Because of its addictiveness over time, it is understandable that Meakins made an attempt to find an alternative, but the use of morphine suggests the serious level of pain Tweedsmuir endured.

On May 6, 1938, Tweedsmuir started out for the West again, but stopped briefly in Winnipeg to see Johnnie.[22] He arrived in Saskatoon late Sunday evening, May 8. His primary purpose was to visit the almost thirty-year-old University of Saskatchewan, to learn more about the university's contribution to combatting the effects of drought, and to encourage the academic and intellectual life of western Canada. The following day he toured various departments and displayed "the same absorbing interest he has shown in other aspects of Canadian life."[23]

From Saskatoon he headed southwest to the town of Swift Current, spending Tuesday afternoon inspecting development work at the local airport and at the Dominion Experimental Farm. George Spence, the director of rehabilitation under the Prairie Farm Rehabilitation Administration (PFRA), guided the governor general around. Demonstrations of the newest equipment prompted questions. In fact it was noted that in "a natural manner, he mixed with all, ... constantly asking questions," which was observed to be a sincere and evident desire to learn as much as possible.[24] From his tour, Tweedsmuir learned that there had been improvement in the region, with a good amount of water behind a dam that last year was "dust-dry."[25]

From Swift Current, Spence accompanied Tweedsmuir on another dusty drive, to the village of Val Marie, a tiny settlement near the American border, on the edge of what is now Grasslands National Park. Biographer Janet Adam Smith described the visit as a "shot in the arm" to the village.[26] Tweedsmuir inspected a dam being built under the auspices of the PFRA, as part of a project to irrigate some twenty thousand acres.[27] At the site the special guest had lunch with the men working on the dam. Believing that protocol required a separate wash station, officials had had one set up. It remained unused. Tweedsmuir insisted on lining up and washing for lunch with everyone else.[28]

The next day they were driven west to the Cypress Hills, which straddle the border with Alberta. It is an area infamous for a massacre of Assiniboine Indians in 1873.[29] Along the way they stopped to visit a sheep rancher Tweedsmuir had met at the Royal Winter Agricultural Fair in Toronto, and to visit the Gilchrist Brothers Whitemud ranch, where he was given lunch.[30] On their return northeast to Maple Creek, fifty-mile-per-hour winds whipped dust into thick clouds, creating a "darkness like midnight."[31] The old-timers said it was the worst dust storm they had ever seen. From Maple Creek a special train carried Tweedsmuir and his party to Swift Current, where they rejoined the mainline and spent a restful Friday journeying eastward toward a Regina hazy from the dust, arriving at 10 p.m.[32]

The following morning Tweedsmuir was driven east to the Qu'Appelle Valley, making planned and unplanned stops, often to chat with Great War veterans. He visited many of the small towns in the area: Qu'Appelle, historic Fort Qu'Appelle,[33] Lebret, and Indian Head, as well as another Dominion Experimental Farm.[34] Along the way he met with the Catholic missionaries, the local archbishop, and nuns, and met the last surviving member of the jury at the Louis Riel trial, a Mr. E.J. Brooks.[35] He visited hospitals and a sanatorium in Lebret, where he toured the children's pavilion and was presented a pipe holder by a young patient who had carved it with his jackknife.[36]

The large native population received equal attention, with Tweedsmuir making a number of visits to First Nations' schools. As an honorary Cree chief, he met two hereditary Cree chiefs in full dress and emphasized his special responsibility toward them, noting he would make a personal report to the king during his planned trip to England in the summer. Later, he also held an impromptu talk with three Sioux bandmembers from Fort Qu'Appelle, who stated that their reserve had lost their horses during the winter because of a lack of feed. A promise was made to look into the matter, though we have no record of the outcome. He then returned to Government House in Regina.[37]

The viceregal train rolled out of Regina the next day, arriving in Winnipeg around 6 p.m. (May 15). After inspecting the St. John Ambulance Corps and attending church service, where he read the lesson, he had another opportunity to visit with his son, talking until midnight. Departure was difficult, as he felt they were such close companions.[38] Among other activities before he left, he attended the opening of the Dominion Drama Festival.

On his return from the Prairies, Tweedsmuir forwarded a report of his observations to the prime minister, but he was anxious to inform him in person about the more optimistic mood he had observed in the West, especially its southern parts, where the drought had been particularly severe.

The governor general left Ottawa for Toronto on Friday, May 20, to attend the dedication of Holy Blossom Congregation's new temple on Bathurst Street that evening. The new structure was magnificent, he thought, and the service at which he read the lesson was "very beautiful and dignified."[39] In the souvenir pamphlet marking the dedication, there was a note from the governor general in which he noted the "untold misery and oppression" of Jews in many parts of the world, but he remarked that the new synagogue "bears witness" that "they have not lost, and they will not lose, their ancient faith and fortitude." He added, "those of our Jewish friends who live in Canada are free to maintain the great traditions of their race, and can continue to make their contribution to the happiness and culture of mankind."[40]

The following day Tweedsmuir was driven to Hamilton, where he addressed a crowded Canadian Club luncheon, then returned to Toronto. The day after, he attended the seventy-ninth running of the King's Plate horse races. As he presented the plate to the winning jockey, he was momentarily overcome by emotion. The jockey bore a striking resemblance to his brother Alastair, who had been killed in the First World War.[41]

After his return to Ottawa, he remained barely a week before leaving on May 30 for Peterborough, about 250 kilometres west of the capital.

He received a "wonderful welcome" there, and later boarded the *Bessie Butler*, travelling westward through the canal and river system. As the boat reached each set of locks or a village, there were "hordes of people," children, veterans, and representatives of the Women's Institutes asking for Lady Tweedsmuir.[42] He was told that no governor general had been that way since Lord Lansdowne (1883–1888). Travel on the canal was endlessly enjoyable, with the slower pace, he felt, doing him "a world of good." They finally arrived at Lake Simcoe and the town of Orillia, an area he described in his familiar, complimentary superlatives, as "the richest [and the] loveliest," and an "extraordinarily loyal part of Canada."[43]

From Orillia Tweedsmuir and his small party boarded a train to return to the governor's summer residence in Quebec City, arriving on June 6. The next weeks were a combination of visits around the province, with some time off to indulge in personal pastimes. He attended a garden party hosted by Lieutenant-Governor Ésioff-Léon Patenaude at Government House (known then as Spencerwood, though it would later be called by its older name, Bois de Coulonge), and enjoyed a pleasant afternoon in the wide, two-storey, colonnaded structure, with its beautiful grounds leading down to the river.[44] During this period he also hosted dinner at the Citadel, which was attended by Premier Duplessis.

On June 14, the commander in chief travelled by car to inspect the military base at Valcartier. The next day it was a ride over bumpy roads to Bishop's College in Lennoxville, an English-speaking area in the Eastern Townships of Quebec. At Bishop's he received an honorary degree (D.C.L.).[45] In his address he spoke of the monarchy and the Commonwealth, and explained the concept of kingship. He made explicit comparison between the values of hereditary monarchy and the dictatorships in Europe.[46]

> [E]ven when the character of the monarch was despised, the office was immensely respected.... [Kingship] focuses the historic consciousness of the nation.... It is the point around which coheres the nation's sense of a continuing personality.... [A] hereditary monarchy such as ours prevents any violent changes which weaken attachment; ...

[it] has, of course, its drawbacks, but as a practical method
it has the enormous advantage that it is beyond popular
caprice. It operates automatically and unconsciously like
a process of nature, and therefore it has the strength of a
natural process.... In reverencing our [k]ing we reverence
what is best in ourselves.[47]

After this engagement Tweedsmuir looked forward to a piscatorial
weekend on the Montmorency River, with his son Johnnie, who was
joining him from Winnipeg, and with Ferris Greenslet, a partner in his
American publisher, Houghton Mifflin.

Peterborough Museum and Archives

*Tweedsmuir, accompanied by the mayor of Peterborough, Ontario, approaches
the war memorial to lay a wreath, May 1938. Tweedsmuir saw such ceremonies
as important acts of public commemoration, but they also had very personal
significance, too, and he performed them in virtually every community he visited.*

Later in June he travelled to the United States to receive honorary degrees from Harvard and Yale, returning to Quebec City on June 25. His only plan was to "lie doggo" and rest before sailing for England and joining Susan.[48] He wrote to her that his gastritis continued "grumbling away in the background," but, ever hopeful, he looked forward to the ocean voyage home, anticipating some positive effect on his health.

He returned to Ottawa to prorogue Parliament, it being noted in Hansard that he had postponed his departure for England to do so. It was a point appreciated by King,[49] and indicative of Tweedsmuir's dedication — dedication that was generally recognized in other quarters, too. King George VI was much impressed with his representative's "tireless activity," and felt certain it would have a very positive impact both within Canada and in terms of relations with the United States.[50]

The five-day voyage over the Atlantic was rough, though, and Tweedsmuir looked forward to reaching his home near Oxford. He must have sunk into Elsefield as into a comfortable old sofa, with a sense of relief and comfort that was only magnified by his constant ill health. Despite cold and cloudy weather, he found his home "looking very beautiful ... [with] the same smells that Broughton [a boyhood family home] used to have."[51] It made him feel better. A few days to relax and reflect, with no official engagements except at Edinburgh University, where he was installed as chancellor, added to his sense of well-being. His reflection yielded one resolution, which was "not to

Peterborough Museum and Archives/983-023

The governor general on board the Bessie Butler, flagship of the Trent Canal system, in the locks at Buckhorn in Central Ontario, June 1938.

go back to Canada until I get my inside[s] in decent order."[52] He arranged to see Lord Dawson of Penn, a doctor to the royal family, within the first week. Until he saw him, he would make no other plans.

Following his appointment with Dawson on July 11, Tweedsmuir advised his prime minister that the doctor had recommended a treatment of four or five weeks at Ruthin Castle, a clinic in north Wales. This was a possibility that he and Mackenzie King must have discussed previously, and which is implied in his letter: "I know that you agree to my extending my leave."[53] King encouraged him to stay longer if it would help.

The extension meant cancellations he regretted, including another trip to western Canada and a meeting with President Roosevelt for the August 18 opening of the Thousand Islands International Bridge, at Gananoque, Ontario.[54] Toward the end of August, King, himself bedridden, with lumbago and sciatica, wrote Tweedsmuir that if more rest would put him in better shape, he should stay, adding that the public, knowing of his poor health, "would wish and expect it."[55] The rest did help, and Tweedsmuir continued to put on weight.

While away he secured a positive reply regarding the possibility of a royal visit, and his thoughts turned to the planning of it, something that would consume much of his time and energy over the coming winter. It was now the end of September, and he had been away from Canada for three months. For the moment the world seemed a bit safer too. British prime minister Neville Chamberlain had returned from Munich, and his now infamous meeting with Hitler, declaring "peace in our time." It was time to return home to Canada.

The governor general was welcomed at Quebec City by his honorary aides-de-camp on October 7. He boarded his rail car almost immediately, bound for Montreal, where he was met during a brief stop by Sir Edward Beatty and Jack McConnell, and then he proceeded on to Ottawa. The prime minister, the leader of the opposition, and many others met him, in a display of respect and affection. He would not stay off the road for long, however. Central Ontario, Toronto, and western Ontario were his destinations.

The first major stop reflected the still large rural and agricultural character of the country. A province-wide ploughing match was under-way at Lake Simcoe, near Barrie, with an estimated seventy thousand people in attendance.[56] Tweedsmuir was persuaded to try his hand behind a plough. The ploughman in charge of the team of two large draught horses slipped the leather harness over Tweedsmuir's head and instructed him to grab the plough handles. A rather unsure smile crossed Tweedsmuir's face. With a jerk, the horses were led off, with the governor, looking more in tow than in charge, stepping awkwardly over the chewed, up ground behind them. The scene was captured on newsreel and shown in cinemas. The popular governor general was at his good-natured best, mixing with people and taking obvious delight in the experience. He and his party were then driven to a local hall where they were served lunch at what "was a happy and successful occasion" for the locals.[57]

From Lake Simcoe the viceregal party travelled south to Toronto, where they attended "a big popular concert" attended by about 7,500 people.[58] The next afternoon, October 14, Lady Tweedsmuir received

National Film Board of Canada. All rights reserved

Tweedsmuir thanks a young man who had helped him handle a pair of horses to plough a few feet of ground at a ploughing match near Barrie, Ontario, in October 1938.

an honorary degree from the University of Toronto for her contributions to Canada, especially those with respect to the Women's Institutes and the Prairie Libraries Scheme, which sent forty thousand books to libraries throughout the rural areas of the Prairies.[59] She "made a really excellent speech," according to her husband, countering professional historians' criticism of the Women's Institutes local histories, which she supported and which became known as the Tweedsmuir Histories. That evening the couple presided over a ball, held in a small drawing-room, for forty debutantes.

The following day the governor general received an honorary doctor of laws degree from the University of Western Ontario, in London. Tweedsmuir's address focused on Canada's frontiers, but not just the physical ones. He declared: "Every university should live on the frontier of thought, and by research and speculation be steadily pressing forward the kingdom of knowledge."[60] He gave as one example what he had seen first hand in the drought areas of the Prairies; pushing the frontier of knowledge, he remarked, was helping to attenuate the problems there, "to make Prairie farming weatherproof, to so readjust it that in a bad year a farmer [would] not be ruined." He referred to the North, its current developments and its promise. As governor general, he said, his primary task was "to interest Canadians in Canada — in all Canada," and concluded by encouraging his youthful audience to be "alive to the opportunities ... in the physical and intellectual spheres, to enlarge the boundaries of knowledge."

They arrived back at Ottawa on the morning of October 16, welcomed by summer-like temperatures. He had a month at home, attending to other duties, resting and writing, before he left Ottawa again, departing on November 15, heading ultimately to Quebec City. He spent the first evening, though, in Montreal, where he took part in a full-dress parade inspection of one of the oldest French-Canadian militia regiments, *les Fusiliers de Mont-Royal*.[61] The following day included a stop in Trois Rivières, where he was welcomed by Mayor Atchez Pitt and Quebec Minister of Lands and Forests John Bourque. Tweedsmuir replied to their remarks, speaking in both French and English, then moved on to lay a wreath at the cenotaph in Place Boucher. This was followed by inspections of local veterans and Scouts, as well as the cadets of LaSalle Academy, and, finally, a meeting with Bishop Comptois.

The following week included a day trip up the Ottawa Valley to the town of Renfrew,[62] then a return to Toronto for the annual Royal Winter Fair, which, he proudly commented to friends, had "the best show of stock

John Phillips/Library and Archives Canada/C-28759

Susan Tweedsmuir examines books collected for her Prairie Libraries Scheme. In total some forty thousand books were collected for distribution.

in the world."[63] The viceregal couple returned to Ottawa on Thursday, November 24. The last day of 1938, Tweedsmuir spent resting in bed, to be ready for a New Year's levee he held at the Parliament Buildings on January 2. On January 3 he travelled west of Ottawa to another Scottish namesake town, Perth, where he officially opened a new hospital.[64]

Midwinter a flu afflicted Tweedsmuir, along with many in the household at Rideau Hall, causing him to be bedridden a good deal of the time. On his healthier days, he made short trips, including ones to Kingston and Montreal. In Kingston on February 3, he gave a talk at the Royal Military College. There the governor general planned to "speak to the lads about Lawrence" (of Arabia). One of the 270 cadets present recalls Tweedsmuir winding up his talk by describing the visits Lawrence would make to Elsefield on his motorcycle. He then stated: "Gentlemen, I have never been a hero worshipper, but I would gladly have followed Lawrence over the edge of the world."[65] Another junior cadet, who didn't attend the mess dinner, recalled others who did being impressed "that [Tweedsmuir] would understand his audience so well."[66]

Library and Archives Canada/PA-203294

Susan Tweedsmuir was an active member and supporter of the Women's Institutes and unveiled a plaque honouring the WI founder, Adelaide Hunter-Hoodless.

343

On the trips to Montreal Tweedsmuir made with his wife over the next couple of weeks, he paid another visit to McGill on February 10, opened a new art gallery on February 13, and addressed the annual Boy Scout Association dinner on the February 18. At McGill, he toured several departments and had lunch with Principal Lewis Douglas. He also chaired the last in a series of three lectures hosted by McGill, under the overall title "The State in Society,"[67] and gave the closing address before an audience of some 1,300. Tweedsmuir's primary message was to warn of the dangers in the "artificial isolation of branches of thought, the value of which lies in their organic interconnection." He summarized the dangers:

> The first is intellectual barrenness. If you have a closed system of thought, there is no chance of development. Your subject is never fertili[z]ed by contact with the real world.... You can see this danger in political science.... You find it in economics. You find it in law.... A second danger ... is that, lacking the impulse to compare derived from cognate studies, we can accumulate a mass of facts without any adequate interpretation or evaluation. That is already too true of certain social studies.... A third danger is that ... which we may call ideological intolerance.... If I adopt certain views, legal, political, economic, in isolation, without understanding their historical background, I shall tend to take them for absolute truths, valid everywhere and at any time.... Finally, ... isolationism leads to the most abominable jargon.[68]

It was an assessment and advice that supported Douglas's efforts through the three lectures to counter "the collectivist viewpoint," that is, the view of the socialists, who, he believed, dominated the social sciences faculty.[69] Tweedsmuir's comments were, regardless of Douglas's strategy, an integral part of his humanist approach, as amply expressed in other speeches.

The next several weeks were filled with regular duties: final planning for the royal visit; another trip to the West Coast; and a quick trip to Toronto, where he was made an honorary bencher at Osgoode Hall, and opened a new wing.[70] On the evening of March 12, the Tweedsmuirs boarded rail coaches loaned for their use while the governor general's usual coaches were being prepared for the visit of the king and queen.

The expected "English spring" of the West Coast did not disappoint — fog and light rain were forecast for their arrival on March 16. The main engagement the day after arrival was at the University of British Columbia, to receive an honorary doctor of laws degree. Chancellor R.E. McKechnie bestowed the degree "to a beloved household name."[71] Tweedsmuir delivered what he described as a "harangue,"[72] really a survey of the role of applied science and scientific research in modern society, and an appeal to the students to consider their careers in the field.[73] He made the case as well for pure science. He outlined the practical value of investing in research that returned a thousandfold in so many areas of importance to Canada, and lauded the work of the new National Research Council. Skirting the edges of policy, which he admitted he was approaching, he noted no country is "fully awake" to the possibilities of science and that the "research items in our budgets are ludicrously small." The timing and topic were significant, as discussion of war intensified and the student newspaper ran a survey questionnaire ten days later: "War — yes or no?"[74]

Over the next few weeks, the Tweedsmuirs delighted in their surroundings, and a return to Vancouver Island, which was "delectable," though the governor general's health kept him from enjoying it to the full.[75] His wife was worried, writing to her mother that "John isn't very well."[76]

Their return journey to Ottawa included a couple brief but busy stops. In Calgary they dined at the exclusive Ranchmen's Club, where an exception was made to the men-only rule, to allow Lady Tweedsmuir to attend. Winnipeg was "bitterly cold with a wind that would blow the horns off a cow," Susan wrote, using local idiom. While in Winnipeg Tweedsmuir met with Philip Chester and toured the entire Hudson's Bay Company office, making a lasting impression on the staff by his knowledge and genuine interest in their work.[77] Later he unveiled a statue to Ralph Connor, pen name for the Reverend Dr. Charles W. Gordon, a Presbyterian minister who had written many best-selling novels about the country and its early days of pioneering.[78] What linked Tweedsmuir to Connor was not just writing but also John Buchan's co-author of *The Kirk in Scotland* (1930), George Adam Smith, who knew the Presbyterian minister and had written the "Introduction" to his 1901 novel, *Black Rock*.[79]

Back into Ontario the train veered south after edging Lakes Superior and Huron, finally stopping at Guelph, where it was snowing. Tweedsmuir addressed the students of the Agricultural College there and Susan spoke at a luncheon, which this time her husband found rather long, likely because of his "detestable digestion." They moved on to London, Ontario, where they attended the finals of the Dominion Drama Festival.

After "a slow and bumpy journey," they arrived back to milder weather in Ottawa on the evening of April 15, with Rideau Hall and Ottawa preparing for the royal visitors. While King George VI and Queen Elizabeth were in Canada through mid-May to mid-June, Tweedsmuir remained largely in the background, explaining: "I cease to exist as [v]iceroy, and retain only a shadowy legal existence as [g]overnor [g]eneral-in-[c]ouncil." He was present for some events, but once the royal couple left Ottawa, so did he — though he left to travel to Quebec to do some fishing.

In late August the Tweedsmuirs' son Johnnie was completing his year at a Hudson's Bay Company post on Baffin Island. His parents travelled with Tweedsmuir's sister, Anna, to Churchill, Manitoba, on Hudson's Bay, to meet him. They stopped along the way in The Pas, where the mayor, Ben Dembinsky, presented his council.[80] The stop also included a visit to the local First Nations reserve and a brief meeting with Chief Louis McGillivray, who presented the governor general with a letter "containing both words of welcome and ... complaint and a petition of rights."[81]

The Tweedsmuirs returned south to the main rail line, then travelled west, stopping at Grande Prairie, Alberta, before continuing on to British Columbia's Peace River District, where they were welcomed at Tupper Creek by Sudeten German refugees from Czechoslovakia. It was particularly touching, the governor general commented, to hear the refugee settlers singing "God Save the King," which they had learned by memory,

South Peace Regional Archives/2003.14.08

The governor general with T.W. Lawlor, mayor of Grande Prairie, Alberta, where the viceregal train stopped in August 1939.

South Peace Regional Archives/2003.14.05

Susan Tweedsmuir and Mrs. Lawlor inspecting war veterans at the train station in Grande Prairie, Alberta, August 1939.

although they didn't really know what the words meant.[82] They were Social Democrats and anti-Nazi, and had been at risk; most were Catholic but there was one Jewish family among those at Tupper.[83] Tweedsmuir had suggested the Canadian government accept five thousand Sudetens, but ultimately, only just over one thousand arrived, half of whom settled around Tupper while the other half settled around St. Wahlburg, northwest of Saskatoon, Saskatchewan.[84]

The viceregal couple's visit with the Sudeten refugees was but a taste of how the conflict in Europe was to affect Canada. Barely had they left when Hitler invaded Poland, launching the infamous *blitzkrieg* on September 1. Britain declared war on Nazi Germany on September 3. Canada's war declaration came one week later. From that point on, a significant part of Tweedsmuir's travel was the result of his role as commander in chief.

His oldest and youngest sons joined the Canadian Militia. In November he flew to Camp Borden where Alastair was training. The return flight to Ottawa enchanted Tweedsmuir: "I have never seen anything more beautiful than the flight back over the Algonquin Park and the Upper Ottawa Valley. It was an amazing sunset, and we seemed to be swinging along in a sea of gold dust."[85]

That sunset also marked the beginning of the end for the Tweedsmuir's tenure in Canada. New Year's Day, 1940, was the governor general's last levee. "There is always something melancholy about doing something for the last time," he wrote, "even when you are glad."[86] It was time to plan for the "start [of] my melancholy farewell tours." He was thinking of heading west again in the latter half of March. However, Mackenzie King visited him at Rideau Hall on Tuesday evening, January 23, and told His Excellency that he intended to ask for a dissolution and call an election, to seek a full mandate for the war.[87] There had been rumours, perhaps expectations, that there would be a national government in this war situation. Still, when the governor general read the Speech from the Throne on Friday, January 25, the announcement of dissolution came "as a complete surprise to everyone."[88] Tweedsmuir had to delay his trip west until after the results of the election called for March 26.[89] Until then he had only a few engagements between Ottawa, Toronto, and Montreal.

On February 1 the viceregal couple travelled to Montreal to attend a charity ball. Tweedsmuir spent the following morning with the Sulpician Brotherhood, who impressed him. At midday he spoke at a luncheon of the Canadian Forestry Association, complimenting them on their having "forced the question of forest conservation upon the attention of Canada, so that it has become a matter of major public interest."[90] There was a need to care for national assets, for future generations, he stated, and it was important, too, to use it for the training of the country's youth, such as was being done with the fire protection program the association had organized and that he had seen in northern British Columbia.

When they returned to Ottawa on the evening of February 2, a Father D'Arcy, head of the Jesuit College at Oxford, and an old friend, returned with them. The weekend was a Catholic one. Tweedsmuir attended a dinner at the apostolic delegate's home on Saturday, along with Mackenzie King, Cardinal Villeneuve, and new missionary bishops. Sunday evening, the cardinal had a lengthy discussion with Tweedsmuir about Thomist philosophy, Aristotle, and the most fitting basis "for the reconstruction of the social order."[91] Tweedsmuir wrote to his sister on Monday about the weekend, and other news.[92] It was his last.

Part V

Encouraging Excellence

CHAPTER 16

Literary Governor General

Honours in Canada, and most Commonwealth countries, flow from the Crown. They recognize excellence in many aspects of life, including public service, military service, the arts and literature, and giving selflessly to others. We have already read how formal honours, in the form of orders of chivalry carrying titles, were the first point of collision between Tweedsmuir and his prime minister, and how they were finally put aside once and for all; but there nonetheless remained an important role for the governor general to play in honouring Canadians. In addition to travelling the country, meeting Canadians and engaging them through his speeches, the governor general also encourages excellence: "celebrating in public," and, thus, helping to build pride in and encourage service to one's country, and to humanity, in and through "all forms of cultural endeavour."[1] Governors general must, as one Canadian academic noted, be involved in this aspect of the national life "to anchor themselves in the public's mind and in public life."[2]

Literature and the arts are a significant part of the national fabric, both reflecting and developing national character. Tweedsmuir expressed the belief that literature could be "a true formative force in our national life."[3] Indeed, this was a theme of conversation between the governor general and prime minister when the two men met in the library at Rideau Hall the day after Tweedsmuir's arrival in Ottawa. Tweedsmuir concurred with King's view that "more could be achieved [through culture] for the unity of Canada generally, than in almost any other way."[4] These were all words that would find voice a decade later in the Royal Commission on National Development in the Arts, Letters, and Sciences.[5] Tweedsmuir added that he was more than prepared to do what he could. King was flattering but sincere in his rejoinder that he "felt [Buchan's] presence in Canada, in that particular, would mean very much to our country."[6]

The excitement generated by the appointment of a best-selling author as governor general was palpable, and has already been described in earlier chapters. Expectations were certainly high in the country, but whereas in Britain and the United States, the focus was principally on his qualities as a statesman and his potential for enhancing Anglo-American relations, expectations in Canada rested mainly on his primary public reputation, as a man of letters. Literary and arts organizations, journalists, libraries and universities, all expected an influential boost to their status from the appointment of this erudite, articulate author and independent scholar. From other writers there were congratulations, but from readers there were concerns his appointment might mean an interruption for the pen of John Buchan.

Representative of the arts community, *Saturday Night* editor Bernard Sandwell noted the "experimental side" of Buchan's appointment and the expected, raised status for writers. Sandwell also highlighted Buchan's Scottish roots. The impact of Buchan's appointment transcended English Canada on both points, however. Ottawa journalist Fulgence Charpentier wrote of the new governor general for his French-Canadian readers, knowing that there was interest in the writer, something that might partly be explained by the sympathies and historic connection between the Scots and the French.

One of the most enthusiastic groups receiving word of John Buchan's appointment as governor general was the Canadian Authors Association (CAA), founded in 1921. Members of the CAA, including Charles G.D. Roberts, "the father of Canadian poetry," had undertaken a literary tour of England and Scotland in July 1933.[7] The group was hosted by the British prime minister of the day, Ramsay MacDonald, toasted by Rudyard

Kipling and G.K. Chesterton at a luncheon at Claridge's, and welcomed by the Canadian high commissioner and the visiting Canadian prime minister, R.B. Bennett.[8] At Oxford University, the tour was hosted by John Buchan, Sir Gilbert Murray, and Poet Laureate John Masefield. One of the tour group, a founding member of the CAA, was Winnipeg professor W.T. Allison, who talked with Buchan at Oxford University. On receiving news of Buchan's appointment, Allison enthused that they all greatly approved of the appointment.[9]

The CAA, under its president, Dr. Pelham Edgar, sent a telegram to the governor general–designate with a request that he grant them the kindness of accepting their offer to make him the CAA's honorary president. Buchan accepted.[10] It was more than fitting that the first organization for which Buchan agreed to serve as patron after being appointed governor general was a literary one.

Edgar informed Buchan about the CAA's activities in Canada, which included "Book Week." Buchan liked the idea, lightheartedly noting in his reply that as a writer he took a special interest "in the promotion of the habit of book buying."[11] He added: "The reading habit is vital to the future of a nation, for how else can you have a diffusion of thought and knowledge in the widest commonality?" He hoped Book Week would also "stimulate interest in Canada's own literature, for which, in my belief, there is a great future," concluding that "an intelligent and interested public is the best hope for the production of good books."[12] These were views to excite anyone involved in the field of literature in Canada.

When the authorial governor general arrived in Canada, Pelham let the honorary CAA president settle in, but not long, before he approached him with a specific proposal. Many years earlier, in 1927, the CAA had asked the Canadian government to establish an award "for the most notable work published each year by a resident Canadian"; it was a proposal to help celebrate the diamond jubilee of Confederation.[13] The idea had been sparked after Toronto-based writer Mazo de la Roche had won a literary prize of ten thousand dollars from the American publication the *Atlantic Monthly*.[14] She was subsequently feted by the CAA at a special banquet. That almost decade-old CAA idea and the fortuitous

1933 meeting in England with John Buchan fused into opportunity after Buchan was announced as Canada's next governor general.

CAA president Edgar Pelham "recalled John Buchan's strong encouragement of Canadian literature."[15] Discussion and consultation occurred. A.H. Robson spoke with W.A. Deacon, who was the *Mail and Empire's* book review editor. Medals were the trend in awards at the time. They signalled recognition, even if no money was included, which, it had to be admitted, would have been difficult to find in the midst of the Depression. Pelham "believed Lord Tweedsmuir would be happy to endow some medals as further stimulation," and made arrangements to present the proposal to the governor general.[16]

Tweedsmuir consented to the plan and granted permission to use the name of his office "in perpetuity, provided the Association took full responsibility for financing, judging, and all other administration."[17] The Governor General's Literary Awards were born. Initially, they took the form of medals only. Lyn Harrington, author of a CAA history, wrote that Buchan "saw no need to back up his rhetoric with a hundred thousand dollars."[18] It was quite consistent with Buchan's character and approach that he would see recognition as stimulating interest in the books as the most important reward — a position that was also usefully consonant with the inadequacy of the Rideau Hall budget and the small likelihood there was of obtaining any funding from a federal government still wrestling with the economic depression.[19]

The first awards for excellence in literature were for fiction and non-fiction. The Royal Society was asked to supply judges for the first books nominated in 1936, but, Harrington notes, their tardiness resulted in the awards only being presented in April 1937. The prize for fiction went to Bertram Brooker for *Think of the Earth*, while the prize for non-fiction was given to Thomas B. Roberton for *T.B.R. — Newspaper Pieces*.[20] It was, perhaps, a result of the excitement of the launch of these awards — and, in particular, the awarding of the initial fiction medal to Brooker, a member of the Arts and Letters Club of Toronto — that helped spark revival of the Club's newsletter, *LAMPS*, which Brooker began editing.[21]

In 1937 an additional category was created; a medal was awarded for the best book in the genres of poetry or drama, with medals being given as well for both fiction and non-fiction. A leading poet of the day, Sir Charles G.D. Roberts, was among the judges; Stephen Leacock, Laura G. Salverson, and E.J. Pratt were the winners for non-fiction, fiction, and poetry respectively.[22] Through succeeding decades, the awards have signalled the arrival of Canadian literary talent, many of whom have been destined for international renown.[23]

At the launch of the awards, and, in fact, for the first twenty-three years, there were no awards for French-language works, though two titles translated from the French won during the first decade. This situation, raises questions about how literature — or culture, generally —was seen at the time in terms of whether or not it had a role to play in contributing to national unity, despite the fact that this point was one that the governor general and prime minister had discussed and agreed upon.[24]

Why, one could ask, did Tweedsmuir permit the imprimatur of his office to be borrowed by an organization that claimed to represent the country's literary culture, despite being unilingual? It seems especially puzzling considering the fact that Tweedsmuir believed that "*la langue et la littérature françaises constituent une richesse non seulement pour le Canada français mais encore pour le Canada anglais.*"[25] He had certainly been well advised to respect the French culture by King George V, but it was also in his nature to reach out.[26] He had, for example, attended a literary congress in Quebec City, spoken in French, and encouraged the development of French language and literature.

Had he questioned the Canadian Authors Association about the gap in the new awards, or was it considered? Could the fact that Quebec already had a provincial government award for literature, *le Prix David*, established in 1923, be a factor? To understand such a seemingly incongruous situation, it is important to consider the context of the time.

The Catholic Church dominated Quebec society and cultural life, the English dominated business outside agriculture, and the provincial government was bound by both. To the extent that Tweedsmuir encouraged the development of French language literature, it was within a very conservative environment, which emphasized a rural way of life. The literature of this period has been described as *la littérature du terroir*,[27] and it was dominated by Monsignor Camille Roy. There was a certain, imposed homogeneity to Quebec's literary landscape at the time. It was natural, then, and expected, that the senior figure in the Church would meet with a governor general interested in Quebec culture. Hence, Tweedsmuir's reference at the congress in Quebec City that he was *"guidé surtout par les oeuvres de mon ami, Mgr Camille Roy, le grand seigneur de la littérature canadienne."*[28]

A more important factor, however, was, likely, the insular anglophone world of the CAA. There had been a French-language association of writers established by Victor Barbeau in 1936, *la Société des écrivains canadiens*, which had links to the CAA; indeed members of the *Société* attended CAA dinners when they were held in Montreal.[29] *La Société* delegated one of their bilingual members, Germaine Guèvremont, to establish and maintain contact with the CAA and to try to increase awareness of Quebec literature in English Canada. Little happened, however, and it would not be until 1959 that categories for French-language works would be included in the Governor General's Literary Awards; this was when the recently established Canada Council, a federal government agency, took over the administration of the awards from the CAA.

The prospect of John Buchan's arrival, and his subsequent time in Canada, spurred sales of his books, a financial bonus, especially for a position that, at the time, could be a draw on the incumbent's personal finances. Increased book sales and a literary governor general provided a fillip not just for Buchan, though; they acted as a spur for any organization connected to the literary and publishing worlds.

In February, not long after Tweedsmuir had opened the new Parliament with the Speech from the Throne, he travelled to Montreal to, among other activities, speak an encouraging word to the CAA. He received compliments from King on his address.[30] The opportunities he would have to address bookish crowds, and others, of course, would reveal his own philosophy and outlook about what constituted "great literature." It was, he stated emphatically, the foundation of Western civilization, and he regarded the whole ever more preciously and in need of defence the more threatening the violent ideologies and dictators became and the more modernism entered into the arts and letters.[31]

One nascent organization to benefit from the new atmosphere Buchan's presence created was the Association of Canadian Bookmen (ACB), founded in February 1936.[32] It was intended to represent those involved with books, whether authors, retailers, publishers, or readers. Tweedsmuir was supportive and accepted the request to serve as their patron, as he had for the CAA. There was undoubtedly some duplication of membership between the two organizations.[33] One of the primary activities of the ACB was organizing book fairs, which combined the interests of its membership. The first fair was held at the King Edward Hotel in Toronto in November that year, though Tweedsmuir could not attend the opening.

On his second trip west, in the late autumn of 1936, Tweedsmuir addressed the inaugural meeting of the Western Canada section of the ACB, held in the ballroom of Government House in Winnipeg. To about 150 attentive listeners, which included *Winnipeg Free Press* editor and University of Manitoba chancellor John Dafoe, he referred to Canada's rich literary heritage from Britain and France, and expressed confidence that Canada would produce great literature. There was, however, an important qualification.

Great literature depended on preserving the classical traditions. Part of that tradition was critical thinking: thinking that demanded a "keen, alert, enjoying mind, with an edge on it," as he described it.[34] He contrasted this tradition with the one encouraged by the captivating ideologies of fascism and communism, ideologies that were, he believed, the intolerant antitheses of an inquiring mind. The loose use of political phrases, and slogans little or misunderstood, dulled the mind, he told his audience. It is cant, he said, and it is rampant as well in the fields of economics, philosophy, and religion. The situation is exacerbated by the imprecise use of words, which should "fit [their] meanings and no more; it should be exactly as thought," he advised, citing Cardinal Newman and Aldous Huxley as examples.[35] Tweedsmuir referred to Sigmund Freud and the impact of psychoanalysis, which was an influential force during the period. "Too many writers are carried away with it, and the result is enormous novels filled with a jumble of psychology, not reality."[36] He cautioned again that readers need to be aware of cant and clear their own minds of it. He then set his base for reader and author alike: "Integrity of thought and purity of speech are the two standards … of production and the full enjoyment of good literature."[37]

A year later Tweedsmuir addressed at length and in detail a larger group of the ACB, at a dinner in Montreal, "of more than five hundred, and two hundred were turned away."[38] In a survey of Western thinkers and writers, he outlined his own thoughts, essentially for defeating the onslaught of ideologies undermining the intellectual heritage and foundations of Western [c]ivilization. It was an elaboration on his theme of cant, "mental and emotional insincerity":

> If literature is to be a true formative force in our national life, then our readers must have the right attitude towards it. They must approach it with a keen enjoying temper, and with a proper edge to their mind.... The first requisite is a mind in hard training — a mind with a just sense of values, with quick perceptions and with complete intellectual honesty.... Cant ... means the use of unrationali[z]ed concepts out of laziness or a blind following of fashion.... Emotionally it means a parade of feelings which we do not really possess.... All of us at times have to dissemble — to pretend to assent to something which we do not quite understand, to simulate feelings which we do not altogether share.... Cant goes much deeper; when we are guilty of it we have somehow battered ourselves into a belief that we think or feel as we profess to think or feel, because the edge of our mind has been blunted. It is what Plato called "the lie in the soul."[39]

He illustrated his point from public life, where politics is "conducted by a kind of shorthand [in which] [c]reeds are telescoped into formulas and slogans and catchwords."[40] "The danger begins," he emphasized, "when we accept these slogans without understanding what is behind them." He asked his audience: "[H]ow many of us have ever considered what we mean by [democracy]?"[41] A lack of understanding of such a fundamental concept was dangerous, he believed. Equally, the uninformed use of terms such as "planning" and "planned economy" (which had become popular through their use in the Soviet Union) was also dangerous, since these were words that sowed confusion, because there was a lack of knowledge generally, of what was meant by them, not to mention what outcomes they proposed. Through an assessment of Hegel and Marx — "it would be a very good thing if people read *Das Kapital* before talking about it" — he emphasized the importance of critical thinking, of the need to refresh and restate political creeds.[42] Critical thinking was required for a healthy society and polity, he stated.

He returned then to a related and equally unfavourable development that was influencing writers at this time, Freud and psychoanalysis. For Buchan, the subconscious explored by Freud and others was "the underworld of the soul." He noted that their work "produced results of enduring value," but that there was a tendency "to overemphasize certain of their discoveries, and ... to fall under the bondage of formulas" which became fashionable. Others gave "undue importance" to psychoanalysis for answering life's questions. But the impact was far-reaching. "Worse," Tweedsmuir lamented, "the novelists got hold of the thing and produced vast shapeless works which were simply a rubbish-heap."[43] There were distinctions, however, as he complimented Virginia Woolf, "a fine artist" who could handle the "delicate psychology." The problem was that too many just dug through the material from the subconscious, which did not produce art but was "the raw stuff of art — *ta pro tragodias*." This may partly be why Buchan did not particularly like literary society. It would be consistent for another reason, which his son William suggested "was due to [his father's] sense that intellect was a gift from God and must be trained and not allowed to 'run free in idle speculation or serve its owner as a means of self-flattery.'"[44]

Tweedsmuir appealed to his audience to "keep close to the classics," but he qualified it. "I do not mean the Latin and Greek only," he said, "but the classics of any tongues with which we are familiar."[45] The speech was both a call to strengthen critical thought as a buttress against threats from ideologies demanding unthinking obedience and to check the modernism that was now taking hold in literature. It was not, however, just to writers of philosophy, history, or novels that he addressed his appeal for a return to the classics. Three days prior to his address to the Montreal ACB dinner, he had given a lengthy speech in Toronto, applied to another field of the arts.

Aside from being given a category (shared with drama) in the newly minted Governor General's Literary Awards, poets and poetry received special attention from the governor general, who had, as John Buchan, written verse himself, publishing *Poems, Scots and English* in 1917. He gave an evening lecture at Convocation Hall, University of Toronto, late in November 1937, at a meeting, held under the auspices of the *Canadian Poetry Magazine*, "to foster an interest in Canadian poetry."[46] To a capacity crowd of some 1,500, his lengthy address was a journey through "master poets," from ancient to modern times, including English and French poets, as well as, among others, Homer and Aeschylus, Racine, Corneille and Hugo, Chaucer, Shakespeare, Coleridge, Arnold and Tennyson.[47] It was philosophical, historical, critical, and serious, but not without an element of fun. While the minor poets have their charm, Tweedsmuir's task that evening was to counter what he believed to be "a tendency to forget about the masters, or to treat them disrespectfully."

"[D]efine a masterpiece, a classic," he said, "by its enduring charm, for age does not wither it, and by its universal appeal, which is not limited by race or nationality."[48] He lamented "the dearth of great [writers], both in English and in French literature," resulting in lesser, younger, and impatient figures today finding "consolation in affecting to despise [the greats]." He attributed this attitude to their lack of knowledge and familiarity with the masters, combined with their character to "*feel* acutely."[49]

Despite his criticisms he expressed sympathy for those attempting to engage in "social regeneration." "No great poetry," he said, "can be deaf to the 'still sad music of humanity.'" He advised, however, that "every lover of poetry should be also a critic," if they are to enjoy the form to its fullest. Passing from the poets to their critics, Tweedsmuir argued that the problem with contemporary criticism "is that the critics are so ignorant."

As for Canada, which had already produced good poets, he said, he wanted to see the nation's "poetic impulse … create its own idiom," based on the masterpieces, the "eternal background which will at once inspire and dignify our own reading of life." It was the masterpieces, he reminded his audience, that provide the common canvas of references for a civilization. He cited Greek and Roman poets, the Bible, and Scottish ballads as all producing "thoughts deep and grave," which in turn infused the literature of a nation to "produce gravity and dignity both in the character and in the speech of the ordinary citizen." Tweedsmuir cautioned: "If the Bible should go out of the national memory and its place be taken by the jargon of a crude popular science, or the jingles and captions of popular forms of entertainment, then what a fall would be there."[50]

Tweedsmuir continued in a professorial form to instruct and raise the standards of criticism. When some piece of contemporary poetry is described as "unparalleled since Donne," the advice is straightforward: recall Donne and actually compare. Tweedsmuir noted that Donne was "cited today more than he [was] read." But not all was "deep and grave." In an attempt to demonstrate the genius of Shakespeare and of great poetry (that he defined as "the only possible words in the only possible order"), he attempted a translation of the great poet's "O Mistress Mine," from *Twelfth Night*, into Hollywood-American:

> Hud! Sweeties, where you gettin' to?
> Your big boy's here and pettin' you,
> And he's the guy that rings the bell.
> Say, kid, quit hikin' and sit nice,
> For shakin' feet don't cut no ice,
> The goopiest mutt can tell.[51]

"Horrible isn't it?" he wrote humorously to Stanley Baldwin, "but a perfectly literal translation."[52]

He concluded his lecture with a recognition that Canada already had good poets, recognizing "with pride the reality [of its] poetic impulse" and wanting to see Canada "provide its special version" to match its "prairies and forests and mountains and northern wilds."[53] Canada, he said, "must make her own music." He commended again that it be measured against the values and qualities of the masterpieces. "No nation can cut itself off from the past."

At the end of 1937, Tweedsmuir observed that "[t]here seems to be a kind of literary revival going on in Canada."[54] It was, indeed, a change from the "agonizingly slow development of literary life since the 1920s," as one Canadian writer and critic described that period.[55] Tweedsmuir's observation was, obviously, prompted by the literary-related activity he had either been a part of, observed, or encouraged. His presence in Canada was in itself a catalyst to a more positive environment and outlook for writers and poets in Canada. Tweedsmuir's support and encouragement, however, was not exclusively directed to organized groups. Individual writers received his support and encouragement, while the fact of his presence and speeches inspired others.

John Buchan read emerging new fiction and provided encouragement where he believed it due.[56] He had, as his son William noted, "a writer's sympathy with other writer's aspirations, however feeble their achievement and since they thought to send him their books, he would thoughtfully give them a place on his shelves."[57] His scouting and his sympathies did not cease in Canada.

In the fall of 1937, Tweedsmuir had written to George Blackwood, publisher of *Blackwood's Magazine* in Britain, asking about "the admirable man writing Nova Scotia stories."[58] Thomas Raddall's outlook would have appealed to Tweedsmuir as much as his writing ability. Raddall maintained a strong loyalty to his region, using it to inspire his stories: "I was determined," he wrote, "to remain in Nova Scotia and to write about my own country and people."[59]

Raddall had first been published in *Blackwood's* in 1933, after having had the same story rejected by *Maclean's* magazine in Canada five years earlier. He went on to publish many more articles in *Blackwood's*. George Blackwood replied to Tweedsmuir's initial letter and provided his old contributor with Raddall's contact information. Tweedsmuir subsequently wrote to the young Raddall in March 1938: "I have long been an admirer of your *Blackwood* stories … and I hope on my next tour of the Maritimes to have the pleasure of making your acquaintance."[60]

Raddall readily agreed. He was expressive in his reply for "the very kind things" Tweedsmuir had said about his writing. "[Y]our interest is a most encouraging surprise."[61] "I strive for bones and blood in my tales," Raddall wrote, "because I hope to reflect in some measure the life and mood of our people."[62] The "[p]raise from John Buchan is very high praise indeed" and the two exchanged further correspondence.[63]

Tweedsmuir praised Raddall's "rare gift of swift, spare, clean-limbed narrative," "a plot … which issues in a dramatic climax."[64] It was, he wrote, in the same school as Scott, Stevenson, Maupassant, Kipling, and Conrad. Especially, Tweedsmuir loved the sense of adventure emanating from both historic and modern Nova Scotia. But the old life of the province was "being broken into by an ugly modernity," and it was from this "contrast of old and new that [Raddall] gets much of his drama."[65] Tweedsmuir was active in his exchanges with Raddall, encouraging him by proposing themes for books.[66]

The result of the connection between Tweedsmuir and Raddall was that George Blackwood proposed in January 1939 that the short stories that Raddall had published in *Blackwood's* be compiled, with a foreword written by Lord Tweedsmuir. Raddall, obviously, "was delighted."[67] The volume was published by William Blackwood & Sons later in 1939. Blackwood subsequently gave permission for publishing it in Canada, in 1943, by McClelland & Stewart, under the title *The Pied Piper of Dipper Creek and Other Tales*. It included the "Foreword" by the then late Lord Tweedsmuir that had appeared in the original Blackwood publication. The book won the Governor General's Literary Award for fiction for 1943.

Raddall's success — he published twenty-seven books of fiction and non-fiction, two more of which were also winners of Governor General's Literary Awards, for non-fiction,[68] and he received the endorsement from an author as successful as Buchan — did not, however, save him from obscurity in Canada today. As John Bell notes, like Buchan, Raddall "has been given short shrift by modernist critics," but unlike Buchan, Raddall is no longer in print.[69]

Another writer from the Maritimes, though he began his authorial career many years after Tweedsmuir's death in February 1940, served as an aide-de-camp to the governor general in 1938 and 1939. David Walker, Scottish-born, had been a career military officer, with the Black Watch, and had already served in India and Sudan when he received word at his then-current posting in Perth, Scotland, that a post of aide-de-camp in Canada was being vacated. He was excited about the prospect of serving the governor general because, since childhood, Walker wrote, he had been "gobbling up" John Buchan's adventure stories.[70] This statement is contradicted, however, by the fact that in almost the same breath he writes that the "allure was not to serve the famous John Buchan, [but, rather,]it was [the allure of] plain Canada, that immense and wonderful land of rugged legend."[71] Regardless, the amount of personal time he spent with Tweedsmuir left a legacy of inspiration.

Walker described Tweedsmuir as "a brilliant and amusing raconteur, the best storyteller I ever met, and his visual memory was astounding."[72] Despite criticizing his love of "honorific plums," Walker notes he "was infallibly kind and good company with people, young and old, never speaking down to them out of an encyclopedic knowledge and profound intelligence.... I liked and admired him for many things, most of all his fortitude."[73]

The latter description was a reference to what Walker observed of Tweedsmuir, whom he described as being in "constant discomfort with an ulcer and other ailments."[74] Fortitude was a quality Walker would come to understand after his own experiences in the 1939–45 war, reflecting back on Tweedsmuir's own type of imprisonment imposed by poor health and yet remaining so productive.

Walker left Canada in 1939 to serve on active duty when the war started. He was captured in June 1940 and spent the remainder of the war in a series of German prison camps, from which he made several successful escapes but was recaptured each time. He lived adventure of the kind that he had read about in John Buchan's books. During his last period of imprisonment, at Colditz Castle in the summer of 1944, Walker began to write poetry and told himself that after the war he was going to write, though he was not sure about what.[75] He could not then appreciate at the time that he was living much of what he would write about.

In 1948 Walker and his wife, Willa (Magee) from Montreal, whom he had married in 1939, returned to Canada, to St. Andrews, New Brunswick. As he had told himself during that summer of 1944, he began to write fiction. In 1950 he produced *Geordie*, about a young Scot who defies early taunting to become athletic, participates in Highland games, then goes on to the Olympics. *Geordie* was made into a movie in 1955. By that time, however, he had written two other novels, *The Pillar* and *Digby*, in 1952 and 1953 respectively. The former aide-de-camp to the governor general who had established the Governor General's Literary Awards won the award for fiction those two years in a row!

Shifting our attention from the east coast to Toronto, 1939, we find a young man, twenty-three, married, with his wife expecting a child. An aspiring writer, Kenneth Millar had a teaching job lined up for September, but in June of 1939, he was going to attend a high school commencement where the governor general, the famous writer John Buchan, was to give an address. It was a critical choice to attend. The governor's talk included a version of the classic fable of the tortoise and the hare, but in the version related, the hare won. Tweedsmuir's presence and talk inspired Millar to do something toward his desired career.[76] He soon after won a typewriter in a radio quiz contest and promised himself that "he'd make money someday by writing."[77] Indeed, his first professional publication, a poem entitled "Fatal Facility," appeared a month later in *Saturday Night*.[78] Subsequent publication, however, would take time.

Millar's first novel, *The Dark Tunnel*, appeared in 1944. It was influenced by *The Thirty-Nine Steps* and has been described as "a hybrid of old-fashioned puzzle-mystery, Buchanesque spy adventure, and Chandleresque exposé of sexual perversion."[79] Millar, writing under the pseudonym Ross Macdonald, subsequently became a master of detective novels. With his main character, Lew Archer, he gained fame for "the finest series of detective novels ever written by an American."[80] Millar's career may have begun with inspiration from Buchan, but certainly did not continue nor end with similarity to Buchan, who would not have approved of the graphic quality and lewdness.

* * *

Tweedsmuir continued his own writing while in Canada, to the extent that his professional duties permitted. He completed *Augustus*, a historical biography of Augustus Caesar, in 1937, a book of recognized scholarship and referenced within classics classes in Canadian universities through to at least the last decade of the twentieth century. It was dedicated "To My Friend William Lyon Mackenzie King: Four Times Prime Minister of Canada," an inscription to endear him to King, who wrote immediately to thank Tweedsmuir "from the bottom of my heart" for "the gift of this child of your mind."[81] King found it fascinating reading.[82] Tweedsmuir subsequently attended a book fair in December in Montreal, where he autographed copies in front of a large poster with the title and John Buchan's name underneath, and depicting busts of the ancient Roman leader.[83]

Subsequent to *Augustus*, Tweedsmuir began to focus on other projects, one of which was a form of autobiography, "a kind of spiritual autobiography," as he described it, published as *Memory Hold-the-Door* in 1941.[84] His energy remained high, despite poor health, and Canada had inspired him, particularly the North, the idea of frontier, the health problems of the indigenous population, and the romance of the country's history. He began work on two Canadian books, both inspired by his travels and his love for the country.

One was a novel set mostly in the Canadian North, *Sick Heart River*.[85] It dealt with the search in the North for a missing New York-based French-Canadian banker, who has had a nervous breakdown. It describes the dismal health, depression, and poor conditions of First Nations peoples and how one of John Buchan's main characters, Sir Edward Leithen, finds redemption in sacrificing his own health (diagnosed with advanced tuberculosis in London before setting out on this last adventure), and ultimately his life, to help a tuberculosis-ridden, depressed Hare First Nation community back to physical and mental health. It was reviewed by a young Robertson Davies, with the prejudices of the time evident with regard to the Natives, for *Saturday Night* magazine. Davies noted "evidences of fatigue … not the John Buchan who wrote *Greenmantle* and *Huntingtower*. But it is a fine and thrilling story none the less."[86]

The second book Tweedsmuir was writing was for children, *Lake of Gold*. It was an attempt to fill a void, having noted that the history books used in school "are perfectly deadly, and there is really nothing to engage the imagination of a child, and yet there are few more romantic stories in the world."[87] It was not a popular success when it was published in 1941, selling less than two-thirds of the twenty-five thousand print run.[88] Nor did it live up to critical acclaim, being described as "didactic" and "better history than it is fiction," "so pedestrian in tone and style that it is difficult to believe that it came from the author of fast-paced spy stories."[89]

Sick Heart River has, regrettably, not been included in anthologies of Canadian literature nor considered a Canadian novel, but it remains in print. *Lake of Gold*, on the other hand, was never reprinted, but has been assessed as the first of its genre in Canada: "the first recognized Canadian fantasy" of "realistic fiction for children," though also described as being written "by a visitor."[90] It was, however, still being talked about, favourably, in 2011.[91]

As though his own projects were not enough, Tweedsmuir was approached by others with proposals for writing. For example, in the spring of 1938 a nephew of former prime minister Sir Robert Borden tried to persuade Tweedsmuir to write a biography of his uncle. Though Tweedsmuir had known and respected Borden, he declined, noting Borden had left a considerable autobiography, which might be published that fall. Indeed, two volumes of memoirs were published in 1938 by Macmillan in Toronto. He suggested to Borden's nephew that Arthur Meighen might be a good choice to write "the life."[92]

Tweedsmuir's legacy to Canada's literary development is undeniable. At a broad level, he established the Governor General's Literary Awards (the "GGs") and supported and encouraged the Canadian Authors Association, the Association of Canadian Bookmen, and Canadian poets. As a public intellectual, he stimulated discussion about what constitutes good and great literature and poetry. At an individual level, Thomas Raddall, David Walker, and Kenneth Millar were or became well-known writers of their time and had support or drew inspiration from John Buchan's presence in Canada. How many others may have been inspired? Canada, in turn, inspired him, yielding *Sick Heart River* and *Lake of Gold*. But this renowned literary governor general did not ignore other areas of the cultural field in Canada.

CHAPTER 17

Patron and Intellectual Promoter

During the first substantive meeting between governor general and prime minister, the day after Tweedsmuir arrived in Ottawa, Mackenzie King expressed his hope the governor general would become honorary president of the National Gallery. The point was made during the discussion about the importance of culture in helping to contribute to national unity. Tweedsmuir replied that "he was most anxious to help in all these cultural matters."[1] He accepted the National Gallery honorific position shortly thereafter, and many others besides.[2] In fact, during his first week he agreed to be patron or honorary member of at least thirty organizations, with the number mounting to about sixty-five in the first month. Susan Tweedsmuir became patron or honorary member of at least forty-five organizations and groups within the first two months. They were of course, advised by their staff, and guided by precedent.

On November 7, two days after arriving in Ottawa, the governor general maintained a tradition and was sworn in as the Chief Scout of Canada. It was a tradition that he gladly accepted because of his interest in the development of young people as good citizens. While most organizations had made their requests for patronage or honorary membership to Tweedsmuir within his first year, there were still some making requests, and being accepted, through 1939. By the end of that last year, Their Excellencies were patrons of over 220 organizations, ranging from the temporary, such as the American Association for the Advancement of Science Conference in Ottawa in 1938, through very small groups, such as the Upper Canada College Camera Club, and local groups like the Montreal Children's Library, to large, national organizations such as the St. John Ambulance, the Red Cross, and of course the Boy Scouts and the Girl Guides.[3] Veterans organizations figured prominently, matching Tweedsmuir's own experience and his dedication to the memory of those who died and to those who survived the Great War. A visit with these varied groups and institutions would often be added to a program or itinerary of viceregal travels, giving Their Excellencies the opportunity to connect with them.

The lending of the name of the governor general or his (or her) spouse as patron to a group or organization is, of course, a message of encouragement, a sign of the worthiness of what that group or organization represents. This action also sets an example to others. A viceregal recommendation provides recognition for the organization and can motivate others to contribute to it in some form. It is a recognition of the pursuit of that which makes society better: what might be described as excellence of objective. Tweedsmuir's personal reputation, particularly his celebrity status as a best-selling author, greatly enhanced the effect of his support. This was of particular importance for the many organizations, often small and with limited budgets, that were volunteer-based and had charitable objectives. Others, like the science conference, served specific purposes, which would have attracted Tweedsmuir's interest and support.

Tweedsmuir's arrival as governor general was highly anticipated in the Canadian world of letters obviously, but the other cultural fields would hope for some beneficial effect as well. Aside from agreeing generally about the importance of culture contributing to national unity, Tweedsmuir believed the cultural sphere was important to provide proportion and a better balance to both individuals and society. His own interests and limited time, however, meant that he could not give equal attention to all fields.

The Gazette (Montreal), November 13, 1939

The governor general and Lady Tweedsmuir were patrons of more than two hundred organizations. As president of the Canadian Red Cross Society, Tweedsmuir lent his support for an appeal for funds in the first months of war.

During his first week in Ottawa, one of the many organizations he accepted to be patron of was the Dominion Drama Festival. In this he was successor to Lord Bessborough, who had established the festival with a group of theatre representatives who met with him at Rideau Hall in October 1932.[4] Tweedsmuir's frequent correspondent and fellow Scottish peer, Lord Crawford, had written a word in support of the festival. He was perhaps conscious that although his friend had a natural draw to letters, he also displayed a certain lack of excitement about the theatre.[5] "[P]ray don't forget," Crawford counselled, "to encourage the Dramatic Societies, which Bessborough did so much to create and which may wane for lack of friendly recognition from high quarters."[6]

Tweedsmuir did not forget, and attended the festivals held in Winnipeg in 1938 and in London, Ontario, in 1939. He also provided support by securing judges from Britain and the United States. One year he tried to secure Noel Coward as a judge. Though that did not work out, it demonstrated his support to try to enhance both the profile of the festival and the experience of those involved in it.

He applied his ever-productive mind, though, beyond the stage, to a relatively newer medium: the screen. Recall that Alfred Hitchcock directed a film adaptation in 1935 of John Buchan's novel *The Thirty-Nine Steps*, and that as a member of Parliament Buchan had taken initiatives to help establish a film institute in Britain. Of course Hollywood was the epitome of excellence for moviemaking and was in its prime at the time, so competing with it was not possible. Still, Tweedsmuir thought that, perhaps, it might be possible to use the benefits of Canada's position between America and Britain, along with its own resources and talent, to foster a film industry in Canada, too.

So, on a weekend in mid-January 1940, as Ottawa experienced a winter thaw and while the war had not yet really heated up, the governor general hosted a party at Rideau Hall. Afterwards, he wrote to his sister that he was trying to interest Canada's richest people "in a scheme … to establish a Hollywood in British Columbia."[7] The idea, however it came to him, had a strong appeal. Among the people at Rideau Hall that weekend was Sam McLaughlin, the millionaire head of General Motors in Canada, who Tweedsmuir hoped to interest in the idea. The timing of the scheme was linked to a couple of factors.

The British Films Act of 1938 had cut out film productions in the Dominions from being included in Britain's quota system.[8] Such productions were alleged to be of poor quality, even though they included aspiring young actors like James Mason, Vivian Leigh, Ray Milland, Rex Harrison, and Madeleine Carroll. Previously, the ten-year-old Films Act of 1927, designed to rescue the British film industry from being overwhelmed by Hollywood, had included productions made in the Dominions. At the end of that ten-year period, 20 percent of the films that distributors and exhibitors handled had to be British, defined as a film in which 75 percent of the salaries went to British subjects, including a British writer, and that was produced within the British Empire. It was this situation that motivated Hollywood film-makers to move north, to British Columbia in particular, producing the low-budget movies nicknamed "quota-quickies." After the changes introduced by the 1938 Films Act, however, the "branch-plant" movie-making moved away.

Thinking of this situation, with the film industry in Britain working "at a fairly good pitch," in contrast to the situation in Canada, Tweedsmuir wanted to help ensure that they did not "let it drop again."[9] He was undoubtedly also thinking of the role that film could play in the war effort. It was, therefore, a good time to try to light a new cinematic spark in Canada, but not branch-plant based.

Tweedsmuir had spoken with a number of British-born actors now living or working in Hollywood. Sir Cedric Hardwicke and Charles Laughton, both stars of the successful 1939 big-budget film *The Hunchback of Notre Dame*, as well as the dashing Ronald Colman (*Beau Geste*, *Prisoner of Zenda*), among others, were all "keen" about the idea.[10] Another movie star had stayed at Rideau Hall in December 1938, the young Douglas Fairbanks, causing the governor general's residence to be besieged by journalists.[11]

We don't know what Sam McLaughlin's reaction was to this scheme, and there was not much time for Tweedsmuir to follow up. The emerging champion of a "Hollywood in B.C." died within the month. Had he lived longer, would he have been able to persuade McLaughlin and others to financially support his scheme and see his vision realized? We can speculate that it may have been possible because the automobile millionaire had great admiration for Tweedsmuir, something demonstrated later by his agreement to purchase John Buchan's library at Elsfield from Lady Tweedsmuir in 1955, which he then donated to Queen's University in Kingston, Ontario. Intermediary in the arrangement was another prominent Canadian and admirer and acquaintance of Tweedsmuir, Leonard Brockington, who was the first head of the Canadian Broadcasting Corporation and the rector of Queen's University from 1947 to 1966.[12]

Obviously, we can never know for sure whether McLaughlin or others would have been persuaded to support the scheme, or whether Tweedsmuir broached the subject with Mackenzie King or would have tried to persuade the government to support it in some way. Nonetheless, over half a century later, Vancouver, British Columbia, was nicknamed "Hollywood North," and Tweedsmuir's vision seemed prescient indeed, more recent declines in the industry notwithstanding.[13]

In another field of the visual arts, we do not have any indication of his views on the medium, but there is evidence of him having had an indirect hand in contributing to the launch of a great career. A young immigrant to Canada had set up a photography studio in Ottawa in 1932, and through other interests became involved with the Ottawa Little Theatre. The son of Governor General Bessborough was also involved with it. The connection resulted in the young Bessborough persuading his father to be photographed. Consequently, by the time Lord Tweedsmuir arrived, the young photographer was known to the staff at Rideau Hall.

Yousuf Karsh was "commanded to appear," to take an official photograph of the new governor general.[14] Things went well, and the following summer, he was again invited to photograph the governor general, this time during the visit of President Roosevelt at Quebec City. The visit presented a significant opportunity for Karsh, but it was one in which he would be competing with perhaps fifty other photographers. The comptroller at Rideau Hall, Major Mackenzie, advised Karsh to remain on the terrace until most of the dignitaries and others had left. As Karsh relates: "Patience was rewarded, for an hour or two later, the [p]resident emerged on the arm of his son James, accompanied by Lord Tweedsmuir and Mr. Mackenzie King."[15] Karsh asked if he could take a picture and pretended to do so as they posed. When they had relaxed after that more formal shot, and "Tweedsmuir began to tell one of the Scottish stories for which he was famous," Karsh photographed a truly natural pose of the three men. It was here that Karsh met the prime minister for the first time, a connection that developed back in Ottawa and helped the young photographer's career; two years later, Karsh took a very famous photograph of a very famous wartime leader, Winston Churchill.

Tweedsmuir generally supported the role of the performing arts — stage and screen — but for the visual arts he expressed rather more definite views, similar to those for poetry and literature, both of which could be said to rest on an aesthetic and classical base. He had "a passion for landscape," for which Canada provided more than ample possibilities, and he encouraged the development of "a modest form of portrait painting," which he saw as "in accord with the historic Canadian tradition, both French and English."[16] His more conservative views were openly admitted. There are, he said, "certain much-belauded masters whom I do not appreciate at all, and there is a good deal of art criticism of which I cannot understand a single word."[17] Still, he observed that there were various schools of painting in Canada, "some of them traditional, some of them revolutionary, but all deeply interesting."[18] But, to be a nation "in the full sense of the word," he noted, Canada's richness in material assets must be complemented with "assets of the mind and the spirit," which painting could contribute.

Similar to poetry, he believed visual art had a purpose to beautify life. His view of what constituted art reflected his optimism. A fallen world does not need to dwell on its fallenness, but could aspire to that which is good, that which is beautiful. Of course he knew well the underside of life, growing up with the poor in various parishes in Scotland; and he knew equally well the ugliest, most vile and tragic side of life through war. However, Tweedsmuir's view was counter to much of modernist art, which seeks to convey social commentary or reform. He believed that art should inspire. He drew an analogy to a great painter who would not paint the picture of "a cancerous cripple, or, if he does, he does not expect people to look at it."[19] Notwithstanding this, his approach to art and artistic expression did not ignore the fact that art could also express a darker side of humanity, just as he said that poetry could not be "deaf to the 'still sad music of humanity.'"

As we read in his speeches to the Canadian Authors Association and the Association of Canadian Bookmen, Tweedsmuir promoted intellectual clarity and a mind "with an edge"; these were qualities he believed were necessary not only for producing the best in writing but also to get the most out of reading as well. A strong contributing component to that was, obviously, education, in the formal sense, the object of which, he said, was "to train the mind, not to crowd the memory."[20] It would, he thought, "not be possible to exaggerate" the value of teaching, whose "business [was] to create citizens in the fullest sense of the word."[21] The role of a university, in particular, was important, since it was "the guardian of the central wisdom of humankind, a trustee of humane learning."[22] This is a message he repeated.[23] Specifically, the university had two duties: to transmit knowledge and to advance knowledge.

> [The university] has to train the student's mind, and also ... provide [him] with the special equipment which will enable him to earn a living; it has to give him as a basis a liberal education, and to add to that a professional technique.... Our purpose is to combine humanism with technique. By humanism I mean the study of man in all his relations, as thinker, as artist, as social and moral being; and by technique I mean the study of what might be called brute fact. Now, I believe that all true education requires a humane foundation. By humane learning I mean simply the disinterested pursuit of truth for its own sake, apart from any incidental advantages. The humanities should be broadly defined. They are not only art, literature, history,

philosophy and religion; they are each and every science provided it is pursued in a certain way.[24]

Education was a lifelong interest of John Buchan, particularly because of its importance in developing both the character and the minds of young people. Recall that when he was partner in Thomas Nelson & Son (1907–1929), as editor and literary advisor, the company was involved in printing educational texts. Indeed, Buchan edited a 675-page history of English literature, in which he wrote three chapters in the section on the nineteenth century.[25] It was intended, as Buchan wrote in the preface, to "occupy a middle place between the mere summary of the textbook and the more elaborate compendium … and … should be at once a manual for the student and a book which could be used with profit by the general reader."[26]

As the member of Parliament for the Scottish Universities (1927–1935), John Buchan had promoted education issues. He was, at the same time, writing regularly for a magazine called *The Graphic*. In one article, published in 1931, he addressed the problem of the student who had graduated but has no specific prospect for a job — a rather contemporary-sounding problem![27] When he arrived in Canada, his interest in education continued and he sought to learn about the situation in his new Canadian home. To a meeting of educators in March 1937, he said, "I am still in the position of a learner [but] I hope I may have something useful to say about [the education problems in Canada] before I finish my term of office here."[28] He did, however, have firm views about what the foundations of education should be and of the distinctions within it.

He noted some of the challenges he was observing in Canada, such as the need for national education to be highly organized, and the difficulties presented by distances and by the fact that the country was still, in significant part, a "pioneer land." This latter point raised a particular problem for education, he believed, in that much practical training was still in demand and needed. Therefore the question was how to "strike a just balance between the academic and the practical; how to combine education in the broadest sense, which is the training of the mind and character, with the acquisition of the special technique which enables a boy to earn his livelihood."[29]

During his travels across the country, Tweedsmuir visited many schools and universities, not a few of the latter of which conferred honorary degrees on him.[30] He addressed faculty and students, and had many discussions with the heads of the universities and others about education questions. Some of the university leaders and various educators visited with the governor general while they were in Ottawa. By the end of 1938, while he may have considered he was a "learner," he began developing several ideas.

He had already had discussions with officials at McGill University in Montreal, prior to the installation of the new principal, Lewis Douglas, in January 1938, and then continued discussions with Douglas.[31] In November 1938 Tweedsmuir met with C.D. Ellis, a professor of physics from King's College, London, who was visiting Canada and studying the state of education.[32] Subsequent to his fact-finding travels, Ellis found

© National Film Board of Canada. All rights reserved.

Tweedsmuir discussed ways of enhancing the academic and intellectual life of the country with many. Here he shares a lighter moment with Dr. Henry Cody (right), president of the University of Toronto, during the visit of Cordell Hull (left), U.S. secretary of state, who received an honorary degree from the university on October 22, 1937.

the "most striking feature is the excellence in the teaching."[33] However, he believed there was a need to introduce Ph.D. programs at universities in western Canada, where, at the time, only the University of Manitoba had one. The situation presented dangers, the first of which was that this gap, along with a lack of research opportunities and grants, resulted in many students moving to the United States. There would in future be economic development in the western provinces, he said, and the universities had a role to play in it. If they were not to "become intellectually just a northern and frontier fringe of the States," then they must develop Ph.D. programs.[34] Tweedsmuir's interest was piqued.

In an effort to see how Canada could avoid becoming just a northern fringe of the United States, Ellis went to the United States, where he planned to meet a Dr. Keppel of the Carnegie Corporation in New York. The Carnegie Corporation, with the Carnegie Foundation, provided funding for the promotion of education in the United States and the British Dominions and colonies.[35] Ellis promised that he would update Tweedsmuir on that meeting.[36]

Tweedsmuir incorporated Ellis's information into his accumulating knowledge. He had been impressed enough by what he had seen and learned himself of the Canadian universities, but he assessed the situation as being far from its full potential. In his various discussions, he learned there was much duplication among the universities, which was costly, at a time — the Depression was still afflicting the country — when funding was difficult. Reflecting on how these issues might be dealt with, Tweedsmuir thought of the experience in Britain, where there had been two university commissions in the past century, "both of which had admirable results."[37] He was ready to set out some specific ideas.

In December he wrote to Principal Lewis Douglas, now just a year in the position, and in January 1939 he wrote to the principal of Queen's University in Kingston, Ontario, Robert Wallace. He proposed to meet with Dr. Cody, the president of the University of Toronto, but illness prevented Cody from meeting, so Tweedsmuir wrote to him in February.

He sought the opinion of all three regarding his proposal that a "universities commission" be established to look at ways "to weave a great deal of vigorous local intellectual life into a national organism."[38] The purpose of the commission would be to deal with issues such as duplication of programs and resources, and the lack of Ph.D. degrees in the West. He thought that these efforts might also pull the universities away from a "narrow utilitarian outlook." The commission would also propose solutions to what were observed to be "a cluttering up of rival institutions" in the Maritimes, where the origins of many universities were religious. He informed each of his correspondents that he had been communicating with the others, and suggested that the three "should talk about the matter."[39] If they were all agreed about the need for a commission, it would be easier to obtain the support of other universities, including the Catholic ones, and then "the [g]overnment would, I have no doubt," Tweedsmuir wrote optimistically, "give it the imprimatur of a [r]oyal [c]ommission."[40] He believed also that some of the "public-spirited rich" might well be persuaded to provide money if this initiative went ahead, since it would be seen to be impressive and practical. In the meantime, while awaiting developments, he continued to inform himself.

Terence Macdermot, the headmaster of Upper Canada College, had lunch with the governor general in early January. Tweedsmuir solicited his thoughts on a university commission. Macdermot replied within days, enthusiastic that someone was championing such an idea.[41] He set out a list of ten problem areas, ranging from entrance qualifications, the comparative value of degrees, the specialized functions of universities, the desirability of a university press, the relationship between English- and French-speaking universities, and the need for a federal education office. He recognized, however, that the British North America Act, which gave the provinces jurisdiction over education, presented an obstacle to "any effort to centralize education and to steer university policy from outside the province," but he believed that just outlining some of the issues would in itself be useful.[42] Tweedsmuir replied that Macdermot's list would "be most useful."[43]

Meanwhile, replies were being received from Douglas, Wallace, and Cody. They were generally positive, but Tweedsmuir was discovering that Canada was not Britain. Both Douglas and Wallace raised the federal-provincial jurisdictional issue Macdermot had mentioned. Wallace also highlighted the potential difficulties regarding institutions "under denominational auspices," and suggested that the provincial

Kaiden-Kazanjian Studios Inc./Library and Archives Canada/C-090174

Tweedsmuir proposed establishing a universities commission to examine ways
"to weave a great deal of vigorous local intellectual life into a national organism."

ministers of education should be informed because their support would be valuable in paving the way to set up a royal commission.[44] Douglas, on reflection, concurred with Tweedsmuir's proposal, adding that there may also be "some other questions" that could be touched on in discussion with Wallace and Cody.[45] Cody would soon be spending a weekend at Rideau Hall and Tweedsmuir would continue discussions with him. The three university heads seemed to agree on one point: each suggested that the matter be put on the agenda of the next National Conference of Canadian Universities, which was to be held in May. Wallace wrote to the secretary, "suggesting the general subject of the [c]ommission for the May gathering."[46] He added that an item already on the agenda dealt with inter-university co-operation, and that perhaps the idea of a universities commission could be raised then.

Maintaining momentum, Tweedsmuir tried to move the others past the obstacles they saw in the jurisdictional issues and the religious-based institutions. In March he sent Douglas, Wallace, and Cody each a letter with "a few notes on the kind of question which a universities commission might discuss."[47] The subjects for discussion were set out in nine points, and reflected much of the information Tweedsmuir had gathered from his contacts and discussions, points which he believed were "ripe for discussion, and the settlement of which [was] important for the [u]niversity life of Canada": i) making generally available information about activity in all the universities; ii) creating uniform qualification for entrance, a goal that implicated the secondary schools; iii) introducing post-graduate studies and Ph.D. programs, especially in the West; iv) specializing the functions of the different universities; v) associating university training with requirements for government service; vi) improving the relationship between English- and French-speaking universities; vii) creating a Federal Bureau of Education; viii) significantly increasing the number and value of scholarships; and ix) creating a university press. The responses were mixed.

Cody said the points "will be presented to the Executive of the Conference, and very probably discussed in the general conference to be held at McGill in May."[48] Douglas, "on reflection," however, changed his mind, and "for a number of reasons" thought it inadvisable to include the issue of a universities commission on the conference agenda.[49] Some of the issues he thought would raise conflicts. He was apologetic for not having made the time yet to meet with Cody and Wallace, but wanted to discuss the matter further with them. He believed that if they could agree on the terms of reference for a commission, they would avoid "much discussion and no effective action" at the conference. As for Wallace, he sounded a note similar to one made by Douglas: some of the points "would commend themselves more than others to members of the Canadian Universities Conference," while other points might attract "considerable opposition."[50] However, he proposed, as an alternative, to present the idea "as an argument for a survey, either in the form of a [c]ommission or otherwise." He committed to contacting the secretary of the Conference to suggest that time be allowed to present this idea.

The Eighteenth National Conference of Canadian Universities was held at McGill on May 29 and 30, 1939, with seventeen universities and colleges attending, along with representatives of the American National Association of State Universities, the National Research Council, and the Canadian Student Assembly. Several of the issues to be discussed were those raised in Tweedsmuir's discussions with Cody, Douglas, Wallace, Macdermot, and Ellis, including Wallace's point that an existing agenda item would be relevant for raising their subject: the increasing cost of education; national scholarships and bursaries; and Dominion co-operation in educational problems.[51] Another topic on the agenda would also have greatly appealed to Tweedsmuir: the responsibility of the university in a democratic society.

During the first session, dealing with the increasing cost of education, the vice-principal of McGill, Dr. W.E. McNeill, helped set a higher tone, quoting, among others, Lord Tweedsmuir, and warning of the "perpetual temptation to think more of the material than the spiritual, the temporal than the eternal, to choose the easy path of showy worldly success instead of the difficult road of truth and wisdom."[52]

All of one morning was devoted to Dominion co-operation in education, with T.H. Matthews of McGill, Dr. Spence of the University of Manitoba, and Terence Macdermot all speaking to the issue. Proposals were made that went in the direction of the discussions Tweedsmuir had

had with the key academic representatives. Matthews suggested some central agency, specifically proposing the government establish a Dominion Council of Education "to consider the general problems of Canadian education," and at the same time establish a commissioner of education.[53]

Spence and Macdermot dealt with co-operation in university matriculation. The latter attacked the jurisdictional issue head-on, referring to "our educational provincialism." The discussion that ensued resulted in a motion proposed by Wallace, one he had suggested to Tweedsmuir, that "a commission be appointed by the [e]xecutive to consider the whole question of entrance to the universities, … to co[-]operate with all existing educational associations … and to report at the next meeting of the Conference." The motion was seconded and carried. It was a start — a start, however, that would be interrupted by war.

As an interesting aside to the focused discussion on the future of universities in Canada, the correspondence Tweedsmuir carried on with Cody, Douglas, and Wallace included several other initiatives and offers of assistance. In discussion with Montreal businessman Jack McConnell, Tweedsmuir, as "Visitor" to McGill, offered to Principal Douglas to forward to Lord Nuffield, founder of the Morris Motor Company and a philanthropist in Britain, a proposal to establish a school of aeronautical engineering at McGill, presumably to seek additional financial assistance for the venture.[54] Cody agreed to Tweedsmuir's proposal that Moritz Bonn be invited to lecture at the University of Toronto.[55] Bonn was a well-known German professor who had been driven from Nazi Germany because he was Jewish. Cody also made reference to a visit from Stanley Baldwin, now Earl Baldwin of Bewdley, arranged for April, when Baldwin would give a lecture and receive an honorary degree.[56] Given Tweedsmuir's close connection with Baldwin, it is likely that he facilitated this visit.

While the National Conference of Canadian Universities was underway at McGill, Tweedsmuir was addressing another aspect of education. On May 29 he laid the cornerstone for the Ottawa Technical School. Eight months later, on January 19, 1940, he attended the opening of the school and addressed those gathered for the event. He discussed the importance of technical knowledge and its practical application. But, he continued, for technical knowledge to be really practical, it must be "combined with a reasonable standard of general culture, with something of a liberal education."[57] It was this mixing that reflected, for him, the importance of the classics in education. Education was, of course, about young people and young adults, but there were other avenues the governor general used to express his deep interest in encouraging the development of youth.

As Chief Scout of Canada, the governor general ensured he saw Cubs and Scouts across the country as he travelled, just as Lady Tweedsmuir did the Girl Guides. It was an organization he valued, and he saw it as one of the real projects of genius of the time. He had known its founder, Robert, Lord Baden-Powell, in South Africa. His use of "we" and "our" as he spoke of the organization and its objectives and plans showed how closely he identified with it.

We know of his annual addresses to the Boy Scouts Association dinner. There were, of course, common themes. In the final words of his first address to the association, on May 1, 1936, he set out a basic principle he espoused: "I do not care how long a man may live; in one sense he should never grow old. If we get out of touch with our world we cease to be any use in it, and I have always believed that the best way of keeping abreast of our times is to keep in touch with youth."[58]

With each succeeding year, he emphasized the importance of developing and encouraging the Scouts to be physically, mentally, and morally strong. His addresses became more explicit as dangers grew. His 1939 speech was broadcast from his bed in Ottawa because he was too ill to travel.[59] He began by suggesting some maxims of life, the first of which was the importance of being prepared to take risks, though he cautioned that it was necessary not to do so foolishly. "There is no more hopeless motto for youth," he advised, "than 'Safety first.'"[60] The second maxim was that intelligence was vital; using one's brains was crucial, especially when confronted with increasing confusion and disillusion. The third point to hang on to, he stressed, was the need to have some faith and purpose, "to carry us through the darkest days"; [61] but one must also be critical, he told his audience:

There are many isms today to perplex us — Naziism,
Communism, Fascism, and so forth — [but] there is only
one ism which kills the soul, and that is pessimism.… I
was once the [w]arden of an ancient Border castle which
stands in a narrow pass, through which flows the river
Tweed. I have often thought that that old keep typified
some of the greatest duties of human life.… These two
duties are before every man, and they were never more
vital in the world than today. We have to hold the pass,
for many precious things are in danger. We have to hold
the pass and defend our liberties and our heritage of
civili[z]ation. But we have also to hand on the light.…
We must hand that on to our successors not only undi-
minished, but increased, for the only way in which we
can pay our debt to the past is by putting the future in
debt to ourselves.[62]

The speech evoked a grateful reply from Baden-Powell. It was, the
Scouting founder wrote, "one of the most inspiring [speeches] that has ever
been given to the Scouts in Canada."[63] He regretted Tweedsmuir's health
had prevented him from delivering the speech in person, but it being
broadcast meant it was heard "far and wide," and would, Baden-Powell
believed, "have far-reaching effects for good." Half a year later, Canada was
at war, and many young men and women would be asked "to hold the
pass" in many ways.

The Scouts' Association annual dinner in February 1940 was held
in Toronto. The Chief Scout's address was read out to the audience by
a spokesman. It seems, with its abrupt ending, not to have been completed as its author would have wished. On February 6, Tweedsmuir
had fallen at Rideau Hall, suffered a concussion, and was unable to
attend. He had planned on leaving Canada in the autumn, as scheduled, so this would have been his last dinner in any case. The war had
started, circumstances had changed, but not Tweedsmuir's optimism
and encouragement for the Scouting movement. "You have given me
far more than I have been able to give you."[64] He praised the volunteers

and the leaders for their work, "a most unselfish and worthy form of public service."

As well as praise, he also offered the movement some ideas. He had written in his speech that since this was his last address to them, he was "going to venture to offer you a few suggestions as to the lines on which our future work should develop." There was scope for increasing the numbers, and he wanted to see an end to the trend of the organization weakening "as adolescence proceeds." He asked if, with the developments of air travel and the importance of aircraft for both the development of Canada's North and for the war, there could not be something in the program to include the air. He suggested that we should "link up our Scout training more closely with the practical problems which are facing our growing youth." "The problems of youth," he wrote, "are more difficult today than ever before, and they are not going to be easier when this war is over." These few suggestions were consistent with his approach, but most important was forming good citizens, of good character, led by intelligent and critical thinking.

Tweedsmuir encouraged individuals and organizations to excel in whatever their endeavours. Indeed, we could say that his own standard was excellence. He sometimes advised, sometimes admonished, his listeners or interlocutors to look beyond their own fields of interest or specialization, to provide proportion and balance to their perspectives and to enrich their own lives and that of society.

In the field of engineering, the governor general gave an address to the jubilee dinner of the Engineering Institute of Canada. Contrary to many people, who viewed engineering projects as blights on a beautiful countryside, he observed that "[n]ature has a wonderful power of absorbing human inventions."[65] But, he advised, "at the same time, the constructive powers of man must keep in some kind of harmony with nature"; the engineer, he added, "should be also something of the artist."[66] He concluded with a visionary comment of their "high mission" in a "land whose horizons are not limited, and whose development no man can assess."[67]

In medicine — a field Tweedsmuir knew from the inside, as it were — he praised the "rank and file," as well as the outstanding figures, some of whom had gone to Britain and the United States to pursue their careers. He was impressed by the physicians he had met on the Prairies, individuals who "often [had] a brilliant college record [who were] surrendering professional ambitions for the day-to-day work of relieving pain and sickness in poverty-stricken districts."[68] Their reward, he added, returning to a consistent theme, was in "the consciousness of faithful service."

He spoke, too, of the importance of preventive medicine because "[m]an is a septic animal and if he is given a chance he poisons himself and his neighbours," an increasing problem in an ever more closely settled and connected world.[69]

He also noted that the success of treating many diseases of early life would mean that those of later life, like rheumatic diseases, "nerve strain" (how mental illnesses were often described at the time), and "cancer, will bulk more prominently."

Tweedsmuir was made an Honorary Fellow of the Royal College of Physicians and Surgeons of Canada in October 1936. At the time of his induction, he talked of how Canada was at the intersection of the medical profession; it benefitted from the influences from England, Scotland, and France, and "the great avenue that joins you to the United States."[70] He lauded the value of the national, provincial, and local medical associations to help keep abreast of new ideas, noting the necessity of maintaining awareness of the latest developments in medical research and equipment; doing so was, he noted, a duty the physician owes his patients and himself.[71] Commenting on the success medical sciences had made in reducing diseases of early life, he observed that such progress would likely result in diseases of later life, such as cancer, looming larger. He advocated for research campaigns, highlighting the need for research into rheumatic diseases, which cause significant lost working days and which could, therefore, have a "direct bearing upon our economic welfare."[72] Taking short cuts or searching for some "easy panacea" was not advised, he told his audience. "You have to fight the quack," likely speaking from experience in his search for intestinal peace, "just as the statesman has to fight the theorist, and the economist the charlatan."[73]

In the fall of 1938, following Tweedsmuir's return to Canada from Britain, where he had undergone lengthy treatment at a clinic in north Wales, he spoke to the Ottawa Medical Society dinner, reflecting on his time there. With bouts of humour, he offered two suggestions, noting that they were those "of a layman, [and] made with all deference and modesty."[74] The first involved the advisability of providing more information to the public, but "directed to the prevention of needless anxieties and false hopes," so that they do not believe that cancer can be cured "out of a bottle or a tube."[75] His second reflection stressed the indivisibility of body and mind, and stemmed from a quotation from Plato.[76] He had addressed the issue of mental illness numerous times, and he did so again, pleading that a "good doctor should be — and indeed always has been — something of a psychologist."[77]

He commented also that just as some physicians had been renowned writers, some had excelled in other fields. As a historian, Tweedsmuir was conscious of the fact that Canada was a relatively young country, but it was, nonetheless, one with a romantic history, and he stressed the need to preserve it. So it was that Tweedsmuir drew the attention of his listeners to the work of a Dr. Clarence Webster of Shediac, New Brunswick, who had been active in archival work and the conservation of historic monuments. After a very successful medical career, including studies at Edinburgh, Leipzig, and Berlin, Dr. Webster had retired and "became a really distinguished historian, and … done invaluable work in restoring and preserving archives and monuments in the Maritime Provinces," a point noted also by *Saturday Night* magazine.[78] To recognize his contribution, Tweedsmuir proposed him for an honorary doctorate from Edinburgh University. It was curious that he would not have suggested this to one of his contacts at one of the Canadian universities, though we do not know if he did. Tweedsmuir was by this time chancellor of the University of Edinburgh, however, and since Webster had studied at Edinburgh, perhaps he felt that it would be appropriate for that institution to award Webster the honour.

It was not just the professions that Tweedsmuir was concerned with, however. We have noted his encouragement of farmers and of the Dominion government's agricultural research and development that was aimed at mitigating the dual disasters of drought and depression. He was, in fact, so proud of the work done there that he had wanted Roosevelt to visit and see it.

And along with his efforts to celebrate Canada and Canadians, Tweedsmuir was also moved to try to aid those he felt were in need of assistance. It was the plight of his fellow citizens that moved Tweedsmuir in his speeches and actions to instill in citizens a greater sense of charity and duty to help those less fortunate. The Thirties was a time when government assistance was just beginning and was not what we know today. It was a time when churches, religious orders, ethnic organizations, and other charitable groups played a more significant role. The Great Depression greatly exacerbated difficult conditions, compounding the difficult situation of many war veterans, who had been wounded physically or mentally.

The Tweedsmuirs' active support for charitable causes began almost immediately upon their arrival in Ottawa. They quickly lent support for the Poppy Campaign, and they did even more each year thereafter. "Some of the returned men," the governor general said during the campaign in 1936, "have been compelled by the effects of their war service to fall out of the battle line of life. The work you are doing is keeping the spirit of hope alive. You are aiding them to find their place in the world again."[79]

The Depression had placed even greater distress on families. Tweedsmuir described "men and women, wanted by economic insecurity, [who] have begun to lose their nerve, and [who] look out upon the world with hopeless eyes. We have not only to succour the body but to revive the spirit."[80] While governments struggled to cope with financing and providing services, there was much still to be done by everyone. The private citizen, he said encouragingly, "is beginning to see that sympathy which does not issue in practical deeds is no virtue at all."[81] It was a humanitarian call to those citizens better off to help restore and revive society.

CHAPTER 18

"Touched Nothing
Which He Did Not Adorn"[1]

In 1939 Lillian Killick, John Buchan's long-time secretary, commented that His Excellency was writing "a very odd book, so unlike him, so introspective."[2] She was referring to *Sick Heart River*, a novel with a familiar Buchan character, Sir Edward Leithen, which was mostly set in the Canadian North. Though Tweedsmuir was maintaining his myriad activities through the last months of 1939, amidst his preoccupation with the war and his duties as commander in chief visiting military units, there were a number of indicators of what seems to have been a shift in his psychological state.

"I am getting homesick now for the first time," he wrote to his sister in late November.[3] It was a stark admission. He attributed it to the "Peebles letters," from his sister and brother who lived in that Scottish Borders village. It may also have been partly attributable to the fact that he knew he was into the last year as governor general.

John Buchan's appointment as governor general had been for five years. Christmas 1939, the first Christmas of the war, would be his last in Canada. Aware of this government members and other individuals began to inquire whether his time might not be extended.

"I am going to have great difficulties," he wrote, "about my term of office, for there is a very strong effort being made to make me stay for the duration of the war!"[4]

It was argued that with the war, it would be a poor time for a change. He began receiving letters expressing regret about his foreseen departure, but he was convinced he must not extend his time. Regardless of how he felt, it was not assured he would be able to leave. He had written formally to King George VI, setting out his wish not to remain in Canada beyond his five-year term, but there was at the back of his mind the thought that the king might think it unwise to make any changes during wartime.[5] He would have to try all avenues to attain the outcome he believed necessary.

He wrote to Violet Markham at the end of November 1939 that if she happened to be writing to Mackenzie King, requesting that she "tactfully suggest" and pass on his views about his not staying on.[6] King's friendship with Markham ensured an understanding and sympathetic hearing. A little over a week later, he had a lengthy and candid conversation with his prime minister, who had asked him to stay on.

Tweedsmuir set out various reasons why he believed he should not continue. He started, but not with his underlying reason. His high level of energy and breadth of interests, he confessed, had caused concern about the precedent that might be set as to expectations. "[W]ithout being vain he could say that he had done many things which a successor would find it very difficult to do," including travelling extensively, delivering numerous talks (he had made some thirty or more speeches to Canadian Clubs within a short time after he had arrived), and involving himself closely with the universities.[7] It "would be difficult, [he suggested,] to find other men who could fill these different roles providing they came to be looked upon as, in a sense, apart from the position of [governor general]."[8] His personal qualities had given him an authority in his own right, complementing the authority inherent in the office of governor general. The office in turn leveraged his other activities, which were not necessarily part of the viceregal role; regardless, all his roles aimed at similar objectives — the betterment of the individual and society, and, in the unique context of the time, the defence of Western civilization. It is interesting that in his statement about his successors he was in fact questioning the model he had established. Would he have offered the same explanation had his health been better? We cannot know, but we do know he has inspired several of his successors.

Finally, he turned to his underlying reason. "[W]hat he really needed [he said] was to take a cure that would run over several months," likely thinking of the improvement following his rest at Ruthin Castle in 1938.[9] He indicated that if he continued on, "he was running risks that might prove very prejudicial."[10] It was an ominous, and prescient, statement. Finally, he told his prime minister, he felt he could not ask his wife to stay on longer, though she would, if that was what he asked her to do. Tweedsmuir then asked Mackenzie King if he would write King George directly, and suggested the approach to take: the prime minister should say that he wanted him to stay, as did the people, but, nevertheless, the prime minister advised that he should return, citing the reasons they had just discussed. Clearly, Mackenzie King was sympathetic, and moved past his selfish motivation for wanting Tweedsmuir to stay, as he admitted.[11] He agreed to do it "at once."

Tweedsmuir then thought it important that he should provide more detail himself to the Palace about his reasons for desiring to depart on schedule, but was too stoic to reference his health. He wrote to Alexander Hardinge, asking the private secretary to put his case before the king.[12] He mentioned that he had had a long talk with the prime minister, who was "completely convinced." He elaborated in writing the reasons he had expressed to King, and added an outline of why he believed this a good time to make a transition to a new governor general, countering any renewal argument based on exigencies of the war. In describing what was, in fact, his uniqueness as a governor general, he noted that his extensive speaking had included discussions of issues beyond the usual "governor generalities"; perhaps he wanted to recall the controversies he had caused and also the disapproval of the Palace when his detailed articles on his journey down the Mackenzie River had appeared in the London *Sunday Times*. His third reason was his consideration for his wife, who was "never well in the Canadian winter," and who was now concerned about her family in wartime England. After five years of "an immense amount of valuable work," he did not think it fair to ask her to stay longer. As for changing governors general during wartime, Tweedsmuir argued this would, in fact, be the best time, since a new appointee "could slip easily into the saddle after the formal reception, and would not have to do as I did, and make some thirty or forty speeches in the first two months." In other words the activities would be more routine and there would not be the same expectations, there would be less of a legacy from the previous governor general. Summing up, he wrote that his "principal task in Canada [was] now over," and that he would just be "marking time" if he did remain, acknowledging though that those official wartime functions could be useful in their own way. The statement belied his own activities in the interest of Canada that were continuing, regardless of the war.

A couple of days later, King provided Tweedsmuir a copy of the letter he proposed to send to His Majesty. It was a formally worded letter, as one would expect, yet rather warm. In his accompanying note, he offered that if Tweedsmuir wanted to talk privately rather than write a return note he would immediately visit him at Government House.[13] Tweedsmuir preferred to write, thanking King for "exactly what I should like to see written," and stating that he believed it would facilitate his own request to King George.[14] He had only one more point to make, and that was that he was blessed with "good spirits," even when his health made him uncomfortable, but now it would be even better for him to know that he would be able, "within a reasonable time … to give [his] whole attention to getting well." All of this confirmed that health was truly uppermost in his mind, a point he had made to Violet Markham in his letter to her at the end of November.[15] It was confirmed further in a letter Tweedsmuir sent to Neville Chamberlain just before Christmas, in which he cited his health as the only reason for not wanting to extend his time in Canada.[16]

The prime minister immediately dispatched his letter to the king. He emphasized that an extension would not be in Lord Tweedsmuir's best interests, especially considering his health. The anxieties of the war would, he added, affect Lady Tweedsmuir and other family members, which in turn could further prejudice the governor's health. King therefore "reluctantly … and definitely advise[d] against any thought of the extension of Lord Tweedsmuir's term."[17] The next day, King wrote again to Tweedsmuir, that it was with "sadness and feeling of regret at even the thought of a severance of our official relations."[18]

His Majesty accepted. Sir Alexander Hardinge notified the Canadian prime minister of the king's decision in the first week of the new year

(1940),[19] and then sent a letter to Tweedsmuir in which he acknowledged the health issue and stated that "in view of all the circumstances, you should not be invited to accept an extension of your term of office beyond September of this year."[20] Hardinge added that "the [k]ing feels that the regret expressed by Mr. Mackenzie King at having to make this recommendation must be very gratifying to you." With this matter confirmed, the Palace and the prime minister agreed they had ample time to consider a successor.

In the meantime, however, word leaked to the media that Tweedsmuir's time would not be extended, mainly due to his health. King George was not pleased. "His Majesty [trusted] that the report is inaccurate."[21] Tweedsmuir replied protectively of his prime minister, explaining that "our Canadian journalists are terribly inexact." He attributed the inexactitude to the fact that few journalists wrote shorthand, and therefore they likely misreported King, who was, Tweedsmuir emphasized, "very particular about etiquette and is the last man, I think, to anticipate the [k]ing's decision."[22] By way of explanation, Tweedsmuir suggested two phrases the prime minister may have said and how it was possible for either one to be misrepresented.[23]

With this matter now formally put to rest, the king's private secretary sent another letter, three days after the previous one, to raise the issue of a successor, an issue Tweedsmuir had also raised in his private correspondence of December 7.[24] Given the unpleasant experience over the selection and nomination of John Buchan as governor general, fomented by then opposition leader Mackenzie King, the Palace was cautious. After summarizing the delicate situation of 1935, Hardinge had two questions for Tweedsmuir: 1) "[I]s there any likelihood of a General Election taking place before your term of office expires, in which there is a probability of a change of Government?" and 2) "[D]o you think that Mr. Mackenzie King would object to being asked to consult the Leader of the Opposition before submitting any names?" The questions were supported by advice in the file from 1935, which Hardinge relayed to Tweedsmuir.

Tweedsmuir replied in detail, explaining that his prime minister would be wise to ask for a dissolution of Parliament then, for several reasons. He assured Hardinge that there was very little probability of a situation similar to the time of his own appointment, because "there [was] not much doubt as to the result [of the election]," which he expected to be held before the end of March, with the new Parliament meeting by the end of the following month.[25] As an additional assurance, Tweedsmuir relayed his belief that he was certain King would, "as a matter of courtesy," inform the opposition leader about his proposal for the next governor general. Therefore, he concluded, there would be no repeat of the problems that worried Hardinge.

Tweedsmuir then confidentially and delicately advanced a suggestion for his successor, but ever so politely, indicating that he did "not want the appointment to be too long delayed," believing the delay could be an embarrassment, likely meaning also an inconvenience, to both incumbent and successor. He was in fact sounding out the Palace on behalf of his prime minister, who, not knowing "the personnel at home very intimately," was, Tweedsmuir emphasized, "bound to lean a good deal for advice upon the [governor general] then in office."[26] This, of course, took for granted that the next governor general would be from Britain as well. Is it surprising that this seems to have been taken for granted, given the debate provoked by Buchan's appointment in 1935? Not really, if we consider the context of the war and that, as a result, there was a renewed bond with Britain. The prime minister would not want to open a discussion that could create division in the country.

Tweedsmuir and King had "talked over various people." One of the names Tweedsmuir had put forward just ten days earlier was his former colleague, the betroubled information minister, Lord (Hugh) Macmillan, who had just been removed from the position. Tweedsmuir would not only have wished to help his friend in a fundamental way, but would also, perhaps, have wished to find a face-saving position for him.[27] King raised Macmillan's difficulties and his tarnished reputation at the Information Ministry. Tweedsmuir countered that those issues weren't as important for a position like governor general, though he admitted that there might be concern that Macmillan was, perhaps, too much like a scholar. In this particular case, it seems naive of Tweedsmuir to think Macmillan could have been seriously considered, but his attempt to champion him demonstrates his loyalty to an old colleague.

Tweedsmuir intimated to Hardinge that King seemed to have one name in mind over others, Lord Athlone, who was a cousin of the king. Such a suggestion seems at odds with King's previous thoughts about who was appropriate to serve as governor general, especially considering his attitude to royalty, but in the present circumstances, the royal connection would "be especially welcome."[28] King could see that. Tweedsmuir supported the choice, noting that "many people in Canada have the same notion," and that the Athlones were known for their good work in South Africa. What Tweedsmuir wanted was Hardinge's opinion as to whether Athlone would accept if his name were put forward. If not, then the governor general indicated he could find "ways and means of discouraging my [prime minister] from thinking more about it."

Once it was official that he would be leaving in the fall, Tweedsmuir began to write frequently in his letters to family and friends of his feelings of regret. To his old professor, Gilbert Murray, he wrote that leaving would be difficult, "for I have got my roots down very deep [here]."[29] It would be "like pulling up mandrakes!" he exclaimed to his sister.[30] And from the time the news had leaked to the public, more letters began arriving at Rideau Hall from those asking him to reconsider. He described to his sister the appeals for him to stay longer, coming from "humble folk," Prairie farmers, French Canadians, and others, as "really rather heart-breaking."[31] Some of them wrote that they felt "safe" with him in Canada, though he wasn't quite sure what they meant. This was, in fact, similar to what King had expressed: "The Canadian people would feel a sense of security and satisfaction if he stayed on for the balance of the war."[32] It was a sentiment deriving in significant part from Tweedsmuir's demonstrated confidence, sincere character, and impressive rhetorical abilities to describe in inspiring ways the strength and values of Western civilization, its liberties, and the heritage that needed protecting.

One letter, dated January 7, expressed "infinite regret, shared by all Canadians ... [that] you do not feel strong enough to allow the extension of your term of office."[33] Another closed with a reference to "our beloved [governor general], our fireside friend, John Buchan."[34] One of the most touching letters he received was from Pelham Edgar, head of the Canadian Authors Association. Edgar wrote how distressing it had been to learn that Tweedsmuir's term would not be extended. With emotion he wrote that "you know and love the country and the country knows and loves you in return."[35] He continued, "[t]he energy and intellect you have brought to your task will leave us permanently in your debt.... In war even more than in peace your influence is a national necessity." He extended the "same affection and admiration" to Lady Tweedsmuir.

Arthur Murray, Tweedsmuir's fellow discreet conduit between Roosevelt and the British government, summed up an important aspect: "It may be said with great truth that in winning the affection and admiration of every section of the Canadian people as you have done, you have — at a most important juncture in the life of the British Commonwealth, and in difficult circumstances — thirled Canada to the Mother Country and fashioned strong and lasting bonds between the two."[36] Significantly, and likely because he now knew Tweedsmuir would be leaving as governor general, Murray also wanted to pass on what President Roosevelt had said to him when he was at the White House in 1938, specifically that "Tweedsmuir is the best [governor general] that Canada has ever had."

Despite the mix of emotions he felt, his departure in the fall of 1940 was now definite. January was turning out to be a good month for him, particularly health-wise. The trip to Halifax to review the military installations seemed to have done him a great deal of good and was a fillip to his spirit. He was convinced that "my stupid inside is beginning to behave a little better." It was frustrating, though, because, as he described to his friend Stair Gillon, "I am a strong man for my age, but for this one weakness, and therefore I am apt to do too much, not for the rest of my body, but for my stomach."[37]

January 28 he spent in bed, resting, "according to doctor's orders," and seemed pleased to report to his sister that he was "certainly putting on a little weight."[38] He didn't like that the newspapers in England were describing his health as the reason for his returning, noting that he "could easily have put up with that if it had been necessary." What the papers did say, though, he didn't mind otherwise: "They are remarkably civil in what they say about me."

On the first of February, the Tweedsmuirs were in Montreal for a charity ball, returning the next day, Friday. On Saturday, he wrote to Lord Lothian in Washington and noted that he was having a dinner that coming Tuesday, February 6, for the new American ambassador, James H.R. Cromwell, who had presented his credentials little more than a week earlier. That evening he was hosted for dinner by Monsignor Ildebrando Antoniutti, the apostolic delegate, in the company of Cardinal Villeneuve, new missionary bishops, and Mackenzie King. There was, Tweedsmuir wrote to his sister, "a great deal to be said for the Church of Rome in Canada [because] it is the only Church which has any scholarship in it."[39] But after this last trip to Montreal and his meeting with the Catholic clergy, he became nostalgic, thinking that it would be harder to leave the French in Canada, whom he collectively described as "so extraordinarily affectionate."[40] He wrote a letter to his sister on Monday, telling her about the weekend. He was likely also thinking wistfully of where she was, Peebles, and that he would finally be returning there later that year.

Tuesday, February 6 saw Rideau Hall in preparation for the dinner that evening for the new American ambassador. Sometime around mid-day, however, James Cromwell received a message that the dinner was cancelled. The governor general had had an accident and would be unable to host the evening.

While preparing his bath that morning, Tweedsmuir was reported to have felt faint; he fell and struck his head, suffering a concussion. The faintness was diagnosed as a "cerebral thrombosis," a stroke, which paralyzed his left arm and leg.[41] He lay there unconscious for about an hour before he was discovered and taken to his bed. His physician, Dr. Gordon Gunn, was called. A reassuring announcement from Government House made it into the late afternoon edition of the newspapers and said he was "resting comfortably."[42]

By the next morning, Wednesday, the whole country had been alerted. Reporting on the governor's condition shared the front pages with the war news. Around eleven o'clock, a medical bulletin was issued:

"The Governor-General passed a comfortable night and his condition is showing satisfactory improvement."[43] Behind that somewhat comforting statement, however, was the reality that the situation had been assessed as serious enough that Dr. Gunn decided to call in two specialists from Montreal, Dr. Jonathan Meakins, who had examined Tweedsmuir in the past, and Dr. Wilder Penfield, an internationally renowned neurosurgeon, of Montreal's Neurological Institute at the Royal Victoria Hospital.[44] It was taken as an encouraging sign when they returned to Montreal that evening.

On Thursday, Tweedsmuir had what was described as "rather a restless day."[45] Another medical bulletin was issued at half past noon, stating that His Excellency's condition was giving rise to "grave anxiety." By Friday the seriousness of Tweedsmuir's condition had brought Drs Meakins and Penfield back from Montreal, and the governor general's condition had now displaced the war in the newspaper headlines.

A bulletin was issued, signed by five doctors — Gunn, Meakins, Penfield, a Dr. William Cone of Montreal, and Lieutenant Colin Russel of the Royal Canadian Army Medical Corps: "His Excellency's condition became more critical through the night, and this morning at Government House an emergency trephining operation was performed which has temporarily relieved the increased intracranial pressure."[46]

The success of the emergency operation allowed a decision to be made to transport Tweedsmuir to the Montreal Neurological Institute, where Dr. Penfield and his team could operate. Just before three o'clock, Friday afternoon, Tweedsmuir was taken by ambulance to Ottawa's Union Station, accompanied by other vehicles carrying some of the doctors as well as Susan Tweedsmuir, their son Alastair, and some staff. Mackenzie King met Lady Tweedsmuir at the station and spoke briefly with her. Within ten minutes of their arrival, the train had pulled out and the track to Montreal was ordered cleared. The engine had two white flags on the front, signalling that it was a "special." An ordinary coach was attached just behind the engine, "to absorb the shock between the private coaches and the engine."[47] As the train passed through the various towns and villages, concerned people stood on both sides of the track as it passed.[48]

Dr. Wilder Penfield and Dr. William Cone, assisted by others, operated twice on Tweedsmuir after he was transported to the Neurological Institute. A bulletin was issued at 11:05 p.m., after the second operation: "His Excellency had a sub-temporal decompressive operation this evening.... There has resulted a slight but definite improvement but his condition must be considered critical."[49] Another bulletin was issued Saturday morning around ten o'clock, stating, the "Governor-General passed a better night and is more active although he remains unconscious."[50] Cables, telegrams, and letters arrived at Rideau Hall and at the Neurological Institute, asking about the governor's condition and expressing concern and sympathy. Susan Tweedsmuir, spending most of the time at the Institute, received a message of concern from President Roosevelt. She was also given support in Montreal by the parents-in-law of one of the aides-de-camp, David Walker.[51]

Late Sunday afternoon a further cranial operation had to be performed to relieve another blockage. It was a success. "The signs of pressure were receding in a reassuring manner," said the doctors' statement, but then, "at 5:58 p.m. he had a sudden arrest of respiration which was due to pulmonary embolism resulting from a clot which had formed in the veins of the legs."[52]

Lord Tweedsmuir, the beloved governor general, better known as the best-selling author John Buchan, died at 7:13 on Sunday evening, February 12, 1940.

As soon as it was learned that Lord Tweedsmuir had died, the Montreal radio station CBM interrupted the popular Jack Benny program with a brief announcement and two minutes silence. The station played sombre chamber music for the remainder of the evening.[53] Lady Tweedsmuir, in Montreal, received a telegraph of sympathy that Sunday evening from President Roosevelt, who had been following developments closely.

Radio programming on the national network of the CBC was interrupted that evening at ten o'clock as the prime minister went on air, "in fulfillment of a sad duty," to inform the country of the news. "In the passing of His Excellency, the people of Canada have lost one of the greatest and most revered of their [governors general], and a friend who from the day of his arrival in this country dedicated his life to their service."[54] He "brought wisdom, experience, grace of words, and a generosity of heart, which found expression in a wide human sympathy and understanding," and he "came to know and to share the feelings and the aspirations of the Canadian people in all parts of the Dominion."[55]

The following day King issued a statement to the press. "Canada was proud," he wrote, "to have in her midst a great scholar who touched life at so many places and touched nothing which he did not adorn."[56] Praising Tweedsmuir's speeches as "models of matter and form," King said Tweedsmuir gave to those he addressed "an inspired vision of the strength of democracy and of the true meaning of nationhood." His "great arts and talents ... were devoted to an understanding of the people, and to the interpretation of all that was best in French and English, East and West, new Canada and old Canada." The prime minister summarized parts of Tweedsmuir's career, concluding that he had "expressed the wish that he might be truly called a Canadian," then added what would have pleased Tweedsmuir: "Hundreds of thousands of our citizens who came under the influence of his wise gentleness and his humble courtesy were more than willing to claim him as their own."

King George sent a cable to the prime minister, who made it public. The king shared the grief of "the Dominion whose welfare [Tweedsmuir] had so much at heart and to whose service he devoted himself in the face of ill health with unfailing energy and courage."[57] A seven-day mourning period was proclaimed.

Letters of sympathy and tributes deluged Rideau Hall, not just from within Canada but from abroad as well. The newspapers carried tributes from all quarters and printed details and highlights of his time and accomplishments in Canada, giving details of the man and his "typical" day at Rideau Hall, which reflected his enormous capacity for work and his concentration, though he always interspersed his work with morning and afternoon walks, which Ottawa residents and neighbours of Rideau Hall recalled.[58]

Federal, provincial, and municipal political leaders, as well as religious leaders, issued statements, as did the lieutenant-governors of the provinces and many groups of which he had been patron. The leader of the opposition Conservative Party, Dr. R.J. Manion, speaking over the CBC from Fort William, Ontario, lamented that the loss of Tweedsmuir's "advice and counsel will be keenly felt," especially while Canada was at war. He recalled Tweedsmuir's qualities and experience as diplomat, civil servant, and member of Parliament, as well as his "broad human sympathies and his knowledge of human nature," and his encouragement of people engaged in charitable causes. But he did not forget the "joy and pleasure" that John Buchan had given as a legacy through his novels and historical works. Ernest Lapointe, Mackenzie King's Quebec deputy, said Canada had lost "a friend who devoted himself entirely to its service, with remarkable intelligence and tact." He highlighted Tweedsmuir's "vast culture" and reputation as a "wise and experienced administrator," and spoke of his "breadth of vision and patriotism of a great man of state." Tweedsmuir's speeches and his example inspired us, Lapointe stated, and helped to "flourish our respect for the constitutional system of government and our faith in our future as a nation."

Religious leaders of the major churches had wide and high praise, beyond their spiritual domain. Tweedsmuir was recalled as "one of the most brilliant and versatile figures of our time," who "endeared himself alike to the greatest and the humblest";[59] a "beloved [governor general]," who was "[p]ossessed of rare and singular gifts of mind and heart ... [and made] an enduring contribution to the life of this nation and Empire, and to the world."[60] His statesmanship made him "a real interpreter" between Canada and Britain and between the Empire and the United States;[61] he was "a keen psychologist, a scholar of the highest rank and brilliance, [and] a wise and prudent diplomat" who "exercised an enlightened prestige."[62] A "remarkable author," too, he became "still greater through the delicacy of his sentiments [and], [w]ith a penetrating mind of great scope, he seemed a stranger to nothing that could preoccupy human thought, [his] Christianity and culture joined in the expression of spiritual values."[63] "[I]n him French-Canadians [lost] a sincere friend."[64]

Tweedsmuir's American publisher, Houghton Mifflin, wrote that he had devoted "himself so thoroughly to Canada and its people that at his untimely death in February there was an unparalleled sense of personal loss north of the border, and, south of it, a widespread feeling that a vital figure had disappeared from the continent."[65]

The editors of the *Ottawa Journal* summed up Tweedsmuir's character and approach: "He would have prepared us by deeper concern for things spiritual and intellectual, and by allegiance, above all, to the

National Film Board of Canada. Photothèque/Library and Archives Canada/PA-123494

"Canada was proud to have in her midst a great scholar who touched life at so many places and touched nothing which he did not adorn." Lord Tweedsmuir's body lies in state in the Senate Chamber of Parliament, February 13, 1940.

tradition of human dignity and liberty."[66] One of the editors, Grattan O'Leary, observed in the large crowds their "instinctive recognition that this was a great man."[67]

It was written that Canada had lost "an able administrator and brilliant mind," but Ottawa's citizens had also lost a friend, "likeable and genuine," whom they might meet on the street, the ski trail, at the theatre, or in church. "They got to know him as a man," though he never lost "the abiding dignity of the [g]overnor [g]eneral's [o]ffice." "He had indeed walked with kings but retained the common touch." An officer cadet at the Royal Military College remembers "everyone was very upset as he was considered a kindly caring man, more a man of the people than his immediate predecessors."[68]

Tweedsmuir's body lay in state in the Centre Block of the Parliament Buildings. A state funeral was held on Wednesday, February 14, in the afternoon, at St. Andrew's Presbyterian Church on Wellington Street. Government offices were closed. Military personnel lined Parliament Hill and Wellington Street on that cold and snowy day, as the coffin made its way, at the slow march, to the church, then back again to Union Station, where it was taken to Montreal for cremation and the final journey by ship to the United Kingdom. A memorial service was held in Westminster Abbey, and others in Oxford, Edinburgh, and Glasgow.[69] The ashes of Lord Tweedsmuir, John Buchan, are buried at Elsefield, near Oxford.

Epilogue

John Buchan, Lord Tweedsmuir, is an inspiration — as much today as he was more than seventy years ago, whether for governors general or individual citizens.

I first discovered "JB" while conducting unrelated research at Library and Archives Canada in Ottawa. During the course of that research, I came across documents referring to the royal visit in 1939. I subsequently picked up this thread, as a hobby, and through it discovered the significant role that Governor General Lord Tweedsmuir played in initiating that historic event.

I began reading his correspondence in the archives, and some of his books, both his novels and his history titles. My initial attraction to him grew stronger, for many reasons: his sense of being Canadian himself; his sensitivity to Canada, to its French and British heritage, in the crucial first decade after the passage of the 1931 Statute of Westminster; his closeness to its people; his motivating principles; his integrating approach as governor general, which was both visionary and practical at the same time; his role as public intellectual; and what seemed to me to be his eminent good sense and the basic goodness of his character.

When I recalled that my maternal grandfather had had a book by John Buchan on his shelf (*The King's Grace*, 1935), my interest and instincts were strengthened, because of my respect for my grandfather, a gentle, public-spirited immigrant from Norway who arrived in Canada at the turn of the last century. He had written his name in the book, a book he bought, I believe, because he was loyal to his adopted country and wished to learn more about this famous new governor general and what he wrote about King George V in the king's silver jubilee year.

I did not start with the idea of writing a book; however, after my initial research and after writing an article on the 1939 royal visit, I did wish to share what I had found, and wanted to reveal, or rather reintroduce, to Canadians this remarkable individual and his contributions to Canada and to the strengthening of Western civilization's basic principles. After writing several articles in various journals, newspapers, and magazines over the next few years, I decided it was time to put them together and add to the research.

The framework I have used to examine Tweedsmuir's time as governor general has two broad areas: the governmental and the cultural, each of which, in turn, is made up of the various roles a governor general plays. It was Tweedsmuir's energy and ability to operate effectively in all the various roles that enabled him to accomplish so much and that helped draw unparalleled admiration. That he continues to draw admiration and spark inspiration more than seventy years later from more contemporary successors to that office is testimony to this ability, to his classical humanist character, and to his enduring, even endearing, qualities.

Through these chapters we have gotten to know a man of deep humanity, high principle and intelligence, enormous energy despite constant illness, natural optimism (something he possessed almost to a fault), and love of the outdoors. His presence in Canada created a new, positive atmosphere.

His humanity and compassion were evident in his reaching out to Canadians, on a broad level as well as on an individual level, as we saw with his visits to the drought-stricken Prairies, his personal assistance to an old Scottish immigrant friend no longer able to farm, and his encouragement Canadians to be generous in helping to look after the needs of veterans and of families struck by the effects of the economic depression.

It was evident as well in his public and private support to the Jews, who were suffering violent persecution in Europe. The wreaths that he laid at the cenotaphs in most every city, town, or village he visited were displays of public commemoration but also very solemn and sincere personal acts. Having himself experienced trauma and personal loss due to war, he knew the "poison of militarism," although he also recognized the need to be able to defend one's country.

His contribution to Canada's cultural life is undeniable; particularly notable is the establishment of the Governor General's Literary Awards, and the support and inspiration he gave to writers, individually and collectively. He and his wife, Susan, were patrons of many arts and letters organizations, encouraging excellence of effort and objective in all. Admittedly not modernist in his tastes, he sympathized with those working for "social regeneration" through their art, but advocated drawing inspiration from the deep well of our classical heritage. To the heads of Canada's largest universities, he proposed establishing a universities commission, to examine ways of enhancing the academic and intellectual life of the country, which was a broader objective he strove for.

As governor general he recognized the limitations on public pronouncements imposed by his office — "governor generalities" he called them — but did not allow that to restrain him from addressing broad areas of policy. Indeed, he frequently addressed social or other issues he believed needed airing in his talks, sometimes testing the limits of what was acceptable to the prime minister and even the king himself. His eloquent, informed, and articulate comments on a wide range of issues stimulated debate, and at times controversy.

As a statesman within Canada, he addressed and influenced governmental institutions and institutional structures, whether by assisting the prime minister to organize his office and Cabinet business more effectively, thereby helping to establish a part of Canada's modern machinery of government, or by meeting with members of Parliament and ministers to discuss issues of the day.

Tweedsmuir's personal reputation and qualities gave him an authority in his own right, and this complemented and enhanced the authority inherent in the office. He used all his authority to pursue the many roles he developed as governor general in the new context of that office created by the Statute of Westminster, and in his role as interpreter of Canada, Britain, and the United States to each other.

As an international statesman, Tweedsmuir functioned as a "best bridge," a role that was at once strategic and practical, direct and indirect, official and unofficial. He tapped his broad network of friends and contacts in the upper echelons of American politics, business, media, and education to stay attuned to opinion-makers, making a proposal that foreshadowed future intelligence work in the United States as part of the war effort. He provided encouragement as well as practical advice to those in decision-making roles, on both sides of the Atlantic, which helped enhance Britain's image in the United States, the country he saw as critical to helping shape the post-war world. His personal relationship with Roosevelt and with leaders of the British government allowed him to serve as a valuable unofficial channel between them. Relations between Britain and America were stronger because of the multi-faceted role Tweedsmuir played.

What is striking is how familiar to us in Canada today many of the issues that Tweedsmuir addressed in his actions and public speeches are, and how relevant many of his messages remain.

National unity and the strength of regionalism remain dominant political issues. The call Tweedsmuir made for greater national feeling, above that of the local or regional focus, finds echo today. The separatist movement in Quebec has intensified, and the resource-based richness of the Prairie provinces has strengthened their hand in dealing with the federal government. Given the different jurisdictions embedded in our constitutional makeup, the federal-provincial give and take will remain. It was to this basic issue that Tweedsmuir frequently turned his mind, identifying what unifies the country. He used his office to that end — the governor general as *trait d'union*. For him, at the time, the North sparked one vision as a potential unifying factor for the country. Could it still? Whether or not it does, the principle behind Tweedsmuir's vision, valid today, is to focus on what can unify, and, if not overcome, at least, diminish the divisions and the centrifugal forces in Canadian society.

The extent of Canada's natural resources was only beginning to be explored in the 1930s, especially in the North. The concept of frontier excited Tweedsmuir, whether defined geographically or spiritually. The North still fits the definition of frontier, on both counts, stirring the imagination. He envisaged future development with the application of technology, particularly aircraft, but spoke of the need for conservation of our natural resources, a point on which he respected the role of the conservation-minded Native peoples. About the latter, he expressed concern and cautions to the prime minister about their health, a concern still with us.

Tweedsmuir's active and productive mind continually yielded ideas for encouraging many aspects of Canada's development. In some areas he was prescient indeed, such as in his efforts to create a Hollywood in British Columbia, something he tackled after the war had started and within the last month of his life. In pursuit of excellence and in order to encourage the greatest potential for contributing to society, he promoted a balance between the physical and the spiritual, the practical and the cultural. The material development of a sovereign nation would be incomplete if not complemented by cultural development. The material side must be side by side with the spiritual. Canada, he said, "must make her own music."

He extolled public service as the highest calling, and spoke to the challenge of attracting good and talented people into public life. He was an example himself. The complement to citizens involving themselves in public service, he stressed, was citizens informing themselves about public affairs, and, beyond that, about international affairs. This, he believed, was necessary to ensure the health of the democratic system of government and the preservation of its underlying principles.

In developing engaged, informed citizens, Tweedsmuir stressed the role of education. However, he also noted that, whether for youth or adults, education should focus on developing and training the mind, not just crowding the memory. He encouraged individuals to read widely, but to have a mind "with an edge," to think critically, and to rid the mind of cant. There was purpose in each speech, and always a core of *humanitas*. He reminded us we are not just individuals, but also citizens. If we pay attention only to our own needs and wants and do not take an interest in public affairs, we may find some day that this self-limitation causes our lives to be adversely imposed upon by the public affairs we have ignored.

In certain of his public addresses, Tweedsmuir identified developments that he assessed as dangerous to either society or the development of youth, cautioning, for example, against "the trashy psychology" that recommends never reprimanding or checking children, because such an approach does not prepare them for the realities of life.

He used technology to advance his objectives, but warned that we must remain in control of technology, this "gigantic machine" we have created; we must use it or we will be used by it, with negative consequences for our humanity. He warned of the dangers of over-specialization, of isolation of thought, in academic disciplines or in the professions, without recognizing the "organic interconnection" of the various fields and sub-fields.

While even more disproportionate now than then, the U.K.-U.S. "special relationship" nonetheless remains an important one in world affairs. It was John Buchan's belief that this key alliance would prevail and shape the post-war world. He envisioned federal groupings, based on geography or shared principles such as respect for just law, as a more effective way of preventing war than an ineffectual international organization like the League of Nations had been, despite the idealism at its origin.

John Buchan, Lord Tweedsmuir, was an exceptional and influential leader: he helped strengthen the unity and sovereignty of Canada, while also working to reinforce the country's loyalty to the sovereign — all at an exceptional time in the country's constitutional history; he helped lighten the burden at a difficult time in Canada's social and economic history; and he helped strengthen a critical alliance for freedom at a dangerous time in the world's history. He established a new model for the role of governor general after the Statute of Westminster. John Buchan — model governor general, and model citizen.

Notes

Preface

1. Vincent Massey, *What's Past Is Prologue: The Memoirs of Vincent Massey* (Toronto: Macmillan Company of Canada, 1963), 328.

2. Robert Speaight, *Vanier* (Toronto: Collins, 1970), 488. Some of the traits included their strong Christian beliefs, military experience (though Vanier was a career soldier), loyalty to the Crown and the concept of constitutional monarchy, belief in the importance of history, love of physical activity and the outdoors, and health issues. (See "Chapter 24: Themes of Office," 439, where Vanier is referenced as quoting Tweedsmuir.)

3. Adrienne Clarkson, *Heart Matters* (Toronto: Viking Canada, 2006), 217. See also the *National Post*, May 16, 2000, in which Clarkson expounds on travel, saying that she "won't let up" and hopes to understand the country better and wants Canadians to know their country better. Comments are made on how she challenged established conventions in her speeches, actions, and comments while governor general, while being very cognizant of her constitutional role (see J. William Galbraith, "Viceregal Advocate: Does Adrienne Clarkson Go Too Far?" *Ottawa Citizen*, February 5, 2000; and John Bentley Mays, "Clarkson Follows Buchan to the North," *National Post*, April 3, 2000.

4. Clarkson, *Heart Matters*, 206.

5. Aaron Wherry, "Keep Calm and Carry On," *Maclean's*, October 10, 2011, 19.

6. There has been no separate, detailed exploration of Buchan's time in Canada written from a Canadian perspective, though there are "Canadian"

chapters in two British biographies of Buchan: Janet Adam Smith, *John Buchan* (London: Rupert Hart-Davis, 1965); and Andrew Lownie, *John Buchan: The Presbyterian Cavalier* (London: Constable, 1995). There have been, through the 1960s onward, criticisms of Buchan, based largely on characters in his novels and because he was seen to represent "the Empire" in the post-war period of decolonization. These criticisms have no foundation as will be seen in the succeeding chapters.

7. I am indebted to Dr. Paul Benoit for his four-part concept of the Crown; see his article "The Crown and the Constitution," *Canadian Parliamentary Review* 25, no. 2 (Summer 2002): 2-3.

8. Ibid.

9. Ibid.

Introduction

1. House of Commons, *Debates,* March 27, 1935, 2144.

2. Ibid.

3. Mackenzie King Diary (MKD), March 26, 1935, Library and Archives Canada (LAC).When the *Ottawa Journal* contacted King for comment, he made no reply but "was inwardly delighted."

4. Tweedsmuir "was a surprisingly small man," noted Sydney Checkland in *Voices Across the Water* (Aberdeen: Aberdeen University Press, 1989), 124. General Roger Rowley, an Ottawa resident and friend of Buchan's sons, recalls a similar physical impression but adds there was a "wiry toughness" to him (Roger Rowley, interview by author, Ottawa, February 28, 1998).

5. Checkland, *Voices Across the Water,* 124.

6. See John Buchan, *Memory Hold-the-Door* (*MHTD*) (London: Hodder & Stoughton, 1940), chaps. 1 and 2; Andrew Lownie, *John Buchan: The Presbyterian Cavalier* (London: Constable, 1995), chap. 1; and Janet Adam Smith, *John Buchan* (London: Rupert Hart-Davis, 1965), chap. 1.

7. Smith, *John Buchan,* 27.

8. Ibid., 30-31.

9. See Gilbert Murray, preface to *The Clearing House: A Survey of One Man's Mind*, by John Buchan, edited by Susan Buchan (London: Hodder & Stoughton, 1946), vii.

10. See David Crackanthorpe, "*The Yellow Book* and John Buchan," *The John Buchan Journal* (*JBJ*), no. 41 (Spring 2010): 9-16, for a description of *The Yellow Book*, its content, role at the time, and John Buchan's relationship to it.

11. Smith, *John Buchan,* 75.

12. Ibid., 75-78.

13. Ibid., 83.

14. Quoted in Smith, *John Buchan*, 115.

15. See Thomas Pakenham, *The Boer War* (New York: Random House, 1979), 587; Peter Warwick, ed., *The South African War* (London: Longman, 1980), 415; and Buchan, *MHTD*, 108. From October 1901, when Buchan arrived, to April 1902, the number of deaths in the camps declined steadily from 34 percent for Europeans and 20 percent for Africans to 3 percent and 6 percent respectively. Schools for children were also established in the camps.

16. Smith, *John Buchan*, 118.

17. See Lownie, "The Creche," *Presbyterian Cavalier*, 70-85; and Smith, "Milner's Young Men," *John Buchan*, 106-145.

18. See David Crackanthorpe, "The Great Estate," *JBJ*, no. 38 (Summer 2008): 21-28.

19. John Buchan, *The Thirty-Nine Steps* (Edinburgh and London: William Blackwood and Sons, 1915), 1.

20. See Smith, *John Buchan*, 149; and Buchan, *MHTD*, 126-127.

21. John Buchan, *A Lodge in the Wilderness* (Edinburgh and London: Thomas Nelson and Sons, 1922), 332.

22. See Edwin Lee, "The Vision Splendid," *JBJ*, No. 27 (Autumn 2002): 6-22; and, in the same issue, Michael Redley, "John Buchan and East Africa": 23-33. Buchan's biographers, Smith and Lownie, each also deal with *A Lodge in the Wilderness*.

23. Buchan, *MHTD*, 112.

24. W. Forbes Gray, ed., *Comments and Characters by John Buchan* (Edinburgh and London: Thomas Nelson and Sons, 1940), 95.

25. In 1910 Buchan published the novel *Prester John*; in 1911, *Sir Walter Raleigh*; 1912, *The Moon Endureth*, a collection of his short stories; and in 1913, *The Marquis of Montrose*.

26. See, for example, Smith, *John Buchan*, 180-184; Lord Stewartby, "John Buchan and Parliament," *JBJ*, no. 31 (Autumn 2004): 9-18; and Michael Redley, "Making Democracy Safe for the World: A Note on John Buchan's Political Career," *JBJ*, no. 17 (Autumn 1997): 31-37, for Buchan's political views and the difficulties he had with partisan politics.

27. Smith, *John Buchan*, 191.

28. John Buchan, *The Powerhouse* (1916, reprint, London: Pan Books, 1961), 39.

29. John Charteris, *At GHQ* (London: Cassell and Company, 1931), 196.

30. See John Buchan, *Canadian Occasions* (*CO*), (Toronto: Musson Book Company, 1941), 183; and Buchan, *MHTD*, 172, 180-181, and 183, for Buchan's abhorrence of war.

31. In addition to references to F.S. Oliver in the Buchan biographies by Smith and Lownie, see Antony Hornyold, "John Buchan and the FSOs," *JBJ*, no. 40 (Autumn 2009): 3-13; and Michael Pollard, "'The Same Breed' or 'An Odd Brotherhood'?" *JBJ*, no. 40 (Autumn 2009):14-24.

32. Smith, *John Buchan*, 227.

33. See J. William Galbraith, "A Promised Land: The Buchans in Canada — 1924," *JBJ*, no. 40 (Autumn 2009): 34.

34. See Michael Redley, "John Buchan at Milton Academy," *JBJ*, no. 22 (Spring 2000): 22-32.

35. Buchan, *MHTD*, 261.

36. Redley, "John Buchan at Milton Academy": 25.

37. Buchan, *MHTD*, 222.

38. See Smith, *John Buchan*, chap. 11 (299-334); Lownie, *Presbyterian Cavalier*, chap. 12 (206-230); Andrew Lownie, "John Buchan: Conservative Politician," *JBJ*, no. 35 (Autumn 2006): 31-34; and Lord Stewartby, "John Buchan and Parliament": 9-18. See also Buchan, *MHTD*, 219-243.

39. Buchan, *MHTD*, 223.

40. Ibid., 220.

41. Buchan, *CO*, 94.

42. Gray, ed., *Comments and Characters*, 95.

43. Smith, *John Buchan*, 317-319.

44. Ibid., 303.

45. Stewartby, "John Buchan and Parliament": 17.

46. Buchan, *MHTD*, 231.

47. See Smith, *John Buchan*, chap. 11; and Lownie, *Presbyterian Cavalier*, chap. 12.

48. Smith, *John Buchan*, 307, 315; and Lownie, "John Buchan: Conservative Politician": 33.

49. See Lownie, "John Buchan: Conservative Politician": 33; and Smith, *John Buchan*, 322-323.

50. Smith, *John Buchan*, 322; and Lownie, "John Buchan: Conservative Politician": 33.

51. Lownie, "John Buchan: Conservative Politician": 31.

52. Smith, *John Buchan*, 338-339.

53. Margaret MacMillan, *Paris 1919* (New York: Random House, 2003), 44.

54. Ibid., 45. MacMillan writes: "The British were taken aback by the new assertiveness in their empire."

55. See, for example, Robert M. Dawson, ed., *The Development of Dominion Status, 1900–1936* (Oxford: Frank Cass & Co., 1965), 54-65; and Robert Bothwell, Ian Drummond, and John English, *Canada, 1900–1945*

(Toronto: University of Toronto Press, 1987), 235-38. For a description of the military actions, see MacMillan, *Paris 1919*, 451-452.

56. Dawson, ed., *Dominion Status*, 103-132.
57. Ibid., 331. The Balfour report is reproduced in Section V of Dawson's book.
58. Buchan, *MHTD*, 163.
59. Quoted in Smith, *John Buchan*, 301.
60. See Bothwell, Drummond, and English, *Canada, 1900–1945*, 206-207. Mackenzie King had asked Governor General Byng for a dissolution of Parliament, to avoid a defeat in the House of Commons, but was refused. King resigned and Byng then offered Conservative leader Arthur Meighen the opportunity to form a government. Meighen did but it lasted less than a week. Meighen could not muster a majority in Parliament, and asked Byng for the dissolution that had been refused to King. It was an issue that set King firmly in his suspicions of British governors.
61. Dawson, ed., *Dominion Status*, 333.
62. Ibid., 402-403.
63. For example, see the letters and telegrams from Chambly Canton, QC; Toronto; Moose Jaw and Regina, SK; and Vancouver, B.C.: all RBP, LAC.
64. "Ottawa Has Authority to Nominate Native Son As Rideau Hall Tenant," *Toronto Star*, December 3, 1930.
65. Letters from two individuals, RBP, LAC.
66. Bennett to George Smith, president of the Native Sons of Canada, March 29, 1935, RBP, LAC.
67. *New York Times*, February 11, 1931.
68. The Statute of Westminster, 1931, along with related Acts and comments, is included in the appendices of K.C. Wheare, *The Statute of Westminster and Dominion Status*, 4th ed. (London: Oxford University Press, 1949).
69. The six Dominions were: the Dominion of Canada; the Commonwealth of Australia; the Dominion of New Zealand; the Union of South Africa; the Irish Free State; and Newfoundland.
70. Dawson, ed., *Dominion Status*, 412.
71. Ibid.
72. Blair Neatby, *The Politics of Chaos: Canada in the Thirties* (Toronto: Macmillan, 1972), 164.
73. House of Commons, *Debates*, April 1, 1935. The CCF was the predecessor to the New Democratic Party (NDP).
74. *The Economist* (London), April 6, 1935.
75. Neatby, *Politics of Chaos*, 165.
76. The term "Bennett buggies" was the nickname given to automobiles that had been hitched to horses because the people couldn't afford to repair

them or put gas in them. The author remembers hearing from his grand-parents about men who would come to the door of their house asking for work in exchange for food, lodging, or a little money.

77. J.H. Thompson and A. Seager, *Canada, 1922–1939: Decades of Discord* (Toronto: McClelland & Stewart, 1985), 97.

78. *The Canadian Almanac and Legal and Court Directory, 1935* (Toronto: Copp Clark, 1935), 341.

79. See Bothwell, Drummond, and English, *Canada, 1900–1945*, 246-249, for figures and a detailed description of the period.

80. See Thompson and Seager, *Canada, 1922–1939*; the reference is from the caption on the photograph between pages 146 and 147.

81. James Struthers, "The Great Depression," CanadianEncyclopedia.com, *www.thecanadianencyclopedia.com/articles/great-depression* (accessed September 23, 2011).

82. Paul Martin, "Address," in *Minutes from the Eighteenth National Conference of Canadian Universities, McGill University, Montreal, May 29, 1939*. Martin, an MP, noted "that the stage through which we are passing is one which indicates that more and more the state will be called upon to intervene and engage in new activities" (Queen's University Library LA417.5 N2 1939).

83. House of Commons, *Debates*, April 3, 1930. See also the brief description in Bothwell, Drummond, and English, *Canada, 1900–1945*, 260.

84. Bothwell, Drummond, and English, *Canada, 1900–1945*, 260. References to the emerging importance of radio are made in the entry for R.B. Bennett in the Dictionary of Canadian Biography Online (P.B. Waite, "R.B. Bennett," Biographi.ca, *http://biographi.ca/009004-119.01-e.php?id_nbr=7997* (accessed October 9, 2011)).

85. Waite, "R.B. Bennett."

86. See Dawson, ed., *Dominion Status*, 126-127; and Waite, "R.B. Bennett."

87. Donald V. Smiley, ed., *The Rowell-Sirois Report*, The Carleton Library No. 5, (Toronto: Macmillan Canada, Toronto, 1978), 166.

88. Ibid.

89. J.T. Morley, "Co-operative Commonwealth Federation," CanadianEncyclopedia.com, *www.thecanadianencyclopedia.com/index.cfm?PgNm=TCE&Params=A1ARTA0001902* (accessed October 9, 2011).

90. The Manitoba Historical Society, "Memorable Manitobans: James Shaver Woodsworth (1874–1942)," MHS.Mb.ca, *www.mhs.mb.ca/docs/people/woodsworth_js.shtml*; and Kenneth McNaught, "James Shaver Woodsworth," CanadianEncyclopedia.com, *www.thecanadianencyclopedia.com/index.cfm?PgNm=TCE&Params=A1ARTA0008704* (accessed October 9, 2011).

91. House of Commons, *Debates,* May 22, 1919, 2698.

92. "Titles in Canada in 1917." This pamphlet was a compilation of "Canadian press comment on the acceptance or refusal of hereditary and other non-Canadian honours," originally deposited in the Library of Parliament (now part of LAC).

93. See Christopher McCreery, *The Canadian Honours System,* (Toronto: Dundurn Press, 2005), 36.

94. This is a thesis found in Jane Errington, *The Lion, the Eagle, and Upper Canada* (Montreal and Kingston, ON: McGill-Queen's University Press, 1994). See, for example, page 7.

95. Mackenzie King was, however, conflicted when, after the war, he wrestled with the question of whether or not to accept the Order of Merit, a direct award from King George VI. Ultimately, he accepted.

96. For a detailed history of Canada's honours system, see McCreery, *Canadian Honours System.*

97. See Bothwell, Drummond, and English, *Canada, 1900–1945,* chap. 16.

98. Ibid., 257.

99. Michael Dupuis, "The Response of the *Toronto Daily Star* to the 'On-to-Ottawa' Trek and Dominion Day Riot in Regina," *Canadian Journal of Media Studies* 6, no. 1 (March 2010), *http://cjms.fims.uwo.ca/issues/06-01/dupuis.pdf* (accessed August 7, 2011). See also Bothwell, Drummond, and English, *Canada, 1900–1945,* 256.

100. The PFRA received royal assent in April 1935 in response to the widespread drought, farm abandonment, and land degradation of the 1930s. Source: Agriculture and Agri-Food Canada, "Prairie Farm Rehabilitation Administration (PFRA)," *www4.agr.gc.ca/AAFC-AAC/display-afficher.do?id=1187374232064&lang=e* (accessed July 4, 2008).

101. Smiley, *Rowell-Sirois Report,* 171.

102. *Canadian Almanac, 1935, 344.*

103. Ibid. Calculations were derived from figures cited in the *Almanac.* Figures are based on the twelve-month period ending March 31, 1934, and are for the value of merchandise imports for consumption. Compiled by the External Trade Branch of the Dominion Bureau of Statistics.

104. Ibid. The values are of exports of Canadian produce.

105. Source: Foreign Affairs and International Trade Canada, *www.international.gc.ca/history-histoire/world-monde/1921-1939.aspx?lang=eng* (accessed September 25, 2011).

Chapter 1

1. MKD, March 26, 1935, LAC. The exact date was May 28, 1919. Markham had met King in 1905 in Ottawa, introduced by Sir Wilfrid Laurier, who had even suggested King should marry Miss Markham! Markham provided King with financial and moral support after his and the Liberals' election defeat in 1911.

2. MKD, May 28, 1919, LAC. The "English manner" that King observed was likely a generic reference to Buchan's British style. It might have perhaps been due to his ignorance of Buchan's Scottish background, or it could also have been an indication of Buchan's adoption of English ways, including an Oxford accent.

3. John Buchan, "The Causal and the Casual in History," *Men and Deeds* (London: Peter Davies, 1935), 3-20.

4. Smith, *John Buchan*, 246.

5. MKD, September 14, 1924, LAC; Deuteronomy 34: 1-4.

6. MKD, September 15, 1924, LAC.

7. Ibid.

8. Smith, *John Buchan*, 249-250; Lownie, *Presbyterian Cavalier*, 244-245.

9. Smith, *John Buchan*, 249.

10. Bessborough to Bennett, September 18, 1934, RBP, LAC.

11. Wigram to Bennett, October 29, 1934, RBP, LAC.

12. Ibid.

13. The desired appointment was the then chief justice of the Australian High Court, Sir Isaac Isaacs, who indeed became governor general.

14. Cited in J.R. Mallory, "The Appointment of the Governor General," *Canadian Journal of Economics and Political Science* 26, no. 1 (February 1960): 98.

15. Cited from numerous newspaper clippings (Montreal, Ottawa, and Toronto), in RBP, LAC.

16. MKD, December 18, 1934, LAC.

17. Ibid.

18. Mallory, "Appointment of the Governor General," 103.

19. George VI's private secretary, Sir Alexander Hardinge, January 8, 1940, Buchan Papers (BP), LAC. Hardinge, in discussing the method of selecting Tweedsmuir's successor in 1940, noted that the previous situation was similar, in that a general election was in the offing.

20. The information in this and succeeding paragraphs is taken largely from Mackenzie King's diary entry for February 21, 1935 (MKD, LAC).

21. It was a rather distant connection in that her father was a grandson of a niece of the first duke.

22. MKD, February 21, 1935, LAC; and House of Commons, *Debates*, February 21, 1935, 1062.
23. MKD, March 7, 1935, LAC.
24. Bessborough to Bennett, February 28, 1935, RBP, LAC.
25. MKD, March 1, 1935, LAC.
26. George V's position is noted in a letter from Buchan to Stair Gillon, May 24, 1935, BP, LAC.
27. MKD, March 14, 1935, LAC.
28. Bennett to Bessborough, March 16, 1935, RBP, LAC.
29. Bessborough to Bennett, March 18, 1935, RBP, LAC.
30. Violet Markham to Buchan, March 24, 1935, BP, LAC; and Violet Markham to Susan Buchan, March 28, 1935, BP, LAC.
31. Lownie, *Presbyterian Cavalier*, 243.
32. Mallory, "Appointment of the Governor General," 105.
33. Clive Wigram to Bessborough, telegram, March 22, 1935, External Affairs, LAC.
34. Cable and original petition, March 23, 1935, RBP, LAC; cable stamped March 24, 1935, by the Code Section, Department of External Affairs (External Affairs, LAC).
35. King George V to Bennett, cyphered telegram, March 26, 1935, RBP, LAC.
36. Clive Wigram to Bennett, cyphered messages, March 26, 1935, RBP, LAC.
37. Clive Wigram to Bennett, April 3, 1935, RBP, LAC.
38. Bennett to Clive Wigram, handwritten message, for "Immediate, Secret, Cypher," March 26, 1935, RBP, LAC.
39. MKD, March 26, 1935, LAC.
40. Ibid.
41. Ibid.
42. Ibid.
43. Ibid.

Chapter 2

1. *Globe* (Toronto), March 27, 1935.
2. *Winnipeg Free Press*, March 28, 1935.
3. Senate, *Debates*, March 27, 1935.
4. Ibid.
5. Meighen to George Perley and Perley to Meighen, March 28 and 29, 1935, respectively, both RBP, LAC. Meighen wrote tersely of the "humiliating position" he had found himself in. The announcement should have been made simultaneously in the House and the Senate: "I am sure it was

just an oversight," he offered stiffly in closing. Sir George apologized but only after throwing some of the blame back to Meighen: "I am sorry that you were not in Council when I read the proposed announcement to our Colleagues."

6. *Globe* (Toronto), March 28, 1935.

7. Bennett to Buchan, cable, March 28, 1935, RBP, LAC.

8. Buchan to Bennett, cable, April 9, 1935, RBP, LAC.

9. *Telegraph-Journal* (Saint John, NB), April 3, 1935.

10. See, for example, Lownie, *Presbyterian Cavalier*, 244.

11. *Globe* (Toronto), March 28, 1935.

12. G.E. (Ted) Beament, telephone conversation with the author, June 7, 1995.

13. Smith, *Buchan*, 386.

14. Earl Johnson, telephone conversation with the author, June 15, 1995.

15. Strome Galloway, undated typed note and conversations with the author, February 5 and March 3, 1998. Similar comments were recalled by Lt. Col. Clifford Smith, conversation with the author, Ottawa, May 28, 1994; and Émile Colas, conversation with the author, Montreal, June 15, 1996.

16. See Carl Berger, ed., introduction to *Imperial Relations in the Age of Laurier* (Toronto: University of Toronto Press, 1969), for a summary of the background to imperialist sentiment in Canada.

17. MKD, February 13, 1935, LAC. King considered these two men "loose cannons."

18. Senate, *Debates,* March 27, 1935, 208-211. The following section is based on these debates, which were subsequently reported in newspapers across the country, along with editorial comment.

19. Sir Isaac Isaacs was a chief justice of the Australian High Court.

20. Neither Dandurand nor Lemieux, however, lived to see the day; Lemieux died in 1937 and Dandurand in 1942.

21. MKD, November 5, 1935, LAC.

22. Eugene Forsey, *A Life on the Fringe* (Toronto: Oxford University Press, 1990), 100.

23. Senate, *Debates*, March 27, 1935, 211.

24. *Le Soleil* (Quebec City), March 28, 1935.

25. *Le Devoir* (Montreal), April 1, 1935. *Le Devoir* asserted, naively or otherwise, that if a Canadian were governor general, the country might avoid involvement.

26. Henri Bourassa, *Great Britain and Canada: Topics of the Day* (Montreal: C.O. Beauchemin & Fils, 1902), 134.

27. House of Commons, *Debates*, April 1, 1935, 2283-2284.

28. House of Commons, *Debates*, May 20, 1935, 2866.

29. C.R. Hodgins to Bennett, April 6, 1935, RBP, LAC. See also, "letter," *Globe* (Toronto), April 13, 1935.

30. John Taylor, "letter," *Daily Colonist* (Victoria, B.C.), April 4, 1935, 4. A Mr. A.D. Martin referred to Henri Bourassa's speech in the House of Commons to bolster his own views that it was time for Canada to define the status of her citizens and to adopt her own flag, as the Australians and South Africans had already done (A.D. Martin, "letter," *Daily Colonist* (Victoria, B.C.), April 6, 1935, 4).

31. The 1936–1937 edition of *Canadian Who's Who* contains, for example, the names of W.T. Galbraith (no relation to the author), a veterinary surgeon in London, Ontario; and Edward T. Kenney, B.C. merchant and member of the provincial legislature.

32. George Smith, national president of the Native Sons of Canada, to George Perley, acting prime minister, telegram, March 27, 1935, External Affairs, LAC.

33. Ibid.

34. Perley to George Smith, carbon copy of letter, March 29, 1935, External Affairs, LAC.

35. "Letter," *Daily Colonist* (Victoria, B.C.), April 2, 1935.

36. "Editorial," *Globe* (Toronto), April 5, 1935. J.H.C. Sangster wrote that the important question was not where the man was born but rather how much good he could do for Canada (*Daily Colonist* (Victoria, B.C.), April 7, 1935).

37. *Saturday Night*, November 9, 1935.

38. *La Presse* (Montreal), May 21, 1935.

39. Buchan, *MHTD*, 243.

40. Fulgence Charpentier (former diplomat and journalist), interview with the author, Ottawa, June 4, 1994.

41. King to Buchan, July 19, 1935, BP, LAC.

42. *Winnipeg Free Press*, March 28, 1935.

43. Violet Markham to Buchan, April 16, 1935, BP, LAC.

44. Ezra Pound to Buchan, August 13, 1935, BP, LAC.

45. *Vancouver Sun*, March 27, 1935.

46. MKD, May 17, 1935, LAC. See also, King to Buchan, July 19, 1935, BP, LAC.

47. "Editorial," *Globe* (Toronto), May 17, 1935.

48. Markham to Buchan, April 16, 1935, BP, LAC.

49. Several people old enough to remember Tweedsmuir's time in Canada, and queried by the author in the 1990s, were not aware that he was also John Buchan, or had only a vague notion that Tweedsmuir was a writer.

50. "Editorial," *Globe* (Toronto), May 17, 1935.

51. Susan Tweedsmuir, comp., *Wife and Friends* (London: Hodder & Stoughton, 1947), 268. George V awarded Buchan the Knight Grand Cross of the Order of St. Michael and St. George (GCMG), an order of chivalry generally awarded to senior public servants.

52. MKD, April 6, 1935, LAC.

53. MKD, May 7, 1935, LAC.

54. Ibid.

55. King to Buchan, July 19, 1935, BP, LAC.

Chapter 3

1. *Telegraph-Journal* (Saint John, NB), April 4, 1935; and Buchan to Susan Buchan, July 8 and 11, 1935, BP, LAC.

2. Tweedsmuir to Vanier, July 4, 1935, External Affairs, LAC.

3. Tweedsmuir's reply to Vanier is quoted in a letter from the Canadian High Commission to the Department of External Affairs, July 5, 1935, External Affairs, LAC.

4. Bessborough to Buchan, April 17, 1935, RBP, LAC.

5. Bennett to Ramsay MacDonald, February 7, 1931, RBP, LAC.

6. *The Economist* (London), November 2, 1935. *The Economist*, watching affairs in Canada with interest, commented that "the new Parliament will be unhealthy, as the Government majority will be unwieldy and the Opposition, composed of groups with hopelessly divergent views, too weak to be effective."

7. MKD, October 15, 1935, LAC.

8. Ibid.

9. Bennett to Howard Ferguson, the Canadian high commissioner in London, telegram, October 15, 1935, External Affairs, LAC.

10. Buchan to Bennett, telegram, October 16, 1935, External Affairs, LAC.

11. Bennett to King, October 16, 1935, RBP, LAC; and Bennett to Buchan, telegram, October 16, 1935, External Affairs, LAC.

12. Lownie, *Presbyterian Cavalier*; and J.A. Smith, *John Buchan*. The Buchans' other children were older and settling into their own lives: Alice, twenty-seven, was married to Brian Fairfax-Lucy in 1933; and Johnnie, twenty-four, was in the Colonial Service in Uganda. William, nineteen, was attending Eton, staying with family friends Alan and Elizabeth Cameron, Elizabeth (Bowen) being a novelist (Victoria Glendinning, *Elizabeth Bowen: Portrait of a Writer* (London: Wiedenfeld and Nicolson, 1977)). Other baggage, servants, chauffeur, and their cars preceded them (William Buchan, *John Buchan: A Memoir* (Toronto: Griffin House, 1982), 208-209;

and Lownie, *Presbyterian Cavalier*, 250-151).

13. A photo showing this appeared in the *Daily Times-Journal* (Fort William, ON), November 8, 1935.
14. King to Tweedsmuir, telegram, November 1, 1935, BP, LAC.
15. Tweedsmuir to Stanley Baldwin, November 16, 1935, BP, LAC.
16. MKD, November 2,1935, LAC.
17. Ibid.
18. Ibid.
19. Roger Rowley, interview with the author, Ottawa, February 28, 1998. This is also how a young Scout in Montreal described Tweedsmuir when he attended a Scout Jamboree ("frail, not robust," "wiry"): Charles Scot-Brown, interview with the author, Toronto, June 15, 1998.
20. Descriptions in this and following paragraphs are taken from the November 4, 1935, editions of the following newspapers: *Le Soleil* (Quebec City); the *Montreal Gazette*; and the *Ottawa Citizen*.
21. Claude Bissell, *The Young Vincent Massey* (Toronto: University of Toronto Press, 1981), 237; and Vincent Massey's memoir, *What's Past Is Prologue*, 540.
22. See MKD, November 2, 1935, LAC.
23. See Massey, *What's Past Is Prologue*, 222; and MKD, February 14 and October 6, 1935, LAC. In fact, King could hardly stand Massey, going to great lengths to minimize the time he had to spend with him, despite Massey being president of the National Liberal Federation and a lead in the election campaign. Almost two weeks before the October 14 election, Massey had interrupted the Liberal leader in his railway car. This was "the last straw" for King, who had previously even changed his phone and locked his doors to have privacy from Massey. Both men recorded the incident in similar terms, so the accuracy and severity of the friction that existed is not in doubt.
24. King George V, commission document for installation of Tweedsmuir as governor general of Canada, External Affairs, LAC.
25. Mackenzie King's speech was reprinted in various newspapers; e.g., the *Globe* (Toronto), November 4, 1935.
26. Tweedsmuir, Speeches, BP, LAC. His remarks were also reported in newspapers of the day; e.g., the *Ottawa Citizen*, November 4, 1935.
27. MKD, November 2,1935, LAC.
28. Ibid.
29. Ibid.
30. Many newspapers commented on this, as did Mackenzie King in his diary of that day.
31. MKD, November 2, 1935, LAC.

32. *Telegraph-Journal* (Saint John, NB), November 2, 1935.

33. William Buchan, *John Buchan*, 207.

34. *Calgary Herald*, November 4, 1935.

35. *Leader-Post* (Regina, SK), November 5, 1935.

36. *Daily Colonist* (Victoria, B.C.), November 3, 1935.

37. *Saturday Night*, November 9, 1935.

38. Ibid.

39. *Telegraph-Journal* (Saint John, NB), November 2, 1935.

40. John O. Herrem is the author's maternal grandfather.

41. Roger Rowley, interview with the author, Ottawa, February 28, 1998.

42. H.L. Stewart, "Baron Tweedsmuir," *Halifax Herald*, November 2, 1935.

43. These descriptions are from newspapers, magazines, and newsreel coverage.

44. MKD, November 4, 1935, LAC.

45. Much of this section is described from newsreel footage of the events, viewed at the National Film Board Archives, Montreal, May 10, 2002.

46. MKD, November 4, 1935, LAC.

47. H. Willis-O'Connor, *Inside Government House* (Toronto: Ryerson Press, 1954), 78; and Raymond Willis-O'Connor (son of H. Willis-O'Connor), interview with the author, June 4, 1996.

48. *Ottawa Citizen*, November 4, 1935.

49. Tweedsmuir to Helen Buchan (his mother), November 5, 1935, BP, LAC.

50. MKD, November 4, 1935, LAC.

51. Tweedsmuir to Helen Buchan, November 5, 1935, BP, LAC.

52. Ibid; and Tweedsmuir to Caroline Grosvenor (his mother-in-law), November 8, 1935, BP, LAC.

Chapter 4

1. MKD, November 4, 1935, LAC.

2. Quoted in Smith, *John Buchan*, 377.

3. King to Buchan, July 19, 1935, BP, LAC.

4. Ibid.

5. MKD, November 5, 1935, LAC. King strongly suspected that Vincent Massey had spoken about the subject with Tweedsmuir when they met in Quebec City a couple of days earlier; Massey was on his way to London to replace Howard Ferguson.

6. King to Buchan, July 19, 1935, BP, LAC.

7. MKD, November 5, 1935, LAC. In confiding this incident to his diary, King privately regretted having used such harsh words.

8. Ibid.

9. Ibid.

10. MKD, November 11, 1935, LAC.

11. MKD, December 6, 1935, LAC.

12. MKD, December 24, 1935, LAC.

13. MKD, December 31, 1935, LAC.

14. Ibid. There would be at least one meeting in February, where, King noted, "It was really the first time that he has come around to speaking of these matters in a perfectly natural and human way" (MKD, February 20, 1936, LAC).

15. MKD, March 25, 1936, LAC.

16. King to Tweedsmuir, handwritten letter, March 26, 1936, BP, LAC. This is a very introspective, emotional letter, in which King was trying to reach out to Tweedsmuir, to have their relationship the way he had imagined it. "There must not be room for possibility of misunderstanding on any score," King concluded.

17. Tweedsmuir to King, March 27, 1936, BP, LAC.

18. King to Tweedsmuir, handwritten letter, March 27, 1936, BP, LAC. King hoped someday there would be "a room which will be worthy of according a place to so prized a treasure." King reached out for that dreamy relationship with Buchan that he ached for.

19. See, for example, MKD, March 25, 1936, and October 9 and 20, 1937, LAC.

20. Tweedsmuir to King, December 13, 1935, BP, LAC.

21. MKD, December 26, 1935, LAC. King's diary entry makes no reference to Tweedsmuir's mid-December letter, and is written in such a way that it seems he was hearing Tweedsmuir's offer of assistance for the first time.

22. Ibid.

23. Ibid.

24. MKD, January 8, 1936, LAC.

25. MKD, December 26, 1935, LAC.

26. Ibid.

27. MKD, December 27, 1935, LAC.

28. MKD, December 29 and 30, 1935, LAC.

29. Tweedsmuir to King, December 31, 1935, BP, LAC.

30. Document attached to Tweedsmuir's December 31, 1935, letter to King, BP, LAC.

31. MKD, May 21, 1927, LAC.

32. Referred to in Burgon Bickersteth's letter to Tweedsmuir, January 4, 1936, BP, LAC.

33. MKD, December 31, 1935, LAC. King thought Skelton's "extreme radical sympathies spoil[ed] his judgement" (See MKD, December 26, 1936, LAC).

34. There is, however, no mention of this in King's diary.
35. Burgon Bickersteth to Tweedsmuir, January 4, 1936; and Burgon Bickersteth, memo to King regarding organization of PMO, 1927, BP, LAC.
36. Burgon Bickersteth gave the example of Norman Rogers, who had acted as "a sort of super-secretary" to King for a couple of years beginning in 1927, but left, less for health reasons, Bickersteth believed, than because King hadn't known how to use him effectively. Rogers was elected to Parliament in 1935 and became a trusted minister in King's government, serving first as minister of labour, 1935 to 1939, then as minister of defence, from 1939 until his death in a plane crash in 1940.
37. Tweedsmuir, three-page undated document with brief outline of program for the opening of Parliament on February 6, 1936, BP, LAC.
38. MKD, January 6, 1936, LAC.
39. For example, Tweedsmuir could not believe no minutes were kept of Cabinet meetings and that ministers were not provided with relevant documents beforehand.
40. MKD, January 6, 1936, LAC.
41. The two men got on well, as is indicated by the fact that Tweedsmuir referred Bickersteth to a friend in New York City who could provide accommodation there (Bickersteth to Tweedsmuir, January 4, 1936, BP, LAC).
42. See J.L. Granatstein, *The Ottawa Men: The Civil Service Mandarins 1935–1957* (Toronto: Oxford University Press, 1982), 94, 189, and 213. Norman Robertson, who had joined the Department of External Affairs in 1929, was assigned to the Prime Minister's Office in 1937, but only briefly, because his skills on the trade side were needed. He was replaced by Jack Pickersgill, who had recently joined External Affairs.
43. Hardinge to Tweedsmuir, February 1, 1938, BP, LAC.
44. King to Tweedsmuir, August 25, 1938, BP, LAC.
45. Arnold D.P. Heeney, *The Things That Are Caesar's* (Toronto: University of Toronto Press, 1972), 56.
46. See MKD, July 16, 1935, LAC. The quote is from the diary entry for July 22, 1936. See also, for example, the diary entry for July 28, 1938.
47. King to Arnold Heeney, July 13, 1938, cited in Heeney, *Things That Are Caesar's*, 73; the contents of the letter described in some detail on page 42.
48. King to Tweedsmuir, September 6, 1938. The quote is in MKD, September 4, 1938, LAC.
49. King to Tweedsmuir, September 20, 1938, BP, LAC.
50. "[M]any of my early duties as secretary to the [C]abinet took the form of personal service to the [p]rime [m]inister," wrote Heeney, *Things That Are Caesar's*, 56-57, 73-74. Bickersteth had cautioned against this. Heeney

refused, to his credit, to carry out work related to King's role as leader of the Liberal Party, which King resented.

51. Heeney, *Things That Are Caesar's*, 45.

52. See J. William Galbraith, "John Buchan in Canada: Writing a New Chapter in Canada's Constitutional History," in *John Buchan and the Idea of Modernity*, edited by Kate Macdonald and Nathan Waddell, Literary Texts and the Popular Marketplace: 4 (London: Pickering & Chatto, 2013).

53. Tweedsmuir to Violet Markham, March 9, 1936, BP, LAC.

54. King to Tweedsmuir, January 21, 1936, BP, LAC.

55. Tweedsmuir to Violet Markham, March 9, 1936, BP, LAC.

56. House of Commons, *Debates*, February 6, 1936. Issues raised in the Speech from the Throne included, "Canada's most urgent national problem," unemployment; a plan for closing the camps established for homeless single men, believed to have been a cause of the 1935 "Regina riot"; a Canada-United States trade agreement; amending the British North America Act regarding Dominion-provincial financial arrangements; greater government authority over the Canadian National Railways and the Bank of Canada; an inquiry into radio broadcasting; and the "seriousness of the international situation."

57. Tweedsmuir to Baldwin, March 24, 1936, BP, LAC.

58. Tweedsmuir to Violet Markham, March 9, 1936, BP, LAC.

59. Granatstein, *Ottawa Men*, 333.

60. Tweedsmuir to Susan Tweedsmuir, September 17, 1936, BP, LAC.

61. Tweedsmuir to Baldwin, March 24, 1936, BP, LAC.

62. Ibid.

63. Queen's Encyclopedia, "Brockington, Leonard (1888–1966)," *Queensu.ca*, *www.queensu.ca/encyclopedia/b/brockingtonleonard.html* (accessed April 15, 2013). Brockington was born in Wales in 1888, and immigrated to Edmonton in 1912. He practised law but had a wide interest in the arts. He was a member of the first Canada Council and was rector of Queen's University.

64. Leonard Brockington, "John Buchan in Canada," in *Wife and Friends*, 273.

65. Ibid.

66. Tweedsmuir to King, June 20, 1936, BP, LAC. Tweedsmuir had a conflict hosting a delegation of about sixty Presbyterian ministers from "the old country," with which King would have sympathized.

67. Tweedsmuir to King, June 26, 1936, BP, LAC. See also House of Commons, *Debates*, June 23, 1936, 4156-4157.

68. Tweedsmuir to King, June 26, 1936, BP, LAC.

69. Tweedsmuir to Susan Tweedsmuir, October 16, 1936, BP, LAC.

70. Tweedsmuir to Susan Tweedsmuir, October 26, 1936, BP, LAC.

71. Hardinge to Tweedsmuir, October 15, 1936, BP, LAC.

72. Tweedsmuir to Hardinge, October 27, 1936, BP, LAC.

73. Baldwin to Tweedsmuir, October 26, 1936, BP, LAC; and BBC News: World Edition, "BBC Timeline," BBC.co.uk, *http://news.bbc.co.uk/2/hi/uk_news/2701463.stm* (accessed April 26, 2009). For additional details, see Graham Stewart, *Burying Caesar: Churchill, Chamberlain and the Battle for the Tory Party* (London: Phoenix, 2000), 264-269.

74. MKD, October 21, 1936, LAC. King's partisan bias also reveals itself in his repetition of this opinion: "The Tory Government in Britain want[s] to do something but [is] using Canada to pull its chestnuts out of the fire" (MKD, December 4, 1936, LAC).

75. Baldwin to Tweedsmuir, October 26, 1936, BP, LAC.

76. MKD, November 8, 1936, LAC. Subsequent quotes in the next paragraphs are also from diary entries for this date.

77. Ibid.

78. Tweedsmuir to Baldwin, November 9, 1936, BP, LAC.

79. MKD, December 4, 1936, LAC.

80. The "request and consent" refers to the Statute of Westminster, 1931, 22 & 23 Geo. V, c. 4.

81. See, for just one example, the *Toronto Star*, December 3 and 4, 1936.

82. MKD, December 4, 1936, LAC. "[W]ith the best of intentions, Tweedsmuir would have been seeking to further the wishes of the British [g]overnment in the matter of having Canada assert herself much more forcibly than I have decided it wise she should."

83. MKD, December 6, 1936, LAC.

84. Ibid.

85. Ibid.

86. Ibid.

87. Victoria Wilcox, "Prime minister and governor-general: Mackenzie King and Lord Tweedsmuir, 1935–1940" (master's thesis, Queen's University, 1978), 185, microfiche, LAC.

88. MKD, December 6, 1936, LAC. King notes that at the reference to Byng, Tweedsmuir "closed his eyes." King confidently attributed this to Tweedsmuir "being anxious to be loyal to the memory of his friend."

89. Ibid.

90. Ibid.

91. Tweedsmuir to Caroline Grosvenor, December 10, 1936, BP, LAC. In this letter Tweedsmuir wrote that he had never been "off the telephone or cable with Mr. Baldwin" in the last few days. The new technology was, in

the urgent circumstances, replacing letters, which had yet to be regularly transported by air.

92. Ibid.

93. Tweedsmuir to Stair Gillon, December 7, 1936; and Lord Crawford to Tweedsmuir, January 20, 1936, both BP, LAC.

94. Tweedsmuir to Caroline Grosvenor, December 10, 1936, BP, LAC.

95. Crawford to Tweedsmuir, January 20, 1937, BP, LAC

96. "Editorial," *Ottawa Citizen*, January 22, 1936.

97. Peacock to Tweedsmuir, December 30, 1936, BP, LAC. Edward Peacock, originally from Canada, then financial advisor to Edward VIII, agreed that the crisis resulted in the "Imperial Cabinet sitting in constant session." He and Hardinge believed that this was a positive thing (Hardinge to Tweedsmuir, December 22, 1936, BP, LAC).

98. MKD, December 9 and 11, 1936, LAC.

Chapter 5

1. Tweedsmuir to Baldwin, March 24, 1936, BP, LAC.

2. Ibid.

3. Tweedsmuir believed the League "too grandiose and its machinery far too slow and complicated" but, "*faute de mieux*," it had to carry on. He suggested it be supplemented by regional pacts, such as a modified Treaty of Locarno, the 1925 agreement guaranteeing the borders between France, Belgium, and Germany, and demilitarizing the Rhineland. Over the longer term, he envisioned a modified League as part of a new international order (See Tweedsmuir to Caroline Grosvenor, May 12, 1936, BP, LAC).

4. MKD, June 11, 1936, LAC.

5. Stewart, *Burying Caesar*, 260. For example, Sir Austen Chamberlain, who had won the Nobel Peace Prize for his role in negotiating the Treaty of Locarno, was a supporter of the League, but he viewed regional arrangements as a strategy for containing Germany in the short term.

6. Tweedsmuir to King, June 20, 1936, BP, LAC. For details of the speech, see House of Commons, *Debates*, June 18, 1936, 3862-3873.

7. House of Commons, *Debates*, June 18, 1936, 3868-3869. These factors included, "too much geography ... maintaining government over vast areas and unity among sections thousands of miles apart ... a real interest in the peace and prosperity of the world ... international trade essential for us ... it is necessary to emphasize the obvious when men speak as if it were only in and through the League of Nations that we can take our

part in international affairs ... but our direct relations with Britain and the United States and other countries are of daily and vital import."

8. Tweedsmuir to King, June 20, 1936, BP, LAC.

9. Groups of concerned citizens included the decade-old Canadian Institute of International Affairs (CIIA), the more academic-oriented Canadian Institute on Economics and Politics, as well as the League of Nations Society. For a detailed history of the CIIA, see E.D. Greathed, in the bibliography, and publications of proceedings of the Canadian Institute on Economics and Politics, also referred to in the bibliography.

10. Malcolm Macdonald to Tweedsmuir, May 7, 1936, BP, LAC.

11. King to Tweedsmuir, August 24, 1936, BP, LAC.

12. Ibid. King had confided to his diary on June 14, 1936, that his duty was to "keep this country out of war above all else and, next, to do all that is possible to have war restricted within as narrow limits as possible between European countries."

13. Tweedsmuir to King, August 31, 1936, BP, LAC.

14. Tweedsmuir to Caroline Grosvenor in London, September 16, 1936, BP, LAC.

15. Ibid.

16. This is a point that Churchill also highlighted (See Winston Churchill, *The Gathering Storm*, Vol. 1 of *The Second World War* (Boston: Houghton Mifflin, 1948), 207).

17. See House of Commons, *Debates*, April 1, 1935, 2287 and 2302 respectively, for the quotes.

18. King to Tweedsmuir, August 24, 1936, BP, LAC.

19. MKD, August 25, 1936, LAC.

20. *Globe* (Toronto), August 22, 1936.

21. *Globe* (Toronto), August 22 and September 4, 1936.

22. *Globe* (Toronto), August 22, 1936, 1. There was extensive newspaper coverage and editorial comment for a couple of weeks during Elibank's speaking tour.

23. MKD, August 6, 1936, LAC.

24. Tweedsmuir, "Speech, Vancouver, August 1936," BP, LAC. Press reports were describing the barbarous Japanese invasion of China; there were also reports of the civil war in Spain, Italy's conquest of Abyssinia, and Germany's rearmament.

25. *Daily Province* (Vancouver), August 27, 1936.

26. August 27, 1936: Articles from the *Mail & Empire* (Toronto), the *Globe* (Toronto), the *Montreal Star*, the *Union Advocate* (Newcastle, NB) and, other papers: all from RBP, LAC (indicating interest on Bennett's part).

27. Tweedsmuir to King, August 31, 1936, BP, LAC.

28. Possibly because none of King's ministers raised concerns and they were dealing with controversial remarks by Lord Elibank, which still occupied the press.

29. Tweedsmuir, quoted in the *Globe* (Toronto), September 4, 1936.

30. *Globe* (Toronto), September 4, 1936.

31. The quotes in these paragraphs are taken from King's diary (MKD, September 4, 1936, LAC).

32. Ibid.

33. Ibid.

34. Ibid.

35. Ibid.

36. King to Tweedsmuir, handwritten letter, September 4, 1936, BP, LAC.

37. "Editorial," *Globe* (Toronto), September 5, 1936.

38. King to Tweedsmuir, September 8, 1936, BP, LAC.

39. Tweedsmuir to King, September 8, 1936, BP, LAC.

40. Tweedsmuir to King, September 29, 1936, BP, LAC.

41. MKD, September 24, 1936, LAC.

42. MKD, September 24, 1936, LAC. John Buchan had written about the Dundonald crisis in his biography of Minto (John Buchan, *Lord Minto: A Memoir* (Boston: Houghton Mifflin, 1924), 150-152).

43. Tweedsmuir to King, September 29, 1936; similar sentiments were expressed in Tweedsmuir's letter to Caroline Grosvenor, September 16, 1936, BP, LAC.

44. King to Tweedsmuir, October 2, 1936, BP, LAC.

45. Ibid.

46. See, for example, Ramsay MacDonald to Tweedsmuir, December 7, 1936, BP, LAC. MacDonald noted the "unity of spirit" of the Empire still required a great effort to weld the Dominions into it. Lord Crawford noted the anxiety in England over the attitudes prevalent in Quebec, but took heart, however, from the "brilliant reception" Tweedsmuir had received on his arrival at Quebec City, and hoped that a number of factors might contribute to reconciling Quebec to Europe. Among the factors noted by Crawford were Tweedsmuir's speeches in French, following those of the French-speaking wife of his predecessor, Lord Bessborough, and also the "very striking tour" recently of the archbishop of Quebec in France (Crawford to Tweedsmuir, January 1937, BP, LAC).

47. House of Commons, *Debates*, January 25, 1937, 237.

48. House of Commons, *Debates*, February 15, 1937, 902.

49. This is described in J.W. Dafoe, "Canadian Foreign Policy — Public Opinion," in *World Currents and Canada's Course: Lectures Given at the Canadian*

Institute on Economics and Politics, August 7th to 20th, 1936, edited by Violet Anderson (Toronto: Thomas Nelson and Sons, 1937), 146-147.

50. House of Commons, *Debates*, February 19, 1937, 1053-1057.

51. Tweedsmuir to King, February 20, 1937, BP, LAC.

52. King to Tweedsmuir, February 21, 1937, BP, LAC.

53. Halifax, Earl of, *Fulness of Days* (London: Collins, 1957), 205.

54. Tweedsmuir to King, April 7, 1937, BP, LAC.

55. See, for example, MKD, April 16, 1937, LAC: "It seemed to me that the speech [by Baldwin that King heard on the radio] on the whole was not at all exceptional. It relieved my mind as to what might be expected of myself in some addresses overseas." Other similar references to King's worrying about speeches are found in King's diaries (MKD, April 10, and May 21 and 22, 1937, LAC).

56. Tweedsmuir to King, with notes attached, April 7, 1937, BP, LAC.

57. See, for example, Arnold Heeney, *The Things That Are Caesar's*. Heeney noted that those, like himself, who worked closely with King knew that King's "attachment to Britain and things British was pervasive." King's diary (see, for example, MKD, April-June 1937, LAC) reveals, indeed, his respect for the institutions and form of government Canada inherited from Britain, as well as his strong belief that his rebel grandfather contributed to the gift of responsible government in Canada and throughout the Commonwealth. In this respect King was like the United Empire Loyalists, who fled the United States wishing to remain loyal to the Crown but not wanting to recreate English, class-based society in Canada (see Errington, *The Lion, the Eagle, and Upper Canada*, 272).

58. King to Tweedsmuir, April 7, 1937, BP, LAC.

59. MKD, April 10, 1937, LAC.

60. MKD, May 4, 1937, LAC. King took great metaphysical pride in his role of doing justice to the memory of his grandfather. On May 12, 1937, King recorded in his diary that he had been "thinking continuously of my grandfather, how he sought to establish liberty and service as the foundation stone of the Empire, and the bond between the Sovereign and the people" (MKD, LAC).

61. MKD, May 4, 1937, LAC.

62. Tweedsmuir to King, May 27, 1937, BP, LAC.

63. Tweedsmuir, "Speech to the Canada Club dinner, London, U.K., May 27, 1935," in *Canadian Occasions*, Buchan, 13.

64. Tweedsmuir to King, May 27, 1937; and June 14, 1937, BP, LAC.

65. As the issue was pursued subsequently, King was concerned about his political career because he faced considerable opposition from within

his own party. While he believed that at a strategic level he was being pro-British in his approach, he thought he would be accused of being pro-American, and would face the possibility of a Liberal defeat similar to that suffered in 1911 due to the issue of reciprocity with the United States. He consoled himself that Tweedsmuir at least knew the truth (Mackenzie King to Tweedsmuir, November 18, 1937, BP, LAC). King received strong encouragement from Tweedsmuir, whose handwritten letter to King included a biblical quotation that would strike a chord (Nehemiah, 6: 11). He praised King as the "only statesman in Canada with the larger outlook." He was emphatic that King had faced these sorts of challenges before and won, "and you are going to do it again." The emotional support was valuable, but just as important were the reasons why Tweedsmuir didn't think 1911 would be repeated, including that the British government now shared the same view and that Canadians were becoming more aware "that closer relations with America are the surest guarantee of the world's peace" (Tweedsmuir to King, November 18, 1937, BP, LAC).

66. Tweedsmuir, Speech, May 12, 1937, Ottawa, BP, LAC. The speech was given extensive press coverage across the country.

67. King, "Speech, Ottawa, May, 25, 1937," in the *Winnipeg Free Press*, May 25, 1937.

68. Tweedsmuir to Baldwin, April 2, 1938, BP, LAC.

69. Tweedsmuir to Susan Tweedsmuir, May 25, 1938, BP, LAC.

70. Robert Rhodes James, *Anthony Eden* (London: Weidenfeld and Nicolson, 1986), 177.

71. Described in F.J. Hatch, *The Aerodrome of Democracy: Canada and the British Commonwealth Air Training Plan, 1939-1945*, (Ottawa: Directorate of History, Department of National Defence, 1983), 7-8.

72. House of Commons, *Debates*, May 24, 1938, 3183.

73. King to Tweedsmuir, July 20 and 23, 1938, BP, LAC.

74. Tweedsmuir to King, July 12, 1938, BP, LAC.

75. King to Tweedsmuir, July 20 and 23, 1938, BP, LAC.

76. King to Tweedsmuir (in England), July 20, 1938, BP, LAC.

77. See Tweedsmuir to Anna (his sister), July 14, 1938, BP, LAC. In his letter he noted that he was having "most valuable talks" with Prime Minister Chamberlain, former prime minister Stanley Baldwin, Sir Thomas Inskip (minister for the coordination of defence), Lord Halifax (foreign secretary), Sir Samuel Hoare (home secretary), and Anthony Eden, who had resigned as foreign secretary in February. As well as talking with politicians, Tweedsmuir also spoke with the archbishop of Canterbury.

78. King to Tweedsmuir (in Britain), July 23, 1938, BP, LAC.

79. Ibid.
80. King to Tweedsmuir (in Britain), August 25, 1938, BP, LAC.
81. King to Tweedsmuir (in Britain), September 6, 1938, BP, LAC.

Chapter 6

1. Susan Tweedsmuir, comp., *Wife and Friends*, 273.
2. Buchan, *MHTD*, 13.
3. Ibid. The first chapter of Buchan's memoir describes this process.
4. Tweedsmuir, Speech, September 1937, Charlottetown, Prince Edward Island, printed in Buchan, *CO*, 30.
5. Ibid., 31.
6. Buchan, *MHTD*, 47. For example, Buchan notes that at Oxford he "discovered a new loyalty."
7. Buchan, *CO*, 31.
8. Ibid.
9. See Buchan, "Canada and the Empire," *Scottish Review*, March 5, 1908, reprinted in Gray, ed., *Comments and Characters*, 95.
10. Gray, ed., *Comments and Characters*, 99.
11. Ibid., 290-291.
12. Tweedsmuir to Baldwin, March 24, 1936, BP, LAC.
13. Tweedsmuir, "Speech to the St. Andrew's Society, Winnipeg, November 30, 1936," in Buchan, *Canadian Occasions*, 45.
14. Ibid.
15. Tweedsmuir, "Speech to the Canadian Institute of Mining, March 17, 1937," Speeches, BP, LAC.
16. Buchan's opinions and views were shared by friends and parliamentary colleagues. One correspondent, Leopold Amery, British secretary of state for Dominion affairs, toured Canada in 1928 and spoke on the subject of Empire. Referring to Lord Durham as the beginning of the current phase of the Empire, Amery stated: "At every stage in that chapter the growth of national sentiment and of national life in Canada has been indissolubly bound up with growth and the deepening of the sentiment of Imperial unity" (Leopold S. Amery, *My Political Life* (London: Hutchinson, 1953), 459).
17. See Murray Donnelly, *Dafoe of the Free Press* (Toronto: Macmillan of Canada, 1968), 44. Dafoe viewed the post of governor general as "a symbol of colonialism and he continued to attack the office throughout his career."
18. Buchan, "English Life," N.p. (1926), n.p., BP, LAC.
19. Ibid.

20. See A.R.M. Lower, "Quebec Nationalism," *Winnipeg Free Press*, November 26, 1936. Imperialist views prevailing at the time included those who revelled in the fact that Canada was part of the only super-power at the time, the British Empire, and others who saw Canada as only subordinate to the Empire, even a non-entity without it. Historian Arthur Lower wrote of the current in English-speaking Canada that "in an emergency put the Empire before Canada." This, Lower argued, was the suspicion that many French-speakers in Quebec harboured and was an obstacle to them developing a commitment to Canada.

21. Edward, D. Greathed, "Antecedents and Origins of the Canadian Institute of International Affairs," in *Empire and Nations: Essays in Honour of Frederic H. Soward*, edited by H.L. Dyck and H.P. Krosby (Toronto: University of Toronto Press, 1969), 91-115.

22. Canadian Institute on Economics and Politics (CIEP), *Canada, The Empire and The League: Lectures Given at the Canadian Institute on Economics and Politics, July 31 to August 14, 1936* (Toronto: Thomas Nelson & Sons, in association with the National Council of YMCAs of Canada, 1936); CIEP, *World Currents and Canada's Course: Lectures Given at the Canadian Institute on Economics and Politics, August 7th to 20th, 1936* (Toronto: Thomas Nelson and Sons, 1937).

23. CIEP, *Canada, The Empire and The League*, 136. The Imperial Federation "project" was a movement dating from the 1880s that aimed to create a closer union of Britain with its self-governing colonies such as Canada but which for all intents and purposes died after the First World War.

24. Frank H. Underhill, "The Outline of a National Foreign Policy," in *World Currents and Canada's Course*, 136-137.

25. Donnelly, *Dafoe of the Free Press*, 44. Dafoe's apparent respect for and contact with Tweedsmuir must have tempered his views.

26. *Winnipeg Free Press*, March 28, 1935.

27. Shuldham Redfern to King, September 17, 1937, Rideau Hall, LAC.

28. King to Shuldham Redfern, September 21, 1937, Rideau Hall, LAC.

29. Ibid. The dropped portion reads that the prime minister "said very truly the other day that he disliked the facile use of words like 'Fascism' and 'Communism' as terms of abuse, since the taunt of Fascism was used too often against a perfectly reasonable attempt to maintain law and order, and the taunt of Communism to decry some rational scheme of social reform." While a plausible argument against those who would quickly and ignorantly cast exaggerated criticisms about some policies or projects, the references were unacceptable when Canada was at war with Nazi Germany, which was allied to Communist Russia; the references were omitted when

a collection of Tweedsmuir's speeches were published after his death in 1940 (Buchan, *CO*, 256).

30. A list of the head table and other attendees was reported in the *Gazette* (Montreal), October 13, 1937.

31. Tweedsmuir. Quotations are from two typed drafts of speeches, with handwritten comments. Speeches, BP, LAC.

32. See House of Commons, *Debates,* April 1, 1935; *The Economist* (London), April 6, 1935; CIEP, *Canada, The Empire and The League* (1936); and *World Currents and Canada's Course* (1937). For an excellent critical analysis of Canada's characteristics and early evolution under the direct and indirect influences of Britain and the United States, see Errington, *The Lion, the Eagle, and Upper Canada*, 272.

33. MKD, October 12, 1937, LAC. Mackenzie King noted: "I could see Cahan and Jim Macdonnell & other Tories seated in front of me did not like it any too well."

34. Ibid.

35. Ibid.

36. Tweedsmuir, "Speech to Bishop's College, Lennoxville, QC, June 15, 1938," in Buchan, *Canadian Occasions*, 99.

37. "Canada Asked to Take Own Stand" was the *Globe and Mail* headline, though it was not printed on the front page. It was similar to other headlines in other papers: "Own Attitude": *Ottawa Citizen* and *Leader-Post* (Regina); "Fix Own Policy": *Vancouver Daily Province*; and "Own Foreign Policy": *Gazette* (Montreal): all headlines from October 13, 1937.

38. See, for example, the *Vancouver Sun*, October 13, 1937. The *Sun* was very critical, even conspiratorially suspicious, not sure whether they suspected such "a sweeping statement" was done with the tacit approval of the British government or if it may have constituted a warning for Canada "to pay up or get out," which recalled the controversy raised by Lord Elibank (see Chapter 5). The newspaper's editors believed in any case that Tweedsmuir, not a man given "to idle and fatuous talk," had said either too much or too little, but that he "should amplify" his points.

39. *Winnipeg Free Press*, October 13, 1937. In examining the reasons why Canada could afford to take an independent stand, the conservative-leaning *Ottawa Journal* noted that Canada's independence derived from the protection offered by Britain and the U.S. Munroe Doctrine; Canada, in its opinion, had no strength of its own.

40. In its editorial "La paix mondiale," *La Presse* in Montreal, consistent with many opinions in French Canada, expressed the opinion that the speech encouraged citizens to pursue peace in international affairs. *Le Soleil,*

Organe du parti libéral, in Quebec City, concentrated on the governor general's encouragement of citizens to interest themselves in international affairs so they could better judge their politicians. October 13, 1937.

41. *Winnipeg Tribune*, October 13, 1937. The *Tribune* editors noted that those same people who were alarmed by Tweedsmuir's remarks on defence in Calgary the year before would "now throw their nightcaps in the sky and cheer hoarsely.... Then, it was 'interference' in Canada's affairs; today it will be a great declaration of independence — 1776 and all that." These people, the editors continued, "have heard of the Durham Report and even the Statute of Westminster, but they are still fighting the battles of the American Revolution and the Papineau Rebellion."

42. Tweedsmuir to Helen Buchan, October 14, 1937, BP, LAC.

43. Ernest Watkins, *R.B. Bennett* (Toronto: Kingswood House, 1963), 142.

Chapter 7

1. Tweedsmuir to Susan Buchan, November 6, 1936, BP, LAC.

2. MKD, October 26, 1936, LAC.

3. See "First Time in History," *Ottawa Citizen*, November 3, 1936.

4. Tweedsmuir to Susan Buchan, November 6, 1936, BP, LAC.

5. *Ottawa Citizen*, November 10, 1936, with the article dated November 9.

6. Tweedsmuir to Hardinge, February 22, 1938, BP, LAC.

7. Hardinge to Tweedsmuir, April 5, 1938, BP, LAC.

8. Tweedsmuir to Hardinge, April 8, 1938, BP, LAC.

9. Recalled in a letter from Tweedsmuir to Crawford, November 26, 1938, BP, LAC.

10. MKD, May 29, 1938, LAC.

11. Ibid. Tweedsmuir's meeting and the general subject of their talks are also briefly mentioned in letters from him to Susan Tweedsmuir and Anna Buchan, both May 30, 1938, BP, LAC.

12. Whereas Mackenzie King's motivation in proposing the 1936 visit had been negative, to detract the public's attention from Mrs. Simpson, Tweedsmuir's motivations in proposing the 1939 visit were positive.

13. MKD, May 29, 1938, LAC.

14. Tweedsmuir to Chamberlain, March 26, 1938, Neville Chamberlain Papers, Birmingham University Library Special Collections (NCP, BULSC).

15. House of Commons, *Debates*, June 30, 1938, 4511. Mackenzie King explained how, three months previous, he had asked the governor general to postpone sailing to England until the first week of July, because of the "probable length of the session."

16. House of Commons, *Debates,* July 1, 1938, 4511.
17. Tweedsmuir to King, July 15, 1938, MKP, LAC.
18. Ibid.
19. Tweedsmuir to King, July 25, 1938, BP, LAC.
20. Mackenzie King was pleased to receive word from Tweedsmuir in England about a possible visit to Canada by the king. He believed that such a visit, including an informal one to the United States, "would be very much all to the good" (King to Tweedsmuir, July 23, 1938, BP, LAC).
21. Tweedsmuir to Anna Buchan, October 10, 1938, BP, LAC.
22. Ibid.
23. Hardinge to Tweedsmuir at Ruthin Castle, telegram, September 12, 1938, BP, LAC.
24. Hardinge to Tweedsmuir, in response to Tweedsmuir's reply, September 16, 1938, BP, LAC.
25. Tweedsmuir to Crawford, November 26, 1938, BP, LAC.
26. MKD, October 8, 1938, LAC. King also notes that he had made the suggestion (of the king holding a meeting of his Privy Council in Canada) to Tweedsmuir before the governor left for England.
27. Tweedsmuir to Anna Buchan, October 10, 1938, BP, LAC. The announcement gave "great pleasure to Canada," according to Tweedsmuir. The wording change and other details are described in MKD, October 8, 1938, LAC.
28. Tweedsmuir to Chamberlain, October 27, 1938, BP, LAC.
29. Tweedsmuir to Anna Buchan, November 20, 1938, BP, LAC.
30. Tweedsmuir to Hardinge, December 6, 1938, BP, LAC.
31. Tweedsmuir commented to his predecessor as governor general that it was a "pretty skillful" schedule, believing that the only real complaint could come from Montreal, which only had the king and queen for half a day, but that could be rationalized by the fact it was not a capital city (Tweedsmuir to Bessborough and to Crawford, both January 4, 1939, BP, LAC).
32. Lord Crawford also advised that the young sovereigns "must not be overdone, though," he added, "they are pretty tough" (Crawford to Tweedsmuir, November 12, 1938, BP, LAC).
33. Tweedsmuir to Anna Buchan, November 14, 1938, BP, LAC.
34. Crawford to Tweedsmuir, November 12, 1938, BP, LAC.
35. Tweedsmuir to Crawford, November 26, 1938, BP, LAC.
36. Tweedsmuir to Anna Buchan, November 7, 9, and 14, 1938, BP, LAC. Recalling the issue of who should meet the king, one of Tweedsmuir's aides-de-camp at the time, David Walker, was categorical in his 1984 autobiography: "The answer was fairly obvious. It should be the governor general, who would then slip into a sort of limbo while the prime minister

accompanied his king across Canada" (Walker, *Lean, Wind, Lean* (London: Collins, 1984), 125).

37.   MKD, November 25, 1938, LAC.

38.   Tweedsmuir to Hardinge, November 17, 1938, BP, LAC.

39.   MKD, November 25, 1938, LAC.

40.   Tweedsmuir to Hardinge, November 29, 1938, BP, LAC.

41.   Tweedsmuir to Hardinge, December 6, 1939, BP, LAC.

42.   Tweedsmuir to Hardinge, January 10, 1939, BP, LAC.

43.   Tweedsmuir to Hardinge, January 10, 1939, BP, LAC. The alternative was that he, Tweedsmuir, would meet Their Majesties aboard the *Repulse*, while the prime minister would be first to greet them on Canadian soil. Again, however, he twisted, cutting off his own argument by noting that the territorial waters in which the *Repulse* would lie would be considered Canadian soil in any case. The Palace itself would undoubtedly have been sensitive to the "advice" of King, knowing how far he could take issues, recalling both the 1926 King-Byng affair and King's attitude regarding the appointment of Bessborough's successor.

44.   Hardinge to Tweedsmuir, February 8, 1939, BP, LAC. The "certain cases" referred to were the lord lieutenants of the counties in Britain, who represent the king and who, when the king arrives, meet him and then go into the background. Hardinge was "nervous about what people [would] say if the [g]overnor [g]eneral [did] not appear at Quebec."

45.   Tweedsmuir to King, February 21, 1939, BP, LAC. The two possible courses of action involved, on the one hand, Tweedsmuir staying in Ottawa to await the royal couple, and on the other hand, him travelling to Quebec to greet them. If King favoured the former, Tweedsmuir assured him that "you have only to say that ... I should not appear at Quebec and the matter is settled." If, however, King believed there were some benefit to be had in Tweedsmuir travelling to Quebec to be on hand to greet the royal couple, if King thought there might be "some validity in Hardinge's arguments" and that, "properly managed," for example, if he flew back to Ottawa, it might add to the drama of the event, Tweedsmuir would be amenable to that course of action also. He concluded, "Whatever your decision I shall most gladly accept."

46.   King to Tweedsmuir, Feburary 24, 1939, BP, LAC.

47.   MKD, February 28, 1939, LAC. "Tories like Hardinge, Lascelles and the Tory Court do not wish any Liberal Administration to figure prominently with the King and Queen. Lascelles has been loaded up against me during the time Bennett was in office here; Hardinge knows that I dislike him. They both made up their minds to reduce my part to as small a one as possible...."

48. Hardinge to Tweedsmuir, typed copy of telegram, March 17, 1939, BP, LAC.

49. Walker, *Lean, Wind, Lean*, 125.

50. See, for example, Tweedsmuir to Hardinge, November 17, 1938, BP, LAC. This was an opinion he would have formed during his three years as governor general.

51. For more detail, see J. William Galbraith, "Fiftieth Anniversary of the 1939 Royal Visit," *Canadian Parliamentary Review* 12, no. 3 (Autumn 1989): 7-11.

52. O.D. Skelton to Shuldham Redfern, December 5, 1938, MKP, LAC.

53. Tweedsmuir to Anna Buchan, January 30, 1939, BP, LAC.

54. Among the correspondents who expressed this were Bessborough, Amery, and Crawford. Lord Crawford wrote that in the existing international context, the visit "could well prove epoch-making" if a crisis were to break out while the king and queen were in Canada (Crawford to Tweedsmuir, March 2, 1939, BP, LAC).

55. Hardinge to Tweedsmuir, April 20, 1939, BP, LAC.

56. Tweedsmuir to Anna Buchan, January 30, 1939, BP, LAC.

57. Tweedsmuir to King, December 17, 1938, BP, LAC.

58. King to Tweedsmuir, February 22, 1939; and Tweedsmuir to King, February 23, 1939, BP, LAC.

59. Tweedsmuir to King, February 28, 1939, BP, LAC.

60. MKD, March 2, 1939, LAC.

61. Tweedsmuir to Hardinge, March 1, 1939, BP, LAC.

62. Hardinge to Tweedsmuir, March 19, 1939, BP, LAC.

63. Tweedsmuir to Massey, December 29, 1938, BP, LAC.

64. Ibid.

65. Hardinge to Tweedsmuir, November 4, 1938, BP, LAC.

66. Tweedsmuir to C.D. Howe, November 24, 1938, BP, LAC.

67. Tweedsmuir's report from his trip to the Arctic in the summer of 1937 had been published in the *Sunday Times* in November that year. His attempt in that instance to make Canada better known in Britain had drawn the ire of the Palace, the king not being pleased that his representative was acting as something of a publicity agent due to his facility for writing, and putting other governors at a disadvantage (See Chapter 14).

68. Tweedsmuir to Hardinge, March 6, 1939; and Hardinge to Tweedsmuir, March 23, 1939, BP, LAC.

69. R.K. Carnegie, *And The People Cheered* (Ottawa: Legionary Library, 1940), 58-59.

70. Ibid., 58.

71. Tweedsmuir to Anna Buchan, March 12, 1939, BP, LAC.

72. Susan Tweedsmuir to Caroline Grosvenor (her mother), May 9, 1939, BP, LAC.

73. Tweedsmuir to Anna Buchan, May 15, 1939, BP, LAC.

74. Smith, *John Buchan*, 454.

75. House of Commons, *Debates*, May 19, 1939, 4617. The nine bills were: an act respecting a trade agreement between Canada and the United States; an act bringing into effect provisions of a Canada-U.S. convention providing emergency regulation of water levels in Rainy Lake and other boundary waters in the Rainy Lake watershed; two acts to encourage the co-operative marketing of wheat and of agricultural products; an act providing for the supervision and regulation of trading in grain futures; an act to amend the Pensions Act; an act to amend the Criminal Code; an act to provide youth employment training; and a supply bill.

76. Gustave Lanctôt, *The Royal Tour, 1939* (Toronto: E.P. Taylor Foundation, 1964), 15.

77. Walker, *Lean, Wind Lean*, 124.

78. Lanctôt, *Royal Tour*, 15.

79. See Galbraith, "Fiftieth Anniversary of the 1939 Royal Visit."

80. Two agreements were ratified with the Great Seal of Canada, the legislation to implement which the king had granted royal assent to only a few hours earlier. Both were agreements with the United States: i) a trade agreement signed in Washington the previous November; and ii) the convention regarding the boundary waters of the Rainy River district in northwestern Ontario, signed the previous September in Ottawa.

81. Lanctôt, *Royal Tour*, 19. The official historian of the tour noted "a new official procedure was established, which asserted and recognized Canada's equality of political status within the British Empire."

82. Lanctôt, *Royal Tour*, 25.

83. The success of the tour can also be measured for its effect on the king and queen. Back in England not even two months, Prime Minister Neville Chamberlain related to Tweedsmuir that the king showed increased self-confidence. Lady Tweedsmuir received an eight-page letter from the queen, and the governor general a six-page letter, each handwritten (Tweedsmuir to King, July 20, 1939, MKP, LAC).

Chapter 8

1. *New York Times*, March 27, 1935.

2. "The Many-Sided Buchan," *New York Times*, March 27, 1935.

3. *Time*, October 21, 1935.

4. Violet Markham to Susan Buchan, March 28, 1935, BP, LAC.

5. Violet Markham to Buchan, April 16, 1935, BP, LAC. See also, Edmond S. Ions, *James Bryce and American Democracy* (London: Macmillan, 1968), 339.

6. *New York Times*, March 27, 1935.

7. *The Graphic* (London), May 10, 1930.

8. *New York Times*, March 27, 1935.

9. MKD, November 6, 1935, LAC.

10. See Smith, *John Buchan,* 327. Baldwin respected and sought advice from Buchan who had also helped draft many of Baldwin's speeches.

11. Tweedsmuir to Caroline Grosvenor, May 25, 1936, BP, LAC.

12. See, for example, Jim Beach, "Origins of the Special Intelligence Relationship: Anglo-American Intelligence Co-operation on the Western Front, 1917– 1918," *Intelligence and National Security* 22, no. 2 (April 2007), 229-249.

13. Tweedsmuir to King, May 31, 1936, BP, LAC.

14. Roosevelt to Tweedsmuir, June 5, 1936, Roosevelt Papers (RP), FDR Library (FDRL).

15. Tweedsmuir to Caroline Grosvenor, June 8, 1936, BP, LAC.

16. Tweedsmuir to King, May 31 and July 9, 1936, BP, LAC.

17. Tweedsmuir to King, July 15, 1936, BP, LAC.

18. King to Tweedsmuir, July 18, 1936, BP, LAC.

19. Attributed to Michael Adeane in a letter from Susan Tweedsmuir to her family in England, August 4, 1937, BP, LAC.

20. King to Tweedsmuir, August 2, 1936, BP, LAC.

21. Lord Tweedsmuir, William Lyon Mackenzie King, and Franklin Delano Roosevelt, "Speeches at Quebec City, July 31, 1936," audio recording, Sound and Moving Image Division, LAC.

22. Ibid.

23. Tweedsmuir to King, August 4, 1936, BP, LAC.

24. Ibid.

25. Crawford to Tweedsmuir, September 23, 1936, BP, LAC.

26. Cited in correspondence from King to Tweedsmuir, August 24, 1936, BP, LAC.

27. King to Tweedsmuir, August 2, 1936, BP, LAC.

28. Ibid.

29. Ibid.

30. Tweedsmuir to Susan Tweedsmuir, September 12, 1936, BP, LAC.

31. "Franklin D. Roosevelt established the modern tradition of delivering an oral State of the Union beginning with his first in 1934." Source: Gerhard Peters, "State of the Union Addresses and Messages," Presidency.ucsb.edu (*www.presidency.ucsb.edu/sou.php*, accessed December 5, 2009).

32. Roosevelt to Tweedsmuir, February 20, 1937, BP, LAC.
33. King to Tweedsmuir, March 15, 1937, BP, LAC.
34. Ibid.
35. *New York Times*, March 28, 1937.
36. Roosevelt to Tweedsmuir, February 20, 1937, BP, LAC.
37. *New York Times*, April 1, 1937.
38. Frank Freidel, *Franklin D. Roosevelt: A Rendezvous with Destiny* (Boston: Little, Brown, 1990), 260.
39. United States Congress, Congressional Record, 75th Cong., 1st sess., April 1, 1937, Senate.
40. United States Congress, Congressional Record, 75th Cong., 1st sess., April 1, 1937, House of Representatives.
41. *New York Times*, April 2, 1937.
42. Tweedsmuir to Baldwin, April 8, 1937, BP, LAC.
43. Tweedsmuir to King, May 14, 1937, BP, LAC. Information on the conference is from other letters, sent to Tweedsmuir from his former parliamentary colleagues, John Simon, Leopold Amery, and Ramsay MacDonald.
44. Tweedsmuir to Stair Gillon, April 9, 1937, BP, LAC.
45. Tweedsmuir to Arthur Murray, April 3, 1937, BP, LAC.
46. Tweedsmuir, "Midway Report," July 1, 1937, BP, LAC. It is not specified to whom it was addressed, but it may have been sent to the Palace.
47. Ibid.
48. *New York Times*, March 31 and April 1 and 2, 1937.
49. Canadian Press, *New York Times*, April 2, 1937.
50. There are also many books that have dealt with this theme; see, for example, the discussion in D. Cameron Watt, chap. 4, "1934–1940," *Succeeding John Bull: America in Britain's Place, 1900–1975* (Cambridge, UK: Cambridge University Press, 1984).
51. Ronald Lindsay, quoted in a letter from Tweedsmuir to Helen Buchan, April 5 and 6, 1937, BP, LAC.
52. Leopold Amery to Tweedsmuir, April 8, 1937, BP, LAC.
53. MKD, April 4, 1937, LAC.
54. Ibid.
55. Tweedsmuir to Baldwin, April 8, 1937, BP, LAC
56. Ibid.
57. Ibid.
58. Smith, *John Buchan*, 473.
59. Tweedsmuir to King, April 7, 1937, BP, LAC.
60. King to Tweedsmuir, April 7, 1937, BP, LAC.
61. MKD, April 9 and 16, 1937, LAC.

62. MKD, April 16, 1937, LAC.

63. MKD, August 8, 1937, LAC.

64. Buchan, *CO*, 63.

65. Tweedsmuir to King, May 14, 1937, BP, LAC.

66. Text of speech cited in the *New York Times* and *Ottawa Citizen*, July 2, 1937.

67. Ibid.

68. *New York Times*, July 2, 1937.

69. Tweedsmuir to Gilbert Murray, October 8, 1937, BP, LAC.

70. Roosevelt to Tweedsmuir, September 24, 1937, BP, LAC.

71. Roosevelt, "Speech, Chicago, October 5, 1937," Speeches, RP, FDRL.

72. Ibid. Roosevelt biographer Conrad Black notes how Roosevelt pushed public opinion forward using such methods as this speech. Black then goes on to explain that, although nothing had really changed, opinion did move, and this movement would allow Roosevelt to follow it in policy. Black describes this strategy as "astonishingly subtle and skillful," and notes that, among the British leadership, only King George VI seemed to recognize it (Conrad Black, note to the author, January 8, 2007).

    There was, however, earlier analysis published by Harold Levine and James Wechsler. In it the authors note the "educative" efforts of Roosevelt to help "create a setting favourable to war propaganda" (348). They add: Roosevelt was "confiden[t] that popular opinion was ready for stiffer words; and the words themselves were intended to make popular opinion more receptive to acts." See *War Propaganda and the United States* (New Haven, CT: Yale University Press for the Institute for Propaganda Analysis, 1940; reprinted, New York: Garland Publishing, 1972), 349.

73. Most major papers across the United States, and some not so major ones, had comments. The *New York Times* summarized many of the commentaries, as well as international reactions, in its edition of October 6, 1937.

74. Freidel, *Franklin D. Roosevelt*, 264.

75. Tweedsmuir to Baldwin, October 11, 1937. He expressed the same point to Gilbert Murray, October 8, 1937, BP, LAC.

76. Tweedsmuir to Gilbert Murray, October 8, 1937, BP, LAC.

77. See U.S. Department of State, "Press Release no. 94, October 6, 1937," Peace and War: United States Foreign Policy, 1931–1941, Ibiblio.org, *www .ibiblio.org/hyperwar/Dip/PaW/094.html*; and Secretary of State Cordell Hull to Norman Davis, U.S. delegate to the Nine-Power conference in Brussels, *www.mtholyoke.edu/acad/intrel/interwar/hull31.html* (accessed July 10, 2007). The Nine-Power Treaty was signed in Washington, D.C., on

February 6, 1922, by the United States, Great Britain, Canada, Australia, New Zealand, The Netherlands, Portugal, Japan, and China; its purpose was to guarantee Chinese independence.

78. Tweedsmuir to King, October 11, 1937, BP, LAC.

79. MKD, October 19, 1937, LAC. Cordell Hull received the honorary degree October 22, 1937.

80. MKD, October 20, 1937, LAC.

81. Ibid.

82. Ibid. Applying sanctions involved the danger of provoking Japan to seize even more territory, in order to supply itself with required military-related materials, but refraining from applying sanctions, which was the U.S. position, could be misinterpreted as a pacifist attitude by Japan, which would then feel itself free to continue its aggression. It seemed a lose-lose situation. Regardless, Britain and the United States both agreed on the need to become ever more prepared.

83. Tweedsmuir to Gilbert Murray, October 8 and 27, 1937, BP, LAC.

84. Tweedsmuir to Chamberlain, October 25, 1937; Tweedsmuir's letter is referred to in Chamberlain's response to Tweedsmuir, November 19, 1937, BP, LAC.

85. Tweedsmuir to King, October 11, 1937, BP, LAC

86. Chamberlain to Tweedsmuir, November 19, 1937, BP, LAC.

87. Chamberlain's attitude toward the Americans was well known and described by many historians. See, for example, his remarks from a July 1939 letter he sent to Tweedsmuir, in regard to the U.S. neutrality legislation and Congress: "Their behaviour over the neutrality legislation is enough to make one weep, but I have not been disappointed for I never expected any better behaviour from these pig-headed and self-righteous nobodies" (Quoted in Watt, *Succeeding John Bull*, 88, n. 76).

88. Chamberlain to Tweedsmuir, November 19, 1937, BP, LAC.

89. MKD, October 29, 1937, LAC. King continued in this vein, his attitude and arrogance showing in his diary entry for March 15, 1938, when he writes of the absurdity "of this business of governor generals [*sic*] from the Old Land whom one has appointed oneself."

90. Tweedsmuir to Anna Buchan, January 13, 1938, BP, LAC.

91. Tweedsmuir to Anna Buchan, January 20, 1938, BP, LAC.

92. See Embassy of the United States, Ottawa, Canada, "Chiefs of the United States Mission to Canada," Canada.usembassy.gov, *http://canada.usembassy .gov/ambassador/past-ambassadors.html* (accessed September 1, 2012).

93. Conrad Black, *Franklin Delano Roosevelt: Champion of Freedom* (New York: Public Affairs, 2003), 439.

94. *Times* (London), February 21, 1938; and Robert Rhodes James, *Anthony Eden* (London: Weidenfeld and Nicolson, 1986), 173-195.

95. Tweedsmuir to Halifax, March 5, 1938, BP, LAC.

96. David E. Koskoff, *Joseph P. Kennedy: A Life and Times* (Upper Saddle River, NJ: Prentice-Hall, 1974), 122.

97. Halifax to Tweedsmuir, March 15, 1938, BP, LAC.

98. Koskoff, *Joseph P. Kennedy*, 122-124.

99. Nicholas John Cull, *Sellling War* (Oxford: Oxford University Press, 1995), 20. Lindsay's failure would have been all the more poignant in view of former Foreign Secretary Eden's direction in March 1937 to report on how best to "retain the goodwill of the United States Government and public opinion" (Cited in Cull, *Selling War*, 13).

100. Tweedsmuir to Chamberlain, January 23, 1939, BP, LAC.

101. Ibid.

102. Chamberlain to Tweedsmuir, February 7, 1939, BP, LAC.

103. King to Tweedsmuir, February 22, 1939, BP, LAC. See also MKD, February 22, 1939, LAC.

104. Tweedsmuir to Lothian, April 25, 1939, BP, LAC.

105. J.R.M. Butler, *Lord Lothian* (London: Macmillan, 1960), 12. For additional information, see D.M. Abbott, "John Buchan and Lord Lothian," *JBJ*, no. 26 (spring 2002): 37-39.

106. See Black, *Roosevelt*, 505.

107. Tweedsmuir to Anna Buchan, January 30, 1939, BP, LAC.

108. For example, Jean Monnet, as a private businessman, was better placed than many government officials to see what information was really being provided, and he had the added benefit, he also believed, of not being biased or jaded by unjustified optimism or the fear of great responsibility (Jean Monnet, *Mémoires*, 2 vols. (Paris: Livre de Poche, 1976), vol. 1, 164).

109. Ibid., 163-175.

110. Freidel, *Franklin D. Roosevelt*, 309.

111. Ibid. See also reference to "Roosevelt's secret message to Chamberlain via [Arthur] Murray" in Watt, *Succeeding John Bull*, 87.

112. Tweedsmuir to Roosevelt, October 31, 1938, RP, FDRL.

113. Tweedsmuir to King, November 7, 1938, BP, LAC.

114. Tweedsmuir to Roosevelt, October 31, 1938, RP, FDRL.

115. Roosevelt to Tweedsmuir, November 3, 1938, BP, LAC.

116. Tweedsmuir to Anna Buchan, October 31, 1938, BP, LAC.

117. See Shuldham Redfern to King, March 30 and April 29, 1938, MKP, LAC; and Shuldham Redfern to H.R.L. Henry, April 25, 1938, BP, LAC.

118. Tweedsmuir to King, April 23, 1938, MKP, LAC.

119. King, Note to file, May 5, 1938, MKP, LAC. Redfern had been planning to inform the press but, as he noted to the prime minister and Under-Secretary Skelton, the boards of Harvard and Yale did not disclose the names of recipients of honorary degrees until the actual ceremony, and therfore he would make no mention of the degrees. The reason for attending would certainly have been suspected by anyone reading the announcement!

120. Tweedsmuir to Anna Buchan, June 25, 1938, BP, LAC.

121. Ibid. Young was the *Time* magazine Man-of-the-Year in 1929. He had been asked to participate in the Second Reparations Conference after the First World War (See "Heroes: Man-of-the-Year," *Time*, January 6, 1930, *www.time.com/time/magazine/article/0,9171,738364-1,00.html* (accessed Dec 6, 2009)).

122. Tweedsmuir to Susan Tweedsmuir, June 25, 1938, BP, LAC.

123. Quoted in Marc Eliot, *Walt Disney* (New York: Carol Publishing, 1993), 105. This was ten years after *Steamboat Willie* opened at the Colony movie theatre in New York City; *Snow White* had just been released the previous December, to wide acclaim, and was honoured with a special Academy Award.

124. Several letters from Tweedsmuir describe these days: to King, June 25, 1938; to Susan Tweedsmuir, June 25, 1938; and to Anna Buchan, June 25, 1938: all BP, LAC.

125. *Ottawa Citizen*, June 22, 1938.

126. Tweedsmuir to Roosevelt, April 30, 1938, BP, LAC.

127. Roosevelt to Tweedsmuir, May 12, 1938, and vice versa, May 25, 1938, BP, LAC.

128. Roosevelt to Tweedsmuir, August 31, 1938, BP, LAC.

129. Ibid.

130. Violet Markham to Tweedsmuir, January 17, 1939, BP, LAC.

131. Hardinge to Tweedsmuir, November 14, 1938, BP, LAC.

132. Tweedsmuir to Hardinge, November 29, 1938, BP, LAC.

133. Tweedsmuir to Hardinge, January 14, 1939, BP, LAC.

134. Ibid.

135. Ibid.

136. Ibid.

137. Hardinge to Tweedsmuir, February 8, 1939, BP, LAC.

138. Hardinge to Tweedsmuir, February 8, 1939, BP, LAC.

139. Tweedsmuir to Chamberlain, March 11, 1939, CP, UBLSC.

140. Hardinge to Tweedsmuir, March 31, 1939, BP, LAC.

141. King to Tweedsmuir, July 21, 1939, MKP, LAC.

Chapter 9

1. Leopold Amery to Tweedsmuir, April 8, 1937, BP, LAC. Amery held direc-torships in some German companies and hence travelled to Germany through the 1930s (he was not in government in those years).

2. Graham Stewart describes the "temporary calm in international affairs," *Burying Caesar*, 270.

3. Tweedsmuir to King, May 5, 1937, BP, LAC.

4. Bessborough to Tweedsmuir, November 26, 1937, BP, LAC.

5. For background to the Nine-Power Treaty, see Office of the Historian, Bureau of Public Affairs, United States Department of State, "Milestones: 1921–1936 – The Nine-Power Treaty," History.state.gov, *http://history.state .gov/milestones/1921-1936/NavalConference* (accessed April 17, 2013).

6. MKD, October 29, 1937, LAC.

7. Ibid.

8. Bessborough to Tweedsmuir, November 26, 1937, BP, LAC.

9. Ibid. See also Edward (Lord) Halifax, *Fulness of Days* (London: Collins, 1957), 183-184; Winston Churchill, *The Gathering Storm*, Vol. 1 of *The Second World War* (Boston: Houghton Mifflin, 1948), 249-250; and Stewart, *Burying Caesar*, 281. The trip was subsequently seen as confirming Halifax's appeasement credentials and part of conspiring against Foreign Secretary Anthony Eden, increasingly opposed to Chamberlain's policy.

10. John Simon to Tweedsmuir, November 24, 1937, BP, LAC.

11. Tweedsmuir to John Simon, December 11, 1937, BP, LAC.

12. Robert Rhodes James, *Anthony Eden* (London: Weidenfeld and Nicolson, 1986), 173-195. For a more contemporary view, see Keith Feiling, *The Life of Neville Chamberlain* (London: Macmillan, 1947), 336-339; and Robert Rhodes James, *Victor Cazalet* (London: Hamish Hamilton, 1976), 208.

13. James, *Anthony Eden*, 200-202; and Feiling, *Neville Chamberlain*, 339. King George VI's private secretary, Alexander Hardinge, informed Tweedsmuir that the Eden-Chamberlain differences "came to a head" over Italy's veiled threat to open discussions with Germany (Hardinge to Tweedsmuir, April 5, 1938, BP, LAC). Tweedsmuir correspondents Lord Crawford and Leopold Amery believed that maintaining contact with Italy was the way to avoid the drift toward a war in which Britain alone might face Germany, Italy, and Japan.

14. Tweedsmuir to Stair Gillon, March 26, 1938, BP, LAC.

15. Halifax to Tweedsmuir, February n.d., 1938, BP, LAC. That occasion never arose due to Tweedsmuir's death in February 1940. Halifax didn't publish his memoirs until 1957, though they are not particularly illuminating on this point.

16. James, *Anthony Eden*, 187-195; James, *Victor Cazalet*, 208; Churchill, *The Gathering Storm*, 251-254; and Stewart, *Burying Caesar*, 284-285.

17. Tweedsmuir to Chamberlain, March 26, 1938, NCP, UBLSC.

18. Chaim Weizmann, Letter 264: Weizmann to Colonial Secretary Ormsby-Gore in London, January 20, 1938, *Letters*, Vol. 18, general editor: Barnet Litvinoff; volume editor: Aaron Kliem (Jerusalem: Israel Universities Press, 1979), 292-297; Weizmann, Letter 285: Weizmann to Lord Tweedsmuir, February 22, 1938, *Letters*, Vol. 18, 320-321. Weizmann became the first president of Israel.

19. See Norman Rose, *The Gentile Zionists* (London: Frank Cass, 1973), 5, n. 37. The committee had been formed in 1929 by members of Parliament who supported the establishment of a Jewish homeland, including Tweedsmuir's close friend Leopold Amery (also a friend of the Weizmanns), Walter Elliot, a fellow Scot and friend, and another MP, Victor Cazalet, who later served as joint chairman of the Committee with Buchan and who became very close to Weizmann. In its first few months, the committee was concerned with how the government would respond to a commission investigating Arab-Jewish riots in Palestine. The committee agreed it should publish a letter in the (London) *Times*, signed by Balfour, former prime minister Lloyd George, and the respected South African statesman Jan Smuts. The letter appeared on December 20, 1929. Historian Norman Rose describes it as "a remarkable exercise in public relations" (*Gentile Zionists*, 6). John Buchan assisted Weizmann in drafting that letter as well as another, just over three months later, signed by Weizmann himself, reacting to the commission's report. The latter was published in short version in the *Times* and in full in the (Manchester) *Guardian* (N. Rose, *Gentile Zionists*, 5-8). On a number of occasions, when the British government didn't pursue or follow through on implementing partition, Cazalet became outraged and let his parliamentary colleagues know (See James, *Victor Cazalet*, 197, 214-215).

20. This and the British commitment to protecting its imperial life-line to the East through the Mediterranean were reported together in the *Toronto Star*, October 21, 1937.

21. Weizmann, Letter 264: Weizmann to Colonial Secretary Ormsby-Gore in London, January 20, 1938, *Letters*, Vol. 18, 292-297.

22. Ibid. Also quoted in Norman Rose, *Chaim Weizmann: A Biography* (New York: Viking Penguin, 1986), 335. The quote is from the Old Testament book of Exodus, 1:8, and refers to the story of Joseph, who was sold by his brothers to the Egyptians. Joseph was accepted by Pharaoh for the good things he had done for the Egyptians and was

made a governor. As a result Pharaoh let the Jews live in Egypt. After Joseph died, however, and a new Pharaoh ruled Egypt, he forgot about all this, began to feel threatened by the Jews, and so wished to "get them up out of the land."

23. Weizmann, Letter 285: Weizmann to Lord Tweedsmuir, February 22, 1938, *Letters*, Vol. 18, 320-321.

24. Tweedsmuir's response was received within a week of Weizmann writing his letter on February 22, assuming it took the mail about five to seven days for the letter to reach Ottawa by ship and rail.

25. Tweedsmuir, Letter 297: Tweedsmuir to Weizmann, March 5, 1938, in *Letters*, Vol. 18, by Chaim Weizmann, 320-321, n. 5.

26. Tweedsmuir to Halifax, March 5, 1938, BP, LAC.

27. Crawford to Tweedsmuir, January 20, 1938, BP, LAC.

28. Chaim Weizmann, *Trial and Error* (London: Hamish Hamilton, 1950), 178.

29. Weizmann, Letter 285: Weizmann to Tweedsmuir, February 22, 1938, *Letters*, Vol. 18, n.p. "Balfour" refers to the British statesman Arthur Balfour, a former prime minister (1902–1905) who, while foreign secretary (1916–1919), had his name attached to the November 1917 "Balfour Declaration," which set out British government support for partitioning Palestine and creating a homeland for the Jewish people.

30. Andrew Roberts, *The Holy Fox* (London: Weidenfeld and Nicolson, 1991), 128. For another example of Halifax's compassion, notwithstanding Weizmann's pressure, see Weizmann's memoir, *Trial and Error*, 496.

31. Halifax to Tweedsmuir, March 15, 1938, BP, LAC.

32. N. Rose, *Gentile Zionists*, 159.

33. Weizmann, Letter 307: Weizmann to Lord Halifax, March 14, 1938, *Letters*, Vol. 18, 337-341.

34. N. Rose, "Partition: The Withdrawal," *Gentile Zionists*, 151-177.

35. Weizmann, Letter 307: Weizmann to Lord Halifax, March 14, 1938, *Letters*, Vol. 18, 337-341.

36. Ibid., Letter 318: Weizmann to Mrs. Blanche Dugdale, a leading, non-Jewish supporter of a Jewish homeland, April 4, 1938, 349-351.

37. Weizmann, *Trial and Error*, 496; N. Rose, *Chaim Weizmann*, 520; and Jehuda Reinharz, *Chaim Weizmann: the Making of a Statesman*, Studies in Jewish History, Vol. 2 (Oxford and New York: Oxford University Press, 1993), 536.

38. Weizmann, *Trial and Error*, 402, 494-495. See also James, *Victor Cazalet*, 214, where Cazalet writes he was "seeing Weizmann every day" by 1939.

39. James, *Victor Cazalet*, 165.

40. N. Rose, *Gentile Zionists*, 159, n. 43.

41. Chaim Weizmann, Weizmann to Lady Tweedsmuir, February 12, 1940, *The Letters and Papers of Chaim Weizmann*, Series A: Letters, Vol. 19: January 1939–June 1940, general editor: Barnet Litvinoff; volume editor: Norman Rose (Jerusalem: Israel Universities Press, 1979), 227.

42. N. Rose, *Chaim Weizmann*, 221. Rose also includes in this list Leopold Amery, as well as Victor Cazalet, Churchill, Lloyd George, and Ormsby-Gore. It is clear from this type of comment, and many other similar comments and actions described in this book, that Buchan was not anti-Semitic; an anti-Semite would not have provided such extensive support, both privately and publicly, to Jews, both individually and collectively.

43. Roberts, *Holy Fox*, 128-129.

44. Weizmann, *Trial and Error*, 497.

45. Ibid.

46. N. Rose, *Chaim Weizmann*, 222-223.

47. Tweedsmuir to Halifax, March 5, 1938, BP, LAC.

48. Tweedsmuir to Anna Buchan, March 14, 1938, BP, LAC.

49. Tweedsmuir to Anna Buchan, March 14 and May 30, 1938, BP, LAC.

50. MacMillan, *Paris 1919*, 493. MacMillan's reassessment in 2001 notes that "Hitler did not wage war because of the Treaty of Versailles, although he found its existence a godsend for his propaganda.... Even if Germany had been left with its old borders, ... [Hitler] would still have wanted more." Tweedsmuir, his correspondents, and most others realized toward the end of 1938 and through the spring of 1939 that Hitler could not be appeased. Regardless of contemporary assessments, the belief in 1937 and 1938 was that the Treaty was largely to blame.

51. Tweedsmuir to Hardinge, March 16, 1938; and to Anna Buchan, March 19, 1938, both BP, LAC.

52. MKD, March 12, 1938, LAC.

53. Leopold Amery to Tweedsmuir, March 29, 1938, BP, LAC.

54. King's response would have been that Canada was not part of Europe and would confine itself to its affairs to the extent possible (MKD, March 14, 1938, LAC).

55. Chamberlain to Tweedsmuir, April 11, 1938, BP, LAC.

56. Tweedsmuir to King, April 23, 1938, MKP, LAC.

57. MKD, April 25, 1938, LAC.

58. At a dinner hosted by the British high commissioner in Ottawa, Sir Francis Floud, in honour of a visit by Lord and Lady Stanley, son of a former governor general, King used the occasion for "saying an appreciative word of Chamberlain and his colleagues."

59. Tweedsmuir to Anna Buchan, March 28, 1938, BP, LAC.

60. Tweedsmuir to Chamberlain, March 26, 1938, NCP, UBLSC; Tweedsmuir to Chamberlain, May 11, 1938, NCP, UBLSC; and Tweedsmuir to Anna Buchan, March 28, 1938, BP, LAC.

61. Chamberlain to Tweedsmuir, April 11, 1938, in which Chamberlain notes he received a letter from former Canadian prime minister Bennett, BP, LAC.

62. James, *Anthony Eden*, 174. It was a belief influenced by his experience at the 1937 Commonwealth Prime Ministers Conference, held in London to coincide with the coronation of George VI, and which had a "conspicuously pacifist tone." See also Peter Clarke, *Hope and Glory: Britain, 1900–1990* (London: Allen Lane, Penguin Press, 1996), 187; and Richard Lamb, *The Ghosts of Peace: 1935–1945* (London: Michael Russell, 1987), 48.

63. Tweedsmuir refers to these telegrams in a letter to Susan Tweedsmuir, June 6, 1938, BP, LAC.

64. For example, on May 16, 1938, Hardinge sent a five-page note to Tweedsmuir dealing with the German threat to Czechoslovakia, air expansion policy, and an agreement with Ireland, BP, LAC.

65. King to Tweedsmuir, September 6, 1938, BP, LAC.

66. Tweedsmuir to Stair Gillon, September 29, 1938, BP, LAC.

67. King to Tweedsmuir, September 16, 1938, BP, LAC.

68. Tweedsmuir to Chamberlain, September 29, 1938, NCP, UBLSC.

69. Chamberlain to Tweedsmuir, October 7, 1938, BP, LAC.

70. Tweedsmuir to Chamberlain, October 27, 1938, BP, LAC.

71. Ibid.

72. Tweedsmuir to Stair Gillon, October 27, 1938, BP, LAC.

73. Tweedsmuir to Halifax, November 5, 1938, BP, LAC.

74. Ibid.

75. "Billingsgate" was a derogatory term, derived from the name of a fish market in London and referring to the vulgar or offensive language often heard there.

76. Extracts from Chamberlain's speech in the British House of Commons were printed in the *New York Times*, November 2, 1938.

77. Winston Churchill, *The Gathering Storm*, 326, and *Their Finest Hour*, Vol. 2 of *The Second World War* (Boston: Houghton Mifflin, 1949), 550-551.

78. *New York Times*, November 8, 1938. The *Times* reported that a by-election in Dartford, Kent, resulted in the Labour candidate, a Jennie Adamson, winning, and noted that she stated that she won "because the electors disapprove of the government's foreign policy and are ashamed of Mr. Chamberlain's betrayal of Czechoslovakia and democracy."

79. *New York Times*, November 5, 1938.
80. Tweedsmuir to Roosevelt, October 31, 1938, BP, LAC.
81. *New York Times*, November 5, 1938.
82. *New York Times*, November 6, 1938.
83. Crawford to Tweedsmuir, November 12, 1938, BP, LAC.
84. Crawford to Tweedsmuir November 12, 1938, BP, LAC. For this shift in opinion, see also James, *Anthony Eden*, 196.
85. Tweedsmuir to Anna Buchan, November 7, 1938, BP, LAC.
86. Tweedsmuir to Crawford, November 26, 1938, BP, LAC.
87. Ibid.
88. Irving Abella and Harold Troper, *None Is Too Many* (Toronto: Lester & Orpen Dennys, 1986), 40.
89. Tweedsmuir to Crawford, November 26, 1938, BP, LAC.
90. See Lita-Rose Betcherman, *The Swastika and the Maple Leaf* (Don Mills, ON: Fitzhenry & Whiteside, 1975), 167. Four of the eleven chapters in the book focus specifically on fascist activities in Quebec; the other chapters also contain material on the movement in that province.
91. Michael Brown, "Zionism in the Pre-Statehood Years: The Canadian Response," in *From Immigration to Integration; The Canadian Jewish Experience*, edited by Ruth Cline and Frank Dimant (Toronto: B'nai Brith Canada, Institute for International Affairs, 2001), 121-134.
92. Ibid.
93. Tweedsmuir to Anna Buchan, April 11, 1938, BP, LAC.
94. *Gazette* (Montreal), April 12, 1938.
95. A copy of the "Dedication Souvenir to commemorate the opening of the new Holy Blossom Temple," was provided to the author on June 17, 2008, by Holy Blossom Temple, Toronto.
96. See, for Canadian government policy during this period, Abella and Troper, *None Is Too Many*, chaps. 1 and 2.
97. Patricia Clavin, "The Way to Make History: British Historians and the Shaping of American Foreign Policy, 1940–1945," in *Transatlantic Encounters: Public Uses and Misuses of History in Europe and the United States*, edited by D.K. Adams and M. Vaudagna (Amsterdam: VU University Press, 2000), 119-143.
98. Moritz Bonn to Tweedsmuir, December 15, 1938, BP, LAC.
99. Tweedsmuir to Anna Buchan, November 13, 1939, BP, LAC. At the same time as Bonn visited, the head of McGill University was also at Rideau Hall.
100. Mortiz J. Bonn, *The Wandering Scholar* (New York: John Day, 1948), 403; and Clavin, "The Way to Make History." While Bonn's autobiography makes only brief references to his work in propaganda for Germany

during the last years of the First World War and of his "information" activities in the United States during the Second World War, historian Patricia Clavin accessed private papers that confirm and clarify Bonn's work on behalf of the British.

101. Moritz Bonn to Tweedsmuir, December 15, 1938, BP, LAC.

102. Moritz Bonn to Tweedsmuir, December 15, 1938, BP, LAC. Bonn used benign card game analogies for a deadly situation, describing Chamberlain "as a gentlemen bridge player playing poker against card sharks and not wanting to see them in that light."

103. Tweedsmuir to Violet Markham, December 28, 1938, BP, LAC.

104. Tweedsmuir to Baldwin, December 12, 1938, BP, LAC.

105. Leopold Amery to Tweedsmuir, December 28, 1938, BP, LAC.

106. Crawford to Tweedsmuir, December 16, 1938, BP, LAC. Crawford described the German reaction to Chamberlain's moderate response to the Nazis' undiplomatic name-calling of former British prime minister Stanley Baldwin, whom the Nazis had labelled as a "gutter-snipe" and a "street arab." The Germans, including their ambassador in London, boycotted an international press dinner, of which they were the joint hosts. Crawford had many other anecdotes exposing the Nazis as "bandits," such as their forcing a Nobel Prize–winning, Jewish Viennese professor of pharmacology to hand over his £3,000 prize money from a bank in Oslo.

107. Ibid.

108. Tweedsmuir to Violet Markham, December 23, 1938, BP, LAC.

109. Ibid.

110. Bessborough to Tweedsmuir, December 6, 1938, BP, LAC. Bessborough also passed along the latest political humour making the rounds, about a conversation between Hitler, Mussolini, and Roosevelt. Mussolini said he would not be satisfied with less than half the world, while Hitler said that was impossible anyway because the Almighty had promised him the whole world, to which Roosevelt replied that he had promised no such thing!

111. Tweedsmuir to Violet Markham, December 28, 1938, BP, LAC.

112. Ibid.

113. Tweedsmuir to Anna Buchan, January 9, 1939, BP, LAC.

114. Tweedsmuir to Violet Markham, February 3; to Crawford, April 30; and to Anna Buchan, November 14, 1938, and February 6, 1939, BP, LAC.

115. Chamberlain to Tweedsmuir, February 7, 1939, NCP, UBLSC.

116. Leopold Amery to Tweedsmuir, January 24, 1939, BP, LAC.

117. Crawford to Tweedsmuir, January 24, 1939, BP, LAC.

118. Tweedsmuir to Hardinge, January 14, 1939, BP.

119. Bessborough to Tweedsmuir, April 4, 1939, BP, LAC.

120. Tweedsmuir to Anna Buchan, March 20, 1939, BP, LAC.
121. Hardinge to Tweedsmuir, March 30, 1939, BP, LAC.
122. Ibid.
123. Tweedsmuir to Anna Buchan, April 2, 1939, BP, LAC.
124. Tweedsmuir to Bessborough, April 28, 1939, BP, LAC.
125. Tweedsmuir to King, August 2, 1939, BP, LAC.
126. Tweedsmuir to King, August 10, 1939, BP, LAC.
127. Tweedsmuir to Stair Gillon, September 1, 1939, BP, LAC.

Chapter 10

1. Tweedsmuir to Hugh Macmillan, U.K. minister of information, September 11, 1939; and to Stair Gillon, September 23, 1939, both BP, LAC.
2. Mackenzie King, *Canada at Britain's Side* (Toronto: Macmillan Company of Canada, 1941), 14.
3. MKD, September 9, 1939, LAC.
4. The process is described in detail in Mackenzie King's diaries around these dates, in King's book *Canada At Britain's Side*, and also in Arnold Heeney's memoirs, *The Things That Are Caesar's*, 57.
5. "Proclamation," *Canada Gazette*, September 10, 1939, *www.collectionscanada .gc.ca/databases/canada-gazette/093/001060-119.01-e.php?document_id_ nbr=8420&image_id_nbr=301989&f=p&PHPSESSID=qod94dp57c1e1m v2qn9l9l3655* (accessed September 3, 2012).
6. The *Toronto Star* observed that the declaration of war was "another precedent in Canada's constitutional evolution." Other papers noted with varying positions and font sizes on their front pages that Canada was at war: The *Winnipeg Free Press*, "Historic Document Is Signed by King"; The *Halifax Herald*, "Canada Is At War"; *La Presse*, "Proclamation de l'état de guerre contre l'Allemagne." All newspapers dated September 11, 1939.
7. The *Winnipeg Free Press* noted the king's approval, while others, such as the *Ottawa Citizen* and Montreal's *La Presse*, referred only to the governor general. The *Halifax Herald* used both versions in different articles on the front page.
8. *New York Times*, September 11, 1939.
9. *Ottawa Citizen*, September 11, 1939.
10. Two days after Britain's declaration of war, impatience with Canada's delay was evident, as can be seen, for example, in the editorial of the *Ottawa Citizen*, September 5, 1939.
11. For a brief description of Mackenzie King's approach to conscription, see Bothwell, Drummond, and English, *Canada, 1900–1945*, 315.

12. Hardinge to Tweedsmuir, September 30, 1939, BP, LAC.

13. Some of the planes had been previously ordered by England and New Zealand; the order was valued at approximately eleven million dollars (See MKD, September 9, 1939, LAC).

14. As far back as 1920, Roosevelt condemned isolationism (See Black, *Roosevelt*, 126).

15. MKD, September 5 and 10, 1939, LAC. Information about the U.S. proclamations was widely reported in the press (See, for example, the *Ottawa Citizen*, September 6 and 8, 1939).

16. Tweedsmuir to Stair Gillon, Septermber 1, 1939; and to Lord Lothian, September 12, 1939, both BP, LAC.

17. Tweedsmuir to Stair Gillon, September 23, 1939; and to Ashley Cooper, November 14, 1939, both BP, LAC.

18. Tweedsmuir to Stair Gillon, September 23, 1939, BP, LAC

19. Ibid.

20. Robert Calder, *Beware the British Serpent: The Role of Writers in British Propaganda in the United States 1939–1945* (Montreal and Kingston, ON: McGill-Queen's University Press, 2004), 21. See also, among many other works: Nicholas John Cull, *Selling War* (Oxford: Oxford University Press, 1995), 6-9; Niall Ferguson, *Empire* (New York: Basic Books, 2003), for example, pages 88-89, 95, and 343-344; and Walter Johnson, *William Allen White's America* (New York: Henry Holt and Company, 1947), 520.

21. For a contemporary perspective, see Harold Lavine and James Wechsler, *War Propraganda and the United States*, 363. For American skepticism about the British Empire, see the same work, 225.

22. Calder, *Beware the British Serpent*, 41.

23. Cull, *Selling War*, 19.

24. Tweedsmuir to Roosevelt, September 8, 1939, RP, FDRL. Tweedsmuir also kept Ambassador Lord Lothian informed of his planned visit to Roosevelt, noting that because of the delicate situation, it might have to be cancelled (Tweedsmuir to Lothian, September 12, 1939, BP, LAC).

25. Ted Morgan, *FDR* (New York: Simon and Schuster, 1985), 513.

26. The power of public opinion in the United States was well known to John Buchan, who had written about it as early as 1930 (See *The Graphic*, May 10, 1930, BP, LAC).

27. In "Storms of Criticism Over Issuing War News," *Ottawa Citizen*, December 18, 1939, Macmillan was described as "a distinguished jurist who [was] well known in Canada." See also Macmillan's autobiography, *A Man of Law's Tale: The Reminiscences of the Rt. Hon. Lord Macmillan* (London: Macmillan, 1952), 140, where he describes "the honour which I

valued most highly of all was that which was paid to me by the Dominion of Canada"; and, especially, chapter 9, "The Ministry of Information."

28. Macmillan, *A Man of Law's Tale*, 166.
29. Macmillan, "The Pilgrim Trust," *A Man of Law's Tale*; and Smith, *John Buchan*, 25-26, and 327, n. 116, for a brief explanation of and reference to the Pilgrims.
30. Cull, *Selling War*, 6.
31. Tweedsmuir to Macmillan, September 5, 1939, BP, LAC; and MKD, September 6, 1939, LAC.
32. Tweedsmuir to Macmillan, September 11, 1939, BP, LAC.
33. Macmillan, *A Man of Law's Tale*, 165.
34. Macmillan to Tweedsmuir, September 10, 1939, BP, LAC.
35. A.C. Cummings, *Ottawa Citizen*, September 7, 1939. Tweedsmuir sarcastically attributed the problem-plagued and bloated Information Ministry "to the genius of Sam Hoare"; see Tweedsmuir to Leopold Amery, October 31, 1939, BP, LAC. See also Calder, *Beware the British Serpent*, 74; Macmillan, *A Man of Law's Tale*, chap. 9; and Lord Crawford's comment about there being "no material for the storyteller," in other words for the press, Crawford to Tweedsmuir, December 28, 1939, BP, LAC.
36. Aside from the reference in Tweedsmuir's September 11, 1939, letter to Macmillan, see also John Wheeler-Bennett, *Special Relationships: America in Peace and War* (London: Macmillan, 1975), 76-77.
37. Tweedsmuir to Macmillan, September 11, 1939, BP, LAC.
38. Ibid. Also informative in this regard are several articles by Peter Buitenhuis, *The Great War of Words: British, American, and Canadian Propaganda and Fiction, 1914–1933* (Vancouver: University of British Columbia Press, 1987), chaps. 7 and 10; and R. Jeffreys-Jones, "The Role of British Intelligence in the Mythologies Underpinning the OSS and Early CIA," *Intelligence and National Security* 15, no. 2 (Summer 2000): 5-19.
39. Cull, *Selling War*, 10. See also Clavin, "The Way to Make History," 124. This was a period when John Buchan was serving as chairman of Reuters, a position that was a legacy of his having been a government information representative on the board of Reuters.
40. Lavine and Wechsler, *War Propraganda*, 363.
41. Tweedsmuir to Macmillan, September 11, 1939, BP, LAC. This book is quoted in Calder, *Beware the British Serpent*, 56. Calder notes that none of the propaganda instruments used by Britain was "as problematic as that of lecturers and visitors to the United States." Other references to Rogerson's book and its impact are found in Lavine and Wechsler, *War Propraganda*.
42. Quoted in Calder, *Beware the British Serpent*, x.

43. Ibid., especially chapter 8, "Unheralded Ambassadors from England."

44. Ibid., 59, 61.

45. Ibid., especially 58-62.

46. Ibid., especially chap. 4, "Making the War Seem Personal: British Authors in the United States."

47. Tweedsmuir to Macmillan, September 11, 1939, BP, LAC.

48. Macmillan to Tweedsmuir, September 23, 1939, BP, LAC.

49. See Donald Read, *The Power of News: The History of Reuters* (Oxford: Oxford University Press, 1992), 431. John Buchan had been appointed as the British government's representative to the board of directors of Reuters during the war (1916–1917), and in 1919 was invited by the chairman, Sir Roderick Jones, to become a director, which Buchan remained until 1935. In a January 1938 message to Reuters employees, for the launch of an in-house magazine, Tweedsmuir recalled his close connection with the company and wrote of Reuters as "a great service, a service of truth and world peace. Its task has never been more important than today, not even in the Great War." Source: John Entwistle, group archivist, Reuters Ltd., email to the author, June 12, 2001.

50. Macmillan to Tweedsmuir, September 23, 1939, BP, LAC.

51. Clavin, "The Way to Make History," 120 and 126.

52. Tweedsmuir to Macmillan, September 11, 1939, BP, LAC. The eleven were: Hugh Bullock, a "distinguished member of the New York Stock Exchange"; Ferris Greenslet, a partner in Houghton Mifflin; Granville Clarke [sic]; Walter Stewart; Thomas Watson, the president of the International Chamber of Commerce; David Winton of Minneapolis, "the great lumberman"; Douglas Freeman; William Allen White of Kansas; William Clayton of Texas, "the largest cotton exporter in the U.S.A.," and a man who would subsequently join a group of thirty men to sign "A Summons to Speak Out," a declaration published in leading newspapers throughout the United States that called for U.S. intervention in the war on the side of Britain (See M.L. Chadwin, *The Hawks of World War II* (Chapel Hill, NC: University of North Carolina Press, 1968), 36); Bob Lovett, "a youngish man, but is probably the most respected financial authority in Wall Street"; and V. Cameron.

53. See Michael Redley, "John Buchan and *The Great Illusion*," *JBJ*, no. 37 (Autumn 2007): 33, and the reference to the use of non-official channels.

54. See, for example, Chadwin, *The Hawks of World War II*, 21-22 (White), 36 (Clayton), and 149 (Clark). See also the biography on Clark by Norman Cousins, and J.G. Clifford, eds., *Memoirs of a Man: Grenville Clark* (New York: W.W. Norton & Company, 1975), 319; for White see

The Autobiography of William Allen White (New York: Macmillan, 1946), and also Douglas Fairbanks Jr., *The Salad Days* (New York: Doubleday, 1988), 431.

55. Referred to in Lownie, *Presbyterian Cavalier*, 159.

56. Johnson, *William Allen White's America*, 309. Johnson notes that after the Paris Peace Conference in 1919, White travelled to London, where he had a "chance to renew his friendship with Norman Angell, Frederick Whyte, H.G. Wells, and John Buchan." Frederick Whyte became director of the American Division in the Ministry of Information at the beginning of the Second World War. See pages 521 and 527 for examples of White's correspondence with President Roosevelt regarding public opinion.

57. *Ottawa Citizen*, November 23, 1936.

58. Arrangements are found in a letter from Lothian to Tweedsmuir, September 13, 1939, BP, LAC; and in Tweedsmuir's response to Lothian, October 9, 1939, BP, LAC. The account of their meeting is in a letter from Tweedsmuir to Macmillan, October 26, 1939, BP, LAC. The first Stephenson biographer, H.M. Hyde, notes that Stephenson worked "intimately" and "informally" with Lothian (H.M. Hyde, *The Quiet Canadian: The Secret Service Story of Sir William Stephenson* (London: Hamish Hamilton, 1962), 48, 57).

59. Tweedsmuir to Chamberlain, September 19, 1939, NCP, UBLSC.

60. Lothian to Tweedsmuir, September 13, 1939, BP, LAC. See also Butler, *Lord Lothian*, 272. Stories of the situation in Britain are described in letters to Tweedsmuir from Crawford (November 2, 1939); from Violet Markham (October 23, 1939); and from Leopold Amery (October 9, 1939): all letters BP, LAC. These letters describe such problems as, for example, evacuation plans from London being ignored; the excessively large and ineffectual Ministry of Information; and the strange and costly plans for distribution of fish in the event that all fish markets were simultaneously bombed and distribution therefore disrupted.

61. Tweedsmuir to Chamberlain, September 19, 1939, NCP, UBLSC.

62. See Stewart, *Burying Caesar*, especially page 393, for a broad commentary on Chamberlain's inadequacy. Also, senior Conservative MP Leopold Amery wrote to Tweedsmuir; describing the Cabinet, he noted that its weakness, in addition to being structural, was personal; he referred specifically to Chamberlain, calling him a "civilian of civilians," who "detests war" and functions out of "a sense of duty and not with any passionate or joyous thirst for victory," October 10, 1939, BP, LAC. Violet Markham wrote to Tweedsmuir that Chamberlain was "a very poor judge of character," October 23, 1939, BP, LAC.

63. Tweedsmuir to Chamberlain, September 19, 1939, NCP, UBLSC.

64. Tweedsmuir's correspondent Lord Crawford, a man described as a Conservative elder statesman (Paul Addison, *Churchill: The Unexpected Hero* (Oxford: Oxford University Press, 2005), 158), had also been very critical of Churchill, but he too had come round to seeing Churchill as the "only figure in the [C]abinet with the virtue of uncompromising aggressive victory."

65. Chamberlain to Tweedsmuir, September 25, 1939, NCP, UBLSC.

66. See, for example, Black, *Roosevelt*, 423; Freidel, *Roosevelt*, 313; and Stewart, *Burying Caesar*, 284-285.

67. Chamberlain to Tweedsmuir, September 25, 1939, NCP, UBLSC.

68. Ibid.

69. Tweedsmuir to Chamberlain, October 16, 1939, NCP, UBLSC.

70. The Nazi leader's logic, based not unreasonably on Britain's and France's respective records of appeasement, had led him to conclude that since those countries had declared war to save Poland, and since Poland was lost, there was no need for them to continue fighting (Sir Llewellyn Woodward, *British Foreign Policy in the Second World War*, Vol. 1 (Oxford: Oxford University Press, 1970), 13). Churchill dealt with this offer from Hitler in Volume 1 of his history of the Second World War, noting that Hitler had not appreciated the profound change that had occurred in Chamberlain's views and in the policies of the British Commonwealth (Churchill, *The Gathering Storm*, 454-455). See also, Stewart, *Burying Casear*, 391-392.

71. Tweedsmuir to Chamberlain, October 16, 1939, NCP, UBLSC; and Tweedsmuir to Alexander Hardinge, October 2, 1939, BP, LAC. Also, Winston Churchill, *Churchill In His Own Voice* (Audio cassette. Abridged edition. New York: Caedmon Audio, Harper, 1994).

72. Chamberlain to his sister Hilda, October 1, 1939, NCP, UBLSC. Chamberlain also mentioned in the letter that he took the same view as Churchill as regards the Russian-German relationship. Chamberlain was still receiving vast numbers of letters (2,450 in a three-day period during the first week of October), three-quarters of which wanted to "stop the war in one form or another," giving him concern about those he termed, perhaps surprisingly given his recent record, the "peace-at-any-price people" (Chamberlain to sister Ida, October 8, 1939, NCP, UBLSC). Chamberlain had, indeed, turned away from his previous ways, writing, "[t]he difficulty is that you cannot believe anything Hitler says … the only chance of peace is the disappearance of Hitler and that is what we are working for."

73. Tweedsmuir to Lothian, December 12, 1939, BP, LAC. Lothian had sought Tweedsmuir's opinion on it; see, for example, Lothian to Tweedsmuir, December 8, 1939, BP, LAC.

74. One year later, however, it was the British who produced a film that was a success in the United States. The Ministry of Information released *London Can Take It*, about the Blitz, but it was narrated by Americans and distributed by Warner Brothers in the United States, thus disguising its origins. The impact was significant on American public opinion (See Black, *Roosevelt*, 582).

75. Tweedsmuir to Halifax, January 1, 1940, BP, LAC.

76. Tweedsmuir to Alexander Hardinge, October 2, 1939, BP, LAC.

77. Ibid.

78. *Gazette* (Montreal), November 13, 1939. The role for women was changing. As the armed forces grew in size, industry was deprived of workers, resulting in calls for greater numbers of women to be hired to replace the men. See Churchill, *The Gathering Storm*, 555; and for Canada, see Bothwell, Drummond, and English, *Canada, 1900–1945*, 379.

79. Hardinge to Tweedsmuir, November 12, 1939, BP, LAC.

80. *New York Times*, November 12, 1939.

81. Butler, *Lord Lothian*, 270. Churchill described American public opinion in terms of "tides and currents" (Cited in Black, *Roosevelt*, 327). See also Hull, *Memoirs*, 733-735.

82. Black, *Roosevelt*, 437. As Black recounts, a proposal by Congressman Louis Ludlow to require a referendum for a declaration of war was defeated by 209 to 188, demonstrating significant support for what Black justly describes as "fantastic naïveté."

83. Tweedsmuir to Macmillan, October 26, 1939, BP.

84. Tweedsmuir to Macmillan, September 11, 1939; to Lothian, September 12, 1939; and Lothian to Tweedsmuir, September 13, 1939, in which he replied: "I agree entirely with your views about propaganda in the United States." All BP, LAC.

85. Roosevelt to Tweedsmuir, October 5, 1939, RP, FDRL.

86. Shuldham Redfern to O.D. Skelton, N.d., External Affairs, LAC.

87. O.D. Skelton to Loring Christie, October 14, 1939, External Affairs, LAC.

88. Loring Christie to O.D. Skelton, October 17, 1939, External Affairs, LAC. Christie "believed there were no fundamental differences between American interests and those of the British Empire. A tacit alliance with the United States should be the supreme objective of British policy" (Bothwell, Drummond, and English, *Canada, 1900–1945*, 233).

89. Ibid.

90. Corliss Lamont, ed., *The Thomas Lamonts in America* (New York: A.S. Barnes and Company, 1962), 92. Buchan had met Lamont in 1917 when Lamont was "an unofficial advisor to President Woodrow Wilson's U.S.

Government Mission, headed by Colonel E.M. House." References in the Lamont memoir to various common friends are found on pages 93, 98, 99, and 119. Buchan's friendship with Lamont is also referred to in "Willard Connely and the Buchans," *JBJ*, no. 37 (Autumn 2007): 13-17.

91.   Black, *Roosevelt*, 134, 200.

92.   Tweedsmuir to King, October 25, 1939, BP, LAC. The meeting with Rockefeller, whom Tweedsmuir described as "a wonderful type of public-spirited citizen," had been arranged by King, who had worked for the Rockefellers during the First World War and who had maintained contact with them. Conant would later become a member of a highly secret group established by Roosevelt to investigate the development of the atom bomb. The other names, while not mentioned explicitly, can be inferred from a variety of other correspondence. See also Cousins and Clifford, eds., *Memoirs of a Man*, 319.

93.   Tweedsmuir to Macmillan, October 26, 1939, BP, LAC.

94.   Wheeler-Bennett, *Special Relationships*, 67.

95.   Tweedsmuir to Macmillan, October 26, 1939, BP, LAC. Tweedsmuir's use of the slang for illicit drugs is in itself interesting because it reveals he was conscious of the real commodity he was dealing with — intelligence, which has been compared to a drug to which government officials become addicted.

96.   See F.H. Hinsley et al., *British Intelligence in the Second World War*, Vol. 1 (London: Her Majesty's Stationery Office, 1979), 312; Vol. 4 (1990), 143; William Stevenson, *A Man Called Intrepid* (New York: Ballantine Books, 1976), chap. 16; and Hyde, *The Quiet Canadian*, 2, 3, 50, and 73.

97.   Hyde, *The Quiet Canadian*, 48 and 57. Stephenson biographer, William Stevenson, however, writes that "[Lothian] was bypassed." Though both biographers worked with Intrepid's organization, Hyde's account seems the stronger in light of the fact that *Time* magazine, in July 1940, described Lothian as "the most popular British [a]mbassador" in Washington since James Bryce at the beginning of the 1900s, and in light of views Lothian expressed to Tweedsmuir in correspondence and with the content of Lothian's speeches which counter reasons Stevenson gives for Lothian being bypassed (mainly because he had been an appeaser).

98.   Wheeler-Bennett, *Special Relationships*, 155.

99.   Stevenson, writing in the context of the attitudes of Roosevelt and the American public toward Britain, referred to "such private counsellors as William Allen White" who would help encourage American support for Britain (*Intrepid*, 137). White, like many other Americans, was at first skeptical, after the years it had spent in appeasement of Germany,

of British conviction to prosecute a war, and believed Britain would lose soon in any case. It took the fall of France in May 1940 and the work of the Ministry of Information, and, more particularly, the work of Ambassador Lothian, to convince America that the defeat of Britain was a threat to the United States.

100. David Dimbleby, and David Reynolds, *An Ocean Apart: the Relationship Between Britain and America in the Twentieth Century* (New York: Random House, 1988), 138-139.

101. Robert P. Browder, and Thomas G. Smith, *Independent: A Biography of Lewis W. Douglas* (New York: Alfred A. Knopf, 1986), 148.

102. Fairbanks, *Salad Days*, 307-309. Tweedsmuir had invited Fairbanks to Ottawa in December 1938, most likely to discuss extending to the United States the planned visit to Canada the following spring by King George VI and Queen Elizabeth. It was an idea that Fairbanks had apparently suggested previously. Tweedsmuir wrote to his sister, Anna Buchan, that it was "useful to have someone like him on the Pacific coast to keep the British Flag flying" (Tweedsmuir to Anna Buchan, December 19, 1938, BP, LAC).

103. Brian Connell, *Knight Errant: A Biography of Douglas Fairbanks Jr.* (London: Hodder & Stoughton, 1955), 80; and a brief Canadian Press wire service article dated December 17, 1938, that appeared in Canadian newspapers and even the *New York Times* on December 18, 1938. Ultimately, the proposed film went nowhere, but Fairbanks's social and political contacts in Britain continued to grow, as did his interest in world affairs.

104. "Lord Lothian's Job," *Time*, July 8, 1940.

105. Lavine and Wechsler, *War Propaganda*, 220.

106. Cull, *Selling War*; and Watt, *Succeeding John Bull*, 97-98. Both are cited in Roberts, *Holy Fox*. See also Calder, *Beware the British Serpent*.

107. Wheeler-Bennett, *Special Relationships*, quotations from pages 68 and 93 respectively.

108. The assessment of the New York-based Institute for Propaganda Analysis was expressed in its May 1940 publication of Lavine and Wechsler's *War Propaganda and the United States*, 225.

109. Smith, *John Buchan*, 367. See also Roberts, *Holy Fox*, 282.

110. *New York Times*, October 26, 1939; and A.P. Baker, *History of the Pilgrims* (London: Profile Books, 2002).

111. Lord Lothian (Philip Kerr), *The American Speeches of Lord Lothian*, (Oxford: Royal Institute of International Affairs, Oxford University Press, 1941). Lothian died in December 1940.

112. Lothian, *Speeches*.

113. Noted in Calder, *Beware the British Serpent*, 42.

114. The contemporary assessment (May 1940) by Lavine and Wechsler, *War Propaganda*, 181, notes this distinction and how Lothian's focus on democracy and shared values contradicted the views of Chamberlain and others in the British government documents whose writings were "attired in imperialist phrases." Lothian's approach, with the support of and input from Tweedsmuir, was the more successful.

115. *New York Times*, October 27, 1939.

116. Garet Garrett, *Defend America First: the Anti-War Editorials of The Saturday Evening Post 1939–1942* (Caldwell, ID: Caxton Press, 2003), 32.

117. Tweedsmuir to Macmillan, September 11, 1939, BP, LAC.

118. Lothian biographer J.R.M. Butler wrote that the ambassador's views were to avoid propaganda in America and never to presume to "teach them their duty" (Butler, *Lothian*, 266). There is, however, no real discussion of the development of these views. Wheeler-Bennett, *Special Relationships*, 93, describes Lothian's "thesis" for approaching the United States and expresses it as the zenith of the ambassador's courage and wisdom. Tweedsmuir contributed to Lothian's approach and helped Lothian to express it so effectively with this first important speech.

119. *Ottawa Citizen*, October 28, 1939.

120. Lothian, *Speeches*.

121. Tweedsmuir to Hardinge, January 20, 1940, BP, LAC; Tweedsmuir to Chamberlain, November 2, 1939, NCP, UBLSC; see also Butler, introduction to *Lothian*.

122. Tweedsmuir to Macmillan, October 26, 1939, BP, LAC.

123. Tweedsmuir to Lothian, February 3, 1940, BP, LAC.

124. Lothian, *Speeches*. Subsequent speeches were delivered to the *New York Herald Tribune* Forum, October 26, 1939; Swarthmore College, Pennsylvania, November 11; the fiftieth anniversary celebration for Barnard College, November 14; at the Library of Congress for deposit of Magna Carta, November 28; and to the Chicago Council of Foreign Relations, January 4.

125. Tweedsmuir to Lothian, February 3, 1940, BP, LAC.

126. Roberts, *Holy Fox*, 276-284.

127. Calder, *Beware the British Serpent*, chaps. 1 and 2.

Chapter 11

1. C.P. Stacey, *Six Years of War: The Army in Canada, Britain, and the Pacific*, Vol. 1 of *The Official History of the Army of Canada In the Second World*

War (Ottawa: Minister of National Defence, Queen's Printer, 1955), 4; and C.P. Stacey, *The Canadian Army 1939–1945: An Official Historical Summary* (Ottawa: Minister of National Defence, King's Printer, 1948), 1-2. Subsequent figures in this paragraph are also from this source.

2. See, for example, *Globe* (Toronto), August 24, 1936.
3. Stacey, *Canadian Army*, 1.
4. Ibid., 11. See also House of Commons, *Debates*, Fifth (Special War) Session, September 7, 1939, 19; and MKD, September 8, 1939, LAC.
5. House of Commons, *Debates*, Fifth (Special War) Session, September 7, 1939, 19.
6. *Ottawa Citizen*, September 9, 1939.
7. Tweedsmuir to Hardinge, October 2, 1939, BP, LAC. Tweedsmuir, who undoubtedly echoed reports and information he received both officially and unofficially, noted the poor condition of the Defence Department "owing to the chaos" it had been in. For official renderings of the situation, see C.P. Stacey, *Arms, Men & Governments: War Policies of Canada* (Ottawa: Queen's Printer, 1970); and, by the same author, *Six Years of War*, chap. 1.
8. Tweedsmuir to Stair Gillon, September 23, 1939, BP, LAC.
9. Betcherman, *The Swastika and the Maple Leaf*, especially pages 86, 93, and 94.
10. Tweedsmuir to Chamberlain, October 31, 1939, NCP, UBLSC.
11. Directorate of Staff Duties, General Staff, Department of National Defence, "The Recruiting Problem in the Province of Quebec: A Military Appreciation," Ottawa, June 7, 1941. DND, DHH-112.3S2.
12. Stacey, *Six Years of War*, app. B.
13. Tweedsmuir to Leopold Amery, October 31, 1939, BP, LAC. The importance of air power was a prevailing opinion: "the Navy could lose the war but only the Air Force could win it" (Churchill, *Their Finest Hour*, 458).
14. Tweedsmuir to Chamberlain, November 1939 2, NCP, UBLSC.
15. Ibid.
16. Described in Hatch, *The Aerodrome of Democracy*, chap. 1. See also Churchill, *The Gathering Storm*, chap. 13 and app. D, for Churchill's warnings about German air power surpassing that of Britain and France.
17. Greenhous et al., *The Crucible of War*, 13 and 18.
18. Cited in Hatch, *The Aerodrome of Democracy*, 5.
19. Ibid., 7-8.
20. Tweedsmuir to Susan Tweedsmuir, in England for a holiday, May 25, 1938, BP, LAC.
21. Hatch, *The Aerodrome of Democracy*, 13.

22. Described in Tweedsmuir's letters to Sir Alexander Hardinge, November 9, 1939, BP, LAC; and to Anna Buchan, November 6 and 20, 1939, BP, LAC.

23. Tweedsmuir to Anna Buchan, November 6, 1939, BP, LAC.

24. Tweedsmuir to Chamberlain, November 2, 1939, NCP, UBLSC.

25. Ibid.

26. Ibid.

27. These details are described in Hatch, *The Aerodrome of Democracy*, 17.

28. MKD, October 31, 1939, LAC.

29. Tweedsmuir to Chamberlain, November 2, 1939, NCP, UBLSC.

30. MKD, October 31, 1939, LAC.

31. Tweedsmuir to Crawford, November 25, 1939, BP, LAC.

32. King to Tweedsmuir, December 12, 1939, BP, LAC. See also Hatch, *The Aerodrome of Democracy*, 21-26; and Greenhous et al., *The Crucible of War*, 20-23.

33. MKD, December 10, 1939, LAC.

34. MKD, December 14, 1939, LAC.

35. MKD, December 16, 1939, LAC.

36. Ibid.

37. Ibid.

38. Ibid.

39. "British Air Training Plan," Department of National Defence, Directorate of History and Heritage, n.d.

40. MKD, December 16, 1939, LAC. Buchan biographer Janet Adam Smith noted Tweedsmuir's private secretary, Shuldham Redfern, did not have a similar observation (Smith, 460). However, Mackenzie King records that Redfern was not in the room at the time of signing, and therefore would have only briefly seen the air marshal pass by (MKD, December 16, 1939, LAC).

41. Ibid.

42. *Ottawa Citizen*, December 18, 1939.

43. Ibid.

44. King to Tweedsmuir, handwritten letter, December 24, 1939, BP, LAC.

45. Chamberlain to Tweedsmuir, December 27, 1939, BP, LAC.

46. Tweedsmuir to Chamberlain, December 16, 1939, BP, LAC.

47. Tweedsmuir to Chamberlain, December 16, 1939, BP, LAC.

48. Hardinge to Tweedsmuir, December 21, 1939, BP, LAC.

49. Tweedsmuir to Anna Buchan, January 29, 1940, BP, LAC.

50. Bothwell, Drummond, and English, *Canada, 1900–1945*, 319.

51. Other leaders, such as Churchill, confirmed this assessment later, noting that Purvis was "a man of outstanding ability" and "enjoyed the confidence of the Americans to a remarkable degree" (Churchill, *Their Finest Hour*,

555; and Hyde, *The Quiet Canadian*, 27). Purvis also later assisted William Stephenson, head of British Security Coordination in New York City.

52. Tweedsmuir to Chamberlain, October 16, 1939, NCP, UBLSC; the *Gazette* (Montreal), November 8, 1939; and the *Canadian Who's Who* (London: Times Publishing, 1936).
53. *Ottawa Citizen*, November 9, 1939.
54. Tweedsmuir to D.M. Spencer, January 25, 1940, BP, LAC.
55. Cited in Black, *Roosevelt*, 654.
56. *New York Times*, October 2, 1939.
57. See, for example, the *Gazette* (Montreal), and the *Globe and Mail* (Toronto), November 4, 1939.
58. Tweedsmuir to Hardinge, November 9, 1939, BP, LAC. There is no other indication in the correspondence as to the identity of the individual.
59. Tweedsmuir to Duncan M. Spencer, January 25, 1940, BP, LAC. This is the same individual Tweedsmuir had recommended to Lord Macmillan back in September as the principal contact to help put together a group of Americans to keep a "watching brief" for Britain's cause.
60. Attached to a letter from Tweedsmuir to Graham Towers, January 25, 1940, BP, LAC.
61. It is unknown what the outcome was of this information forwarded to Duncan M. Spencer and the governor of the Bank of Canada.
62. Tweedsmuir to Anna Buchan, November 27, 1939, BP, LAC.
63. Tweedsmuir to Anna Buchan, November 20, 1939, BP, LAC.
64. "Johnnie" went on to command the Hastings and Prince Edward Regiment, based in Belleville, ON, in the Italian campaign.
65. Tweedsmuir to Stair Gillon, January 19, 1940, BP, LAC.
66. J.H. Beith to Tweedsmuir, December 23, 1939, BP, LAC.
67. Ibid.
68. Tweedsmuir, Speech to Blackwatch Regiment, Montreal, October 27, 1939, BP, LAC.
69. Tweedsmuir to J.H. Beith, January 9, 1940, BP, LAC.
70. Ibid.
71. Ibid. The British had their own concerns in this regard, as Tweedsmuir's friend Lord Crawford indicated in a letter dated December 28, 1939 (BP, LAC): "Our Brass-hats out there must be conscious of all this — how boredom produces staleness, and how staleness breeds worse things; and I hope they are closely watching this phase of army psychology."
72. Tweedsmuir to J.H. Beith, January 9, 1940, BP, LAC.
73. The first type was "some man of affairs whose words carry weight," such as George Lloyd, who was from a Birmingham industrial family, had become

a lord, and who, in May 1940, would be named by Churchill as secretary of state for the colonies. The second type of person could be a Scotsman, Tweedsmuir thought, to appeal to "the hordes of our fellow countrymen here" — a recommendation that suggested Beith himself. Beith would in fact travel to the United States "on detached duty," an ambiguous term describing "the role of so many of the touring British writers" (See Calder, *Beware the British Serpent*, 82-83). Tweedsmuir named two other Scotsmen, Walter Elliot, a friend of Tweedsmuir who had been made the minister of health, and Iain Colquhoun, from a long line of Scottish baronets (see Lownie, "John Buchan," *JBJ*, no. 32 (Autumn 2006)). Finally, he proposed "a practical idealist who can give, with discretion, some notion of our ultimate war purpose," suggesting a Professor Norwood of St. John's College, Oxford.

74. Quotes in this paragraph are taken from MKD, January 15, 1940, LAC.
75. Tweedsmuir to Chamberlain, January 10, 1940, NCP, UBLSC.
76. The speech was widely reported. See for example "Ranks Closing for Battle," *Ottawa Citizen*, January 10, 1940; and the *New York Times*, 1, 4, January 10, 1940.
77. Tweedsmuir to Chamberlain, January 10, 1940, NCP, UBLSC.
78. Chamberlain to his sister Hilda, January 13, 1940, NCP, UBLSC.
79. Chamberlain to his sister Ida, October 22, 1939; and January 20 and 27, 1940: all NCP, UBLSC.
80. Canadian Community Newspapers Association, "Book of Honour," www .ccna.ca (accessed August 17, 2011). After the war Thompson went on to become recognized as the dean of the public relations profession in Canada.
81. Gary Evans, *John Grierson and the National Film Board: The Politics of Wartime Propaganda* (Toronto: University of Toronto Press, 1984), 57. See also MKD December 5, 1939, LAC.
82. MKD, December 14, 1939, LAC.
83. MKD, December 8, 1939, LAC.
84. Brockington contributed to a book by Tweedsmuir's widow, Susan Tweedsmuir, comp., *Wife and Friends*, (see page 304). Brockington also acted as intermediary between Lady Tweedsmuir and automaker Sam McLaughlin, persuading the latter to purchase Buchan's library from the Tweedsmuir home in Elsefield. McLaughlin donated it to Queen's University in Kingston, Ontario (See Queen's University Archives; *JBJ* (Spring 2005); and Heather Robertson, *Driving Force: The McLaughlin Family and the Age of the Car* (Toronto: McClelland & Stewart, 1995)).
85. MKD, December 20 and 21, 1939, LAC.

86. See Evans, *John Grierson*, 56-58. Grierson had also been an advisor to the Imperial Relations Trust and had earlier been tasked to travel to the Dominions to report on film production, with the objective of suggesting how relations between Britain and the Dominions could be strengthened if war erupted.

87. Tweedsmuir to Halifax, January 1, 1940, BP, LAC.

88. See MKD, November 15, 16, 1939, LAC; and December 5, 6, and 8, 1939, LAC. King's attitudes and the related political environment are described in Evans, *John Grierson*, 56-58.

89. Tweedsmuir to Stair Gillon, October 27, 1939, BP, LAC.

90. See for example, the *Gazette* (Montreal), November 13-15, 1939. In "The Day After Tomorrow," *Winnipeg Free Press*, December 1, 1939, the paper reported that a group of experts "[was] at work on details of the peace." A speech by Chamberlain delivered on January 10, which is discussed later in this chapter, also deals with the future. See Roberts, *Holy Fox*, 251-252 for comments with regard to Lord Halifax, who was also minister responsible for war aims.

91. Reference to the post-war phase and to Keynes's plan was made in an editorial of the *Ottawa Citizen*, December 18, 1939.

92. David Reynolds, *The Creation of the Anglo-American Alliance, 1937-41: A Study in Competitive Co-operation* (Chapel Hill, NC: University of North Carolina Press, 1982), 70.

93. Tweedsmuir to Baldwin, December 28, 1939, BP, LAC.

94. Tweedsmuir to Anna Buchan, January 1, 1940, BP, LAC.

95. *Halifax Herald*, January 6, 1940. Material in this paragraph was gleaned from articles in the *Halifax Herald*, January 5, 6, 8, and 10, 1940, and from the Tweedsmuir correspondence.

96. Tweedsmuir to Stair Gillon, January 19, 1940, BP, LAC.

97. Tweedsmuir to Anna Buchan, January 8, 1940, BP, LAC. Other details of his Halifax visit are contained in a letter Tweedsmuir sent to Neville Chamberlain, January 10, 1940, NCP, UBLSC.

98. Tweedsmuir to Anna Buchan, January 15, 1940, BP, LAC.

99. Tweedsmuir to King, January 10, 1940, BP, LAC.

100. Tweedsmuir to Anna Buchan, January 15, 1940, BP, LAC.

101. The law firm was Root, Clark, Buckner & Ballantine, 31 Nassau Street. Clark became a special assistant to Secretary of War Henry L. Stimson in the autumn of 1941 after he recommended Stimson to Roosevelt (Clark and Roosevelt were both young lawyers in the law firm Carter, Ladyard and Milburn (Cited in Black, *Roosevelt*, 561)). He has been described as a "statesman incognito" because of his behind the scenes work (J. Garry Clifford, "Grenville Clark: World Peace Through World Law," harvardsquarelibrary

.org (*www.harvardsquarelibrary.org/unitarians/clark_grenville.html*, accessed April 14, 2013). Elihu Root won the Nobel Peace Prize in 1912 and founded the U.S. Council on Foreign Relations in 1918.

102. Tweedsmuir to Grenville Clark, January 15, 1940, BP, LAC.

103. Grenville Clark continued to be an active advocate of world government, publishing three editions, with Louis B. Sohn, of *World Peace Through World Law*, through Harvard University Press, in 1960, 1962, and 1966. This from an individual who also believed in preparedness, supporting conscription in the United States for both world wars.

104. Tweedsmuir to Grenville Clark, January 15, 1940, BP, LAC. Clark was also one of seven directors of Harvard University, along with Dr. Conant, with whom Tweedsmuir had met in New York and maintained communication.

105. See King, *Canada at Britain's Side*, 20; the *Ottawa Citizen*, December 18, 1939, quoting Conservative leader Dr. R.J. Manion as saying Canada "should create a competent body to study and prepare for the problems of peace"; and the *Gazette* (Montreal), December 18, 1939, quoting principal-elect of McGill University, F. Cyril James, who warned of "economic problems and other post-war responsibilities which could not be overemphasized," especially the reorganization and adaption of the Canadian war economy to a peacetime economy.

106. Tweedsmuir to Macmillan, October 26, 1939, BP, LAC.

107. Tweedsmuir to Leopold Amery, October 31, 1939, BP, LAC. Amery did, however, presciently envisage the possibility of a post-war Germany willing "to live and let live as a member of a European Commonwealth."

108. Office of the Historian, Bureau of Public Affairs, United States Department of State, "Milestones: 1937-1945: The Atlantic Conference and Charter, 1941," http://history.state.gov (*http://history.state.gov/milestones/1937–1945/AtlanticConf* (accessed March 4, 2013)).

109. Hardinge to Tweedsmuir, December 21, 1939, BP, LAC.

110. By the time Hardinge died in May 1960, he had lived to see the creation of the European Coal and Steel Community in 1951, and in 1957, the creation of both the European Economic Community (or Common Market) and the European Atomic Energy Community. All of these "communities" eventually became the European Union.

111. Tweedsmuir to Hardinge, January 20, 1940, BP, LAC; and Tweedsmuir to Chamberlain, November 2, 1939, NCP, UBLSC.

112. Tweedsmuir to Stair Gillon, January 19, 1940, BP, LAC.

113. Tweedsmuir to Grenville Clark, January 23, 1940, BP, LAC. Additional comments can also be found in Tweedsmuir to Cecil, January 24, 1940, BP, LAC.

114. Tweedsmuir to Grenville Clark, January 23, 1940, BP, LAC.

115. This theme of leadership passing from Britain to the United States is dealt with extensively, with several quotes from Tweedsmuir, in Niall Ferguson, *Empire: The Rise and Demise of the British World Order and the Lessons for Global Power* (New York: Basic Books, 2002).

116. Cousins and Clifford, eds., introduction to *Memoirs of a Man*, and page 22.

117. Kenneth Rose, *The Later Cecils* (London: Weidenfeld and Nicolson, 1975), 152-153; and MacMillan, *Paris 1919*, 87.

118. Nobel Foundation. "Nobel Peace Prize 1937: Robert Cecil," nobelprize. org (*www.nobelprize.org/peace/laureates/1937/chelwood-bio.html*, accessed March 2006). See also K. Rose, *The Later Cecils,* 127-184.

119. In his 1987 biography of Murray (*Gilbert Murray, OM, 1866–1957* (Oxford: Oxford University Press, 1987)), Duncan Wilson writes, referring to this period in Murray's life, that the "voluminous correspondence on [League of Nations Union] affairs shows how Murray was till the end looked to for his opinion and counsel" (387–388). An account of Cecil's activity is found in his semi-autobiographical book, *A Great Experiment* (London: Jonathan Cape, 1941), 390. See also, K. Rose, *The Later Cecils*. It is an interesting historical twist that Cecil and Moritz Bonn both participated in the Paris Peace Conference, but on opposite sides, then in the first months of the next war were both connected, on the same side, to Buchan. See also Roberts, *Holy Fox*, 252.

120. Tweedsmuir to Grenville Clark, January 23, 1940, BP, LAC.

121. Carnegie Endowment for International Peace, "100 Years of Impact: A Timeline of the Carnegie Endowment for International Peace," www.carnegieendowment.org (*carnegieendowment.org/about/timeline100/index.html*, accessed March 2006). The first president Carnegie chose for his foundation was Elihu Root, of the same law firm as Grenville Clark. He served until 1925.

122. Tweedsmuir to Grenville Clark, January 23, 1940, BP, LAC.

123. Tweedsmuir to Cecil, January 24, 1940, BP, LAC.

Chapter 12

1. This is a point he expressed during his speech at a Canada Club dinner in London two months after his appointment (See "Speech to Canada Club dinner, London, U.K.," in Buchan, *Canadian Occasions*, 9).

2. Tweedsmuir to Baldwin, March 24, 1936, BP, LAC.

3. Buchan, *Minto*, 180.

4. Jean I. Wright and Marion W. DeBoice, both daughters of Alec Fraser, "letters," *JBJ*, no. 6 (Autumn 1986): 30-32. Fraser's letter is referred to in a letter from Tweedsmuir to John Edgar, January 11,1936, BP, LAC.

5. J.W. Jeffrey, letter to the author, June 8, 1995; and later phone conversation.

6. John (Jack) W. Jeffrey, William's son, letter to the author, June 8, 1995. William Jeffrey was invited to Rideau Hall early in 1936 for an afternoon and each year after, until the war. Jeffrey was made to feel comfortable; as he later repeated to his son, Tweedsmuir enjoyed the visits: "I could not contemplate month after month of 'Your Excellency this and Your Excellency that' without being able to schedule a few hours talking about the past with someone with whom I can be on a first name basis."

7. There are many references to this aspect of his character, observed by those who worked for him and by friends. Buchan refers to this himself in his memoir, *Memory Hold-the-Door*, see 40-41, 93, 111, and 147.

8. Details taken from *La Presse* (Montreal), November 23 and 25, 1935. Houde was first elected mayor in 1928, defeated in 1932, then elected mayor once again in 1934. He would be defeated again in 1936 and re-elected mayor in 1938.

9. Reuben Gold Thwaites, ed. *The Jesuit Relations and Allied Documents: Travels and Explorations of the Jesuit Missionaries in New France, 1610–1791.* Vol. 57, *Lower Canada, Abenakis, Louisiana, 1716–1727* (Cleveland: Burrows Brothers, 1896–1901). Originals scanned and transcribed by Thom Mentrak; formatted and organized by Raymond A. Bucko for Creighton University, *http://puffin.creighton.edu/jesuit/relations/relations_67.html*, accessed June 29, 2008), no. 3. "Claude de Ramezay was born at La Gaise, France, in 1657, the descendant of a noble Scottish family (Ramsay, Gallicized to Ramezay)."

10. This can be roughly translated as: "In order to get to the heart of French Canada, there could be no better way than through the quality of being Scottish."

11. Details of the speech in *La Presse* (Montreal), November 25, 1935.

12. Buchan, *Canadian Occasions*, 18.

13. Ibid., 21.

14. Ibid., 22. He explained that other cultures have their own value for their own people and "on them I pass no criticism, except to say that they do not mix well with ours." The "great tradition" of Western civilization, reaching back to Greco-Roman times, was a deep well of inspiration for arts and letters, but it was being forgotten, as he addressed in a later speech, "Return to Masterpieces," delivered at the University of Toronto in November 1937. These foreign cultures came from regions of the world — Eastern Europe, Africa, and Asia, for which he used the terms common for the time, "Slav, Mongol, Negroid" — which he believed did

not share the same two and a half thousand year heritage; he did not wish to see artists drawing on these foreign cultures when "Western" masterpieces were being ignored. It was a period when he saw the Nazi barbarism threatening the basis of Western civilization.

15. Ibid., 155.
16. Tweedsmuir to John Edgar, December 3, 1935, BP, LAC.
17. Ibid.
18. Tweedsmuir to Stair Gillon, December 3, 1935, BP, LAC.
19. Tweedsmuir to John Edgar, January 11, 1936, BP, LAC. Edgar was in a nursing home, suffering from nervous problems, which today would be diagnosed as some form of mental illness.
20. Buchan to John Edgar, December 3, 1935, BP, LAC.
21. Details from Tweedsmuir to John Edgar, January 11, 1936, BP, LAC; and Tweedsmuir to Helen Buchan, January 13, 1936, BP, LAC.
22. Buchan, *CO*, 200.
23. Ibid., 199-202.
24. Ibid., 201
25. Tweedsmuir to Stair Gillon, February 4, 1936, BP, LAC.
26. Ibid.
27. Izaak Walton, and Charles Cotton, *The Compleat Angler*, introduction by John Buchan, World's Classics (Oxford: Oxford University Press, 1935).
28. Tweedsmuir, "Speech to Canadian Institute of Mining and Metallurgy, Ottawa, March 19, 1936," in Buchan, *Canadian Occasions*, 203-207.
29. Tweedsmuir to Baldwin, March 24, 1936, BP, LAC.
30. E.H. Bensley, "Lord Tweedsmuir, Osler and the Osler Library," *Osler Library Newsletter* (McGill University, Montreal) 15 (February 1974): 3.
31. Tweedsmuir to Baldwin, March 24, 1936, BP, LAC. He also delivered thirty-two speeches in English during that trip to the Eastern Townships, a significant portion of the population of which was English at the time.
32. Tweedsmuir to Baldwin, March 24, 1936, BP, LAC.
33. Ibid.
34. Tweedsmuir to Stair Gillon, May 23, 1936, BP, LAC. These two lines are from Sir Walter Scott's (1771–1832) epic poem *Marmion* (1808), Canto VI, Stanza XVII.
35. Crawford to Tweedsmuir, April 9, 1936, BP, LAC.
36. Tweedsmuir to Caroline Grosvenor, May 12, 1936; and to John Edgar, May 25, 1936, both BP, LAC.
37. Tweedsmuir to Caroline Grosvenor, May 12, 1936, BP, LAC.
38. Ibid.
39. Tweedsmuir to Gillon, May 23, 1936, BP, LAC.

40. Tweedsmuir to King, May 15, 1936, BP, LAC.

41. William Lyon Mackenzie King, *Industry and Humanity: A Study in the Principles Underlying Industrial Reconstruction* (Toronto: Houghton Mifflin, 1918), 568.

42. Tweedsmuir to Stair Gillon, May 23, 1936, BP, LAC.

43. William Lyon Mackenzie had moved to Queenston in the early 1820s and there started to publish the *Colonial Advocate*, a paper through which he expressed his views to reform the oligarchic government structure and which ultimately culminated in his leading the Rebellion of 1837.

44. Niagara Parks, "Museum History," Niagaraparksheritage.com, *www .niagaraparksheritage.com/mackenzie-printery/museum-history.html*, accessed August 16, 2009).

45. Tweedsmuir to King, May 15, 1936, BP, LAC.

46. MKD, June 18, 1938, LAC. See also Niagara Parks, "Museum History."

47. There are no references in King's diary to Tweedsmuir's suggestion to him on this, either after Tweedsmuir's May 15, 1936, letter, or the official opening of the house on June 18, 1938. It would not have been proper for King himself to promote the house's restoration by public funds, but it could certainly be promoted by others and it is not unreasonable to think that Tweedsmuir may have pursued the issue or spoken with Niagara Parks Commission officials about it.

48. Tweedsmuir to King, May 31, 1936, BP, LAC.

49. Ibid.

50. Tweedsmuir to Baldwin, March 24, 1936, BP, LAC.

51. Tweedsmuir to John Edgar, May 25, 1936, BP, LAC.

52. Tweedsmuir to Caroline Grosvenor, May 25, 1936, BP, LAC.

53. Tweedsmuir to Caroline Grosvenor, June 8, 1936, BP, LAC.

54. Tweedsmuir to King, June 26, 1936, BP, LAC.

55. King to Tweedsmuir, July 4, 1936, BP, LAC.

56. Meakins was a professor of medicine at McGill University in Montreal who had practised and conducted research at Johns Hopkins University in the United States and at the University of Edinburgh. Meakins would likely have hit it off with the governor general, since he had also served in the Canadian Army Medical Corps during the First World War.

57. Tweedsmuir to an unidentified correspondent, most likely a family member in England, July 14, 1936, BP, LAC.

58. Tweedsmuir to King, July 15, 1936, BP, LAC.

59. Tweedsmuir to unidentified correspondent, July 14, 1936, BP, LAC.

60. Colonel Toody Munro, interview with the author, June 14, 1994, Ottawa. Munro recalled the challenges of managing the horse-drawn carriage when

taking the governor general to Parliament Hill on impossibly icy streets one winter day.

61. Crawford to Tweedsmuir, July 16, 1936, BP, LAC.
62. Tweedsmuir to John Edgar, July 24, 1936, BP, LAC.
63. Tweedsmuir to King, July 15, 1936, BP, LAC.
64. Lady Tweedsmuir to family, August 4, 1936, BP, LAC.
65. *La Presse* (Montreal), August 4, 1936.
66. Tweedsmuir to King, August 4, 1936, BP, LAC.

Chapter 13

1. Tweedsmuir, "Speech to the Engineering Institute of Canada, June 15, 1937," in Buchan, *Canadian Occasions*, 195-198.
2. King to Tweedsmuir, August 24, 1936, BP, LAC. The appointments of lieutenant-governors was and is the responsibility of the prime minister, who appoints them taking into account the suggestions coming from the provinces concerned.
3. Tweedsmuir to King, August 17, 1936, BP, LAC; and MKD, September 10, 1936, LAC.
4. Reported in the *Edmonton Journal*, August 13, 1936.
5. Ibid.
6. Details are taken from the *Edmonton Journal*, August 13, 1936.
7. He repeated similar words in a letter to King: "the most wonderful optimism and courage" (Tweedsmuir to King, August 17, 1936, BP, LAC).
8. *Edmonton Journal*, August 13, 1936. The welcome and receiving line for about three hundred local citizens could be trying. It was evident to a reporter that even the handshaking was becoming "strenuous" for Tweedsmuir as he was observed changing hands a number of times.
9. Tweedsmuir to King, August 17, 1936, BP, LAC. King called the lieutenant-governor to ask if he would accept (MKD, September 10, 1936, LAC).
10. Tweedsmuir to Helen Buchan, August 29, 1936 BP, LAC.
11. Details from a letter, Tweedsmuir to King, August 17, 1936, BP, LAC, and articles in the *Vancouver Daily Province*, August 17, 1936.
12. *Vancouver Daily Province*, August 17, 1936.
13. Tweedsmuir to King, August 31, 1936, BP, LAC.
14. *Vancouver Daily Province*, August 17, 1936. Hutchison, who was then thirty-five years old, went on to become associate editor of the *Winnipeg Free Press*, editor of the *Victoria Daily Times*, then editor of *the Vancouver Sun*, and was to win the Governor General's Literary Award for non-fiction three times.

15. Ibid. For reference to Buchan meeting Laurier, see Buchan, *MHTD*, 84.

16. "Viceroy Gives Brilliant Sketches of Great And Near Great," *Vancouver Daily Province*, August 20, 1936.

17. *Vancouver Daily Province*, August 20, 1936.

18. Ibid.

19. Buchan's *Prester John* was published in 1910. *Munsey's Magazine* was a leading popular fiction magazine at the turn of the last century and into the first decades of the twentieth century. See Richard Cary, "Ben Ames Williams and Robert H. Davis: The Seedling in the Sun," *Colby Library Quarterly* 6, no. 7 (September 1, 1963): 302-327, *http://digitalcommons .colby.edu/cgi/viewcontent.cgi?article=1753&context=cq&sei-redir=1&ref erer=http%3A%2F%2Fwww.google.ca%2Fsearch%3Fclient%3Dsafa ri%26rls%3Den%26q%3Dbob%2Bdavis%2Bmunsey%27s%2Bmagazine% 26ie%3DUTF-8%26oe%3DUTF-8%26redir_esc%3D%26ei%3DjMxZUOb fOsTn0QGrxIGgBw#search=%22bob%20davis%20munseys%20maga zine%22* (accessed September 19, 2012).

20. "Bob Davis Compares Tweedsmuir and Stevenson," *Vancouver Daily Province*, August 21, 1936.

21. *Vancouver Daily Province*, August 21, 1936.

22. *Vancouver Daily Province*, August 22, 1936.

23. "Richard Hannay Off Again," *Vancouver Daily Province*, Sunday magazine, 4, August 22, 1936.

24. *Vancouver Daily Province*, August 24 and 25, 1936, especially the editorial of August 25, that reflects the impression the Tweedsmuirs were making.

25. For information on the Fairbridge Farm School, see Jon Lawrence and Pat Starkey, *Child Welfare and Social Action in the Nineteenth Century and Twentieth Centuries: International Perspectives* (Liverpool, UK: Liverpool University Press, 2001), chaps. 3 and 4; and for information on the Solarium, which is now called the Children's Health Foundation of Vancouver Island, see *http://childrenshealthvi.org/about-us/our-history* (accessed August 20, 2011), and also Dr. C. Wace, "The Queen Alexandra Solarium for Crippled Children," *Canadian Medical Association Journal* 21, no. 6 (December 1929), 702-706, *www.ncbi.nlm.nih.gov/pmc/articles/ PMC381561/pdf/canmedaj00086-0058.pdf* (accessed August 20, 2008).

26. Described in the *Vancouver Daily Province*, August 27, 1936.

27. For background, see Michael Duffy, "The Old Contemptibles," Firstworldwar .com, *www.firstworldwar.com/atoz.oldcontemptibles.htm* (accessed October 3, 2010).

28. Tweedsmuir to King, August 31, 1936, BP, LAC. See also Chapter 5 for further details.

29. The text of the speech was reported in the newspapers and reproduced in Buchan, *CO*, 24-25. Other details were related in the *Vancouver Daily Province*, August 27, 1936. Tweedsmuir was as laudatory in private about Vancouver, describing it as "the most incredibly beautiful city" to his mother, August 29, 1936, BP, LAC.

30. *Vancouver Daily Province*, August 28, 1936. Tweedsmuir met a Mr. Dickson, the son of a gardener he had known in Scotland, who was now head gardener of Stanley Park, the thousand-acre sanctuary of lush forest and gardens named after Canada's sixth governor general, Lord Stanley (1888–1893).

31. *Vancouver Daily Province*, August 27, 1936. Delighted with the turnout, he gave a brief talk to the assembled youth, lauding them on their training, saying how fortunate they were "to live in a country like this, with wild nature next door to you," encouraging them to increase their numbers, and reminding them that the future of Canada lies in their hands.

32. Tweedsmuir hoped the spirit of the pioneers who had built the first church in Vancouver would continue to inspire the congregation for many generations (Quoted in the *Vancouver Daily Province*, Vancouver, August 31, 1936). Other details are in the same article and a reference in a letter to Mackenzie King, August 31, 1936, BP, LAC.

33. Tweedsmuir to Susan Tweedsmuir, September 8, 1936, BP, LAC. Waterton Lakes Park was linked in 1932 with Glacier National Park in Montana (U.S.A.) to form the Waterton-Glacier International Peace Park, an act that struck a chord with Tweedsmuir.

34. Tweedsmuir to Susan Tweedsmuir, September 8, 1936, BP, LAC. See also John Robert Colombo, *Canadian Literary Landmarks* (Toronto: Dundurn, 1984), 260.

35. Tweedsmuir to Caroline Grosvenor, September 16, 1936, BP, LAC.

36. Tweedsmuir to Susan Tweedsmuir, September 11, 1936, BP, LAC.

37. The Alsask population then was about seven hundred. Details of this visit and the town from an article by Marion Fraser in *Captured Memories* (N.p.: Alsask History Book Committee, 1983), 249-250; letter from Tweedsmuir to Susan Tweedsmuir, September 11 and 12, 1936, BP, LAC; letters by Alex's daughters, Jean Wright and Marion DeBoice, and a September 15, 1936 *Calgary Herald* article about the visit: all printed in *JBJ*, no. 6 (Autumn 1986), 30-32; and from a visit by the author to Alsask in August 2004.

38. Tweedsmuir subsequently assisted the family — with finances for one of the daughters to go to teacher's college in Saskatoon; and an introduction to the RCMP for the son, who made his career with the Mounted Police. Tweedsmuir also made inquiries, hoping to secure Alec "a little post in

the Government Service, and some journalistic work." The state of Alec's health, though, would not have made any work easy. He died a year and a half later, on March 20, 1938. When Tweedsmuir received news of his friend's deteriorating health, then death, he wrote to his sister in Scotland that he was glad "to have been able to do something to sweeten his last years" (Tweedsmuir to Anna Buchan, March 19 and added to on March 22, 1938, BP, LAC).

39. Tweedsmuir to King, September 29, 1936, BP, LAC.
40. Tweedsmuir to his son Alastair, September 15, 1936, BP, LAC.
41. Tweedsmuir to Susan Tweedsmuir, September 17, 1936, BP, LAC.
42. Ibid.
43. Tweedsmuir to Susan Tweedsmuir, September 20, 1936, BP, LAC.
44. Tweedsmuir to Susan Tweedsmuir, September 22, 1936, BP, LAC.
45. Buchan, *CO*, 27.
46. Ibid., 27-28.
47. Grey Owl had returned the previous February from an almost four-month-long speaking tour in England. He was believed at the time to be a North American "Indian," but in fact had been born Archie Belaney, in England.
48. Tweedsmuir to Stair Gillon, November 5, 1936, BP, LAC.
49. Tweedsmuir to King, September 29, 1936, BP, LAC.
50. Jane Billinghurst, *The Many Faces of Archie Belaney: Grey Owl* (Vancouver: Greystone Books, 1999), 117.
51. Tweedsmuir to Susan Tweedsmuir, September 20, 1936, BP, LAC.
52. Ibid.
53. Tweedsmuir to King, October 12, 1936, BP, LAC.
54. Buchan, *CO*, 123-124.
55. Buchan, *CO*, 122.
56. Ibid., 125-126.
57. Ibid., 127.
58. Tweedsmuir to Susan Tweedsmuir, October 26, 1936, BP, LAC.
59. Tweedsmuir to Susan Tweedsmuir, November 2, 1936, BP, LAC.
60. Buchan, *CO*, 183.
61. Ibid., 173.
62. Tweedsmuir to Stair Gillon, November 5, 1936, BP, LAC.
63. Tweedsmuir, Speeches, BP, LAC.
64. *Edmonton Journal*, November 23, 1936.
65. Ibid. Information in this paragraph is taken from various articles in the newspaper.
66. *Edmonton Journal*, November 24, 1936.
67. Ibid.

68. Ibid. Details of the event and full text of speech included in the newspaper.
69. Tweedsmuir, Speeches, BP, LAC.
70. *Edmonton Journal*, November 24, 1936. The three examples were: a person starting a career for which he is not suited; the facts changing to the extent that "the old creed becomes simply irrelevant"; and, an individual's mind developing such that "a new world suddenly opens before him and a new interest arises."
71. Tweedsmuir to Susan Tweedsmuir, handwritten letter from Edmonton, November 25, 1936, BP, LAC. Edmonton claimed its pride in making Tweedsmuir the first governor general in Canada to fly! In fact, Lord Willingdon, governor general 1926–1931, had been the first to fly, from Ottawa to Montreal (See Office of the Governor General of Canada, "Former Governors General: The Viscount Willingdon," gg.ca, *www.gg.ca/ document.aspx?id=14615* (accessed October 10, 2010)).
72. *Regina Leader-Post*, November 28, 1936.
73. Reported in the *Winnipeg Free Press*, November 28, 1936; and *the Ottawa Citizen*, November 27, 1936. Newspaper coverage of Lloyd George's published opinions and the controversy they stirred was widespread over several days.
74. *Regina Leader-Post*, November 26, 1936.
75. Tweedsmuir to Stair Gillon, December 7, 1936, BP, LAC.
76. Ibid.
77. *Winnipeg Free Press*, December 1 and 2, 1936.
78. *Winnipeg Free Press*, December 1, 1936.
79. Tweedsmuir to Susan Tweedsmuir, December 7, 1936, BP, LAC.
80. See J.B.M. "A Scot Among Scots," *Winnipeg Free Press*, November 28, 1936. Among the dignitaries were Lieutenant-Governor W.J. Tupper, Premier John Bracken, Chief Justice James Emile Prendergast, Mayor John Queen, and the head of the new Canadian Broadcasting Corporation, Leonard Brockington.
81. Buchan, *CO*, 45. More details of the speech are in Chapter 6.
82. *Winnipeg Free Press*, December 2, 1936.
83. Ibid.
84. Buchan, *CO*, 71.
85. Ibid.
86. Ibid., 73.
87. Ibid., 75.
88. Hubbard, *Ample Mansions*, 162.
89. *Winnipeg Free Press*, December 3, 1936. For details of the speech he gave, see Chapter 16.

90. *Winnipeg Free Press*, December 3, 1936.

91. Tweedsmuir to Susan Tweedsmuir, December 7, 1936, BP, LAC.

92. Tweedsmuir to Susan Tweedsmuir, December 10, 1936, BP, LAC.

93. Willis-O'Connor to Lady Tweedsmuir, December 7, 1936, BP, LAC. See also Col. H. Willis-O'Connor, *Inside Government House*, (Toronto: Ryerson Press, Toronto, 1954), 163.

94. Buchan, *CO*, 136-140.

95. Tweedsmuir, Speeches, March 17, 1937, BP, LAC.

96. Buchan, *CO*, 105-113.

97. Ibid., 108-109.

98. Ibid., 111.

99. This was at Echo Beach Fishing Club, a private club founded by Ottawa businessmen in the 1880s. They caught well over fifty trout between them, though the weather was extreme, from "blazing sun to snow flurries" (Tweedsmuir to King, May 14, 1937, BP, LAC).

100. Tweedsmuir to King, May 27, 1937, BP, LAC.

101. Details of the activities in and around Toronto were described in the *Toronto Star,* May 20-25, 1936.

102. Tweedsmuir to King, May 27, 1937, BP, LAC.

103. *Halifax Herald*, June 7-9, 1937.

104. *Halifax Herald*, June 11, 1937.

105. *Halifax Herald*, June 12, 1937.

106. This incident, as well as the second one while climbing Bear Rock along the Mackenzie River, were referenced in a Reuters telegram, dated July 30, 1937, BP, LAC. King, still in London after the coronation of George VI, heard of the incident and cabled immediately to express concern. Tweedsmuir replied nonchalantly that he hadn't given it much thought until he received "a flood of cables from home" (Tweedsmuir to King, June 14, 1937, BP, LAC).

107. Buchan, *CO*, 196.

108. Ibid., 198.

109. Ibid., 212.

110. In an incisive commentary, an eminent historian at the time, Arthur Lower, asked: "What is it that is waiting to be born in the province of Quebec? Is it just a new version of old-fashioned nationalism? Is it mere economic discontent? Are the hammer-blows of the industrial revolution breaking something? Is the shell of medievalism cracking?... Are the secular influences of the turbulent world beyond the threshold beginning to work their will?" (A.R.M. Lower, "Quebec Nationalism," *Winnipeg Free Press*, November 26, 1936).

111. Tweedsmuir to King, October 12, 1936, BP, LAC. Leopold Amery, who, as secretary of state for Dominion affairs had completed a tour in Canada in 1926, was even more blunt, blaming an unfortunate lack of mixing between English and French in part on "the incurable laziness of the English-speaking Canadians about learning French." Leopold S. Amery, *My Political Life* (London: Hutchinson, 1953), 464.

112. Tweedsmuir to King, October 12, 1936, BP, LAC.

113. Tweedsmuir to King, July 3, 1937, BP, LAC.

114. Translation: On us depends the preservation of the purity of the language, a language of which the glory rests on its purity, its precision, its exquisite clarity.

115. Tweedsmuir to King, July 3, 1937, BP, LAC. The text, in French, is in Buchan, *CO*, 243-247.

116. Tweedsmuir to King, July 3, 1937, BP, LAC.

117. Professor Lower cited a francophone Quebec MP, who described most of the younger clergy in Quebec as nationalist. The dangers of this Quebec nationalism and separatism would, Lower wrote, ultimately pit these younger nationalists against the Church as an institution, since the Church could not conceivably "welcome a philosophy which is closer to Nazism than to Italian Fascism" ("Quebec Nationalism," *Winnipeg Free Press*, November 26, 1936).

118. Tweedsmuir to King, July 3, 1937, BP, LAC.

119. Ibid.

120. Tweedsmuir to Stair Gillon, June 19, 1937, BP, LAC.

121. Tweedsmuir to King, July 3, 1937, BP, LAC.

122. King to Tweedsmuir, July 10, 1937, BP, LAC.

123. The references to fishing on Lake of the Woods and meeting Richardson are in a handwritten note from Tweedsmuir to HBC Governor Ashley Cooper, July 14, 1937, HBC Archives, Provincial Archives of Manitoba (HBCA/PAM).

124. *Calgary Herald*, July 8, 1937.

125. Details in this paragraph were provided by Mr. and Mrs. E.A. Wood in two letters to the author, June 20 and July 10, 1995. Other activities included laying a wreath at the cenotaph and opening a Rover Den for the senior group of Scouts.

126. Mr. E.A. Wood, letter to the author, July 10, 1995. At a reception at the armouries, the governor general was presented with an archery set, crafted by E.A. Wood, from Cuban cottonwood, with a quiver of birchbark containing four distinct arrows. Wood could not be there, so Tweedsmuir sent an aide-de-camp and his wife's lady-in-waiting to visit him in his workshop to thank him for the gift, which was to hang in the study at Rideau Hall.

127. Canadian Press, July 16, 1937, from Red Deer, AB, appearing in newspapers on July 17.

128. H.F. Lambert, "The Harry Snyder Canadian Expedition, 1937," *Canadian Alpine Journal* 25, (June 1938): n.p.

Chapter 14

1. The North provided isolated places where human endurance was tested or thriller adventure occurred (for example, John Buchan, *A Prince of the Captivity* (London: Hodder & Stoughton, 1933); and John Buchan, *The Island of Sheep/The Man from the Norlands* (Edinburgh and London: Thomas Nelson and Sons, 1936)).

2. John Buchan, *The Last Secrets* (Boston and New York: Houghton Mifflin, 1924), 303.

3. Ibid., vii.

4. The Oxford University Exploration Club website gives 1929 as the date the club was founded, whereas Shackleton's book (see next note) gives 1927.

5. Edward Shackleton, *Arctic Journeys* (London: Hodder & Stoughton, 1937), 35. Buchan was also on the Council of the Oxford University Museum (See Tweedsmuir to Ken Sandford, March 19, 1936, BP, LAC).

6. Shackleton, *Arctic Journeys*, 33. The Oxford-sponsored group consisted of six individuals, including the fifty-one-year old Dr. Noel Humphreys, an experienced explorer who led the expedition, and a member of the Royal Canadian Mounted Police, Sergeant Stallworthy, who had long experience in Arctic travel. Shackleton described the latter participant as "undoubtedly the greatest help we could have received," because none of the others had any polar experience. Stallworthy travelled to England to assist with the preparations.

7. Ibid., iv.

8. General Crerar to Tweedsmuir, February 17, 1936, BP, LAC. It is important to recall that at that time, the term "British" generally still included Canada; the evolution of the constitutional implications of the Statute of Westminster would take more time to work their way into practical affairs of a completely separate identity.

9. Tweedsmuir to Shackleton, March 31, 1936, BP, LAC.

10. Tweedsmuir to unidentified correspondent, April 30, 1936, BP, LAC.

11. The British-Canadian Arctic Expedition was sponsored by Cambridge University (See University of Calgary, "Arctic Expedition: The British-Canadian Expedition, 1936–1940," ucalgary.ca, *www.ucalgary.ca/arcticexpedition/baffintomelville* (accessed December 4, 2010)).

12. Graham, W. Rowley, *Cold Comfort: My Love Affair With the Arctic* (Montreal and Kingston, ON: McGill-Queen's University Press, 1996), 3.

13. Graham Rowley, letter to the author, April 29, 1998; and Graham Rowley, telephone conversation with the author, May 5, 1998. As Rowley noted in his autobiography, this period was also "the end of an era in polar exploration" (Rowley, preface to *Cold Comfort*).

14. Tweedsmuir, Speech to the Dominion Land Surveyors' Luncheon, Ottawa, February 3, 1936. Speeches, BP, LAC.

15. Shackleton to Tweedsmuir, March 17, 1936, BP, LAC. The pole of inaccessibility is defined as the "location that is the most challenging to reach owing to its remoteness from geographical features which could provide access. The term describes a geographic construct, not an actual physical phenomenon. Subject to varying definitions, it is of interest mostly to explorers" (http://www.geog.ucsb.edu/events/department-news/1084/poles-of-inaccessibility/, accessed May 1, 2013).

16. Robert Bentham to Tweedsmuir, March 25, 1936, BP, LAC. The appeal was because time was growing short in which to make arrangements, since the SS *Nascopie* was sailing in July to service northern posts.

17. Tweedsmuir to Shackleton, March 31, 1936, BP, LAC.

18. The following year the young Shackleton wanted to arrange a speaking tour in Canada and asked Tweedsmuir if he would write a letter of introduction for him to the Canadian Clubs. Again, however, Tweedsmuir replied that "it would be quite improper" for him to write such a letter. He suggested Shackleton contact Charles Camsell, deputy minister of mines and resources, who would help him out (Tweedsmuir to Shackleton, June 30, 1937, BP, LAC).

19. Notes written for Mackenzie King, as thoughts for developing speeches while the prime minister was in London in the spring of 1937 for the Imperial Conference and the coronation of King George VI (attachment to letter from Tweedsmuir to King, April 7, 1937, BP, LAC).

20. Ibid.

21. Tweedsmuir, Report, July 1, 1937, BP, LAC.

22. *Sunday Times* (London), December 5, 1937.

23. Thomas Wood, introduction to *Down North: Life in the Arctic*, by Anthony Onraet (London: Jonathan Cape, 1944).

24. R.H.G. Bonnycastle, "Lord Tweedsmuir as Mountaineer," *Canadian Alpine Journal* 28, no. 2 (1942–1943), 203.

25. See Tweedsmuir to George Allen, September 2, 1937, HBCA/PAM, for reference to Ashley Cooper's visit to Tweedsmuir.

26. Canadian Press, *Winnipeg Free Press*, July 24, 1937.

27. The books were: *Almayer's Folly* (Joseph Conrad); *Tragedy of Korosko* (Conan Doyle); *The Wallet of Kai Lung* (Ernest Bramah); *A Passage to India* (E.M. Forster); *The Regent* (Arnold Bennett); and *Sylvia Scarlett* (Compton Mackenzie). See *New York Times*, July 7, 1937.

28. Tweedsmuir to HBC Governor Ashley Cooper, September 6, 1937, BP, LAC; and *Sunday Times* (London), December 5, 1937.

29. Shuldham Redfern, in Susan Tweedsmuir, comp., *Wife and Friends*, 239-240.

30. Stirling McNeil, interview with the author, June 14, 2001, Ottawa. McNeil had also been tasked with drawing up a list of and brief notes on the men in the RCMP detachment area, for use by Tweedsmuir so he could know in advance the names and main points about the officers. The first list McNeil submitted, however, was rejected because of one, too brief entry: the individual was described as "Scotch and proud of it!" The attempted appeal to Tweedsmuir's roots was judged inappropriate, and the list had to be retyped.

31. McNeil, interview, June 14, 2001.

32. Tweedsmuir's speech was reported in the *Winnipeg Free Press*, July 26, 1937.

33. Archdeacon Fleming, in *A Gentleman Adventurer: The Arctic Diaries of Richard Bonnycastle*, edited by Heather Robertson (Toronto: Lester & Orpen Dennys, 1984), 19.

34. See Wood, introduction to *Down North*; and Margaret Bourke-White, *Portrait of Myself* (New York: Simon and Schuster, 1963), 153-154.

35. Cited from Wood, introduction to *Down North*; and Redfern, in *Wife and Friends*, 238.

36. Redfern, in *Wife and Friends*, 240.

37. *Sunday Times* (London), December 5, 1937.

38. *Ottawa Journal*, and *Winnipeg Free Press* respectively, July 27, 1936.

39. L.J. Burpee, "Canada's Awakening North," *National Geographic*, June 1936, 767.

40. Charles Camsell, *Son of the North* (Toronto: Ryerson Press, 1954), 242.

41. William Clark Bethune, *Canada's Western Northland* (Ottawa: King's Printer, 1937), 6. The Department of Mines and Resources was established on December 1, 1936. Previously, its work had been included in the former Department of Mines, Interior, Indian Affairs and Immigration. See the annual *Report of the Department of Mines and Resources*, for the fiscal year ended March 31, 1937.

42. B. Hunt, ed., *Rebels, Rascals & Royalty: The Colourful North of LACO Hunt*, (Yellowknife, NT: Outcrop, 1983), 85.

43. Buchan, *Sick Heart River* (1941; reprint, Oxford and New York: Oxford University Press, World's Classics, 1994), 322.

44. Bourke-White, *Portrait of Myself*, 157-158.

45. *Sunday Times* (London), December 5, 1937.

46. *Ottawa Journal*, July 29, 1937.

47. Bonnycastle, "Lord Tweedsmuir As Mountaineer," 205-206.

48. Ibid. Bonnycastle, who had been followed up by one of the priests from the mission at Fort Norman, told the priest to return to Fort Norman to get men and ropes and return as soon as possible. He then had one of the other men from the party and one of the young Natives with them climb up the front to get to Rivers-Smith and Macdonald and try to help them either hang on until the ropes arrived or to help them work their way down if they could.

49. Ibid., 206.

50. *Globe and Mail* (Toronto); and *Winnipeg Free Press*, both July 30, 1937.

51. *Winnipeg Free Press*, August 2, 1937; and, with less detail, Redfern, in *Wife and Friends*, 242.

52. *Ottawa Journal*, August 3, 1937.

53. Redfern, in *Wife and Friends*, 243.

54. Walter E. Gilbert, *Arctic Pilot: Life and Work on North Canadian Air Routes* (Toronto: Thomas Nelson & Sons, 1940), 200. The first airmail deliveries along the Mackenzie River occurred in 1929, a development that was reported on by Frederick B. Watt (see Watt, "The New Gentlemen Adventurers," *The Rotarian* 37, no. 2 (August 1930), 9-11, *http://books .google.ca/books?id=6kUEAAAAMBAJ&pg=PA50&lpg=PA50&dq =the+rotarian+1930+frederick+watt&source=bl&ots=wuttSenQTO& sig=J4jHrBo0urURX4W62W9qqjZBCoQ&hl=en&ei=9i0hTefpJ9Skn QeDt5DkDQ&sa=X&oi=book_result&ct=result&resnum=1&ved=0CBg Q6AEwAA#v=onepage&q=the%20rotarian%201930%20frederick%20 watt&f=false* (accessed December 22, 2010).

55. Gilbert, *Arctic Pilot*, 201.

56. *Winnipeg Free Press*, August 3, 1937.

57. Wood, introduction to *Down North*.

58. Tweedsmuir to Cooper, September 6, 1937, BP, LAC.

59. Bethune, *Canada's Western Northland*, 12.

60. Tweedsmuir to Cooper, September 6, 1937, BP, LAC. Also recounted in *Sunday Times* (London), December 5, 1937.

61. *Sunday Times* (London), December 12, 1937.

62. Ibid.

63. Tweedsmuir to George Macleod, January 17, 1940, BP, LAC. Reverend Macleod headed a project called "The Iona Community," established in Iaon, by Oban, in Scotland. Macleod had written to Tweedsmuir to ask him to support their request to the Pilgrim Trust for funds for the community. Tweedsmuir replied positively, commenting that he was "deeply

interested in it" and that this type of project "is needed everywhere today to vitalise [sic] the Church."

64. Noted in J. William Galbraith, "His Excellency's Excellent Adventure," *Up Here* (Yellowknife, NT), May/June, 1996. Much later governments would agree with this assessment. They tried to move the residents of Aklavik to the new model town of Inuvik in the 1950s, but Aklavik is still there, proud to be "the town that wouldn't die."

65. *Sunday Times* (London), December 12, 1937; and Buchan, *Sick Heart River*, 118-120.

66. Tweedsmuir to Cooper, September 6, 1937, BP, LAC.

67. Ibid.

68. Described in Department of Mines and Resources annual reports; and in Bethune, *Canada's Western Northland*.

69. Harry Snyder, "Exploring Upper Nahanni River and Snyder Mountains in 1937," *Canadian Geographic*, October 1937, 168-191. Snyder's explorations in the North led him to try and have what are now called the Mackenzie Mountains named after himself. The title, accompanying map, and text all refer to the Snyder Mountains.

70. Ibid.

71. *Sunday Times* (London), December 12, 1937.

72. Snyder, "Exploring Upper Nahanni," 188.

73. Tweedsmuir to Stair Gillon, September 7, 1937, BP, LAC.

74. Hunt, *Rebels, Rascals & Royalty*, 86.

75. Guy Rhoades, *Ottawa Journal*, February 12, 1940.

76. The area is still described in much the same way as when John and Susan Tweedsmuir were there. See Shanagan Webservices Inc., "Burns Lake," BritishColumbia.com, *www.britishcolumbia.com/regions/towns/?townID= 3589* (accessed November 10, 2008).

77. Tweedsmuir to Stair Gillon, September 7, 1937, BP, LAC.

78. Susan Tweedsmuir, "Tweedsmuir Park: The Diary of a Pilgrimage," *National Geographic*, April 1938, 451-476.

79. Ibid., 453, 468.

80. Tweedsmuir to George Allen, September 2, 1937, HBCA/PAM.

81. Tweedsmuir to Cooper, September 6, 1937, BP, LAC.

82. Text of broadcast (no date) but it would have to have been early September 1937, BP, LAC.

83. *Sunday Times* (London), December 12, 1937.

84. Richard H.G. Bonnycastle, "'Down North' with the Governor-General," *The Beaver* (since April/May 2010, known as Canada's History), September 1937, 14-16.

85. Snyder, "Exploring Upper Nahanni," 169-191.

86. Margaret Bourke-White, "A 10,000 Mile Tour of Canada's Northwest With Lord Tweedsmuir," *Life*, October 25, 1937, 40-47.

87. Wood, introduction to *Down North*.

88. Hardinge to Tweedsmuir, December 20, 1937, BP, LAC.

89. Ibid.

90. Tweedsmuir to Hardinge, January 3, 1938, BP, LAC.

91. Tweedsmuir, "Down North," report attached to letter to the HBC Governor Ashley Cooper, September 6, 1937, HBCA/PAM.

Chapter 15

1. Tweedsmuir to Stanley Baldwin, October 11, 1937, BP, LAC.

2. Buchan, *CO*, 29-33.

3. Ibid., 92.

4. Ibid., 185.

5. Ibid., 186.

6. Ibid., 188-190.

7. Tweedsmuir to Anna Buchan, January 24, 1938, BP, LAC.

8. Tweedsmuir to Anna Buchan, January 13, 1938, BP, LAC.

9. See R.P. Browder, and T.G. Smith, *Independent*, 132. He was the first American appointed principal, though his father was born in Canada and his grandfather was a governor of McGill from 1910 to 1918.

10. *La Presse* (Montreal), January 7, 1938.

11. Tweedsmuir, "Speech, February 5, 1938," in Buchan, *Canadian Occasions*, 141-143.

12. Tweedsmuir to Anna Buchan, February 3, 1938, BP, LAC.

13. Tweedsmuir to Anna Buchan, March 7, 1938, BP, LAC.

14. Buchan, *CO*, 88-89.

15. Tweedsmuir to Anna Buchan, March 28, 1938, BP, LAC.

16. The event and Tweedsmuir's speech were reported in the *Gazette* (Montreal), March 22, 1938. He spoke at Moyse Hall on Monday, March 20, 1938.

17. Tweedsmuir, "The Mind of the Citizen," Speeches, March 21, 1938, BP, LAC.

18. Ibid. At the time thirty thousand people were being treated in mental hospitals at an annual cost of more than ten million dollars, and 4 percent of children in school were "doomed to suffer from mental ailments."

19. One of the main problems of research, he said, was to "bring science out of the laboratory into the hospitals and schools." The second point he stressed was the importance of administration, which must understand

the special problems and try to combine the efforts of government and voluntary agencies. Third was the important role of education, which was believed linked to prevention.

20. Tweedsmuir to Anna Buchan, March 28, 1938, BP, LAC.

21. Tweedsmuir to Susan Tweedsmuir, May 5, 1938, BP, LAC.

22. These plans were outlined in a letter to Anna Buchan, April 18, 1938, BP, LAC.

23. *Star-Phoenix* (Saskatoon), May 9, 1938; and *Leader-Post* (Regina), May 10, 1938. He had been greeted by Chancellor Sir Frederick Haultain and President James S. Thomson. Aside from praising the agricultural research, he lauded the work of Dr. A.S. Morton in recording the early history of western Canada.

24. *Leader-Post* (Regina), May 11, 1938.

25. Tweedsmuir to Susan Tweedsmuir, May 15, 1938, BP, LAC.

26. It provided a "shot in the arm," in the sense that the inhabitants began a general cleanup, painting and restoring buildings, fences, and whatever else needed repair (See Smith, *John Buchan*, 393-394).

27. *Leader-Post* (Regina), May 13, 1938.

28. Smith, *John Buchan*, 393.

29. The Cypress Hills massacre is a focus of Guy Vanderhaeghe's 1996 novel, *The Englishman's Boy*, which won the Governor General's Literary Award for fiction.

30. The sheep rancher was William Martin, originally from the borders area of Scotland (See the *Leader-Post* (Regina), May 13, 1938).

31. Tweedsmuir to Susan Tweedsmuir, May 15, 1938, BP, LAC.

32. *Leader-Post* (Regina), May 14, 1938.

33. Fort Qu'Appelle was headquarters for General Middleton during the Riel Rebellion.

34. The Indian Head Research Farm, established in 1887, is still active and is now part of a network of nineteen research centres of the Semiarid Prairie Agricultural Research Centre (SPARC), which is operated by the federal government.

35. *Leader-Post* (Regina), May 16, 1938.

36. Tweedsmuir expressed wonderment at the fine workmanship by the young lad, creating a special moment. He spoke to all 328 patients over the public address system, expressing regret he was unable to see them all (*Leader-Post* (Regina), May 16, 1938).

37. Tweedsmuir to Susan Tweedsmuir, May 15, 1938, BP, LAC.

38. Tweedsmuir to Anna Buchan, May 23, 1938, BP, LAC.

39. Tweedsmuir to Caroline Grosvenor, May 23, 1938, BP, LAC.

40. From copy of "Dedication Souvenir to commemorate the opening of the new Holy Blossom Temple," provided to the author by Holy Blossom Temple, Toronto, June 17, 2008.
41. Tweedsmuir to Anna Buchan, May 23, 1938, BP, LAC.
42. Tweedsmuir to King, June 8, 1938, MKP, LAC; and Tweedsmuir to Susan Tweedsmuir, June 6, 1938, BP, LAC.
43. Tweedsmuir to Susan Tweedsmuir, June 2, 1938, BP, LAC.
44. See Hubbard, *Ample Mansions*, 35-40.
45. Tweedsmuir to Susan Tweedsmuir, June 15, 1938, BP, LAC.
46. Buchan, *CO*, 94-101.
47. Ibid., 98-101.
48. Tweedsmuir to Susan Tweedsmuir, June 20, 1938, BP, LAC.
49. King wrote that he appreciated that Tweedsmuir "had had Parliament fully in mind" (King to Tweedsmuir, July 20, 1938, BP, LAC).
50. Hardinge to Tweedsmuir, June 18, 1938, BP, LAC.
51. Tweedsmuir to Anna Buchan, July 9, 1938, BP, LAC.
52. Ibid.
53. Tweedsmuir to King, July 12, 1938, MKP, LAC.
54. Ibid.; and King to Tweedsmuir, July 20, 1938, BP, LAC.
55. King to Tweedsmuir, August 25, 1938, BP, LAC.
56. Referenced in a letter from Tweedsmuir to Anna Buchan, October 17, 1938, BP, LAC. It was also the subject of an untitled newsreel shown in cinemas (Untitled newsreel showing Tweedsmuir at ploughing match, National Film Board of Canada, October 13, 1938; viewed by the author at the National Film Board Archives, Montreal, Canada, February 2001).
57. William H. Milne, letter to the author, November 23, 1999. His wife's family had a tea room business and catered the luncheon.
58. Tweedsmuir to Anna Buchan, October 17, 1938, BP, LAC.
59. Little has been written about this initiative of Susan Tweedsmuir's until recently (See Geoffrey Little, "'The people must have plenty of good books': The Lady Tweedsmuir Prairie Library Scheme, 1936–40," Spectrum, library.concordia.ca, *http://spectrum.library.concordia.ca/974102/*, accessed September 20, 2012).
60. Tweedsmuir, "Speech to the University of Western Ontario, London, ON, October 15, 1938," Speeches, BP, LAC.
61. Details in this paragraph are taken from the *Gazette* (Montreal), November 16-17, 1938.
62. Mrs. Nora Wade, "letter," *JBJ*, no. 6 (Autumn 1986): 30.
63. Tweedsmuir to Stair Gillon, December 12, 1938, BP, LAC.
64. Archival material, Perth County Museum, Perth, ON.

65. W.K. Lye, letter to the author, July 30, 1998. The same expression found its way into Tweedsmuir's autobiography, *Memory Hold-the-Door*, which he would have been writing at this time and which Lye may have subsequently seen.

66. A. Britton Smith, letter to the author, March 17, 1998.

67. There were three lectures, plus Tweedsmuir's closing address, all of which were delivered at McGill University and published by Oxford University Press in 1940 under the title *The State in Society* (Toronto, Oxford, and New York: Oxford University Press, 1940). The first lecture was delivered on January 23, and the last, along with the closing address, on February 10, 1939. The three lecturers were: Robert Warren, professor of economics, Princeton University; Leo Wolman, professor of economics, Columbia University; Henry Clay, economic advisor to the Bank of England and former professor of social economics at the University of Manchester.

68. Ibid., 116-117.

69. See Browder and Smith, *Independent*, 36; and for a description of how the Depression changed the political makeup of McGill, see Paul Walters, "Between the Wars: Hard Times and Turmoil," *McGill Reporter* (McGill University, Montreal), October 14, 2011, 11, *http://publications.mcgill .ca/reporter/files/2011/10/HISTORY-ISSUE.pdf* (accessed November 19, 2011).

70. Tweedsmuir, Speeches, BP, LAC.

71. University of British Columbia, "The Degree of Doctor of Laws *(Honoris Causa)* Conferred at Special Congregation March 17th, 1939. His Excellency the Right Honourable Lord Tweedsmuir, Governor-General of Canada," Library.UBC.ca, *www.library.ubc.ca/archives/hdcites/hdcites1 .html* (accessed November 20, 2010).

72. Tweedsmuir to Anna Buchan, March 20, 1939, BP, LAC.

73. See Tweedsmuir, "A Vice-Regal Congregation," *The Graduate Chronicle of the Alumni Association of the University of British Columbia* (Vancouver), April 5, 1939: 6, 8, *www.library.ubc.ca/archives/pdfs/chronicle/AL_CHRON_ 1939_04_05.pdf#search=%22tweedsmuir%22*, accessed November 21, 2010. He encouraged these young men and women to consider research as a possibility for "a satisfying life's work ... of profound public importance."

74. The survey asked: "Are you in favour of military action to check the expansion of totalitarian states?"; "If England becomes involved in a war should Canada should enter the war?"; "Would you go to war if Canada faced invasion?"; and "Would you favour conscription of (a) Manpower; (b) Wealth?" (Canadian University Press, "War — Yes or No?" *Ubyssey* (University of British Columbia, Vancouver), March 24, 1939: 4, *www.library.ubc.ca*

/archives/pdfs/ubyssey/UBYSSEY_1939_03_24.pdf#search=%22war%22, accessed November 21, 2010).

75. Tweedsmuir to Caroline Grosvenor, April 4; and Tweedsmuir to Anna Buchan, April 2, 1939, both BP, LAC.

76. Susan to Caroline Grosvenor, April 10, 1939, BP, LAC.

77. Philip Chester to Tweedsmuir, April 11, 1939, BP, LAC. The memory of his tour down the Mackenzie River two years before, in which he had travelled as a guest of the Company, was still very fresh. In a subsequent letter to Chester, he complimented them all with his usual, sincere superlatives (Tweedsmuir to Chester, April 17, 1939, BP, LAC).

78. For a short biography and list of books, see Manitoba Historical Society, "Memorable Manitobans: Charles William Gordon [Ralph Connor] 1860–1937," MHS.MB.ca, *www.mhs.mb.ca/docs/people/gordon_cw.shtml* (accessed April 20, 2013). Gordon was listed as one of nineteen millionaires in Winnipeg in 1910 (Cited from Manitoba Historical Society, "Memorable Manitobans: Winnipeg's Millionaires, 1910," MHS.MB.ca, *www.mhs.mb.ca/docs/people/millionaires1910.shtml* (accessed November 21, 2010)).

79. Ralph Connor, *Black Rock* (New York: Mershon, 1901), 247.

80. Ray Horsefield, "An Affair of State," *The Beaver*, Spring 1979, 44-47.

81. Ibid.

82. Tweedsmuir to Stair Gillon, September 1, 1939, BP, LAC.

83. Walter Schoen, email to the author, September 9, 2007; and Walter Schoen, letter to the author, including old photograph reprint, November 22, 2007. Mr. Schoen's family was among those who settled around Tupper. Given Canadian government policy at the time, which precluded Jewish immigration, it was easier to consider the Sudetens as refugees than the Jews (See also Abella and Troper, *None Is Too Many*, 48-49, for a discussion of the Sudeten issue).

84. In encouraging the government, Tweedsmuir presented his argument as an opportunity; he focused on those skilled in the glass industry, suggesting a new industry might be created in Canada, where all the raw materials for making glass were found (Tweedsmuir to Anna Buchan, November 14, 1938, BP, LAC). He had also written to the British foreign secretary, Lord Halifax, and to the Canadian high commissioner in London, Vincent Massey (Tweedsmuir to Halifax, December 9, 1938, BP, LAC), likely unaware that much discussion had already gone on after the Munich agreement that gave the Sudetenland to Hitler. There were, in fact, very few glass workers among the five hundred refugees at Tupper; rather, the group included textile workers, leather workers, shoe-makers, blacksmiths,

office workers, and others (Walter Schoen, email to the author, September 9, 2007).

85. Tweedsmuir to Anna Buchan, November 27, 1939, BP, LAC.

86. Tweedsmuir to Anna Buchan, January 1, 1939, BP, LAC.

87. MKD, January 23, 1940, LAC. Tweedsmuir thought the French wording of the speech from the throne was "inelegant"; King offered to have Lapointe go over it but he didn't have time.

88. Tweedsmuir to Stair Gillon, January 19, 1940, BP, LAC.

89. Ibid.

90. Buchan, *CO*, 34.

91. *Ottawa Journal*, February 12, 1940.

92. Tweedsmuir to Anna Buchan, February 5, 1940, BP, LAC.

Chapter 16

1. Paul Benoit, "The Crown and the Constitution," *Canadian Parliamentary Review* 25, no. 2 (Summer 2002): 2-3.

2. David E. Smith, "The Crown and the Constitution: Sustaining Democracy?" (paper presented at the conference, "The Crown in Canada: Present Realities and Future Options," Ottawa, Canada, June 10, 2010).

3. Tweedsmuir, "Address to the Association of Canadian Bookmen, November 27, 1937," in Buchan, *Canadian Occasions*, 248.

4. MKD, November 5, 1935, LAC.

5. The royal commission was also referred to as the Massey Commission, after its chair, Vincent Massey. It was created by Order-in-Council on April 8, 1949, and submitted its report two years later (See Canada, *Royal Commission on National Development in the Arts, Letters, and Sciences, 1949–1951*, (Ottawa: King's Printer, 1951), *www.collectionscanada.gc.ca/massey/h5-400-e.html*, accessed August 21, 2011).

6. MKD, November 5, 1935, LAC.

7. See Lyn Harrington, *Syllables of Recorded Time: The Story of the Canadian Authors Association, 1921–1981* (Toronto: Dundurn Press, 1981), chap. 10, and page 263.

8. E.M. Pomeroy, *Sir Charles G.D. Roberts: A Biography* (Toronto: Ryerson Press, 1943), 322-323.

9. *Winnipeg Tribune*, March 27, 1935. William Talbot Allison had been a Presbyterian pastor, a poet, and literary critic for several newspapers (Source: The Manitoba Historical Society, "Memorable Manitobans: William Talbot Allison (1874–1941)," MHS.MB.ca. *www.mhs.mb.ca/docs/people/allison_wt.shtml*, accessed May 29, 2011).

10. Harrington, *Syllables of Recorded Time*, 263.
11. Ibid., 79.
12. Ibid.
13. Harrington, *Syllables of Recorded Time*, 263. The quote is found in John Coldwell Adams, *Sir Charles God Damn: The Life of Sir Charles G.D. Roberts* (Toronto: University of Toronto Press, 1986), 201.
14. Adams, *Sir Charles God Damn*.
15. Harrington, *Syllables of Recorded Time*, 263.
16. Ibid.
17. Ibid., 263-264.
18. Ibid., 263.
19. It was not until after the Canada Council took over administration of the awards from the Canadian Authors Association in 1959 that monetary awards were added.
20. Source: The Canada Council. Roberton had died in 1936; his collection of articles was composed posthumously.
21. *LAMPS* (Arts and Letters Club, Toronto), Spring 1938, *www.artsandletters private.ca/lampsletters/lampsletters_1938.pdf* (accessed August 1, 2011). John Buchan had visited the Arts and Letters Club in November 1924 as a guest of Vincent Massey (See Margaret McBurney, *The Great Adventure: 100 Years at the Arts and Letters Club* (Toronto: Arts and Letters Club, 1997), 56).
22. Leacock was a professor of economics at McGill University and had written *My Discovery of the West*. The fiction award went to Laura G. Salverson for *The Dark Weaver*, the poetry award was given to E.J. Pratt for *The Fable of the Goats*.
23. Early recipients included, in the 1950s: Pierre Berton, Morley Callaghan, and Farley Mowat; and in the 1960s: Marshall McLuhan, Mordecai Richler, Leonard Cohen, Yves Thériault, and Margaret Laurence.
24. French-language works translated into English, however, sometimes won an award. The first was in 1940 for *Thirty Acres* (*Trente arpents*) by Ringuet (Phillippe Panneton); the next was in 1947 for *The Tin Flute* (*Bonheur d'occasion*) by Gabrielle Roy (Source: Yvan G. Lepage, "Une ambassadrice des lettres québecoise," *Revue de critique et de théorie littéraire* 5, no. 1 (winter 2010), *www.revue-analyses.org/index.php?id=1576*, accessed August 4, 2011).
25. Free translation: "The French language and literature is a treasure not only for French Canada but also for English Canada" (Tweedsmuir, "Speech to the *Congrès de la langue française*, Quebec City, 1937," in Buchan, *Canadian Occasions*, 243).

26. George V had counselled his new representative "to be sympathetic to the French people of Canada, and jealously to respect their traditions and their language" (Buchan, *MHTD*, 243).

27. See Jean-Louis Lessard, "Le terroir," litterature-quebecoise.org, *www .litterature-quebecoise.org/terroir.htm* (accessed August 4, 2011). This was the period of the now classic *Maria Chapdelaine* by Louis Hémon.

28. Buchan, *CO*, 244-245. Tweedsmuir said he was guided by the words of his friend, Monsignor Camille Roy, the master of Canadian literature.

29. See Lepage, "Une ambassadrice des lettres québecoise."

30. Referred to in a letter from King to Tweedsmuir, February 18, 1936, BP, LAC; and in MKD, February 20, 1936, LAC.

31. For a general discussion, see Kate Macdonald and Nathan Waddell, editors, *John Buchan and the Idea of Modernity* (London: Pickering and Chatto, 2013).

32. The date is implied by a document listing organizations of which Lord and/ or Lady Tweedsmuir were patrons. The date of acceptance for the CAA was February 25, 1936 (See Governor General's Office Records, LAC).

33. Perhaps in part because of both some duplication of membership and some duplication of effort, the ACB survived just three years, being dissolved in April 1939. The time of dissolution can be inferred from the date that Tweedsmuir's patron status was cancelled, April 21, 1939, which is noted in a listing of organizations of which Lord and/or Lady Tweedsmuir were patrons (See Governor General's Office Records, LAC).

34. *Winnipeg Free Press*, December 3, 1936.

35. Cardinal John Henry Newman (1801–1890), an Anglican priest who converted to Catholicism, is now venerated and respected for his writing, especially the classic *Apologia* (National Institute for Newman Studies, "Newman Reader: Venerable John Henry Cardinal Newman, "*www.newman reader.org/*; and Kevin Knight, "John Henry Newman," Newadvent.org, *www.newadvent.org/cathen/10794a.htm*, accessed August 2, 2011). Aldous Huxley (1894–1963), was the author of *Brave New World* (1932), but also wrote widely on philosophy, travel, the arts, religion, et cetera (David Pearce, "Brave New World? A Defence of Paradise-Engineering," *www.huxley.net/ index.html*; and Literature Network, "Aldous Huxley," Online-literature .com, *www.online-literature.com/aldous_huxley/*, accessed August 2, 2011).

36. *Winnipeg Free Press*, December 3, 1936.

37. Ibid.

38. Tweedsmuir to Baldwin, December 11, 1937, BP, LAC. The speech was delivered on November 27, 1937 (See Buchan, *CO*, 248-256).

39. Buchan, *CO*, 248-249.

40. Ibid., 249.
41. Ibid.
42. Ibid., 253.
43. Ibid., 255.
44. William Buchan, *John Buchan*,156.
45. Buchan, *CO*, 256.
46. Ibid., 229-242. The speech was delivered on November 24, 1937.
47. The number is from a letter from Tweedsmuir to Stanley Baldwin, December 11, 1937. A figure of "approximately 1,500" is given as the hall's capacity by "Convocation Hall Tickets," Ticketmaster.ca, *www.ticketmaster.ca/Convocation-Hall-tickets-Toronto/venue/131080 Ticketmaster*, "Convocation Hall Tickets," while 1,700 is given as the capacity at Office of Space Management, University of Toronto, "Convocation Hall," osm.utoronto .ca, *http://osm.utoronto.ca/conhall/rental.html* (both sites accessed August 2, 2011). The information in this and subsequent paragraphs about this speech are from Buchan, *CO*.
48. Buchan, *CO*, 230.
49. Ibid., 232.
50. Ibid., 235. Tweedsmuir would no doubt have been saddened by the predictive quality of his statement as we think of common phrases and references from television shows such as *Friends* or *The Simpsons*.
51. Buchan, *CO*, 239.
52. Tweedsmuir to Baldwin, December 11, 1937, BP, LAC. The Shakespeare version, from *Twelfth Night*, Act II, Scene iii is:

> "Oh Mistress mine! where are you roaming?
> Oh! stay and hear, your true love's coming,
> That can sing both high and low.
> Trip no further pretty sweeting.
> Journeys end in lovers meeting,
> Every wise man's son doth know."

53. Buchan, *CO*, 241.
54. Tweedsmuir to Stanley Baldwin, December 11, 1937, BP, LAC.
55. Quoted in Douglas George Fetherling, "Thomas Raddall, note" in *The Canadian Encyclopedia*, 2nd ed. (Edmonton, AB: Hurtig Publishers, 1988). An article written in 1929 questioned "Is There a Canadian Literature?" (1929); it is cited in David Staines, ed., *The Canadian Imagination: Dimensions of a Literary Culture* (Cambridge, MA: Harvard University Press, Cambridge, Mass., 1977), 10.

56. Kate Macdonald, *John Buchan: A Companion to the Mystery Fiction* (Jefferson, NC, and London: McFarland & Company, 2009), 181.

57. William Buchan, *John Buchan*, 23.

58. Thomas H. Raddall, *In My Time* (Toronto: McClelland & Stewart, 1976), 183.

59. Ibid., 182.

60. Tweedsmuir to Thomas Raddall, March 10, 1937, quoted in John Bell, "Tweedsmuir as Patron: John Buchan and the *Blackwood's* Stories of Thomas H. Raddall," *JBJ*, no. 6 (Autumn 1986), 15. From an initial, limited search, it is unknown whether Tweedsmuir and Raddall actually met.

61. Raddall to Tweedsmuir, March 15, 1938, Thomas Raddall Selected Correspondence, Dalhousie University Library, (TRSC/DUL), *www.library .dal.ca/archives/trela/letters/53blackwood26jul43.htm#r53blackwood 26jul43n3* (accessed October 10, 2011).

62. Ibid.

63. Raddall to Tweedsmuir, March 15, 1938, cited in Bell, "Tweedsmuir as Patron," 16.

64. John Buchan, foreword to *The Pied Piper of Dipper Creek and Other Tales*, by Thomas, H. Raddall, (Toronto: McClelland & Stewart, 1943), v.

65. Ibid., v-vi.

66. Raddall to Blackwood, July 26, 1943, TRSC/DUL. *www.library.dal.ca/ archives/trela/letters/53blackwood26jul43.htm#r53blackwood26jul43n3* (accessed October 10, 2011); Raddall refers to Tweedsmuir making a suggestion similar to one Raddall had in his discussions with Blackwood. Also, in a letter to a Miss Rogers, a graduate student working on a thesis about Raddall, Raddall wrote, "Tweedsmuir was urging me to bring out a book of historical short stories about Nova Scotia" (March 2, 1954); and "In 1947 McClelland & Stewart published a volume of my historical short stories, indeed the volume for which Lord Tweedsmuir had pleaded, entitled 'The Wedding Gift.' Here again the town is Liverpool in colonial days" (Source: TRSC/DUL, *www.library.dal.ca/archives/trela/letters/680rogers 21mar54.htm* (accessed October 10, 2011)).

67. Raddall, *The Pied Piper*, 186.

68. The awards were given in 1948 for *Halifax, Warden of the North* and in 1957 for *The Path of Destiny*, a Canadian history book used in schools.

69. Bell, "Tweedsmuir as Patron."

70. Walker, *Lean, Wind, Lean*, 97.

71. Ibid.

72. Ibid., 99.

73. Ibid.

74. Ibid.

75. Ibid., 151.

76. The Tweedsmuir version of the classic fable gave Millar a metaphor for his and his wife's careers. Margaret, also a writer, signed with Random House in 1943 (Cited from Tom Nolan, *Ross Macdonald: A Biography* (New York: Scribner, 1999), 48, 66). See also Witold Rybczynski, *Globe and Mail* (Toronto), September 2, 2000, D14, in which he recounts Millar's inspiration from Buchan.

77. Nolan, *Ross Macdonald*, 48.

78. Karl-Eric Lindkvist, "Articles," Ross Macdonald Files, hem.passagen.se, *http://hem.passagen.se/caltex/newsart.html* (accessed May 7, 2011).

79. Nolan, *Ross Macdonald*, 66-67.

80. Quotation from author and playwright William Goldman (Source: Wikipedia, "Ross Macdonald," en.wikipedia.org, *http://en.wikipedia.org/wiki/Ross_Macdonald*, accessed August 3, 2011).

81. King to Tweedsmuir, October 20, 1937, BP, LAC. The reference to King's periods as prime minister echoes the famous nineteenth-century British prime minister William Ewart Gladstone.

82. King to Tweedsmuir, November 3, 1937, BP, LAC.

83. His publisher, C.J. Musson, and his wife, Susan, were also in attendance with him. A photograph shows him autographing a copy for Sir Andrew McPhail, long-time professor of the history of medicine at McGill and founder of the *Canadian Medical Association Journal* (*Ottawa Citizen*, December 3, 1937).

84. Tweedsmuir to Violet Markham, November 27, 1939, BP, LAC.

85. John Buchan, *Sick Heart River*, 221. It was published in the United States under the title *Mountain Meadow*.

86. Robertson Davies, review of *Sick Heart River*, *Saturday Night*, May 3, 1941, 16.

87. Quoted in Smith, *John Buchan*, 434.

88. Lownie, *Presbyterian Cavalier*, 287. Lownie notes the book was published in 1941 but "had only sold 15,000 of the 25,000 print run by the following spring when the price was reduced."

89. Sheila Egoff and Judith Saltman, *The New Republic of Childhood: A Critical Guide to Canadian Children's Literature in English* (Toronto: Oxford University Press, 1990), 244.

90. Ibid., 231.

91. Lorne Elliott, Interview by Shelagh Rogers, *The Next Chapter*, CBC Radio 2, May 2, 2011. In the interview Elliott discussed books he liked, including *Lake of Gold*, which he thought better than *Sick Heart River*.

92. Tweedsmuir to Susan Tweedsmuir, May 2, 1938, BP, LAC.

Chapter 17

1. MKD, November 5, 1935, LAC.
2. Tweedsmuir's date of acceptance is noted in a listing of organizations of which he and/or Lady Tweedsmuir were patrons (See Governor General's Office Records, LAC).
3. Ibid.
4. See David Gardner, "Dominion Drama Festival," *Canadian Encyclopedia*, thecanadianencyclopedia.com, *www.thecanadianencyclopedia.com/index .cfm?PgNm=TCE&Params=A1ARTA0002346* (accessed October 28, 2011).
5. Kenneth Hillier, chairman of the John Buchan Society, expressed the opinion that theatre did not hold great interest for Buchan, and, indeed, it has been included as one of his, very few, "blind spots" (John Buchan Weekend conference at Gladstone's Library, Wales, November 12, 2011). I thank Ken for identifying material in support of this: "... but plays bored John" (Susan Tweedsmuir, comp., *Wife and Friends*, 69); "My parents were interested in the theatre though not so besotted [as Anna and Alice herself]" (Alice Buchan, *A Scrap Screen* (London: Hamish Hamilton, 1979), 131).
6. Crawford to Tweedsmuir, January 15, 1936, BP, LAC.
7. Tweedsmuir to Anna Buchan, January 15, 1940, BP, LAC.
8. This section is based on information from David Spencer, *Dreaming in the Rain: How Vancouver Became Hollywood North By Northwest* (Vancouver: Arsenal Press, 2003), 15-26; David Absalom, "It's Not Just Michael Powell," British Films of the 30s, 40s and 50s, *www.britishpictures.com* (accessed April 20, 2013); Seth Feldman, "The Canadian Film Industry," in *Seeing Ourselves: Media Power and Policy in Canada*, edited by Helen Holmes and David Taras (Toronto: Harcourt, 1992), 87-96; and Zaza Fig, "Marriage Between Governments and the Canadian Film Industry: For Better or Worse" (essay submitted to the Department of English, University of Arhus, Denmark, May 10, 2002).
9. Tweedsmuir to Anna Buchan, January 15, 1940, BP, LAC.
10. Ibid.
11. Tweedsmuir to Anna Buchan, December 19, 1938, BP, LAC.
12. The library was actually moved to Douglas Library at Queen's University in 1966 (See H. Home, "John Buchan at the Douglas Library," *JBJ*, no. 30 (Spring 2004); a brief reference is also made in Robertson, *Driving Force*, 402).
13. "Hollywood North," which is how British Columbia is now often referred to, reflects the impressive growth of the film industry in Canada generally and in B.C. in particular. For figures on this growth and size, see *www .hollywoodnorthpr.com* (accessed September 24, 2012).

14. Yousuf Karsh, *In Search of Greatness: Reflections of Yousuf Karsh* (Toronto: University of Toronto Press, 1962), 62.
15. Ibid., 63-64.
16. Tweedsmuir, "Speech at the opening of the Montreal Art Gallery, February 1939," Speeches, BP, LAC.
17. Ibid.
18. Ibid.
19. Tweedsmuir to Anna Buchan, November 7, 1938, BP, LAC.
20. Tweedsmuir, "Speech to the Ontario Educational Association, Toronto, March 29, 1937," in Buchan, *Canadian Occasions*, 108.
21. Ibid., 113.
22. Ibid., 126; See also Tweedsmuir, "Speech at the centenary of Victoria University, Toronto, October 10, 1936," Speeches, BP, LAC. Tweedsmuir received an honorary degree at Victoria University.
23. This echoed words he spoke at the University of Toronto, November 27, 1935 ("Speech at University of Toronto, Toronto, November 27, 1935," in Buchan, *Canadian Occasions*, 159).
24. Tweedsmuir, *The Interpreter's House* (London: Hodder & Stoughton, 1938), 8-9. This is the text of Tweedsmuir's speech at his installation as chancellor of Edinburgh University, July 20, 1938. These were words he had also used in his address to the Ontario Educational Association in Toronto, March 29, 1937.
25. John Buchan, ed., *A History of English Literature* (New York: Thomas Nelson and Sons, 1932), 675.
26. Ibid., v.
27. John Buchan, MP, "When a Man Leaves College: What to Do with the Young Man Who Wakes Up at the End of His University Years to the Need of Earning His Bread and Butter," *The Graphic*, April 11, 1931, BP, LAC.
28. Tweedsmuir, "Speech to the Ontario Educational Association, Toronto, March 29, 1937," in Buchan, *Canadian Occasions*, 107.
29. Ibid., 108.
30. Those that are recorded include McGill University (Montreal); University of Toronto; McMaster University (Hamilton, ON); Bishop's College (now Bishop's University, Lennoxville, QC); University of Manitoba (Winnipeg); Victoria University (Toronto); Queen's University (Kingston, ON); University of Western Ontario (London, ON); and University of British Columbia (Vancouver).
31. As well as being present at Douglas's installation as principal at McGill in January 1938, the Tweedsmuirs and Douglases also met when they were both guests of Montreal businessman and philanthropist Jack McConnell in March 1938 at his log home in the Laurentians, north of Montreal.

32. C.D. Ellis to Tweedsmuir, February 7, 1939, BP, LAC.

33. Ibid. This letter had attached to it "Memorandum to Dr. Keppel from C.D. Ellis."

34. Ellis proposed a union of the four western universities "for the purpose of controlling the Ph.D. degree."

35. During Keppel's time as president, the Carnegie Corporation provided more than $150 million in funding. "Funds have been provided for specific undertakings and long-time projects in the fields of library service, fine arts, scientific and educational research, general education, and for colleges and universities." "The 1941 Rumford Award of the American Academy of Arts and Sciences," *Science Magazine*, October 24, 1941, 384, *www.sciencemag .org/content/94/2443/384.1.extract* (accessed August 21, 2011).

36. On February 7, 1939, Professor Ellis wrote to the governor general to update him on his visit with the Carnegie Foundation and forwarded the two memoranda he had submitted to Dr. Keppel.

37. Tweedsmuir to Lewis Douglas, December 13, 1938; and Tweedsmuir to Wallace, January 7, 1939, both BP, LAC.

38. Henry Cody to Tweedsmuir, February 20, 1939, BP, LAC. Tweedsmuir letters to Lewis Douglas (McGill), December 13, 1938; Robert Wallace (Queen's), January 7, 1939; and Henry Cody (University of Toronto), February 16, 1939, are referred to in Cody's reply.

39. Tweedsmuir to Douglas, December 13, 1938; and Tweedsmuir to Wallace, January 7, 1939, both BP, LAC.

40. Tweedsmuir to Douglas, December 13, 1938; and Tweedsmuir to Wallace, January 7, 1939, both BP, LAC.

41. Terence Macdermot to Tweedsmuir, January 7, 1939, BP, LAC.

42. Ibid.

43. Tweedsmuir to Terence Macdermot, January 13, 1939, BP, LAC.

44. Robert Wallace to Tweedsmuir, January 11, 1939, BP, LAC.

45. Lewis Douglas to Tweedsmuir, December 16, 1939, BP, LAC.

46. Henry Cody to Tweedsmuir, February 20, 1939, BP, LAC.

47. Lewis Douglas to Tweedsmuir, March 10, 1939, BP, LAC. Tweedsmuir's letters to Cody and Wallace on March 8, 1939, and to Douglas, are referenced in Douglas's reply.

48. Henry Cody to Tweedsmuir, March 9, 1939, BP, LAC.

49. Lewis Douglas to Tweedsmuir, March 10, 1939, BP, LAC.

50. Robert Wallace to Tweedsmuir, March 10, 1939, BP, LAC.

51. See *Minutes from the Eighteenth National Conference of Canadian Universities*, 10 (Queen's University Library, LA417.5 N2 1939).

52. Ibid., 17.

53. Ibid., 62. Matthews drew a comparison with the Office of Education in the United States and the American Council on Education.

54. Lewis Douglas to Tweedsmuir, March 10 and 23, 1939, BP, LAC. The Nuffield Foundation continues today: *www.nuffieldfoundation.org/* (accessed November 19, 2011). Recall that Tweedsmuir had been given the honorary title of "Visitor" during his first visit there in November 1935.

55. Henry Cody to Tweedsmuir, February 20, 1939, BP, LAC.

56. Henry Cody to Tweedsmuir, February 20 and March 9, 1939, BP, LAC.

57. Tweedsmuir, "Speech given at Ottawa Technical School, Ottawa, January 19, 1940," Speeches, BP, LAC.

58. Tweedsmuir, "Speech to the Boy Scouts Association dinner, Montreal, May 1, 1936," in Buchan, *Canadian Occasions*, 135.

59. Tweedsmuir to Stair Gillon, February 18, 1939, BP, LAC.

60. Buchan, *CO*, 144.

61. Ibid., 146.

62. Tweedsmuir, "Speech to Boy Scouts Association dinner, Montreal, February 18, 1939," in Buchan, *Canadian Occasions*, 146.

63. Baden-Powell to Tweedsmuir, March 26, 1939, BP, LAC.

64. Buchan, *CO*, 148.

65. Tweedsmuir, "Speech, Montreal, June 15, 1937," in Buchan, *Canadian Occasions*, 197.

66. Ibid., 197, 198.

67. Ibid., 198.

68. Tweedsmuir, "Speech to the Canadian Medical Association, Ottawa, June 24, 1937," in Buchan, *Canadian Occasions*, 212-213.

69. Ibid., 213.

70. Tweedsmuir, "Speech to the Royal College of Physicians and Surgeons of Canada, Ottawa, October 31, 1936," in Buchan, *Canadian Occasions*, 217.

71. Tweedsmuir, "Speech to the Ontario Medical Association, London, ON, May 27, 1936," in Buchan, *Canadian Occasions*, 210.

72. Tweedsmuir, "Speech to the Canadian Medical Association, Ottawa, June 24, 1937," in Buchan, *Canadian Occasions*, 215.

73. Ibid., 216.

74. Tweedsmuir, "Speech to the Ottawa Medical Society Dinner, Ottawa, October 29, 1938," in Buchan, *Canadian Occasions*, 224.

75. Ibid.

76. Ibid., 224-225. The quote from Plato was: "This is the greatest error in the treatment of sickness, that there are physicians for the body and physicians for the soul, and yet the two are one and indivisible."

77. Ibid., 225.

78. Tweedsmuir to Sir Thomas Holland, November 25, 1938, BP, LAC. *Saturday Night* magazine described Webster as "the most energetic advocate of the preservation of historic sites in the Maritime Provinces" (Cited from *Canadian Who's Who, 1936–1937*).

79. *Ottawa Citizen*, November 6, 1936.

80. "His Excellency Praises Welfare Services Pool," *Ottawa Citizen*, October 23, 1936.

81. Ibid.

Chapter 18

1. Mackenzie King, *Tributes to the Late Lord Tweedsmuir: Governor General of Canada* (Ottawa: King's Printer, 1940).

2. Quoted in Lownie, *Presbyterian Cavalier*, 285.

3. Tweedsmuir to Anna Buchan, November 27, 1939, BP, LAC.

4. Tweedsmuir to David Walker, November 23, 1939, David H. Walker Fonds, Correspondence, University of New Brunswick Archives and Special Collections, University of New Brunswick.

5. Referred to in Tweedsmuir to Stair Gillon, December 1, 1939, BP, LAC.

6. Tweedsmuir to Markham, November 27, 1939, BP, LAC.

7. MKD, December 6, 1939, LAC.

8. Ibid.

9. Ibid.

10. Ibid.

11. Ibid.

12. Tweedsmuir to Hardinge, December 7, 1939, BP, LAC. This letter provides the best summary of Tweedsmuir's time in Canada. In a more truncated form, he repeated to close friends his reasons for not staying (See Tweedsmuir to Stair Gillon, December 1, 1939; to Violet Markham, November 27, 1939; to Crawford, November 25, 1939; to Leopold Amery, December 8, 1939: all BP, LAC).

13. King to Tweedsmuir, December 12, 1939, BP, LAC.

14. Tweedsmuir to King, December 13, 1939, BP.

15. Tweedsmuir to Violet Markham, November 27, 1939, BP.

16. Tweedsmuir to Chamberlain, December 16, 1939, NCP, BULSC.

17. King to His Majesty, George VI, December 12, 1939, BP, LAC.

18. King to Tweedsmuir, December 13, 1939, BP, LAC.

19. Hardinge to King, January 3, 1940, BP, LAC.

20. Hardinge to Tweedsmuir, January 5, 1940, BP, LAC.

21. Hardinge to Tweedsmuir, January 8, 1940, BP, LAC. Hardinge had added

a *post scriptum* to his letter in which he noted: "The [k]ing has noticed, in the meantime, a report in the [p]ress that Mr. Mackenzie King has already given out the decision that your time will not be extended. His Majesty trusts that the report is inaccurate."

22. Tweedsmuir to Hardinge, January 26, 1940, BP, LAC.
23. Tweedsmuir explained: "What I think must have happened is that he was asked if my time was not to be extended, and that he said something like: 'H.E. thinks he ought to leave in September, for reasons with which I agree,' or 'H.E. feels that he ought to go at the end of his term if the King permits'" (Tweedsmuir to Hardinge, January 26, 1940, BP, LAC).
24. Harding to Tweedsmuir, January 8, 1940, BP, LAC.
25. Tweedsmuir to Hardinge, January 26, 1940, BP, LAC.
26. Ibid.
27. MKD, January 15, 1940, LAC.
28. Tweedsmuir to Hardinge, January 26, 1940, BP, LAC.
29. Tweedsmuir to Gilbert Murray, January 23, 1940, BP, LAC.
30. Tweedsmuir to Anna Buchan, January 15, 1940, BP, LAC.
31. Ibid.
32. MKD, December 6, 1939, LAC.
33. Albert Mansbridge to Tweedsmuir, January 7, 1940, BP, LAC. Mansbridge lived in England but must have lived in Canada at some point since he seems to express himself as Canadian. Tweedsmuir had sent a Christmas card to the Mansbridges, so must have known or met them.
34. Donald A. Parker to Tweedsmuir, January 19, 1940, BP, LAC. Parker lived in a small town in Saskatchewan (the name of the town is illegible in the letter), and had received an autographed copy of Buchan's *Oliver Cromwell*, along with a letter. Perhaps this was someone he met on his travels who had expressed an interest in Cromwell or that part of English history. It would be in keeping with Tweedsmuir's character to demonstrate such a kindly act.
35. Pelham Edgar to Tweedsmuir, January 24, 1940, BP, LAC.
36. A. Murray to Tweedsmuir, February 1, 1940, BP, LAC.
37. Tweedsmuir to Stair Gillon, January 19, 1940, BP, LAC.
38. Tweedsmuir to Anna Buchan, January 29, 1940, BP, LAC.
39. Tweedsmuir to Anna Buchan, February 5, 1940, BP, LAC.
40. Ibid.

Bibliography

Primary Sources

Bennett, Richard Bedford. Bennett Papers. Library and Archives Canada (RBP)

Buchan, John. John Buchan Papers. Library and Archives Canada (BP)

Canada. Department of External Affairs Records. Library and Archives Canada

Canada. Department of Mines and Resources. Library and Archives Canada

Canada. Department of National Defence/Directorate of History and Heritage. Library and Archives Canada (DND/DHH)

Canada. Department of the Secretary of State Records. Library and Archives Canada

Canada. Governor General's Office Records. Library and Archives Canada

Canada. House of Commons, *Debates*. Library and Archives Canada

Canada. Senate, *Debates*. Library and Archives Canada

Chamberlain, Neville. Papers. University of Birmingham Library, Special Collections. University of Birmingham (NCP/UBLSC)

Holy Blossom Temple Archives. Holy Blossom Temple (Toronto)

Hudson's Bay Company. Hudson's Bay Company Archives. Provincial Archives of Manitoba (HBCA/PAM)

King, William Lyon Mackenzie. Mackenzie King Diaries. Library and Archives Canada (MKD)

____. Mackenzie King Papers. Library and Archives Canada (MKP)

McLure, Lena. Fonds. Public Archives and Records Office of Prince Edward Island

National Conference of Canadian Universities. Minutes. Eighteenth National Conference. May 29-30, 1939. Queen's University Library LA417.5 N2 1939

National Film Board of Canada Archives (NFBA)
Perth County Museum, Perth, ON
Raddall, Thomas. Thomas Raddall Fonds. Selected Correspondence. Dalhousie University Library. Dalhousie University (DUL/TRSC)
Roosevelt, Franklin, D. Papers. Franklin D. Roosevelt Library, Hyde Park, New York (RP/FDRL)
United States Congress. Congressional Records. Library of Congress
Walker, David H. Fonds. University of New Brunswick Archives and Special Collections. University of New Brunswick (UNBA)

Interviews and Correspondence with individuals who recall or met Tweedsmuir

G.E. Beament, Q.C., Ottawa; Fulgence Charpentier, Ottawa; Émile Colas, Montreal; Hugh Douglas, Ottawa; Larry Ellis, Manotick, ON; Colonel Strome Galloway, Ottawa; John W. (Jack) Jeffrey, Victoria, B.C.; Earl Johnson, Ottawa; Lorne Johnson, Ottawa; Robert L. Lane, Ottawa; W.K. Lye, Oakville, ON; Charles Lynch, Ottawa; Judge John Matheson, Rideau Ferry, ON; William H. Milne, Toronto; Maj. (ret'd) George D. Mitchell, Ottawa; Col. Toody Munro, Ottawa; Dr. Graham Rowley, Ottawa; Gen. Roger Rowley, Ottawa; Walter Schoen, Dawson Creek, B.C.; Charles Scot-Brown, Toronto; Robert Short, Ottawa; A. Britton Smith, Kingston, ON; Lt. Col. Clifford Smith, Ottawa; Ernest Smith, Ottawa; James C. Stewart, Kingston, ON; Alfred Wahab, Ottawa; Verna Wallace, Ottawa; Raymond Willis-O'Connor, Ottawa; Mr. and Mrs. E.A. Wood, Red Deer, AB; Douglas B. Wurtele, Ottawa.

Individual Sources

"The 1941 Rumford Award of the American Academy of Arts and Sciences." *Science Magazine*, October 24, 1941, 384.

Abbott, D.M. "John Buchan and Lord Lothian." *John Buchan Journal*, no. 26 (Spring 2002): 37-39.

Abella, Irving, and Harold Troper. *None Is Too Many: Canada and the Jews of Europe*. Toronto: Lester & Orpen Dennys, 1986.

Absalom, David. "It's Not Just Michael Powell." British Films of the 30s, 40s and 50s. *www.britishpictures.com*

Adams, John Coldwell. *Sir Charles God Damn: The Life of Sir Charles G.D. Roberts*. Toronto: University of Toronto Press, 1986.

Addison, Paul. *Churchill: The Unexpected Hero*. Oxford: Oxford University Press, 2005.

Bibliography

Alsask History Book Committee. *Captured Memories: A History of Alsask and Surrounding School Districts. Bonnie Briar, Clifton Bank, Eastside, Lloyd George, Merid, Roslyn, Stonyhurst, Westside, and Wolf Willow.* N.p.: Alsask History Book Committee, 1983.

Amery, Leopold S. *The Unforgiving Years: 1929–1940.* Vol. 3 of *My Political Life.* London: Hutchinson, 1955.

"Arctic Expedition: The British-Canadian Expedition, 1936–1940." ucalgary.ca, *www.ucalgary.ca/arcticexpedition/baffintomelville*

Beach, Jim. "Origins of the Special Intelligence Relationship? Anglo-American Intelligence Co-operation on the Western Front, 1917–18." *Intelligence and National Security* 22, no. 2 (April 2007): 229-249.

Beaverbrook, Lord [Max Aitken]. *Friends.* London: William Heinemann, 1959.

Bell, John. "Tweedsmuir as Patron: John Buchan and the *Blackwood's* Stories of Thomas H. Raddall." *John Buchan Journal*, no. 6 (Autumn 1986): 15-16.

Benoit, Paul. "The Crown and the Constitution." *Canadian Parliamentary Review* 25, no. 2 (Summer 2002): 2-3.

Bensley, E.H. "Lord Tweedsmuir, Osler, and the Osler Library." *Osler Library Newsletter* 15 (February 1974): 3.

Benson, Nathaniel. *None of It Came Easy: The Story of James Garfield Gardiner.* Toronto: Burns & MacEachern, 1955.

Berger, Carl. *The Sense of Power: Studies in the Ideas of Canadian Imperialism, 1867–1914.* Toronto: University of Toronto Press, 1970.

———, ed. *Imperial Relations in the Age of Laurier.* Toronto: University of Toronto Press, 1969.

Betcherman, Lita-Rose. *The Swastika and the Maple Leaf: Fascist Movements in Canada in the Thirties.* Don Mills, ON: Fitzhenry & Whiteside, 1975.

Billinghurst, Jane. *The Many Faces of Archie Belaney: Grey Owl.* Vancouver: Greystone Books, 1999.

Bissell, Claude. *The Young Vincent Massey.* Toronto: University of Toronto Press, 1981.

Black, Conrad. *Render Unto Caesar: The Life and Legacy of Maurice Duplessis.* Toronto: Key Porter Books, 1998.

———. *Franklin Delano Roosevelt: Champion of Freedom.* New York: Public Affairs, 2003.

Black, Mrs. George, (As told to Elizabeth Bailey Price). *My Seventy Years.* Toronto and New York: Thomas Nelson and Sons, 1938.

Bonn, Mortiz J. *The Wandering Scholar.* New York: John Day, 1948.

Bonnycastle, Richard H.G. "Lord Tweedsmuir As Mountaineer." *Canadian Alpine Journal* 28, no. 2 (1942–1943): 200-209.

Bothwell, Robert, Ian Drummond, and John English. *Canada 1900–1945*. Toronto: University of Toronto Press, 1998.

Bothwell, Robert, and William Kilbourn. *C.D. Howe: A Biography*. Toronto: McClelland & Stewart, 1979.

Boutilier, Beverly, and Alison Prentice. *Creating Historical Memory: English-Canadian Women and the Work of History*. Vancouver: University of British Columbia Press, 1997.

Bourassa, Henri. *Great Britain and Canada: Topics of the Day*. Montreal: C.O. Beauchemin & Fils, 1902.

Bourke-White, Margaret. "A 10,000-Mile Tour of Canada's Northwest With Lord Tweedsmuir." *Life*, October 25, 1937, 40-47.

_____. *Portrait of Myself*. New York: Simon & Schuster, 1963.

"British Air Training Plan." Ottawa: Department of National Defence, Directorate of History and Heritage, n.d.

British Columbia Film Commission. "Industry Profile." BCFilmCommission .com, *www.bcfilmcommission.com/about_us/industry_profile.php*

Brooker, Bertram, ed. *Lamps* (Toronto), Spring 1938, *www.artsandlettersprivate .ca/lampsletters/lampsletters_1938.pdf*

Browder, Robert P., and Thomas G. Smith. *Independent: A Biography of Lewis W. Douglas*. New York: Alfred A. Knopf, 1986.

Brown, Michael. "Zionism in the Pre-Statehood Years: The Canadian Response." In *From Immigration to Integration: The Canadian Jewish Experience*, edited by Ruth Cline and Frank Dimant. Toronto: B'nai Brith Canada, Institute for International Affairs, 2001.

Buchan, Alice. *A Scrap Screen*. London: Hamish Hamilton, 1979.

Buchan, Anna. *Unforgettable, Unforgotten*. London: Hodder & Stoughton, 1945.

_____. *Farewell to Priorsford: A Book By and About Anna Buchan*. London: Hodder & Stoughton, 1950.

Buchan, John. *Augustus*. London: Hodder & Stoughton, 1937.

_____. *Canadian Occasions*. Toronto: Musson, 1941.

_____. *The Clearing House: A Survey of One Man's Mind*. Arranged by Lady Tweedsmuir. Preface by Gilbert Murray. London: Hodder & Stoughton, 1946.

_____. *Comments and Characters*. Edinburgh and London: Thomas Nelson and Sons, 1940.

_____. *The Interpreter's House*. London: Hodder & Stoughton, 1938.

_____. *The Island of Sheep* [*The Man from the Norlands*]. London: Hodder & Stoughton, 1936.

_____. *Lake of Gold*. Toronto: Musson, 1941.

_____. *The Last Secrets: The Final Mysteries of Exploration*. Boston: Houghton Mifflin, 1924.

_____. *A Lodge in the Wilderness*. Edinburgh and London: Thomas Nelson and Sons, 1922.

_____. *Lord Minto: A Memoir*. Boston: Houghton Mifflin, 1924.

_____. *The Marquis of Montrose*, Edinburgh and London: Thomas Nelson & Sons, 1913.

_____. *Memory Hold-The-Door*. Toronto: Musson, 1940.

_____. *Men and Deeds*. London: Peter Davies, 1935.

_____. *The Moon Endureth: Tales and Fancies*. Edinburgh: William Blackwood & Sons, 1912.

_____. "Oliver Cromwell." *Canadian Defence Quarterly* 14, no. ? (Summer 1937): n.p.

_____. *The Powerhouse*. 1916. Reprint, London: Pan Books, 1961.

_____. *A Prince of the Captivity*. London: Hodder & Stoughton, 1933.

_____. *Prester John*. Edinburgh: William Blackwood & Sons, 1910.

_____. *Sick Heart River*. Toronto: Musson, 1941.

_____. *Sir Walter Raleigh*. Edinburgh and London: Thomas Nelson & Sons, 1911.

_____. *The Thirty-Nine Steps*. Edinburgh: William Blackwood & Sons, 1915.

_____. "A Vice-Regal Congregation." *The Graduate Chronicle of the Alumni Association of the University of British Columbia* (Vancouver), April 5, 1939, 6, 8, *www.library.ubc.ca/archives/pdfs/chronicle/AL_CHRON_1939_04_05 .pdf#search=%22tweedsmuir%22*

_____. "When a Man Leaves College: What to Do with the Young Man Who Wakes Up at the End of His University Years to the Need of Earning His Bread and Butter." *The Graphic*, April 11, 1931.

_____, ed. *A History of English Literature*. New York: Thomas Nelson and Sons, 1932.

Buchan, William. *John Buchan: A Memoir*. Toronto: Griffin House, 1982.

Buitenhuis, Peter. *The Great War of Words: British, American and Canadian Propaganda and Fiction, 1914–1933*. Vancouver: University of British Columbia Press, 1987.

"Burns Lake." BritishColumbia.com. 2013, *www.britishcolumbia.com/regions/ towns/?townID=3589*

Burpee, L.J. "Canada's Awakening North." *National Geographic*, June 1936, 749–776.

Butler, J.R.M. *Lord Lothian*. London: Macmillan, 1960.

Calder, Robert. *Beware the British Serpent: The Role of Writers in British Propaganda in the United States, 1939–1945*. Montreal and Kingston, ON: McGill-Queen's University Press, 2004.

Camsell, Charles. *Son of the North*. Toronto: Ryerson Press, 1954.

Canada. *Royal Commission on National Development in the Arts, Letters, and Sciences, 1949–1951.* Ottawa: King's Printer, 1951, *www.collectionscanada .gc.ca/massey/h5-400-e.htm*

Canadian Geographical Society. "Royal Visit." *Canadian Geographic,* July 1939.

The Canadian Almanac and Legal and Court Directory, 1935. Toronto: Copp Clark, 1935.

Canadian Institute on Economics and Politics. *Canada, The Empire and The League: Lectures Given at the Canadian Institute on Economics and Politics, July 31 to August 14, 1936.* Toronto: Thomas Nelson & Sons, in association with the National Council of YMCAs of Canada, 1936.

_____. *World Currents and Canada's Course: Lectures Given at the Canadian Institute on Economics and Politics, August 7th to 20th, 1936.* Toronto: Thomas Nelson and Sons, 1937.

Canadian University Press. "War — Yes or No?" *Ubyssey* (University of British Columbia,Vancouver), March 24, 1939, 4, *www.library.ubc.ca/archives/pdfs/ ubyssey/UBYSSEY_1939_03_24.pdf#search=%22war%20*

Canadian Who's Who, 1937. Toronto: University of Toronto Press, 1938.

Carnegie Endowment for International Peace, "100 Years of Impact: A Timeline of the Carnegie Endowment for International Peace." Carnegieendowment .org, *carnegieendowment.org/about/timeline100/index.html*

Carnegie, R.K. *And The People Cheered.* Ottawa: Legionary Library, 1940.

Carr, Emily. *Hundreds and Thousands: The Journals of Emily Carr.* Toronto and Vancouver: Clarke, Irwin & Company, 1966.

Chadwin, Mark Lincoln. *The Hawks of World War II.* Chapel Hill, NC: University of North Carolina Press, 1968.

Charteris, Brig.-Gen. John. *At GHQ.* London: Cassell and Company, 1931.

Checkland, Sydney. *Voices Across The Water: An Anglo-Canadian Boyhood.* Aberdeen: Aberdeen University Press, 1989.

Churchill, Winston S. *Churchill In His Own Voice.* Audio cassette. Abridged edition. New York: Caedmon Audio, Harper, 1994.

_____. *Their Finest Hour.* Vol. 2 of *The Second World War.* Boston: Houghton Mifflin, 1949.

_____. *The Gathering Storm.* Vol. 1 of *The Second World War.* Boston: Houghton Mifflin, 1948.

Clarke, Peter. *Hope and Glory: Britain 1900–1990.* London: Allen Lane, Penguin Press, 1996.

Clavin, Patricia. "The Way to Make History: British Historians and the Shaping of American Foreign Policy, 1940–45." In *Transatlantic Encounters: Public Uses and Misuses of History in Europe and the United States,* edited by D.K. Adams and M. Vaudagna. Amsterdam: VU University Press, 2000.

Clifford, J. Garry. "Grenville Clark: World Peace Through World Law." harvardsquarelibrary.org, *www.harvardsquarelibrary.org/unitarians/clark_ grenville.htm*

Colombo, John Robert. *Canadian Literary Landmarks*. Toronto: Dundurn Press, 1984.

Connell, Brian. *Knight Errant: A Biography of Douglas Fairbanks Jr*. London: Hodder & Stoughton, 1955.

Cousins, Norman, and J.G. Clifford, eds. *Memoirs of a Man: Grenville Clark*. New York: W.W. Norton & Company, 1975.

Crackanthorpe, David. "The Great Estate." *John Buchan Journal*, no. 38 (Summer 2008): 21-28.

____. "*The Yellow Book* and John Buchan." *John Buchan Journal*, no. 41 (Spring 2010): 9-16.

Crowley, Terry. "The Thin Raiment of the North Atlantic Triangle: Canada and the Decision for War, 1938–1939." *London Journal of Canadian Studies* 20 (2004/2005): 27-44.

Cull, Nicholas John. *Selling War: The British Propaganda Campaign Against American 'Neutrality' in World War II*. Oxford: Oxford University Press, 1995.

Dafoe, J.W. "Canadian Foreign Policy — Public Opinion." In *World Currents and Canada's Course: Lectures Given at the Canadian Institute on Economics and Politics, August 7th to 20th, 1936*, edited by Violet Anderson. Toronto: Thomas Nelson and Sons, 1937.

Davis, Kenneth S. *Into the Storm, 1937–1940*. Vol. 4 of *FDR: A History*. New York: Random House, 1993.

Dawson, Robert M., ed. *The Development of Dominion Status 1900-1936*. 1937. Reprint, London: Frank Cass & Co., 1965.

Dickson, Lovat. *Wilderness Man: The Strange Story of Grey Owl*. Toronto: Macmillan of Canada, 1973.

Dimbleby, David, and David Reynolds. *An Ocean Apart: The Relationship Between Britain and America in the Twentieth Century*. New York: Random House, 1988.

Directorate of Staff Duties, General Staff, Department of National Defence. "The Recruiting Problem in the Province of Quebec: A Military Appreciation." Ottawa: King's Printer, 1941.

Donnelly, Murray. *Dafoe of the Free Press*. Toronto: Macmillan of Canada, 1968.

Duffy, Michael. "The Old Contemptibles." Firstworldwar.com, *www.firstworld-war.com/atoz/oldcontemptibles.htm*

Dupuis, Michael. "The Response of the *Toronto Daily Star* to the 'On-to-Ottawa' Trek and Dominion Day Riot in Regina." *Canadian Journal of Media Studies* 6, no. 1 (March 2010): 28-51, *http://cjms.fims.uwo.ca/issues/06-01/dupuis .pdf* (accessed August 7, 2011).

Egoff, Sheila, and Judith Saltman. *The New Republic of Childhood: A Critical Guide to Canadian Children's Literature in English*. Toronto: Oxford University Press, 1990.

Eliot, Marc. *Walt Disney*. New York: Carol Publishing, 1993.

Elliott, Lorne. Interview by Shelagh Rogers. *The Next Chapter*. CBC Radio 2, May 2, 2011.

Embassy of the United States, Ottawa, Canada, "Chiefs of the Unites States Mission to Canada." Canada.usembassy.gov, *http://canada.usembassy.gov/ ambassador/past-ambassadors.html*

Errington, Jane. *The Lion, the Eagle, and Upper Canada*. Montreal and Kingston, ON: McGill-Queen's University Press, 1987.

Evans, Gary. *John Grierson and the National Film Board: The Politics of Wartime Propaganda*. Toronto: University of Toronto Press, 1984.

Fairbanks Jr., Douglas. *The Salad Days*. New York: Doubleday, 1988.

Federated Women's Institutes of Ontario. *Ontario Women's Institute Story*. N.p.: T.H. Best Printing Company, 1972.

Feiling, Keith. *The Life of Neville Chamberlain*. London: Macmillan, 1970.

Feldman, Seth. "The Canadian Film Industry." In *Seeing Ourselves: Media Power and Policy in Canada*, edited by Helen Holmes and David Taras. Toronto: Harcourt, 1992.

Ferguson, Niall. *Empire: The Rise and Demise of the British World Order and the Lessons for Global Power*. New York: Basic Books, 2002.

Fig, Zaza. "Marriage Between Governments and the Canadian Film Industry: For Better or Worse." Paper. Department of English, University of Arhus, Denmark, 2002.

"Foreign Relations: Lord Lothian's Job." *Time*, July 8, 1940, *www.time.com/time/ printout/0,8816,795034,00.html* (accessed December 14, 2007).

Forsey, Eugene. *A Life on the Fringe*. Toronto: Oxford University Press, 1990.

Fraser, Marion. "Untitled submission." In *Captured Memories*. N.p.: Alsask History Book Committee, 1983.

Freidel, Frank. *Franklin D. Roosevelt: A Rendezvous with Destiny*. Boston: Little, Brown, 1990.

Galbraith, J. William. "Fiftieth Anniversary of the 1939 Royal Visit." *Canadian Parliamentary Review* 12, no. 3 (Autumn 1989): 7-11.

____. "His Excellency's Excellent Adventure." *Up Here* (Yellowknife, NT), May/June 1996, n.p.

____. "John Buchan in Canada: Writing a New Chapter in Canada's Constitutional History." In *John Buchan and the Idea of Modernity*, edited by Kate Macdonald and Nathan Waddell. London: Pickering & Chatto, 2013.

____. "A Promised Land: The Buchans in Canada – 1924." *John Buchan Journal,* no. 40 (Autumn 2009): 32-34.

Garrett, Garet. *Defend America First: The Antiwar Editorials of the Saturday Evening Post 1939-1942*. Caldwell, ID: Caxton Press, 2003.

Gilbert, Walter, E., (As told to K. Shackleton). *Arctic Pilot: Life and Work on North Canadian Air Routes*. Toronto: Thomas Nelson & Sons, 1940.

Glendinning, Victoria. *Elizabeth Bowen: Portrait of a Writer*. London: Weidenfeld and Nicolson, 1977.

Goldberg, Vicki. *Margaret Bourke-White: A Biography*. New York: Harper & Row, 1986.

Goldsborough, Gordon. "Memorable Manitobans: James Shaver Woodsworth (1874-1942)." Manitoba Historical Society. April 8, 2011, *www.mhs.mb.ca/docs/people/woodsworth_js.shtml*

Granatstein, J.L. *How Britain's Weakness Forced Canada into the Arms of the United States*. Toronto: University of Toronto Press, 1989.

_____. *The Ottawa Men*. Toronto: University of Toronto Press, 1998.

Gray, W. Forbes, ed. *Comments and Characters by John Buchan*. Edinburgh and London: Thomas Nelson and Sons, 1940.

Greathed, Edward, D. "Antecedents and Origins of the Canadian Institute of International Affairs." In *Empire and Nations: Essays in Honour of Frederic H. Soward*, edited by H.L. Dyck and H.P. Krosby. Toronto: University of Toronto Press, 1969.

Greenhous, B., S.J. Harris, W.C. Johnston, and W.G.P. Rawling. *The Crucible of War, 1939-1945*. Vol. 3 of *The Official History of the Royal Canadian Air Force*. Toronto: University of Toronto Press, in co-operation with the Department of National Defence, 1994.

Grieves, Keith. "Nelson's History of the War: John Buchan as a Contemporary Military Historian 1915-22." *Journal of Contemporary History* 28, no. 3 (July 1993): 533-551.

Grigg, John. *Nancy Astor: A Lady Unashamed*. Boston: Little, Brown and Company, 1980.

Halifax, Edward (Earl of). *Fulness of Days*. London: Collins, 1957.

Hamelin, Marcel, ed. *Les Mémoires du Sénateur Raoul Dandurand (1861-1942)*. Québec: Les presses de l'université Laval, 1967.

Harrington, Lyn. *Syllables of Recorded Time: The Story of the Canadian Authors Association 1921-1981*. Toronto: Dundurn Press, 1981.

Hatch, F.J. *The Aerodrome of Democracy: Canada and the British Commonwealth Air Training Plan, 1939-1945*. Ottawa: Directorate of History, Department of National Defence, 1983.

Heeney, Arnold. *The Things That Are Caesar's: Memoirs of a Canadian Public Servant*. Toronto: University of Toronto Press, 1972.

Henshaw, Peter. "A 'Murky and Distorted Genius': John Buchan on Cecil Rhodes, 1901–1940." *John Buchan Journal*, no. 35 (Autumn 2006): 21-30.

Hinsley, F.H. et al. "Intelligence on the German Economy, September 1939 to the Autumn of 1940." Vol. 1 of *British Intelligence in the Second World War: Its Influence on Strategy and Operations*. London: Her Majesty's Stationery Office, 1979.

_____. *Security and Counter-Intelligence*, Vol. 4 of *British Intelligence in the Second World War: Its Influence on Strategy and Operations*. Cambridge and New York: Cambridge University Press, 1990.

Home, H. "John Buchan at the Douglas Library." *John Buchan Journal*, no. 30 (Spring 2004): n.p.

Horn, Michiel, ed. *The Dirty Thirties: Canadians in the Great Depression*. Toronto: Copp Clark, 1972.

Hornyold, Antony. "John Buchan and the FSOs." *John Buchan Journal*, no. 40 (Autumn 2009): 3-13.

Horsefield, Ray. "An Affair of State." *The Beaver* (since April/May 2010, known as *Canada's History*), Spring 1979, 44-47.

Hubbard, Robert H. *Rideau Hall*. Montreal and Kingston, ON: McGill-Queen's University Press, 1977.

_____. *Ample Mansions: The Viceregal Residences of the Canadian Provinces*. Ottawa: University of Ottawa Press, 1989.

Hull, Cordell. *The Memoirs of Cordell Hull*. 2 vols. New York: Macmillan, 1948.

Hunt, Barbara, ed. *Rebels, Rascals & Royalty: The Colourful North of LACO Hunt*. Yellowknife, NT: Outcrop, 1983.

Hyde, H. Montgomery. *Neville Chamberlain*. London: Weidenfeld and Nicolson, 1976.

_____. *The Quiet Canadian: The Secret Service Story of Sir William Stephenson*. London: Hamish Hamilton, 1962.

Ions, Edmund. *James Bryce and American Democracy*. London: Macmillan, 1968.

James, Robert Rhodes. *Anthony Eden*. London: Weidenfeld and Nicolson, 1986.

_____. *Victor Cazalet: A Portrait*. London: Hamish Hamilton, 1976.

Jeffreys-Jones, Rhodri. "The Role of British Intelligence in the Mythologies Underpinning the OSS and Early CIA." *Intelligence and National Security* 15, no. 2 (Summer 2000): 5-19.

Johnson, Walter. *William Allen White's America*. New York: Henry Holt and Company, 1947.

Karsh, Yousuf. *In Search of Greatness: Reflections of Yousuf Karsh*. Toronto: University of Toronto Press, 1962.

Keenleyside, Hugh L. *Memoirs*. Vol. 1. Toronto: McClelland & Stewart, 1981.

Keenleyside, H.L., James Eayrs, Gaddis Smith, et al. *The Growth of Canadian Policies in External Affairs*. Durham, NC: Duke University Press, 1960.

King, William Lyon Mackenzie. *Canada at Britain's Side*. Toronto: Macmillan Company of Canada, 1941.

____. *Industry and Humanity: A Study in the Principles Underlying Industrial Reconstruction*. Toronto: Houghton Mifflin, 1918.

Knight, Kevin. "John Henry Newman." Newadvent.org. April 27, 2013, *www.newadvent.org/cathen/10794a.htm*

Koskoff, David E. *Joseph P. Kennedy: A Life and Times*. Upper Saddle River, NJ: Prentice-Hall, 1974.

Kruse, J. *John Buchan and the Idea of Empire*. Lampeter, Ceredigion, UK: Edwin Mellen Press, 1989.

Lamb, Richard. *The Ghosts of Peace: 1935–1945*. Norwich, UK: Michael Russell, 1987.

Lambert, H.F. "The Harry Snyder Canadian Expedition, 1937." *Canadian Alpine Journal*, no. 25 (1937): n.p.

Lamont, Corliss, ed. *The Thomas Lamonts in America*. South Brunswick, NJ, and New York: A.S. Barnes and Company, 1962.

Lanctôt, Gustave. *The Royal Tour, 1939*. Toronto: E.P. Taylor Foundation, Toronto, 1964.

Lavine, Harold, and James Wechsler. *War Propraganda and the United States*. New Haven, CT: Yale University Press, in association with the Institute for Propaganda Analysis, 1940. Reprint, New York and London: Garland Publishing, 1972.

Lawrence, Jon, and Pat Starkey. *Child Welfare and Social Action in the Nineteenth Century and Twentieth Centuries: International Perspectives*. Liverpool, UK: Liverpool University Press, 2001.

Lee, Edwin. "The Vision Splendid: A Synthesis of John Buchan's *A Lodge in the Wilderness*." *John Buchan Journal*, no. 27 (Autumn 2002): 6-22.

Lepage, Yvan G. "Une ambassadrice des lettres québecoise." *Revue de critique et de théorie littéraire* 5, no. 1 (Winter 2010): n.p., *www.revue-analyses.org/index.php?id=1576*

Lindkvist, Karl-Eric. "Articles." The Ross Macdonald Files, *http://hem.passagen.se/caltex/newsart.html*

Literature Network. "Aldous Huxley." Online-literature.com, *www.online-literature.com/aldous_huxley/*

Little, Geoffrey. "'The people must have plenty of good books': The Lady Tweedsmuir Prairie Library Scheme, 1936–40." Spectrum.library.concordia.ca. February 11, 2013, *http://spectrum.library.concordia.ca/974102*

Lothian, Lord (Philip Kerr). *The American Speeches of Lord Lothian*. Oxford: Royal Institute of International Affairs, Oxford University Press, 1941.

Lownie, Andrew. "John Buchan: Conservative Politician." *John Buchan Journal*, no. 35 (Autumn 2006): 31-34.

_____. *John Buchan: The Presbyterian Cavalier*. London: Constable, 1995.

Macdonald, Kate. *John Buchan: A Companion to the Mystery Fiction*. Jefferson, NC, and London: McFarland & Company, 2009.

Macdonald, Kate and Nathan Waddell, eds. *John Buchan and the Idea of Modernity*. London: Pickering and Chatto, 2013.

Macdonald, Malcolm. *Canadian North*. Oxford: Oxford University Press, 1942.

Macmillan, Hugh. *A Man of Law's Tale: The Reminiscences of the Rt. Hon. Lord Macmillan*. London: Macmillan, 1952.

MacMillan, Margaret. *Paris 1919*. New York: Random House, 2003.

Mahl, Thomas, E. *Desperate Deception: British Covert Operations in the United States, 1939-44*. Dulles, VA: Brassey's, 1998.

Mallory, J.R. "The Appointment of the Governor-General: Responsible Government, Autonomy, and the Royal Prerogative." *Canadian Journal of Economics and Political Science* 26, no. 1 (February 1960): 96-107.

Manitoba Historical Society. "Memorable Manitobans: Charles William Gordon [Ralph Connor] 1860-1937." MHS.MB.ca. June 9, 2012, *www.mhs.mb.ca/docs/people/gordon_cw.shtml*

Manitoba Historical Society. "Memorable Manitobans: Winnipeg's Millionaires, 1910." MHS.MB.ca. August 8, 2011, *www.mhs.mb.ca/docs/people/millionaires1910.shtml*

Markham, Violet. *Return Passage*. Oxford: Oxford University Press, 1953.

_____. *Friendship's Harvest*. London: M. Reinhardt, 1956.

Massey, Vincent. *On Being Canadian*. Toronto: J.M. Dent & Sons (Canada), 1948.

_____. *What's Past Is Prologue*. Toronto: Macmillan Company of Canada, 1963.

Masters, Anthony. *Nancy Astor: A Life*. London: Weidenfeld and Nicolson, 1981.

McBurney, Margaret. *The Great Adventure: 100 Years at the Arts and Letters Club*. Toronto: Arts & Letters Club of Toronto, 1997.

McCreery, Christopher. *The Canadian Honours System*. Toronto: Dundurn Press, 2005.

McKenty, Neil. *Mitch Hepburn*. Toronto: McClelland & Stewart, 1967.

Monnet, Jean. *Mémoires*. 2 vols. Paris: Le Livre de Poche, 1976.

Morgan, Ted. *FDR*. New York: Simon and Schuster, 1985.

National Institute for Newman Studies. "Newman Reader: Venerable John Henry Cardinal Newman." 2007, *www.newmanreader.org*

Neatby, H. Blair. *The Politics of Chaos: Canada in the Thirties*. Toronto: Macmillan Company of Canada, 1972.

_____. *The Prism of Unity, 1932-1939*. Vol. 3 of *William Lyon Mackenzie King*. Toronto: University of Toronto Press, 1976.

Niagara Parks, "Museum History." Niagaraparksheritage.com, *www.niagaraparks heritage.com/mackenzie-printery/museum-history.html*

Nobel Foundation. "Nobel Peace Prize 1937: Robert Cecil." Nobelprize.org, *www.nobelprize.org/peace/laureates/1937/chelwood-bio.html*

Nolan, Tom. *Ross Macdonald: A Biography*. New York: Scribner, 1999.

Office of the Governor General of Canada. "Former Governors General: The Viscount Willingdon." Governor General of Canada, *www.gg.ca/document .aspx?id=14615*

Office of the Historian, Bureau of Public Affairs, United States Department of State, "Milestones: 1937–1945 – The Atlantic Conference and Charter, 1941." History.state.gov, *http://history.state.gov/milestones/1937–1945/AtlanticConf*

____. "Milestones: 1921–1936 – The Nine-Power Treaty." History.state.gov, *http://history.state.gov/milestones/1921-1936/NavalConference*

"Our History." Children's Health Foundation of Vancouver Island, *http://childrenshealthvi.org/about-us/our-history*

Pakenham, Thomas. *The Boer War*. New York: Random House, 1979.

Pearce, David. "*Brave New World*? A Defence of Paradise-Engineering." 2008, *www.huxley.net/index.html*

Pennington, Doris. *Agnes Macphail: Reformer*. Toronto: Simon & Pierre, 1989.

Peters, Gerhard. "State of the Union Addresses and Messages." *The American Presidency Project, www.presidency.ucsb.edu/sou.php* (accessed December 5, 2009).

"Poles of Inaccesibility." UC Santa Barbara, Department of Geography, http://www.geog.ucsb.edu/events/department-news/1084/poles-of-inaccessibility/ (accessed April 29, 2013).

Pollard, Michael. "'The Same Breed' or 'An Odd Brotherhood'?" *John Buchan Journal*, no. 40 (Autumn 2009): 14-22.

Pomeroy, E.M. *Sir Charles G.D. Roberts: A Biography*. Toronto: Ryerson Press, 1943.

Prang, Margaret. *N.W. Rowell: Ontario Nationalist*. Toronto: University of Toronto Press, 1975.

"Proclamation." *Canada Gazette*, September 16, 1939, 793, *www.collectionscanada .gc.ca/databases/canada-gazette/093/001060-119.01-e.php?document_id_ nbr=8420&image_id_nbr=301989&f=p&PHPSESSID=qod94dp57c1e1mv 2qn9l9l3655*

Raddall, Thomas, H. *In My Time*. Toronto: McClelland & Stewart, 1976.

____. *The Pied Piper of Dipper Creek and Other Tales*. Foreword by Lord Tweedsmuir. Toronto: McClelland & Stewart, 1943.

Read, Donald. *The Power of News: The History of Reuters*. Oxford: Oxford University Press, 1992.

Redley, Michael. "John Buchan and East Africa." *John Buchan Journal*, no. 27 (Autumn 2002): 23-33.

_____. "John Buchan and *The Great Illusion*" *John Buchan Journal*, no. 37 (Autumn 2007): 33-35.

_____. "John Buchan at Milton Academy." *John Buchan Journal*, no. 22 (Spring 2000): 22-32.

_____. "Making Democracy Safe for the World: A Note on John Buchan's Political Career." *John Buchan Journal*, no. 17 (Autumn 1997): 31-37.

Roazen, Paul. *Canada's King: An Essay in Political Psychology*. Oakville, ON: Mosaic Press, 1998.

Reinharz, Jehuda. *Chaim Weizmann: The Making of a Statesman,* Studies in Jewish History. Vol. 2. Oxford and New York: Oxford University Press, 1993.

Reynolds, David. *The Creation of the Anglo-American Alliance, 1937–41: A Study in Competitive Co-operation*. Chapel Hill, NC: University of North Carolina Press, 1982.

Roberts, Andrew. *The Holy Fox: The Life of Lord Halifax*. London: Phoenix Giant, 1997.

Roberts, Priscilla. "Lord Lothian and the Atlantic World." *Historian* 66, no. 1 (March 2004): 97-127, *www.encyclopedia.com/printable.aspx-?id-1G1:135425232* (accessed December 14, 2007).

Robertson, G.R. "The Long Gaze." In *The Unbelievable Land*, edited by Norman Smith. Ottawa: Queen's Printer for Northern Affairs and National Resources, and the Northern Service of the CBC, 1963.

Robertson, Heather. *Driving Force: The McLaughlin Family and the Age of the Car*. Toronto: McClelland & Stewart, 1995.

Robertson, H., ed. *A Gentleman Adventurer: The Arctic Diaries of Richard Bonnycastle*. Toronto: Lester & Orpen Dennys, 1984.

Roosevelt, Franklin Delano. *Franklin D. Roosevelt and Foreign Affairs*. Vol. 3: September 1935–January 1937. Edited by Edgar B. Nixon. Hyde Park, NY: Franklin D. Roosevelt Library; Cambridge, MA: Belknap Press, Harvard University Press, 1969.

Rose, Kenneth. *The Later Cecils*. London: Weidenfeld and Nicolson, 1975.

Rose, Norman. *Chaim Weizmann: A Biography*. New York: Elisabeth Sifton Books, Viking Penguin, 1986.

_____. *The Gentile Zionists*. London: Frank Cass, 1973.

_____. "The Seventh Dominion." *Historical Journal* 14, no. 2 (June 1971): 397-416.

Rowley, Graham W. *Cold Comfort: My Love Affair With the Arctic*. Montreal and Kingston, ON: McGill-Queen's University Press, 1996.

Rumilly, Robert. *Henri Bourassa*. Montreal: Les Editions de l'Homme, 1953.

Saywell, John T. *Just Call Me Mitch: The Life of Mitchell F. Hepburn*. Toronto: University of Toronto Press, 1991.

Shakespeare, William. *Twelfth Night*.

Scott, Sir Walter. *Marmion*.

Shackleton, Edward. *Arctic Journeys: The Story of the Oxford University Ellesmere Land Expedition, 1934–35*. London: Hodder & Stoughton, 1936.

Smiley, Donald, V., ed. *The Rowell-Sirois Report*. The Carleton Library, No. 5. Toronto: McClelland & Stewart, 1963.

Smith, David E. "The Crown and the Constitution: Sustaining Democracy?" Paper presented at the conference, "The Crown in Canada: Present Realities and Future Options," Ottawa, Canada, June 10, 2010.

Smith, Janet Adam. *John Buchan*. London: Rupert Hart-Davis, 1965.

_____. *John Buchan and His World*. London: Thames and Hudson, 1979.

Snyder, Harry. "Exploring Upper Nahanni River and Snyder Mountains." *Canadian Geographic*, October 1937, 168-191.

Soward, F.H., J.F. Parkinson, N.A.M. MacKenzie, and T.W.L. MacDermot. *Canada in World Affairs: The Pre-War Years*. Toronto: Oxford University Press, issued under the auspices of the Canadian Institute of International Affairs, 1941.

Speaight, Robert. *Vanier: Soldier, Diplomat & Governor-General: A Biography*. Toronto: Collins, 1970.

Spencer, David. *Dreaming in the Rain: How Vancouver Became Hollywood North By Northwest*. Vancouver: Arsenal Press, 2003.

Stacey, C.P. *Arms, Men & Governments: War Policies of Canada*. Ottawa: Queen's Printer, 1970.

_____. *Six Years of War: The Army in Canada, Britain and the Pacific*. Ottawa: Queen's Printer, 1955.

_____. *The Canadian Army, 1939–1945: An Official Historical Summary*. Ottawa: King's Printer, 1948.

Staines, David, ed. *The Canadian Imagination: Dimensions of a Literary Culture*. Cambridge, MA: Harvard University Press, 1977.

Stamp, Robert M. *Kings, Queens and Canadians*. Markham, ON: Fitzhenry & Whiteside, 1987.

Stewart, Graham. *Burying Caesar: Churchill, Chamberlain and the Battle for the Tory Party*. London: Phoenix, 2000.

Stewartby, Lord. "John Buchan and Parliament." *John Buchan Journal*, no. 31 (Autumn 2004): 9-18.

Stevenson, William. *A Man Called Intrepid*. New York: Ballantine Books, 1976.

Thompson, John H., with Allen Seager. *Canada 1922–1939: Decades of Discord*. Toronto: McClelland & Stewart Limited, 1985.

Thwaites, Reuben Gold, ed. *The Jesuit Relations and Allied Documents: Travels and Explorations of the Jesuit Missionaries in New France, 1610–1791.* Vol. 57, *Lower Canada, Abenakis, Louisiana, 1716–1727.* Note 3. Cleveland: Burrows Brothers, 1896–1901. Originals scanned and transcribed by Thom Mentrak; formatted and organized by Raymond A. Bucko for Creighton University, *http://puffin.creighton.edu/jesuit/relations/relations_67.html*

Ticketmaster. "Convocation Hall Tickets." Ticketmaster.ca, *www.ticketmaster.ca/Convocation-Hall-tickets-Toronto/venue/131080 Ticketmaster*

Turner, A.C. *Mr. Buchan: Writer.* Toronto: Macmillan Company of Canada, 1949.

Tweedsmuir, Susan, comp. *John Buchan, By His Wife and Friends.* London: Hodder & Stoughton, 1947.

University of Toronto Office of Space Management. "Convocation Hall." UToronto.ca, *http://osm.utoronto.ca/conhall/rental.html*

U.S. Department of State, "Press Release no. 94, October 6, 1937." Peace and War: United States Foreign Policy, 1931–1941, *www.ibiblio.org/hyperwar/Dip/PaW/094.html*

Vanderhaeghe, Guy. *The Englishman's Boy.* Toronto: McClelland & Stewart, 1996.

Wace, C. "The Queen Alexandra Solarium for Crippled Children." *Canadian Medical Association Journal* 21, no. 6 (December 1929): 702-706, *www.ncbi.nlm.nih.gov/pmc/articles/PMC381561/pdf/canmedaj00086-0058.pdf*

Walker, David, H. *Lean, Wind, Lean.* London: Collins, 1984.

Walters, Paul. "Between the Wars: Hard Times and Turmoil." *McGill Reporter* (McGill University, Montreal) October 14, 2011, 11, *http://publications.mcgill.ca/reporter/files/2011/10/HISTORY-ISSUE.pdf*

Walton, Izaak, and Charles Cotton. *The Compleat Angler.* Introduction by John Buchan. World's Classics. Oxford: Oxford University Press, 1935.

Ward, Norman, and David Smith. *Jimmy Gardiner: Relentless Liberal.* Toronto: University of Toronto Press, 1990.

Warwick, Peter, ed. *The South African War.* London: Longman, 1980.

Watkins, Ernest. *R.B. Bennett.* Toronto: Kingswood House, 1963.

Watt, D. Cameron. *Succeeding John Bull: America in Britain's Place, 1900–1975.* Cambridge, UK: Cambridge University Press, 2008.

Watt, Frederick B. "The New Gentlemen Adventurers." *The Rotarian* 37, no. 2 (August 1930), 9-11, *http://books.google.ca/books?id=6kUEAAAAMBAJ&pg=PA50&lpg=PA50&dq=the+rotarian+1930+frederick+watt&source=bl&ots=wuttSenQTO&sig=J4jHrBo0urURX4W62W9qqjZBCoQ&hl=en&ei=9i0hTefpJ9SknQeDt5DkDQ&sa=X&oi=book_result&ct=result&resnum=1&ved=0CBgQ6AEwAA#v=onepage&q=the%20rotarian%201930%20frederick%20watt&f=false*

Weizmann, Chaim. *The Letters and Papers of Chaim Weizmann*. Series A: Letters. Vol. 18, January 1937–December 1938. General editor: Barnet Litvinoff; volume editor: Aaron Kliem. Jerusalem: Israel Universities Press, 1979.

____. *The Letters and Papers of Chaim Weizmann*. Series A: Letters. Vol. 19, January 1939–June 1940. General editor: Barnet Litvinoff; volume editor: Norman Rose. Jerusalem: Israel Universities Press, 1979.

____. *Trial and Error*. New York: Harper & Brothers, 1949.

Wells, H.G. *The Outline of History: Being a Plain History of Life and Mankind*. 3rd ed. New York: Macmillan, 1921.

Wheare, K.C. *The Statute of Westminster and Dominion Status*. 4th ed. Oxford: Oxford University Press, 1949.

Wheeler-Bennett, John. *King George VI: His Life and Reign*. London: Macmillan, 1958.

____. *Special Relationships: America in Peace and War*. London: Macmillan, 1975.

White, William Allen. *The Autobiography of William Allen White*. New York: Macmillan, 1946.

Wilcox, Victoria M. "Prime Minister and Governor-General: Mackenzie King and Lord Tweedsmuir, 1935–1940." Master's thesis. Queen's University, 1976.

"Willard Connely and the Buchans." *John Buchan Journal*, no. 37 (Autumn 2007): 13-17.

Willis-O'Connor, Col. H. *Inside Government House*. Toronto: Ryerson Press, 1954.

Wilson, Duncan. *Gilbert Murray, OM, 1866–1957*. Oxford: Oxford University Press, 1987.

Winnipeg Tribune. *Golden Memories*. Winnipeg: Central Press, n.d.

Wood, Thomas. "Down North: Lord Tweedsmuir on Tour." *Times* (London), October 12 and 13, 1937.

____. Introduction to *Down North: Life in the Arctic*, by Anthony Onraet. London: Jonathan Cape, 1944.

Woodward, Sir Llewellyn. *British Foreign Policy in the Second World War*. Vol. 1. London: Her Majesty's Stationery Office, 1970.

Index

Index

More Biographies from Dundurn

Winston Churchill and Mackenzie King
So Similar, So Different
by Terrence Reardon
978-1459705890
$35.00

Born just two weeks apart in 1874, Winston Churchill and William Lyon Mackenzie King took different paths to achieve their objective of a parliamentary career, Churchill through military exploits and King via academic excellence. When he became prime minister, King realized that Canada had to progress from a subservient position to an independent one. Thus, when the Second World War broke out, Canada's parliament made its own decision to be a participant.

King had been highly critical of Churchill's vehement anti-Nazi stance in the 1930s. However, when Churchill became prime minister, King and Canada gave him whole-hearted support. King changed his opinion of Churchill, and this developed into almost hero worship as the war progressed.

Not just a chronicle of the relationship between these two men during the fifty years they knew each other, this book also examines their influence on the progress of their countries during that period.

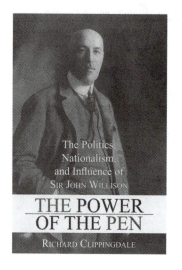

The Power of the Pen:
The Politics, Nationalism, and Influence of Sir John Willison
by Richard Clippingdale
978-1459703728
$30.00

Sir John Willison (1856–1927) was the most influential Canadian journalist in the late nineteenth and early twentieth centuries while the country achieved economic growth, intellectual maturation, and world status. With his incisive pen and clear reasoning, Willison utilized Toronto's *Globe* and *News*, his *Times of London* contributions, his many books and speeches, and his unparalleled connections with key political leaders to establish himself as a major national figure.

Uniquely, Willison was at the heart of both the Liberal and Conservative Parties as a devoted supporter and good friend of Sir Wilfrid Laurier; a first employer, early booster, and continual admirer of William Lyon Mackenzie King; and a close ally of Sir Robert Borden. Willison was a major player in the epochal federal political shifts of 1896, 1911, and 1917 and articulated highly influential views on the nature and evolution of Canadian nationalism and public policy.

DUNDURN

VISIT US AT

Dundurn.com | *@dundurnpress* | *Facebook.com/dundurnpress* | *Pinterest.com/dundurnpress*